Agreement Technologies

Law, Governance and Technology Series

VOLUME 8

For further volumes:
http://www.springer.com/series/8808

Sascha Ossowski
Editor

Agreement Technologies

Co-editors (in alphabetical order):
Giulia Andrighetto
Estefanía Argente
Holger Billhardt
Vicente J. Botti
Cristiano Castelfranchi
Marco Colombetti
Vicente Julián
Sanjay Modgil
Axel Polleres
Juan A. Rodríguez-Aguilar
Jordi Sabater-Mir
Carles Sierra
Francesca Toni
George Vouros
Antoine Zimmermann

Springer

Editor
Sascha Ossowski
University Rey Juan
Carlos, Madrid
Spain

ISBN 978-94-017-8278-4 ISBN 978-94-007-5583-3 (eBook)
DOI 10.1007/978-94-007-5583-3
Springer Dordrecht Heidelberg New York London

Softcover reprint of the hardcover 1st edition 2013

Printed on acid-free paper

Springer is part of Springer Science+Business Media (www.springer.com)

We would like to dedicate this book to the memory of Marc Esteva. His intellectual contributions to the research domain of Agreement Technologies have been numerous. Most of all, however, we value his friendship and his service to the community. The wealth of joyful moments we have shared with Marc over the years will remain constant in our memories. We miss him and will continue to do so.

Foreword

Our species is unique in this world in the range and sophistication of our social abilities. For sure, other animal species can exhibit impressive social skills of a kind – some insects, such as ants and termites, are capable of jaw dropping feats of apparently cooperative activity; and animals such as wolves, hunting in packs, can cooperate to bring down prey that are well beyond the aspirations of any individual animal. But these feats, impressive though they are, pale into insignificance compared to the feats of social magic that we all perform every day of our lives. The social skills we exhibit go far, far beyond animal instinct and evolutionary conditioning. We are capable of routinely communicating rich, complex, abstract ideas across linguistic and cultural divides. We are capable of explicit, rational cooperation on a global scale – think of all the communication, coordination, and cooperation involved in a task such as organising the Olympic games, involving hundreds of nationalities, dozens of languages, millions of people, and years of preparation.

Of all the social skills we possess beyond a common language, it is perhaps our ability to explicitly *reach agreements* with each other that mark us out from the rest of the animal world. A world without agreement would be unimaginable – a world where life was, in the words of the seventeenth century philosopher Thomas Hobbes, "solitary, poor, nasty, brutish, and short". It is our ability to make agreements on matters of common interest, and to implement and police these agreements, that makes the social world that we live in, and the global economy, possible.

For researchers in artificial intelligence, human social skills raise an intriguing challenge: can we build *computers* that are capable of exhibiting these skills? Can we build computers that can cooperate, coordinate, and, more generally, *reach agreements* with each other on our behalf? This question is fascinating because it presents deep scientific and technical challenges, but also raises the prospect of game-changing applications if one is successful. This research question has led to the emergence of a new research area, known as *agreement technologies*. This research area is concerned with the theory and practice of computer systems that can make agreements on behalf of human users or owners in situations where the preferences and beliefs of the participants are different.

The present volume represents the state of the art in agreement technologies. It contains papers that address questions such as how computers can allocate scarce societal resources in a reasonable way; how computers can govern their own artificial social systems; and how we can automate the process of negotiation among rational, self-interested participants. We are, I think it is fair to say, still quite some way from realising the dream of computers that can exhibit the same social skills that we all seem to magically possess. But this volume gives a flavour of where we are on the road to achieving this goal, and clearly demonstrates why this is such a fascinating and rewarding area in which to work.

Oxford, UK Michael Wooldridge

Preface

This book describes the state of the art in the emerging field of Agreement Technologies (AT). AT refer to computer systems in which autonomous software agents negotiate with one another, typically on behalf of humans, in order to come to mutually acceptable agreements. The term "Agreement Technologies" was introduced by Michael Wooldridge in conversations at the AAMAS conference in 2004. It was also used by Nicholas R. Jennings as title for a keynote talk given in 2005. Carles Sierra was among the first to give shape to the field by defining five key areas as technological building blocks for AT in 2007, in the context of the Spanish *Consolider* Project on AT.

The book was produced in the framework of COST Action IC0801 on Agreement Technologies. The Action was funded for 4 years (2008–2012) as part of the European Cooperation in Science and Technology (COST) programme. It comprised about 200 researchers from 25 European COST countries working on topics related to AT, plus 8 institution from 7 non-COST countries (Argentina, Australia, Brazil, Mexico, UAE, USA, and New Zealand). The overall mission of the COST Action was to support and promote the harmonization of nationally-funded high-quality research towards a new paradigm for next generation distributed systems based on the notion of agreement between computational agents, fostering research excellence and sowing the seeds for technology transfer to industry. For this purpose, the Action aimed at improving the quality, profile, and industrial relevance of European research in the emerging field of Agreement Technologies, drawing on relevant prior work from related areas and disciplines.

To achieve its mission, the COST Action defined five Working Groups (WGs) around the key areas of AT, where research results needed to be pooled and coordinated: *Semantic Technologies*, *Norms*, *Organisations*, *Argumentation and Negotiation*, as well as *Trust*. These WGs promoted the interaction among researchers and groups already funded by other national or international initiatives, so as to allow for an effective exchange of knowledge and experience, and to facilitate the dynamic development of sub-communities around specific areas of strategic importance. To this end, two Joint WG Workshops were held each year, usually co-located with a major event in the field (e.g. IJCAI, AAMAS, ESWC, and EUMAS). These workshops included sessions to advance on WG-related topics, as well as sessions and panels on cross-WG topics. As a result, various interrelations between the WGs became apparent, reinforcing the backbone of AT as a new field in its own right. The workshops finally converged into the First International Conference on Agreement Technologies, held in October 2012 in Dubrovnik, Croatia.

This book is the result of the research coordination activities carried out within the framework of COST Action IC0801. It is subdivided into seven parts. Part I is dedicated to foundational issues of Agreement Technologies, examining the notion of agreement and agreement processes from different perspectives. Parts II to VI were put together as a huge collaborative effort within the five WGs of the COST Action, which was coordinated by the respective WG Chairs. Part II outlines the relevance of novel approaches to Semantics and ontological alignments in distributed settings. Part III gives an overview of approaches for modelling norms and normative systems, the simulation of their dynamics, and their impact on the other key areas of Agreement Technologies. Part IV discusses how to design computational organisations, how to reason about them, and how organisational models can be evolved. Part V gives an overview of current approaches to argumentation and negotiation, and how they can be used to inform human reasoning, as well as to assist machine reasoning. Part VI describes different models and mechanisms of trust and reputation, and discusses their relevance for the other key areas of Agreement Technologies. Finally, Part VII provides examples of how the techniques outlined in the previous parts of the book can be used to build distributed software applications that solve real-world problems. Please notice that the parts are supported by a set of video-lectures that can be freely downloaded from the web.

I would like to take the opportunity to thank everybody who contributed to the exciting effort of shaping the vibrant field of Agreement Technologies, whose state of the art is summarised in this book. This includes the researchers and practitioners of the AT community, COST Action IC0801 members and, in particular, the co-editors, chapter authors, and reviewers of this publication. The book is the first one to provide a comprehensive overview of the emerging field of Agreement Technologies, written and coordinated by leading researchers in the field. It is the result of a massive concerted effort – I hope you will enjoy reading it.

Madrid, Spain Sascha Ossowski

Acknowledgements

This publication is supported by

COST – the acronym for European Cooperation in Science and Technology – is the oldest and widest European intergovernmental network for cooperation in research. Established by the Ministerial Conference in November 1971, COST is presently used by the scientific communities of 36 European countries to cooperate in common research projects supported by national funds.

The funds provided by COST – less than 1% of the total value of the projects – support the COST cooperation networks (COST Actions) through which, with EUR 30 million per year, more than 30,000 European scientists are involved in research having a total value which exceeds EUR 2 billion per year. This is the financial worth of the European added value which COST achieves.

A "bottom up approach" (the initiative of launching a COST Action comes from the European scientists themselves), "à la carte participation" (only countries interested in the Action participate), "equality of access" (participation is open also to the scientific communities of countries not belonging to the European Union) and "flexible structure" (easy implementation and light management of the research initiatives) are the main characteristics of COST.

As precursor of advanced multidisciplinary research COST has a very important role for the realisation of the European Research Area (ERA) anticipating and complementing the activities of the Framework Programmes, constituting a "bridge" towards the scientific communities of emerging countries, increasing the mobility of researchers across Europe and fostering the establishment of "Networks of Excellence" in many key scientific domains such as: Biomedicine and Molecular Biosciences; Food and Agriculture; Forests, their Products and Services; Materials, Physical and Nanosciences; Chemistry and Molecular Sciences and

Technologies; Earth System Science and Environmental Management; Information and Communication Technologies; Transport and Urban Development; Individuals, Societies, Cultures and Health. It covers basic and more applied research and also addresses issues of pre-normative nature or of societal importance.

Web: http://www.cost.eu/

ESF provides the COST Office through an EC contract

COST is supported by the EU RTD Framework programme

Contents

Editors' Short Bios

Sascha Ossowski is a Full Professor of Computer Science and the Director of the Centre for Intelligent Information Technologies (CETINIA) at University Rey Juan Carlos in Madrid, Spain. He obtained his M.Sc degree in Informatics from the University of Oldenburg (Germany) in 1993, and received a Ph.D. in Artificial Intelligence from UPM in 1997. His research focuses on the application of distributed AI techniques to real-world problems such as transportation management, smart grids, m-Health, and e-Commerce. He is chair of the COST Action IC0801 on Agreement Technologies, belongs to the board of directors of the International Foundation for Autonomous Agents and Multiagent Systems (IFAAMAS), and is a member of the steering committee of the ACM Annual Symposium on Applied Computing (SAC). He was also co-founder and first chair of the European Association for Multiagent Systems (EURAMAS).

Giulia Andrighetto is a research fellow at the Institute of Cognitive Science and Technologies of the Italian National Research Council (Rome, Italy). Her research is concerned with interdisciplinary studies of cognitive and social phenomena. She is interested in explaining the emergence and evolution of social phenomena, such as social norms and punishment, by integrating empirical findings from cognitive science into a set of operational models. Her publications include the book Minding Norms. Mechanisms and dynamics of social order in agent societies Oxford University Press (forthcoming) and several publications on cognitive social agents, norms representation and reasoning, and agent-based simulation in peer-reviewed international journals.

Estefania Argente was born in Valencia (Spain) and received the M.S. degree in Computer Science from the Universitat Politècnica de València (UPV) in 2000. She obtained her Ph.D. degree in 2008 at the Departamento de Sistemas Informáticos y Compatutación at UPV, where she is currently a lecturer. As member of the GTI-IA researching group, she has been working in the Agreement Technologies Consolider Ingenio project of the Spanish Government (2007–2013), and the Agreement Technologies (AT) European Action COST IC0801 (2008–2012), of which she is co-chair of Working Group 3 – Organisations. She has published more than

60 papers in journals, books, conferences and workshops. Her research interests include agent-oriented methodologies, agent organisations, and normative multi-agent systems.

Holger Billhardt received his M.Sc in Computer Science from the Technical University of Leipzig (Germany) in 1994 and his Ph.D. in Informatics from the Technical University of Madrid in 2003. Since 2001 he has been working at the University Rey Juan Carlos in Madrid in the Artificial Intelligence Group, where he is currently an associate professor of Computer Science. Holger Billhardt has worked in the field of information retrieval and medical informatics. In the last few years, his research has been concerned with multi-agent systems, in particular with enforcement mechanisms (norms, incentives, information provisioning) for regulating the behaviour of software agents in open and dynamic environments. Holger Billhardt is author or co-author of more than 50 research papers. Holger Billhardt has participated in 15 nationally or internationally founded research projects and contracts and he has been member of the organizing committee and the programme committee of several international workshops and conferences.

Vicent J. Botti Navarro is Full Professor at the Departamento de Sistemas Informáticos y Computación of Universidad Politécnica de Valencia (Spain) and head of the GTI-IA research group of this centre. He received his Ph.D. in Computer Science from the same university in 1990. His research interests are multi-agent systems, agreement technologies and artificial intelligence, where he has more than 300 refereed publications in international journals and conferences. He has been and is a principal researcher on nationally and internationally funded projects (CICYT, MC&T, ESPRIT, etc.), and on technology transfer agreements, as well as sitting on various scientific committees in his areas of interest. Currently he is Vice-rector of the Universidad Politécnica de Valencia and the main researcher in the Prometeo project 'Advances on Agreement Technologies for Computational Entities (AtforCE)' and one of the three main researchers in the Consolider Ingenio 2010 project 'Agreement Technologies'.

Cristiano Castelfranchi is a Full professor of "Cognitive Science", University of Siena; director of the Institute of Cognitive Sciences and Technologies CNR, Roma. Cognitive scientist, with a background in linguistics and psychology; also active in the Multi-Agent Systems and Social Simulation communities. Award as ECCAI "fellows" for "pioneering work in the field"; "Mind and Brain" 2007 award Univ. of Torino. Author of several books on social cognition, emotions, language, trust, rehabilitation. Main research topics: Theory of Goals; Cognitive mediators of social phenomena; social image; emotions (shame, envy, pity, guilt...); theory of "values" and "evaluation"; expectations; trust; power; norms and conventions; promises; implicit communication; emergence and functions; collective action; recovery.

Marco Colombetti was born in Milano (Italy) and received the M.S. degree in Electronics Engineering at Politecnico di Milano in 1976. He is Full Professor of Computer Science at Politecnico di Milano and Università della Svizzera italiana, Lugano. He has been involved in many research projects in the field of Artificial

Intelligence, such as the Agreement Technologies (AT) European Action COST IC0801 (2008–2013), of which he is co-chair of Working Group 3 on Organisations. He has been Vice-President of the Italian Association for Artificial Intelligence, and member of the Managing Boards of Fast (the Italian Federation of Scientific and Technical Associations) and of EURAMAS (the European Association for Multi-Agent Systems). His research interests include Agent Communication Languages, Artificial Institutions, Semantic Web and Human Communication and Interaction. He has authored about 120 scientific papers and a book published by MIT Press.

Vicente Julian was born in Valencia, Spain, in 1971. He received his Ph.D. degree in Computer Science from Universidad Politecnica de Valencia in 2002. His Ph.D. dissertation focused on agent methodologies for real time systems. He is a researcher with Grupo Tecnologia Informatica – Inteligencia Artificial at Universidad Politecnica de Valencia. He also holds an Associate Professor position. His research interests are adaptive systems, agreement technologies, and real-time multiagent systems.

Sanjay Modgil completed his Ph.D. in computational logic at Imperial College London, and is currently a lecturer at the Department of Informatics, King's College London (www.dcs.kcl.ac.uk/staff/smodgil/). His research work has focussed on non-monotonic logics, belief revision, argumentation theory, and applications of these logic based models of reasoning in practical technologies, and in particular medical applications. He has contributed to development of the Argument Interchange Format, proof theories for abstract argumentation frameworks, and has led the development of abstract argumentation frameworks that accommodate meta-level reasoning about arguments, and applications of these frameworks to agent reasoning about beliefs, actions and norms. He is currently co-chair of the WG4 group on argumentation and negotiation, within the Agreement Technologies COST Action.

Axel Polleres Ph.D. (2003), Vienna University of Technology; Habilitation (2011) has worked at various universities before joining Siemens Corporate Technologies (CT) as Senior Research Scientist in 2011. Research interests: Knowledge Representation and Management (Querying and Reasoning about Ontologies, Rules, Linked Data/Semantic Web technologies, Web Services) and applications. Axel has been an active participant in several European and national research projects, has published more than 100 articles in journals, books, and conference and workshop contributions, and leads international standardization efforts in Semantic Technologies (co-chair of the W3C SPARQL working group for Siemens AG). Currently, Dr. Polleres works in Siemens CT's research group on Configuration Technologies in Vienna.

Juan A. Rodríguez-Aguilar is a tenured scientist at the Institute of Research on Artificial Intelligence of the Spanish Council for Scientific Research (CSIC). He received an M.Sc in Artificial Intelligence (1998) and a Ph.D. in Computer Science (2001) from the Autonomous University of Barcelona. In 1999 he worked as a researcher for the e-Business group of the Sloan School of Management at the

Massachusetts Institute of Technology (MIT). Between 2001 and 2003 he worked as a researcher for iSOCO S.A., leading the development of auction and optimisation products. He has participated in multiple research projects funded by the European Commission and the Spanish Government, and has published around 150 papers in specialized scientific journals, conferences and workshops. He is an associate editor of the Knowledge Engineering Review journal and the Electronic Commerce Research and Applications journal. He acts as a reviewer of several international journals (JAAMAS, IEEE Internet Computing, Computational Intelligence, etc.) and as PC member of top international conferences (e.g. IJCAI, AAAI, AAMAS).

Jordi Sabater-Mir is a tenured scientist at the Artificial Intelligence Research Institute (IIIA) of the Spanish National Research Council (CSIC), Barcelona, Spain. He holds a doctorate in Artificial Intelligence and has been a postdoctoral Marie Curie fellow at the Institute of Cognitive Sciences and Technologies (ISTC-CNR) in Rome, Italy. His current research is focused on computational trust and reputation models, agent based social simulation and cognitive agents. He has published more than 90 papers in specialised scientific journals, conferences and workshops. He is a member of the EURAMAS board of directors and was the PC chair of EUMAS 2009 in Cyprus. He has co-organized the last nine editions of the workshop on Trust in Agent Societies. http://www.iiia.csic.es/~jsabater.

Carles Sierra is Full Professor at the Institute of Research on Artificial Intelligence of the Spanish National Research Council (CSIC) and Adjunct Professor at the University of Technology, Sydney, Australia. Recently, he has been particularly active in the area of multi-agent systems, especially on methodological aspects and on trust modelling. He has participated in around 40 research projects funded by the European Commission and the Spanish Government, and has published around 300 papers in specialised scientific journals, conferences and workshops. He is a member of the program committees of around a dozen of conferences and workshops per year, and is a member of seven journal editorial boards including AIJ, JAIR and JAAMAS. He has been General Chair of the conference Autonomous Agents 2000 in Barcelona, AAMAS 2009 in Budapest, and PC chair of AAMAS 2004. He has been the local chair for IJCAI 2011 in Barcelona. http://www.iiia.csic.es/~sierra.

Francesca Toni completed her Ph.D. in computational logic at Imperial College London, and is currently a Reader in Computational Logic at the Department of Computing, Imperial College London, where she leads the Computational Logic and Argumentation group (www.doc.ic.ac.uk/~ft/). Her research has focused on logic programming, abduction, non-monotonic reasoning and argumentation, logic-based multi-agent systems. She has contributed to the development of Assumption-Based Argumentation and its application in several settings, from decision-making to negotiation to conflict resolution and trust computing. She is currently co-chair of the WG4 group on argumentation and negotiation, within the Agreement Technologies COST Action, as well as a member of the Management Committee of this action.

George Vouros (B.Sc, Ph.D.) holds a B.Sc in Mathematics, and a Ph.D. in Artificial Intelligence all from the University of Athens, Greece. He started pursuing research in the areas of Expert Systems, and Conceptual Knowledge Representation. Currently he works in the areas of knowledge management, Ontologies (their engineering, alignment, mapping, coordination, learning and evolution), Agent organizations, collaborative agents and their adaptation, and architectures of collaborative agents. His published scientific work includes numerous book chapters, papers in international journals and proceedings of national and international conference papers in the above mentioned themes. He has served as program chair and chair and member of organizing committees of national and international conferences on related topics. After several years in the University of the Aegean, he has moved to the Department of Digital Systems, University of Piraeus.

Antoine Zimmermann (M.Sc, Ph.D.) is an associate professor at École des mines de Saint-Étienne. His research interests are in representing, reasoning, querying and managing contextual knowledge that are distributed and heterogeneous, in open environments. Antoine participated in several international research projects, conference committees and in the OWL 2 and RDF 1.1 W3C working groups. Since 2009, Antoine has jointly chaired the working group on semantics in the COST Action Agreement Technologies.

List of Contributors

Pablo Almajano IIIA-CSIC, Campus UAB, Bellaterra, Barcelona, Spain

Giulia Andrighetto Institute of Cognitive Science and Technologies, CNR, Rome, Italy

Estefanía Argente Departamento de Sistemas Informáticos y Computación, Universitat Politécnica de València, Valencia, Spain

Floris Bex University of Dundee, Dundee, UK

Holger Billhardt University Rey Juan Carlos, CETINIA, Móstoles, Madrid, Spain

Olivier Boissier FAYOL-EMSE, LSTI, Saint-Etienne, France

Vicente Botti Departamento de Sistemas Informáticos y Computación, Universitat Politécnica de València, Valencia, Spain

Ivan Bratko University of Ljubljana, Ljubljana, Slovenia

Jan Broersen Department of Information and Computing Sciences, Universiteit Utrecht, Utrecht, The Netherlands

Carlos Carrascosa Departamento de Sistemas Informáticos y Computación, Universitat Politécnica de València, Valencia, Spain

Pompeu Casanovas Institute of Law and Technology, Faculty of Law, Universitat Autonoma de Barcelona, Barcelona, Spain

Cristiano Castelfranchi Institute of Cognitive Sciences and Technologies – National Research Council, Rome, Italy

António J.M. Castro LIACC, Dep. Eng. Informática, Faculdade de Engenharia, Universidade do Porto, Porto, Portugal

Jesús Cerquides IIIA-CSIC, Campus UAB, Bellaterra, Barcelona, Spain

Carlos I. Chesñevar Universidad Nacional del Sur, Bahía Blanca, Argentina

Zijie Cong University Rey Juan Carlos, CETINIA, Móstoles, Madrid, Spain

Rosaria Conte Institute of Cognitive Science and Technologies, CNR, Rome, Italy

Stephen Cranefield Information Science Department, University of Otago, Dunedin, New Zealand

Natalia Criado Departamento de Sistemas Informáticos y Computación, Universitat Politécnica de València, Valencia, Spain

Carlos E. Cuesta, University Rey Juan Carlos, ETSII, Móstoles, Madrid, Spain

Paul Davidsson Malmö University, Malmö, Sweden
Blekinge Institute of Technology, Blekinge, Sweden

John Debenham QCIS, University of Technology, Sydney, NSW, Australia

Fabien Delecroix Laboratoire d'Informatique Fondamentale de Lille, Université Lille 1, Villeneuve d'Ascq, France

Michał Drozdowicz Systems Research Institute Polish Academy of Sciences, Warsaw, Poland

Wolfgang Dvořák Vienna University of Technology, Vienna, Austria

Sergio Esparcia Departamento de Sistemas Informáticos y Computación, Universitat Politécnica de València, Valencia, Spain

Marc Esteva IIIA-CSIC, Campus UAB, Bellaterra, Barcelona, Spain

Àngela Fàbregues IIIA-CSIC, Campus UAB, Bellaterra, Barcelona, Spain

Marcelo A. Falappa, Universidad Nacional del Sur, Bahía Blanca, Argentina

Falcone, Rino Institute of Cognitive Sciences and Technologies – National Research Council, Rome, Italy

Xiuyi Fan Imperial College London, London, UK

Alberto Fernández University Rey Juan Carlos, CETINIA, Móstoles, Madrid, Spain

Nicoletta Fornara Università della Svizzera italiana, Lugano, Switzerland

Dov Gabbay Department of Computer Science, King's College London, London, UK

Sarah Alice Gaggl Vienna University of Technology, Vienna, Austria

Maria Ganzha Systems Research Institute Polish Academy of Sciences, Warsaw, Poland

Alejandro J. García Universidad Nacional del Sur, Bahía Blanca, Argentina

Antonio Garrido Departamento de Sistemas Informáticos y Computación, Universitat Politécnica de València, Valencia, Spain

Adriana Giret Departamento de Sistemas Informáticos y Computación, Universitat Politécnica de València, Valencia, Spain

María P. González Universidad Nacional del Sur, Bahía Blanca, Argentina

Thomas F. Gordon Fraunhofer FOKUS, Berlin, Germany

Jana Görmer Department of Informatics, TU Clausthal, Clausthal, Germany

Davide Grossi Department of Computer Science, University of Liverpool, Liverpool, UK

Marie Gustafsson Friberger Malmö University, Malmö, Sweden

Stella Heras Departamento de Sistemas Informáticos y Computación, Universitat Politécnica de València, Valencia, Spain

Ramón Hermoso University Rey Juan Carlos, CETINIA, Móstoles, Madrid, Spain

Andreas Herzig Logic, Interaction, Language, and Computation Group, IRIT, Université Paul Sabatier, France

Johan Holmgren Blekinge Institute of Technology, Blekinge, Sweden

Enrique de la Hoz Computer Engineering Department, Universidad de Alcalá, Escuela Politécnica, Alcalá de Henares, Madrid, Spain

Jomi Fred Hübner Federal University of Santa Catarina, Florianópolis, Brazil

Andreas Jacobsson Malmö University, Malmö, Sweden

Gordan Ježić Faculty of Electrical Engineering and Computing, University of Zagreb, Zagreb, Croatia

Andrew Jones Department of Informatics, King's College London, London, UK

Jaume Jordán Departamento de Sistemas Informáticos y Computación, Universitat Politécnica de València, Valencia, Spain

Vicente Julián Departamento de Sistemas Informáticos y Computación, Universitat Politécnica de València, Valencia, Spain

Kristi Kirikal Tallinn University of Technology, Tallinn, Estonia

Martin Kollingbaum Department of Computing Science, University of Aberdeen, Aberdeen, UK

Andrew Koster IIIA-CSIC, Campus UAB, Bellaterra, Barcelona, Spain

Mario Kušek Faculty of Electrical Engineering and Computing, University of Zagreb, Zagreb, Croatia

João Leite CENTRIA, Departamento de Informática, Universidade Nova de Lisboa, Lisbon, Portugal

Henrique Lopes Cardoso LIACC / Dep. Eng. Informática, Faculdade de Engenharia, Universidade do Porto, Porto, Portugal

Miguel A. López-Carmona Computer Engineering Department, Universidad de Alcalá, Escuela Politécnica, Alcalá de Henares, Madrid, Spain

Maite López-Sánchez University of Barcelona, Barcelona, Spain

Emiliano Lorini Logic, Interaction, Language, and Computation Group, IRIT, Université Paul Sabatier, Toulouse, France

Ignac Lovrek Faculty of Electrical Engineering and Computing, University of Zagreb, Zagreb, Croatia

Michael Luck Department of Informatics, King's College London, London, UK

Marin Lujak University Rey Juan Carlos, CETINIA, Móstoles, Madrid, Spain

Jordi Madrenas IIIA-CSIC, Campus UAB, Bellaterra, Barcelona, Spain

Samhar Mahmoud Department of Informatics, King's College London, London, UK

Iván Marsá-Maestre Computer Engineering Department, Universidad de Alcalá, Escuela Politécnica, Alcalá de Henares, Madrid, Spain

Felipe Meneguzzi Pontifícia Universidade Católica do Rio Grande do Sul, Faculdade de Informática, Porto Alegre, Brazil

John-Jules Meyer Department of Information and Computing Sciences, Universiteit Utrecht, Utrecht, The Netherlands

Boris Mikhaylov IIIA-CSIC, Campus UAB, Bellaterra, Barcelona, Spain

Sanjay Modgil Kings' College London, London, UK

Maxime Morge Laboratoire d'Informatique Fondamentale de Lille, Université Lille 1, Villeneuve d'Ascq, France

Martin Možina University of Ljubljana, Ljubljana, Slovenia

Pablo Noriega IIIA-CSIC, Campus UAB, Bellaterra, Barcelona, Spain

Timothy J. Norman Department of Computing Science, University of Aberdeen, Aberdeen, UK

Eugénio Oliveira LIACC, Dep. Eng. Informática, Faculdade de Engenharia, Universidade do Porto, Porto, Portugal

Nir Oren University of Aberdeen, Aberdeen, UK

Sascha Ossowski University Rey Juan Carlos, CETINIA, Móstoles, Madrid, Spain

Fabio Paglieri Goal-Oriented Agents Lab (GOAL), Istituto di Scienze e Tecnologie della Cognizione, CNR, Roma, Italy

Jeff Z. Pan University of Aberdeen, King's College, Aberdeen, UK

Marcin Paprzycki Systems Research Institute Polish Academy of Sciences, Warsaw, Poland

Xavier Parent Individual and Collective Reasoning (ICR) group, University of Luxembourg, Luxembourg, Luxembourg

Toni Penya-Alba IIIA-CSIC, Campus UAB, Bellaterra, Barcelona, Spain

José-Santiago Pérez-Sotelo University Rey Juan Carlos, CETINIA, Móstoles, Madrid, Spain

Jan A. Persson Malmö University, Malmö, Sweden

Vedran Podobnik University of Zagreb, Faculty of Electrical Engineering and Computing, Zagreb, Croatia

Axel Polleres Siemens AG Österreich, Vienna, Austria

Marc Pujol-González IIIA-CSIC, Campus UAB, Bellaterra, Barcelona, Spain

Martin Purvis Information Science Department, University of Otago, Dunedin, New Zealand

Maryam Purvis Information Science Department, University of Otago, Dunedin, New Zealand

Chris Reed University of Dundee, Dundee, UK

M. Birna van Riemsdijk Electrical Engineering, Mathematics and Computer Science (EEMCS), Delft, The Netherlands

Ana Paula Rocha LIACC, Dep. Eng. Informática, Faculdade de Engenharia, Universidade do Porto, Porto, Portugal

Inmaculada Rodríguez University of Barcelona, Barcelona, Spain

Juan A. Rodríguez-Aguilar IIIA-CSIC, Campus UAB, Bellaterra, Barcelona, Spain

Mario Rodrigo Departamento de Sistemas Informáticos y Computación, Universitat Politécnica de València, Valencia, Spain

Bruno Rosell IIIA-CSIC, Campus UAB, Bellaterra, Barcelona, Spain

Antonino Rotolo CIRSFID – Faculty of Law, University of Bologna, Bologna, Italy

Jean-Christophe Routier Laboratoire d'Informatique Fondamentale de Lille, Université Lille 1, Villeneuve d'Ascq, France

Jordi Sabater-Mir IIIA-CSIC, Campus UAB, Bellaterra, Barcelona, Spain

Giovanni Sartor EUI, Florence/CIRSFID – Faculty of Law, University of Bologna, Bologna, Italy

Bastin Tony Roy Savarimuthu Information Science Department, University of Otago, Dunedin, New Zealand

Marco Schorlemmer IIIA-CSIC, Campus UAB, Bellaterra, Barcelona, Spain

Michael I. Schumacher University of Applied Sciences Western Switzerland, Sierre, Switzerland

Carles Sierra IIIA-CSIC, Campus UAB, Bellaterra, Barcelona, Spain

Moser Silva Fagundes University Rey Juan Carlos, CETINIA, Móstoles, Madrid, Spain

Guillermo R. Simari Universidad Nacional del Sur, Bahía Blanca, Argentina

Jose M. Such Departamento de Sistemas Informáticos y Computación, Universitat Politécnica de València, Valencia, Spain

Stefan Szeider Vienna University of Technology, Vienna, Austria

Paweł Szmeja Systems Research Institute Polish Academy of Sciences, Warsaw, Poland

Charalampos Tampitsikas Università della Svizzera italiana, Lugano, Switzerland

Kuldar Taveter Tallinn University of Technology, Tallinn, Estonia

Francesca Toni Imperial College London, London, UK

Leendert van der Torre ICR Group, University of Luxembourg, Luxembourg, Luxembourg

Paolo Torroni University of Bologna, Bologna, Italy

Denis Trček Faculty of Computer and Information Science, University of Ljubljana, Ljubljana, Slovenia

Tomas Trescak IIIA-CSIC, Campus UAB, Bellaterra, Barcelona, Spain

Cássia Trojahn INRIA and LIG, Grenoble, France

Krunoslav Tržec Ericsson Nikola Tesla, Zagreb, Croatia

Luca Tummolini Institute of Cognitive Science and Technologies, CNR, Rome, Italy

Paolo Turrini University of Luxembourg, Luxembourg, Luxembourg

Joana Urbano LIACC, Dep. Eng. Informática, Faculdade de Engenharia, Universidade do Porto, Porto, Portugal

Matteo Vasirani University Rey Juan Carlos, CETINIA, Móstoles, Madrid, Spain

Laurent Vercouter INSA de Rouen, Saint-Etienne du Rouvray, France

Serena Villata INRIA Sophia Antipolis, Sophia Antipolis, France

Daniel Villatoro IIIA-CSIC, Campus UAB, Bellaterra, Barcelona, Spain

George Vouros Department of Digital Systems, University of Piraeus, Piraeus, Greece

Katarzyna Wasielewska Systems Research Institute Polish Academy of Sciences, Warsaw, Poland

Stefan Woltran Vienna University of Technology, Vienna, Austria

Antoine Zimmermann École Nationale Supérieure des Mines, FAYOL-ENSMSE, LSTI, Saint-Étienne, France

Acronyms

A&A	Agent & Artifact
AAOL	Autonomous Agents in Organized Localities
ABA	Assumption-Based Argumentation
ABC4MAS	Assembling Business Collaborations for Multi Agent Systems
ABM	Agent Based Modelling
ABML	Argument-Based Machine Learning
ACL	Agent Communication Language
AF	Argumentation Framework
AGM	Alchourron, Gardenfors and Makinson
AI	Artificial Institution
AI	Artificial Intelligence
AIF	Argument Interchange Format
AiG	Agents in Grid
AJAX	Asynchronous JavaScript and XML
ALS	Advanced Life Support
ANTE	Agreement Negotiation in Normative and Trust-enabled Environments
AOCC	Airline Operations Control Centre
AOCP	Airline Operations Control Problem
AOM	Agent-Oriented Modelling
AOSE	Agent-Oriented Software Engineering
API	Application Programming Interface
ArgDSS	Argument-based Decision Support Systems
ASP	Answer Set Programming
AT	Agreement Technologies
ATE	Agreement Technologies Environment
AUML	Agent Unified Modelling Language
B2B	Business-to-Business
B2C	Business-to-Consumer
BDI	Belief-Desire-Intention
BLS	Basic Life Support

BOID	Beliefs, Obligations, Intentions and Desires
BPEL	Business Process Execution Language
CA	Combinatorial Auction
CArtAgO	Common ARTifact infrastructure for AGents Open environments
CBB	Consumer Buying Behavior
CBR	Case-Based Reasoning
CGO	Core Grid Ontology
CIC	Client Information Center
CPU	Core Processing Unit
CSP	Constraint Satisfaction Problem
CTD	Contrary-To-Duty
CWA	Closed World Assumption
DAI	Distributed Artificial Intelligence
DAML	Darpa Agent Markup Language
DDL	Distributed Description Logic
DEC	Discrete Event Calculus
DeLP	Defeasible Logic Programming
$DIO(DE)^2$	DIagnostic and DEcision-theoretic framework for DEontic reasoning
DL	Description Logic
DLP	Description Logic Programs
DM	Decision Making
EI	Electronic Institution
EIDE	Electronic Institutions Development Environment
EL	Execution Layer
EMA	Emergency Medical Assistance
EMIL	EMergence In the Loop
EMS	Emergency Medical Services
ERP	Enterprise Resource Planning
FCFS	first-come, first-served
FET	Future and Emerging Technologies
FIPA	Foundation for Intelligent Physical Agents
FOAF	Friend Of A Friend
FORe	Functional Ontology of Reputation
GCI	Global Computing Initiative
GCII	Global Computing II
GORMAS	Guidelines for ORganisational Multi-Agent Systems
GPS	Geographic Positioning System
GRDDL	Gleaning Resource Descriptions from Dialects of Languages
GUI	Graphical User Interface
HTML	HyperText Markup Language
I/O	Input/Output
IA	Institutional Agent
ICL	Individual Context Layer
ICT	Information and Communication Technologies

IDDL	Integrated Distributed Description Logic
ILP	Induction Logic Programming
IM	Institution Manager
IST	Information Science Technologies
IT	Information Technology
JADE	Java Agent DEvelopment Framework
KR	Knowledge Representation
LREP	Reputation Language
MA	Mixed Auctions
MAGNET	MultiAgent NEgotiation Testbed
MANET	Multi-AGent Normative EnvironmenTs
MAS	Multiagent System
MASDIMA	Multi-Agent System for DIsruption MAnagement
MDP	Markov Decision Process
ML	Machine Learning
ML	Mechatronic Layer
MMUCA	Mixed Multi-Unit Combinatorial Auction
MMUCATS	MMUCA Test Suit
$\mathcal{M}$oise	Model of Organisation for multI-agent SystEms
MSM	Minimal Service Model
N3	Notation3
NAO	Network of Aligned Ontologies
NoA	Normative Agent
norMAS	normative Multi-Agent Systems
OAEI	Ontology Alignment Evaluation Initiative
OASIS	Organization for the Advancement of Structured Information Standards
OCeAN	Ontology CommitmEnts Authorizations Norms
OCMAS	Organisation-Centred Multi-Agent System
OCML	Operational Conceptual Modelling Language
ODR	Online Dispute Resolution
OE	Organisational Entity
OMAS	Open Multi-Agent Systems
OMI	Organisation Management Infrastructure
OML	Organisation Modelling Language
OMS	Organisation Management System
OS	Operating System
OS	Organisational Specification
OSGi	Open Services Gateway Initiative
OU	Organisational Units
OWA	Open World Assumption
OWL	Web Ontology Language
P2P	Peer-to-Peer
P3P	Platform for Privacy Preferences
PDA	Proactive Dialogical Agent

P-DL	Package-based Description Logics
PIUP	Partial Identity Unlikability Problem
PLING	Policy Languages Interest Group
PnP TCM	Plug and Play Transport Chain Management
PPC	Pay Per Click
PS	Performative Structure
PSA	Persuasive Selling Agent
QAD	Qualitative Assessment Dynamics
RDF	Resource Description Framework
RDFS	RDF Schema
RFQ	Request For Quotation
RIF	Rule Interchange Format
RoP	Range of Perception
SAT	Boolean SATisfiability problem
SAWSDL	Semantic Annotations for WSDL
SCF	Supply Chain Formation
SCL	Social Context Layer
SESA	Semantically Enabled Service-Oriented Architectures
SF	Service Facilitator
SIOC	Semantically Interlinked Online Communities
SLA	Service Level Agreement
SM	Scene Manager
SMA	Sequential Mixed Auction
SOA	Service Oriented Architecture
SPARQL	SPARQL Protocol and RDF Query Language
SPPCA	Semantic Pay-Per-Click Agent
SQL	Structured Query Language
SRM	Supplier Relationship Management
SWRL	Semantic Web Rule Language
THOMAS	MeTHods, Techniques and Tools for Open Multi-Agent Systems
TM	Transition Manager
T-MAS	Task-oriented Multi-Agent Systems
TMC	Technology Management Centre
TOE	Dempster-Shafer Theory of Evidence
UBL	Universal Business Language
UML	Unified Modelling Language
URI	Uniform Resource Identifier
VAF	Value-based Argumentation Framework
VI	Virtual Institution
VIXEE	Virtual Institution eXEcution Environment
VO	Virtual Organisation
VOF	Virtual Organisation Formalisation
VOM	Virtual Organisation Model
VSM	Vector-Space Model
VW	Virtual World

VWBT	Virtual World Builder Toolkit
W3C	World Wide Web Consortium
WDP	Winner Determination Problem
WRL	Web Rule Language
WSDL	Web Service Description Language
WSML	Web Service Modeling Language
WSMO	Web Service Modeling Ontology
WUI	Web-based User Interface
XACML	eXtensible Access Control Markup Language
XHTML	eXtensible Hypertext Markup Language
XML	eXtensible Markup Language
XSLT	eXtensible Stylesheet Language Transformation
YARS2	Yet Another RDF Store version 2

Part I
Foundations

Most would agree that large-scale open distributed systems are an area of enormous social and economic potential. In fact, regardless of whether they are realised for the purpose of business or leisure, in a private or a public context, people's transactions and interactions are increasingly mediated by computers. The resulting networks are usually large in scale, involving millions of interactions, and are open for the interacting entities to join or leave at will. People are often supported by software components of different complexity, sometimes termed *agents* to stress their capability of representing human interests. There is currently a paradigm shift in the way that such systems are build, enacted, and managed: away from rigid and centralised client-server architectures, towards more flexible and decentralised means of interaction.

The vision of *Agreement Technologies* (AT) are next-generation open distributed systems, where interactions between *computational agents* are based on the concept of *agreement*. Two key ingredients to such systems are needed: first, a normative context that defines rules of the game, or the "space" of agreements that the agents can possibly reach; and second, an interaction mechanism by means of which agreements are first established, and then enacted.

In recent years, researchers from the field of Multiagent Systems, Semantic Technologies, as well as Social Sciences have joined together to work towards that vision. Autonomy, interaction, mobility and openness are the characteristics that the AT paradigm covers from a theoretical and practical perspective. Semantic alignment, negotiation, argumentation, virtual organizations, learning, real time, and several other technologies are in the sandbox to define, specify and verify such systems.

In addition, the wide range of social theories available to-date offers many different solutions to problems found in complex (computer) systems. So, deciding which theories to apply as well as how and when, becomes a major challenge. And, in particular, this kind of interdisciplinary research is needed to work towards a more robust understanding of the notion of agreement and all the processes and mechanisms involved in reaching agreements between different kinds of agents, thus putting the AT paradigm on more solid conceptual foundations.

This Part discusses how notions related to agreements and processes leading to agreements are used in different fields of Science and Technology. Chapter 1 takes the perspective of *Computer Science*. It argues that computing requires certain *implicit* agreements between programmers and language designers. As the complexity of software systems grows, *explicit* agreements within the design and development team are of foremost importance. Still, when software entities become more autonomic and adaptive, these explicit agreements cannot be determined offline any longer, and need to be established and tracked on-the-fly. This calls for a new computing paradigm that allows for agreements that are both explicit and dynamic. Chapter 2 contributes a perspective from the field of *Law*. Agreements have been the basis for private and civil law for about two millennia. Logical and empirical approaches have often led to competing and mutually ignoring results. The chapter suggests that the Internet and new scenarios created by the Web pose new challenges to both approaches, and that in this context AT may not only help in bridging the gap between both theoretical approaches, but may also foster new ways of implementing regulations and justice in societies where both humans and agents interact with one another. The contribution of Chap. 3 sets out from a *Cognitive Science* perspective. It first offers a bird's-eye view of several topics of interest in agreement theory for social science. A socio-cognitive analysis of the distinction between "being in agreement" and "having an agreement" is put forward, and multiple paths leading to agreement are explored in this context. Finally, a point is raised that may be of particular interest to the vision of AT in the long run: a certain level of disagreement is actually desirable, even in the most well-ordered social system.

Sascha Ossowski
Editor Part "Foundations"

Chapter 1
Agreement Technologies: A Computing Perspective

Sascha Ossowski, Carles Sierra, and Vicente Botti

1.1 Introduction

In the past, the concept of agreement was a domain of study mainly for philosophers and sociologists, and was only applicable to human societies. However, in recent years, the growth of disciplines such as social psychology, socio-biology, social neuroscience, together with the spectacular emergence of the information society technologies, have changed this situation. Presently, agreement and all the processes and mechanisms involved in reaching agreements between different kinds of agents are also a subject of research and analysis from technology-oriented perspectives.

In Computer Science, the recent trend towards large-scale open distributed software systems has triggered interest in computational approaches for modelling and enacting agreement and agreement processes. Today, most transactions and interactions at business level, but also at leisure level, are mediated by computers and computer networks. From email, over social networks, to virtual worlds, the way people work and enjoy their free time has changed dramatically in less than a generation. This change has meant that IT research and development focuses on aspects like new Human-Computer Interfaces or enhanced routing and network

S. Ossowski (✉)
CETINIA, University Rey Juan Carlos, Madrid, Spain
e-mail: sascha.ossowski@urjc.es

C. Sierra
IIIA – CSIC, Barcelona, Spain
e-mail: sierra@iiia.csic.es

V. Botti
Departamento de Sistemas Informáticos y Computación, Universitat Politècnica de València, Valencia, Spain
e-mail: vbotti@dsic.upv.es

S. Ossowski (ed.), *Agreement Technologies*, Law, Governance and Technology Series 8, DOI 10.1007/978-94-007-5583-3_1,

management tools. However, the biggest impact has been on the way applications are thought about and developed. These applications require components to which increasingly complex tasks can be delegated, components that show higher levels of intelligence, components that are capable of interacting in sophisticated ways, since they are massively distributed and sometimes embedded in all sorts of appliances and sensors. These components are often termed *software agents* to stress their capability to represent human interests, and to be autonomous and socially-aware. In order to allow for effective interactions in such systems that lead to efficient and mutually acceptable outcomes, the notion of *agreement* between computational agents is central.

Over the last few years, a number of research initiatives in Europe and the USA have addressed different challenges related to the development and deployment of large-scale open distributed systems. One of the most related to the Action's goals was the Global Computing initiative (GCI) launched in 2001 as part of the FP6 IST FET Programme. The vision of the call, also contained in the Global Computing II (GCII) initiative, was to focus research on large-scale open distributed systems: a timely vision given the exponential growth of the Internet and the turmoil generated in the media and scientific fora of some international initiatives like the Semantic Web, and the peak of Napster usage in 2001 with more than 25 million users. Most projects had a highly interdisciplinary nature, and a large number of groups from theoretical computer science, agents, networks and databases worked together in a fruitful way. The focus of GCI was on three main topics: analysis of systems and security, languages and programming environments, and foundations of networks and large distributed systems. Along these lines, GCI projects dealt with formal techniques, mobility, distribution, security, trust, algorithms, and dynamics. The focus was ambitious and foundational, with an abstract view of computation at global level, having as particular examples the Grid of computers or the telephone network. The focus on GCII shifted towards issues that would help in the actual deployment of such big applications, namely, security, resource management, scalability, and distribution transparency.

Other approaches for large distributed systems (although with a limited degree of openness) include Peer-to-Peer (P2P) systems, where nodes in a graph act both as clients and servers and share a common ontology that permits easy bootstrapping and scalability, or Grid applications where the nodes in a graph share and interchange resources for the completion of a complex task. The Semantic Web proposal that has received large funding in the European Union and the USA is generating standards for ontology definition and tools for automatic annotation of web resources with meta-data. The size of the Semantic Web is growing at a fast pace. Finally, the increasing availability of web services has enabled a modular approach to solve complex systems by combining already available web services. The annotation of those through standards like WSDL or BPEL permits the automatic orchestration of solutions for complex tasks. Combinations of Semantic Web and Web services standards have been carried out (SAWSDL, SESA) by standardization bodies such as the W3C and OASIS. And finally a strong social approach to developing new collaborative web applications is at the heart of the Web 2.0 and 3.0 initiatives (Flickr, Digg).

There are diverging opinions regarding the similarities and differences between services, agents, peers, or nodes in distributed software systems. The terms usually imply different degrees of openness and autonomy of the system and its elements. Nevertheless, our stance is that the commonality is rooted in the interactions that can, in all cases, be abstracted to the establishment of *agreements for execution*, and a subsequent *execution of agreements*. In some cases these agreements are implicit, in others they are explicit, but in all cases we can understand the computing as a two-phase scenario where agreements are first generated and then executed.

This chapter is organised as follows. Section 1.2 analyses the concept of agreement from a Computing perspective, discussing the different types of agreements and agreement processes related to software. It also outlines challenges that need to be addressed as software components become increasingly adaptive and autonomic. Section 1.3 introduces the field of Agreement Technologies, where the complex patterns of interaction of software agents are mediated by the notion of agreement. It describes and relates the different technologies and application areas involved, and provides pointers to subsequent parts and chapters of this book. Finally, Sect. 1.4 provides an outlook and concludes.

1.2 Agreement from a Computing Perspective

The Computing Curricula 2005 Overview Report[1] defines Computing quite broadly as

> [...] any goal-oriented activity requiring, benefiting from, or creating computers. Thus, computing includes designing and building hardware and software systems for a wide range of purposes; processing, structuring, and managing various kinds of information; doing scientific studies using computers; making computer systems behave intelligently; creating and using communications and entertainment media; finding and gathering information relevant to any particular purpose, and so on. The list is virtually endless, and the possibilities are vast.

However, the same report acknowledges that “Computing also has other meanings that are more specific, based on the context in which the term is used”. In the end, the open distributed systems mentioned in the introduction are software systems as well, so in this section we take a foundational stance and look into the role of agreement and agreement processes in relation to programs and software development. We also identify challenges that will need to be addressed in an open world where software components become increasingly adaptive and autonomic.

[1] http://www.acm.org/education/curric_vols/CC2005-March06Final.pdf

1.2.1 *Agreement and Software*

Software development has traditionally been based on implicit agreements between programmers and language designers. Thanks to the formal semantics of programming languages specified by their designers, programmers are aware of the meaning of the computational concepts used to write and execute a program. For instance, programmers who use some imperative programming languages share the meaning of the concept of variable, value or loop as well as the notion of program state and state transition. There is no need for direct interaction between programmers and language designers – the meaning of the programming constructs is *fixed* before a particular program is designed, and will certainly remain *unchanged* during the execution of the program.

As software systems become bigger and more complex, more dynamic and explicit agreements between project leaders and programmers are needed, in order to establish and document the relationships between the different software components. These agreements (e.g. in the form of specifications of interface and behaviour) become then the basis for the subsequent implementation and verification of the resulting software product. They are established *dynamically* at design-time, as project leaders and programmers need to interact and discuss the component specifications. However, once such agreements are reached for all elements of the software system, they necessarily remain *unchanged* at execution-time.

But, when software systems and their elements become open, adaptive, and autonomic, it turns out to be impossible to explicitly define such agreements at design-time. Some software elements may need to interact with others that their programmer was unaware of at design-time. In addition, they cannot rely on complete functional descriptions of the elements that they interact with, as certain behaviours may vary at run-time in response to changes in the environment. Therefore, agreements need to forged *dynamically* at run-time, and there must be mechanisms for re-assessing and *revising* them as execution progresses.

Such agreements will need to rely on an explicit description of the interoperation between two independent pieces of code. They will certainly be multi-faceted and refer to different issues: to the meaning of the exchanged input/output variables, to the protocol to follow during the interaction and its exceptions, to the constraints to be respected during the computation (e.g. time, accuracy), etc. They will need to be generated at run-time by the two pieces of code themselves, perhaps by means of some particular type of built-in interaction between the software entities. This view requires that the interaction between two components starts by the generation (or perhaps selection) of the interoperation agreement, followed by a subsequent phase in which the actual interoperation of the parties takes place. Agreements can then evolve in a long term interoperation by further interaction between the computational entities. Agreements should become the basic run-time structures that determine whether a certain interaction is correct, in a similar way as type-checking currently determines if the values in a call to a procedure are correct. In summary, software components need to be "interaction-aware" by explicitly representing and reasoning about agreements and their associated processes.

1.2.2 Challenges

Software components willing to participate in open systems need extra capabilities to explicitly represent and generate agreements on top of the simpler capacity to interoperate. To define and implement these new capabilities, a large number of unsolved questions must be tackled that require a significant research effort and in some cases a completely new and disruptive vision. Following Sierra et al. (2011), in the sequel we briefly outline a few areas where new solutions for the establishment of agreements need to be developed. They are key to supporting the phase in which autonomous entities establish the agreements to interoperate.

1.2.2.1 Semantics

The openness in the development of agents, components, or services creates the need for semantic alignments between different ontologies. Every component may have an interface defined according to a (not necessarily shared) ontology. Although standards are in place for ontology representation (e.g. OWL) there is currently no scalable solution to establish agreements between software entities on the alignment of their semantics. The sheer dimension of some ontologies and the large number of them available on the web makes it impossible to solve the alignment problem entirely by hand, so robust computational mechanisms need to be designed. Techniques that might bring light into the problem include: data mining of background knowledge for the alignment algorithms, information flow methods to align concepts, or negotiation techniques to allow agents or services to autonomously negotiate agreements on the meaning of their interactions. Agreements on semantics are of a very fundamental nature and their establishment is key for the success of truly open software systems in the long run (Kalfoglou and Schorlemmer 2003).

1.2.2.2 Norms

The entities that interact with each other may have a behaviour that changes along time, and there may be different contexts within which to reach agreements. A way this context is defined and constrained is through the definition of conventions and norms regulating the interaction. What set of norms to use in an interaction is a matter of agreement between the entities. These and other considerations require that the code of entities be highly adaptive to its environment so that agreements including a normative context can be correctly interpreted and executed. This is not the case in current software development. For instance, most current approaches to service programming assume a static environment, and the classical approaches to code verification still focus on static verification techniques. Adaptive code is a necessity for the design of open distributed applications. In particular, programming will need to face issues like norm adoption and behaviour learning. Agreements are explicit and declarative, and thus they open the door to using model checking and logic based approaches, like BDI. These techniques may make open entities norm-aware and endow them with the capacity to build cognitive models of their environment. For recent discussions see Andrighetto et al. (2012).

1.2.2.3 Organisations

Many tasks require the recruiting of agents or services to form teams or compound services. These software entities bring in different capabilities that, when put together, may solve a complex task. How many entities have to be involved and what tasks have to be associated to each one of them are difficult questions. Traditional planning systems and balancing algorithms are not well adapted due to the large search space and the high dynamics and uncertainty of an open environment where software entities may join or leave or stop behaving cooperatively at any time. Thus, new techniques need to be developed to underpin agreements between open and possibly unreliable computational resources in order to forge stable co-operation for the time needed to solve a task.

Business process modelling systems and languages (e.g. BPEL or BPEL4WS) (Ko et al. 2009) have made the interaction between activities and entities the central concept in software design. A detailed workflow regulates the activities and the combination of roles in an organisation as well as their associated data flow. The interaction between entities is modelled as a precise choreography of message interchanges. However, current approaches assume that the orchestration and choreography is external to the entities and static. In an open world the way entities will interact and be combined has to be determined on-the-fly. And this choreography in an evolving world must necessarily be part of the agreement between entities. Agreeing on the workflow of activities implies reaching agreements on the role structure, the flow of roles among activities, and most importantly the normative system associated to the workflow. In a sense the signing of an agreement between two entities is the decision on what workflow to follow. Techniques from the field of coordination models and languages are particularly promising in this context (Ossowski and Menezes 2006).

1.2.2.4 Negotiation

Most programming languages and methodologies base their semantics on a compositional view of code. Knowing the behaviour of the components, and how they are combined, we can know the overall behaviour. This approach is to a large extent not applicable to open software systems where the behaviour of the components cannot be totally known or analysed, and can only be observed. They are black boxes. Even though the behaviour of an entity can be restricted by the normative context and the agreements signed, it is not completely determined at component definition time. Moreover, setting agreements does not give total guarantees on behaviour: autonomy and self-interest may mean agents refrain from honouring their commitments if there is a potential gain in so doing. New and radically different approaches are required to deal with this problem.

The interaction between software components depends on two types of dynamics. First, open systems evolve, new entities appear and disappear, and thus new agreements have to be set. Second, the rules of the game that regulate the interaction between two entities might change due to the establishment of new agreements between them and due to agreements with third parties. This dynamics is a true challenge as many traditional research solutions are based on a static world view (e.g. game theory, classic planning). Given that the entities are autonomous and black boxes to each other the only way agreements can be reached is via negotiation of its terms and conditions. Negotiation is the key technique to achieving a composition of behaviours capable of dealing with the dynamics of open software systems (Jennings et al. 2001; Kraus 1997). Some of the challenges are how to efficiently negotiate the terms of an agreement, how to explore large spaces of solutions, how to establish trade-offs between the dimensions of the agreements or how to use the experience of human negotiation in software development. Computational models from the field of argumentation will also be relevant in facilitating and speeding up the process of reaching such agreements.

1.2.2.5 Trust

There are two basic security dimensions over open networks. The first is how to guarantee identity, and this is to a large extent solved by cryptographic methods. The second is how to guarantee behaviour. Entities sign agreements and these agreements have to be honoured by the signatories. In the case where the entities' code is available for inspection, recent results on Proof Carrying Code techniques provide an answer (Hermenegildo et al. 2005; Necula and Lee 1997). These techniques permit the mobile code itself to define properties of its behaviour and to carry a formal proof that it satisfies the behaviour. Source code and properties are input to compilers that generate executable code and certificates which permit to verify that the code has not been tampered with. However, when the code is not mobile, as in the area of web services (where the service is executed remotely), the possibility of fraud and malevolent behaviour creates a security threat to applications. No definitive solution has been found yet.

Trust models summarise the observations of the execution of agreements and allow entities to decide whether to sign agreements again with the same entity or which entity to prefer for particular tasks (Jøsang et al. 2007). Reputation measures are needed to bootstrap the signing of agreements between entities. There are two challenges that need to be addressed to guarantee behaviour: on semantics of the agreements and on social relations between entities. Trust and reputation models need to take into account semantic aspects of the agreements to permit entities to understand the relationship between past experiences and new ones. Social network measures are needed to understand the intentions of the entities and therefore predict their behaviour (e.g. they may be cheating to favour a friend). In this sense, the relationships built over time among entities and/or their principals may also provide guarantees of behaviour (Sierra and Debenham 2006).

1.3 Agreements Among Software Agents

In this section, we shift our attention to open distributed systems whose elements are *software agents*. There is still no consensus where to draw the border between programs or objects on the one hand and software agents on the other (Franklin and Graesser 1997; Wooldridge 1997). Perhaps the most commonly accepted characterisation of the term was introduced by Wooldridge and Jennings (1995), who put forward four key hallmarks of agenthood:

- *Autonomy*: agents should be able to perform the majority of their problem solving tasks without the direct intervention of humans or other agents, and they should have a degree of control over their own actions and their own internal state.
- *Social ability*: agents should be able to interact, when they deem appropriate, with other software agents and humans in order to complete their own problem solving and to help others with their activities where appropriate.
- *Responsiveness*: agents should perceive their environment (which may be the physical world, a user, a collection of agents, the INTERNET, etc.) and respond in a timely fashion to changes which occur in it.
- *Proactiveness*: agents should not simply act in response to their environment, they should be able to exhibit opportunistic, goal-directed behaviour and take the initiative where appropriate.

For the purpose of this chapter (and this book in general), we remark that, in order to show the aforementioned properties, the interactions of the software agent with its environment (and with other agents) must be guided by a reasonably complex program, capable of rather sophisticated activities such as reasoning, learning, or planning.

Our vision is a new paradigm for next-generation open distributed systems, where interactions between software agents are based on the concept of agreement. It relies on two main ingredients: firstly, a normative model that defines the "rules of the game" that software agents and their interactions must comply with; and secondly, an interaction model where agreements are first established and then enacted. Agreement Technologies (AT) refer to a sandbox of methods, platforms, and tools to define, specify and verify such systems. This book compiles the state of the art of research activities in Europe, and worldwide, working towards the achievement of the aforementioned goal.

This part of the book analyses the notion of agreement and agreement processes from different viewpoints, in particular from a perspective of Philosophy and

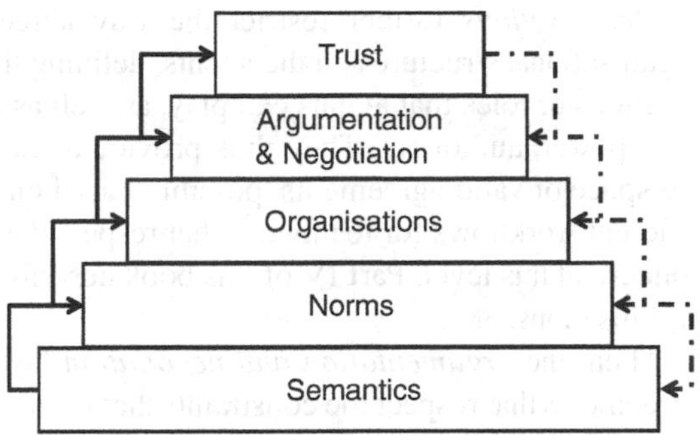

Fig. 1.1 AT tower

Sociology of Law (Chap. 2) and of Cognitive and Social Science (Chap. 3), thus contributing to putting AT on solid conceptual foundations. Parts II–VI describe in detail the different technologies involved, while Part VII provides examples of real-world applications of AT and their potential impact. In what follows, we give a short overview of the different technologies involved in AT and relate them to each other. We also outline how, by gluing together these technologies, novel applications in a variety of domains can be constructed.

1.3.1 Agreement Technologies

The basic elements of the AT sandbox are related to the challenges outlined in Sect. 1.2.2, covering the fields of semantics, norms, organisations, argumentation and negotiation, as well as trust and reputation. However, we are dealing with open distributed systems made up of software agents, so more sophisticated and computationally expensive models and mechanisms than the ones mentioned in Sect. 1.2.2 can be applied.

The key research fields of AT can be conceived of in a tower structure, where each level provides functionality to the levels above, as depicted in Fig. 1.1.

Semantic technologies constitute the bottom layer, as semantic problems pervade all the others. Solutions to semantic mismatches and alignment of ontologies are essential, so agents can reach a common understanding on the elements of agreements. In this manner, a shared multi-faceted "space" of agreements can be conceived, providing essential information to the remaining layers. Part II of this book is dedicated to semantic technologies.

The next level is concerned with the definition of *norms* determining constraints that the agreements, and the processes leading to them, should satisfy. Thus, norms can be conceived of as a means to "shaping" the space of valid agreements. Norms may change over time, so support for the adaptation of the behaviour of software agents and of the normative system itself is to be provided. Part III of this book provides a survey of the field of norms.

Organisations further restrict the way agreements are reached by imposing organisational structures on the agents, defining the goals and capabilities of certain positions or roles that agents can play, as well as a set of relationships among them (e.g. power, authority). They thus provide a way to efficiently design and evolve the space of valid agreements, possibly based on normative concepts. Determining efficient workflows for teamwork that respect the organisational structures is also a concern at this level. Part IV of this book describes the state of the art in the field of organisations.

Then, the *argumentation and negotiation* layer provides methods for reaching agreements that respect the constraints that norms and organisations impose over the agents. This can be seen as choosing certain points in the space of valid agreements. Again, support for dynamicity is of foremost importance, so agreements can be adapted to changing circumstances. Part V of this book gives an overview of computational argumentation and negotiation models.

Finally, the *trust and reputation* layer provides methods to summarise the history of agreements and subsequent agreement executions in order to build long-term relationships between the agents. They keep track of as to how far the agreements reached respect the constraints put forward by norms and organisations. Trust and reputation are the technologies that complement traditional security mechanisms by relying on social mechanisms that interpret the behaviour of agents. Part VI of this book describes the state of the art in this field.

Even though one can clearly see the main flow of information from the bottom towards the top layers, results of upper layers can also produce useful feedback that can be exploited at lower levels. For instance, as mentioned above, norms and trust can be conceived as a priori and a posteriori approaches, respectively, to security. Therefore, in an open and dynamic world it will certainly make sense for the results of trust models to have a certain impact on the evolution of norms.

In fact, such “direct relations” between layers are manifold, and different chapters of this book study them in detail. Chapter 15 is devoted to analysing the complex relationship between norms and trust. In Chap. 16 an overview of the existing work in the field of argumentation and norms is presented. Chapter 25 discusses how argumentation can be used in trust and reputation models and vice versa. Chapter 26 is devoted to relating ontologies, semantics and reputation, presenting several approaches to the problem of how agents can talk about trust and reputation among them. Finally, Chap. 28 analyses how reputation can influence different dimensions of an organization.

Some techniques and tools are orthogonal to the AT tower structure. The topics of environments and infrastructures (García-Fornes et al. 2011), for instance, pervade all layers. In much the same way, coordination models and mechanisms (Omicini et al. 2004; Ossowski 2008) are not just relevant to the third layer of Fig. 1.1, but cross-cut the other parts of the AT tower as well. Where appropriate, these tools and techniques are presented within the context of a particular application within Part VII of the book.

1.3.2 Key Domains

There is no limitation per se regarding the domains where AT can be successfully applied. Still, in this section we have chosen three broad areas that we believe are particularly attractive in the context of this book: firstly, because the problems and challenges in these areas are of significant socio-economic relevance, so that applications based on AT can actually make a difference; and secondly because applications in these fields usually require the simultaneous use of several of the AT building blocks, thus illustrating the integration of the different layers outlined in the previous section.

E-Commerce is certainly a major application domain for AT, as the challenges for efficiently supporting business transactions neatly fit the building blocks of AT: negotiation and argumentation are often essential for agreeing on effective deals, transactions take place within a specific normative and organisational context, trust models are pervasive in electronic marketplaces, semantic matching and alignment is crucial to find and compare goods in a meaningful manner, etc. Part VII provides several examples of AT-based applications for e-Commerce. Chapters 32 and 36 describe applications that support Business-to-Business interactions in a dynamic and adaptive manner (to this respect, see also the comments on crowdsourcing in Chap. 2). Chapters 30 and 37 show how AT, and in particular argumentation models, can be used in Business-to-Consumer scenarios for customer support and product guidance, respectively.

Transportation Management is another candidate domain for applying AT-based solutions. Transportation is certainly a large-scale open distributed system, where the self-interested behaviour of agents (drivers, passengers, etc.) is organised by a set of norms (traffic rules), some transport modes are more reliable (trustworthy) than others, etc. In this context, Chap. 31 describes the on-the-fly generation and adaptive management of transport chains using AT. Chapter 35 illustrates how AT can be used to effectively manage fleets of ambulances. Another strand of work in the transportation field refers to next-generation intelligent road infrastructures. For instance, vehicle-to-vehicle and vehicle-to-infrastructure communication can be used for novel approaches to intersection management based on negotiation and auctions (Vasirani and Ossowski 2012), and semantic technologies are essential for dynamically locating and selecting traffic information and management services (Fernández and Ossowski 2011).

AT are particularly well-suited for *E-Governance* applications as well, as it provides methods and tools for modelling, simulating, and evaluating processes and policies involving citizens and public administrations. Chapters 33 and 34 show how the electronic institution framework (Arcos et al. 2005) (see also Chap. 18) can be used to build a detailed model of real-world water rights markets, including negotiation and grievance procedures, as well as to simulate and evaluate their dynamics.

A plethora of other domains are candidates to become the playground for AT in the future. Among them, the field of *smart energy grids* is currently receiving much attention. In the energy grids of tomorrow, thousands or even millions of small-scale producers of renewable energy (solar, wind, etc.) will be distributed across the transmission as well as distribution networks and – taking into account certain norms and regulations – may decide to act together temporarily as *virtual power plants*. Through *demand side management* strategies (which may involve negotiation and trust models), neigbourhoods could coordinate (shift) their demands so as to adapt to the contingencies of intermittent renewable generation (see Ramchurn et al. (2012) for an overview). Some interesting overlap with the transportation domain becomes apparent when challenges such as coordinating the recharging process of large groups of electric vehicles, or employing the unused battery capacity of vehicles as a huge distributed storage facility come into play (Vasirani and Ossowski 2013).

1.4 Outlook and Conclusion

In this chapter we have analysed the relevance of the notion of agreement and agreement processes from a Computing perspective. Open distributed systems are going to be the norm in software development, and the interoperation of software entities will need to rely on a declarative concept of agreement that is autonomously signed and executed by the entities themselves. We have presented a number of challenges for representation languages and programming techniques that need to be addressed in order to adequately support this type of software development. We then introduced Agreement Technologies as a sandbox of methods, platforms, and tools to define, specify and verify next-generation open distributed systems where interactions between software agents are based on the concept of agreement. The building blocks of AT comprise otherwise disparate research areas, such as semantics, norms, organisations, argumentation and negotiation, as well as trust and reputation. We show how they can be integrated into a natural tower structure, and provide examples of domains of socio-economic relevance, where new types of innovative applications were built by gluing together these technologies.

In this book we describe the state of the art of research and applications in the field of Agreement Technologies. Besides further progress in the development of methods and tools in the AT key areas, and an even tighter coupling of them, we would like to point to some complementary lines of work to be addressed in the future. First of all, a deeper integration of AT with the fields of programming and software engineering should be sought. This will require further formalisation and standardisation of AT, perhaps based on a graded notion of agreements and a set of alternative agreement processes of different complexity, so as to be able to balance expressiveness and computational complexity depending on the requirements of a particular setting. The analysis of the relation of AT to Semantic Web standards put forward in Chap. 4 constitutes a step in this direction.

Another exciting enterprise refers to efforts for smoothening the boundary between the human space and the computational space, by extending the AT paradigm to include not just software agents but also *human agents*. For this purpose, the AT sandbox needs to be extended, so as to support systems in which humans work in partnership with highly inter-connected computational agents. Adaptation of the normative context, adjustable autonomy and recognition of user intentions are some of the characteristics that should be covered from a theoretical and practical perspective. Semantics, norms, argumentation, learning, behavioural modelling and human-agent collaboration are additional building blocks needed for the specification, enactment, and maintenance of such systems. The v-mWater application of Chap. 34, for instance, is specifically geared towards supporting the interaction between humans and software agents. Also, Chap. 21 on argumentation makes some steps in this direction: it not only describes methods and techniques for argumentation to aid machine reasoning but also shows how methods and techniques for argumentation can aid human reasoning.

Acknowledgements The term "Agreement Technologies" was introduced by Michael Wooldridge in conversations at the AAMAS conference in 2004. It was also used by Nicholas R. Jennings as title for a keynote talk given in 2005. Carles Sierra was among the first to give shape to the field by defining five key areas as technological building blocks for AT in 2007.

This work was partially supported by the Spanish Ministry of Science and Innovation through the project "Agreement Technologies" (CONSOLIDER CSD2007-0022, INGENIO 2010). The authors would like to thank Matteo Vasirani for inspiring discussions on the challenges of extending Agreement Technologies to mixed societies of human and software agents.

References

Andrighetto, G., G. Governatori, P. Noriega, and L. van der Torre. 2012. Dagstuhl Seminar Proceedings 12111: Normative Multi-Agent Systems. http://www.dagstuhl.de/12111.

Arcos, J.L., M. Esteva, P. Noriega, J.A. Rodríguez, and C. Sierra. 2005. Engineering open environments with electronic institutions. *Journal on Engineering Applications of Artificial Intelligence* 18(2): 191–204.

Fernández, A., and S. Ossowski. 2011. A multiagent approach to the dynamic enactment of semantic transportation services. *IEEE Transactions on Intelligent Transportation Systems* 12(2): 333–342.

Franklin, S., and A. Graesser. 1997. Is it an agent, or just a program? A taxonomy for autonomous agents. In *Intelligent agents III, agent theories, architectures, and languages*. Lecture Notes in Computer Science, vol. 1193, 21–35. Heidelberg: Springer.

García-Fornes, A., J. Hübner, A. Omicini, J.A. Rodríguez-Aguilar, and V. Botti. 2011. Infrastructures and tools for multiagent systems for the new generation of distributed systems. *Engineering Applications of AI* 24(7): 1095–1097.

Hermenegildo, M., E. Albert, P. López-García, and G. Puebla. 2005. Abstraction carrying code and resource-awareness. In *Principle and practice of declarative programming (PPDP-2005)*, 1–11. New York: ACM.

Jennings, N., P. Faratin, A. Lomuscio, S. Parsons, C. Sierra, and M. Wooldridge. 2001. Automated negotiation: prospects, methods and challenges. *International Journal of Group Decision and Negotiation* 10(2): 199–215.

Jøsang, A., R. Ismail, and C. Boyd. 2007. A survey of trust and reputation systems for online service provision. *Decision Support Systems* 43(2): 618–644.

Kalfoglou, Y., and M. Schorlemmer. 2003. IF-Map – an ontology-mapping method based on information-flow theory. In *Journal on Data Semantics I*. Lecture Notes in Computer Science, ed. S. Spaccapietra, S. March, and K. Aberer, vol. 2800, 98–127. Heidelberg: Springer.

Ko, R.K.L., S.S.G. Lee, and E.W. Lee. 2009. Business process management (bpm) standards: A survey. *Business Process Management Journal* 15(5): 744–791.

Kraus, S. 1997. Negotiation and cooperation in multi-agent environments. *Artificial Intelligence* 94(1–2): 79–97.

Necula, G.C., and P. Lee. 1997. Proof-carrying code. In *24th symposium on principles of programming languages (POPL-1997)*, 106–109, New York: ACM.

Omicini, A., S. Ossowski, and A. Ricci. 2004. Coordination infrastructures in the engineering of multiagent systems. In *Methodologies and software engineering for agent systems – the agent-oriented software engineering handbook*, 273–296. Boston/London: Kluwer.

Ossowski, S., and R. Menezes. 2006. On coordination and its significance to distributed and multi-agent systems. *Concurrency and Computation: Practice and Experience* 18(4): 359–370.

Ossowski, S. 2008. Coordination in multi-agent systems – towards a technology of agreement. In *Multiagent system technologies (MATES-2008)*. Lecture Notes in Computer Science, vol. 5244, 2–12. Heidelberg: Springer.

Ramchurn, S., P. Vytelingum, A. Rogers, and N. Jennings. 2012. Putting the "Smarts" into the smart grid: A grand challenge for artificial intelligence. *Communications of the ACM* 55(4), 86–97.

Sierra, C., and J. Debenham. 2006. Trust and honour in information-based agency. In *Proceedings of the 5th international conference on autonomous agents and multi agent systems*, 1225–1232. New York: ACM.

Sierra, C., V. Botti, and S. Ossowski. 2011. Agreement computing. *Künstliche Intelligenz* 25(1): 57–61.

Vasirani, M., and S. Ossowski. 2012. A market-inspired approach for intersection management in urban road traffic networks. *Journal of Artificial Intelligence Research (JAIR)* 43: 621–659.

Vasirani, M., and S. Ossowski. 2013. A proportional share allocation mechanism for coordination of plug-in electric vehicle charging. *Journal on Engineering Applications of Artificial Intelligence*. http://dx.doi.org/10.1016/j.engappai.2012.10.008.

Wooldridge, M., and N. Jennings. 1995. Intelligent agents – theory and practice. *Knowledge Engineering Review* 10(2): 115–152.

Wooldridge, M. 1997. Agents as a rorschach test: A response to franklin and graesser. In *Intelligent agents III, agent theories, architectures, and languages*. Lecture Notes in Computer Science, vol. 1193, 47–48. Heidelberg: Springer.

Chapter 2
Agreement and Relational Justice: A Perspective from Philosophy and Sociology of Law

Pompeu Casanovas

2.1 Introduction: Relational Justice

In Chap. 1, Ossowski, Sierra and Botti (Ossowski et al. 2012) introduced the issue of computing agreements. This chapter addresses the issue of legal agreements in a complementary way. The web fosters *personalization* and *democratization* (D'Aquin et al. 2008). I will refer to these legal forms as *relational justice*. From a theoretical point of view, let's assume broadly that relational justice intersects with *relational law* – the concrete social and economic bonds among the parties in business, companies, corporations or other organizations. User-centered strategies of the next Semantic Web generation – the so-called *Web of Data* – fit well into this perspective, in which rights and duties belong to a new regulatory framework because the networked information environment is transforming the marketplace and the relationship with the state. Cloud computing, cooperation, multiple use of mobile phones, crowdsourcing, and web services orientation constitute the next step for the World Wide Web. This is the social environment of the relational justice field, where scenarios and contexts are shaped from a hybrid use of different technologies by a multitude of different users (including MAS).

However, from the legal point of view, all that seems new can sink into the deep waters of the legal ocean. What does "agreement" mean in this kind of ecological environment? How can it be understood and theorized? *And how does it link with what "agreement" means in the rich legal tradition?*

This chapter, planned as a conceptual and historical overview, deals with the latter question. The issue around the concept of agreement in law is addressed in Sect. 2.2. Section 2.3 shows three different ways of theorizing agreements

P. Casanovas (✉)
Institute of Law and Technology, Faculty of Law, Universitat Autonoma de Barcelona, 08193, Barcelona, Spain
e-mail: pompeu.casanovas@uab.cat

S. Ossowski (ed.), *Agreement Technologies*, Law, Governance and Technology Series 8, DOI 10.1007/978-94-007-5583-3_2,

in the legal theory of the twentieth century. Section 2.4 describes the origins and development of relational law. Finally, I will discuss some implications for agreement technologies in Sect. 2.5.

2.2 Agreement in Law

One of the most popular online legal Dictionaries differentiates two different meanings of "agreement" in law: "1) any meeting of the minds, even without legal obligation; 2) another name for a contract including all the elements of a legal contract: offer, acceptance, and consideration (payment or performance), based on specific terms."[1] These two meanings are carried on by a multitude of different legal words, which can be nuanced regarding to the specific terms and conditions of the agreement.[2] The "languages" of law, the symbols through which law is expressed, conveyed and formulated, encompass all forms of ancient and modern natural languages (Mellinkoff 1963), and foster legal dictums and mottos – the ancient (and not always consistent) *brocards*. For example *Conventio vincit legem* (Agreements overrule statutes), *Conventio facit legem* (Agreements make the law), or *Pacta sunt servanda* (Agreements must be kept).

It is worthwhile highlighting the strength of agreements in ancient and medieval law. In pre-modern societies ties among relatives, social groups and the community had the additional value of being a survival bond in everyday life (Watson 1989). We can understand then the non-intuitive point of a value-correlated chain between the two legal meanings pointed out, the epistemic and the behavioral one – the *implicit* cognitive agreement about something, and the *explicit* proactive and intentional agreement on some plan of action or expected behavior.

From the political point of view, the problem may be formulated as the limitation of the ruler's power (usually the monarch, but often the tyrant). From the legal point of view, it goes as the birth of the obligation to fulfill the agreement because of the existence of this same agreement. When might it be enforced? At what moment does the *obligatio* appear, the binding power that qualifies as enforceable the link between the subjects of the agreement? And, even more important, can regulatory effects of agreements exist outside of legal formalism?

---

[1] http://legal-dictionary.thefreedictionary.com/agreement

[2] (I) Agreement as concurrence: *accord, amity, arrangement, assent, common assent, common consent, common view, community of interests, concord, conformance, congruence, congruency, congruity, consent, consentaneity, consentaneousness, consentience, consonance, cooperation, good understanding, harmony, meeting of the minds, mutual assent, mutual promise, mutual understanding, oneness, reciprocity of obligation, settlement, unanimity, understanding, uniformity, unison, unity*. (II) Agreement as contract: *alliance, arrangement, bargain, binding promise, bond, commitment, compact, concordat, concordia, contractual statement, convention, covenant, deal, engagement, legal document, mutual pledge, obligation, pact, pledge, settlement, transaction, understanding, undertaking.*

This was the origin of the theory of *causality* in law, as explained by Lorenzen (1919):

> Roman law, even in the last stage of its development, did not enforce an agreement unless it could be brought under certain well-defined heads of contracts or pacts. In the time of Justinian all agreements would become actionable by being clothed in the form of a *stipulation*, which for practical purposes may be regarded as equivalent to a written form. (...). In all real contracts the obligation arose not from the agreement of the parties but from the delivery of property or the performance of the plaintiff's promise, that is, in our terminology, from an executed consideration.[3]

In other words, *nude pacts* were not enforceable unless they entered into a more concrete formal way, in a process of ritualization in which certain use of words and *mise en scene* to produce artificial effects close to religion and magic were due.[4] These legal grounds were the *causa* of the contract. An agreement had to show an underlying "cause" to become a contract. There were no contracts *sine causa*, "without cause".

> With us an agreement is actionable unless there is some reason why it should not be so. With the Romans an agreement was not actionable unless there was some reason why it should be so. (Buckland, quoted by Lorenzen (1919))

I think that at least three consequences can be drawn from this statement: (i) asserting what a legal agreement is or could be is a theoretical issue, in which jurists have been involved since Roman times; (ii) defining 'agreement' as a concept means activating at the same time a certain degree of inner knowledge of the legal system in which the definition works; (iii) discrete categories of agreement are at odds with the continuum between nude pacts and more coercive forms of contracts.

Taxonomies are entrenched with the concrete performance of types of agreements susceptible to variations. A set of "nearly considered" contracts do exist either in the Roman or in contemporary Civil Law.[5] Lorenzen's conclusion is nowadays a common belief.[6] What happened, then?

---

[3]In the Common Law consideration is the correlative of causa in the Civil Law. "Something of value given by both parties to a contract that induces them to enter into the agreement to exchange mutual performances." http://legal-dictionary.thefreedictionary.com/consideration

[4]But see the warning by MacCormack (1969) on going too far in the "magical" interpretation of law in pre-modern societies

[5]Cf. Radin (1937). The Institutes of Justinian (III, 13) divided obligations "into four species"; *ex contractu, quasiex contractu; ex maleficio, quasi ex maleficio*, i.e. contract, quasicontract; tort, quasi-tort. Gaius, (about 150 A.D.) listed only contract, tort and an unclassifiable miscellaneous group, *ex variis causarum figuris.*

[6]"There is in reality no definable 'doctrine' of causa. The term 'causa' includes a variety of notions which may equally well be derived from the nature of a juristic act and from considerations of equity" (Lorenzen 1919). See also Orestano (1989).

The most natural explanation is the emergence of the modern State in the Seventeenth century, and the formulation of the legal framework of the Rule of Law in the nineteenth century. One of the main contributors to the doctrine of causality in law was Jean Domat (1625–1696), the French jurist who at the same time, within the *Traité des loix*,[7] organized in one single legal body the public order system of Louis XIV. There is a direct line from this theoretical body and the French Civil Code (1804), through which Napoléon intended the political reconstruction of the nation-state, stemming from the administrative organization of the Ancien Régime.[8]

Dialogue as a source of law disappeared from legal thought with the construction of the Monarchic state.[9] Since 18th century agreements as covenants or pacts adopted other legal forms and had other roles, either grounding civil codes in the new private space or constitutions in the public one. From 19th century onwards, what lies behind the gradual compulsory enforcement of a legal agreement is the compulsory force of the State under the Rule of Law.

2.3 Agreement in Legal Theory

Legal theory in the 20th c. took this mutual embedment between law and the state seriously. Although it may come as a surprise, thinking simultaneously of a theory of both law and the state was not commonplace on jurisprudence until the last third of 19th c., after the unification of the German State in 1871.

Perhaps the first full theory of this kind is Georg Jellinek's *Allgemeine Staatslehre* (1900). It was clear for him, following previous Romanist (i.e. von Jhering, Gerber) and Germanist (i.e. von Gierke) scholars, that the State could be considered a moral person, capable of holding rights and duties. If this is so, the private notion of agreement could be expanded to the public sphere: as subjects of law, states would behave and act as a person, and the regulatory value of agreements between private persons – their 'subjective rights' – would be defined by the 'objective' laws of the states in the public sphere.

---

[7]The Traité des Loix is the preface of *Les lois civiles dans leur ordre naturel* (1689), in which Domat equated Roman and Civil Law with rational order and with Christian principles. Law is *Raison écrite*.

[8]See the intellectual and personal genealogy from Domat (16th c.), Pothier (17th c.), and the nine drafters of the Civile Code (19th c.) in Arnaud (1973). See also Tarello (1978).

[9]I have developed this subject in Casanovas (2010). For a specific study on the transformation of humanist dialectics and rhetoric in 16th c. and 17th c., cf. Ong (1958) and Fumaroli (1980).

2.3.1 Hans Kelsen

This is the path trodden by Hans Kelsen's *Reine Rechtslehre* (The Pure Theory of Law) as well. In its last version, as late as 1960, he still fights the 'fiction' of freedom of self-determination as a source of law.[10]

To me, this denial is not what counts or is important in Kelsen's approach, for what he was really questioning through the critique of the concept of autonomy was the concept of legality itself. Why can we qualify an act legal or illegal? How to define the obligation to do or not do something as legal? Kelsen would set up his theory of norms to answer these kind of questions. He conceived it as a complementary balance between norms – "schemes of interpretation", "the meaning of acts of will" – and normative decisions, in which the link between norms and facts would be performed by the formal quality of their normative content – the property of *validity*. Norms had to be legally 'valid' to acquire a 'binding' character and be applied. In such a conception, the State was conceived as a logical *prius*, in a pure neo-Kantian way.

It is not my aim to go deeper into this. It is worth noticing that Kelsen broadened the space in which to discuss legal issues on different grounds other than plain jurisprudence. Instead of discussing at only the level of positive legal doctrine, he would have shown the need to structure a coherent theory about the tools employed to describe and operate within legal systems. And nevertheless, his conceptual framework remained solidly anchored to the same doctrinal bases he tried to overcome. As Ross (2011) (1936) would put it on the first edition of the full version of the theory (1935), in Kelsen's view "legal science is not social theory but *normative cognition*, doctrine [emphasis added, P.C.]".

2.3.2 Alf Ross

However, although he wanted legal theory to be a non-doctrinal social science clearing up old and broad legal concepts, Ross remained close to Kelsen as regards to the reflecting value of agreements as a source of law. His argument is interesting to follow, because in his major work he would compare agreements to promises:

> If it has been agreed that in order to gain admittance to a private night club a person must utter a meaningless word, this word in itself will remain meaningless even if by agreement it functions as a directive to the doorkeeper. The position is exactly the same in pronouncing a promise. In itself, abstracted from the legal order, the expression 'I promise' is meaningless. It would just do as well to say abracadabra. But by the effect the legal order attaches to the formula it functions as a directive to the judge and can be used by private parties for the exercise of their autonomy (Ross 1959).

---

[10]"The fictiousness of this definition of the concept of the subject of law is apparent. (...). The legal determination ultimately originates in the objective law and not in the legal subjects subordinated to it. Consequently there is no full self-determination even in private law." (Kelsen 1967: 170–171; see 258 as well)

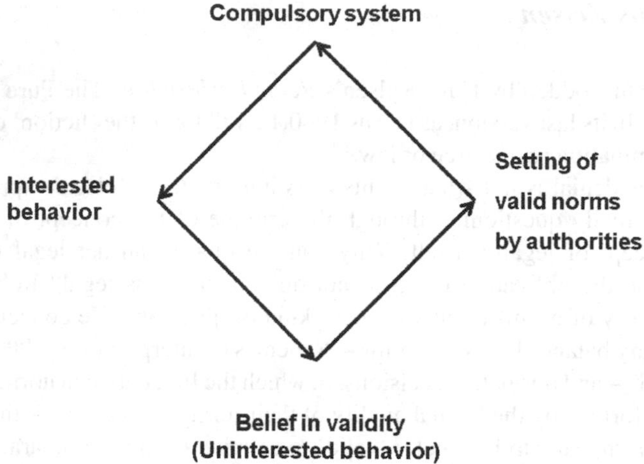

Fig. 2.1 Compliance with the law (Source: Ross (1946))

Should we substitute doorkeeper for judge, the private nightclub for the legal order and abracadabra for the 'will' of an agreement (or a promise) and we would obtain a quite precise – and unintended kafkian – image of Ross' legal theory. "A legal rule is neither true nor false; it is a directive" (ibid.) addressed to judge, that is to say, an utterance "with no representative meaning but with intent to exert influence" (ibid.).[11] What counts then is the binding force- of a "national legal order", which is an integrated body of rules whose function is to carry out the exercise of this physical force.

We need two more ideas to complete the picture: (i) Compliance with rules and rule enforcement are related through patterns of behavior, operating in judges' mind or in the legal consciousness of the population, which eventually would agree to comply with the law according to the dynamics shown in Fig. 2.1; (ii) 'validity' is an empirical property of rules related to the judges' behavior, for "valid law is never a historical fact, but a calculation, with regard to future" (ibid.). 'Validity' stands for the binding force of the law, but it is not an inter-normative property, for it cannot be derived from norms but stems from the social behavior itself – "the relation between the normative idea content and the social reality" (ibid.).

Ross' positions and the so-called Scandinavian realism have been recently revisited by legal theorists. For our purposes, I will single out only two revisions. The first one points at what Ross left out of the legal system: reasoning through the "intermediate legal concepts" of jurisprudence, the semantics of law. The second is

[11]The interested reader is invited to follow the late formulation of the argument in Ross (1968): "Directives which are impersonal and heteronomous-autonomous include the rule of games and similar arrangements grounded on agreements."

in a sense complementary to the former one. It states the proximity between social positivism and Ross's approaches to fundamental problems, mainly the problem of validity of legal rules.

By intermediate legal concepts are meant "those concepts through which legal norms convey both legal consequences and preconditions of further legal effects" (Sartor 2009a). Sartor uses the term *inferential links* (broader than legal norms, or rules) to describe how legal concepts (but other concepts as well, e.g. moral or social) can carry on and transfer meaning. He is embracing then the Fregian view according to which the meaning of a term results from the set of inferential links concerning the *sentences* in which the term occurs (ibid.).

This view was advanced by Ross in a famous paper, Tû-Tû (1957), in which he figured out a fictional society with concepts representing fictional facts or states of mind (tû-tû).

> FOR ANY (x) IF x eats of the chief's food THEN x is tû-tû, which really means, connecting this factual precondition to deontic conclusions FOR ANY (x) IF x eats of the chief's food THEN x should be purified, or x is forbidden from participating in rites.

Ross aims at stating that these kind of intermediate terms are also fictional, because they are not adding any deontic meaning to the whole reasoning and they are not needed to represent any semantic content. This reproduces the abracadabra argument for promises: doctrines about *ownership*, or other legal concepts such as *claims* or *rights*, are just meaningless terms to facilitate the deontic conclusions in a legal order. From a theoretical point of view they are useless, and we should get rid of them. This task "is a simple example of reduction by reason to systematic order" (Ross 1957).

We encounter here the rejection of the "magic" power of words, one of the subject-matters of Hägerström philosophy (Pattaro 2010). However, asserting that the concept of right has no substance is quite different from stating that it does not carry any meaning.

Sartor is proposing an alternative solution, setting an inferential field for legal meanings to encompass dogmatic concepts as well within the legal system. As I will show later on, this position has to do with the possibility to reasoning with ontologies in the web. However, it takes into account also what we may call the *pervasiveness* and *resilience* of some fundamental legal concepts that bridge the common understanding of what law is about.

2.3.3 H.L.A. Hart

Law expressed through its common or natural language, the semantics of law, constitutes the timber of perhaps the most influential work of legal theory in the 20th century, Herbert Hart's *The Concept of law* (1961) (Hart 1960).

I will chose an indirect approach here, because I will bring to the fore the second revision I mentioned above. It deals with the natural language in which Ross expressed his analysis, and it comes from the new generation of the Scandinavian legal theory that he helped to build. Eng (2011) explains that the most central technical term in Alf Ross's book *Om ret og retfærdighed* (1953) (translated as *On Law and Justice*, 1959) is *gældende ret* (valid law, in Danish).[12] This corresponds to the Norwegian term *gjeldende rett* and the Swedish term *gällande rätt*.

Those Scandinavian terms have been translated into English as *validity*, but have different uses which express a broader and more context-sensitive meaning. In Latin languages, e.g., *gældende ret* has been translated by *derecho vigente*, *diritto vigente* or *droit en vigueur* for it points at the efficacy of the legal rules as well.

Hart made the review of Ross's book, pointing at the differences between their theories. Shortly after, he published *The Concept of Law* (1960), in which he sets up a broad conceptual framework to elucidate the meaning of the most common legal concepts assuming that law is embedded into society and it *rules* over their members, including the members of the ruling elite.

Social and legal rules are differentiated, because in complex societies rules with social content adopt a legal form, according to which secondary rules – of change, adjudication, and recognition – operate over the primary ones, controlling the production, enforcement and implementation of new rules, and solving possible conflicts among them. The rule of recognition plays then the same fundamental role as the set of directives than Ross would call "sources of law"[13] (and Kelsen, *Grundnorm*).

For our purposes, I will pinpoint only three points of the Hart model: (i) Hart maintains separate the "internal" and "external" points of view about rules, depending upon the degree of commitment and operability (according to different social roles in the system, citizen, judge, expert etc. ...)[14]; (ii) the "rule of recognition" is in fact a complex criterion of identification that might encompass different kind of behaviors and rule interpretations (depending on the legal system we are facing); (iii) if the "rule of recognition" might be used not only to identify individual rules but to indicate also whether or not they are 'legal', then this criterion is not only about the 'validity' of rules but about the *existence* of the whole system as well.

Officers, civil servants, are kept separate from members of the community (the 'civil society'), following the empiricist dual pattern for sovereignty obedience/sovereign common since *The Leviathan* (1651) in political philosophy. Secondary rules have to be accepted by, and are really addressed to, state officers. Conceptual understanding of the rules is the common path to their compliance.

---

[12] Eng (2011) recalls that in Ross' theory, the term *gældende ret* refers to "(i) normative meaning-content in the form of directives (ii) that have the property of being part of the judge's motivation when he is reaching a decision in the case at hand".

[13] In Ross's theory, sources of law "are understood to mean the aggregate of factors which exercises influence on the judge's formulation, of the rule on which he bases his decision." (Ross 1959)

[14] According to Hart, "the observer may, without accepting the rules himself, assert that the group accepts the rules, and thus may from outside refer to the way in which they are concerned with them from the internal point of view." (Hart 1960)

Social interactions are glued together by the dynamics of the internal and external point of view, which goes necessarily through the semantics of language. This position seems to open a gap between social positivism, as it is conceived by Hart, and Ross. Nevertheless, a closer look at the grounds of both positions lead to a unified and coherent conception of the law, referring not only to the validity of legal rules, but to their *existence*, as interpretive schemes are 'shared' by groups, be they lawyers, the population or (especially) judges (Eng 2011). Interestingly, legal positivists discussed on the content of "agreements as concurrence", but accorded the same relative value to "agreements as contracts".

2.4 Agreement in Socio-legal Theory

I have presented so far the conceptualization of agreements in the classical theory of law of the 20th c. But, before going further in the argumentation, let's go to the socio-legal side of legal theory. I will not describe in this section the traditions of pure sociology or psychology, but only the so-called Legal Realist tradition of the thirties, and some Law and Society approaches that followed up regarding relational law.

2.4.1 Karl Llewellyn

As his late editor, Frederik Schauer (Llewellyn 2011) has recently reminded, according to Llewellyn's *The Bramble Bush* (1930b), rules are no more than "pretty playthings". Rule reckonability would lay in multiple *situated* forms, adapted to what Llewellyn calls *situated concepts, working practices, devices.*[15]

Llewellynesque has become a common expression in legal theory to characterize informal writing. But I think that it would be misleading to believe that his loose and sometimes bizarre expressions are merely rhetoric. I have plotted in Fig. 2.2 the structure of the legal realist approach he was advancing in 1930 (Llewellyn 1930a).

Following Pound, *law-in-action* is opposed to *law-in-books*, and *paper rules* are opposed to *working rules*. There is no mechanical way to decide whether a rule is legal or not: this is left to the variable conditions set by the actors and to the conventions accepted by the market or the social community in which legal acts and rules operate. In a way, then, language is experienced and reflected as *felt* or *accepted* within rules, but meaning is a function of too many variables to be

---

[15]"[...] I am not going to attempt a definition of law. (...). I have no desire to exclude anything from matters legal. (...). I shall instead devote my attention to the *focus* of matters legal. I shall try to discuss a *point of reference*; a point of reference to which I believe all matters legal can most usefully be referred." (Llewellyn 1930a)

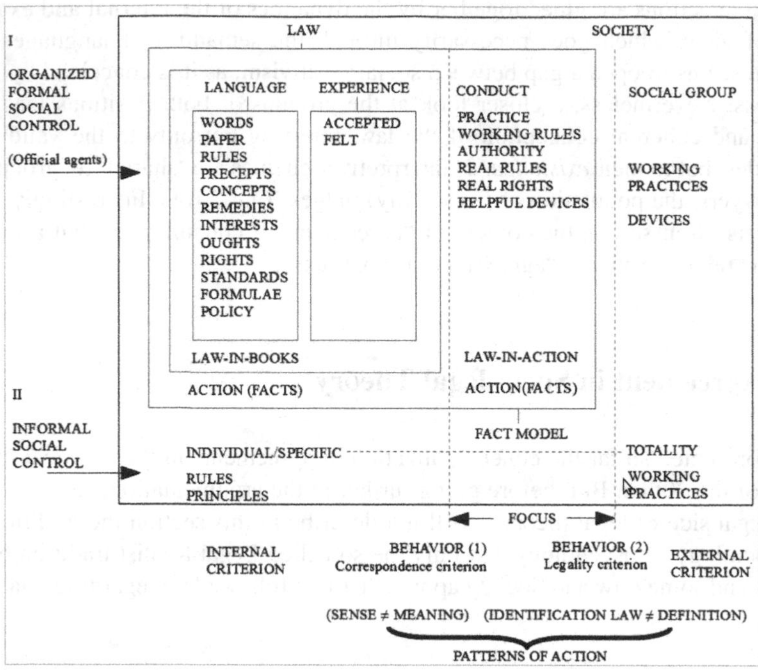

Fig. 2.2 Legal realism approach, based on Llewellyn's (1930a)

structured as an object (in a contract e.g.). There is no way to fix a stable meaning, as there is no way to fix a stable legal standard or value. The internal criterion for meaning or legality is doubled and revamped by externalities, first within the legal community, and then within the open society (market sectors, organizations, and the political community).

It is worthwhile noting the division between informal and formal control (performed by the law, especially through organized judicial institutions and behavior). But this comes from the first-hand knowledge that Llewellyn possessed of Max Weber's sociology and of German legal philosophy.

It seems to be a common bond between public law and legal philosophy. Jellinek, Kelsen, Hart, Ross ... were all public law scholars. Llewellyn, on the contrary, was the Chief Reporter of the USA Uniform Code of Commerce from its inception in 1940 until his death in 1962. The code was his main contribution, and it was a revolutionary one. Sections 1–201(3) of the U.C.C defines *agreement* as "the bargain of the parties in fact as found in their language or *by implication from other circumstances* including course of dealing or usage of trade or course of performance as provided in this Act. [emphasis added P.C.]"

American scholars have underlined the significance of this legal change with respect the understanding of contract as a formal promise (Blair 2006–2007; Breen 2000; Patterson 1989). It is a departure from previous Holmes, Landell and Willinston's interpretations of the offer-acceptance-consideration model.[16] Patterson (1989) has extracted the underlying conception of language – contract terms do not have a plain meaning, and written contract terms might not have priority over all unwritten expressions of agreement:

> Under the Code, as Llewellyn conceived it, the meaning of contract terms was not a function of intent, mercantile or otherwise. In construing the meaning of a contract, a court should focus not on what the parties mentally intended by their words but on what the trade took the words to mean. (…) Llewellyn believed that there should be no unitary concept of contract or agreement, *only a myriad of ways that parties could come to agreement against the background of commercial practice.* [Emphasis added P.C.]

2.4.2 Relational Law

Coming from legal realism, socio-legal scholars have embraced a pluralist perspective and they do not refer to a validity criterion or a validity rule to describe norms or rules as social artifacts. The legal field is defined, e.g., as "the ensemble of institutions and practices through which law is produced, interpreted, and incorporated into social decision-making. Thus, the field includes legal professionals, judges, and the legal academy" (Trubek et al. 1994). From this behavioral perspective, they actually do not embrace one version of legal pluralism but many, based on multiple regulatory forms that I have summarized elsewhere (Casanovas 2002). Pluralisms lead to different social approaches and methodologies. However, legal theory and social studies have been often seen as opposite.

One of the reasons for such a situation lies on the first stages of relational law. Legal realists understood that law was 'relational' as an adversarial shift from the existing approaches and as a self-affirmative action. Llewellyn (1931) posed it as "Pound's development of 'relation' as a status-like element constantly latent and now re-emergent in our order". Roscoe Pound, in a series called "The end of Law as Developed in Juristic Thought" (1914, 1917) – the Harvard papers that constituted the bases for *The Spirit of the Common Law* (1921) – explained the history of the Common Law tradition as opposed to the Roman Civil Law tradition:

> The idea of relation, and of legal consequences flowing therefrom, pervades every part of Anglo-American law. (…). The action for use and occupation may only be maintained where a relation exists. *When the relation does exist, however, a train of legal consequences follows* (Pound 1917).

[16]As Breen (2000) puts forward, under the Code: (i) "the context of an agreement – the unspoken background of beliefs and understandings formed by repetition within an industry and familiarity among individuals, which are taken for granted by the parties involved – becomes central to the meaning of the contract. Contextual evidence is thus fully recognized as an 'effective part' of the agreement itself." (ii) Art. 2 states that "the meaning of a written agreement is determined not only by the language used by [the parties] but also by their action[s], read and interpreted in the light of commercial practices and other surrounding circumstances" (U.C.C. Id. § 1–205 cmt. 1.).

Therefore, the "spirit" of Anglo-American Law would be *relational* (and not authoritative), bottom-up (more than top-down), and collective (as opposed to the individual trend of natural law philosophy). However, more recently, this way of constructing a broad legal perspective contrasting other concurrent ones has twisted in favor of particular approaches. This is the second step for relational law.

'Relational' is considered a common property that emerges from the existing social and economic bonds among companies, providers, customers, consumers, citizens (or digital neighbors). It seems to be a pervasive quality, perhaps straddling too many genres and fields, from psychology to jurisprudence, and from political science to business managing and marketing studies.[17]

Relational refers to the capacity to set up a common space of mutual relations – a shared regulatory framework – in which some reciprocity is expected with regard to goods, services, attitudes and actions. Thus, relational law is more based on trust and dialogue than on the enactment of formal procedures or on the enforcement of sanctions. This has been proved especially useful regarding the analysis of norms – e.g. in consumer research studies (Johar 2005), in B2B relationships (Blois and Ivens 2006), in relational governance (Ott and Ivens 2009).

Either Macauley (1963), MacNeil (1974, 1983, 1985, 2001) or Blumberg (2005) stress a view of contracts as relations rather than as discrete transactions looking at the evolving dynamics of the different players and stakeholders within their living constructed shared contexts. "Relational norms",[18] "relational exchange norms", and "relational contract" are concepts widely used since. By the term "relational thinking" it is meant an approach emphasizing the complex patterns of human interaction that inform all exchanges (MacNeil 1985). But in fact this does not mean getting rid of a more conventional notion of what law is or how lawyers think (for a good comprehensive summary of MacNeil's works, see Campbell (2001)). More recent studies confirm that there is no simple opposition or alternate choice, but different combinations in between: legal contracting and regulatory governance may intertwine, substitute each other, or co-apply (Cannon et al. 2012; Fisher et al. 2011; Gundlach et al. 1995; Poppo and Zenger 2002).

This means that relational regulatory systems and models are complex, and that their strength certainly stems from sources other than the normative power of positive law only. But, again, legal drafting, contracting and sentencing matter and can play changing roles within the system. I will call *regulatory systems* this set of coordinated individual and collective complex behavior which can be grasped through rules, values and principles that nowadays constitute the social framework

[17]'Relational' has been applied not only to contracts but to *sovereignty* (Stacey 2003), *rights* (Minow and Shandley 1996), *copyright* (Craig 2011), *governance* (Chelariu and Sangtani 2009; Zeng et al. 2008), and *conflicts* (Wallenburg and Raue 2011), broadening up the field from private law to the public domain.

[18]MacNeil (1983) distinguishes five relational norms – role integrity, preservation of the relation, harmonization of relational conflict, propriety of means, and supracontract norms.

Fig. 2.3 Linked data and the semantic Web (Source: Hendler (2009))

<table>
<tr><td colspan="2">Web 3.0</td></tr>
<tr><td rowspan="2">Web 2.0</td><td>Semantic Web (RDFS, OWL)</td></tr>
<tr><td>Linked Data (RDF, SPARQL)</td></tr>
</table>

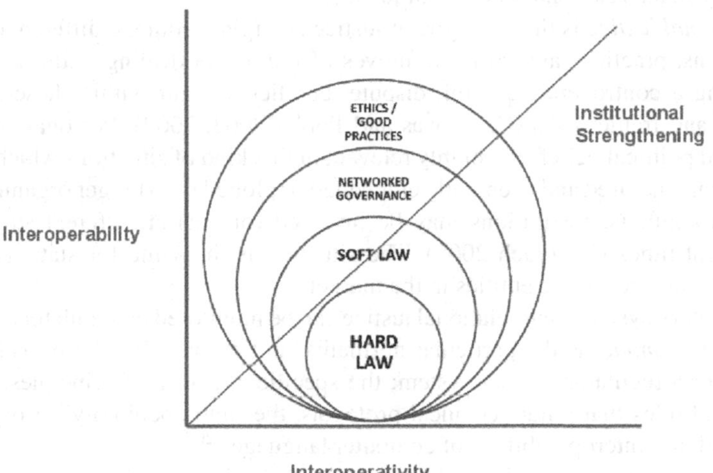

Fig. 2.4 Scheme of regulatory spaces, interoperability/interoperativity axes (Source: Casanovas and Poblet (2012))

of the law. I will call *regulatory models* the set of structured principles, norms and rules that can be designed to control and monitor the interaction between technology and regulatory systems. I will call *relational justice* the set of procedural devices to manage and eventually solve disputes and conflicts within the framework of dialogue as a source of law.

This is the third step for relational law: when social patterns, networked governance, ethical principles and legal systems are entrenched through the regulatory protocols of technological environments. This is properly the field in which Online Dispute Resolution developments (ODR), privacy by design, security by design or identity patterns take place and will operate in the next stage of the web (ubiquitous computing, cloud computing, open data, XML standardization etc. …). In this third sense, relational law refers to the point in which the Social Web (2.0) and the Web of Data (3.0) intersects with the way of regulating systems and end users behavior alike (be the users considered as citizens, consumers, companies or political organizations). A visualization of what I mean by the third stage of relational law may arise in the overlapping of Figs. 2.3 and 2.4.

2.4.3 Regulatory Systems, Relational Justice, Regulatory Models

Regulatory systems are broader than their legal side because they include all aspects set by players in the social, political and economic games at stake. They are situated, flow-driven, and work specifically in a multitude of similar but differently evolving scenarios. As long as they contain procedural ways to solve and manage conflicts as well, they shape relational systems of justice.[19]

Relational justice is thus the type of justice emerging from the different conceptualizations, practices and strategic moves of the actors dealing with, managing, or solving a controversy, quarrel, dispute, conflict or fight within these situated contexts and frameworks (Casanovas and Poblet 2008, 2009). Personal attitudes, moral and political beliefs are highly relevant in this kind of situations which can be initially unstructured and eventually embedded or plotted onto bigger organizational or social conflicts. Institutions may be involved (or not) at different stages and at different times (Lederach 2005). The situation is the same for state agencies, companies and corporate entities in the market.

Regulatory systems and relational justice can be monitored by regulatory models. A *regulatory model* is the particular normative suit encased by platforms built up to monitor a regulatory social system; the specific structure of principles, values, norms and rules that guide technical protocols, the 'interoperativity' of organized teams and the 'interoperability' of computer languages.[20]

These concepts – relational law, relational justice, regulatory systems and regulatory models – have to be spelled out further. They have to be carefully distinguished from virtual or *electronic institutions, corporate governance*, all forms of *networked governance* and *ethical* informatics. From this point of view, agents, networks and principles are components of social regulatory systems and they have to be taken into account by the specific regulatory models built up to control and monitor the technology applied to particular fields – ODR platforms, security platforms, digital rights management, mobile applications etc. for e-commerce, e-administration, e-security etc. Figure 2.4 shows a possible structure for regulatory models, in which hard law (enforceable norms), soft law (non-enforceable norms), networked governance (administrative, managerial norms), and ethics and good

[19] A regulatory system can be a broad social system, with several groups, networks and professional people involved. It can be described and explained by means of statistical measures (using social indicators e.g.) and qualitative methods. We had the opportunity, e.g., to describe the social system of mediation in Catalonia. Results are available in Catalan and Spanish at http://www.llibreblancmediacio.com. Chapter 16 of the Spanish version contains the state the art of ODR (years 2008–2009, Poblet et al. 2011), and the prototype of an electronic institution for mediation (developed by Noriega et al. (2010)).

[20] I prefer to maintain separate *interoperativity* (referred to human coordinated or collective behaviour to team up) and *interoperability* (compatibility of computer languages).

practices (prudential norms, technical protocols) are ordered along the axes of interoperability and interoperativity. As stated by Axel Polleres (2012): "Best practices and norms on the Web are indeed largely not (yet) being made explicit".

2.5 Discussion: Dialogue as a Source of Law

I have summarized so far the perspective of legal theory and socio-legal approaches on agreements. My brief description did not intend to be exhaustive. Three legal theories and three stages of relational law have been exposed. It is time to come back to the starting point and finish with a more open discussion on some issues that can be raised from them.

The starting points are the following: (i) a continuum line between the two poles of agreement – as a "meeting of the minds" and "agreement as a contract" (see Sect. 2.2); (ii) a history of agreements in modern and contemporary societies that reverse the value and role of agreements in ancient (and face to face) societies (Sect. 2.2); (iii) the prominent role of the state and public law in the value accorded to agreements in contracts under the rule of law (Sect. 2.3); (iv) agreement in classical theories of law about the existence of a system based on the "legal" (i.e. "valid") use of the physical force by the state (or the final ruler) (Sect. 2.4); (v) the agreement in classical theories of law on describing theoretically the legal space as a single normative system with a criterion of validity; (vi) agreement between Hart and Ross on the existence of the legal system, the existence of a method to test the validity of norms, and (most important) a "shared acceptance" or "common understanding" of law by state officers (e.g. judges) and the civil population (Sects. 2.3.2–2.3.3); (vii) the clash of such a perspective with more behavioral and empirical approaches, to contracts from a *myriad of ways that parties could come to agreement* (Llewellyn), and the importance of context and working practices of the field (Sect. 2.4); (viii) the shift towards relational contracts, and networked and corporate governance in the second step of the relational conception of law, in which positive statutes, acts and sentences are components of the regulatory framework (Sect. 2.4.2); (ix) the emergence of concepts such as regulatory systems, relational justice, regulatory models; and the entrenchment of technological environments and regulations in the next stage of the Web (Sect. 2.4.3).

I will address four final issues related with these points: (i) crowdsourcing; (ii) the relationship between agreement and disagreement; (iii) the notion of 'legally valid norm', (iv) and democratic values.

All issues have to do with the idea of dialogue in the cloud. We might consider as cloud services infrastructures, platforms, or software. According to the NIST standards the cloud model is composed of five essential characteristics, three service models, and four deployment models (Srivastava et al. 2011). For example the five essential characteristics are: on-demand self-service, broad network access, resource pooling, rapid elasticity, and measured service.

As information grows on the net, *personalization* and *empowerment* of users becomes an issue, because knowledge is increasingly produced through cooperation and participation. The Web fosters participation, but at the same time, risks or threats to citizens are higher too. Crowdsourcing is one side; identity management is the other side of the picture. Trust and security come along. The *Internet meta-system layer*, as was put forward by Cameron (2005), coexists with the Linked Open Data movement. Perhaps for the first time, then, regulations have to cope with a semantic structure which organizes them as metadata.

2.5.1 Crowdsourcing

Originally this term was coined to refer to distributive labor. Different types have been recently distinguished in recent times. Most of the more successful examples, like Wikipedia, may be defined as non-profit collective aggregation of information stemming from micro-tasks widely distributed across the Web, and freely performed by people. Therefore, it implies much more than a new way to collect information or to respond to labor offers or contests, following the Amazon Mechanical Turk or Microworks.com models, because (i) it points at the personalization of services and applications, (ii) it creates a link between Web 2.0 and 3.0 (the Web of Data), for it creates the conditions to transform the aggregation of individual information into the clustering, classification and enhancement of collective knowledge, (iii) it broadens up and enhances a democratic way of living and behaving in the global world.

This is the main reason why people use it when they need it, reacting to events that concern them or into which they want to get involved. No measures based on routine or loyal customer behavior are accurate enough to capture this public dimension. The broad democratic political model to be implemented cannot be taken for granted, as the integration between the regulatory forms of law, relational governance and what Petrie (2010) calls *Emerging Collectivities* (EC) has to be thought about from new bases. Crowdsourcing can be expanded then into *crowdservicing* (Davies 2011).

2.5.2 Agreement and Disagreement

Classical positivist theories (including Ross') assumed the existence of a united central state – a national order – and a legal order as a *common project* to explain obedience or acceptance of norms. Both aspects are interconnected, and point at a legal theory as a privileged approach. However, *power*, not empowerment, is the subject-matter or *idée force* that guides the argumentation process in classical legal theories.

This is not to criticise. Hobbes, Kelsen, Ross or Hart had to tackle the problem of violence and survival in a convulsing world. As Abizadeh has shown (2011), the primary source of war, according to Hobbes, is not necessity, greed or even glory, but weakness, human disagreement. Disagreements can turn into *deep disagreements*; and this is an existential stage in which argumentation and rationality stop, for they undercut the conditions essential to arguing (Fogelin 1985).

However, philosophical argumentation is *nonpreemptive*: "philosophical issues are always such that arguments of prima facie cogency can be built up for a cluster of mutually incompatible thesis" (Rescher 1978). This is the case for legal theory as well.

The notion of "genuine disagreement" was used by Dworkin (1986) to challenge what he called "the semantic sting" – that lawyers follow certain linguistic criteria for judging propositions of law. Therefore, Hart (and other positivists) would derive the use, the pragmatics of law from the semantics of legal language, a mistake that would prevent them from properly explaining theoretical disagreements.

Dworkin's criticism raised a passionate debate in legal philosophy, especially after Hart's posthumous *Postcript* to *The Concept of Law* (second edition, 1994), where Hart defended what was called *inclusive positivism*, a reassessment of his philosophy as a method for descriptive (non normative or interpretative) jurisprudence (see the essays contained in Coleman, 2001; especially Endicott 1998; Raz 2001).

Dworkin pointed indeed at the nature of Hart's linguistic endorsement. What does *sharing* a rule of recognition exactly mean to officers? As regards citizens, where did the *common understanding* of law or the acceptance of a primary rule comes from?

Pettit has recently followed the same procedure of refining the meaning of natural language to better define what the content of a norm is. He fills what he calls "the norm-normative gap" – the fact that a norm is such a norm and not a mere behavioral pattern "since people give acceptance or approval to those who conform with the regularity and or reject or disapprove of those who deviate" (Pettit 2010). This is Hart's *internal* point of view, which Pettit elaborates to assess meaning to the norm of honesty as a particular case – "norms come about as a result of rationally intelligible adjustments between the parties" (ibid.).

The question of emergence of norms is an important one and can be studied empirically, because there is not a single general answer for the problem (see e.g. McAdams 2010 for a different solution). At this level, it makes sense to distinguish carefully between two meanings of agreement: *B-agreements* (being in agreement) and *H-agreements* (having an agreement) (Paglieri 2012).

From the cognitive and social sciences it makes complete sense to flesh out these concepts by seeking micro-foundations for agents' behavior as well (Castelfranchi 2003). Emergence of meaning and interoperability is another dimension of the problem, with a variety of approaches – specifying the conditions under which two individuals (or one individual at two points in time) will infer they share a diffuse referent (Chaigneau et al. 2012); or conceiving semantic interoperability as a coordination problem between the world, information systems, and human users (grounding semantics, semiotic dynamics) (Steels 2006).

Philosophy can support theories and empirical testing on analytical grounds. We can find a correlative example on H-agreements in Black (2007), preferring the offer-acceptance model over the undertaking-based model.

From the analytical point of view, *agreements in language* and *agreements of language* should be kept separate. Wittgenstein made a substantial contribution when code or symbolism are involved distinguishing in his late works *agreement in judgment* and *agreement in opinion*. To disagree means having the capacity to agree, first, in a common communicative ground. Agreement in judgment would mean that what is shared is the language as a 'form of life'; the role inter-subjective agreement plays for the possibility of linguistic communication.

As said, these kinds of fundamental questions can and should be faced not only from the philosophical point of view but from the empirical one. The assumption that obedience or acceptance of norms has an "internal" side that can be solved only by refining the natural meaning; *id est*, that normative agreements "emerge" naturally from the social body, is a strong assumption that can be put under the light of knowledge acquisition through data analysis.

Clearly, assumptions on the general picture – the sovereign state, the division onto citizens and officers ... – played a role (and a major one) in the classical legal theory approach to agreements and rules.

2.5.3 Validity and Regulatory Models

Equally, in the new scenarios raised by crowdsourcing, cloud computing, and relational law and justice, assumptions on the whole context have an impact on the way agreements and norms are faced. We generally deal with complex environments, in which power is fragmented and divided into multiple sources of authority, with different levels and degrees of compulsory force, and different jurisdictions.

In networked governance, legality anchors the intended behavior of state agencies, their relationships, and their relationships with citizens (see Fig. 2.4). Hard and soft laws are commonly differentiated by the existence of legal norms. But legality is *situated* within national, communitarian (European), or international borders. In the cloud, nevertheless, the sixty million controversies that e-Bay has to solve every year, e.g., occur in what we could understand as a *dereferenced legality*. There is a procedure to be implemented and followed that is eventually grounded on the conditions of dialogue between the parties, and the incentives and disincentives at stake (e.g. reputation), not because there is no other way to enforce a final ruling, but because actually the technological nature of the web can implement a new balance between public power and personal empowerment.

This state of affairs recalls the situation of agreements in pre-modern societies, in absence of the state but with a strong need to maintain the balance of a living social regulation (see Sect. 2.2). Online Dispute Resolution procedures consist of ordered steps and the structure of rational agreements – usually between only two different sides (Lodder and Zeleznikow 2010). However, there are other scenarios regarding public goods (e.g. ecological conflicts, polluters etc.) in which non-binding voluntary agreements are most effective if selective, because power is still an issue even in non-enforceable, i.e. non-legally binding, situations (Glachant 2007). This is the first argument in favor of considering dialogue as a primary source of law.

I will elaborate this position stemming from a second argument on the emergence of validity as a result of agreements. My position is that this is so when bindingness is put aside through the *same conditions* in which it appears in a conventional legal reasoning process. Validity, legal bindingness is not strictly needed, but it is a factor that co-exists with other scenarios in the web. Let's elaborate on that.

Semantics has a long history in law as well, since Hohfeldian jural schemes. Hohfeld, von Wright, Alchourrón and Bulygin, Lindahl, McCarty, Sergot, among many others, built up a normative space in which it was held to perform the distinction of legal from non-legal norms (or deontic effects from other modal ones). One of the last contributions is due to Ross (2011) and (Sartor 2008, 2009a,b). Following Ross's suggestions on inference (see Sect. 2.3.2) Sartor dwells on *semantic* inference. He claims that "that certain features of a norm entail the norm's legal validity on the basis of their ability to justify the norm's legal bindingness (through the mediation of legal validity". This means (i) that a norm is automatically enforceable if it is legal, (ii) that legality is a deontic property that "supervenes" in a process of legal reasoning; (iii) that legality is a moral property (in a broad sense).

However, if legal bindingness depend on a test on the acceptability of premises in an argumentation process, i.e., is considered strictly dependent on validity as an evaluative concept, then, I think that bindingness requires a theory of democracy (broader than legal theory) to fix the acceptable criteria and values to be implemented in a legal reasoner. The political side of validity cannot be avoided, even accepting Sartor's moral distance. Even the late Ross asserted that "feelings of validity" are "the very foundation of all politically organized life" (Ross 1968).

I do not consider legality as a moral property, but as a political one; i.e., it not only applies through legal reasoning, but through the diverse moves of negotiating agreements (and at the different layers of the possible disputes as well), soft law, good practices and ethical codes that constitute the line of *institutional strengthening*; that is to say, the resulting vector of a regulatory space which is broader than the application of legal norms. If this is so, validity goes along a continuum that cannot be only linearly determined by a unilateral process of reasoning, but by a set of variable procedures that are themselves negotiated, discussed, evaluated, and eventually changed, in a dialogical process among different agents or stakeholders (the notion of "meta-agreements" points at this situation).

In a context of dereferenced legality, what immediately pops up is not the rationality of the argumentation or the enforceability of the agreement, but the effective satisfacing behavior of both (or more) parties, be they optimal or suboptimal.

There is still a third related argument in favor of considering dialogue as a source of law.

Many years ago, Valente and Breuker (1994) suggested that ontologies could help to bridge the gap between Artificial Intelligence and Legal Theory, and in fact many legal ontologies have been constructed since then. Sartor correctly states that conflicts between inferential and ontological approaches need to be considered "as a dialectical balance and co-evolution", and this would require that lawyers and ontological engineers "have the ability to continuously adjust their onto-terminological constructions as the law evolves" (Ross 1968).

I think the analysis can go a bit further: reconciling ontologies and inferential schemes requires an adjustment not only on legal but on social basis as well. Therefore, I would suggest the adjustment be produced by taking into account the democratic values carried out by citizen participation and the evolution of the Web of Data. This means that a double and, if possible, coordinated process of dialogue has to take place – between personal, local (or singular) knowledge, and expert, global (or general) knowledge.

2.5.4 Democratic Values

Democratic values are consubstantial to crowdsourcing, privacy, data protection, and the transparency and accountability principles that inform Linked Open Data, but they are not strictly necessary for constructing artificial societies or MAS. This means that they have to be *consciously* designed, reflected and implemented, because I do not think they can be simply derived from any theoretical legal model alone. This goes back to dialogue and participation as a source both of legitimacy and legality.

A political reading, or a pragmatic epistemological position, emphasizes, as e.g. Brandom (2008) does, that the possibility of disagreement and dissent is a condition of democracy. Disagreement is then viewed as "[...] an absolutely essential element of discursive practice. Without the right to disagree, there is no language".

Besides, from a linguistic point of view, it seems that free speech and dissent have (even through "non politically correct language") a positive effect on the evolution of democratic systems (Stromer-Galley and Muhlberger 2009). Diversity of opinion seems to reinforce models of deliberation on the web too (Karlsson 2010). However, I would not defend the existence of an implicit common law model to articulate a linguistic model of normativity as a political ground for the rule of law in the WWW. There are other means of looking for collective aggregation of information or knowledge than assuming normative restrictions at the speaker level.

The proposal of an I-thou structure of normative scorekeeping and discursive updating instead of a I-we structure (Brandom), or the "we-mode social groups" hypothesis put forward by Tuomela (2007) stress the function of collective action in the construction of a common social order based on agreement (implicit or explicit).

Nevertheless, from the legal point of view, it is my contention that the basic question posed by Sunstein (1994) some time ago is still a good starting point to reflect on the implementation of a democratic model, because it poses an intermediate, down to earth coordination level between the individual and collective dimensions:

> How is law possible in a heterogeneous society, composed of people who sharply disagree about basic values? (...) Much of the answer to this puzzle lies in an appreciation of how people who disagree on fundamental issues can achieve *incompletely theorized agreements on particular cases.*

People disagree everywhere and on everything, and very likely they will keep disagreeing everywhere and on everything. But (and this is Sunstein's strong point) they do not need to agree on general principles to reach agreements: "people from divergent starting-points, or with uncertainty about their starting-points, can converge on a rule of a low-level judgment".

More recently, Sunstein has warned against the biased reasoning trends and polarization to which the blogosphere is prone. There is an ongoing interesting discussion on *meta-agreements* – the conceptualization of issues at stake, the context of sets of judgments over multiple interconnected propositions – and *single-peakedness* – individuals rationalize their preferences in terms of a common issue dimension – to overcome the well-known voting paradoxes (List 2007; Ottonelli and Porello 2012).

I still think that there is no valid argument against the capacity to produce new knowledge through the empowerment of individual participation in the web. Developing these theses falls out of the scope of the present chapter. However, I hope to have shown that both theoretical and empirical approaches are needed to face them in a consistent manner.

Acknowledgements The research presented in this paper has been partially developed within the framework of the projects INNPACTO IPT-2011-1015-43000, and CAPER, EU FP7 SECURITY-2010-1.2-1 Project 261712. I am grateful to John Zeleznikow and Pauline Stanton for their kind invitation at Victoria University, Melbourne, where this chapter has been finally written under the Salvador de Madariaga fellowship PR2011-0550 *Relational law, Models of Justice and the Semantic Web*.

References

Abizabeh, A. 2011. Hobbes on the causes of war: A disagreement theory. *The American Political Science Review* 105(2): 298–315.

Arnaud, A. J. 1973. Essai d'analyse structurale du Code Civil français. La règle du jeu dans la paix bourgeoise. Préf. de Michel Villey. Postface de Georges Mounin, LGD, Paris.

Black, O. 2007. Two theories of agreement. *Legal Theory* 13: 1–22.

Blair, A. 2006–2007. You don't have to be Ludwig Wittgenstein: How Lewellyn's concept of agreement should change the law of open-quantity contracts. *Seton Hall Law Review* 37: 67–126.

Blois, K., and B. Ivens. 2006. Measuring relational norms: Some methodological issues. *European Journal of Marketing* 40(3/4): 352–365.

Blumberg, P. I. 2005. The Transformation of modern corporation law: The law of corporate groups. *Connecticut Law Review* 37: 605–615.

Brandom, R. B. (Pritzlaff, T.) 2008. Freedom is a matter of responsibility and authority: An interview with Robert B. Brandom. *European Journal of Political Theory* 7(3): 365–381.

Breen, J. M. 2000. Statutory interpretations and the lessons of Llewellyn. *Loyola Law Review* 33: 263–451.

Cameron, K. 2005. *The laws of identity ... as of 5/11/2005*. Microsoft Corp.

Campbell, D. 2001. *The relational theory of contract: Selected works of Ian MacNeil*. London: Sweet & Maxwell.

Cannon, J. P., R. S. Achrol, and G. T. Gundlach. 2012. Contracts, norms, and plural form governance. *Journal of the Academy of Marketing Science* 28(2): 180–194.

Casanovas, P. 2002. Dimensiones del pluralismo jurídico. In *IX Congreso Internacional de Antropología*. Barcelona: FAAEE.

Casanovas, P. 2010. Legal electronic institutions and ONTOMEDIA: Dialogue, inventio, and relational justice scenarios. In *AI approaches to the complexity of legal systems (AICOL I–II)*. LNAI, vol. 6237, ed. P. Casanovas, U. Pagallo, G. Sartor, and G. Ajani, 184–204. Heidelberg/Berlin: Springer.

Casanovas, P., and M. Poblet. 2008. Concepts and fields of relational justice. In *Computable Models of the Law: Languages, Dialogue, Games, Ontologies*. LNAI, vol. 4884, ed. P. Casanovas, G. Sartor, N. Casellas and R. Rubino, 323–342. Berlin/Heidelberg: Springer.

Casanovas, P., and M. Poblet. 2009. The future of law: Relational law and next generation of web services. In *The future of law and technology: Looking into the future*, Selected Essays, ed. M. Fernández-Barrera, et al., 137–156. Florence: European Press Academic Publishing.

Casanovas, P., and M. Poblet, et al. 2012. D WP7.1. EU Project CAPER. http://www.fp7-caper.eu/.

Castelfranchi, C. 2003. Grounding we-intentions in individual social attitudes. In *Realism in action*, Essays in the Philosophy of Social Sciences, ed. M. Sintonen, P. Yliskoski, and K. Miller, 195–213. Amsterdam: Kluwer.

Chaigneau, S., E. Canessa, and J. Gaete. 2012. Conceptual agreement theory. *New Ideas in Psychology* 30: 179–189.

Chelariu, C., and V. Sangtani. 2009. Relational governance in B2B electronic marketplaces: An updated typology. *Journal of Business & Industrial Marketing* 24(2): 108–118.

Craig, C. J. 2011. *Copyright, communication and culture: Towards a relational theory of copyright law*. Cheltenham: Edward Elgar.

Davies, J. 2011. From crowdsourcing to crowdservicing. *IEEE Internet Computing* 15(3): 92–94.

D'Aquin M., E. Motta, M. Sabou, S. Angeletou, L. Gridinoc, V. Lopez, and D. Guidi. 2008. Toward a new Generation of Semantic Web Applications. *IEEE Intelligent Systems* (23)3: 20–28.

Dworkin, R. 1986. *Law's empire*. Cambridge: Harvard University.

Endicott, T. A. O. 1998. Herbert Hart and the semantic sting. *Legal Theory* 4: 283–300.

Eng, S. 2011. Lost in the system or lost in translation? The exchanges between Hart and Ross. *Ratio Juris* 24(2): 194–246.

Fischer, T., T. Huber, and J. Dibbern. 2011. Contractual and relational governance as substitutes and complements – explaining the development of differential relationships. In: *The 19th European Conference on Information Systems*, Helsinki, Finland. Reprinted in: Theory-guided modeling and empiricism in information systems research, ed. A. Heinzl, O. Wendt, and T. Weitzel, 65–84. Physica-Verlag: Heidelberg.

Fogelin, R. J. 1985. The logic of deep disagreements. *Informal Logic* 7(1): 1–8.

Fumaroli, M. 1980. L'Âge de l'éloquence: rhétorique et *res literaria* de la Renaissance au seuil de l'époque classique. Paris: Droz.

Glachant, M. 2007. Non-binding voluntary agreements. *Journal of Environmental Economics and Management* 54: 32–48.

Gundlach, G. T., R. S. Achrol, and J. T. Mentzer. 1995. The structure of commitment in exchange. *Journal of Marketing* 59(1): 78–93.

Hart, H. L. A. 1960. In *The concept of law, second edition, 1994, with a postcript*, ed. P. A. Bulloch and J. Raz. Oxford: Oxford University.

Hendler, J. 2009. Web 3.0 emerging. *IEEE Computer* 42(1): 111–113.

Johar, G. T. 2005. The price of friendship: When, why, and how relational norms guide social exchange behavior. *Journal of Consumer Psychology* 15(1): 22–27.

Kelsen, H. 1967. *The pure theory of law*. Trans. M. Knight, 1960. Berkeley: University of California.

Karlsson, M. 2010. What does it take to make online deliberation happen? – A comparative analysis of 28 online discussion forums. In *Proceedings of the fourth international conference on online deliberation*, Leeds, 30 June–2 July, ed. F. De Cindio, A. Macintosh, and C. Peraboni, 142–156.

Lederach, J. P. 2005. *The moral imagination: The art and soul of making peace*. Oxford: Oxford University.

List, C. 2007. Deliberation and agreement. In *Deliberation, participation and democracy: Can the people govern?*, ed. Shawn W. Rosenberg, 64–81. Basingstoke: Palgrave Macmillan.

Lodder, A., and J. Zeleznikow. 2010. *Enhanced dispute resolution through the use of information technology*. Cambridge: Cambridge University.

Lorenzen, E. G. 1919. Causa and consideration in the law of contracts. *The Yale Law Journal* 28(7): 621–646.

Llewellyn, K. N. 1930a. A realistic jurisprudence – The next step. *Columbia Law Review* 30(4): 431–465.

Llewellyn, K. N. 1930b. *The bramble bush: On our law and its study*. New York: Columbia University Press.

Llewellyn, K. N. 1931. What price contract? An essay in perspective. *The Yale Law Journal* 40(5): 704–751.

Llewellyn, K. N. 2011. *The theory of rules*, ed. F. Schauer. Chicago: University of Chicago Press.

Macauley, S. 1963. Non-contractual relations in business: A preliminary study. *American Sociological Review* 28: 55–67.

MacCormack, G. 1969. Formalism, symbolism, and magic in early Roman law. *Tijdschrift voor Rechtsgeschiedenis* 37: 439–468.

MacNeil, I. R. 1974. The many futures of contract. *Southern California Law Review* 47: 691–896.

MacNeil I. R. 1983. Values in contract: Internal and external. *University of Northwestern Law Review* 79: 340–418.

MacNeil I. R. 1985. Relational contract: What we do and do not know. *Wisconsin Law Review* 3: 483–525.

MacNeil, I. R. 2001. *The relational theory of contract*, ed. David Campbell. London: Sweet & Maxwell.

McAdams, R. H. 2010. Resentment, excuse and norms. In *The hart-fuller debate in the twenty-first century*, ed. P. Cane, 249–257. Hart: Oxford/Portland.

Mellinkoff, D. 1963. *The language of the law*. Boston: Little Brown.

Minow, M., and M. L. Shandley. 1996. Relational rights and responsibilities: Revisioning the family in liberal political theory and law, hypathia. *Journal of Feminist Philosophy* 11(1): 4–29.

Noriega, P., et al. 2010. Prototipo de institución electrónica de mediación. In Poblet, M. et al. Tecnologías para la mediación en línea: estado del arte, usos y propuestas. In *Libro Blanco de la Mediación en Cataluña*, ed. P. Casanovas, J. Magre, and E. Lauroba. Barcelona: Department Justicia-Huygens.

Ong, W. 1958. *Ramus, method, and the decay of dialogue: From the art of discourse to the art of reason*. Cambridge: Harvard University.

Orestano, R. 1989. *Edificazione del Giuridico*. Bologna: Il Mulino.

Ossowski, S., C. Sierra, and V. Botti. 2012. Agreement technologies – A computing perspective (in this volume, Chap. 1).

Ott, C. M., and B. Ivens. 2009. Revisiting the norm concept in relational governance. *Industrial Marketing Management* 38: 577–583.

Ottonelli, V., and D. Porello. 2012. On the elusive notion of meta-agreement. *Politics Philosophy Economics* March 29, 2012 1470594X11433742 (forthcoming, published online).

Paglieri, F. 2012. Agreements as the Grease (not the glue) of society – A cognitive and social science perspective (in this volume, Chap. 3).

Pattaro, E. 2010. I will tell you about Axel Hägerström: His ontology and theory of judgment. *Ratio Juris* 23(1): 123–156.
Patterson, D. M. 1989. Good faith, lender liability, and discretionary acceleration: Of Llewellyn, Wittgenstein, and the uniform commercial code. *Texas Law Review* 68: 169–211.
Petrie, C. 2010. Plenty of room outside the firm. *IEEE Internet Computing* 14(1): 92–95.
Pettit, P. 2010. How norms become normative. In *The hart-fuller debate in the twenty-first century*, ed. P. Cane, 227–247. Oxford/Portland: Hart.
Poblet, M., P. Noriega, J. Suquet, S. Gabarró, and J. Redorta. 2011. Tecnologías para la mediación en línea: estado del arte, usos y propuestas. In *Libro Blanco de la Mediación en Cataluña*, ed. P. Casanovas, J. Magre, and E. Lauroba, 943–1008 . Barcelona: Department Justicia-Huygens.
Polleres, A. Agreement technologies and the semantic web (in this volume, Chap. 4).
Poppo, L., and T. Zenger. 2002. Do formal contracts and relational governance function as substitutes or complements? *Strategic Management Journal* 23: 707–725.
Pound, R. 1917. The end of law as developed in juristic thought II. *Harvard Law Review* 30(3): 201–225.
Pound R. 1921. *The spirit of the common law*. Francestown: Marshall Jones.
Radin, M. 1937. The Roman law of quasi-contract. *Virginia Law Review* 37(3): 241–255.
Raz, J. 2001. Two views of the nature of the theory of law. In *Hart's postcript, Essays on the postcript to the concept of law*, ed. J. L. Coleman, 1–37. Oxford: Oxford University.
Rescher, N. 1978. Philosophical disagreement. *Review of Metaphysics* 32(2): 217–251.
Ross, A. 1946. *Towards a realistic jurisprudence: A criticism of the dualism in law*. Copenhagen: E. Munksgaard.
Ross, A. 1957. Tû-Tû. *Harvard Law Review* 70(5): 812–882.
Ross, A. 1959. *On law and justice*. Berkeley: Berkeley University.
Ross, A. 1968. *Directives and norms*. London: Routledge & Kegan Paul.
Ross, A. 2011. The 25th anniversary of the pure theory of law (1935). *Oxford Journal of Legal Studies*, 31(2): 243–272.
Sartor, G. 2008. Legal validity: An inferential analysis. *Ratio Juris* 21(2): 212–247.
Sartor, G. 2009a. Understanding and applying legal concepts: An inquiry on inferential meaning. In *Concepts in law*, ed. J. C. Hage and D. von der Pfordten, 35–54. Heidelberg: Springer.
Sartor, G. 2009b. Legal concepts as inferential nodes and ontological categories. *Artificial Intelligence and Law* 17: 217–251.
Srivastava, P., S. Singh, A. Pinto, S. Verma, V. K. Chaurasiya, and R. Gupta. 2011. An architecture based on proactive model for security in cloud computing. In *Proceedings of the IEEE-ICRTIT, MIT, Anna University*, Chennai, 661–666.
Stacey, H. 2003. Relational sovereignty. *Stanford Law Review* 55(5): 2029–2059.
Steels, L. 2006. Semiotic dynamics for embodied agents. *IEEE* 21(3): 32–38.
Stromer-Galley, J., and P. Muhlberger. 2009. Agreement and disagreement in group deliberation: Effects on deliberation satisfaction. *Future Engagement, and Decision Legitimacy, Political Communication* 26: 173–192.
Sunstein, C. R. 1994. Political conflict and legal agreement, the tanner lectures on human values, Harvard University, November 29th, December 1st. *The Tanner Lectures on Human Values* 17(1996): 137–249.
Tarello, G. 1978. *Storia della cultura giuridica moderna. Assolutismo e codificazione del diritto*. Bologna: Il Mulino.
Trubek, D. M., Y. Dézalay, R. Buchanan, and J. R. Davis (1994). Global restructuring and the law: Studies of the internationalization of legal fields and the creation of transnational Arenas. *Case Western Reserve Law Review* 44(2): 407–498.
Tuomela, R. 2007. *The philosophy of sociality: The shared point of view*. Oxford: Oxford University.
Valente, A., and J. Breuker. 1994. Ontologies: The missing link between legal theory and AI & law. In *Legal knowledge based systems JURIX 94: The foundation for legal knowledge systems*, ed. A. Soeteman, 38–150. Lelystad: Koninklijke Vermande.

Wallenburg, C., and J. S. Raue. 2011. Conflict and its governance in horizontal cooperations of logistics service providers. *International Journal of Physical Distribution & Logistics Management* 41(4): 385–400.
Watson, A. 1989. Artificiality, reality and Roman contract law. *Tijdschrift voor Rechtsgeschiedenis [Legal History Review]* 7, –2(1989): 147–156.
Zeng, J., J. K. Roehrich, and M. A. Lewis. 2008. The dynamics of contractual and relational governance: Evidence from long-term public-private procurement arrangement. *Journal of Purchasing & Supply Management* 14: 43–54.

Chapter 3
Agreements as the Grease (Not the Glue) of Society: A Cognitive and Social Science Perspective

Fabio Paglieri

3.1 Introduction

There is widespread consensus on the key importance of agreements for the smooth and efficient functioning of society: the most frequently used metaphor to capture their relevance describes agreements as the glue of society, that which keeps us together. While I fully endorse the idea that agreements are essential to social life, I think the glue metaphor is misleading in regard to their true function. In these introductory remarks, I will try to propose an alternative view on what agreements are for, which will serve to frame the rest of the discussion in this chapter.

The glue idea is problematic in that it suggests that the ultimate reason why agreements exist and agents comply with them is a need to stick together in more or less permanent social groups. Whereas there is little doubt that such a need is present and paramount in people's mind (overwhelming evidence is reviewed in Baumeister and Leary (1995)), I doubt it is the terminal aim of their social engagements. On the contrary, sticking together is instrumental to other, more pragmatic objectives, which can be obtained only by joining forces with other agents. At the practical level, the primary function of agreement is *to get things done*, that is, to enlist the cooperation of other parties to allow a single agent to achieve a goal that would otherwise be impossible to satisfy. So, from a pragmatic perspective, the ultimate function of agreements is to be the grease of society, to wit, the means by which individual efforts are harnessed and harmonized in a coherent overall plan, like the cogs in a complex mechanical device.

Of course, in order to realize this function, agreements typically also serve to keep us together (gluing society), but this is, adaptively speaking, a means, not

F. Paglieri (✉)
Goal-Oriented Agents Lab (GOAL), Istituto di Scienze e Tecnologie della Cognizione, CNR, Via S. Martino della Battaglia 44, 00185 Roma, Italy
e-mail: fabio.paglieri@istc.cnr.it

S. Ossowski (ed.), *Agreement Technologies*, Law, Governance and Technology Series 8, DOI 10.1007/978-94-007-5583-3_3,

an end: agreements are meant to keep us together only because, and as long and as far as, doing so serves to get things done more efficiently. By the same token, agreements (at least a type of them – see next section) are primarily about actions and goals, to specify what different agents ought to do in order to fulfill some larger plan. Obviously there are also a lot of agreements on beliefs, but these are again instrumental to agreements on actions: either they are needed to allow coordinated action, or they facilitate it (e.g., sharing moral values facilitate cooperation, by helping to identify who belongs to one's own group and by aligning individual attitudes; on the importance of in-group dynamics for the evolution of cooperation, see Bowles (2006) and Carletta (1996)).

This action-oriented view of the function of agreements is important not only to better describe their relevance in human society, but also to understand what makes them so important in future and emerging technologies. The kind of agreement technologies described in this volume do not regard cohesion and cooperation of autonomous agents as an end in itself, but rather as a necessary means to improve and extend the practical value of distributed technologies. This suggests that agreements are the grease, not the glue, of society, for both natural and artificial agents.

Building on this pragmatic approach to agreements, in what follows I will discuss the difference between "being in agreement" and "having an agreement", propose a socio-cognitive analysis of both notions, mention in passing a variety of ways by which agreement might emerge (e.g., norms, argumentation, organizations, etc.), highlight a typical circularity that all these "paths to agreement" have in common (to wit, they simultaneously presuppose and facilitate/produce agreement among the parties), and finally make few cursory remarks on the fact that disagreement is not only/necessarily nefarious for social interaction. Along the way, I will also endeavor to highlight how these insights could be relevant to the technologies discussed in the remaining parts of the book.

3.2 Two Meanings of Agreement: B-Agreements and H-Agreements

In everyday language, the word "agreement" is used in two related but different ways: it is used to describe states of affairs upon which two or more agents independently share the same mental attitudes (being in agreement on something), and it is also used to designate actions, plans, and projects that two or more agents are committed to bring about, while mutually acknowledging each other's commitment to do so (having an agreement on something). These two senses of agreement are by no means identical, as the following two examples illustrate:

1. Adam and Eve agree on Paris being the capital of France.
2. Adam and Eve agree on visiting Paris during their honeymoon.

In (1), Adam and Eve are in agreement on what city is the capital of France without having an agreement (and the resulting commitment) to that effect, whereas in (2) they do have an agreement to visit Paris during their honeymoon, whether or not they are in agreement that this option is the best possible one – in fact, it is easy to conceive plausible scenarios where neither of them think Paris to be the optimal location for their honeymoon, and yet they end up having an agreement to go there (e.g., as a compromise between diverging sets of preferences).

Let us call the state of being in agreement on something a *B-agreement*, and the state of having an agreement on something an *H-agreement*. Almost invariably, B-agreements are about beliefs, while H-agreements concern goals and actions. This is not a logical necessity, but rather a linguistic and psychological constraint. Regarding B-agreements, of course it is possible for two or more agents to have exactly the same goals and plans independently from each other and without any H-agreement to that effect. However, in this case we do not speak of the agents as "agreeing" on such goals and plans. Consider the following cases:

3. Adam and Eve agree on running the NY marathon next year.
4. Both Adam and Eve intend to run the NY marathon next year.

These sentences do not have the same meaning: in particular, (3) is immediately interpreted as referring to an H-agreement (Adam and Eve made some pact to run the NY marathon), and not as indicating a mere B-agreement, in which Adam and Eve happens to have the same goal of running the NY marathon, without necessarily implying any mutual understanding or obligation to do so. In contrast, (4) remains ambiguous between these two interpretations, and could be correctly understood as indicating either an H-agreement or a B-agreement between the parties. This tells us that everyday language does not use the notion of (B-)agreement to refer to independently shared motivational attitude (goals, plans, desires, etc.), but only to independently shared doxastic attitudes (beliefs, opinions, tastes, etc.).

What about the possibility of H-agreements on beliefs? Intuitively, this seems also forbidden by linguistic conventions, as the following examples demonstrate:

5. Adam and Eve have an agreement on Paris being the capital of France.
6. Adam and Eve have an agreement on hydrogen not being a metal.

Both sentences strike us as bizarre, if not outright ungrammatical – possibly (6) more than (5). This is because the facts of the matter (the capital of France, the nature of hydrogen) do not depend on Adam and Eve having an agreement, and, even more crucially, their beliefs about such facts also are not produced by any H-agreement. What Adam and Eve end up believing depends on their doxastic processes, and these are not subject to H-agreements – we cannot agree to believe something just because we stipulated to do so.[1] Hence, H-agreements typically do

[1]Even doxastic voluntarism (Ginet 2001; Wansing 2006) entails a much more nuanced view of our volitional control over belief formation, and it is anyway a highly controversial position in epistemology, where the dominant view is that beliefs cannot be willed or decided (doxastic

not refer to beliefs, opinions, or states of affairs, but rather to motivational and behavioral concepts.

Another key difference between B-agreements and H-agreements is that the latter entails a commitment to act in certain ways (to fulfill the agreement between the parties), whereas no commitment is implied by B-agreements. The mere fact that two or more agents share the same mental attitude towards a certain state of affairs does not commit them to anything, not even to maintain such attitude. Dialogical commitments, as they are understood in argumentation theories (see for instance Van Eemeren and Grootendorst 2004; Walton and Krabbe 1995), do not constitute an exception to this rule: in an argument, an agent becomes committed to a certain position after stating or accepting it, but this should not be regarded as a commitment on a B-agreement. There are three independent reasons for that claim: first, the dialogical commitment is incurred even if the other party does not agree on what was stated by the arguer (in fact, disagreement on statements is typical in the initial and intermediate stages of an argument); second, the arguer is committed to prosecuting the argument in ways that do not contradict what s/he previously stated or accepted (unless s/he retracts it), but this is a behavioral constraint, and not an obligation to believe whatever was stated or accepted (indeed, when we accept something "for the sake of the argument", we are precisely accepting a commitment to argue consistently with a position that we do not necessarily believe); third, and most crucially, the commitment is generated by a speech act (asserting something, or publicly assenting to it), and not by whatever mental attitude might have justified making such speech act (for more details on the complex relationships between dialogical commitments and mental attitudes, see Paglieri (2010)).

Prima facie, H-agreements might seem to imply a recursive B-agreement: whenever we have an H-agreement, we are in B-agreement about having it, and we are also in B-agreement that we are in B-agreement on that, and so on. However, there is more to it than just recursion or common knowledge, as it becomes obvious thinking about cases where B-agreement seems unavoidable. For instance, all people with normal vision are in B-agreement that there are many stars in the night sky, and all such people also are in B-agreement that they all B-agree on such fact. However, it would be improper to say that we have an H-agreement to that effect, a sort of

irresistibility; Woods 2005). Alternatively, one might object that certain facts, to wit, conventional facts, such as Paris being the capital of France, are precisely the product of an agreement to believe in that particular fact. I think this view of conventions is fundamentally wrong: conventions are agreements to act in certain ways, and the resulting coordinated efforts of all the agents endorsing a convention creates an objective (social) reality, to which people's beliefs refer in the usual way. As a case in point, that Paris is the capital of France is a (social) fact, no less real than the non-metallic nature of hydrogen, and believing it does not depend on any worldwide agreement to do so. However, the fact that Paris is the capital of France does depend on a worldwide agreement to act accordingly to such notion, but this is an H-agreement on actions, not beliefs. For further details on the relationship between conventions and agreements, see Gilbert (1983, 1993) and Andrighetto et al. (2009).

collective pact to consider the night sky full of stars: the reason why it would be improper is because we cannot help but being in B-agreement on that fact, whereas having an H-agreement involves an act of choice – more subtly, it involves the possibility of doing otherwise, of disagreeing instead of agreeing. This is linked to the reason why only having an H-agreement entails commitment: we cannot be committed to something that we cannot help thinking or doing, hence we cannot have an H-agreement on something we cannot help but B-agreeing to. This is of course true also for H-agreements on actions, as our intuitions on the following three situations will clarify:

7. While under hypnosis, Adam had an agreement with the hypnotist to give him 10.000 $.
8. While being held at gunpoint, Adam had an agreement with his robber to give him 10.000 $.
9. While his son was held for ransom, Adam had an agreement with the kidnappers to give them 10.000 $.

In (7), it is clearly improper to speak of "having an agreement" with the hypnotist; the expression sounds odd also in (8), where it could be used only ironically, to stress that Adam in fact had no proper H-agreement, and was instead forced to do the robber's bidding; but in (9), having an agreement with the kidnappers sounds just right, precisely because here we perceive more clearly that Adam could have done otherwise, albeit at great personal costs (namely, risking his son's life).

The upshot is that having an H-agreement on *X* is not just being in B-agreement that we are in B-agreement on *X*, that is, it is not just a meta-B-agreement. It entails something more, to wit, the choice of endorsing the commitment implied by accepting an H-agreement. Notice that the commitment is there even in the absence of any explicit promise, contract, etc. (see Gilbert 1993), since at a basic level it just depends on the expectation that neither party will deviate from the agreement without informing the others, once such agreement has been acknowledged (for further details and references on the relationship between promises, expectations and agreements, see Andrighetto et al. (2009)). Also notice that various agents involved in a collective effort, to which H-agreements typically are instrumental, need not have identical or even convergent goals. Consequently, having an H-agreement with another party does not entail having the same goal of that party, not even with respect to the behavior for which the H-agreement is relevant. An important consequence is that most H-agreements are not fair, in the sense of granting all parties the same chances of reaping the same amount of benefits.

The distinction between B-agreements and H-agreements is relevant not only on conceptual grounds, but also because it helps in making sense of the vast and sometimes ambiguous literature on agreements in cognitive science, social science, and Distributed Artificial Intelligence, where both notions have been used in different contexts and domains. For instance, discourse analysis in computational linguistics and cognitive science heavily relies on agreement between different informants and/or coders, in order to validate the generality of their subjective assessment or linguistic intuitions on discourse segments (for an authoritative review, see Carletta 1996): in this context, the emphasis is clearly on B-agreements, since the point is whether or not independent agents will converge on the same intuition about a given linguistic element, without any H-agreement among them. The same is true for most developmental studies on B-agreements in children, where the emphasis is on independent convergence or divergence of beliefs, and not on H-agreements between the parties (e.g., Wainryb et al. 2004). In contrast, studies on the psychology of negotiation (for a review, see Bazerman et al. 2000) look at how individual differences and social context affect the likelihood and the nature of H-agreements between negotiators, such that all parties will commit to a shared plan or course of action. Similarly, research in economics tends to focus on H-agreements, for instance in the study of bargaining impasses (Crawford 1982; Svejnar 1986), but the economic effects of B-agreements (or lack thereof) have also been studied, for instance in looking at how differences of opinions among traders dramatically influence stock markets (Hong and Stein 2006). H-agreements are also highly relevant in political science, for instance as the target state of deliberative democracy (Gutmann and Thompson 2004); however, inasmuch as the need to give reasons to justify public deliberations is grounded in the level of B-agreement within a given population, this too has received attention in this domain (e.g., the seminal survey on agreements and disagreements about democratic principles conducted by Prothro and Grigg (1960)). As for the philosophy of law (see also Casanovas 2013, this volume), the definition of what an agreement is, for instance in international law, clearly identifies it as an H-agreement (Widdows 1979); yet, a fair share of attention has also been given to differences of opinion on foundational issues, such as lack of B-agreement on what justice and law are (Waldron 1999).

Both notions have also been studied in computer science, so that agreement technologies actually span the divide between B-agreements and H-agreements (for a review, see Ossowski 2008, as well as the rest of this volume). As a case in point, consider first approaches to consensus and cooperation that focus on aligning the individual states of multiple networked agents or nodes to a desired target point: here consensus is defined as "an agreement regarding a certain quantity of interest that depends on the state of all agents" (Olfati-Saber et al. 2007, p. 215), and this clearly refers to a B-agreement. In contrast, multi-agent approaches using argumentation and negotiation to foster agreements among independent agents (e.g., Belesiotis et al. 2010; Heras et al. 2012; see also Part V of this volume) focus on H-agreements, inasmuch as their aim is to facilitate agreements on plans for action. Obviously, focusing on either notion does not imply overlooking the importance of the other, since aligning the agents' internal states to a state of B-agreement is typically instrumental to enable H-agreements on shared plans and collaborative actions – both in artificial agents and in humans. However, it is still the case that failing to acknowledge the crucial distinction between B-agreements and H-agreements may lead to confusion, ambiguity, and much talking at cross purposes, especially in a domain characterized by a significant degree of interdisciplinarity.

3.3 Paths to Agreement: Multiplicity and Circularity

If there is one thing which ought to be clear after browsing through the pages of this volume, it is that there are many ways of reaching an agreement – be it of the B- or the H- type. Agents can agree by sharing the same language and vocabulary (Semantics, Part II of this volume), by following a common set of rules (Norms, Part III), by being part of the same, internally structured social group (Organizations, Part IV), by discussing their respective positions (Argumentation and Negotiation, Part V), by delegating tasks to other agents and relying on their compliance and by assessing each other's features via socially shared mechanisms of interpersonal validation (Trust and Reputation, Part VI). This is true not only for artificial agents, but for humans as well: so it is no accident that many agreement technologies described in this volume are inspired by theories and models developed in cognitive and social science (e.g., on trust, norms and reputation, see Conte and Castelfranchi (1995), Conte and Paolucci (2002), and Castelfranchi and Falcone (2010)) and in philosophy (e.g., on argumentation, see Walton and Krabbe (1995) and Walton et al. (2008)).

Paths to agreement are not only multifarious: they also share a typical *circularity*, in that they all simultaneously presuppose and facilitate/produce agreement among the parties. Let us take norm-based agreements as a case in point: for norms to be efficacious, it is necessary (albeit not sufficient) that all parties are in B-agreement on their contents and have an H-agreement on their normative force – which does not necessarily imply automatic compliance with the norms, just accepting to be subjected to it, including when the norm is violated. In the absence of such agreements, norms are virtually useless – some would even say that they are not norms in any meaningful sense, just vacuous principles devoid of any efficacy. However, once norms are in place, they do facilitate further agreements among the parties of the normative pact, in the ways explored elsewhere in this volume (Part III, in particular). The same is true for many other paths to agreement, and this does not constitute a vicious circularity, but rather a self-sustaining loop in agreement dynamics. Whether or not current agreement technologies avail themselves of such loop is an intriguing question, one that, to my knowledge, has not been explored so far. The first impression is that agreement technologies by and large fail to exploit this beneficial circularity in agreement formation, mostly because the level of agreement presupposed by norms, arguments, trust relationships, etc., is often hardwired in the system, rather than emerging spontaneously, as it is often the case in human societies. Whether or not this impression is correct, how to design and implement self-sustaining agreement technologies is an open challenge for this research domain.

3.4 Should We Fear Disagreement?

From what has been said so far and the widespread emphasis on the virtues of agreement, it is evident that agreements are considered highly desirable features of social interaction: the more they are, and the greater their efficacy, the better for all parties involved – or so it would seem. Does it also follow that disagreements are invariably bad, something we should always try to get rid of, possibly in a permanent way? Answering this question again requires making use of the distinction between B-agreements and H-agreements. In general, it is fair to say that lack of H-agreements (for the sake of brevity, H-disagreements) is a problem for society, because it blocks the possibility of reaping the benefits of cooperation: as a case in point, think of the substantial costs of negotiation impasses in bargaining situations (see Crawford 1982; Svejnar 1986). However, a certain level of differences of opinion (B-disagreements) is inevitable in any dynamic social group, especially if its members enjoy high degrees of autonomy; moreover, such a variety of views is often beneficial to the group itself, inasmuch as it allows the exploration of several possible courses of action and avoid premature fixation on sub-optimal plans. Indeed, the accuracy of so called "wisdom of crowds" has been linked to the variety of opinions represented within a group, and to the independence of judgment of its members: lacking one or both of these parameters, the collective ability to converge on a correct belief or find an effective plan of action dramatically decreases (for discussion, see Surowiecki 2004).

So it would seem that well-functioning social groups do not eradicate B-disagreements among their members, but rather develop effective methods to negotiate H-agreements when (and only when) consensus is required on a given matter. This delicate balance between ad hoc agreement formation and a permanent reservoir of disagreement conveys important lessons also for agreement technologies. Schematically, a well-adapted "agreement ecology" includes both techniques for removing disagreements, and *renewable sources of further disagreement*. However, the current emphasis in agreement technologies is unbalanced towards the first factor, while paying much less attention to the second. This runs the risk of killing the goose that laid the golden eggs, that is, designing agent societies in which the volume of agreements rapidly escalates, without at the same time maintaining a healthy level of baseline disagreement. This can be avoided in many ways, and sometimes it is the structure of the task that feeds disagreement into the system: for instance, agreement technologies aimed at supporting interaction between buyers and sellers (see Part VII for several examples) can safely focus all their efforts in facilitating agreement, since the parties themselves will automatically bring within the interaction different opinions and conflicting goals. However, the more autonomous artificial agents become, the more designers need to worry about preserving their autonomy of judgment. This will entail the fascinating challenge of designing dynamic sources of disagreement, and not just automatic methods for agreement formation.

3.5 Conclusions

In this chapter we took a random walk across a variety of studies in cognitive and social science on the multifaceted notion of agreement. This was not meant to provide any systematic review of the extensive literature on the topic, but rather to offer the occasion for some reflections on specific aspects of agreement dynamics. In particular, I defended a pragmatic view of agreements as the grease of social interaction, discussed the difference between being in agreement and having an agreement, outlined how both notions have received attention across various domains in cognitive and social sciences, analyzed the self-sustaining loop between agreements and methods for agreement formation (norms, argumentation, organizations, etc.), and emphasized the beneficial role of disagreement in social dynamics and thus the need to preserve pools of disagreement even in the most agreeable societies. Hopefully, this brief overview will offer some food for thought, in relation to the impressive scope of agreement technologies described in the rest of the volume.

References

Andrighetto, G., L. Tummolini, C. Castelfranchi, and R. Conte. 2009. A convention or (tacit) agreement betwixt us. In *Normative multi-agent systems. Dagstuhl seminar proceedings 09121*, ed. G. Boella, P. Noriega, G. Pigozzi, Verhagen, H. http://drops.dagstuhl.de/opus/volltexte/2009/1919.

Baumeister, R., and M. Leary. 1995. The need to belong: desire for interpersonal attachments as a fundamental human motivation. *Psychological Bulletin* 117(3): 497–529.

Bazerman, M., J. Curhan, D. Moore, K. Valley. 2000. Negotiation. *Annual Review of Psychology* 51: 279–314.

Belesiotis, A., M. Rovatsos, and I. Rahwan. 2010. Agreeing on plans through iterated disputes. In *Proceedings of 9th international conference on autonomous agents and multiagent systems, AAMAS 2010*, ed. W. van der Hoek, G. Kaminka, Y. Lespérance, M. Luck, and S. Sen, 765–772. Toronto: ACM.

Bowles, S. 2006. Group competition, reproductive leveling, and the evolution of human altruism. *Science* 314: 1569–1572.

Carletta, J. 1996. Assessing agreement on classification tasks: The kappa statistics. *Computa-tional Linguistics* 22(2): 249–254.

Casanovas, P. 2013. Agreement and relational justice: A perspective from philosophy and sociology of law. In *Agreement technologies*, ed. S. Ossowski, 19–42. Berlin: Springer, this volume.

Castelfranchi, C., and R. Falcone. 2010. *Trust theory: A socio-cognitive and computational model.* Chichester: Wiley.

Conte, R., and C. Castelfranchi. 1995. *Cognitive and social action*. London: UCL.

Conte, R., and M. Paolucci. 2002. *Reputation in artificial societies: Social beliefs for social order.* Boston: Kluwer.

Crawford, V. 1982. A theory of disagreement in bargaining. *Econometrica* 50(3): 607–638.

Gilbert, M. 1983. *On social facts*. London: Routledge.

Gilbert, M. 1993. Is an agreement an exchange of promises? *The Journal of Philosophy* 54(12): 627–649.

Ginet, C. 2001. Deciding to believe. In *Knowledge, truth, and duty*, ed. M. Steup, 63–76. Oxford: Oxford University Press.

Gutmann, A., and D. Thompson. 2004. *Why deliberative democracy?* Princeton: Princeton University Press.

Heras, S., V. Botti, and V. Julián. 2012. An abstract argumentation framework for supporting agreements in agent societies. In *Proceedings of the HAIS 2010*, ed. E. S. Corchado Rodriguez, et al., Part II, 177–184. Berlin: Springer.

Hong, H., and J. Stein. 2006. Disagreement and the stock market. *Journal of Economic Perspectives* 21(2): 109–128.

Olfati-Saber, R., A. Fax, and R. Murray. 2007. Consensus and cooperation in networked multi-agent systems. *Proceedings of the IEEE* 95(1): 215–233.

Ossowski, S. 2008. Coordination and agreement in multi-agent systems. In *Proceedings of the CIA-2008*, ed. M. Klusch, M. Pechoucek, and A. Polleres, 16–23. Berlin: Springer.

Paglieri, F. 2010. Committed to argue: on the cognitive roots of dialogical commitments. In *Dialectics, dialogue and argumentation. An examination of Douglas Walton's theories of reasoning*, ed. C. Reed and C. W. Tindale, 59–71. London: College Publications.

Prothro, J., and C. Grigg. 1960. Fundamentals principles of democracy: Bases of agreement and disagreement. *The Journal of Politics* 22(2): 276–294.

Surowiecki, J. 2004. *The wisdom of crowds: Why the many are smarter than the few and how collective wisdom shapes business, economies, societies and nations*. London: Little/Brown

Svejnar, J. 1986. Bargaining power, fear of disagreement, and wage settlements: Theory and evidence from the U.S. Industry. *Econometrica* 54(5): 1055–1078.

Van Eemeren, F., and R. Grootendorst. 2004. *A systematic theory of argumentation: The pragma-dialectical approach*. Cambridge: Cambridge University Press.

Wainryb, C., L. Shaw, M. Langley, K. Cottam, and R. Lewis. 2004. Children's thinking about diversity of belief in the early school years: Judgments of relativism, tolerance, and disagreeing persons. *Child Development* 75(3): 687–703.

Waldron, J. 1999. *Law and disagreement*. Oxford: Clarendon.

Walton, D., and E. Krabbe. 1995. *Commitment in dialogue: Basic concepts of interpersonal reasoning*. Albany: SUNY.

Walton, D., C. Reed, and F. Macagno. 2008. *Argumentation schemes*. Cambridge: Cambridge University Press.

Wansing, H. 2006. Doxastic decisions, epistemic justification, and the logic of agency. *Philosophical Studies* 128: 201–227.

Widdows, K. 1979. What is an agreement in international law? *British Yearbook of International Law* 50: 117–149.

Woods, J. 2005. Epistemic bubbles. In: *we will show them: essays in honour of Dov Gabbay*, ed. S. Artemov, H. Barringer, A. d'Avila Garcez, L. Lamb, and J. Woods, vol. II, 731–774. London: College Publications.

Part II
Semantics in Agreement Technologies

In an open and large scale distributed system such as the ones covered by Agreement Technologies, where local agents are mostly autonomous, applications, services, communication devices, social entities, etc. are likely to comply with very different data models, knowledge representation, functionalities and so on. Thereby, in order to make them interact appropriately to reach common goals, there is a need for agents to carry and offer an explicit semantic interface in such a way that agents can mutually "understand" each other. However, when agents can enter and leave the system at any time and have their own objectives with different capabilities, it is not reasonable to assume that they all adhere to a single view of the world. Thus, heterogeneity is a strong obstacle to reaching agreements to interoperate properly. Yet, semantic technologies provide good solutions to unlock the barriers towards interoperability.

In this part, we present a number of existing tools, both theoretical and practical, that enable interoperability in Agreement Technologies by exploiting existing contributions from the fields collectively called "semantic technologies". We insist on the fact that in spite of the term *semantics*, which is related to the *meaning* of things, semantic technologies do not enable software to truly *understand* the underlying meaning. However, these technologies are developed to *approximate* real comprehension by way of knowledge representation, automated reasoning, logical formalisms, ontologies, rule systems, ontology matching, and so on.

As it is expected that Agreement Technologies will be commonly deployed over—or interact with—the World Wide Web, we give a special attention to the standards proposed to enable the vision of the *Semantic* Web. Indeed, we start the part with a chapter on this matter (Chap. 4) where we present the Resource Description Framework (RDF), the Web Ontology Language (OWL), the SPARQL RDF Query Language (SPARQL) and the Rule Interchange Format (RIF) as they can be used in the context of Agreement Technologies. These standards are based on logical formalisms which define unambiguously what can be inferred from a data set or ontology, and what are valid results from a query. However, strictly conforming to these formalisms in the context of distributed, open and heterogeneous systems almost certainly leads to inconsistencies, undesired or invalid conclusions, untrusted inferences, etc. Therefore, we describe non-standard logical frameworks that were proposed to extend classical knowledge representation formats to the case of distributed, open, multi-contextual, heterogeneous sources of information (Chap. 5). In addition to that, when integrating independent knowledge sources, it is generally necessary to match the terms or symbols used in distinct representations. This task, known as *ontology matching*, has to be performed when autonomous agents, adhering to different terminologies, need to interact for the first time. Chapter 6 surveys some of the techniques used to reach semantic agreement via ontology matching and argumentation.

All the technologies mentioned so far are generic in the sense that they are agnostic with respect to the application setting in which they are used. Consequently, they can be applied to all the fields covered by Agreement Technologies, particularly Multi-Agent Systems (MAS), (semantic) Web services, or Grid and Cloud computing, where semantic interoperability is crucial. To show how semantics play a role in these domains, we describe existing contributions in those fields, showing:

- How Semantic Web technologies can be leveraged to ensure norms and commitments in a MAS (Chap. 7);
- How semantic matchmaking enables brokering e-business services in MAS for content discovery in telecommunication environment (Chap. 7);
- How Web services can be combined automatically or semi-automatically based on semantic descriptions and matching techniques (Chap. 8);
- How ontologies make easier access to adequate computational sources in Grid computing (Chap. 9).

Outline of the Part

The organisation of the part is summarised in the diagram of Fig. 1. The chapters can be grouped in two main parts, one presenting generic approaches originated from semantic technologies (Chaps. 4–6) and one showing applications of these technologies in various fields of Agreement Technologies (Chaps. 7–9).

More precisely, in Chap. 4, we present how Semantic Web technologies can be used in Agreement Technologies. In Chap. 5, we present logical formalisms that have been proposed to define the semantics and reasoning tasks in a multicontextual setting, as it is the case in large scale, distributed, open systems that Agreement Technologies are dealing with. In Chap. 6, we present the models of aligning heterogeneous ontologies, especially insisting on how to reach agreement on alignments between local knowledge. In Chap. 7, we present how multi-agent systems take advantage of semantic technologies to treat problems of commitment and norms.

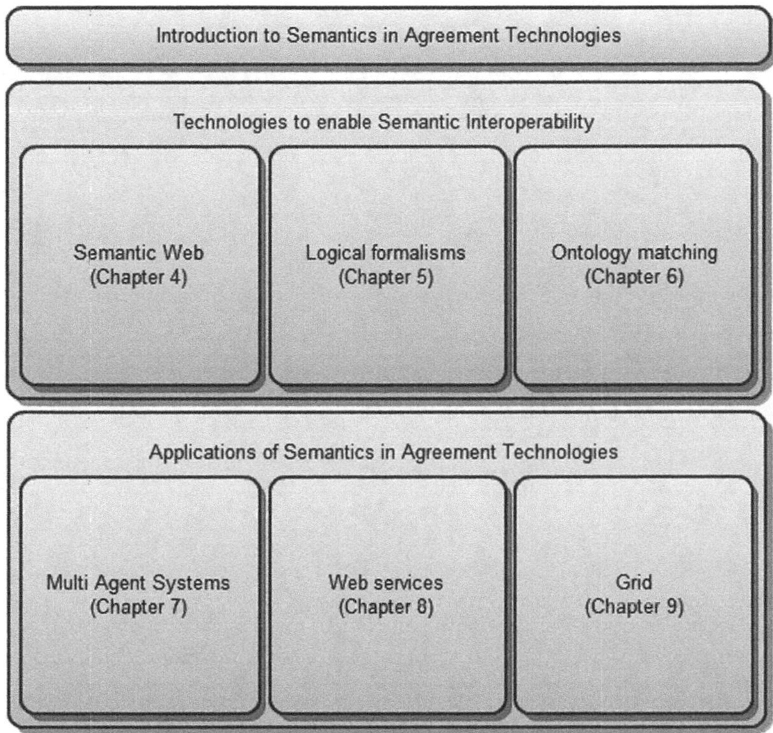

Fig. 1 Organisation of Part II

In Chap. 8, we present how semantics enable discovery, interoperability and matchmaking at the service level. In Chap. 9, we present how semantic technologies, especially ontologies, help describing meta information in Grid computing to improve resource discovery and usage.

Antoine Zimmermann, George Vouros and Axel Polleres
Editors Part "Semantics"

Chapter 4
Agreement Technologies and the Semantic Web

Axel Polleres

4.1 Introduction

In this chapter we discuss the relationship between Agreement Technologies and the Semantic Web. We especially focus on how Semantic Web standards play a role in the Agreement Technologies stack, but also refer to issues related to Linked Data and the Web of Data.

We start the chapter with an overview of Semantic Web standards. Then, the scientific foundations for Semantic Web standards are discussed. Finally, Sect. 4.4 relates the work on semantic technologies to other fields of Agreement Technologies, from the point of view of Semantic Web standards.

4.2 Semantic Web Standards

The Semantic Web is growing up. Over the last few years, technologies and standards for building up the architecture of this next generation of the Web have matured and are being deployed on large scale in many live Web sites. The underlying technology stack of the Semantic Web consists of several standards endorsed by the World Wide Web consortium (W3C) that provide the formal underpinnings of a machine-readable "Web of Data" (Polleres and Huynh 2009):

- A uniform exchange syntax: the eXtensible Markup Language (XML)
- A uniform data exchange format: the Resource Description Framework (RDF)
- Ontologies: RDF Schema and the Web Ontology Language (OWL)

A. Polleres (✉)
Siemens AG Österreich, Siemensstrasse 90, 1210 Vienna, Austria
e-mail: axel.polleres@siemens.com

S. Ossowski (ed.), *Agreement Technologies*, Law, Governance and Technology Series 8, DOI 10.1007/978-94-007-5583-3_4,

- Rules: the Rule Interchange Format (RIF)
- Query and transformation languages: XQuery, SPARQL

4.2.1 The eXtensible Markup Language (XML)

Starting from the pure HTML Web which mainly facilitated the exchange of layout information for Web pages only, the introduction of the eXtensible Markup Language (XML) in its first edition in 1998 (Bray et al. 1998) was a breakthrough for Web technologies. With XML as a uniform exchange syntax, any semi-structured data can be modeled as a tree. Along with available APIs, parsers and other tools, XML allows one to define various other Web languages besides HTML. XML nowadays is not only the basis for Web data, but also for Web services (Fensel et al. 2006) and is used in many custom applications as a convenient data exchange syntax. Schema description languages such as XML Schema (Thompson et al. 2004) can be used to define XML languages; expressive query and transformation languages such as XQuery (Chamberlin et al. 2007) and XSLT (Kay 2007) allow for querying specific parts of an XML tree, or for transforming one XML language into another.

4.2.2 The Resource Description Framework (RDF)

The *Resource Description Framework* (RDF) – now around for over a decade already as well – is the basic data model for the Semantic Web. It is built upon one of the simplest structures for representing data: a directed labeled graph. An RDF graph is described by a set of triples of the form ⟨*Subject Predicate Object*⟩, also called *statements*, which represent the edges of this graph. Anonymous nodes in this graph – so called-blank nodes, akin to existential variables – allow one to model incomplete information. RDF's flat graph-like representation has the advantage of abstracting away from the data schema, and thus promises to allow for easier integration than customised XML data in different XML dialects: whereas the integration of different XML languages requires the transformation between different tree structures using transformation languages such as XSLT (Kay 2007) or XQuery (Chamberlin et al. 2007), different RDF graphs can simply be stored and queried alongside one another, and as soon as they share common nodes, form a joint graph upon a simple merge operation. While the normative syntax to exchange RDF, RDF/XML (Beckett and McBride 2004), is an XML dialect itself, there are various other serialisation formats for RDF, such as RDFa (Adida et al. 2008), a format that allows one to embed RDF within (X)HTML, or non-XML representations such as the more readable Turtle (Beckett and Berners-Lee 2008) syntax; likewise RDF stores (e.g., YARS2 Harth et al. 2007) normally use their own, proprietary internal representations of triples, that do not relate to XML at all.

4.2.3 RDF Schema and the Web Ontology Language (OWL)

Although RDF itself is essentially schema-less, additional standards such as RDF Schema and OWL facilitate formal descriptions of the relations between the terms used in an RDF graph: i.e., the predicates in an RDF triple which form edges in an RDF graph (properties) and types of subject or object nodes in an RDF graph (classes). Formal descriptions of these properties and classes can be understood as logical theories, also called ontologies, which allow systems to infer new connections in an RDF graph, or link otherwise unconnected RDF graphs. Standard languages to describe ontologies on the Web are

- RDF Schema (Brickley et al. 2004) – a lightweight ontology language that allows one to describe essentially simple class hierarchies, as well as the domains and ranges of properties; and
- The Web Ontology language (OWL) (Smith et al. 2004) which was first published in 2004 and recently has been extended with additional useful features in the OWL 2 (Hitzler et al. 2009) standard.

OWL offers richer means than RDF Schema to define formal relations between classes and properties, such as intersection and union of classes, value restrictions or cardinality restrictions. OWL 2 offers even more features such as, for instance, the ability to define keys, property chains, or meta-modeling (i.e., speaking about classes as instances).

4.2.4 The Rule Interchange Format (RIF)

Although ontology languages such as OWL (2) offer a rich set of constructs to describe relations between RDF terms, these languages are still insufficient to express complex mappings between ontologies, which may better be described in terms of rule languages. The lack of standards in this area had been addressed by several proposals for rule languages on top of RDF, such as the Semantic Web Rule language (SWRL) (Horrocks et al. 2004), WRL (Angele et al. 2005), or N3 (Berners-Lee and Connolly 2008; Berners-Lee et al. 2008). These languages offer, for example, support for non-monotonic negation, or rich sets of built-in functions. The importance of rule languages – also outside the narrow use case of RDF rules – has finally lead to the establishment of another W3C working group in 2005 to standardise a generic Rule Interchange Format (RIF). RIF has recently reached proposed recommendation status and will soon be a W3C recommendation. The standard comprises several dialects such as (i) RIF Core (Boley et al. 2010), a minimal dialect close to Datalog, (ii) the RIF Basic Logic Dialect (RIF-BLD) (Boley and Kifer 2010) which offers the expressive features of Horn rules, and also (iii) a production rules dialect (RIF-PRD) (de Sainte Marie et al. 2010). A set of standard datatypes as well as built-in functions and predicates (RIF-DTB) are defined in a separate document (Polleres et al. 2010). The relation of RIF to OWL and RDF is detailed in another document (de Bruijn 2010) that defines the formal semantics of combinations of RIF rule sets with RDF graphs and OWL ontologies.

4.2.5 Query and Transformation Language: SPARQL

Finally, a crucial puzzle piece which pushed the recent wide uptake of Semantic Web technologies at large was the availability of a standard query language for RDF, namely SPARQL (Prud'hommeaux and Seaborne 2008), which plays the same role for the Semantic Web as SQL does for relational data. SPARQL's syntax is roughly inspired by Turtle (Beckett and Berners-Lee 2008) and SQL-99 (1999), providing basic means to query RDF such as unions of conjunctive queries, value filtering, optional query parts, as well as slicing and sorting results. The recently re-chartered SPARQL1.1 W3C working group[1] aims at extending the original SPARQL language by commonly requested features such as aggregates, sub-queries, negation, and path expressions.

4.3 Scientific Foundations for Semantic Web Standards

The work in the respective standardisation groups is partially still ongoing or has only finished very recently. In parallel, there has been plenty of work in the scientific community to define the formal underpinnings for these standards:

- The logical foundations and properties of RDF and RDF Schema have been investigated in detail (Gutiérrez et al. 2004; Muñoz et al. 2007; Pichler et al. 2008). Correspondence of the formal semantics of RDF and RDF Schema (Hayes 2004) with Datalog and First-order logic have been studied in the literature (Bruijn and Heymans 2007; Bruijn et al. 2005; Ianni et al. 2009).
- The semantics of standard fragments of OWL have been defined in terms of expressive Description Logics such as $\mathcal{SHOIN}$(D) (OWL DL) (Horrocks and Patel-Schneider 2004) or $\mathcal{SROIQ}$(D) (OWL 2 DL) (Horrocks et al. 2006), and the research on OWL has significantly influenced the Description Logics community over the past years: for example, in defining tractable fragments like the $\mathcal{EL}$ (Baader 2003; Baader et al. 2005) family of Description Logics, or fragments that allow for reducing basic reasoning tasks to query answering in SQL, such as the DL-Lite family of Description Logics (Calvanese et al. 2007). Other fragments of OWL and OWL 2 have been defined in terms of Horn rules such as DLP (Grosof et al. 2003), OWL^{-} (de Bruijn et al. 2005),

[1] http://www.w3.org/2009/sparql/wiki

pD* (ter Horst 2005), or Horn-SHIQ (Krötzsch et al. 2007). In fact, the new OWL 2 specification defines tractable fragments of OWL based on these results: namely, OWL 2 EL, OWL 2 QL, and OWL 2 RL (Motik et al. 2009).
- The semantics of RIF builds on foundations such as Frame Logic (Kifer et al. 1995) and Datalog. RIF borrows, e.g., notions of Datalog safety from the scientific literature to define fragments with finite minimal models despite the presence of built-ins: the *strongly-safe* fragment of RIF Core (Boley et al. 2010, Sect. 6.2) is inspired by a similar safety condition defined by Eiter, Schindlauer, et al. (Eiter et al. 2006b; Schindlauer 2006). In fact, the closely related area of decidable subsets of Datalog and answer set programs with function symbols is a very active field of research (Baselice et al. 2009; Calimeri et al. 2009; Eiter and Simkus 2010).
- The formal semantics of SPARQL is also very much inspired by academic results, such as by the seminal papers of Pérez et al. (2006, 2009). Their work further lead to refined results on equivalences within SPARQL (Schmidt et al. 2010) and on the relation of SPARQL to Datalog (Polleres 2006, 2007). Angles and Gutierrez (2008) later showed that SPARQL has exactly the expressive power of non-recursive safe Datalog with negation.

4.4 Semantic Web Standards in Agreement Technologies

Herein we relate the work on semantic technologies to other fields of Agreement Technologies, from the point of view of Semantic Web standards.

4.4.1 Policies, Norms and the Semantic Web "Trust Layer"

Policies (as far as they are subject to standards in the W3C) are typically considered as rules and constraints that model intended behaviours. Within W3C, the Policy Languages Interest Group (PLING)[2] is the forum to coordinate efforts around policy languages, frameworks and use cases for policies. The affected standards range from standard protocols to exchange policies, e.g., P3P (Cranor et al. 2006), to concrete rules languages that should eventually allow to describe and exchange such policies such as the Rule Interchange Format (RIF), cf. RIF's Use Cases and Requirements document (Paschke et al. 2008, Sect. 10) for a concrete example. Apart from W3C's activities, the most prominent and established industry standard for describing and exchanging policies is probably OASIS' eXtensible Access Control Markup Language (XACML) (Moses 2005).

---

[2] http://www.w3.org/Policy/pling/

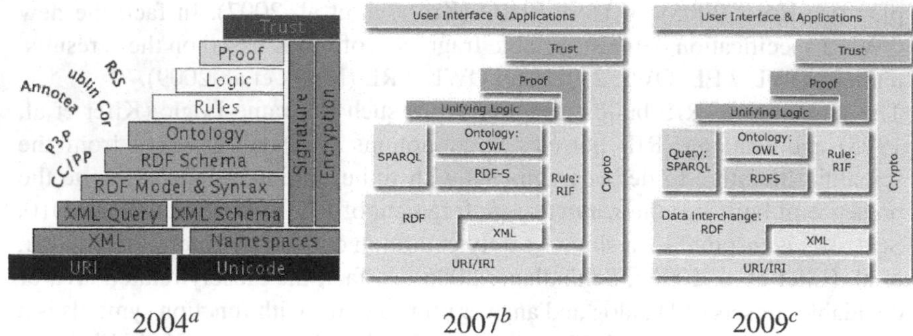

2004[a] 2007[b] 2009[c]

[a]http://www.w3.org/2004/Talks/0319-RDF-WGs/sw_stack.png

[b]http://www.w3.org/2007/Talks/0130-sb-W3CTechSemWeb/layerCake-4.png

[c]http://www.w3c.it/talks/2009/athena/images/layerCake.png

Fig. 4.1 Development of the semantic web layer cake

Norms, in contrast are probably rather what one may call *agreed policies* in a community, whereas policies can also be something individual (my privacy policies in a social network, mail filtering policies, etc.). With this definition in mind, *policies* on the (Semantic) Web build the foundation for privacy of personal or organisational data, whereas *norms* are more important in terms of establishing best practices (e.g., how to publish data).

Formalisation of both (private and organisational) policies and (community) norms would be useful for various applications (be it Web applications or federated applications across enterprises) such as checking compliance or conformance, alignment of policies, or checking internal consistency or redundancies of policies made explicit. Formal languages are not being used yet to describe norms and best practices in the standardisation bodies themselves, though. Normative documents such as the W3C patent policy (Weitzner 2004) or best practices documents such as the ones for publishing RDF vocabularies (Berrueta and Phipps 2008), the Web content accessibility guidelines (Caldwell et al. 2008), or conformance clauses in most standards documents are formulated in natural language only.

Now as to how far questions on policies and norms relate to the "trust layer" in the Semantic Web layer cake, policy languages are indeed to play a major role there, although a lot of questions (how to enable provenance, signatures, etc.) around this trust layer are still largely discussed on a lower level than modeling actual policies. It can probably be expected that the single "trust layer" as it exists in the various incarnations of the infamous Semantic Web "layer cake" (see Fig. 4.1) will end up being split into different building blocks and standards, just like it was the case for the Ontology and Rules layers: as these "layers" got populated they have split up in different interplaying standards that are not necessarily strictly layered anymore (RIF, OWL, RDFS, SPARQL). The standardisation process in W3C is still two layers down, before the trust layer will be tackled, and we may expect the simplifying "layer" picture to change even more drastically over the next few years.

4.4.2 *Evolution of Norms and Organisational Changes*

In many cases the evolution of norms and policies and organisational change are mainly about merging and aligning existing policies and norms. This issue becomes increasingly important in scenarios such as big enterprise mergers where automated support for the alignment of norms and policies would be a real cost-saver. So, one could ask the latter question the other way around as well, i.e., whether research in ontology matching, alignment and merging (for an overview, see Euzenat and Shvaiko 2007) can possibly contribute to gaining more insights on how to deal with the alignment of policies and norms. What should be stressed here is that "ontology alignment" should be viewed broadly, Description Logics based ontology languages are likely not sufficiently expressive to express both semantic models and policies, but rule languages and other formalisms are necessary. Unifying semantics of Description Logics and Rules are a widely discussed topic in the literature over the past few years (cf. Eiter et al. 2006a, 2008 for an overview).

4.4.3 *Semantic Web Languages Versus Norm-Based or Organisation-Based Programming Languages*

There is still a huge potential in terms of making the existing Semantic Web standards themselves interplay better, and this is where research will probably still have to solve some problems, before the "trust layer" of the Semantic Web can at all be populated with standards. While protocols and languages like P3P and XACML are emerging, it will become an issue of how to tie these with domain ontologies in RDFS and OWL, or how to embed rule based descriptions of policies (e.g., given in RIF) in formal descriptions of policies and norms. Still, what is important to observe is that all these languages and standards are being used by communities of increasing sizes already. The main question is thus not how to promote or establish new languages and standards to even increase the existing "language zoo", but in closing gaps between the existing standards, or building frameworks that make them interplay smoothly. Wherever research in norm-based or organisation-based programming languages can contribute here, there are good chances for practical impact.

4.4.4 *What Can We Learn from Standardisation Efforts in the Semantic Web Area?*

In a narrow view, one could claim that the "Semantic Web" is actually all about standardisation since it is an activity which emerged within the World Wide Web consortium – a standardisation body. There are important lessons to be learned from these standardisation efforts in the Semantic web area: the bottom-up population of an architectural idea (symbolised by the "Semantic Web Layer cake" in Fig. 4.1) by standards is beginning to being picked up at wide scale: RDF is becoming increasingly popular on the Web and light-weight ontologies such as FOAF[3] or SIOC (Bojārs et al. 2007) are used to publish increasingly structured content on the Web following the so called "Linked Data" principles (Berners-Lee 2006), indeed making a big fraction of the Web machine-understandable. Those ontologies being widely used on the emerging Web of Data (Polleres and Huynh 2009) are not necessarily complex. For instance, SIOC, an ontology for describing online communities and their conversations consists only of a handful of concepts and relations, but most of the effort of the SIOC-project went into finding agreement on these common terms and promoting the ontology's usage on the Web, e.g., by writing exporters and tools.[4] It is such efforts which enable practical deployment of Semantic Web technologies Thus, the lesson learned is that standards and technologies make only as much sense as they are eventually being deployed, following Metcalfe's law that the value of telecommunications technologies – and this law seems to apply even more so to Web technologies – increases proportionally with the square of its users. Technologies that help enforcing policies or establish norms on the Web will need to follow the same principles.

4.4.5 Implicit Versus Explicit Norms on the Semantic Web

Best practices and norms on the Web are indeed largely not (yet) being made explicit, and indeed it is questionable whether doing so would have measurable benefits. Many "de facto standards" on the Web did not emerge from standardisation bodies at all, but rather from "grass roots efforts". Standardisation bodies can still help by "rubber-stamping" agreed technologies to make them usable beyond specialised communities. In fact, standardisation processes like within W3C with mechanisms such as member submissions for proposing technologies that have been proven useful in practice for standardisation try to encompass such movements.

References

Adida, B., M. Birbeck, S. McCarron, and S. Pemberton. 2008. RDFa in XHTML: Syntax and Processing. W3C Recommendation, W3C. Available at http://www.w3.org/TR/rdfa-syntax/.

Angele, J., H. Boley, J. de Bruijn, D. Fensel, P. Hitzler, M. Kifer, R. Krummenacher, H. Lausen, A. Polleres, and R. Studer. 2005. Web Rule Language (WRL). W3C Member Submission. http://www.w3.org/Submission/WRL/.

[3]http://xmlns.com/foaf/spec/

[4]http://www.sioc-project.org/

Angles, R., and C. Gutierrez. 2008. The expressive power of sparql. *In international semantic web conference (ISWC 2008)*. Lecture Notes in Computer Science, vol. 5318, 114–129. Karlsruhe: Springer.

Baader, F. 2003. Terminological cycles in a description logic with existential restrictions. In *Proceedings of the eighteenth international joint conference on artificial intelligence (IJCAI2003)*, Acapulco, Mexico, 325–330.

Baader, F., S. Brandt, and C. Lutz. 2005. Pushing the el envelope. In*Proceedings of the nineteenth international joint conference on artificial intelligence (IJCAI2005)*, 364–369. Edinburgh: Professional Book Center.

Baselice, S., P. A. Bonatti, and G. Criscuolo. 2009. On finitely recursive programs. *TPLP* 9(2): 213–238.

Beckett, D., and T. Berners-Lee. 2008. Turtle – Terse RDF triple language. W3c Team Submission, W3C. Available at http://www.w3.org/TeamSubmission/turtle/.

Beckett, D., and B. McBride. 2004. RDF/XML syntax specification (Revised). W3c Recommendation, W3C. Available at http://www.w3.org/TR/REC-rdf-syntax/.

Berners-Lee, T. 2006. Linked data – Design issues. Available at http://www.w3.org/DesignIssues/LinkedData.html.

Berners-Lee, T., and D. Connolly. 2008. Notation3 (N3): A readable RDF syntax. W3c Team Submission, W3C. Available at http://www.w3.org/TeamSubmission/n3/.

Berners-Lee, T., D. Connolly, L. Kagal, Y. Scharf, and J. Hendler. 2008. N3logic: a logical framework for the world wide web. *Theory and Practice of Logic Programming* 8(3): 249–269.

Berrueta, D., and J. Phipps. 2008. Best practice recipes for publishing rdf vocabularies. W3C Working Group Note. http://www.w3.org/TR/swbp-vocab-pub/.

Bojārs, U., J. G. Breslin, D. Berrueta, D. Brickley, S. Decker, S. Fernández, C. Görn, A. Harth, T. Heath, K. Idehen, K. Kjernsmo, A. Miles, A. Passant, A. Polleres, L. Polo, and M. Sintek. 2007. SIOC core ontology specification. W3C Member Submission Available at http://www.w3.org/Submission/sioc-spec/.

Boley, H., and M. Kifer. 2010. RIF basic logic dialect. W3C Proposed Recommendation, W3C. Available at http://www.w3.org/TR/2010/PR-rif-bld-20100511/.

Boley, H., G. Hallmark, M. Kifer, A. Paschke, A. Polleres, and D. Reynolds. 2010. RIF core dialect. W3C Proposed Recommendation, W3C. Available at http://www.w3.org/TR/2010/PR-rif-core-20100511/.

Bray, T., J. Paoli, and C. Sperberg-McQueen. 1998. XML Path Language (XPath) 2.0. W3C recommendation, W3C. Available at http://www.w3.org/TR/1998/REC-xml-19980210.

Brickley, D., R. Guha, B. McBride. 2004. RDF vocabulary description language 1.0: RDF schema. Tech. rep., W3C. W3C Recommendation. http://www.w3.org/TR/rdf-schema/.

Bruijn, J. d., and S. Heymans. 2007. Logical foundations of (e)RDF(S): Complexity and reasoning. In *Proceedings of the 6th international semantic web conference and 2nd Asian semantic web conference (ISWC2007+ASWC2007)*, Lecture Notes in Computer Science, no. 4825, 86–99. Busan: Springer. http://www.debruijn.net/publications/frames-rdf-conference.pdf.

Bruijn, J. d., E. Franconi, and S. Tessaris. 2005. Logical reconstruction of normative RDF. In *OWL: experiences and directions workshop (OWLED-2005)*, Galway, Ireland. http://www.debruijn.net/publications/owl-05.pdf.

Caldwell, B., M. Cooper, L. G. Reid, and G. Vanderheiden. 2008. Web content accessibility guidelines (wcag) 2.0. W3C Recommendation, http://www.w3.org/TR/WCAG20/.

Calimeri, F., S. Cozza, G. Ianni, and N. Leone. 2009. Magic sets for the bottom-up evaluation of finitely recursive programs. In *Logic programming and nonmonotonic reasoning, 10th international conference (LPNMR 2009)*. Lecture Notes in Computer Science, ed. E. Erdem, F. Lin, and T. Schaub, vol. 5753, 71–86. Potsdam: Springer.

Calvanese, D., G. D. Giacomo, D. Lembo, M. Lenzerini, and R. Rosati. 2007. Tractable reasoning and efficient query answering in description logics: The *dl-lite* family. *Journal of Automated Reasoning* 39(3): 385–429.

Chamberlin, D., J. Robie, S. Boag, M. F. Fernández, J. Siméon, and D. Florescu. 2007. XQuery 1.0: An XML Query Language. W3C Recommendation, W3C. Available at http://www.w3.org/TR/xquery/.

Cranor, L., B. Dobbs, S. Egelman, G. Hogben, J. Humphrey, M. Langheinrich, M. Marchiori, M. Presler-Marshall, J. Reagle, M. Schunter, D. A. Stampley, and R. Wenning. 2006. The platform for privacy preferences 1.1 (P3P1.1) specification. W3C Working Group Note. Available at http://www.w3.org/TR/P3P11/.

de Bruijn, J. 2010. RIF RDF and OWL compatibility. W3C Propose Recommendation, W3C. Available at http://www.w3.org/TR/2010/PR-rif-rdf-owl-20100511/.

de Bruijn, J., A. Polleres, R. Lara, and D. Fensel. 2005. OWL^{-}. Final draft d20.1v0.2, WSML.

de Sainte Marie, C., G. Hallmark, and A. Paschke. 2010. RIF production rule dialect. W3C Proposed Recommendation, W3C. Available at http://www.w3.org/TR/2010/PR-rif-prd-20100511/.

Eiter, T., G. Ianni, A. Polleres, R. Schindlauer, and H. Tompits. 2006a. Reasoning with rules and ontologies. In *Reasoning Web 2006*. Lecture Notes in Computer Science, ed. P. Barahona, et al., vol. 4126, 93–127. Berline/Heidelberg: Springer. http://www.polleres.net/publications/eit-etal-2006_rowSchool.pdf.

Eiter, T., G. Ianni, R. Schindlauer, and H. Tompits. 2006b. Effective integration of declarative rules with external evaluations for semantic-web reasoning. In *Proceedings of the 3rd European Semantic Web Conference (ESWC2006)*. LNCS, vol. 4011, 273–287. Budva: Montenegro.

Eiter, T., G. Ianni, T. Krennwallner, and A. Polleres. 2008. Rules and ontologies for the semantic web. In *Reasoning Web 2008*. Lecture Notes in Computer Science, ed. C. Baroglio, P. A. Bonatti, J. Maluszynski, M. Marchiori, A. Polleres, and S. Schaffert, vol. 5224, 1–53. Venice: Springer. http://www.polleres.net/publications/eite-etal-2008.pdf.

Eiter, T., and M. Simkus. 2010. FDNC: Decidable nonmonotonic disjunctive logic programs with function symbols. *ACM Transactions on Computational Logic* 11(2): 1–45.

Euzenat, J., and P. Shvaiko. 2007. *Ontology matching*. Heidelberg: Springer.

Fensel, D., H. Lausen, A. Polleres, J. de Bruijn, M. Stollberg, D. Roman, and J. Domingue. 2006. Enabling semantic web services : The web service modeling Ontology. Berlin/New York: Springer. http://www.springer.com/west/home/business/business+information+systems?SGWID=4-170-22-173663112-0.

Grosof, B. N., I. Horrocks, R. Volz, and S. Decker. 2003. Description logic programs: Combining logic programs with description logic. In *12th international conference on world wide web (WWW'03)*, 48–57. Budapest: ACM.

Gutiérrez, C., C. A. Hurtado, A. O. Mendelzon. 2004. Foundations of semantic web databases. In *Proceedings of the twenty-third acm sigact-sigmod-sigart symposium on principles of database systems (PODS 2004)*, 95–106. Paris: ACM.

Harth, A., J. Umbrich, A. Hogan, and S. Decker. 2007. YARS2: A federated repository for querying graph structured data from the web. In *6th international semantic web conference, 2nd Asian semantic web conference*, 211–224. Berlin/New York: Springer

Hayes, P. 2004. RDF semantics, W3C Recommendation 10 February 2004. W3C Recommendation, World Wide Web Consortium (W3C). http://www.w3.org/TR/2004/REC-rdf-mt-20040210/.

Hitzler, P., M. Krötzsch, B. Parsia, P. F. Patel-Schneider, and S. Rudolph. 2009. OWL 2 web ontology language primer. W3c recommendation, W3C. Available at http://www.w3.org/TR/owl2-primer/.

Horrocks, I., and P. F. Patel-Schneider. 2004. Reducing owl entailment to description logic satisfiability. *Journal of Web Semantics* 1(4): 345–357.

Horrocks, I., P. F. Patel-Schneider, H. Boley, S. Tabet, B. Grosof, and M. Dean. 2004. SWRL: A semantic web rule language combining OWL and RuleML. W3C Member Submission. http://www.w3.org/Submission/SWRL/.

Horrocks, I., O. Kutz, and U. Sattler. 2006. The even more irresistible sroiq. In *Proceedings of the tenth international conference on principles of knowledge representation and reasoning (KR'06)*, 57–67. Lake District of the United Kingdom: AAAI.

Ianni, G., A. Martello, C. Panetta, and G. Terracina. 2009. Efficiently querying RDF(S) ontologies with Answer Set Programming. *Journal of Logic and Computation (Special issue)* 19(4): 671–695. doi:10.1093/logcom/exn043.

Kay, M. 2007. XSL transformations (XSLT) version 2.0. W3C Recommendation, W3C. Available at http://www.w3.org/TR/xslt20.

Kifer, M., G. Lausen, and J. Wu. 1995. Logical foundations of object-oriented and frame-based languages. *Journal of the ACM* 42(4): 741–843.

Krötzsch, M., S. Rudolph, and P. Hitzler. 2007. Complexity boundaries for horn description logics. In *Proceedings of the twenty-second aaai conference on artificial intelligence (AAAI)*, Vancouver, 452–457.

Moses, T. 2005. eXtensible access control markup language (XACML) version 2.0. OASIS Standard

Motik, B., B. C. Grau, I. Horrocks, Z. Wu, A. Fokoue, C. Lutz, D. Calvanese, J. Carroll, G. D. Giacomo, J. Hendler, I. Herman, B. Parsia, P. F. Patel-Schneider, A. Ruttenberg, U. Sattler, and M. Schneider. 2009. OWL 2 web ontology language profiles. W3c recommendation, W3C. Available at http://www.w3.org/TR/owl2-profiles/.

Muñoz, S., J. Pérez, and C. Gutiérrez. 2007. Minimal deductive systems for rdf. In *Proceedings of the 4th European semantic web conference (ESWC2007)*, ed. E. Franconi, M. Kifer, and W. May. Lecture Notes in Computer Science, vol. 4519, 53–67. Innsbruck: Springer.

Paschke, A., D. Hirtle, A. Ginsberg, P. L. Patranjan, F. McCabe. 2008. RIF use cases and requirements. W3C Working Draft. Available at http://www.w3.org/TR/rif-ucr/.

Pérez, J., M. Arenas, and C. Gutierrez. 2006. Semantics and complexity of SPARQL. In *International semantic web conference (ISWC 2006)*, 30–43. Berlin/New York: Springer.

Pérez, J., M. Arenas, and C. Gutierrez. 2009. Semantics and complexity of SPARQL. *ACM Transactions on Database Systems* 34(3): Article 16, 45p.

Pichler, R., A. Polleres, F. Wei, and S. Woltran. 2008. Entailment for domain-restricted RDF. In *Proceedings of the 5th European semantic web conference (ESWC2008)*, 200–214. Tenerife: Springer. http://www.polleres.net/publications/pich-etal-2008.pdf.

Polleres, A. 2006. SPARQL rules!. Tech. Rep. GIA-TR-2006-11-28. Universidad Rey Juan Carlos, Móstoles. Available at http://www.polleres.net/TRs/GIA-TR-2006-11-28.pdf.

Polleres, A. 2007. From SPARQL to rules (and back). In *Proceedings of the 16th world wide web conference (WWW2007)*, 787–796. Banff: ACM. Available at http://www2007.org/paper435.php.

Polleres, A., H. Boley, and M. Kifer. 2010. RIF datatypes and Built-Ins 1.0. W3C Proposed Recommendation, W3C. Available at http://www.w3.org/TR/2010/PR-rif-dtb-20100511/.

Polleres, A., and D. Huynh (eds.). 2009. Special issue: The web of data. *Journal of Web Semantics* 7(3): 135. Elsevier.

Prud'hommeaux, E., and A. Seaborne. 2008. SPARQL query language for RDF. W3c Recommendation, W3C. Available at http://www.w3.org/TR/rdf-sparql-query/.

Schindlauer, R. 2006. Answer-set programming for the semantic web. Ph.D. thesis, Vienna University of Technology.

Schmidt, M., M. Meier, and G. Lausen. 2010. Foundations of SPARQL query optimization. In *13th international conference on database theory (ICDT2010)*, Lausanne.

Smith, M. K., C. Welty, D. L. McGuinness. 2004. OWL web ontology language guide. W3c Recommendation, W3C. Available at http://www.w3.org/TR/owl-guide/.

SQL-99. 1999. Information technology – database language SQL- Part 3: call level interface (SQL/CLI). Tech. Rep. INCITS/ISO/IEC 9075-3, INCITS/ISO/IEC. Standard Specification.

ter Horst, H. J. 2005. Completeness, decidability and complexity of entailment for rdf schema and a semantic extension involving the owl vocabulary. *Journal of Web Semantics* 3: 79–115.

Thompson, H. S., D. Beech, M. Maloney, and N. Mendelsohn. 2004. *XML schema Part 1: Structures*, 2nd ed. W3C Recommendation, W3C. Available at http://www.w3.org/TR/xmlschema-1/.

Weitzner, D. 2004. W3c patent policy. Available at http://www.w3.org/Consortium/Patent-Policy/.

Chapter 5
Logical Formalisms for Agreement Technologies

Antoine Zimmermann

5.1 Introduction

Semantic Web standards offer a good basis for representing the knowledge of local agents,[1] the schemata, the functionalities and all things that matter in order to achieve a goal in agreement with other agents. However, the formalisms behind these technologies have limitations when dealing with the distributed, open and heterogeneous nature of the systems concerned by Agreement Technologies. In particular, since agents are inherently autonomous, they define their knowledge according to their own beliefs, which can differ from one another or even be inconsistent with other agents' beliefs. Since the standards of the Semantic Web are not concerned about belief and they do not provide the means to compartment knowledge from distinct sources, the conclusions reached when using the global knowledge of disagreeing agents are inevitably inconsistent. Hence, by virtue of the "principle of explosion", all possible statements are entailed.

For these reasons, a number of logical formalisms have been proposed to handle the situations in which pieces of knowledge are defined independently in various contexts. These formalisms extend classical logics—sometimes the logics of Semantic Web standards—by partitioning knowledge from different sources and limiting the interactions between the parts in the partition in various ways. We collectively call these logics *contextual logics*, although they have been called sometimes *distributed logics* (Borgida and Serafini 2003; Ghidini and Serafini 2000; Homola 2007) or *modular ontology languages* (Cuenca-Grau and Kutz 2007).

---

[1]We use the term "agent" to denote any entity which can act towards a goal, such as a service, an application, a device, or even a person or organisation.

A. Zimmermann (✉)
École Nationale Supérieure des Mines, FAYOL-ENSMSE, LSTI, F-42023 Saint-Étienne, France
e-mail: antoine.zimmermann@emse.fr

S. Ossowski (ed.), *Agreement Technologies*, Law, Governance and Technology Series 8, DOI 10.1007/978-94-007-5583-3_5,

This chapter aims at presenting a variety of proposals for contextual reasoning, where each approach addresses to a certain extent the problems of heterogeneity, inconsistency, contextuality and modularity.

5.2 General Definitions for Contextual Logics

5.2.1 Networks of Aligned Ontologies

In most of the formalisms presented here, it is generally agreed that local knowledge, defined to serve one purpose from one viewpoint, should conform to a classical semantics, that is, the semantics of standard knowledge representation formats. For instance, the ontology that defines the terms used in the dataset of a single semantic website could be defined in OWL and all the conclusions that can be drawn from it are determined according to the W3C specification. Similarly, the functionalities of a single Web service could be described in WSML, and using this description alone would yield the inferences defined by the WSML specification.

To simplify the terminology, we will use the term *ontology* to denote a logical theory in a language which is local to an agent and a specific purpose. An agent may own several ontologies to describe different types of knowledge, such as describing the domain associated with the application's data, describing local policies, functionalities or computational resources. Agreement Technologies are working on systems composed of many software agents, therefore contextual logics provide a semantics to systems of multiple ontologies. Besides, ontologies developed independently are likely to use disjoint sets of terms (or at least, different identifiers for terms). So, if local ontologies are the only constituent of a contextual logic formalism, then there is no possible interaction between the knowledge associated with a context and the knowledge of another. For this reason, we assume that additional knowledge is present to "bind" ontologies together. We call this additional knowledge *ontology alignments*, which provide an explicit representation of the correspondences between ontologies. In practice, an alignment can take many forms, which depend on the actual contextual logic used. In this chapter, we do not discuss how the alignments are produced.[2]

As a result, the structure for which a contextual logic defines a semantics is a graph-like structure that we call a *network of aligned ontologies* (NAO) where vertices are ontologies and edges are alignments. In theory, ontology alignments could express correspondences between more than two ontologies, so the structure should be a hypergraph in general. But practical ontology matching tools always produce binary alignments, so we will often consider that NAOs are standard directed graphs.[3]

---

[2]This is the subject of Chap. 6.

[3]Nonetheless, $\mathcal{E}$-connection is a formalism where non-binary alignments can be expressed, as explained in Sect. 5.6.

5.2.2 Local Semantics

This section recapitulates the definitions that are common to classical logical formalisms, especially introducing the notions of ontology, interpretation, satisfaction and model.

A local ontology is a logical theory, written in a language of a logic. A *logic* is characterised by:

- A syntax, that is a set of symbols and sentences (or formulas) that can be built with them;
- A notion of interpretations, which define a domain of interpretation and associate symbols with structures over the domain;
- A satisfaction relation, which relates interpretations to the sentences they satisfy.

For example, Description Logics allow symbols for atomic concept, roles and individuals, as well as constructs such as $\exists$, $\forall$ to build ABox or TBox axioms. Interpretations must assign a subset of the domain to a concept name, and a set of pairs to a role name. A subsumption axiom $C \sqsubseteq D$ is satisfied by an interpretation if the set denoted by C is contained in the set denoted by D.

An ontology is simply a set of sentences and when an interpretation satisfics all sentences in an ontology, we say that it is a model of the ontology.

For a logic L, we will write Sen_L to denote the set of sentences (or formulas) defined by L; we write Int_L to denote the interpretations; $\models_L$ to denote the satisfaction relation, and given an ontology O, we note $\mathrm{Mod}(O)$ the set of models of O.

5.2.3 Contextual Logics

A contextual logic provides a semantic to networks of aligned ontologies. We describe this particular kind of logics very much like a standard logic is defined, that is, by presenting the syntax, the interpretations and models. First, a contextual logic is defined on top of a set of local logics $\mathbf{L}$, which determine the languages used in local ontologies. The sentences of a contextual logic are of two types: local axioms and cross-ontology correspondences.

First, we assume the existence of a set $\mathbf{C}$ of *context identifiers*. Each context $c \in \mathbf{C}$ is associated with a fixed language $L_c \in \mathbf{L}$. A *local axiom* is written $c{:}\alpha$, where c is a context identifier, and α is a local sentence in the language L_c. A (cross-ontology) *correspondence* is a sentence in an alignment language L_A, which can be of many forms depending on the actual logic used—as we will see later—but expresses a relation between some terms from distinct contexts. Generally, correspondences express binary relations between terms of two ontologies, such that most contextual logics work on correspondences of the form $\langle e_c, e_{c'}, r\rangle$, where e_c (resp. $e_{c'}$) is an entity (term or construct) from context c (resp. c') and r denotes a type of relations, such as equality or subsumption.[4]

A network of aligned ontologies is in fact a set of local axioms together with cross-ontology correspondences. They can be defined as logical theories in a contextual logic. More formally:

Definition 5.1 (Network of aligned ontologies). A *network of aligned ontologies* (or NAO) in a contextual logic $\mathscr{L}$ is a pair $\langle \Omega, \Lambda \rangle$ where:

- $\Omega = (o_c)_{c \in K}$ is a tuple of local ontologies indexed by a finite set of contexts $K \subseteq \mathbf{C}$, such that $o_c \subset \mathrm{Sen}_{L_c}$;
- Λ, called the set of correspondences, is a finite set of formulas in language L_A.

Interpretations in a contextual logic are composed of two parts: (1) a family of local interpretations, which intuitively assigns an interpretation to each ontology in an NAO, and (2) a structure that interprets cross-context knowledge. Formally:

Definition 5.2. $\langle (I_c)_{c \in C}, \Gamma \rangle$ is an interpretation in the contextual logic if and only if $C \subseteq \mathbf{C}$ and for all $c \in C$, I_c is an interpretation in the language L_c. The structure of Γ depends on the alignment language used by the formalism and it varies depending on the contextual logic the same way the structure of an interpretation varies depending on the local logic used.

To be precise, Γ could be described as an object in a mathematical category which depends on the contextual logic. Many definitions are needed to present the theory of categories, so we prefer to keep the definition looser and simply say that Γ is a structure that depends on the contextual formalism. We provide examples thereafter.

Satisfaction in a contextual logic is constrained by the local semantics, which impose the way local axioms are satisfied:

Definition 5.3 (Satisfaction of a local axiom). A local axiom $i{:}\alpha$ is satisfied by an interpretation $(I_c)_{c \in C}$ if $i \in C$ and $I_i \models_{L_i} \alpha$.

This means that a local axiom is satisfied by a contextual interpretation if it assigns a local interpretation to the context of the local axiom, and the local interpretation satisfies (according to the local semantics) the axiom.

Satisfaction of correspondences are not particularly constrained and the exact definition depends on the contextual logic at hand. As correspondences are usually binary, correspondences of the form $\langle e_c, e_{c'}, r \rangle$ typically constrain the relationship between the local interpretations of e_c and $e_{c'}$ according to the relation symbol r. Such constraints often express a form of "equivalence", but even in this restricted setting, semantics vary. A discussion on the semantics of binary correspondences is found in Zimmermann and Euzenat (2006).

---

[4]Chapter 6 gives a more detailed account on how to discover implicit binary correspondences between two ontologies.

Now a model of a network of aligned ontologies necessarily contains a tuple of *local models*. More formally, if $\langle\Omega,\Lambda\rangle$ is a an NAO where Ω is a (finite) set of ontologies and Λ a (finite) set of alignments, and $\mathbf{I} = \langle (I_c)_{c\in C}, \Gamma\rangle$ is a contextual interpretation, then $\mathbf{I}$ is a model of $\langle\Omega,\Lambda\rangle$ iff $I_o \models_{L_o} o$ for each ontology $o \in \Omega$ and $\mathbf{I}$ satisfies all alignments in Λ. So the set of models of the NAO $\mathrm{Mod}(\Omega,\Lambda)$ restricts the possible local models to a subset of the Cartesian product $\mathrm{Mod}(o_1) \times \cdots \times \mathrm{Mod}(o_k)$, with k the cardinality of Ω.

The remainder of the chapter presents various formalisms that instantiate the notion of contextual logic by setting a concrete syntax for correspondences and defining the satisfaction of the alignments. In each section, we summarise the components of the contextual logic.

5.3 Standard Logics as Contextual Logics

Here we show that a standard logic can be used as a simple contextual logics. Let us assume that the local logics are reduced to a single logic and the alignment language is again the same as the ontology language. Correspondences are satisfied if: (1) the domains of interpretation of all local interpretations are the same; (2) all local interpretations agree on the interpretation of identical local terms; and (3) the correspondence is satisfied by the union of the local interpretations.

In fact, this formalisation exactly corresponds to a standard logic where the meaning of the NAO is the same as a single ontology obtained by making the union of all ontologies and alignments. Therefore, from an inference perspective, there is no difference with a single standard logic, as all axioms will influence all ontologies equally, just as if everything was local. However, there can still be an interest in having local axioms compartmentalised, especially to track the provenance of some knowledge, or in a query mechanism that allow requests on a specific context, which SPARQL allows thanks to the dataset structure. Indeed, SPARQL engines are not simply managing single RDF graphs, they are required to work on a structure composed of separated graphs which are labelled with URIs. However, SPARQL is agnostic with respect to how knowledge from one graph influence knowledge in another. It only enables one to query a portion of the knowledge based on the graph identifiers.

Using a standard logic in a multi-contextual setting is common as it is easier to understand and not controversial, although it is very sensitive to heterogeneity and disagreements across contexts. Therefore, other non-standard approaches were proposed that we discuss next.

Local logics: local logics are all the same but can be of any type.

Correspondence syntax: correspondences are expressed as axioms built using the terms of local ontologies.

Contextual interpretation: an interpretation of a network of aligned ontologies in this logic is simply a tuple of local interpretations whereby the domain of interpretation is the same for each context.

Satisfaction of correspondences: since correspondences are standard axioms, the satisfaction of correspondences is as in the local logic.

5.4 Distributed Description Logics (DDL)

Distributed Description Logics (DDL) (Borgida and Serafini 2003) is a formalism which was developed to formalise contextual reasoning with Description Logic ontologies. Therefore, local logics are Description Logics, which is well adapted for the Semantic Web standard OWL. Moreover, cross-context formulas can be defined to relate different terminologies in the form of so called *bridge rules* and written either $i{:}C \xrightarrow{\sqsubseteq} j{:}D$ or $i{:}C \xrightarrow{\sqsupseteq} j{:}D$ where i and j are two different contexts, and C and D are terms from the contextual ontologies O_i and O_j respectively. A bridge rule $i{:}C \xrightarrow{\sqsubseteq} j{:}D$ (resp. $i{:}C \xrightarrow{\sqsupseteq} j{:}D$) should be understood as follows: from the point of view of O_j (i.e., in the context j), C is a subclass (resp. superclass) of D.

Local logics: local logics are description logics.
Correspondence syntax: correspondences take the form of into- ($i{:}C \xrightarrow{\sqsubseteq} j{:}D$) or onto-bridge rules ($i{:}C \xrightarrow{\sqsupseteq} j{:}D$).
Contextual interpretation: DDL interpretations are tuples of local interpretations together with domain relations for each pair of contexts, formally $\langle (I_i),(r_{ij})\rangle$ where I_i are local DL interpretations over domains Δ_i for all i and r_{ij} is a set $r_{ij} \subseteq \Delta_i \times \Delta_j$ for all contexts i and j.
Satisfaction of correspondences: an interpretation $\langle (I_i),(r_{ij})\rangle$ satisfies a bridge rule $i{:}C \xrightarrow{\sqsubseteq} j{:}D$ (resp. $i{:}C \xrightarrow{\sqsupseteq} j{:}D$) iff $r_{ij}(C^{\mathcal{I}_i}) \subseteq D^{\mathcal{I}_j}$ (resp. $r_{ij}(C^{\mathcal{I}_i}) \supseteq D^{\mathcal{I}_j}$).[5]

This formalism allows different contexts to model the same domain in different ways with a reduced risk of causing inconsistencies due to heterogeneity. Yet, it still allows for cross-ontology inferences, such as: $i{:}A \sqsubseteq B$, $i{:}A \xrightarrow{\sqsupseteq} j{:}C$, $i{:}B \xrightarrow{\sqsubseteq} j{:}D$ together entail $j{:}C \sqsubseteq D$. The reasoning procedure for DDL has been implemented in a peer-to-peer system where each peer embed a local reasoner extended with message exchanges based on the bridge rules they detain (Serafini and Tamilin 2005).

5.5 Package-Based Description Logics

In package-based Description Logics (P-DL Bao et al. 2006), local logics are again description logics and cross-ontology knowledge can only take the form of

[5]For a set S, $r_{ij}(S) = \{x \in \Delta^{\mathcal{I}_j} \mid \exists y \in S, \langle x,y\rangle \in r_{ij}\}$.

semantic imports of ontological terms. This formalism was essentially designed to compensate the drawbacks of the OWL import mechanism and improve modularity of Web ontologies. Imports are satisfied when the local interpretation of the imported terms are the same in the importing and imported ontologies.

Local logics: local logics are description logics.

Correspondence syntax: correspondences take the form $O_i \xrightarrow{t} O_j$, which can be read "ontology O_j imports the term t defined in ontology O_i".

Contextual interpretation: in its first definition, P-DL interpretations were simply tuples of local interpretations (Bao et al. 2006). In later publications, the formulation was revised (yet is equivalent) using domain relations as in DDL, imposing furthermore that the domain relations are one-to-one, that r_{ij} is the inverse of r_{ji} and that the composition of r_{ij} with r_{jk} must be equal to r_{ik}, for all i, j and k (Bao et al. 2009).

Satisfaction of correspondences: an interpretation $\langle (I_i),(r_{ij})\rangle$ satisfies an import $O_i \xrightarrow{t} O_j$ iff $r_{ij}(t^{\mathscr{I}_i}) = D^{\mathscr{I}_j}$. In earlier versions of the semantics, the condition was that the local interpretations of an imported term must be equal in both the importing and imported ontology.

5.6 $\mathscr{E}$-Connections

$\mathscr{E}$-connections is another formalism for reasoning with heterogeneous ontologies (Kutz et al. 2004). Again, different ontologies are interpreted distinctly but formally related using particular assertions. Instead of expressing correspondences of ontological terms, an ontology can connect to another by using special terms (called *links*) which can be combined in conjunction with terms from another ontology. The semantics of links is very similar to the semantics of roles in Description Logics, except that instead of relating elements from the same domain of interpretation, they relate two different domains. So, in $\mathscr{E}$-connections, in addition to local interpretations, domain relations are assigned to each link. The difference with DDL is that the domain relations are not unique per pair of interpretations: they are specific to a link, so there can be many over two different interpretation domains. Moreover, links are used like roles in DL, with the difference that using a link imposes that terms from distinct ontologies are used. For instance, one can define the sentence $C_i \sqsubseteq \exists \langle L_{ij} \rangle D_j$, where $\langle L_{ij} \rangle$ denotes a link between ontologies O_i and O_j, C_i denotes a term of O_i and D_j denotes a term of O_j. Finally, a sentence with multiple links can involve terms from more than two ontologies. Therefore, it is not possible in general to represent a NAO in $\mathscr{E}$-connection as a simple directed graph.

In principle, $\mathscr{E}$-connections serve to relate ontologies about very different domains of interest. For instance, an ontology of laboratories could be connected to an ontology of medical staff. However, $\mathscr{E}$-connection is not particularly appropriate to relate ontologies of similar domains, as there is no way to formally express a form of equivalence between terms of distinct ontologies. Also, in $\mathscr{E}$-connection, links have to be defined for each pairs of ontologies, so it is hardly possible to build up an $\mathscr{E}$-connected NAO from automatic ontology matching techniques.

Local logics: $\mathscr{E}$-connections were originally defined on a more general set of local logics, but later results, algorithms, proofs and practical developments were all defined on networks of description logic ontologies.

Correspondence syntax: correspondences exist in the form of local DL axioms where special relations called *links* appear. Links appear in axioms where roles normally would in role restriction constructs such as $\exists R.C$. Axioms with links are tied to a local ontology, but the links relate them to foreign terms. When a DL construct calls for a role with a concept (such as $\exists$, $\forall$, $\leq n$, $\geq n$), a link can be used instead of the role, together with a concept from a foreign ontology. For instance, $i{:}C_i \sqsubseteq \exists R^{ij}.C_j$ indicates a relationship between the term C_i of ontology O_i and the term C_j of O_j.

Contextual interpretation: in addition to a tuple of local interpretations, an $\mathscr{E}$-connection interpretation has a special interpretation that assigns to each link R^{ij} from i to j a domain relation, that is, a subset of $\Delta_i \times \Delta_j$.

Satisfaction of correspondences: since correspondences are essentially DL axioms, they are satisfied in the same way as in DL. However, the difference is in the way concepts constructed from links are interpreted. Concepts with links are interpreted according to the same definitions as in normal DL role restrictions, with the exception that instead of relying on a binary relation over the local domain (that is, a subset of $\Delta_i \times \Delta_i$), they rely on a domain relation (a subset of $\Delta_i \times \Delta_j$).

From a practical perspective, the designers of $\mathscr{E}$-connections provided a set of tools and guidelines to integrate them in the Semantic Web infrastructure (Cuenca-Grau et al. 2006). Notably, they extended the ontology editor SWOOP to model connections and integrated an $\mathscr{E}$-connections reasoner into Pellet,[6] but it no longer supports it.

5.7 Integrated Distributed Description Logics

Integrated Distributed Description Logics (IDDL Zimmermann 2007) is a formalism that addresses similar issues as DDL but takes a different paradigm than other contextual frameworks. Usually, cross-ontology assertions (e.g., bridge rules in DDL, links in $\mathscr{E}$-connections, semantic imports in P-DL) define knowledge from the point of view of one ontology. That is to say that the correspondences are expressing the relations "as witnessed" by a local ontology. On the contrary, IDDL asserts correspondences from an "external" point of view which encompasses both

[6] http://clarkparsia.com/pellet/

ontologies in relation. One consequence of this approach is that correspondences can be manipulated and reasoned about independently of the ontologies, allowing operations like inversing or composing ontology alignments, as first class objects (Zimmermann and Euzenat 2006).

In terms of model theory, this is represented by using an additional domain of interpretation to the whole network of ontologies, as if it was a single ontology. The local domains of interpretation, assigned to all ontologies, are then related to the global domain by way of the so-called *equalizing functions* (ε_i). These functions map the elements of local domains to elements of the global domain. Formally, a correspondence $i:C \xleftrightarrow{\sqsubseteq} j:D$ from a concept C of ontology O_i to concept D of ontology O_j is satisfied whenever $\varepsilon_i(C^{\mathcal{I}_i}) \subseteq \varepsilon_j(D^{\mathcal{I}_j})$.

A reasoning procedure for this formalism has been defined (Zimmermann and Duc 2008), where a central system detaining the correspondences can determine global consistency of a network of ontologies by communicating with local reasoners of arbitrary complexity. This formalism can be used for federated reasoning systems, when the interactions between local ontologies are rather weak. By separating local reasoning and global reasoning, it better prevents interactions between contexts, thus being quite robust to heterogeneity.

Local logics: local logics are description logics.

Correspondence syntax: correspondences take the form of cross-ontology subsumption ($i:C \xleftrightarrow{\sqsubseteq} j:D$), cross-ontology disjointness ($i:C \xleftrightarrow{\perp} j:D$) where C (respectively D) is either a concept or a role, possibly complex, of ontology O_i (O_j respectively).

Contextual interpretation: in addition to a tuple of local interpretations, an IDDL interpretation contains a non empty set Δ called the *global domain of interpretation*, and a tuple of functions $\varepsilon_i : \Delta_i \rightarrow \Delta$ which map elements of local domains to elements of the global domain.

Satisfaction of correspondences: an interpretation $\langle (I_i), (\varepsilon_i), \Delta \rangle$ satisfies a cross-ontology subsumption $i:C \xleftrightarrow{\sqsubseteq} j:D$ whenever $\varepsilon_i(C^{\mathcal{I}_i}) \subseteq \varepsilon_j(D^{\mathcal{I}_j})$ and it satisfies a cross-ontology disjointness $i:C \xleftrightarrow{\perp} j:D$ whenever $\varepsilon_i(C^{\mathcal{I}_i}) \cap \varepsilon_j(D^{\mathcal{I}_j}) = \emptyset$.

5.8 Modular Web Rule Bases

Although this approach is not based on current Semantic Web standards, it is relevant to this survey of formalisms. The framework proposed in Analyti et al. (2011) makes the distinction between global knowledge, local knowledge and internal knowledge. The framework is based on a rule-based language rather than OWL or a Description Logic, and allows one to express and reason modularly over data across the Web. In this framework, each predicate in a rule base is constrained with "uses" and "scope", which in turn determine the reasoning process. It also treats different forms of negation (weak or strong) to include Open-World Assumption (OWA) as well as Closed-World Assumption (CWA) (Analyti et al. 2008). The assumption and type of negation used lead to four different "reasoning modes" (specified s, open o, closed c, normal n). This rule-based framework provides a model-theoretic compatible semantics and allow certain predicates to be monotonic and reasoning is possible with inconsistent knowledge bases.

Local logics: the local logic define "rule bases" as the local theories, which roughly correspond to quadruples of logic programmes (one for each reasoning mode). The authors propose two formal semantics, one based on answer set programming, the other as well-founded semantics.

Correspondence syntax: correspondences take the form of import statements tied to a local rule base r, which abstractly are triples $\langle p, m, i \rangle$ where p is a predicate, m is a reasoning mod (which tells whether weak negation is allowed or if OWA or CWA is used) and i is a set of external rule bases (i.e., $r \notin i$).

Contextual interpretation: there is no particular structure for interpreting import statements. Local interpretations are subsets of a Herbrand base that must satisfy conditions based on the reasoning modes of the predicates.

Satisfaction of correspondences: the notion of model in this formalism requires several formal definitions. To avoid an extensive description, we present the idea informally: intuitively, the meaning of the predicates in a rule base r in reasoning mode m depends on the meaning of the predicates of a rule base r' with reasoning mode m', when r imports terms from r' and the mode m' is "more restrictive" than m (where restrictiveness can be ordered as follows $s < o < c < n$). The detailed semantics is found in Sects. 4 and 5 of Analyti et al. (2011).

Although the formalism behind modular rule bases form a contextual logic, it has features that do not fit well with open, distributed environments. In particular, a rule base can restrict the way other rule bases describe their knowledge. This would be hard to enforce in a system of autonomous agents.

5.9 Other Relevant Formalisms

In this section, we discuss other formalisms that do not fit the general definition of contextual logic provided in Sect. 5.2 but partially address the problem of multi-contextual, heterogeneous and distributed knowledge. In particular, we avoided the presentation of contextual logics where the knowledge *about* context is mixed with the knowledge *inside* a context, as in the seminal approach of McCarthy (1987) or Lenat (1995).

5.9.1 Contextualised Knowledge Repositories

Homola and Serafini (2012) define a contextual logic where cross-context knowledge does not take the form of correspondences between entities in different contexts, but expresses relationships between the contexts themselves. So they split information in a network of ontologies into a tuple of local ontologies and a structure called "meta knowledge", which define a hierarchy of contexts. Contexts and their relationships are described in a DL ontology which describes how knowledge is reasoned with across context. The formalism also provides different dimensions of context, which makes the approach very close to the work of Lenat (1995).

5.9.2 Contextual RDF(S)

Guha et al. (2004) proposed an extension of RDF(S) to incorporate contextual knowledge within RDF model theory. A simpler version of OWL is assumed to be interoperable with the proposed context mechanism. As opposed to the aforementioned formalisms, this contextual version of RDF does not separate the knowledge of different contexts in distinct knowledge bases. On the contrary, context is "reified" such that multiple contexts can be described within the same knowledge base, and context itself can be described. The most basic change in RDFS model-theory introduced by the addition of contexts is that the denotation of a resource is not just a function of the term and the interpretation (or structure), but also of the context in which that term occurs. Most importantly, the proposed context mechanism allows RDF statements to be true only in their context.

5.9.3 Reasoning with Inconsistencies

Robustness to heterogeneity is an important aspect in Agreement Technologies. One of the most problematic consequences of heterogeneity is the occurrence of undesired inconsistencies. Therefore, we believe it useful to investigate formal approaches for handling inconsistencies. There are two main ways to deal with inconsistent ontologies. One is to simply accept the inconsistency and to apply a non-standard reasoning method to obtain meaningful answers in the presence of inconsistencies. An alternative approach is to resolve the error, that is, to repair the ontology or the alignment, whenever an inconsistency is encountered.

Repairing or revising inconsistent ontology is, in principle, a possible solution for handling inconsistency. However, one major pragmatic issue we observe is that some agents may not expose and/or allow repair of their knowledge bases due to various legal or privacy constraints. Also, in a typical Semantic Web setting, importing ontologies from other sources makes them impossible to repair, and if the scale of the combined ontologies is too large then repair might appear ineffective. Other work focus on revising mappings only (Meilicke et al. 2008), but they are meant to be used at alignment discovery time, which we are not discussing in this chapter.

Reasoning with inconsistencies is also possible without revision of the ontology. One effective way of tolerating inconsistencies consists of using paraconsistent logics (Béziau et al. 2007). Paraconsistent logics use a "weaker" inference system that entails less formulas than in classical logics. This way, reasoning can be done in the presence of inconsistency. A paraconsistent extension of OWL was proposed in Huang et al. (2005). Alternatively, defeasible argumentation (Chesñevar et al. 2000) and its implementation Defeasible Logic Programs (DeLP García and Simari 2004) have been introduced to reason and resolve inconsistencies. In this case, the TBox is separated into two subsets, one being *strict*, which means that it must always be used in reasoning, the other being *defeatable*, which means that an argumentation process may defeat them and nullify them for a particular reasoning task.

While we want to tolerate inconsistency when reasoning with an ontology defined in another context, it is not desirable to tolerate local inconsistencies as an agent should normally be self consistent. The system should have a strict logical framework when it only treats local data, that exists in a unique and well understood context. Unfortunately, the approaches mentioned here are not able to distinguish local knowledge and external knowledge. They do not allow specification of the types of mappings we need, and are not capable of treating policies.

5.10 Discussion

With the development of the Semantic Web where more and more knowledge is made available from multiple sources, and subsequently integrated by Linked Data search engines, the need to take into account the context of information has been made much clearer. Still, no contextual formalism has yet managed to gain enough traction to be integrated within standards. Some researchers debates the qualities of each formalisms and compare them, such as Cuenca-Grau and Kutz (2007) and Zimmermann et al. (2009) while others prefer to avoid taking the route to contextual knowledge, advocating pragmatic choices in implementations to counter the effect of heterogeneity, incoherence and scale (Hitzler and van Harmelen 2001; Hogan et al. 2008). Yet, formal justifications are needed to help implementers understand why some practical choices are sensible.

A first step towards an agreed formalism for multi-contextual knowledge is Named Graphs (Carroll et al. 2007) and the SPARQL notion of a dataset (Harris and Seaborne 2012), which many triple stores implement. While these specifications do not make explicit what inferences are allowed from multiple contexts, they acknowledge the need to separate knowledge into identified subsets.

References

Analyti, A., G. Antoniou, and C. V. Damásio. 2011. MWeb: A principled framework for modular web rule bases and its semantics. *ACM Transaction on Computational Logics* 17(2): 46.

Analyti, A., G. Antoniou, C. V. Damásio, and G. Wagner. 2008. Extended rdf as a semantic foundation of rule markup languages. *Journal of Artificial Intelligence Research* 32: 37–94.

Bao, J., D. Caragea, and V. G. Honavar. 2006. On the semantics of linking and importing in modular ontologies. In *Proceedings of the 5th international semantic web conference on the semantic web – ISWC 2006*, Athens, GA, USA, November 5–9, 2006. Lecture Notes in Computer Science, ed. I. F. Cruz, et al., vol. 4273, 72–86. Berlin/Heidelberg: Springer.

Bao, J., G. Voutsadakis, G. Slutzki, and V. G. Honavar. 2009. Package-based description logics. In *Modular ontologies: Concepts, theories and techniques for knowledge modularization*. Lecture Notes in Computer Science, ed. H. Stuckenschmidt, C. Parent, and S. Spaccapietra, vol. 5445, 349–371. Berlin/Heidelberg: Springer.

Béziau, J. Y., W. Carnielli, and D. M. Gabbay. 2007. *Handbook of paraconsistency*. London: College Publications.

Borgida, A., and L. Serafini. 2003. Distributed description logics: Assimilating information from peer sources. *Journal on Data Semantics* 1: 153–184.

Calvanese, D., E. Franconi, V. Haarslev, D. Lembo, B. Motik, S. Tessaris, and A. Y. Turhan (eds.). 2007.*Proceedings of the 20th international workshop on description logics DL'07*, June 8–10, 2007, Brixen/Bressanone, Italy. Bolzano University Press.

Carroll, J. J., C. Bizer, P. Hayes, and P. Stickler. 2007. Named graphs, provenance and trust. In *Proceedings of the 14th international conference on world wide web, WWW 2005*, Chiba, Japan, May 10–14, 2005, ed. A. Ellis and T. Hagino, 613–622. ACM.

Chesñevar, C. I., A. G. Maguitman, and R. P. Loui. 2000. Logical models of argument. *ACM Computing Survey* 32(4): 337–383.

Cruz, I. F., S. Decker, D. Allemang, C. Preist, D. Schwabe, P. Mika, M. Uschold, and L. Aroyo (eds.). 2006. *Proceedings of the 5th international semantic web conference on the semantic web – ISWC 2006*, Athens, GA, USA, November 5–9, 2006. Lecture Notes in Computer Science, vol. 4273. Berlin/Heidelberg: Springer

Cuenca-Grau, B., and O. Kutz. 2007. Modular ontology languages revisisted. In *SWeCKa 2007: Proceedings of the IJCAI-2007 workshop on semantic web for collaborative knowledge acquisition*, Hyderabad, India, January 7, 2007, ed. V. G. Honavar, T. Finin, D. Caragea, D. Mladenic, and Y. Sure.

Cuenca-Grau, B., B. Parsia, and E. Sirin. 2006. Combining OWL ontologies using $\mathscr{E}$-connections. *Journal of Web Semantics* 4(1): 40–59.

García, A. J., and G. R. Simari. 2004. Defeasible logic programming: An argumentative approach. *Theory and Practice of Logic Programming* 4(1–2): 95–138.

Ghidini, C., and L. Serafini. 2000. Distributed first order logics. In: *Frontiers of combining systems 2*. Studies in Logic and Computation, ed. D. M. Gabbay and M. de Rijke, vol. 7, 121–139. Baldock/Philadelphia: Research Studies Press. citeseer.ist.psu.edu/ghidini98distributed.html.

Guha, R. V., R. McCool, and R. Fikes. 2004. Contexts for the semantic web. In *Proceedings of the third international semantic web conference on the Semantic Web – ISWC 2004*, Hiroshima, Japan, November 7–11, 2004. Lecture Notes in Computer Science, ed. F. van Harmelen, S. McIlraith, and D. Plexousakis, vol. 3298, 32–46. Berlin/Heidelberg: Springer.

Harris, S., and A. Seaborne. SPARQL 1.1 query language – W3C working draft 5 January 2012. W3C Working Draft, World Wide Web Consortium (W3C) (2012). http://www.w3.org/TR/2012/WD-sparql11-query-20120105/.

Hitzler, P., and F. van Harmelen. 2010. A reasonable semantic web. *Semantic Web Journal* 1(1). Available from http://www.semantic-web-journal.net/.

Hogan, A., A. Harth, and A. Polleres. 2008. Saor: Authoritative reasoning for the web. In: *Proceedings of the 3rd Asian semantic web conference on the semantic web, ASWC 2008*, Bangkok,

Thailand, December 8–11, 2008. Lecture Notes in Computer Science, ed. J. Domingue and C. Anutariya, vol. 5367, 76–90. Berlin/New York: Springer.

Homola, M. 2007. Distributed description logics revisited. In *Proceedings of the 20th international workshop on description logics DL'07*, June 8–10, 2007, Brixen/Bressanone, Italy, ed. D. Calvanese, E. Franconi, V. Haarslev, D. Lembo, B. Motik, S. Tessaris, and A. Y. Turhan. Bolzano University Press. http://ceur-ws.org/Vol-250/paper_51.pdf.

Homola, M., and L. Serafini. 2012. Contextualized knowledge repositories for the semantic web. *Journal of Web Semantics* 12: 64–87.

Huang, Z., F. van Harmelen, and A. ten Teije. 2005. Reasoning with inconsistent ontologies. In *IJCAI-05, Proceedings of the nineteenth international joint conference on artificial intelligence*, Edinburgh, Scotland, UK, July 30-August 5, 2005, ed. L. P. Kaelbling and A. Saffiotti, 454–459. Professional Book Center.

Kutz, O., C. Lutz, F. Wolter, and M. Zakharyaschev. 2004. $\mathscr{E}$-connections of abstract description systems. *Artificial Intelligence* 156(1): 1–73.

Lenat, D. B. 1995. CYC: a large-scale investment in knowledge infrastructure. *Communications of the ACM* 38(11): 33–38. http://doi.acm.org/10.1145/219717.219745.

McCarthy, J. L. 1987. Generality in artificial intelligence. *Communications of the ACM* 30(12): 1029–1035.

Meilicke, C., H. Stuckenschmidt, and A. Tamilin. 2008. Supporting manual mapping revision using logical reasoning. In *Proceedings of the Twenty-Third AAAI Conference on Artificial Intelligence, AAAI 2008*, Chicago, Illinois, USA, July 13–17, 2008, ed. D. Fox and C. P. Gomes, 1213–1218. AAAI.

Serafini, L., and A. Tamilin. 2005. DRAGO: Distributed reasoning architecture for the semantic web. In *Proceedings of the Second European Semantic Web Conference on the semantic web: Research and applications, ESWC 2005*, Heraklion, Crete, Greece, May 29–June 1, 2005. Lecture Notes in Computer Science, ed. A. Gomez-Perez and J. Euzenat, vol. 3532, 361–376. Springer.

Zimmermann, A. 2007. Integrated distributed description logics. In *Proceedings of the 20th international workshop on description logics DL'07*, Brixen/Bressanone, Italy, June 8–10, 2007, ed. D. Calvanese, E. Franconi, V. Haarslev, D. Lembo, B. Motik, S. Tessaris, and A. Y. Turhan, 507–514. Bolzano University Press. http://ftp.informatik.rwth-aachen.de/Publications/CEUR-WS/Vol-250/paper_37.pdf.

Zimmermann, A., and C. L. Duc. 2008. Reasoning on a network of aligned ontologies. In *Proceedings of the second international conference on web reasoning and rule systems, RR 2008*, Karlsruhe, Germany, October/November 2008, Lecture Notes in Computer Science, ed. D. Calvanese and H. Lausen, vol. 5341, 43–57. Springer.

Zimmermann, A., and J. Euzenat. 2006. Three semantics for distributed systems and their relations with alignment composition. In *Proceedings of the 5th international semantic web conference on the semantic web – ISWC 2006*, Athens, GA, USA, November 5–9, 2006. Lecture Notes in Computer Science, I. F. Cruz, S. Decker, D. Allemang, C. Preist, D. Schwabe, P. Mika, M. Uschold, and L. Aroyo, vol. 4273, 16–29. Berlin/Heidelberg: Springer. http://iswc2006.semanticweb.org/items/Zimmermann2006jw.pdf.

Zimmermann, A., R. Sahay, R. Fox, and A. Polleres. 2009. Heterogeneity and context in semantic-web-enabled HCLS systems. In *Proceedings of teh confederated international conferences on the move to meaningful internet systems: OTM 2009, CoopIS, DOA, IS, and ODBASE 2009*, Vilamoura, Portugal, November 1–6, 2009, Part II. Lecture Notes in Computer Science, ed. D. Calvanese and H. Lausen, vol. 5871, 1165–1182. Springer.

Chapter 6
Reconciling Heterogeneous Knowledge with Ontology Matching

Cássia Trojahn and George Vouros

6.1 Introduction

In open, dynamic and distributed systems, it is unrealistic to assume that autonomous agents or peers are committed to a common way of expressing their knowledge, in terms of one or more ontologies modeling the domain of interest. Thus, before any kind of communication or cooperation, agents must reach an agreement on the meaning of the terms they use for structuring information, conceptualizing the world, or representing distinct entities.

Reaching semantic agreements between ontologies is necessary in (a) distributed settings where autonomous agents do not share common vocabularies and conceptualizations, in (b) peer data management systems where peers are heterogeneous to the data schema they use, and also, as a worth-mentioning refined case of (a), (c) for different ontology alignment and instance matching methods to synthesize their results.

We may distinguish two generic problem cases where reaching semantic agreements (i.e., agreements that preserve the semantics of the representations) between the mapping decisions of heterogeneous agents is of particular value:

1. Two or more agents have the same ontologies and need to produce mappings to the ontology elements of another entity: In this case, entities need to reach agreements concerning the mappings of the ontology elements they share to the ontology elements of the third entity.

C. Trojahn (✉)
INRIA & LIG, Grenoble, France
e-mail: cassia.trojahn@inria.fr

G. Vouros
Department of Digital Systems, University of Piraeus, Piraeus, Greece
e-mail: georgev@unipi.gr

S. Ossowski (ed.), *Agreement Technologies*, Law, Governance and Technology Series 8, DOI 10.1007/978-94-007-5583-3_6,

2. There is a network of entities, whereby each entity is connected to its "known neighbours". Entities do not necessarily share the same ontology. In this setting each entity need to produce mappings between its own ontology and the ontology of each of its neighbours. Entities need to reach agreements on their mappings so that there is a consistent set of mappings in the network as a whole.

Over the years several approaches have been proposed for achieving semantic agreement based on ontology matching in a distributed setting: argumentation-based models, constraint satisfaction methods and probabilistic models. The aim of this chapter is to present a brief overview of the state-of-the-art on these approaches and discuss the main open issues and challenges for future research. We firstly introduce the ontology matching process for semantic agreements (Sect. 6.2) and the notion of argumentation frameworks (Sect. 6.3), and then we present scenarios applying such frameworks (Sect. 6.3.4). Next, we specify the problem of synthesizing different matching methods as a constraint optimization problem and show the benefits of this approach (Sect. 6.4) and we present an approach for peers organized in arbitrary networks to reach semantic agreement on their correspondences (Sect. 6.5). Finally, we discuss some open issues and future research directions on semantic agreement based on ontology matching (Sect. 6.6).

6.2 Producing Correspondences via Ontology Matching

An ontology typically provides a vocabulary describing a domain of interest and a specification of the meaning of terms in that vocabulary, usually identifying elements such as classes, individuals, relations, attributes and axioms. As distributed autonomous agents are designed independently, they may commit to different ontologies to model the same domain. These ontologies may differ in granularity or detail, use different representations, or model the concepts, properties and axioms in different ways. To illustrate this problem, let us consider an e-Commerce marketplace, where two agents, a *buyer* and a *seller*, need to negotiate the price of a digital camera. They use the ontologies o and o', respectively, as shown in Fig. 6.1. These ontologies contain subsumption statements (e.g.,DigitalCamera$\sqsubseteq$Product), property specifications (e.g.,price domain Product) and instance descriptions (e.g.,Nikon price $250). Before starting any kind of negotiation, they need to agree on the vocabulary to be used for exchanging the messages.

Ontology matching is the task of finding correspondences between ontologies (Euzenat and Shvaiko 2007). Correspondences express relationships holding between entities in ontologies, for instance, that an Electronic in one ontology is the same as a Product in another one or that DigitalCamera in an ontology is a subclass of CameraPhoto in another one. A set of correspondences between two ontologies is called an *alignment*. An alignment may be used, for instance, to generate query expressions that automatically translate instances of these ontologies under an integrated ontology or to translate queries with respect to one ontology in to query with respect to the other.

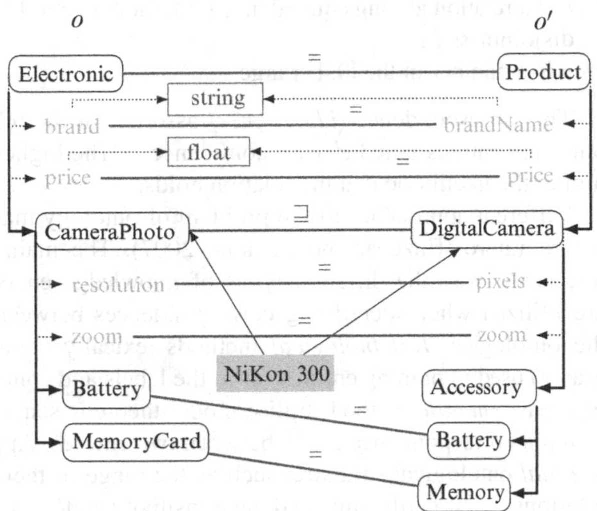

Fig. 6.1 Fragments of ontologies o and o' with alignment A

More specifically, the matching process determines an alignment A' for a pair of input ontologies o and o'. Each of the elements featured in this definition can have specific characteristics which influence the difficulty of the matching task. The input ontologies can be characterized by the input languages they are described by (e.g., OWL Lite, OWL DL, OWL Full), their size (number of concepts, properties and instances) and complexity, which indicates how deeply the hierarchy is structured and how dense the interconnection between the ontological entities is. Other properties such as consistency, correctness and completeness are also used for characterizing the input ontologies. This generic definition of the process can be extended with some input parameters (i.e., thresholds and external resources). For instance, some systems take advantage of external resources, such as WordNet, sets of morphological rules or previous alignments of general purpose (Yahoo and Google catalogs, for instance).

The output **alignment** A' is a set of correspondences between o and o'. Generally, correspondences express a relation r between ontology entities e and e' with a confidence measure n. These are abstractly defined in Euzenat and Shvaiko (2007). Here, we will restrict the discussion to simple correspondences:

Definition 6.1 (Simple correspondence). Given two ontologies, o and o', a simple correspondence is a quintuple:

$$\langle id, e, e', r, n \rangle,$$

whereby:

- id is a URI identifying the given correspondence;
- e and e' are named ontology entities, i.e., named classes, properties, or instances;

- r is a relation among equivalence ($\equiv$), more general ($\sqsupseteq$), more specific ($\sqsubseteq$), and disjointness ($\perp$);
- n is a number in the $[0,1]$ range.

The correspondence $\langle id, e, e', n, r \rangle$ asserts that the relation r holds between the ontology entities e and e' with confidence n. The higher the confidence value, the higher the likelihood that the relation holds.

Different approaches to the problem of ontology matching have emerged from the literature (Euzenat and Shvaiko 2007). The main distinction between each one is the way the different types of knowledge encoded within each ontology are utilized when identifying correspondences between features or structures of the ontologies. *Terminological* methods lexically compare strings (tokens or n-grams) used in naming entities (or in the labels and comments concerning entities), whereas *semantic* methods utilise model-theoretic semantics to determine whether or not a correspondence exists between two entities. Approaches may consider the *internal* ontological structure, such as the range of their properties (attributes and relations), their cardinality, and the transitivity and/or symmetry of their properties, or alternatively the *external* ontological structure, such as the position of the two entities within the ontological hierarchy. The instances (or extensions) of classes could also be compared using *extension*-based approaches. In addition, many ontology matching systems rely not on a single approach. State-of-the-art matching mechanisms result from the composition or synthesis of individual methods, each exploiting a specific type of information concerning ontologies.

Within open, distributed and dynamic environments, ontology matching mechanisms can be used as a basis for semantic agreements between agents. However, creating alignments can be costly and thus the ability to cache or save previously generated alignments may be desirable. Thus, agents may rely on an external **alignment service**, such as the *Alignment server*, built on the Alignment API (Euzenat 2004), which provides functionality to facilitate alignment generation, storage and retrieval. In addition, an agent plug-in has been developed to allow agents based on the JADE/FIPA ACL (*Agent Communication Language*) to interact with the server in order to retrieve alignments that they can use to interpret messages.

However, relying on alignments provided by third parties may not fit with agent's preferences or even privacy issues (i.e., this may allow other agents to infer, and exploit this knowledge in subsequent negotiations). Thus, agents have to agree on which correspondences between their ontologies are mutually acceptable to both agents. As the rationale behind the preferences of each agent may well be private, one cannot always expect agents to disclose their strategy or rationale for communicating (Trojahn et al. 2011).

6.3 Reaching Semantic Agreements by Argumentation

Agents within a distributed environment may have different preferences over correspondences, according to the available knowledge (i.e., kind of ontologies, provenance of the correspondences, etc.). Thus, they may have potentially conflicting preferences over correspondences and agreements between autonomous agents have to be reached. Agreements on alignments can simply be reached by voting or weighting. However, more reasonable ways to reach such agreements takes the form of an argumentation process, where agents iteratively exchange proposals and counter-proposals (arguments) until some consensus is reached.

Different approaches exploit argumentation theory as a way to support the comparison and selection of correspondences within an argumentation process, where correspondences are represented as arguments and argumentation frameworks support the reasoning about their acceptability. Specialized argumentation frameworks for alignment agreements redefine the notion of acceptability, taking into account the confidence of the correspondences (Trojahn et al. 2008) or their support, i.e., the number of votes in favour of a correspondence (Isaac et al. 2008). In this section, before briefly presenting these frameworks, we introduce the notion of argument over correspondences.

6.3.1 Arguments Over Correspondences

The different approaches presented below all share the same notion of argument, which was originally defined in Laera et al. (2006). The general definition of argument is as follows:

Definition 6.2 (Argument). An argument $a \in AF$ is a tuple $a = \langle c, v, h \rangle$, whereby c is a correspondence $\langle e, e', r, n \rangle$; $v \in \mathscr{V}$ is the value of the argument and h is one of $\{+, -\}$, depending on whether the argument is that c does or does not hold.

In this definition, the set of considered values in $\mathscr{V}$ may be based on Trojahn et al. (2011): (a) the types of matching techniques that agents tend to prefer; (b) the type of targeted applications; (c) information about various level of endorsement of these correspondences, and whether or not they have been checked manually. Thus, any type of information which can be associated with correspondences may be used. For example, an alignment may be generated for the purpose of information retrieval; however, this alignment may not be suitable for an agent performing a different task requiring more precision. This agent may therefore prefer the correspondences generated by a different agent for web service composition. Likewise, another agent may prefer human curated alignments rather than alignments generated on the fly.

Arguments interact based on the notion of attack relation:

Definition 6.3 (Attack). An argument $\langle c, v, h \rangle \in \mathscr{A}$ attacks another argument $\langle c', v', h' \rangle \in \mathscr{A}$ iff $c = c'$ and $h \neq h'$.

Therefore, if $a = \langle c, v_1, + \rangle$ and $b = \langle c, v_2, - \rangle$, $a \ltimes b$ and vice-versa (b is the counter-argument of a, and a is the counter-argument of b).

6.3.2 Strength-Based Argumentation Framework (SVAF)

In alignment agreement, arguments can be seen as positions that support or reject correspondences. Such arguments interact following the notion of attack and are selected according to the notion of acceptability. These notions were introduced by Dung (1995). In Dung's model, the acceptability of an argument is based on a reasonable view: an argument should be accepted only if every attack on it is attacked by an accepted argument. Dung defines an argumentation framework as follows:

Definition 6.4 (Argumentation framework (Dung 1995)). An Argumentation Framework (AF) is a pair $\langle \mathscr{A}, \ltimes \rangle$, whereby $\mathscr{A}$ is a set of arguments and $\ltimes$ (attacks) is a binary relation on $\mathscr{A}$. $a \ltimes b$ means that the argument a attacks the argument b. A set of arguments S attacks an argument b iff b is attacked by an argument in S.

In this model, all arguments have equal strength, and an attack always succeeds (or successfully attacks). To attribute different levels of strengths to attacks, Amgoud and Cayrol (1998) has introduced the notion of preference between arguments, where an argument can defend itself against weaker arguments. This model defines a global preference between arguments. In order to relate preferences to different audiences, Bench-Capon (2003) proposes associating arguments to the values which support them. Different audiences can have different preferences over these values. This leads to the notion of *successful attacks*, i.e., those which defeat the attacked argument, with respect to an ordering on the preferences that are associated with the arguments. This allows different audiences with different interests and preferences to be accommodated.

Bench-Capon's framework acknowledges the importance of preferences when considering arguments. However, in the specific context of ontology matching, an objection can still be raised about the lack of complete mechanisms for handling persuasiveness (Isaac et al. 2008). Indeed, many matchers output correspondences with a strength that reflects the confidence they have in the fact that the correspondence between the two entities holds. These confidence levels are usually derived from similarity assessments made during the matching process. They are therefore often based on objective grounds.

To associate an argument to a *strength*, which represents the confidence that an agent has in some correspondence, Trojahn et al. (2008) has proposed the strength-based argumentation framework, extending Bench-Capon's model:

Definition 6.5 (Strength-based argumentation framework (SVAF) (Trojahn et al. 2008)). A SVAF is a sextuple $\langle \mathscr{A}, \ltimes, \mathscr{V}, v, \succeq, s \rangle$ whereby $\langle \mathscr{A}, \ltimes \rangle$ is an AF, $\mathscr{V}$ is a nonempty set of values, $v : \mathscr{A} \rightarrow \mathscr{V}$, $\succeq$ is the preference relation over $\mathscr{V}$ ($v_1 \succeq v_2$ means that, in this framework, v_1 is preferred over v_2), and $s : \mathscr{A} \rightarrow [0, 1]$ represents the strength of the argument.

Each audience α is associated with its own argumentation framework in which only the preference relation $\succeq_\alpha$ differs. In order to accommodate the notion of *strength*, the notion of *successful attack* is extended:

Definition 6.6 (Successful attack (Trojahn et al. 2008)). An argument $a \in \mathscr{A}$ *successfully attacks* (or *defeats*, noted $a\dagger_\alpha b$) an argument $b \in \mathscr{A}$ for an audience α iff

$$a \ltimes b \wedge (s(a) > s(b) \vee (s(a) = s(b) \wedge v(a) \succeq_\alpha v(b)))$$

Definition 6.7 (Acceptable argument (Bench 2003)). An argument $a \in \mathscr{A}$ is *acceptable* to an audience α with respect to a set of arguments S, noted $acceptable_\alpha(a,S)$, iff $\forall x \in \mathscr{A}, x\dagger_\alpha a \Rightarrow \exists y \in S; y\dagger_\alpha x$.

In argumentation, a preferred extension represents a consistent position within a framework, which defends itself against all attacks and cannot be extended without raising conflicts:

Definition 6.8 (Preferred extension). A set S of arguments is *conflict-free* for an audience α iff $\forall a,b \in S, \neg(a \ltimes b) \vee a\dagger_\alpha b$. A conflict-free set of arguments S is *admissible* for an audience α iff $\forall a \in S, acceptable_\alpha(a,S)$. A set of arguments S in the VAF is a *preferred extension* for an audience α iff it is a maximal admissible set (with respect to set inclusion) for α.

In order to determine preferred extensions with respect to a value ordering promoted by distinct audiences, *objective* and *subjective* acceptance are defined (Bench 2003). An argument is *subjectively acceptable* if and only if it appears in some preferred extension for some specific audience. An argument is *objectively acceptable* if and only if it appears in all preferred extension for every specific audience. We will call *objective consolidation* the intersection of objectively acceptable arguments for all audiences and *subjective consolidation* the union of subjectively acceptable arguments for all audiences.

6.3.3 Voting-Based Argumentation Framework (VVAF)

The frameworks described above assume that candidate correspondences between two entities may differ due to the approaches used to construct them, and thus these argumentation frameworks provide different mechanisms with which to identify correspondences generated using approaches acceptable to both agents. However, different alignment generators may often utilise the same approach for some correspondences, and thus the approach used for that correspondence may be significant. Some large-scale experiments involving several matching tools (e.g., the OAEI 2006 Food track campaign (Euzenat et al. 2006)) have demonstrated that the more often a given approach for generating a correspondence is used, the more likely it is to be valid. Thus, the SVAF was adapted and extended in Isaac et al. (2008), to take into account the level of consensus between the sources of the alignments, by introducing the notions of support and voting into the definition of successful attacks. Support enables arguments to be counted as defenders or co-attackers during an attack:

Definition 6.9 (VVAF (Isaac et al. 2008)). A voting-based argumentation framework (VVAF) is a septuple $\langle \mathscr{A}, \ltimes, \mathscr{S}, \mathscr{V}, v, \succeq, s \rangle$ whereby $\langle \mathscr{A}, \ltimes, \mathscr{V}, v, \succeq, s \rangle$ is a SVAF, and $\mathscr{S}$ is a (reflexive) binary relation on $\mathscr{A}$, representing the support relation between arguments. $\mathscr{S}(x,a)$ means that the argument x supports the argument a (i.e., they have the same value of h). $\mathscr{S}$ and $\ltimes$ are disjoint relations.

A simple voting mechanism (e.g., plurality voting) can be used to determine the success of a given attack, based upon the number of supporters for a given approach.

Definition 6.10 (Successful attack (Isaac et al. 2008)). In a VVAF $\langle \mathscr{A}, \ltimes, \mathscr{S}, \mathscr{V}, v, \succeq, s \rangle$, an argument $a \in \mathscr{A}$ successfully attacks (or defeats) an argument $b \in \mathscr{A}$ (noted $a \dagger b$) iff

$$a \ltimes b \wedge (|\{x|\mathscr{S}(x,a)\}| > |\{y|\mathscr{S}(y,b)\}| \vee |\{x|\mathscr{S}(x,a)\}| = |\{y|\mathscr{S}(y,b)\}| \wedge v(a) \succeq v(b)).$$

This voting mechanism is based on simple counting. As some ontology matchers include confidence values with correspondences, a voting mechanism can exploit this confidence value, for example by simply calculating the total confidence value of the supporting arguments. However, this relies on the questionable assumption that all values are equally scaled (as is the case with the SVAF). In Isaac et al. (2008), a voting framework that normalised these confidence values (i.e., strengths) was evaluated, but was inconclusive. Another possibility would be to rely on a deeper justification for correspondences and to have only one vote for each justification. Hence, if several matchers considered two concepts to be equivalent because WordNet considers their identifier as synonyms, this would be counted only once.

6.3.4 Agreement Scenarios

In this section, we present two scenarios of exploiting argumentation to reach agreements. In the first, agents attempt to construct mutually acceptable alignments based on existing correspondences to facilitate communication. Agents argue directly over candidate correspondences provided by an alignment service, with each agent specifying an ordered preference of correspondence types and confidence thresholds. The second scenario focuses on the consensual construction of alignments involving several agents, each of which specialises in constructing correspondences using different approaches. These matching agents generate candidate correspondences and attempt to combine them to produce a new alignment through argumentation. Thus, whilst the first scenario utilises argumentation as a negotiating mechanism to find a mutually acceptable alignment between transacting agents, this latter scenario could be viewed as offering a service for negotiating alignments.

6.3.4.1 Meaning-Based Argumentation

Laera et al. have proposed the meaning-based argumentation approach (Laera et al. 2006, 2007), which allows agents to propose, attack, and counter-propose candidate correspondences according to the agents' preferences, in order to identify mutually acceptable alignments. The approach is based on Bench-Capon's VAF (Bench 2003) to support the specification of preferences of correspondent types within each argument. Thus, when faced with different candidate correspondences (with different types), each agent's preference ordering can be considered when determining if an argument for one correspondence will successfully attack another. Different audiences therefore represent different sets of arguments for preferences between the categories of arguments (identified in the context of ontology matching).

Each agent is defined as follows:

Definition 6.11 (Agent). An agent Ag_i is characterised by a tuple $\langle O_i, F, \varepsilon_i \rangle$, whereby O_i is the ontology used by the agent, F is its (valued-based) argumentation framework, and ε_i is the private threshold value.

Candidate correspondences are retrieved from an alignment service which also provides the justifications G (described below) for each correspondence, based on the approach used to construct the correspondence. The agents use this information to exchange arguments supplying the reasons for their choices. In addition, as these grounds include a confidence value associated with each correspondence, each agent utilises a private threshold value ε to filter out correspondences with low confidence values. This threshold, together with the pre-ordering of preferences, is used to generate arguments for and against a correspondence.

Definition 6.12 (Argument (Laera et al. 2006)). An argument is a triple $\langle G, c, h \rangle$, where c is a correspondence $\langle e, e', r, n \rangle$, G is the grounds justifying a prima facie belief that the correspondence does, or does not hold; and h is one of $\{+, -\}$ depending on whether the argument is that c does or does not hold.

The grounds G that justify a correspondence between two entities are based on the five categories of correspondence types, namely *Semantic* (S), *Internal Structural* (IS), *External Structural* (ES), *Terminological* (T), and *Extensional* (E). These classes are used as types for the values $\mathcal{V}$, i.e., $\mathcal{V} = \{M, IS, ES, T, E\}$, that are then used to construct an agent's partially-ordered preferences, based on the agent's ontology and task. Thus, an agent may specify a preference for terminological correspondences over semantic correspondences if the ontology it uses is mainly taxonomic, or vice versa if the ontology is semantically rich. Preferences may also be based on the type of task being performed; extensional correspondences may be preferred when queries are about instances that are frequently shared. The pre-ordering of preferences $\succeq$ for each agent Ag_i is over $\mathcal{V}$, corresponding to the specification of an audience. Specifically, for each candidate correspondence c, if there exists one or more justifications G for c that corresponds to the highest preferences $\succeq$ of Ag_i (with the respect of the pre-ordering), assuming n is greater than its private threshold ε, an agent Ag_i will generate arguments $x = (G,c,+)$. If not, the agent will generate arguments against: $x = (G,c,-)$.

The argumentation process takes four main steps: (i) each agent Ag_i constructs an argumentation framework VAF_i by specifying the set of arguments and the attacks between them; (ii) each agent Ag_i considers its individual frameworks VAF_i with all the argument sets of all the other agents and then extends the attack relations by computing the attacks between the arguments present in its framework with the other arguments; (iii) for each VAF_i, the arguments which are undefeated by attacks from other arguments are determined, given a value ordering – the global view is considered by taking the union of these preferred extensions for each audience; and (iv) the arguments in every preferred extension of every audience are considered – the correspondences that have only arguments for are included in the a set called *agreed alignments*, whereas the correspondences that have only arguments against them are rejected, and the correspondences which are in some preferred extension of every audience are part of the set called *agreeable alignments*.

The dialogue between agents consists of exchanging sets of arguments and the protocol used to evaluate the acceptability of a single correspondence is based on a set of speech acts (*Support*, *Contest*, *Withdraw*). For instance, when exchanging arguments, an agent sends $Support(c,x_1)$ for supporting a correspondence c through the argument $x_1 = (G,c,+)$ or $Contest(c,x_2)$ for rejecting c, by $x_2 = (G,c,-)$. If the agents do not have any arguments or counter-arguments to propose, then they send $Withdraw(c)$ and the dialogue terminates.

To illustrate this approach, consider the two agents buyer b and seller s, using the ontologies in Fig. 6.1. First, the agents access the alignment service that returns the correspondences with the respective justifications:

- m_1: $\langle zoom_o, zoom_{o'}, \equiv, 1.0\rangle$, with $G = \{T, ES\}$
- m_2: $\langle Battery_o, Battery_{o'}, \equiv, 1.0\rangle$, with $G = \{T\}$
- m_3: $\langle MemoryCard_o Memory_{o'}, \equiv, 0.54\rangle$, with $G = \{T\}$
- m_4: $\langle brand_o, brandName_{o'}, \equiv, 0.55\rangle$, with $G = \{T, ES\}$
- m_5: $\langle price_o, price_{o'}, \equiv, 1.0\rangle$, with $G = \{T, ES\}$
- m_6: $\langle CameraPhoto_o, DigitalCamera_{o'}, \equiv, 1.0\rangle$, with $G = \{ES\}$
- m_7: $\langle resolution_o, pixels_{o'}, \equiv, 1.00\rangle$, with $G = \{ES\}$

Agent b selects the audience R_1, which prefers terminology to external structure ($T \succ_{R_1} ES$), while s prefers external structure to terminology ($ES \succ_{R_2} T$). All correspondences have a degree of confidence n that is above the threshold of each agent and then all of them are taken into account. Both agents accept m_1, m_4 and m_5. b accepts m_2, m_3, while s accepts m_6 and m_7. Table 6.1 shows the arguments and corresponding attacks.

The arguments A, B, G, H, I, and J are not attacked and then are acceptable for both agents (they form the *agreed alignment*). The arguments C and D are mutually attacked and are acceptable only in the corresponding audience, i.e., C is acceptable for the audience b and D is acceptable for the audience s. The same occurs for the arguments E, F, L, M, M, and O. The correspondences in such arguments are seen as the *agreeable alignments*.

Table 6.1 Arguments and attacks

Id	Argument	Attack	Agent
A	$\langle T, m_1, + \rangle$		b, s
B	$\langle ES, m_1, + \rangle$		b, s
C	$\langle T, m_2, + \rangle$	D	b
D	$\langle ES, m_2, - \rangle$	C	s
E	$\langle T, m_3, + \rangle$	F	b
F	$\langle ES, m_3, - \rangle$	E	s
G	$\langle T, m_4, + \rangle$		b, s
H	$\langle ES, m_4, + \rangle$		b, s
I	$\langle T, m_5, + \rangle$		b, s
J	$\langle ES, m_5, + \rangle$		b, s
L	$\langle ES, m_6, + \rangle$	M	s
M	$\langle T, m_6, - \rangle$	L	b
N	$\langle ES, m_7, + \rangle$	O	s
O	$\langle T, m_7, - \rangle$	N	b

6.3.4.2 Solving Conflicts Between Matcher Agents

In Trojahn et al. (2008), alignments produced by different matchers are compared and agreed via an argumentation process. The matchers interact in order to exchange arguments and the SVAF model is used to support the choice of the most acceptable of them. Each correspondence can be considered as an argument because the choice of a correspondence may be a reason against the choice of another correspondence. Correspondences are represented as arguments, extending the notion of argument specified in Laera et al. (2006):

Definition 6.13 (Argument). An argument $x \in AF$ is a tuple $x = \langle c, v, s, h \rangle$, whereby c is a correspondence $\langle e, e', r, n \rangle$; $v \in \mathcal{V}$ is the value of the argument; s is the strength of the argument, from n; and h is one of $\{+, -\}$ depending on whether the argument is that c does or does not hold.

The matchers generate arguments representing their alignments following a *negative arguments as failure* strategy. It relies on the assumption that matchers return complete results. Each possible pair of ontology entities which is not returned by the matcher is considered to be at risk, and a negative argument is generated ($h = -$).

The values v in $\mathcal{V}$ correspond to the different matching approaches and each matcher m has a preference ordering $\succeq_m$ over $\mathcal{V}$ whereby its preferred values are those it associates to its arguments. For instance, consider $\mathcal{V} = \{l, s, w\}$, i.e., *lexical*, *structural* and *wordnet-based* approaches, respectively, and three matchers m_l, m_s and m_w, using such approaches. The matcher m_l has as preference order $l \succeq_{m_l} s \succeq_{m_l} w$. The basic idea is to obtain a consensus between different matchers, represented by different preferences between values.

The argumentation process can be described as follows. First, each matcher generates its set of correspondences, using some specific approach and then the set of corresponding arguments is generated. Next, the matchers exchange their set of arguments with each others – the dialogue between them consists

Table 6.2 Correspondences and arguments generated by m_l and m_s

Id	Correspondence	Argument	Matcher
A	$c_{l,1} = \langle zoom_o, zoom_{o'}, \equiv, 1.0\rangle$	$\langle c_{l,1}, l, 1.0, +\rangle$	m_l
B	$c_{l,2} = \langle Battery_o, Battery_{o'}, \equiv, 1.0\rangle$	$\langle c_{l,2}, l, 1.0+\rangle$	m_l
C	$c_{l,3} = \langle MemoryCard_o Memory_{o'}, \equiv, 0.33\rangle$	$\langle c_{l,3}, l, 0.33, +\rangle$	m_l
D	$c_{l,4} = \langle brand_o, brandName_{o'}, \equiv, 0.22\rangle$	$\langle c_{l,4}, l, 0.22, +\rangle$	m_l
E	$c_{l,5} = \langle price_o, price_{o'}, \equiv, 1.0\rangle$	$\langle c_{l,5}, l, 1.0, +\rangle$	m_l
F	$c_{s,1} = \langle CameraPhoto_o, DigitalCamera_{o'}, \equiv, 1.0\rangle$	$\langle c_{s,1}, s, 1.0, +\rangle$	m_s
G	$c_{s,2} = \langle zoom_o, zoom_{o'}, \equiv, 1.0\rangle$	$\langle c_{s,2}, s, 1.0, +\rangle$	m_s
H	$c_{s,3} = \langle brand_o, brandName_{o'}, \equiv, 1.0\rangle$	$\langle c_{s,3}, s, 1.0, +\rangle$	m_s
I	$c_{s,4} = \langle resolution_o, pixels_{o'}, \equiv, 1.0\rangle$	$\langle c_{s,4}, s, 1.0, +\rangle$	m_s
J	$c_{s,5} = \langle price_o, price_{o'}, \equiv, 1.0\rangle$	$\langle c_{s,5}, s, 1.0, +\rangle$	m_s

Table 6.3 Counter-arguments (attacks) for the arguments in Table 6.2

Id	Correspondence	Counter-argument	Matcher
L	$c_{l,6} = \langle CameraPhoto_o, DigitalCamera_{o'}, \equiv, 0.5\rangle$	$\langle c_{l,6}, l, 0.5, -\rangle$	m_l
M	$c_{l,7} = \langle resolution_o, pixels_{o'}, \equiv, 0.5\rangle$	$\langle c_{l,7}, l, 0.5, -\rangle$	m_l
N	$c_{s,6} = \langle Battery_o, Battery_{o'}, \equiv, 0.5\rangle$	$\langle c_{s,6}, s, 0.5, -\rangle$	m_s
O	$c_{s,7} = \langle MemoryCard_o, Memory_{o'}, \equiv, 0.5\rangle$	$\langle c_{s,7}, s, 0.5, -\rangle$	m_s

of the exchange of individual arguments. When all matchers have received the set of each others' arguments, they instantiate their SVAFs in order to generate their set of acceptable correspondences. The consensual alignment contains the correspondences represented as arguments that appear in every set of acceptable arguments, for every specific audience (objectively acceptable).

In order to illustrate this process, consider two matchers, m_l (lexical) and m_s (structural), trying to reach a consensus on the alignment between the ontologies in Fig. 6.1. m_l uses an edit distance measure to compute the similarity between labels of concepts and properties of the ontologies, while m_s is based on the comparison of the direct super-classes of the classes or classes of properties. Table 6.2 shows the correspondences and arguments generated by each matcher. The matchers generate complete alignments, i.e., if a correspondence is not found, an argument with value of $h = -$ is created. It includes correspondences that are not relevant to the task at hand. For the sake of brevity, we show only the arguments with $h = +$ and the corresponding counter-arguments (Table 6.3). We consider 0.5 as the confidence level c for negative arguments ($h = -$). Considering $\mathscr{V} = \{l, v\}$, m_l associates to its arguments the value l, while m_s generates arguments with value s. m_l has as preference ordering: $l \succ_{m_l} s$, while m_s has the preference: $s \succ_{m_s} l$.

Having their arguments $\mathscr{A}$, the matchers exchange them. m_l sends to m_s its set of arguments $\mathscr{A}_l$ and vice-versa. Next, based on the attack notion, each matcher m_i generates its attack relation $\ltimes_i$ and then instantiates its $SVAFs_i$. The arguments A, D, E, G, H and J are acceptable in both SVAFs (they are not attacked by counter-arguments with $h = -$). F, I, and B ($h = +$) successfully attack their counter-arguments ($h = -$) L, M and N, respectively, because they have highest confidence in their correspondences. C ($h = +$) is successfully attacked by its counter-argument O.

Table 6.4 Interaction steps (dos Santos et al. 2008)

Step	Description
1	Matcher agent m requests the ontologies to be matched to agents b and s
2	Ontologies are sent from m to the argumentation module
3	Matchers $a_1,\ldots,a_n$ apply their algorithms
4	Each matcher a_i communicate with each others to exchange their arguments
5	Preferred extensions of each a_i are generated
6	Objectively acceptable arguments o are computed
7	Correspondences in o are represented as conjunctive queries
8	Queries are sent to m
9	Queries are sent from m to b and s
10	Agents b and s use the queries to communicate with each other

The arguments in the preferred extension of both matchers m_l and m_s are: A, D, E, F, G, H, J, F, I, B and O. While $\langle resolution_o, pixels_{o'}\rangle$, $\langle Battery_o, Battery_{o'}\rangle$ and $\langle CameraPhoto_o, DigitalCamera_{o'}\rangle$ have been accepted, $\langle MemoryCard_o, Memory_{o'}\rangle$ has been discarded.

The argumentation approach presented so far, has been used to provide translations between messages in agent communication (dos Santos et al. 2008), whereas an alignment is formally defined as a set of correspondences between *queries* over ontologies. The set of acceptable arguments is then represented as conjunctive queries in OWL DL (Haase and Motik 2005). A conjunctive query has the form $\bigwedge$ ($\mathrm{P}_i(\mathrm{s}_i)$), where each $\mathrm{P}_i(\mathrm{s}_i)$ represents a correspondence. For instance, $\langle CameraPhoto_o, DigitalCamera_{o'}, \equiv, 1.0\rangle$ is represented as $Q(x)$: $CameraPhoto(x) \equiv DigitalCamera(x)$.

Following the example above, the matching task is delegated to a matcher agent m, that receives the two ontologies and sends them to an argumentation module. This module, made up of different specialised agents $a_1,\ldots,a_n$ (which can be distributed on the web), receives the ontologies and returns a set of DL queries representing the acceptable correspondences. These interactions are loosely based on the Contract Net Interaction Protocol (FIPA 2002). The argumentation process between the specialised matchers is detailed below. Table 6.4 describes the steps of the interaction between the agents.

In fact, only one of the agents should receive the DL queries, which should be responsible for the translations. We consider that the set of objectively acceptable arguments has the correspondences shown in Fig. 6.2, with the respective queries.

Figure 6.3 shows an AUML[1] interaction diagram with the messages exchanged between the agents b and s during the negotiation of the price of the camera. The agents use the queries to search for correspondences between the messages sent from each other and the entities in the corresponding ontologies. In the example, the agent b sends a message to the agent s, using its vocabulary. Then, the agent s converts the message, using the DL queries.

[1] AUML – Agent Unified Modelling Language.

Fig. 6.2 Conjunctive queries

QueryID	Correspondences
$Q_{b1}(x)$	b:CameraPhoto(x)
$Q_{s1}(x)$	s:DigitalCamera(x)
m_1	$Q_{b1} \equiv Q_{s1}$
$Q_{b2}(y)$	b:zoom(y)
$Q_{s2}(y)$	s:zoom(y)
m_2	$Q_{b2} \equiv Q_{s2}$
$Q_{b3}(y)$	b:resolution(y)
$Q_{s3}(y)$	s:pixels(y)
m_3	$Q_{b3} \equiv Q_{s3}$

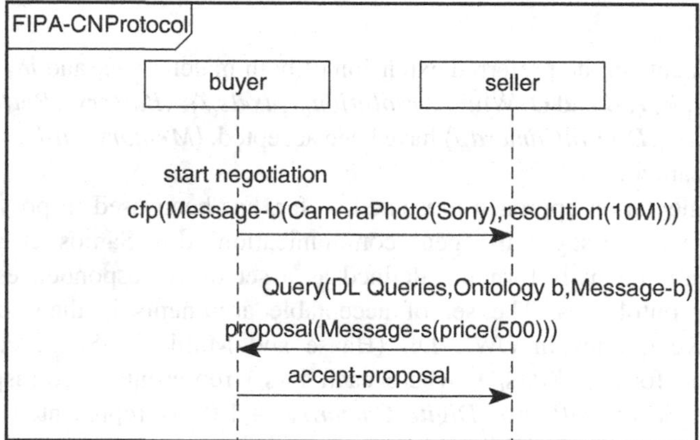

Fig. 6.3 Interaction between buyer and seller agents

6.3.5 Discussion

In the previous sections, we have presented two specific argumentation frameworks designed for ontology alignment agreement, and focused on two scenarios where argumentation is exploited to reach agreements from agents interacting within a multi-agent systems. Before discussing other similar approaches that have been proposed in the literature, we discuss the limitations of the approaches presented so far.

In the meaning-based argumentation proposal (Laera et al. 2007), agents represent audiences with different preferences over justifications on correspondences, delivered by a repository of alignments. Based on Bench-Capon's VAF, each agent can decide, according to its preferences, whether to accept or refuse a candidate correspondence. A first potential limitation of this approach is related to the fact that some conflicts can not be solved in the cases where agents have mutually exclusive preferences (i.e., resulting in an empty agreement, which can compromise the communication). Second, agent's preferences are associated with justifications from repositories of alignments, which may be not available (i.e., very few matcher systems are able to provide such kinds of justifications). Third, it is assumed that agents share the same subset of justifications (although they can express different preferences over them), which can impose some restrictions in an open environment. Finally, the generation of arguments is directed by a single acceptance threshold and preference ordering, what may result in rejecting those correspondences which, whilst not optimal, may reflect the preferences of the agents and eventually be considered acceptable to all the agents.

In Trojahn's proposal (dos Santos et al. 2008), the underlying argumentation framework is based on the strengths of arguments, derived from the confidence associated to correspondences, where stronger arguments successfully attacks weaker arguments. However, there is no objective theory nor even informal guidelines for determining confidence levels and using them to compare results from different matchers is therefore questionable especially because of potential scale mismatches.

Besides the individual limitations of each approach, both of them rely on very basic argument structures. Basically, arguments represent positions in favour or against correspondences and binary attacks are derived from such positions. However, more complex structures of arguments are required to allow exploiting, for instance, inferences on correspondences and establishing more elaborate ways to derive attack relations than the binary ones.

Regarding the other argumentation-based agreement proposals, Doran et al. (2009) propose a modularization approach for identifying the ontological descriptions relevant to the communication, and consequently reduce the number of correspondences necessary to form the alignment, as the use of argumentation can be computationally costly (i.e., the complexity can reach $\Pi_2^{(p)}$-complete in some cases (Doran et al. 2009)). An ontology modularization technique extracts a consistent module M from an ontology O that covers a specified signature $Sig(M)$, such as $Sig(M) \subseteq Sig(O)$. M is the part of O that is said to cover the elements defined by $Sig(M)$. The first agent engaging in the communication specifies the $Sig(M)$ of its ontology O where M is an ontology concept relevant for a task. The resulting module contains the entities considered to be relevant for its task, including the subclasses and properties of the concepts in $Sig(M)$. Thus, by reducing the number of arguments, the time required to generate the alignments can be significantly reduced, even when taking into account the time necessary for the modularization process itself. However, negotiation is based on the meaning-based argumentation process presented above.

In Doran et al. (2010), an approach to overcome the limitation of generating arguments from a single acceptance preference and threshold, in meaning-based argumentation, is proposed. Basically, a function $\phi : \mathscr{V} \rightarrow [0,..,1]$ maps each justification v in $\mathscr{V}$ to a value $0 \leq \phi_i(v) \leq 1$, in such a way that $\phi_i(v)$ represents the minimum confidence threshold for the agents Ag_i to argue in favour of a correspondence with justification v. Thus, an agent determines its orientation on a correspondence on the basis of the minimum confidence threshold for arguing in favour of a correspondence justification and no longer on the ordering of preferences. The preference order then is only used by the VAF when dealing with arguments and attacks. Whilst this approach results in agents relaxing some of their preferences over suitable correspondences, it produces a larger consensus over possible correspondences due to the generation of a greater number of arguments in favour of the candidate correspondences compared to the meaning-based approach.

From a logical perspective, these argumentation approaches do not guarantee that agreed alignments relate the ontologies in a consistent way (i.e., correspondences may generate concepts that are not satisfiable), even if the initial alignments were consistent. In Trojahn and Euzenat (2010), a strategy for computing maximal consistent sub-consolidations, involving both argumentation (using SVAF framework) and logical inconsistency detection, is proposed. It removes correspondences that introduce inconsistencies into the resulting alignment and allows the consistency within an argumentation system to be maintained. The strategy for detecting logical inconsistencies is the one proposed in Meilicke et al. (2009) which identifies the minimal sets of incoherent correspondences and removes them from the original alignment. The algorithm is based on theory of diagnosis, where a diagnosis is formed by correspondences with lowest confidence degrees that introduce incoherence in the alignment.

Finally, in Morge et al. (2006), the authors propose an argumentation framework for inter-agent dialogue to reach an agreement on terminology, which formalizes a debate in which the divergent representations (expressed in description logic) are discussed. The proposed framework is stated as being able to manage conflicts between claims, with different relevancies for different audiences, in order to compute their acceptance. However, no detail is given about how agents will generate such claims.

6.4 Reaching Semantic Agreements via Distributed Constraint Optimization Methods

While argumentation methods have been presented extensively in the previous section, this and the following sections present methods that use constraint optimization and message passing algorithms to reach semantic agreements regarding the computation of correspondences between ontologies. These methods aim at establishing a common vocabulary among autonomous agents or peers, and reconcile semantic disagreements in the alignments computed between ontologies.

For the establishment or development of a common vocabulary among agents, researchers have proposed cognitive models (Reitter and Lebiere 2011), bilateral communication protocols and strategies (Sensoy and Yolum 2009; van Diggelen et al. 2006) for agents, also studying the properties of shared vocabularies (van Diggelen et al. 2004), or the dynamics of their establishment (Baronchelli et al. 2005). In this section, we start from the point where peers have their own ontologies (assumed to be developed/learned independently from the ontologies of others), have computed an initial set of subjective correspondences to acquaintances ontologies using any set of alignment methods, and need to reach consensus as to the meaning of the terms they use, even with distant peers. Therefore, we do not deal with how ontologies have been learned, or how effective alignments can be established between pairs of peers: either using an instance based method (van Diggelen et al. 2006; Williams 2004), a method for tuning the descriptions of concepts (Williams 2004), or other ontology alignment methods, we remain agnostic about specific alignment methods used by the peers and aim at reconciling differences between computed correspondences.

Besides these approaches, there are also several works that aim to preserve the consistency of alignment decisions by locating (minimal) subsets of correspondences that introduce inconsistencies (Jiménez-Ruiz et al. 2009; Meilicke and Stuckenschmidt 2009; Meilicke et al. 2009; Qi et al. 2009). In contrast to these approaches, in this section we consider distributed methods for the computation of agreed correspondences between ontologies.

Focusing on a generic method for reaching semantic agreements between distinct matching methods, this section presents a method for the reconciliation of disagreements by satisfying entities preferences, also addressing scalability, expandability and tolerance to failures of matching methods with which to compute alignments: The method proposed in Spiliopoulos and Vouros (2012) formulates the synthesis of ontology alignment methods as a generic social welfare maximization problem. In doing so, it represents the problem of synthesizing the matching results of different agents as a bipartite factor graph (Kschischang et al. 1998), thus allowing the use of an extension of the max-sum algorithm. The matching methods' synthesis problem is being treated as an optimization problem through local decentralized message passing. While this method concerns the synthesis of individual alignment methods, in the general case it can be applied to settings where agents share the same ontology but are using different methods for computing correspondences to a commonly-known, third ontology.

6.4.1 Problem Specification

As already pointed out, agents within a distributed environment may have different preferences over correspondences, according to the available knowledge (i.e., the kind of ontologies, provenance of the correspondences, etc.). Thus, they may have potentially conflicting preferences over correspondences. Therefore, reaching agreements is necessary.

Such preferences are due to different matching methods, or to different information made available to each matching method. Generally, considering a set of K alignment methods, each method has its own preference concerning any assessed relation r between two ontology entities E_1 and E_2. The synthesis of these K methods aims to compute an alignment of the input ontologies, with respect to the preferences of the individual methods. This has been addressed as a coordination problem (Spiliopoulos and Vouros 2012).

Let us restrict the problem to the alignment of classes. To model it, the method presented considers a set of M interacting agents: each agent is associated to a specific alignment method AM_j and has a state that is described by a discrete variable x_{j-k} corresponding to a class E^i_k in one of the two input ontologies (i = 1,2). The variable x_{j-k} ranges to the classes of the other input ontology that AM_j assesses to be related to E^i_k via a relation r and preference n. Each agent interacts locally with a number of neighboring agents, whereby its utility $U_i(\mathbf{X}_i)$ is dependent on its own state and the states of these agents (defined by the set $\mathbf{X}_i$). The form of this utility function reflects the matching preferences of each agent with respect to the semantics of specifications and the matching preferences computed by the corresponding method. These may be not known to other agents. Agents are organized in a network, where the neighbors of an agent are determined by a set of validity constraints that must be satisfied so that the calculated correspondences conform to the semantics of specifications. The exact constraints, the form of agents utility function and the set of agents neighbors are specified in subsequent paragraphs. Such a network forms a bipartite factor graph, which enables us to view the synthesis of the matching methods as a coordination problem, and use the generic distributed message-passing max-sum algorithm proposed in Farinelli et al. (2008) to find the joint state of agents, $\mathbf{X}^*$, whereby the social welfare of the whole system (i.e., the sum of the individual agents utilities) is maximized:

$$\mathbf{X}^* = argmax \Sigma_{m=1}^{M} U_m(x_m)$$

6.4.2 The Synthesis as a Constraint Optimization Problem

Proceeding to the details of the approach proposed in Spiliopoulos and Vouros (2012), we emphasize that given a set of K alignment methods AM_i, i = 1...K, we address the synthesis of these methods as a coordination problem between self-interested agents that are constructed and organized on-the-fly: the model comprises agents that correspond to ontology entities and alignment mechanisms, and the network topology is determined by inter-agent validity constraints. The problem of synthesizing alignment methods using such a model is different (although closely related) from the one where agents exist in a specific network topology, have different ontologies, local utilities and preferences, and need to align their ontologies consistently by coordinating their computations of correspondences: this problem is addressed in Sect. 6.5.

The next paragraphs describe how the network of acquaintances is being constructed as a factor graph (Loeliger 2004), the validity constraints among agents' states, as well as the exact form of agents' utility function.

Specifically, given the K alignment methods and two ontologies $O_1 = (S_1, A_1)$, $O_2 = (S_2, A_2)$, the situation is represented by a factor graph as follows: the nodes of this factor graph are the utilities (functions) and the states (variables) of agents. Each agent A_{j-i} corresponds to an ontology class E_i^1 of O_1 and to a specific alignment method AM_j. Without any loss of generality it is assumed that agents correspond to the classes in the ontology O_1, which is called the *base ontology* and is being chosen randomly among the two input ontologies. The state of agent A_{j-i} is represented by a variable x_{j-i} that ranges in the subset of classes in O_2 that the method AM_j assesses to be related to E_i^1 via a relation r. Let that set be D_{j-i}. As already said, the problem is formulated for the cases where r is either the equivalence ($\equiv$) or the subsumption (inclusion) ($\sqsubseteq$) relation. The possible values E_i^2 of x_{j-i} may have been assigned confidence values by AM_j. The ordering imposed to D_{j-i} by the confidence values represents the preference of the agent for each possible value of x_{j-i}. In case that classes in D_{j-i} are not associated with confidence values, then the agent considers all possible values of x_{j-i} to be equally preferred. Since each agent A_{j-i} corresponds to the method AM_j and to the element E_i of the base ontology, the factor graph comprises at most $|S_1| \times K$ agents, i.e., at most $2 \times |S_1| \times K$ nodes, in case O_1 is the base ontology. We should point out that if AM_j assesses that there are no classes that can be related to the class E_{i1}, i.e., $D_{j-i} = \emptyset$, then no agent is created for the specific class E_{i1} and matching method AM_j.

Each agent A_{j-i} interacts with a limited number of neighbors: the neighbors of A_{j-i} are those agents that correspond to classes that are direct subsumees of E_i^1 in the base ontology, and the agents that correspond to the class E_i^1 but are associated to different alignment methods or different type of alignment relations r. Formally, the set of neighbors of an agent A_{j-i} is denoted by $N(A_{j-i})$ and it is defined to be

$N(A_{j-i}) = \{A_{u-n} | [n = i \text{ and } j \neq u] \text{ or } [(n \neq i) \text{ and } (E_i^1 \sqsubseteq E_n^1 \text{ in a direct way})]\}$.

In this definition, without loss of generality, we assume that the base ontology is the first ontology.

The states of neighboring agents are interrelated with constraints that affect the values they may take. Let us first show this with an example. Given the two ontologies depicted in Fig. 6.4 (let O_1 be the base ontology) and two alignment methods A and B, the factor graph is as shown in Fig. 6.4c. Given that, as it is also shown in the graph, the method A computes only subsumption relations and the method B computes only equivalences between the two ontologies, the graph comprises eight agents (not all of them are shown in the Figure), each for a method-class combination and a specific type of alignment relation. Specifically, the method proposed in Spiliopoulos and Vouros (2012) considers the generic case where the method A (respectively B) computes for each class E_i^1 of the base ontology the set D_{A-i} (respectively D_{B-i}) of candidate classes from the ontology O_2. Each of the classes in this set is assessed to be related to E_i^1 via the subsumption (respectively equivalence) relation. As already said, the computed sets of classes are sets of possible values for the variables of the corresponding agents, e.g., the first agent for the method A considers values, i.e., classes from the second ontology for the variable x_{A-1} whereby $x_{A-1} \sqsubseteq E_1^1$. Similarly, the first agent for the method B considers values, i.e., classes from the second ontology for the variable x_{B-1} whereby $x_{B-1} \equiv E_1^1$. Clearly, to maintain consistency between their correspondences it must hold that $x_{A-1} \sqsubseteq x_{B-1}$. This is a constraint that must be preserved by the agent

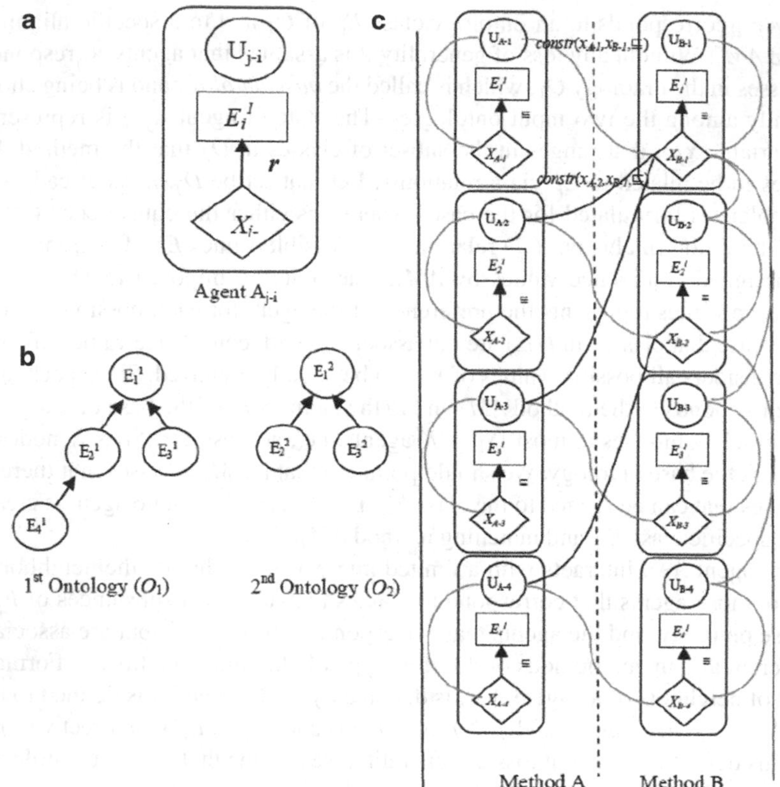

Fig. 6.4 Example ontologies and the resulting graph for two methods A and B

A_{A-1} and it is specified by $constr(x_{A-1}, x-B-1, \sqsubseteq)$. This is depicted in Fig. 6.4c by the curved line that connects the utility U_{A-1} to the variable x_{B-1}. Similarly, since $E_2^1 \sqsubseteq E_1^1$, it must hold that $x_{A-2} \sqsubseteq x_{B-1}$. This is specified by the constraint $constr(x_{A-2}, x_{B-1}, \sqsubseteq)$ for the agent A_{A-2} in Fig. 6.4c.

Constraints are depicted in Fig. 6.4c by curved lines. In case two variables x_{j-i}, x_{u-w} are associated with a specific constraint, then the utility of the agent A_{j-i} is associated with x_{u-w}.

Generally, the constraints between the variables x_{i-j}, x_{u-w} of two agents A_{i-j}, A_{u-w}, are generated as follows (given that the base ontology is the first input ontology):

- If $(E_j^1 \sqsubseteq E_w^1$ and $(x_{u-w} \equiv E_w^1$ and $(x_{i-j} \equiv E_j^1$ or $x_{i-j} \sqsubseteq E_j^1)))$ then $constr(x_{i-j}, x_{u-w}, \sqsubseteq)$. An example of such a constraint is the constraint $constr(x_{A-2}, x_{B-1}, \sqsubseteq)$, discussed in the example above.
- If $(E_j^1 \sqsubseteq E_w^1$ and $(x_{u-w} \sqsubseteq E_w^1$ and $(x_{i-j} \sqsubseteq E_j^1$ or $x_{i-j} \equiv E_j^1)))$ then we can not assume any constraint.

- If ($E_j^1 \equiv E_w^1$ and ($x_{i-j} \equiv E_j^1$ and $x_{u-w} \equiv E_w^1$)) then $constr(x_{i-j}, x_{u-w}, \equiv)$. This constraint drives different methods that compute equivalences to reach an agreement concerning the correspondence of each class.
- If ($E_i^1 \equiv E_w^1$ and ($x_{j-i} \sqsubseteq E_i^1$ and $x_{u-w} \equiv E_w^1$)) then $constr(x_{j-i}, x_{u-w}, \sqsubseteq)$.
- If ($E_i^1 \equiv E_w^1$ and ($x_{j-i} \equiv E_i^1$ and $x_{u-w} \sqsubseteq E_w^1$)) then $constr(x_{u-w}, x_{j-i}, \sqsubseteq)$.
- If ($E_i^1 \equiv E_w^1$ and ($x_{j-i} \sqsubseteq E_i^1$ and $x_{u-w} \sqsubseteq E_w^1$)) then we can not assume any constraint.

It must be pointed out that, without affecting the formulation of the problem, this formulation deals only with constraints that are generated from subsumees to subsumers (i.e., $E_i \sqsubseteq E_w$), and not in the reverse order. The latter choice would generate many more constraints, and therefore, the number of agents neighbors would increase dramatically, thus reducing the efficiency of the max-sum algorithm. Constraints specify how the utility of each agent is affected by its own state and the state of its neighbors. The utility function of an agent A_{j-i} corresponding to the class E_i of the base ontology and to the alignment method AM_j is given by the following formula:

$$U_{j-i}(X) = \gamma_{j-i}(x_{j-i}) - \Sigma_{x_{k-l} \in N(U_{j-i})} \Sigma_{x_{u-w} \in C(x_{k-l}, x_{j-i})} x_{k-l} \otimes x_{u-w}$$

Where $x_{k-l} \otimes x_{u-w}$ is equal to:

- a if $constr(x_{k-l}, x_{u-w}, \equiv)$ but $x_{k-l} \not\equiv x_{u-w}$
- b if $constr(x_{k-l}, x_{u-w}, \sqsubseteq)$ but $x_{k-l} \not\sqsubseteq u - w$
- 0 otherwise

Parameters a and b are set to 1 and 0.2 respectively. Moreover, $\gamma_{j-i}(x_{j-i})$ is the normalized confidence by which the method AM_j maps the class E_i of the base ontology to a class of the other ontology assigned to x_{j-i}. Confidence values of correspondences computed by AM_j (i.e., of values in D_{j-i}) are being normalized by dividing them by the $max_{x_{j-i} \in D_{j-i}}(n_{j-i}(x_{j-i}))$. $N(U_{j-i})$ is the set of the variables connected to the utility U_{j-i}, and $constr(x_{k-l}, x_{u-w}, r)$ denotes the constraint which states that x_{k-l} must be related via r with x_{u-w}. In case a method does not assign a confidence value to any of the assessed correspondences, the confidence for these correspondences is set to be equal to 1. For the correspondences that a method does not assess a value for, the confidence value is set to be 0. Finally, $C(x_{k-l}, xj-i)$ is a set of variables that depend on two given variables, namely x_{k-l}, x_{j-i} and is defined as follows:

$$C(x_{k-l}, x_{j-i}) = \{x_{z-w} \in N(U_{j-i}) | id(x_{z-w}) > id(x_{k-l}) \text{ and } [x_{k-l} \in N(U_{z-w}) \text{ or } x_{z-w} \in N(U_{k-l})]\}$$

where $id(x)$ is an integer that is assigned to a variable by the order in which the corresponding agent is created in the factor graph.

It should be noted that according to the above specifications, the utility function of an agent depends on the states of its immediate neighbors, as well as on the states of the neighbors of their neighbors, based also on an assignment of preferences to the states of these agents. According to experimental results reported in Spiliopoulos and Vouros (2012) and Farinelli et al. (2008), making the utility depend solely on the states of neighbor agents is not sufficient for the algorithm to effectively prevent cycling, causing both the messages and the preferred states of the agents not to converge. The utility function specified above allows agents to take into account not only conflicts with their neighbors, but also conflicts among these neighbors, preventing cycling and driving the algorithm to convergence. While variables converge when they reach a fixed state, messages converge when these are the same with ones sent via a specific edge in a previous cycle of execution.

As pointed out in Spiliopoulos and Vouros (2012), in the current implementation of the algorithm, at each execution cycle agents are ordered randomly, update their messages and state based on the previous messages that they had received, and then propagate their outgoing messages to their neighbors. Therefore, this implementation of the max-sum algorithm simulates asynchronous message passing and the distribution of calculations. For further details about the message passing algorithm, refer to Spiliopoulos and Vouros (2012).

6.4.3 Experimental Findings

To study whether and how the proposed synthesis method satisfies desired properties of a synthesis method (discussed below), results from a series of experiments using three individual methods have been reported in Spiliopoulos and Vouros (2012). The three methods are: the "Classification-Based Learning of Subsumption Relations for the Alignment of Ontologies" (CSR) (Spiliopoulos et al. 2011) method, a Vector-Space Model (VSM) based method and the COCLU lexical matching method (Valarakos et al. 2004). These methods have been chosen due to the different types of correspondence relations they compute, due to the different types of information from ontologies they exploit, as well as due to their fundamentally different approach to the alignment of ontologies.

The testing dataset that was used in Spiliopoulos and Vouros (2012) has been derived from the benchmarking series of the OAEI 2006 contest. This dataset has been used, gold standard correspondences for the CSR method are based on this. Additionally, as the CSR method exploits class properties (in cases where properties are used as class pairs features) and hierarchies of classes (for the generation of training examples), this dataset does not include OAEI 2006 ontologies whose classes have no properties or there are no hierarchical relations between classes.

To sum up the experimental findings, the presented synthesis approach addresses the following desiderata for an ontology alignments' synthesis method:

1. *Generality*: The method addresses the problem as a generic coordination problem among a number of agents. It can be used to synthesize any set of matching methods. In the case where a method does not provide confidence values, the algorithm focuses on the minimization of violations of semantic constrains encoded in the factor graph.
2. *Optimality*: The synthesis solution presented aims to maximize the social welfare of agents, i.e., the sum of their utilities, taking into account the preferences of individual agents and the semantics of specifications. This modeling of the synthesis problem results in a cyclic factor graph, which as stated in the literature (Farinelli et al. 2008) has a near-optimal solution and a very good balance between optimality and scalability.
3. *Scalability*: The method aims to enforce a decentralized solution, where each agent has knowledge of and can directly communicate with a small number of neighbors, which is a small proportion of the total number of (existing or generated) agents. This is true, although the current implementation does not distribute agents in different machines. As the complexity heavily depends on the number of constraints related to an agents function (and thus, on the number of the neighbors of each utility), we need to measure the number of constraints between variables. This number ranges in $[K, K+C\times K]$, when the synthesized methods compute equivalence relations. K is the number of synthesized methods and C is the number of classes that directly subsume the class that the agent tries to map. Usually, which is also the case in our experiments, C is equal to 1. Methods that compute subsumptions do not affect the number of constraints (in some cases they drop the minimum number of constraints further down), as they introduce constraints concerning their own functions.
4. *Expandability*: New individual methods can easily be added to the synthesis model, independently to the other synthesized methods.
5. *Tolerance to failures of individual methods*: It is clear from the experimental results shown in Spiliopoulos and Vouros (2012), that when one of the synthesized methods fails to compute correspondences, not only does the synthesis performs as effectively as the best individual method, but it also improves the effectiveness of the individual methods.
6. *Provision of feedback to the individual methods*: As experimental results in Spiliopoulos and Vouros (2012) show, the synthesis method exploits the correspondences computed by all individual methods to drive individual methods to improve their effectiveness by choosing correspondences that are mostly preferred by them, in conjunction with being consistent with the correspondences computed by the other methods.
7. *Being a semantics-based approach*: As already mentioned, proposed correspondences must form a consistent alignment with respect to the semantics of ontology elements specifications. To do so, the presented model-based synthesis method drives matching methods to compute correspondences that respect a set of validity constraints.

6.5 Reaching Agreements in Arbitrary Networks of Autonomous Peers

Regarding arbitrary networks of peers where each one of them produces correspondences with its immediate neighbors (acquaintances), this section presents on-going research on achieving semantic agreements between these (even distant) peers. This is an important challenge since sensors, or generally, devices produced by different vendors, need to interoperate and share information effectively in ad-hoc networks.

Probabilistic message passing techniques can be used to "enforce" semantic agreements between peers in a peer-to-peer data management system. Therefore, the method proposed in Cudré-Mauroux et al. (2006, 2009) is aimed to be applied in cases where entities connected in a network have different ontologies and produce correspondences to each other. The method proposed in Cudré-Mauroux et al. (2009) takes advantage of the transitive closures of correspondence relations in a cycle of peers to compare a query q to the returned q' via that cycle. Based on computation of the probability of receiving positive feedback from any cycle, they model the (un-)directed networks of correspondences as factor graphs. Based on the sum-prod algorithm (distributed among peers) they compute the posterior probability for any local correspondence participating in a cycle.

Extending the approach reported in Cudré-Mauroux et al. (2009), the work in Vouros (2011) aims to drive peers that are connected in arbitrary networks and that have established correspondences with their acquaintances, with different, even conflicting preferences, to reach matching agreements.

6.5.1 Problem Specification

Let us consider a network of peers represented as a directed graph $G=(V,E)$. Each node in V is a peer P_{node} equipped with a specific ontology O_{node}. Each directed edge (P_{node},P_{neigh}) in E specifies the fact that P_{node} has a specific view of P_{neigh}'s ontology (which can be either a complete, partial, vague or an abstract view, either at the conceptual or at the instances levels, depending on peers actual relation). P_{node} can propagate queries/answers to P_{neigh} by computing correspondences between the elements of O_{node} and O_{neigh}. It must be noticed that P_{node} has its own subjective view of correspondences to O_{neigh}. Thus, in the case where there is also an edge (P_{neigh},P_{node}), then the correspondences computed from P_{neigh} to O_{node} might not be symmetric to those computed by P_{node}. This may happen even in the special case that these peers use the same matching method (because the information that this method exploits may differ in each direction). In such a setting, the problem of computing a coherent set of correspondences between peers in G is rather complicated if we consider that each peer is connected to numerous other peers with distinct ontologies and matching methods (and thus different matching preferences), with the latter being arbitrary connected with others and/or among themselves. This problem includes: (a) The computation of locally coherent correspondences to the ontologies of neighbor peers, and (b) the exploitation of the transitive closure of correspondences between ontologies to reach agreements between (even distant) peers. To describe the proposed approach we distinguish between these, actually highly intertwined, phases towards reaching global agreements to the alignment of ontologies.

6.5.2 Computing Locally Coherent Correspondences

Concerning the computation of locally coherent correspondences of each peer P_{node}, given O_{node} (the ontology of P_{node}) the computation of correspondences from O_{node} to any ontology O_{neigh} of a neighbor peer P_{neigh}, is being addressed as a coordination problem between self-interested agents: This is done using the formulation of the problem and the methods proposed in the Sect. 6.4. Each such tuple (O_{node}, O_{neigh}) is considered as a specific, distinct *alignment case* for P_{node}. Thus, each peer deals with a number of alignment cases that are less or equal to the number of its acquaintances (acquaintances may share ontologies).

Considering that P_{node} has at its disposal a set of K_{node} matching methods $\{AM^i_{node}, i = 1..K_{node}\}$, for each alignment case there is a distinct set of agents, each of which corresponds to a matching method and an ontology element in O_{node}, as already presented in the previous section: Each agent is responsible for deciding on the correspondence of that specific ontology element using a specific alignment method. We call these agents $P_{node} - internal$ (or simply *internal*) agents to emphasize the role of these agents to compute correspondences on behalf of P_{node}. Actually, they may be distant and are organized in a certain way. In the previous section we described how *internal* agents are related in graphs (one per alignment case) via the validity constraints that are enforced between them. Validity constraints must be satisfied so that the calculated correspondences conform to the semantics of ontological specifications. The utility function of each agent, reflects the matching preferences of that agent with respect to the semantics of specifications (i.e., to the constraints enforced). Here, the utility of each agent is also affected by the feedback received from other peers. Specifically, viewing the computation of ontology correspondences from P_{node} to O_{neigh} as a coordination problem between M $P_{node} - internal$ agents, the aim is to find the joined state of agents (i.e., the overall set of correspondences), whereby the social welfare of the whole system (i.e., the sum of the individual agents utilities) is maximized. It must be emphasized that these computations are performed for each distinct alignment case of P_{node}.

6.5.3 Computing Globally Coherent Correspondences

Given the subjective local decisions concerning correspondences, each of the peers propagates these correspondences to the rest of the peers in the network in an iterative and cooperative manner, aiming to detect cycles of correspondences and get feedback on its decisions. Therefore, computed correspondences between elements $(E_i^{node}, E_j^{neigh}, r, n)$ for an alignment case (O_{node}, O_{neigh}) are sent to any of the immediate neighbors P_{neigh} that use O_{neigh}. P_{neigh} in its own turn dispatches received correspondences to the appropriate $P_{neigh} - internal$ agents (i.e., to the agents that are responsible for computing a correspondence for E_j^{neigh}). Computed correspondences for P_{neigh} $(E_j^{neigh}, E_k^{xyz}, r', n')$ are appended to $(E_i^{node}, E_j^{neigh}, r, n)$ and are forwarded to P_{neigh} neighbors, and so on and so forth. The ordered list of correspondences forwarded to a peer shows the correspondences computed along a path and constitutes a *correspondence history*. There are several strategies for propagating correspondences (e.g., until peers are confident enough for their correctness, or until payoffs converge to fixed values): In Vouros (2011) we assume that correspondence histories are propagated in an unrestricted way aiming to detect any cycle of correspondences in the network, for a given number of iterations.

Some correspondences might be (objectively) incorrect, i.e., they might map an element from one ontology to a semantically irrelevant element in another ontology. The goal in Vouros (2011) is not to provide probabilistic guarantees on the correctness of a correspondence as done in Cudré-Mauroux et al. (2009): The aim is to drive peers to re-consider their local correspondences with respect to their preferences, the semantics of specifications, also in accordance to the feedback they receive from other peers via cycles of correspondences, so as to reach agreements. Towards this goal, also in accordance to Cudré-Mauroux et al. (2009), the method proposed in Vouros (2011) takes advantage of the cycles existing in the graph of peers. Given a cycle $(P_{node} \mapsto P_{neigh} \cdots P'_{neigh} \mapsto P_{node})$ it considers that for each correspondence $(E_i^{node}, E_j^{neigh})$ forwarded from P_{node} to P_{neigh}[2] together with the correspondence history, the originator P_{node} must get a correspondence $(E_k^{neigh'}, E_i^{node})$ from the last peer in the cycle, P'_{neigh}. In other words, when P_{node} computes a local correspondence of E_i^{node} to E_j^{neigh}, then P_{neigh}, via the path from P'_{neigh} to P_{node} must propagate a correspondence to the element E_i^{node}, rather than to any other element of O_{node}. In such a case, for each such correspondence, P_{node} counts a positive feedback. If this does not happen, then there are one or more erroneous correspondences (always according to the subjective view of P_{node}) through this path, and P_{node} counts a negative feedback. It must be noticed that erroneous correspondences may still exist when P_{node} gets the expected correspondence but several correspondences along the path compensate their errors: These are detected by the corresponding peers as the correspondence history propagates in the network.

[2]Subsequently we assume r to be the equivalence ($\equiv$) relation and we also simplify the presentation of correspondence histories by not specifying the correspondence relation and confidence degree for each pair of ontology elements.

To summarise the above, according to the proposed approach (Vouros 2011) each peer (a) gets a list of correspondences propagated to it (the correspondence history), and (b) inspects the correspondence history to detect a cycle. This is done by detecting in the correspondence history the most recent correspondence originated from it. Such a correspondence concerns one of its own ontology classes and a specific alignment case. If there is a cycle, the peer propagates the history to the internal agents that (i) correspond to that alignment case and, (ii) are responsible for computing correspondences for that class. These agents incorporate the feedbacks in their decision-making. If there is not any cycle, histories are propagated to all internal agents corresponding to that alignment case. (c) After internal agents computations, the peer propagates correspondence decisions (together with the correspondence histories) to neighbor peers corresponding to the alignment case. Details concerning the propagation of beliefs in internal graphs and between peers, together with the incorporation of feedback to the algorithm are presented in Vouros (2011). It must be pointed out that belief propagation between peers happens seamlessly to the local computations of correspondences by internal agents. So, we may consider that a large, distributed graph comprising the internal agents of peers, spans the whole network of peers.

6.5.4 Measures and Results

Overall, the method proposed in Vouros (2011) addresses the semantic coordination problem in a data management system through payoff propagation, by a distributed extension of the max-sum algorithm. To measure the *degree* or *level* of agreement achieved between peers and the effectiveness of computations, a set of measures has been proposed: $F-score$ (specified by $f-score = 2*(P*R)/(P+R)$) for each alignment case; the level of agreement achieved for each peer, specified by $Level = (F^{+} - F^{-})/PM$, where F^{+} and F^{-} specify the number of positive, respectively negative, feedbacks received; the agreement accuracy for pairs of peers, specified by $Accuracy = Level * f - score$; and the *Message Gain* for achieving this accuracy (and level) given the number of inter-agent messages, specified by $Gain = (Accuracy * sf)/AM$, where sf is a scaling factor. The motivation for these proposed scores is as follows: While $f-score$ shows in a combined way the precision/recall of the correspondences computed per alignment case, the level of agreement shows (independently of the precision/recall achieved) the agreement achieved between peers as a function of positive and negative feedbacks after a specific number of inter-peer messages. Peers may agree to false positive correspondences, as well. To provide a measure of these correspondences, the agreement accuracy measure combines the level of accuracy and the accuracy of computed correspondences. Finally, aiming to show the efficiency of the method, the gain is provided as a function of the accuracy achieved and the number of inter-agent messages.

Experimental results, via typical patterns of peers' behavior in arbitrary networks, show that the method is effective enough, making the best of the correspondences produced by peers, helping peers increase their levels of agreement and the agreement accuracy. The method scales linearly to the number of peers' connections, although the size of ontologies (i.e., the number of possibly corresponding pairs of elements – the possible joined states of agents) affect the performance of the method.

6.6 Concluding Remarks

While the above mentioned methods and the increasing interest of the research community to build methods for reaching semantic agreements in establishing alignments between ontologies (also, closely related to computing emergent semantics) show the increasing interest of the research community on this research topic, there is room for further developments in the area:

- There must be a holistic and generic model for reaching semantic agreements between entities. By holistic we mean approaches that compute consistent alignments using the entire breadth of information available to entities; by generic we mean approaches that are independent of the individual methods used by the distinct entities participating and by the specific problem case considered.
- Approaches must be scalable and applicable to stable, as well as to dynamic settings: where ontologies change non-monotonically, settings in which entities change (or evolve) their matching methods, change matching preferences, may leave or join the system at will.
- Concerning argumentation systems, arguments used by the current methods are rather laconic: they do not justify the correspondence choices made sufficiently enough, so as entities to communicate the (deep) reasons behind computations, in ways that are understandable and exploitable by different entities.
- Graph based approaches seem promising but they need to be studied more as far as their efficiency and efficacy are concerned, especially when these are applied to large-scale settings.
- Finally, the reputation and trust of entities computing the alignments (i.e., the provenance of alignment decisions) need to be integrated into the system (this is another source of information that needs to be taken into account).

Acknowledgements In this chapter, we have extended work by Trojahn et al. published in (Trojahn et al. 2011). We also present on-going work for exploiting message passing algorithms for peers/agents organized in arbitrary large-scale networks to reach semantic agreements.

References

Amgoud, L., and C. Cayrol. 1998. On the acceptability of arguments in preference-based argumentation. In *Proceedings of the 14th conference on uncertainty in artificial intelligence*, 1–7. San Francisco: Morgan Kaufmann.

Baronchelli, A., M. Felici, E. Caglioti, V. Loreto, and L. Steels. 2005. Sharp transition towards shared vocabularies in multi-agent systems. *Statistical Mechanics* 6014: 0509075.

Bench-Capon, T. 2003. Persuasion in practical argument using value-based argumentation frameworks. *Journal of Logic and Computation* 13(3): 429–448.

Cudré-Mauroux, P., K. Aberer, and A. Feher. 2006. Probabilistic message passing in peer data management systems. In *Proceedings of the 22nd international conference on data engineering, ICDE '06*, 41. Washington, DC: IEEE Computer Society. doi:http://dx.doi.org/10.1109/ICDE.2006.118, http://dx.doi.org/10.1109/ICDE.2006.118.

Cudré-Mauroux, P., P. Haghani, M. Jost, K. Aberer, and H. De Meer. 2009. Idmesh: graph-based disambiguation of linked data. In *Proceedings of the 18th international conference on World Wide Web, WWW '09*, 591–600. New York: ACM. doi:http://doi.acm.org/10.1145/1526709.1526789, http://doi.acm.org/10.1145/1526709.1526789.

Doran, P., V. Tamma, T. Payne, and I. Palmisano. 2009. Dynamic selection of ontological alignments: A space reduction mechanism. In *Proceedings of the international joint conference on artificial intelligence*, Pasadena. http://www.aaai.org/ocs/index.php/IJCAI/IJCAI-09/paper/view/551.

Doran, P., V. Tamma, I. Palmisano, and T.R. Payne. 2009. Efficient argumentation over ontology correspondences. In *Proceedings of the 8th international conference on autonomous agents and multiagent systems*, 1241–1242. Richland: International Foundation for Autonomous Agents and Multiagent Systems.

Doran, P., T.R. Payne, V.A.M. Tamma, and I. Palmisano. 2010. Deciding agent orientation on ontology mappings. In *Proceedings of the international semantic web conference (1)*, Lecture notes in computer science, vol. 6496, ed. P.F. Patel-Schneider, Y. Pan, P. Hitzler, P. Mika, L. Zhang, J.Z. Pan, I. Horrocks and B. Glimm, 161–176. Berlin: Springer.

dos Santos, C.T., P. Quaresma, and R. Vieira. 2008. Conjunctive queries for ontology based agent communication in MAS. In *AAMAS (2)*, Estoril, ed. L. Padgham, D.C. Parkes, J.P. Müller and S. Parsons, 829–836. IFAAMAS.

Dung, P. 1995. On the acceptability of arguments and its fundamental role in nonmonotonic reasoning, logic programming and n–person games. *Artificial Intelligence* 77(2): 321–357

Euzenat, J. 2004. An API for ontology alignment. In *Proceedings of the 3rd international semantic web conference*, Hiroshima, 698–7112.

Euzenat, J., and P. Shvaiko. 2007. Ontology matching. Heidelberg: Springer.

Euzenat, J., M. Mochol, P. Shvaiko, H. Stuckenschmidt, O. Svab, V. Svatek, W.R. van Hage, and M. Yatskevich. 2006. Results of the ontology alignment evaluation initiative 2006. In *Proceedings of the first international workshop on ontology matching*, Athens.

Farinelli, A., A. Rogers, A. Petcu, and N.R. Jennings. 2008. Decentralised coordination of low-power embedded devices using the max-sum algorithm. In *Proceedings of the 7th international joint conference on autonomous agents and multiagent systems – vol. 2, AAMAS '08*, 639–646. Richland: International Foundation for Autonomous Agents and Multiagent Systems. http://dl.acm.org/citation.cfm?id=1402298.1402313.

Fipa standard. 2002. FIPA: Contract net interaction protocol specification. http://www.fipa.org/specs/fipa00029/SC00029H.pdf.

Haase, P., and B. Motik. 2005. A mapping system for the integration of owl-dl ontologies. In *Proceedings of the IHIS*, ed. A. Hahn, S. Abels and L. Haak, 9–16. New York: ACM.

Isaac, A., C.T. dos Santos, S. Wang, P. Quaresma. 2008. Using quantitative aspects of alignment generation for argumentation on mappings. In *Proceedings of the OM*, Karlsruhe.

Jiménez-Ruiz, E., B. Cuenca Grau, I. Horrocks, and R. Berlanga. 2009. Ontology integration using mappings: Towards getting the right logical consequences. In *Proceedings of the 6th European semantic web conference on the semantic web: Research and applications, ESWC 2009*, Heraklion, 173–187. Berlin/Heidelberg: Springer. doi:http://dx.doi.org/10.1007/978-3-642-02121-3_16, http://dx.doi.org/10.1007/978-3-642-02121-3_16.

Kschischang, F.R., B.J. Frey, and H.A. Loeliger. 1998. Factor graphs and the sum-product algorithm. *IEEE Transactions on Information Theory* 47: 498–519.

Laera, L., V. Tamma, J. Euzenat, T. Bench-Capon, and T.R. Payne. 2006. Reaching agreement over ontology alignments. In *Proceedings of the 5th international semantic web conference*, Lecture notes in computer science, vol. 4273/2006, 371–384. Berlin/Heidelberg: Springer. doi:10.1007/11926078.

Laera, L., I. Blacoe, V. Tamma, T. Payne, J. Euzenat, and T. Bench-Capon. 2007. Argumentation over ontology correspondences in MAS. In *Proceedings of the 6th international joint conference on autonomous agents and multiagent systems*, 1–8. New York: ACM. doi:http://doi.acm.org/10.1145/1329125.1329400.

Loeliger, H.A. 2004. An introduction to factor graphs. *IEEE Signal Processing Magazine* 21: 28–41.

Meilicke, C., and H. Stuckenschmidt. 2009. An efficient method for computing alignment diagnoses. In *Proceedings of the 3rd international conference on web reasoning and rule systems, RR '09*, 182–196. Berlin/Heidelberg: Springer. doi:http://dx.doi.org/10.1007/978-3-642-05082-4_13, http://dx.doi.org/10.1007/978-3-642-05082-4_13.

Meilicke, C., H. Stuckenschmidt, and A. Tamilin. 2009. Reasoning support for mapping revision. *Journal of logic and computation* 19(5): 807–829.

Morge, M., J.C. Routier, Y. Secq, and T. Dujardin. 2006. A formal framework for inter-agents dialogue to reach an agreement about a representation. In *Proceedings of the 6th workshop on computational models of natural argument (CNMA)*, August 2006, ed. R. Ferrario, N. Guarino and L. Prevot, 1–6. Riva del Garda.

Qi, G., Q. Ji, and P. Haase. 2009. A conflict-based operator for mapping revision. In *Proceedings of the 8th international semantic web conference, ISWC '09*, 521–536. Berlin/Heidelberg: Springer. doi:http://dx.doi.org/10.1007/978-3-642-04930-9_33, http://dx.doi.org/10.1007/978-3-642-04930-9_33

Reitter, D., and C. Lebiere. 2011. How groups develop a specialized domain vocabulary: A cognitive multi-agent model. *Cognitive Systems Research* 12(2): 175–185.

Sensoy, M., and P. Yolum. 2009. Evolving service semantics cooperatively: A consumer-driven approach. *Autonomous Agents and Multi-Agent Systems* 18: 526–555. doi:10.1007/s10458-008-9071-8, http://dl.acm.org/citation.cfm?id=1504399.1504428.

Spiliopoulos, V., and G.A. Vouros. 2012. Synthesizing ontology alignment methods using the max-sum algorithm. *IEEE Transactions on Knowledge and Data Engineering* 24(5): 940–951. doi:http://doi.ieeecomputersociety.org/10.1109/TKDE.2011.42.

Spiliopoulos, V., G. Vouros, and V. Karkaletsis. 2011. On the discovery of subsumption relations for the alignment of ontologies. *Web Semantics: Science, Services and Agents on the World Wide Web* 8(1): 69–88. http://www.websemanticsjournal.org/index.php/ps/article/view/175.

Trojahn, C., and J. Euzenat. 2010. Consistency-driven argumentation for alignment agreement. In *Proceedings of the fifth international workshop on ontology matching (OM-2010) collocated with the 9th international semantic web conference (ISWC-2010)*, Shanghai.

Trojahn, C., P. Quaresma, R. Vieira, and M. Moraes. 2008. A cooperative approach for composite ontology mapping. *LNCS Journal on Data Semantic X (JoDS)* 4900(1): 237–263. doi:10.1007/978-3-540-77688-8.

Trojahn, C., J. Euzenat, T. Payne, and V. Tamma. 2011. Argumentation for reconciling agent ontologies. In *Semantic agent systems: Foundations and applications*, Studies in computational intelligence, vol. XVI, ed. A. Elci, M. Koné and M. Orgun. Berlin: Springer.

Valarakos, A.G., R.G. Valarakos, G. Paliouras, V. Karkaletsis, and G. Vouros. 2004. A name-matching algorithm for supporting ontology enrichment. In *Proceedings of SETNO04, 3rd hellenic conference on artificial intelligence*, 381–389. Berlin/New York: Springer.

van Diggelen, J., R.J. Beun, F. Dignum, R.M. van Eijk, and J.J.C. Meyer. 2004. Optimal communication vocabularies and heterogeneous ontologies. In *AC*, Lecture notes in computer science, vol. 3396, ed. R.M. van Eijk, M.P. Huget and F. Dignum, 76–90. Berlin: Springer. http://dblp.uni-trier.de/db/conf/acom/ac2004.html#DiggelenBDEM04.

van Diggelen, J., R.J. Beun, F. Dignum, R.M. van Eijk, and J.J.C. Meyer. 2006. Anemone: An effective minimal ontology negotiation environment. In *Proceedings of the AAMAS*, ed. H. Nakashima, M.P. Wellman, G. Weiss and P. Stone, 899–906. New York: ACM.

Vouros, G. A. 2012. Decentralized semantic coordination through belief propagation. In *Proceedings of the 1st international conference on agreement technologies (AT-2012), 266–280*. CEUR Vol. 918. http://ceur-ws.org/Vol-918/. The CEUR publication service is provided by RWTH Aachen, Germany.

Williams, A.B. 2004. Learning to share meaning in a multi-agent system. *Autonomous Agents and Multi-Agent Systems* 8: 165–193. doi:10.1023/B:AGNT.0000011160.45980.4b. http://dl.acm.org/citation.cfm?id=964566.964588.

Chapter 7
Semantics in Multi-agent Systems

Nicoletta Fornara, Gordan Ježić, Mario Kušek, Ignac Lovrek, Vedran Podobnik, and Krunoslav Tržec

7.1 Introduction

In this chapter we discuss and report some examples of how *semantic technologies* in general and specific *Semantic Web standards* in particular can contribute to the goal of achieving *interoperability* between independent, loosely coupled, heterogeneous, autonomous software components (that we call agents). These components need to interact, negotiate, compete, or collaborate in order to reach their own goals in an *open framework*, that is, in a framework where those software agents dynamically start or stop to interact with other agents without being specifically programmed for interacting with a specific counterpart. Examples of application domains where this ability is fundamental are eCommerce and eProcurement (for example for the specification of B2B or B2C electronic auctions or e-markets where different parties may buy or sell products in Sardinha et al. (2009) and Milicic et al. (2008)), eBusiness (for example for the dynamic creation of supply chains or virtual enterprises (Collins et al. 2010; Podobnik et al. 2008)), and resource sharing systems (for example systems for data, video, audio, or photo sharing (Bojic et al. 2011; Podobnik et al. 2010a)).

N. Fornara (✉)
Università della Svizzera italiana, via G. Buffi 13, 6900 Lugano, Switzerland
e-mail: nicoletta.fornara@usi.ch

G. Ježić • M. Kušek • I. Lovrek • V. Podobnik
Faculty of Electrical Engineering and Computing, University of Zagreb, Zagreb, Croatia
e-mail: gordan.jezic@fer.hr; mario.kusek@fer.hr; ignac.lovrek@fer.hr; vedran.podobnik@fer.hr

K. Tržec
Ericsson Nikola Tesla, Zagreb, Croatia
e-mail: krunoslav.trzec@ericsson.com

S. Ossowski (ed.), *Agreement Technologies*, Law, Governance and Technology Series 8, DOI 10.1007/978-94-007-5583-3_7,

The problem of interoperability between autonomous components in an open framework has the following two crucial characteristics:

- No assumptions can be made about the internal structure of the interacting parties and about their willingness to satisfy the rules, the norms, the interaction protocols, or the agreements reached with other agents;
- The interacting agents for planning their future communicative and non communicative actions need to have an expectation on the future actions of the other agents and therefore they need to be able to assume that every agent will derive the same conclusions from the information received. Therefore they need to share a *common semantics* for the meaning of the exchanged messages.

In order that the interaction among autonomous parties may lead to states having some global desirable properties, it is crucial to constrain agents' actions with a set of norms, rules, or protocols.

In this chapter in Sect. 7.2 we will present and discuss how Semantic Web Technologies are used for modeling and reasoning on the content of agent communicative acts, on the specification of Artificial Institutions, and on norms and policies definition and enforcement (see Chap. 18 in this book for more details on these concepts). In Sect. 7.3 we will present and discuss how Semantic Web Technologies are used for tackling one of the fundamental problem of open B2C e-markets: the problem of searching for possible matches between requested and available products, where products consists of content delivered over a network by telecommunication services.

7.2 Semantic Technologies for ACL, Institutions, and Norms Specification

One possible proposal, for the realization of *interoperability* in an open framework, is to define an application-independent format for the communication of information (*abstract* and *concrete syntax*), as for instance the one proposed in FIPA-ACL[1] (Agent Communication Language) and most importantly a *commonly accepted semantics*. Usually the semantics of messages is defined compositionally by combining the semantics of the type of the message (as for instance promise, request, inform, agree, refuse) that is application independent, with the semantics of the content of the message that may be partially application independent and partially application dependent.

In the definition of the semantics of those components an important role may be played by *semantic technologies*. One important advantage of adopting Semantic Web technologies is that they are increasingly used in Internet applications and therefore it would be easier to achieve a high degree of interoperability of data and applications. Moreover, given that Semantic Web technologies are becoming

[1] http://www.fipa.org/repository/aclspecs.html.

widely used in innovative applications it will become much easier to teach them to software engineers than convince them to learn and use a logic language adopted by a limited group of researchers. One important standard Semantic Web language is OWL Description Logic (DL).[2] The adoption of this language as a formal language for the specification of messages and their semantics has many advantages: thanks to the fact that it is decidable it is supported by many reasoners (like FaCT++,[3] Pellet,[4] Racer Pro,[5] HermiT[6]), there are many tools for OWL ontology editing (like Protégé, NeOn), and there are libraries for automatic OWL ontology management (like OWL-API, KAON).[7]

Examples of existing approaches that use semantic technologies for the formalization of the content language of FIPA-ACL are: the proposal of using RDF as content language of FIPA-ACL (FIPA 2001), the proposal of using the Darpa Agent Markup Language (DAML) language for expressing the content of messages (Zou et al. 2002), the proposal of using OWL DL as content language of FIPA-ACL (Schiemann and Schreiber 2006), and the proposal of using OWL DL as content language of a commitment-based ACL whose syntax is compatible with FIPA-ACL (Fornara et al. 2012).

A crucial requirement in open system is that the *semantics* of different types of communicative acts and of their content part has to be strongly independent of the internal structure of the interacting agents. The semantics of FIPA-ACL presents the problem of relying heavily on the BDI model of agents and of not taking into account the normative consequences of message exchanges. A successful approach to solving this problem consists in formalizing the effects of making a communicative act under specified conditions with the creation of a new object: the *social commitment* between the speaker and the hearer having a certain content and condition. Formal proposals to treat communicative acts in terms of commitments and to *monitor* their state on the basis of the agents' actions can be found in Colombetti (2000), Singh (2000), Fornara and Colombetti (2002), and Yolum and Singh (2004). In particular in Fornara et al. (2012) a proposal of using OWL DL as content language of a commitment-based ACL and for expressing the semantics of promise communicative acts is presented.

However, expressing the meaning of certain types of communicative acts in terms of social commitments is not enough for completely representing their semantics, that is, for representing all the consequences of sending or receiving certain communicative acts for the future actions of the agents. The point is: why an agent that is a debtor for certain social commitments should plan its actions in order to fulfill or violate them? One possible answer to this question could involve proposing

[2]http://www.w3.org/2007/OWL/wiki/OWL_Working_Group.

[3]http://owl.man.ac.uk/factplusplus/.

[4]http://clarkparsia.com/pellet/.

[5]http://www.racer-systems.com/products/racerpro/.

[6]http://hermit-reasoner.com/.

[7]W3C list of reasoners, editors, development environments, APIs: http://www.w3.org/2007/OWL/wiki/Implementations.

to formalize the *institutional framework* where the interaction takes place, and therefore specify the consequences in terms of reward or sanctions for the fulfilment or violation of social commitments. It is important to remark that in order to be able to apply those rewards or sanctions, it is also necessary to define and realize a *monitoring component* able to detect the fulfilment or violation of social commitments.

The definition of a shared *institutional framework* is also a requirement for defining the meaning of an important type of communicative act: the *declarations*. For example in an electronic auction the agent playing the role of auctioneer may declare open a run of an auction or declare the winner of the run. The institutional framework can be used to define *institutional attributes* (for example the state of an auction) and to define the semantics of a declarative communicative act by means of the changes brought about by this act in the value of institutional attributes, if certain conditions (for example having the required *institutional power*) hold (Fornara and Colombetti 2009).

Nevertheless, for effectively realizing interoperability among autonomous software agents in open, distributed, and competitive scenarios, the definition of a commonly accepted communication language and of an institutional framework that specifies sanctions and institutional concepts may not be enough. As previously remarked, in order to plan their actions the interacting agents need to have an expectation of the future evolution of the state of the interaction. This is possible if the interacting parties commonly accept a set of *rules* or *norms* used to define the *obligations, prohibitions, permissions* of the interacting parties. Some of them may be created and negotiated at run-time by interacting agents with enough reasoning capabilities, but given that negotiating all those rules from scratch may be very expensive in terms of the number of interactions required, and it can be done only by very complex agents, the more complex norms may be completely or partially (at least their structure or template) specified at design time.

It is fundamental to express those norms using a *declarative formal language* because this makes it possible to represent them as data, instead of coding them in the software, with the advantage of making it possible to add, remove, or change the norms that regulate the interaction both at design time or at run-time, without the need to reprogram the interacting agents. Moreover this makes it possible, in principle, to realize agents able to automatically reason about the consequences of their actions and able to interact within different systems without the need to be reprogrammed. Finally their formal specification makes it possible to realize an application-independent *monitoring component* able to keep track of the state of norms on the basis of the events that happen in the system, and an *enforcement component* capable of reacting to norms fulfillment or violation on the basis of specific enforcement rules.

Semantic Web languages play a crucial role as languages for the declarative specification of norms. For example in Fornara and Colombetti (2010) and Fornara (2011) OWL 2 DL and SWRL rules are used to represent and monitor norms and obligations. In those works given that Semantic Web technologies are not devised for modelling and monitoring the state of dynamic systems two problems are tackled: one is related to performing temporal reasoning an important problem given that OWL has no temporal operators; another one is related to successfully monitoring obligations with deadline, that is deducing that when the deadline has elapsed an obligation has to be permanently fulfilled or violated despite the open-world assumption of OWL logic. In Lam et al. (2008) Semantic Web languages are used to represent norm-governed organizations allowing norm conflict (i.e., an action being simultaneously obliged and prohibited), to be captured and studied. Another example is the OWL-based representation of policies presented in Sensoy et al. (2012), it enables both policy-governed decision making and policy analysis within the bounds of decidability.

A crucial open problem related to the choice of using Semantic Web Technologies, and in particular OWL, as formal languages for the specification and development of fundamental components of agreement technologies is the problem of understanding what part of those components it is better and possible to represent in ontologies in order to be able to reason on it and what part of those components it is better to represent in an external application because current semantic web standards do not support its representation. In what follows, some of the issues raised in this section are illustrated by an application in the domain of semantic-aware content discovery.

7.3 Semantic-Aware Content Discovery in Telecommunication Environment

Discovery is the process of searching for possible matches between requested and available products. It is especially important for efficient trading when products do not represent commodities, i.e., their value is not characterized only by their price. An example of such product is content. Efficient discovery processes should identify all the supplies that can fulfill a given demand to some extent, and then propose the most promising ones (Noia et al. 2004; Podobnik et al. 2006, 2007b). Just a few years ago, discovery relied on simple keyword matching. However, nowadays discovery is becoming grounded on novel mechanisms which exploit the semantics of content descriptions. Since these novel mechanisms may lead to a plethora of possible matches, mediation between content requesters (users) and content providers (businesses) is one of the most difficult problems faced in real world B2C e-markets (Podobnik et al. 2007a, 2010b). Thus, the notion of match ranking becomes very important, so matches can be ordered according to some criteria. If supplies and demands were described by simple strings, the only possible match would be identity, resulting in an all-or-nothing approach to matchmaking and ignoring the fact that supplies and demands also have a semantic dimension. This semantic dimension of content could be exploited in order to evaluate "interesting" inexact matches (Noia et al. 2004). Exact (full) matches are usually rare and the true discovery process is aimed at providing a ranked list of the most eligible matches, thus leveraging further interaction (Colucci et al. 2005). Most approaches suggested for semantic discovery to use standard DL reasoning to determine whether one description matches another.

None of these solutions exploit implicit semantics, i.e., patterns and/or relative frequencies of descriptions computed by techniques such as data mining, linguistics, or content-based information retrieval. In order to exploit these techniques, Klusch et al. use the OWLS-MX (Klusch and Kaufer 2009; Klusch et al. 2006), a hybrid semantic matching tool which combines DL-based reasoning with approximate matching based on syntactic information retrieval (IR) similarity computations.

Telecommunication services can be defined as a service which consists of content delivered over network resources. Today, a remarkable selection of diverse content is offered in form of various telecommunication services to users. Consequently, users require efficient mechanisms which can match demands (i.e., content they need) to supplies (i.e., available content) (Podobnik et al. 2009). Here we describe a techno-economic approach to solving this problem, implemented through a multi-agent system representing an electronic marketplace. Stakeholders and processes on the electronic marketplace are based on Telco 2.0 (Yoon 2007) business model – users act as content buyers, content providers as content sellers and telecommunication operators (i.e., telcos) as brokers. The functionality of presented agent-mediated electronic marketplace is realized by applying a semantic-aware content discovery model which uses two-level filtration of available content before a final ranked set of eligible content is recommended to users in response to their requests. The filtration processes do not only consider the semantic information associated with available content, but also consider ratings regarding the actual performance of businesses that act as content providers (with respect to both price and quality) and the prices paid by businesses for advertising their content.

By introducing SPPCA (*Semantic Pay-Per-Click Agent*) auction, we enable content providers to contact telcos and advertise semantic descriptions of the content they provide. Consequently, users can utilize the telco's service of two-level filtration of advertised content to efficiently discover the most suitable. In the first level of filtration, the broker (i.e., the telco) applies a semantic-based mechanism which compares content requested by users to those advertised by content providers (i.e., ranked semantic matchmaking). The content which pass the first level of filtration is then considered at the second level. Here information regarding the actual performance of content providers with respect to both price and quality is considered in conjunction with the prices bid by content providers in the SPPCA auction. At the end, a final ranked set of eligible content is chosen and proposed to the user. The following question may arise here: why does the broker propose the ranked set of eligible content to the user and not just the top-ranked eligible content (or, in other words, why not select just the first content from the top of the list representing the ranked set and then buy that content from corresponding content provider)? Although the latter could be a possible solution, this would violate the CBB (*Consumer Buying Behavior*) model (Guttman et al. 1998) for transactions in the B2C e-markets because it omits the negotiation phase which should happen after the brokering phases and before the purchase and delivery phase. Therefore, the broker proposes the ranked set of eligible content to the user to enable the user to contact more than one content provider and negotiate the terms of purchase with them. When the negotiation phase is completed, the user chooses one content provider and buys the content from it. The chosen content provider can be the content provider of the top-ranked content in the ranked set of eligible content proposed by the broker, but can also be the content provider of lower-ranked content (e.g., the content provider of third-ranked content offers the user the lowest purchase price during the negotiation and the user chooses this content provider because for him/her it is only important that the content is similar to the requested one and that the price is as low as possible). As it is going to be later explained, we are using Contract-Net protocol for the negotiation between users and content providers.

It is important to highlight the fact that telcos, who represent brokers in the proposed service e-market, do not base their recommendations solely on semantic matchmaking, but they also consider the actual performance of businesses which act as content providers, with respect to both price and quality. The performance model of content providers is founded on research regarding trust and reputation in e-business (Fan et al. 2005; Rasmusson and Janson 1999; Tolksdorf et al. 2004; Wishart et al. 2005; Zhang and Zhang 2005).

7.3.1 The Agent-Based Architecture of Electronic Market for Telecommunication Services

A description of the Telco 2.0 service e-market architecture follows along with a demonstration of how it operates. The proof-of-concept prototype is implemented as a JADE (Java Agent DEvelopment Framework) multi-agent system (Bellifemine et al. 2007). In the prototype agents communicate by exchanging ACL (*Agent Communication Language*) messages. Coordination between agents is achieved by applying FIPA (*Foundation of Intelligent Physical Agents*) interaction protocols. Two types of pre-defined FIPA conversation protocols (FIPA Request and FIPA Contract-Net) are used.

Figure 7.1 illustrates the Telco 2.0 service e-market architecture. There are three stakeholders in service e-market: content providers, users and telcos. These stakeholders are in our proposal of service e-market represented with three types of agents: Content Provider Agents, User Agents and Telco Agents, respectively.

In the Fig. 7.1 also four different interactions can be identified:

1. SPPCA auction interaction: between Content Provider Agent and Telco Agent, used for advertising content at the broker;
2. FIPA Contract-Net interaction: between User Agent and Telco Agent, used for discovery of eligible content;
3. FIPA Contract-Net interaction: between User Agent and Content Provider Agent, used for negotiation about content purchase, and;
4. FIPA Request interaction: between Content Provider Agent and Telco Agent, used for requesting content delivery (in form of telecommunication service) to the user.

A more detailed description of agents and interactions follow.

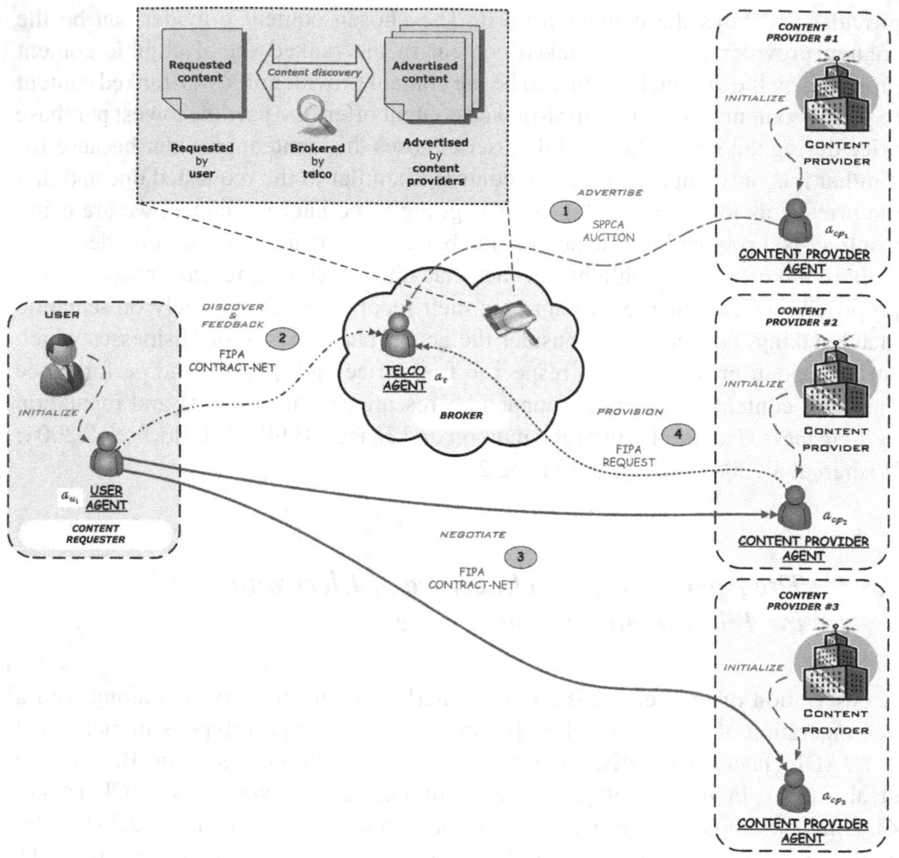

Fig. 7.1 A Telco 2.0 service e-market

7.3.1.1 The Content Provider Agent

In the service e-market agents trade with various types of content C:

$$C = \{c_1, c_2, \ldots, c_{|C|}\}, c \subset C, c_i \subset C : |c_i| = 1$$

which is provided by different content providers CP:

$$CP = \{cp_1, cp_2, \ldots, cp_{|CP|}\}, cp \subset CP, cp_i \subset CP : |cp_i| = 1$$

Content providers are represented in the e-market by Content Provider Agents A_{CP}:

$$A_{CP} = \{a_{cp_1}, a_{cp_2}, \ldots, a_{cp_{|CP|}}\}, a_{CP} \subset A_{CP}, a_{cp_i} \subset A_{CP} : |a_{cp_i}| = 1$$

An a_{cp_i} represents a content provider which offers a certain content c_i. Initially, a_{cp_i} advertise its content (advertised c_i is denoted as c_{adv}) at the broker (i.e., the Telco Agent). An a_{cp_i} accomplishes that by participation in the SPPCA auction (interaction 1 in Fig. 7.1), which enables cp_i to dynamically and autonomously advertise semantic descriptions of its content.

After successfully advertising its c_{adv}, an a_{cp_i} waits to be contacted by an user (i.e., an User Agent) which is interested in the content it is providing. If user purchases the content from a_{cp_i}, the a_{cp_i} requests from user's telco content delivery (in form of telecommunication service) to that user (interaction 4 in Fig. 7.1).

7.3.1.2 The User Agent

Users of telecommunication services U:

$$U = \{u_1, u_2, \ldots, u_{|U|}\}, u \subset U, u_i \subset U : |u_i| = 1$$

are represented in the Telco 2.0 service e-market by agents A_U:

$$A_U = \{a_{u_1}, a_{u_2}, \ldots, a_{u_{|U|}}\}, a_U \subset A_U, a_{u_i} \subset A_U : |a_{u_i}| = 1$$

An a_{u_i} acts on behalf of its owner (i.e., user) in the discovery process of suitable content and subsequently negotiates the utilization of that content. An a_{u_i} wishes to get an ordered list of ranked advertised content which is most appropriate with respect to its needs (requested c_i is denoted as c_{req}). It uses the FIPA Contract-Net interaction protocol (interaction 2 in Fig. 7.1) to contact the broker (i.e., the Telco Agent). After an a_{u_i} receives recommendations from the broker, it tries to contact a desired number of proposed a_{CP} and find the one which offers the best conditions (e.g., the lowest price) for the requested content (interaction 3 in Fig. 7.1).

After the selected content is delivered to the user (in form of telecommunication service), the a_{u_i} sends a feedback message to the broker with information about its level of satisfaction regarding the proposed a_{CP} (completion of interaction 2 in Fig. 7.1).

7.3.1.3 The Telco Agent

The telco t is represented in the e-market by the Telco Agent a_t. An a_t is the only Telco Agent "visible" from outside of telco system and represents a broker between the remaining two types of agents, i.e., A_U and A_{CP}. An a_t enables A_{CP} to advertise their content descriptions (interaction 1 in Fig. 7.1) and recommends ranked sets of eligible content to A_U in response to their requests (interaction 2 in Fig. 7.1). It is assumed that a_t is trusted party which fairly intermediates between content requesters (i.e., users) and content providers.

It is important to highlight the fact that the a_t serves as manager agent which coordinates telco's brokering services and represents the telco in communication with all non-telco agents (i.e., the A_U and A_{CP}). The telco brokering services are in presented proof-of-concept implementation facilitated by three other Telco Agents which are not "visible" from outside the telco system: the SPPCA Auction Agent (a_{SAA}), the Matching Agent (a_{MA}) and the Discovery Agent (a_{DA}).

7.3.2 Content Discovery in Telecommunication Electronic Markets

Figure 7.2 shows a more detailed architecture of a broker in the service e-market. Note that the a_t serves as an interface agent between A_U/A_{CP} and the telco. The SPPCA Auction Agent (a_{SAA}), the Matching Agent (a_{MA}) and the Discovery Agent (a_{DA}) enable the broker functionalities. These agents are allowed to make queries to the telco's databases. The a_{SAA} is in charge of conducting the SPPCA auction. Interaction 1.1 is used for registering/deregistering *CP* in the auction and placing new bids, while the a_{SAA} uses interaction 1.2 to announce a new auction round. The a_{MA} facilitates semantic matchmaking which corresponds to the first level of filtration (f_1) in the content discovery process. It receives semantic descriptions of requested content through interaction 2.1 and forwards a list of semantically suitable content c_{f_1} through interaction 2.2 to the a_{DA} which carries out second-level filtration (f_2) and recommends a ranked set of eligible advertised content $\overrightarrow{c_{f_2}}$ (interaction 2.3). Sometime later, after the selected content is delivered to the user (in form of telecommunication service), the a_{DA} receives feedback information from the $a_{u_{req}}$ (through the a_t) regarding the performance of the $\overrightarrow{cp_{f_2}}$ (cp which offer $\overrightarrow{c_{f_2}}$) (interaction 2.4).

There are two databases at the broker (i.e., telco): the *Content Database* and the *Provider Database*. The Content Database contains information about all the c whose bids are currently active and which therefore participates in SPPCA auction running at this broker. The Provider Database contains information regarding all the cp whose c is advertised at this broker.

Figure 7.3 in more details describes the communication between the three parties involved in the discovery process: u_i (i.e., a_{u_i}) as content requester, telco (i.e., a_t) as broker and cp_i (i.e., a_{cp_i}) as content provider. The presented interactions facilitate a discovery process. The specific parameters in the exchanged messages are described in the following subsections to help clearly present the advertising concept, matchmaking mechanisms and performance evaluation techniques used for designing our content discovery model in the Telco 2.0 service e-market.

Figure 7.4 presents interactions between a_{u_i} and a_t which enable content discovery in the proposed service e-market, while Fig. 7.5 explains how the SPPCA auction, which is part of the discovery process, operates.

The a_{u_i}, by sending CFP (*Call for Proposal*) to a_t, requests two-level filtering of advertised content descriptions to discover which is the most suitable for its

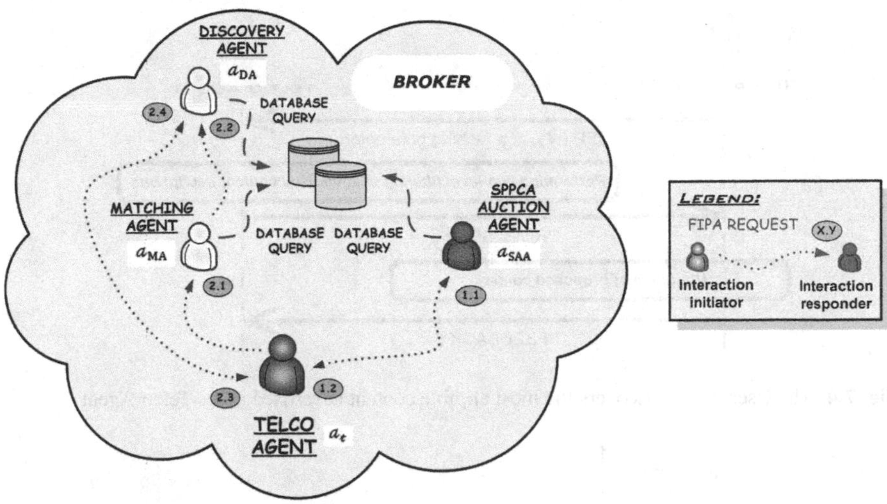

Fig. 7.2 The detailed architecture of a broker in the service e-market

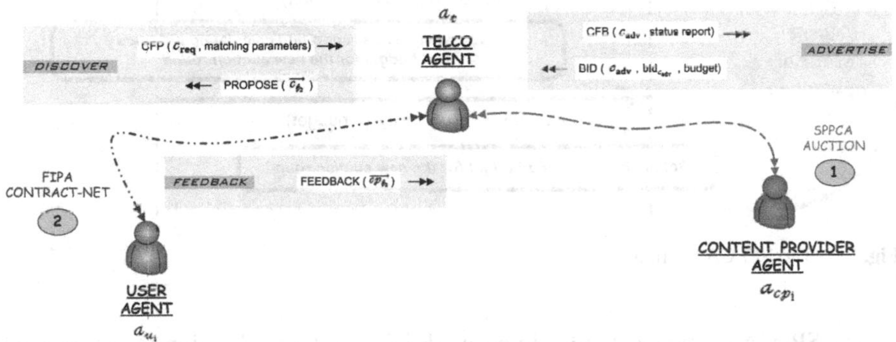

Fig. 7.3 Communication between the User Agent, Telco Agent and Content Provider Agent enabling discovery

needs. Along with the description of requested content c_{req}, the CFP includes the set of matching parameters (to be explained later) that personalize the discovery process according to the user preferences. First-level filtering ($f_1 : C \rightarrow C$) is based on semantic matchmaking between descriptions of content requested by u_i (i.e., a_{u_i}) and those advertised by cp (i.e., a_{CP}). Content which pass the first level of filtering ($c_{f_1} \subset C$) is then considered in the second filtering step. Second-level filtering ($f_2 : C \rightarrow C$) combines information regarding the actual performance of cp_{f_1} (cp which offer c_{f_1}) and prices bid in SPPCA auction by corresponding $a_{CP_{f_1}}$ (a_{CP} that represent cp which offer c_{f_1}). The performance of cp_{f_1} (with respect to both price and reputation) is calculated from the previous A_U feedback ratings. Following filtration, a final ranked set of eligible content ($\overrightarrow{c_{f_2}} \subset c_{f_1}$) is chosen. This set is then recommended to the A_U in response to their requests.

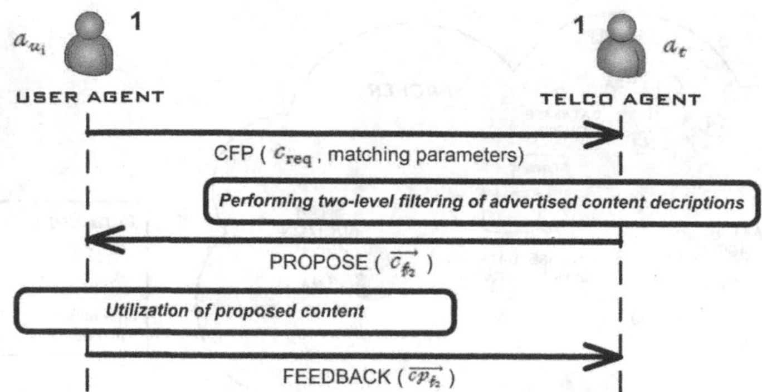

Fig. 7.4 The User Agent discovers the most eligible content advertised at the Telco Agent

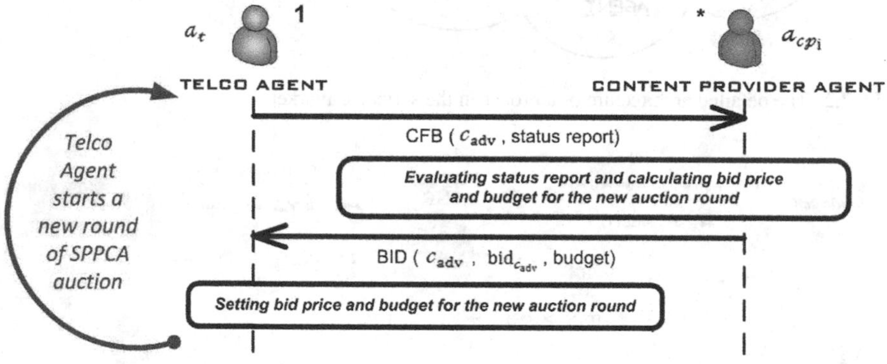

Fig. 7.5 The SPPCA auction

The SPPCA auction is divided into rounds of a fixed time duration. To announce the beginning of a new auction round, the a_t broadcasts a CFB (*Call for Bid*) message to all the a_{CP} which have registered their c_{adv} for participation in the SPPCA auction. Every CFB message contains a status report. In such a report, the a_t sends to the a_{cp_i} information regarding events related to its advertisement which occurred during the previous auction round. The most important information is that regarding how much of the a_{cp_i} budget[8] was spent (the cost of certain advertisement

[8]The notion of budget is very important in the SPPCA scenario because it enables content providers to specify their spend limits for the current auction round. Note that one content provider can have multiple content advertisements simultaneously participating in the same SPPCA auction. If such is the case, all advertisements of the same content provider potentially have different bid values since a content provider can advertise only one content advertisement per BID message, and yet all the advertisements share the same budget. Thus, when multiple BID messages for the same auction round from a single content provider are received, budget values are cumulatively added to a budget balance unique for all advertisements originating from the same content provider. This way, content providers do not need to use complex optimization techniques to optimally distribute

in one auction round is equal to this advertisement's bid price $bid_{c_{adv}}$ multiplied by the number of recommendations of corresponding c_{adv} to various a_U). In response to a CFB message, an a_{cp_i} sends a BID message. In doing so, the a_{cp_i} assures that its c_{adv} will be considered in the discovery processes which will occur during the next auction round. In addition to referencing the corresponding content description c_{adv}, a BID message also contains information specifying the value of the bid $bid_{c_{adv}}$ and information regarding the a_{cp_i} budget.

7.3.2.1 Semantic Matchmaking of Content Descriptions

In the MAS implementing the proposed service e-market, the Semantic Web technology (Antoniou et al. 2007; Leuf 2006) is used to describe content. By applying the Semantic Web concepts (Berners-Lee et al. 2001; Fensel 2003; Hendler 2001), content can be described by OWL[9] (Web Ontology Language), a semantic mark-up language based on DL. OWL provides a reasonable level of flexibility and extensiveness while keeping a balance between expressiveness and decidability. OWL ontology describing content is shown in Fig. 7.6: *Content* is defined by its *Category*, its *InformationType* and its *Theme*. Thc *Category* can be one of the following: *News*, *Music*, *Movies*. Furthermore, the *InformationType* is defined as *Data*, *Audio* or *Video*, where *Audio* is *Voice* or *HighFidelityAudio* (also referred as *CDAudio*) and *Video* is *HighDefinitionVideo* or *InteractionVideo*. The *Theme* is hierarchically organized structure, here represented through hierarchy of continents and countries. The OWL-S[10] (*Web Ontology Language for Services*) is an OWL-based technology originally designed for describing the semantics of services in an unambiguous, computer interpretable mark-up language, but can also been used for describing the semantics of products such as content. The three main parts of an OWL-S ontology are: a *service profile* for advertising and discovering service (the service profile is defined by four parameters: *input*, *output*, *precondition* and *effect*); a *service model*, which gives a detailed description of a service's operation; and a *service grounding*, which provides details on how to interoperate with a service via messages. In our proposal of autonomous content discovery in Telco 2.0 service e-market we use only service profile for description of content: thus, hereafter, the OWL-S service profile will be referred as OWL-S *content profile*. The OWL-S content profile is defined by two parameters: *input* and *output*, which are described by the ontology in Fig. 7.6. The input is

their budget among their multiple content advertisements. The advertisements of every content provider are monitored during the auction round and potentially all advertisements of a certain content provider become inactive until the end of that round if this content provider's budget is spent before the auction round is over. Consequently, this content provider's advertisements are not considered in any of the subsequent content discovery processes during that round.

[9] http://www.w3.org/TR/owl-features/.

[10] http://www.daml.org/services/owl-s.

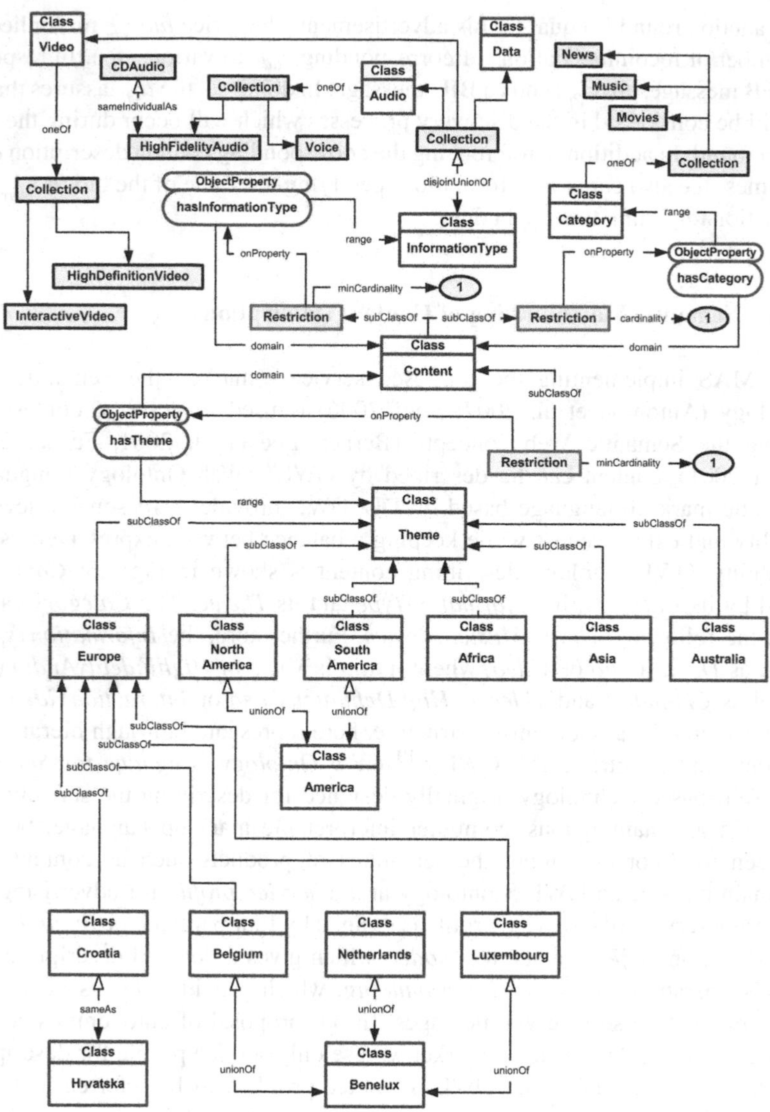

Fig. 7.6 Ontology describing content

described by *hasCategory* and *hasTheme* properties, and output is described by *hasInformationType* property.

The a_{MA} uses OWLS-MX (Klusch and Kaufer 2009), a hybrid semantic matching tool which combines logic-based reasoning with approximate matching based on syntactic information retrieval similarity computations. As the notion of match rankings is important, OWLS-MX enables computation of the degree of similarity

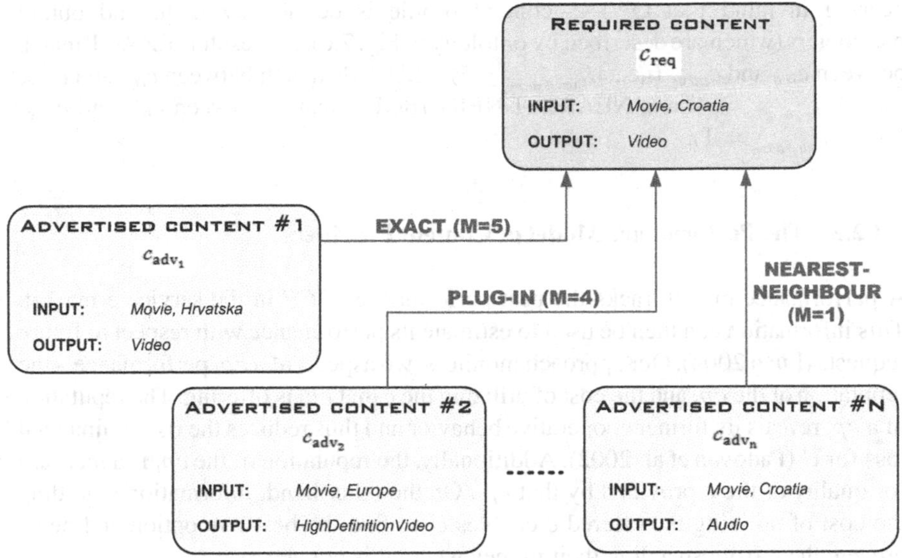

Fig. 7.7 The semantic matchmaking between required and advertised content descriptions

between compared content descriptions, i.e., the comparison is assigned a content correspondence factor (M), which we use as one of the parameters for calculation of a ranked final set of eligible content $\overrightarrow{c_{f_2}}$ in. Such a similarity ranking is highly relevant since it is unlikely that there will always be a content available which offers the exact features requested. Namely, the OWLS-MX matchmaker takes as input the OWL-S content profile of a_{u_i} desired content c_{req} (the c_{req} parameter in Figs. 7.3 and 7.4), and returns a set of relevant content which match the query: c_{f_1}. Each relevant content is annotated with its individual content correspondence factor $M_{c_{req},c_{adv}}$. There are six possible levels of matching. The first level is a perfect match (also called an EXACT match) which is assigned factor $M = 5$. Furthermore, we have four possible inexact match levels which are as follows: a PLUG-IN match ($M = 4$), a SUBSUMES match ($M = 3$), a SUBSUMES-BY match ($M = 2$) and a NEAREST-NEIGHBOUR match ($M = 1$). If two content descriptions do not match according to any of the above mentioned criteria, they are assigned a matching level of FAIL ($M = 0$). The EXACT, PLUG-IN and SUBSUMES criteria are logic-based only, whereas the SUBSUMES-BY and NEAREST-NEIGHBOUR are hybrid due to the additional computation of syntactic similarity values required. A a_{u_i} specifies its desired matching degree threshold, i.e., the M_{min} parameter (one of the matching parameters in CFP message from Figs. 7.3 and 7.4), defining how relaxed the semantic matching is.

A illustration of the hybrid content matching with OWLS-MX by means of simple example follows. Figure 7.7 shows four OWL-S content profiles: the required content description (c_{req}), and three different advertised content descriptions (c_{adv_1}, c_{adv_2} and c_{adv_n}). When OWLS-MX semantic matchmaking rules are applied, bearing in mind that OWL-S content profile is defined by input and output parameters (which are described by ontology in Fig. 7.6), the result is EXACT match between c_{req} and c_{adv_1} (i.e., $M_{c_{req},c_{adv_1}} = 5$), PLUG-IN match between c_{req} and c_{adv_2} (i.e., $M_{c_{req},c_{adv_2}} = 4$) and NEAREST-NEIGHBOUR match between c_{req} and c_{adv_n} (i.e., $M_{c_{req},c_{adv_n}} = 1$).

7.3.2.2 The Performance Model of Content Providers

A performance model tracks the past performance of *CP* in the service e-market. This information can then be used to estimate its performance with respect to future requests (Luan 2004). Our approach monitors two aspects of a cp_i performance – the reputation of the cp_i and the cost of utilizing the c that cp_i is offering. The reputation of a cp_i reveals its former cooperative behavior and thus reduces the risk of financial loss for U (Padovan et al. 2002). Additionally, the reputation of the cp_i is a measure for quality of the c provided by that cp_i. On the other hand, information regarding the cost of utilizing the offered c enables U to find the best-buy option and helps prevent them from spending their money where it is not necessary.

An a_{u_i} gives an a_t feedback regarding all cp_i from $\overrightarrow{cp_{f_2}}$, both from reputation viewpoint called the quality rating ($Q \in [0.0, 1.0]$) and the cost viewpoint called the price rating ($P \in [0.0, 1.0]$) (the FEEDBACK ($\overrightarrow{cp_{f_2}}$) parameter in Figs. 7.3 and 7.4). A rating of 0.0 is the worst (i.e., the cp_i could not provide the content at all and/or utilizing the content is very expensive) while a rating of 1.0 is the best (i.e., the cp_i provides a content that perfectly corresponds to the u_i needs and/or utilizing the content is very cheap).

EWMA-based (*Exponentially Weighted Moving Average*) learning is used for calculating the overall ratings of cp_i.[11] It is computationally simple since the new overall rating can be calculated from the previous overall rating and the current feedback rating (i.e., there is no need to store old ratings which is desirable due to scalability issues). EWMA is defined as follows:

$$\widetilde{x}_t = \xi x_t + (1-\xi)\widetilde{x}_{t-1} \qquad \text{for } t = 1, 2, \ldots$$

where $\widetilde{x}_t$ is the new forecast value of x; x_t is the current observation value (in our case, the new feedback rating); $\widetilde{x}_{t-1}$ is the previous forecast value; $0 \leq \xi \leq 1$ is a factor that determines the depth of memory of the EWMA. As the value of ξ

[11] EWMA-based learning cannot calculate the overall ratings when a content provider is participating for the first time and does not have a history of customer feedback (i.e., there is no entry for the content provider in the Provider Database). Therefore, when a content provider sends a BID message for the first time, the broker not only puts the information about new content advertisement into the Content Database, but also creates a new entry in the Provider Database where the initial quality and price ratings of this new content provider are set to the average values of quality and price ratings of all content providers whose entries already exist in the Provider Database. In such a manner we counter the problem of cold start inherent to EWMA-based learning method.

increases, more weight is given to the most recent values. Every broker (i.e., telco) sets this factor value according to its preferences.

7.3.2.3 Calculating a Recommended Ranked Set of Eligible Content

After an a_t receives a discovery request message (the CFP (c_{req}, matching parameters) message in Figs. 7.3 and 7.4) from an a_{u_i}, the broker (i.e., telco) calculates a ranked set of the best-suitable content $\overrightarrow{c_{f_2}}$. An ordered set $\overrightarrow{cp_{f_2}}$ is then recommended to the a_{u_i} in response to its request (the PROPOSE ($\overrightarrow{cp_{f_2}}$) message in Figs. 7.3 and 7.4). The matching parameters in CFP message are defined as: $\{\alpha, \beta, \gamma, M_{min}\}$. Since the performance model monitors two aspects of the cp_{adv} (i.e., its quality and price), the a_{u_i} defines two weight factors which determine the significance of each of the two aspects in the process of calculating the final proposal (β represents a weight factor describing the importance of content quality at cp_{adv} while γ represents a weight factor describing the importance of content prices at cp_{adv}). Furthermore, an a_{u_i} can specify whether information regarding the semantic similarity of c_{req} and c_{adv} is more important to it or information regarding a cp_{adv} performance. Thus, the a_{u_i} also defines parameter α which is a weight factor representing the importance of the semantic similarity between c_{req} and c_{adv}. The M_{min} parameter is already explained: with it a a_{u_i} specifies its desired matching degree threshold, i.e., defining how relaxed the semantic matching is.

The final rating $R_{c_{adv}}$ of a specific c_{adv} at the end of discovery process is given by:

$$R_{c_{adv}} = \frac{\alpha \cdot \frac{M_{c_{req},c_{adv}}}{5} + \beta \cdot Q_{cp_{adv}} + \gamma \cdot P_{cp_{adv}}}{\alpha + \beta + \gamma} \cdot bid_{c_{adv}}$$

A higher rating means that this particular c_{adv} is more eligible for the user's needs (i.e., c_{req}); α, β and γ are weight factors which enable the a_{u_i} to profile its request according to its owner u_i needs regarding the semantic similarity, quality and price of a c_{adv}, respectively; $M_{c_{req},c_{adv}}$ represents the content correspondence factor M, but only c_{adv} with M higher than threshold M_{min} are considered; $Q_{cp_{adv}}$ and $P_{cp_{adv}}$ represent the quality and price ratings of a particular cp_{adv}, respectively; $bid_{c_{adv}}$ is the bid value for advertising a c_{adv} in the SPPCA auction.

An illustration of the content discovery process by means of simple example shown in Fig. 7.8 follows. The input for the discovery process is the CFP message sent by the a_{u_i} where the following matching parameters, along with the c_{req}, are defined: $\alpha = 5$, $\beta = 2$, $\gamma = 8$ and $M_{min} = 1$. The required content description (c_{req}) and three different advertised content descriptions (c_{adv_1}, c_{adv_2} and c_{adv_n}) are the same as shown in Fig. 7.7. The $Q_{cp_{adv}}$, $P_{cp_{adv}}$ and $bid_{c_{adv}}$ for all the c_{adv} are randomly defined as shown in Fig. 7.8. Thus, c_{adv_1} is advertised by cp_i with a high quality rating, but expensive, opposite of c_{adv_2} which is advertised by cp_i with a lower quality rating, but very cheap. The c_{adv_n} is advertised by cp_i with both quality and price rating somewhere between ratings for cp_is that advertised c_{adv_1} and c_{adv_2}.

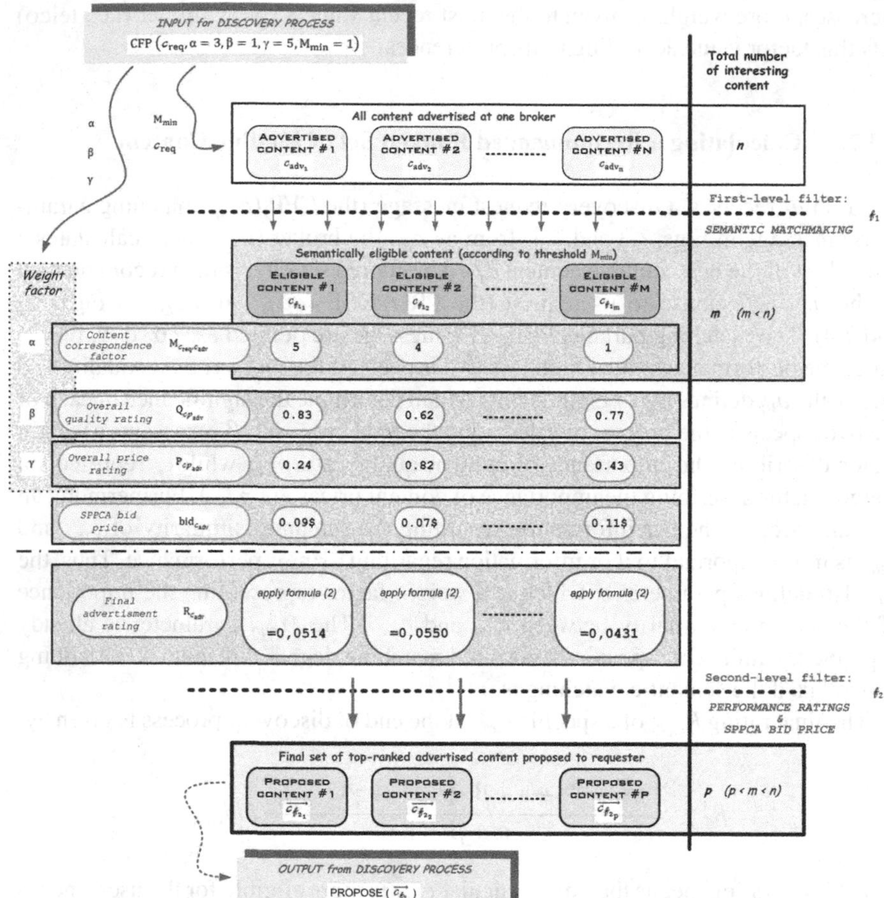

Fig. 7.8 An example of the discovery process

Additionally, the $a_{cp_{advn}}$ made the highest bid in the SPPCA auction, while the $a_{cp_{adv_2}}$ made the smallest bid. The $R_{c_{adv}}$ calculation shows that the best final rating does not achieve the c_{adv_1} whose description is semantically exact in relation to the required content description (c_{req}), but c_{adv_2} whose description is semantically similar to the required content description (c_{req}). This is the consequence of the fact how the a_{u_i} has set the matching parameters (i.e., $\{\alpha, \beta, \gamma, M_{min}\}$): it was looking for a cheap c_{adv} and it was not very concerned with the c_{adv} quality, while semantic matchmaking was rather relaxed.

7.3.3 Conclusion

An agent-based approach for modeling and analysis of telecommunication e-markets based on Telco 2.0 paradigm is proposed. In particular, B2C e-market for content trading by creating a novel auction, SPPCA auction, which merges together provider's content advertising and user's content discovery is presented. The SPPCA auction is modeled to reward low cost and high quality of content providers (i.e., content providers with better performance rating can put smaller bids and stay competitive). By contrast, the SPPCA auction punishes high cost and low quality of content providers (i.e., content providers with lower performance rating must place higher bids to stay competitive). The autonomous semantic-based content discovery based on the SPPCA is a better solution within the telecom sector compared to the keyword-based discovery based on the classic PPC auction which has a several shortcomings. First of all, there is a scalability problem. Namely, there are a huge number of syntactically valid combinations which result in a vast number of concurrent PPC auctions (a separate PPC auction runs for each particular character sequence and, thus, for every possible character sequence there is a separate auction). Another problem is that separate auctions are held for synonyms. From the content providers' point of view, it can be very complex and expensive for them to bid in auctions for all synonyms. From the content requesters' (i.e., users') point of view, it is very complicated to search all synonymous words when they require a particular content. The last disadvantage of the classic PPC auction model we consider here is competitor click fraud. This occurs when one company clicks on a competitor's advertisement to spend their budget with the long term aim of making PPC advertising too expensive for them and therefore removing them as a competitor from the search engine's results. The auction model proposed here, SPPCA auction, solves the shortcomings described above. The first problem of a vast number of concurrent auctions is solved by having one broker (i.e., telco) running only one SPPCA auction and connecting content provider agent's bids with their OWL-S descriptions and not a specific keyword. The second problem of running separate auctions for synonyms is solved by introducing the Semantic Web technology which uses OWL-S descriptions to characterise advertised services. The third problem of competitor click fraud cannot occur in the SPPCA auction model since a requester cannot predict which advertised content will be recommended as response to a request. Namely, the answer to each new discovery request is calculated dynamically and depends on fast-changing variables which are unknown to all entities outside the broker (i.e., telco). Hence, a user cannot purposely cause the broker to charge the targeted content provider by making a discovery request without the intent of utilizing any content.

Acknowledgements This work was partially supported by the Hasler Foundation project n. 11115-KG and by the Swiss State Secretariat for Education and Research project n. C08.0114, as well as projects 036-0362027-1639 "Content Delivery and Mobility of Users and Services in New Generation Networks", supported by the Ministry of Science, Education and Sports of the Republic of Croatia, and "Agent-based Service & Telecom Operations Management", supported by Ericsson Nikola Tesla, Croatia.

References

Antoniou, G., T. Skylogiannis, A. Bikakis, M. Doerr, and N. Bassiliades. 2007. DR-BROKERING: A semantic brokering system. *Knowledge-Based Systems* 20: 61–72. doi:10.1016/j.knosys.2006.07.006. http://dl.acm.org/citation.cfm?id=1224255.1224531.

Bellifemine, F. L., G. Caire, and D. Greenwood. 2007. *Developing multi-agent systems with JADE*. Wiley Series in Agent Technology. Hoboken: Wiley.

Berners-Lee, T., J. Hendler, and O. Lassila. 2001. The semantic web. *Scientific American* 284(5): 34–43. http://www.scientificamerican.com/article.cfm?id=the-semantic-web.

Bojic, I., V. Podobnik, M. Kusek, and G. Jezic. 2011. Collaborative urban computing: Serendipitous cooperation between users in an urban environment. *Cybernetics and Systems* 42(5):287–307. doi:10.1080/01969722.2011.595321. http://www.tandfonline.com/doi/abs/10.1080/01969722.2011.595321.

Collins, J., W. Ketter, and M. Gini. 2010. Flexible decision support in dynamic interorganizational networks. *European Journal of Information Systems* 19(4): 307–318.

Colombetti, M. 2000. A commitment-based approach to agent speech acts and conversations. In *Proceedings of workshop on agent languages and communication policies, 4th international conference on autonomous agents (Agents 2000)*, Barcelona, Spain, 21–29.

Colucci, S., S. Coppi, T. D. Noia, E. D. Sciascio, F. M. Donini, A. Pinto, and A. Ragone. 2005. Semantic-based resource retrieval using non-standard inference services in description logics. In *Proceedings of the thirteenth Italian symposium on advanced database systems, SEBD 2005, Brixen-Bressanone (near Bozen-Bolzano), Italy, June 19–22, 2005*, ed. A. Calì, D. Calvanese, E. Franconi, M. Lenzerini, and L. Tanca, 232–239.

Fan, M., Y. Tan, and A. B. Whinston. 2005. Evaluation and design of online cooperative feedback mechanisms for reputation management. *IEEE Transactions on Knowledge and Data Engineering* 17: 244–254. doi:http://dx.doi.org/10.1109/TKDE.2005.26. http://dx.doi.org/10.1109/TKDE.2005.26.

Fensel, D. 2003. *Ontologies: A silver bullet for knowledge management and electronic commerce*, 2nd ed. Secaucus: Springer.

FIPA. 2001. FIPA RDF Content Language Specification. Techincal report, FIPA. http://www.fipa.org/specs/fipa00011/XC00011B.html.

Fornara, N. 2011. Specifying and monitoring obligations in open multiagent systems using semantic web technology. In *Semantic agent systems foundations and applications, chap. 2*. Studies in Computational Intelligence, 25–46. Berlin: Springer.

Fornara, N., and M. Colombetti. 2002. Operational specification of a commitment-based agent communication language. In *Proceedings of the first international joint conference on autonomous agents and multiagent systems (AAMAS 2002)*, ed. C. Castelfranchi and W. L. Johnson, 535–542. ACM: New York, NY, USA.

Fornara, N., and M. Colombetti. 2009. Specifying artificial institutions in the event calculus. In *Information science reference*. Handbook of Research on Multi-agent Systems: Semantics and Dynamics of Organizational Models, Chap. XIV, 335–366. IGI Global, Hershey: New York.

Fornara, N., and M. Colombetti. 2010. Representation and monitoring of commitments and norms using OWL. *AI Communications* 23(4): 341–356.

Fornara, N., D. Okouya, and M. Colombetti. 2012. Using OWL 2 DL for expressing ACL content and semantics. In *EUMAS 2011 post-proceedings: Selected and revised papers*. Lecture Notes in Computer Science, vol. 7541, ed. M. Cossentino, M. Kaisers, K. Tuyls, and G. Weiss, 97–113. Berlin/Heidelberg: Springer.

Guttman, R. H., A. G. Moukas, and P. Maes. 1998. Agent-mediated electronic commerce: A survey. *The Knowledge Engineering Review* 13(02): 147–159.

Hendler, J. 2001. Agents and the semantic web. *IEEE Intelligent Systems* 16: 30–37. doi:http://doi.ieeecomputersociety.org/10.1109/5254.920597.

Klusch, M., and F. Kaufer. 2009. Wsmo-mx: A hybrid semantic web service matchmaker. *Web Intelligence and Agent Systems* 7(1): 23–42.

Klusch, M., B. Fries, and K. Sycara. 2006. Automated semantic web service discovery with OWLS-MX. In *Proceedings of the fifth international joint conference on autonomous agents and multiagent systems, AAMAS '06*, 915–922. New York: ACM. doi:http://doi.acm.org/10.1145/1160633.1160796. http://doi.acm.org/10.1145/1160633.1160796.

Lam, J. S. C., F. Guerin, W. W. Vasconcelos, and T. J. Norman. 2008. Representing and reasoning about norm-governed organisations with semantic web languages. In *Sixth european workshop on multi-agent systems*, Bath, UK, 18th–19th Dec 2008.

Leuf, B. 2006. *The semantic web: Crafting infrastructure for agency*. Wiley. http://books.google.co.in/books?id=uLmd-219bVsC.

Luan, X. 2004. Adaptive middle agent for service matching in the semantic web: A quantitive approach. Ph.D. thesis, University of Maryland.

Milicic, T., V. Podobnik, A. Petric, and G. Jezic. . The CrocodileAgent: A software agent for SCM procurement gaming. In *New frontiers in applied artificial intelligence*. Lecture Notes in Computer Science, vol. 5027, ed. N. Nguyen, L. Borzemski, A. Grzech, and M. Ali, 865–875. Berlin/Heidelberg: Springer (2008). doi:10.1007/978-3-540-69052-8_90. http://dx.doi.org/10.1007/978-3-540-69052-8_90.

Noia, T. D., E. D. Sciascio, F. M. Donini, and M. Mongiello. 2004. A system for principled matchmaking in an electronic marketplace. *Iternational Journal of Electronic Commerce* 8: 9–37. http://dl.acm.org/citation.cfm?id=1278104.1278107.

Padovan, B., S. Sackmann, T. Eymann, and I. Pippow. 2002. A prototype for an agent-based secure electronic marketplace including reputation-tracking mechanisms. *Iternational Journal of Electronic Commerce* 6: 93–113. http://dl.acm.org/citation.cfm?id=1286994.1287000.

Podobnik, V., K. Trzec, and G. Jezic. 2006. An auction-based semantic service discovery model for e-commerce applications. In *On the move to meaningful internet systems 2006: OTM 2006 workshops*. Lecture Notes in Computer Science, vol. 4277, ed. R. Meersman, Z. Tari, and P. Herrero, 97–106. Berlin/Heidelberg: Springer. doi:10.1007/11915034_32. http://dx.doi.org/10.1007/11915034_32.

Podobnik, V., G. Jezic, and K. Trzec. 2007a. A multi-agent system for auction-based resource discovery in semantic-aware B2C mobile commerce. *International Transactions on Systems Science and Applications* 3(2): 169–182.

Podobnik, V., K. Trzec, G. Jezic, and I. Lovrek. 2007b. Agent-based discovery of data resources in next-generation internet: An auction approach. In *Proceedings of the 2007 networking and electronic commerce research conference (NAEC'07)*, ed. B. Gavish, Riva del Garda, Italy: American Telecommunications Systems Management Association (ATSMA), 28–51.

Podobnik, V., A. Petric, and G. Jezic. 2008. An agent-based solution for dynamic supply chain management. *Journal of Universal Computer Science* 14(7): 1080–1104. http://www.jucs.org/jucs_14_7/an_agent_based_solution.

Podobnik, V., A. Petric, K. Trzec, and G. Jezic. 2009. Software agents in new generation networks: Towards the automation of telecom processes. In *Knowledge processing and decision making in agent-based systems*. Studies in Computational Intelligence, vol. 170, ed. L. Jain and N. Nguyen, 71–99. Berlin/Heidelberg: Springer. doi:10.1007/978-3-540-88049-3_4. http://dx.doi.org/10.1007/978-3-540-88049-3_4.

Podobnik, V., I. Bojic, L. Vrdoljak, and M. Kusek. 2010a. Achieving collaborative service provisioning for mobile network users: The colldown example. *Infocommunications Journal* 65(3): 46–52.

Podobnik, V., K. Trzec, and G. Jezic. 2010b. An agent-Based B2C electronic market in the next-generation internet. In *Encyclopedia of E-business development and management in the digital economy*, ed. In Lee, 227–238. Hershey: Business Science Reference.

Rasmusson, L., and S. Janson. 1999. Agents, self-interest and electronic markets. *The Knowledge Engineering Review* 14: 143–150. doi:10.1017/S026988899914205X. http://dl.acm.org/citation.cfm?id=975771.975776.

Sardinha, A., M. Benisch, N. Sadeh, R. Ravichandran, V. Podobnik, and M. Stan. 2009. The 2007 procurement challenge: A competition to evaluate mixed procurement strategies. *Electronic Commerce Research and Applications* 8: 106–114. doi:10.1016/j.elerap.2008.09.002. http://dl.acm.org/citation.cfm?id=1523524.1523906.

Schiemann, B., and U. Schreiber. 2006. OWL-DL as a FIPA-ACL content language. In *Proceedings of the workshop on formal ontology for communicating agents*, Malaga, Spain.

Sensoy, M., T. J. Norman, W. W. Vasconcelos, and K. Sycara. 2012. Owl-polar: A framework for semantic policy representation and reasoning. *Web Semantics* 12–13: 148–160. doi:10.1016/j.websem.2011.11.005. http://dx.doi.org/10.1016/j.websem.2011.11.005.

Singh, M. P. 2000. A social semantics for agent communication languages. In: *Proceedings of the 1999 IJCAI workshop on agent communication languages*. Lecture Notes in Artificial Intelligence, vol. 1916, 31–45. Berlin: Springer.

Tolksdorf, R., C. Bizer, R. Eckstein, and R. Heese. 2004. Trustable B2C markets on the semantic web. *Computer Systems Science and Engineering* 19(3): 199–206.

Wishart, R., R. Robinson, J. Indulska, and A. Jøsang. 2005. Superstringrep: Reputation-enhanced service discovery. In *Proceedings of the twenty-eighth Australasian conference on computer science – volume 38, ACSC '05*, 49–57. Darlinghurs: Australian Computer Society. http://dl.acm.org/citation.cfm?id=1082161.1082167.

Yolum, P., and M. P. Singh. 2004. Reasoning about commitments in the event calculus: An approach for specifying and executing protocols. *Annals of Mathematics and Artificial Intelligence* 42: 227–253.

Yoon, J. 2007. Telco 2.0: A new role and business model. *IEEE Communications Magazine* 45(1): 10–12.

Zhang, X., and Q. Zhang. 2005. Online trust forming mechanism: Approaches and an integrated model. In *Proceedings of the 7th international conference on electronic commerce, ICEC '05*, 201–209. New York: ACM. doi:http://doi.acm.org/10.1145/1089551.1089591. http://doi.acm.org/10.1145/1089551.1089591.

Zou, Y., T. W. Finin, Y. Peng, A. Joshi, and R. S. Cost. 2002. Agent communication in DAML world. In: *WRAC*. Lecture Notes in Computer Science, vol. 2564, ed. W. Truszkowski, C. Rouff, and M. G. Hinchey, 347–354. Berlin/Heidelberg: Springer.

Chapter 8
Semantic Web Services in Agreement Technologies

Zijie Cong and Alberto Fernández

8.1 Introduction

The addition of semantic information to describe Web Services, in order to enable the automatic location, combination and use of distributed components, is nowadays one of the most relevant research Service Oriented Architecture (SOA) topics due to its potential to achieve dynamic, scalable and cost-effective enterprise application integration and eCommerce.

The process of discovering and interacting with a Semantic Web Service includes candidate service discovery (matching advertised service descriptions against specifications from requesters), service engagement, and service enactment.

Several description frameworks to annotate provided services on the one hand and express service requests on the other have been proposed. They range from logic-based complex and expressive semantic service descriptions (e.g., OWL-S, WSMO) to syntactical ones (WSDL, keywords, tag clouds and textual description), with some approaches in between (SAWSDL). In this context, several frameworks to semantically match service advertisements and requests have been presented in the literature (Klusch et al. 2009; Li and Horrocks 2004; Paolucci et al. 2002).

In such open environments the mechanisms for locating appropriate services have struggled with the additional problem of service mismatches among descriptions. In this work we consider service mismatches at two different levels:

Service description models Services (advertisements and requests) might be described using different languages or models (e.g., OWL-S, WSMO, SAWSDL). Note that most approaches assume the use of the same language or model for both service advertisements and requests.

Z. Cong (✉) • A. Fernández
CETINIA, University Rey Juan Carlos, Madrid, Spain
e-mail: zijie@ia.urjc.es; alberto.fernandez@urjc.es

S. Ossowski (ed.), *Agreement Technologies*, Law, Governance and Technology Series 8, DOI 10.1007/978-94-007-5583-3_8,

Domain ontology concepts Semantic service descriptions rely on the use of domain ontologies. Thus, the second type of mismatch is due to the use of different domain ontologies to specify the concepts used in the descriptions. Domain ontologies can be specified using different ontology languages (RDF(S), OWL, WSML ...), which is an additional difficulty to deal with.

Note that these options can be combined. For instance, two services might share the same service model (e.g., OWL-S) but use different domain ontologies, or they might use the same domain ontology but different service models. It is common to encounter these kinds of problems in real world applications, therefore, alignment mechanisms for both aforementioned mismatch levels need to be integrated in order to improve the practicability of service discovery mechanism.

8.2 Service Descriptions and Matchmaking

8.2.1 Service Description Approaches

In this section we give a brief introduction to several service description approaches and service matchmaking architecture. We include semantic models (OWL-S, WSMO), syntactic models (WSDL), hybrid (SAWSDL), as well as other lighter approaches (keyword-, cloud-, and text-based service descriptions). Figure 8.1 shows a general picture of different expressiveness and communication scenarios of these models.

- Web Ontology Language for Services (OWL-S) is an OWL ontology characterized by three modules: Service Profile, Process Model and Grounding. The service profile is used to describe what the service does; it takes a global view of the service independently of how this function is realized by the service. The process model is used to describe how the service is used; and the grounding is

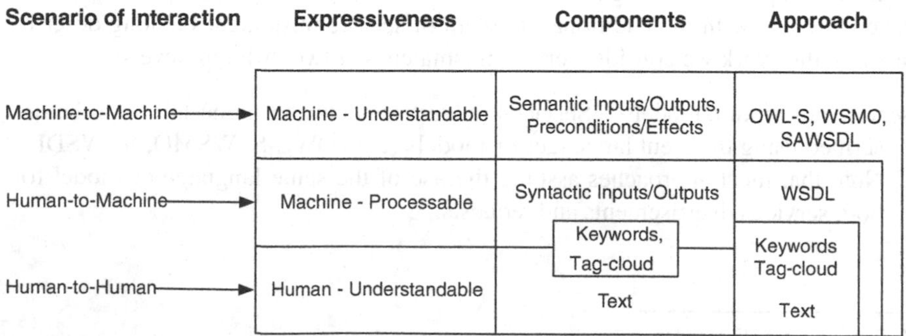

Fig. 8.1 Expressiveness of different service description models

used to describe how to interact with the service. The service profile and process model are thought of as abstract characterizations of a service, whereas the grounding makes it possible to interact with a service by providing the necessary concrete details related to message format, transport protocol, and so on. The service profile is crucial in the web service discovery process since it describes the capabilities of web services.

- Web Service Modeling Ontology (WSMO) is another web service description ontology. Similar to OWL-S, the goal of WSMO is to provide a conceptual underpinning and a formal language for semantically describing Web services in order to facilitate the automation of discovering, combining and invoking electronic services over the Web. WSMO offers four key components with which to model different aspects of Semantic Web Services: ontologies, goals, services, and mediators. Web Service descriptions are defined into WSMO capability by their precondition, postcondition, assumption, effect, and their nonFunctionalProperties (title, subject, natural language description, QoS, etc.).
- Web Service Description Language (WSDL) is an XML format for describing network services as a set of endpoints operating on messages containing either document-oriented or procedure-oriented information. The operations and messages are described abstractly, and then bound to a concrete network protocol and message format to define an endpoint. Related concrete endpoints are combined into abstract endpoints (services).
- Semantic Annotations for WSDL and XML Schema (SAWSDL) introduces three new extension attributes for using in WSDL and XML Schema documents, and discusses some of their possible uses. The extension attribute modelReference is used to specify the association between a WSDL or XML Schema component and a concept in some semantic model. It is used to annotate XML Schema type definitions, element declarations, and attribute declarations as well as WSDL interfaces, operations, and faults. The schema mapping attributes, liftingSchemaMapping and loweringSchemaMapping, are intended for specifying mappings between semantic data and XML. SAWSDL allows service discovery via a direct annotation of the types (simple or complex) and elements that express the content of inputs and outputs of WSDL operations. The addition of these attributes requires no other changes to existing WSDL or XML Schema documents, or the manner in which they had been used previously. Note that it is possible that some of the elements are not semantically annotated.
- WSMO-Lite (Vitvar et al. 2008) provides a lightweight set of semantic service descriptions in RDFS that can be used for annotations of various WSDL elements using the SAWSDL annotation mechanism. These annotations cover functional, behavioral, nonfunctional and information semantics of Web services, and are intended to support tasks such as (semi-)automatic discovery, negotiation, composition and invocation of services.
- Natural language approaches: keywords, tag-clouds and textual description. These approaches are provided primarily for human users or agents with natural language processing capabilities acting on behalf of users.

8.2.2 Service Matchmaking Techniques

Service matchmaking is a critical link in service discovery process. Matchmaking is, essentially, a process that retrieves ideal service advertisements from a service directory according to a service request, which is provided by a user. The fulfillment of the capabilities offered by service advertisements against the requirements specified by service request is expressed in term of *degree of match (DOM)*. The value of DOM can be qualitative or quantitative depending on the matchmaking algorithms and service description model.

Matchmaking algorithms exploit different components in service descriptions. These algorithms, thus, can be divided into two main categories: *logic-based* algorithms utilize semantically annotated elements in service descriptions. By calculating the semantic similarities among elements (usually IOPE) in service requests and advertisements, logic-based algorithms fully exploit the advantage offered by semantic web service description approaches such as OWL-S and WSMO.

One common definition of the degree of match for logic-based approaches is defined as the subsumption relation between two ontological concepts that annotate I/O elements, four degrees of match are then defined (Paolucci et al. 2002):

Exact	if concept *A* and concept *B* are equivalent or *B* is a direct sub-class of *A*
Plug-in	if concept *B* is subsumed by concept *A*
Subsumes	if concept *A* is subsumed by concept *B*
Fail	otherwise

On the other hand, for service descriptions without semantic information, text similarity-based techniques commonly found in information retrieval are used. These algorithms usually calculate the syntactic similarities between sets of keywords, tag-clouds, labels of syntactic inputs and outputs from service requests and advertisements.

Note that for text similarity-based matching, some approaches may map a syntactic element to a concept in a lexical database (e.g., *synset in* WordNet (Miller 1995)), which often can be considered as an ontology as well. Hence, such approaches can also be considered as a semantic matching, but often provides less precision due to the ambiguity of natural language.

Below, we further classify popular matchmaking approaches into five categories with some example matchmakers :

- Logic-based signature(IO) matching: *OWLS-SLR lite (Meditskos and Bassiliades 2010), SeMa2, XSSD, iSeM (Klusch and Kapahnke 2010)*
- Logic-based condition(PE) matching: *SPARQLent (Sbodio et al. 2010), SeMa2, iSem*
- Text similarity-based structural matching: *OWLS-iMatcher (Kiefer and Bernstein 2008), SeMa2*
- Text similarity matching: *OWLS-iMatcher, XSSD, iSeM*

- Others (machine-learning based, concentrate QoS, industrial sector categorization, etc.): *OWLS-MX3, OWLS-SLR lite, iSem*

From this list, one should notice that most of modern matchmakers use hybrid matching, the final DOM is obtained by aggregating most, if not all, DOMs of the above-listed matching techniques.

8.3 Service Description Alignment

As seen in Sect. 8.2, the diversity of service description languages and models is high. Under this wide range of choices, service providers might choose to describe and publish their services in one or more languages that they are familiar with, which may mismatch with the service requester's description language.

To smooth away the heterogeneity problem in service description models, both parties involved in communication need a common model for service discovery. In this section we presents three different options for such a common model.

8.3.1 Translation Among Existing Models

One natural option for service description alignment is to convert services described in one existing model into another, e.g., from WSMO to OWL-S. This usually happens for two models belonging to the same expressiveness level (see Fig. 8.1), otherwise expressiveness of the model from a higher level will be lost.

Among this kind of approach, IRS-III (Domingue et al. 2004) is worth noting. It is the first WSMO compliant system for supporting the Semantic Web Services technologies with storage, publishing and discovery capabilities. The internal representation of a web service in IRS-III is similar to WSMO (in 2004 Hakimpour et al. defined it as a version of WSMO in OCML (Motta 1998)) in most important aspects, such as *goals, functional capabilities, orchestration, mediators and choreography.*

To further enhance the capabilities of IRS-III, Hakimpour et al. presented a translation from OWL-S to WSMO description in Hakimpour et al. (2004), the latter can be used by IRS-III.

This translation consists of two main components:

1. Translator of "OWL-S to WSMO Ontology"
2. Translator of "OWL to OCML"

The first component translates the *service capabilities* defined in OWL-S to WSMO *Web Service*. This process is performed in three phrases:

Functional parameters (IOPE) Inputs and outputs of a service described in OWL-S process model using *hasInput* and *hasOutput* are translated into IRS-III's

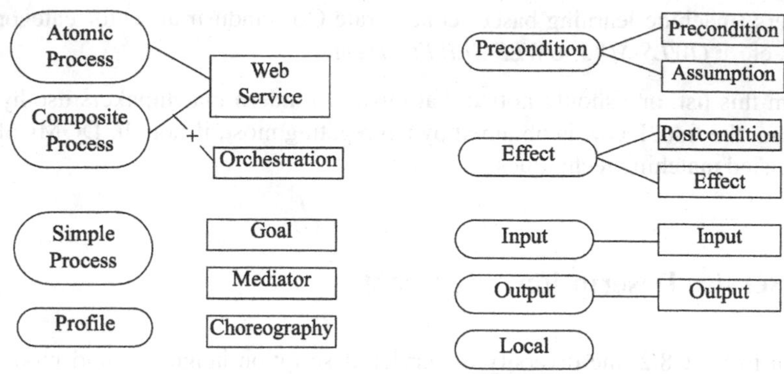

Fig. 8.2 Similarity of the basic elements of OWL-S (in *ovals*) and WSMO (in *boxes*)

has-input-role and *has-output-role*. Preconditions and effects from OWL-S are translated into IRS-III's *Capabilities* which include: *has-preconditions, has-assumption, has-effect* and *has-postcondition*. Overall, the functional parameters OWL-S are translated to *Web Service* in IRS-III and WSMO. Figure 8.2[1] illustrates the similarity of basic elements of two models.

Goals The notion of Goal is essential in IRS-III and WSMO. A goal is a general description of a problem rather than a description of a method that solves a particular problem, which is the focus of the OWL-S process model. During the translation process, user may choose whether to automatically generate a goal and corresponding *mediators* based on the original OWL-S description. Because a goal in IRS-III and WSMO may be associated with several Web Services (translated from OWL-S functional parameters in previous phrase), user may also choose to associate an existing goal with the translated Web Service.

Composition Composite processes in OWL-S are defined as a set of processes and control constructs, e.g., a sequence of processes (using SEQUENCE control construct). The translation of such a process could be done in two ways: (1) using translator developed for the previous version of IRS (IRS-II) to translate composite process into PSM in OCML; or (2) take the advantage of *goal composition* offered by IRS to achieve Web Service composition dynamically in execution time.

Lara et al. has provided a conceptual comparison between OWL-S and WSMO, one may find in their work (Lara et al. 2004) more details about the differences on both conceptual and concrete implementation levels between these two popular semantic web service description approaches.

[1]Figure extracted from Hakimpour et al. (2004)

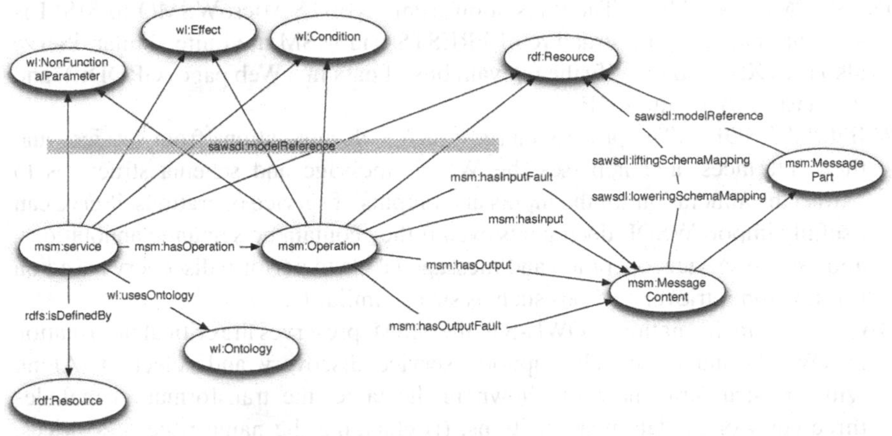

Fig. 8.3 Simplified view of model (MSM) used by iServe

8.3.2 Neutral Model (Intersection)

Some works choose to overcome the heterogeneity problem by introducing a neutral model (or using existing lightweight model, such as the WSMO-Lite used in the SEALS platform (Wrigley et al. 2010)) that covers the elements commonly seen in existing service description approaches.

Pedrinaci et al. utilized such approach in their service publication and discovery system *iServe* (Pedrinaci et al. 2010). Named *Minimal Service Model (MSM)*, this service model is a neutral model which captures some common components found in popular semantic service description approaches, e.g., WSMO, OWL-S and SAWSDL. iServe benefits from MSM thanks to its simplicity, MNM contains only essential elements dedicated to service discovery and invocation tasks.

MSM describes a web service as a set of *Operations*, each *Operation* contains input, output and fault *MessageContent* which is composed of one or more *MessagePart*. To bring the semantics into MSM, SAWSDL vocabularies for relating syntactic elements and semantic models are adopted, namely *sawsdl:modelReference*, *sawsdl:lifting SchemaMapping* and *sawsdl:loweringSchemaMapping*. Other elements related to semantic annotation of the web service are described in WSMO-Lite vocabularies, such as *wl:Condition* and *wl:Effect*, as well as non-functional parameters (*wl:nonFunctional Parameters*). Figure 8.3 depicts a simplified view of the MSM.

When a service advertisement is submitted to iServe, an import plug-in corresponding to the original service description model is invoked to convert the original model to MSM. Currently, service described in OWL-S, WSDL/SAWSDL and hRESTS (Kopecky et al. 2008) or MicroWSMO are supported by iServe.

hRESTS/MicroWSMO The translation from hRESTS/MicroWSMO to MSM is straightforward as the structure of hRESTS and MSM are quite similar. iServe also uses XSLT to identify the relevant bits of data in a Web page (GRDDL), and to translate them into RDF.

WSDL/SAWSDL The process merges SAWSDL annotations from services and their interfaces, and it parses the WSDL message and schema structures to extract the annotations of the inputs and outputs of service operations. iServe can usefully import WSDL documents even if they contain no semantic annotations, and use the service, operation and message labels to perform discovery based on information retrieval methods such as string similarity.

OWL-S Transformation of OWL-S to the MSM, preserves the critical information in OWL-S and effectively supports service discovery and selection. Along with the structural mapping shown in the table, the transformation includes three noteworthy data manipulations: (i) changing the namespace of services, operations, and messages; (ii) changing literal grounding values to useful URIs; and (iii) adding the *rdfs:isDefinedBy* link between the resulting MSM service and the original OWL-S description as promoted by Linked Data principles.

8.3.3 Neutral Model (Union)

Another possible option for a neutral abstract model is a model that is a union of the elements of existing description approaches. Such model may avoid the loss of expressivity seen in intersection neutral model.

Fernandez et al. presented an neutral model in Cong et al. (2011), named "AT-GCM" which contains the following elements: *inputs, outputs, preconditions, effects, keywords, textual description, category and tag cloud.* A formal definition can be seen in Definition 8.1 (Fig. 8.4).

Definition 8.1. Let N be a set of concepts of domain ontologies, a general common model (GCM) for service discovery is a tuple $< \mathscr{I}_{GCM}, \mathscr{O}_{GCM}, \mathscr{P}_{GCM}, \mathscr{E}_{GCM}, K_{GCM}, C_{GCM}, T_{GCM}, TC_{GCM} >$, where:

- $\mathscr{I}_{GCM} =< I_{syn}, I_{sem} >$ is the set of syntactic ($I_{syn} \in a,\ldots,z^*$) and semantic ($I_{sem} \subseteq N$) inputs of the service.
- $\mathscr{O}_{GCM} =< O_{syn}, O_{sem} >$ is the set of syntactic ($O_{syn} \in \{a,\ldots,z\}^*$) and semantic ($O_{sem} \in N$) outputs.
- $\mathscr{P}_{GCM}$ is the set of preconditions. $\mathscr{P}_{GCM} \subseteq N$.
- $\mathscr{E}_{GCM}$ is the set of effects. $\mathscr{E}_{GCM} \in N$.
- $\mathscr{K}_{GCM} =< K_{syn}, K_{sem} >$ is the sets of syntactic and semantic keywords, where $K_{syn} \subseteq \{a,\ldots,z\}^*, K_{sem} \in N$.
- $\mathscr{C}_{GCM}$ is a set of categories of the service, described semantically ($C_{sem} \in N$) (e.g., NAICS or UNSPSC).
- $\mathscr{T}_{GCM}$ is a textual description of the service.
- $\mathscr{TC}_{GCM}$ is a tag cloud. $TCGCM = \{< t,n > |t \in \{a,\ldots,z\}^*, n \in \mathbb{N}.$

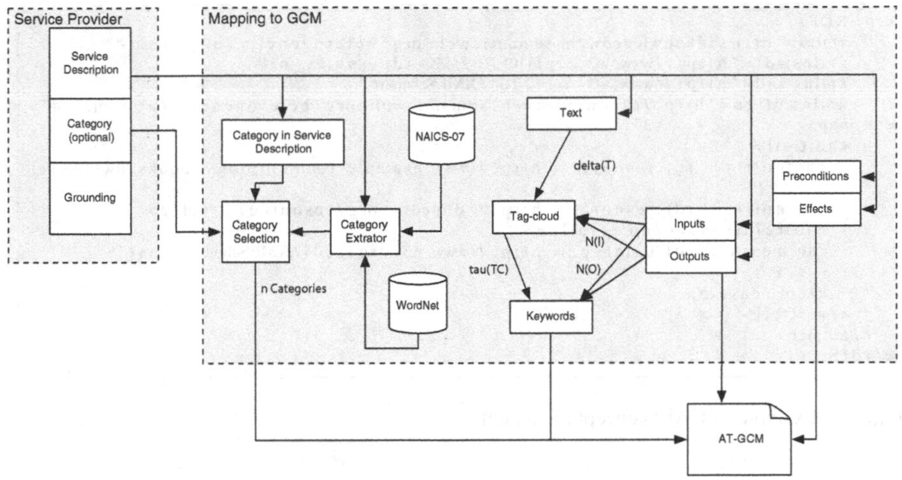

Fig. 8.4 Mapping to original service description to AT-GCM

There are many straightforward mappings that consist of simple associations between parameters in both original models and AT-GCM. For instance, in OWL-S/WSMO $I_{GCM} = < \emptyset, pt(I) >$ because they only provide semantically described inputs $I(I_{sem})$, where $pt(I) = \{t | t = parameterType(i) \forall i \in I\}$. The contrary applies to WSDL, where only the syntactic values are filled ($I_{GCM} = < I, \emptyset >$). However, SAWSDL may contain both syntactic and semantic descriptions explicitly, thus $I_{GCM} = < I_{syn}, I_{sem} >$. The same is applied to the outputs. Trivial mappings apply to preconditions (P_{GCM}), effects (E_{GCM}), categories (C_{GCM}) and textual descriptions (T_{GCM}).

However, some fields (tag-clouds, keywords) may not be explicitly described by a given model but they can be obtained from the rest of the description. Tag-clouds can be calculated from textual descriptions by means of a function $\Delta(T)$, which returns the k most relevant words from the text T as well as their frequency. We adopt information retrieval (IR) techniques to obtain that information through a process of (i) word extraction using TF-IDF or quadgram-based methods (Renz et al. 2003), (ii) stemming/lemmatization, and (iii) filtering out non-relevant terms (chosen heuristically). In addition, the set of input concept names $N(I)$ and output concept names $N(O)$ in semantic descriptions (OWL-S, WSMO, SAWSDL) are considered for the cloud with non-character symbols removed and converted to lowercase. In the case of keyword-based service descriptions (where no text is included), a plain cloud is created with frequency 1 for every keyword in the description.

Keywords can be easily obtained from tag clouds (either original or calculated with Δ), by simply adopting the k most relevant words (function $\tau(TC)$, being TC a tag-cloud). The set of input and output concept names as well as their parameter types ($pt(I)$ and $pt(O)$) are also adopted as syntactic and semantic keywords, respectively.

```
<rdf:RDF
    xmlns="http://knowledgeweb.semanticweb.org/heterogeneity/alignment#"
    xmlns:rdf="http://www.w3.org/1999/02/22-rdf-syntax-ns#"
    xmlns:xsd="http://www.w3.org/2001/XMLSchema#"
    xmlns:align="http://knowledgeweb.semanticweb.org/heterogeneity/alignment#">
<ao:map>
    <ao:Cell>
      <ao:entity1 rdf:resource='http://www.example.com/ontology/books.owl#Novel
          '/>
      <ao:entity2 rdf:resource='http://dbpedia.org/resource/Novel'/>
      <ao:relation>=</ao:relation>
      <ao:measure rdf:datatype='http://www.w3.org/2001/XMLSchema#float'>
          1.0
      </ao:measure>
    </ao:Cell>
  </ao:map>
</rdf>
```

Fig. 8.5 Example of OAEI concept alignment

8.3.4 Concept Alignment

Semantic service descriptions rely on the use of domain ontologies. To deal with this kind of mismatch, ontology alignment is required. The theoretic details of ontology alignment were discussed in Chap. 5.10, in this section, we will present a recommended standard format for representing alignment as well as how service matchmaking system can utilize these alignments.

An alignment between two ontologies O and O' is represented in a quadruple (David et al. 2011): $< e, e', n, R >$ where:

- e and e' are the entities between which a relation is asserted by the mapping (e.g., formulas, terms, classes, individuals)
- n is a degree of trust (confidence) in that mapping
- R is the relation associated to a mapping, where R identifies the relation holding between e and e'.

RDF would be an ideal concrete language for representing the alignments results as they can be published on the web and queried using SPARQL. One option is to use the format of the Ontology Alignment Evaluation Initiative.[2] Figure 8.5 shows an OAEI-like concept alignment segment represented in RDF/XML format, the measure of concept similarity could be obtained by human evaluation or other automated/semi-automated ontology alignment approaches.

In the case where two concepts involved in a service discovery process are contained in different ontologies, or the DOM obtained from the matching algorithm is *fail*, service discovery systems could query the concept alignment repository (e.g., see Fig. 8.5) to attempt to obtain an existing similarity measure using SPARQL. An example of such query is shown in Fig. 8.6.

[2] http://oaei.ontologymatching.org/, an example of OAEI alignment can be found at http://alignapi.gforge.inria.fr/tutorial/tutorial1/results/equal.rdf

```
SELECT ?concept ?measure WHERE {
?alignment ao:entity1 <http://www.example.com/ontology/books.owl#Novel>.
?alignment ao:entity2 ?concept.
?alignment ao:relation ‘‘=’’.
?alignment ao:measure ?measure
}
```

Fig. 8.6 Example of SPARQL query of concept alignment

8.4 Conclusion

In this chapter, we first presented some from among the many existing approaches for describing web services, and related matchmaking process. Among these service description approaches, service provider and requester may describe their own service in two different models or languages, however, common service matchmakers usually assume that the advertisements and request are in the same model or language. An agreement on a common model for both parties involved in the communication is required. Three approaches for dealing with service description model mismatch are presented, along with example systems that realize them: (1) translation among existing models; (2) neutral model built on the intersection of existing models; (3) neutral model built on the union of existing models.

The second focus of this chapter is to present works that deal with domain ontology mismatch, while Chap. 6 presents the ontology alignment techniques, this chapter mainly focused on representation and utilization of the alignment results, in particular OAEI format.

References

Cong, Z., A. Fernandez, C. E. and Soto. 2011. A directory of heterogeneous services. In *Fourth international workshop on resource discovery*, Heraklion.

David, J., J. Euzenat, F. Scharffe, and C. Trojahn dos Santos. 2011. The alignment api 4.0. *Semantic Web* 2(1): 3–10.

Domingue, J., L. Cabral, F. Hakimpour, D. Sell, and E. Motta. 2004. Irs iii: A platform and infrastructure for creating wsmo based semantic web services. In *CEUR workshop proceedings*, vol. 113. Frankfurt: Germany.

Hakimpour, F., J. Domingue, E. Motta, L. Cabral, and Y. Lei. 2004. Integration of owl-s into irs-iii. In *First AKT workshop on semantic web services (AKT-SWS04)*. Milton Keynes: UK.

Kiefer, C., and A. Bernstein. 2008. The creation and evaluation of isparql strategies for matchmaking. *The Semantic Web: Research and Applications*, 463–477. Springer.

Klusch, M., and P. Kapahnke. 2010. isem: Approximated reasoning for adaptive hybrid selection of semantic services. In *The semantic web: Research and applications* 30–44. Heidelberg/Berlin: Springer.

Klusch, M., B. Fries, and K. Sycara. 2009. OWLS-MX: A hybrid Semantic Web service matchmaker for OWL-S services. *Web Semantics: Science, Services and Agents on the World Wide Web* 7(2): 121–133.

Kopecky, J., K. Gomadam, and T. Vitvar. 2008. hrests: An html microformat for describing restful web services. In *IEEE/WIC/ACM international conference on web intelligence and intelligent agent technology, 2008. WI-IAT'08*, vol. 1, 619–625. Los Alamitos: IEEE.

Lara, R., D. Roman, A. Polleres, and D. Fensel. 2004. A conceptual comparison of WSMO and OWL-S. In *Web services*. Lecture Notes in Computer Science, vol. 3250, ed. L.J. Zhang and M. Jeckle, 254–269. Berlin/Heidelberg: Springer.

Li, L., and I. Horrocks. 2004. A software framework for matchmaking based on semantic web technology. *International Journal of Electronic Commerce* 8(4): 39–60. http://www.gvsu.edu/business/ijec/

Meditskos, G., and N. Bassiliades. 2010. Structural and role-oriented web service discovery with taxonomies in owl-s. *IEEE Transactions on Knowledge and Data Engineering* 22(2): 278–290.

Miller, G. 1995. WordNet: A lexical database for English. *Communications of the ACM* 38(11): 39–41.

Motta, E. 1998. An overview of the ocml modelling language. In: *The 8th workshop on methods and languages*. Citeseer.

Paolucci, M., T. Kawamura, T. Payne, and K. Sycara. 2002. Semantic matching of web services capabilities. In *The semantic web-ISWC 2002*, 333–347. Springer: Berlin.

Pedrinaci, C., D. Liu, M. Maleshkova, D. Lambert, J. Kopecky, and J. Domingue. 2010. iserve: A linked services publishing platform. In *CEUR workshop proceedings*, vol. 596. CEUR.org.

Renz, I., A. Ficzay, and H. Hitzler. 2003. Keyword extraction for text characterization. In *Proceedings of 8th International Conference on Applications of Natural Language to Information Systems*, Burg, Germany: GI.

Sbodio, M., D. Martin, and C. Moulin. 2010. Discovering semantic web services using sparql and intelligent agents. *Web Semantics: Science, Services and Agents on the World Wide Web* 8(4):310–328.

Vitvar, T., J. Kopecký, J. Viskova, and D. Fensel. 2008. Wsmo-lite annotations for web services. *The semantic web: Research and applications*, 674–689. Berlin/New York: Springer.

Wrigley, S., K. Elbedweihy, D. Reinhard, A. Bernstein, and F. Ciravegna. 2010. Evaluating semantic search tools using the seals platform? In *International workshop on evaluation of semantic technologies (IWEST 2010), International semantic web conference (ISWC2010)*, China.

Chapter 9
Using Ontologies to Manage Resources in Grid Computing: Practical Aspects

Michał Drozdowicz, Maria Ganzha, Katarzyna Wasielewska, Marcin Paprzycki, and Paweł Szmeja

9.1 Introduction

The aim of this chapter is to discuss practical aspects of the application of ontologies and semantic data processing in management of resources in the Grid. Firstly, issues involved in the development of an ontology of Grid computing are briefly considered. The discussed ontology is used not only to describe Grid resources, but also in Service Level Agreement (SLA) negotiations. Second, it is discussed how an ontology-driven user interface can be developed, to facilitate human-computer (i.e., human-software agent) communication. Third, a solution to the problem of ontology-based agent-agent communication is presented. Finally, the role of ontologies in SLA negotiations is outlined. The chapter begins with top-level description of the system, which is used to illustrate these four main points.

The *Agents in Grid* (*AiG*) project aims to develop a flexible agent-based infrastructure, which is to facilitate intelligent resource management in the Grid. Thus, the project can be considered an attempt to realize the main idea underlining the seminal paper (Foster et al. 2004), where the use of software agents as high-level middleware for the Grid was suggested. In the *AiG* project, it is proposed that flexible management of resources in the Grid can be provided by teams of software agents (Kuranowski et al. 2008a,b). Furthermore, the proposed approach is based on the application of semantic data processing in all aspects of the system. Specifically, ontologies provide the metadata, to be used to describe resources, reason about them, and negotiate their usage. In addition, adaptability and flexibility of the system are to result from the application of other "agreement technologies", being agent negotiations the most prominent one.

M. Drozdowicz (✉) • M. Ganzha • K. Wasielewska • M. Paprzycki • P. Szmeja
Systems Research Institute Polish Academy of Sciences, Warsaw, Poland
e-mail: drozdowicz@gmail.com; maria.ganzha@ibspan.waw.pl; katarzyna.wasielewska@gmail.com; marcin.paprzycki@ibspan.waw.pl; pawel.szmeja@gmail.com

S. Ossowski (ed.), *Agreement Technologies*, Law, Governance and Technology Series 8, DOI 10.1007/978-94-007-5583-3_9,

9.2 System Overview

In the work of Wasielewska et al. (2011), the Grid is considered as an open environment (see also Chap. 7), in which *Agents* representing *Users* interact to, either (a) join a team, or (b) find team(s) to execute job(s) (Dominiak et al. 2008; Kuranowski et al. 2008a). The main assumptions behind the proposed approach were[1]:

- Agents work in teams (groups of agents),
- Each team has a single leader—the *LMaster* agent,
- Each *LMaster* has a mirror, the *LMirror* agent that can take over its job,
- Incoming workers (*Worker* agents) join teams based on *User*-defined criteria,
- Teams (represented by their *LMasters*) accept *Workers* based on team-specific criteria,
- Each *Worker* agent can (if needed) play role of the *LMirror* or the *LMaster*,
- Matchmaking is facilitated by the *CIC* component, represented by the *CIC Agent*.

These assumptions have been summarized in the Use Case diagram in Fig. 9.1.

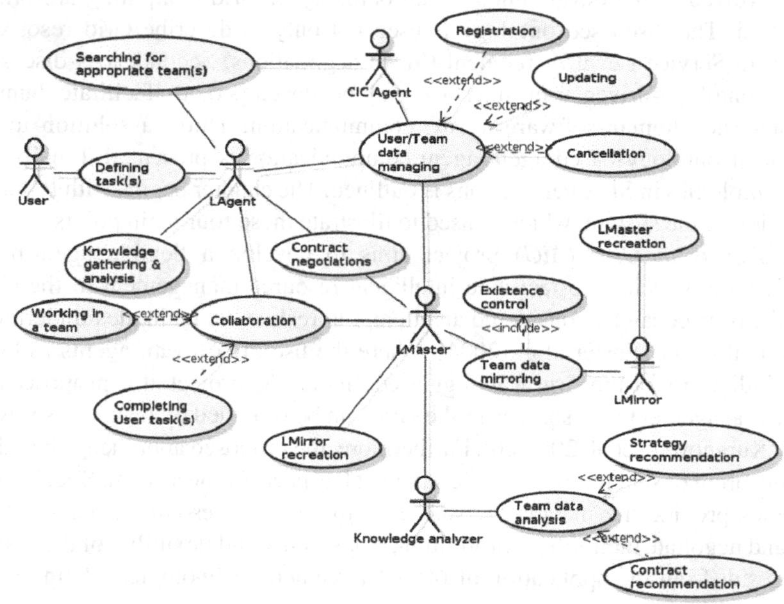

Fig. 9.1 Use case diagram of *AiG* system

[1]For a comprehensive discussion of reasons behind the approach, see Dominiak et al. (2006) and Wasielewska et al. (2011).

Let us now outline interactions between components of the system, i.e., the *User* and its representative, the *LAgent*, and agent teams represented by their leaders—*LMaster* agents (more information can be found in Dominiak et al. (2006)). Since the system is based on semantic data processing, ontologies are used whenever applicable. Here, recall that utilization of ontologies as a method of knowledge representation, and basics of the OWL (Web Ontology Language) were introduced in Chaps. 4 and 5, respectively. Let us now assume that the team "advertisements" describing: (1) what resources they offer, and/or (2) characteristics of workers they would like to "hire", are registered with the *Client Information Center* (*CIC*). Obviously, team advertisements are ontologically demarcated. Specifically, offered resources are represented with individuals (instances), and worker characteristics are represented with OWL class expressions. Let us focus on two main scenarios in the system: the *User* is looking for a team (1) to commission job execution, or (2) to join (to be paid for the usage of her resources). In both cases, the *User* interacts with her *LAgent* via an ontology-driven GUI application, and formulates conditions for (1) job execution, or (2) team joining. Respective descriptions of a desired resource(s) (or characteristics of (an) offered resource(s)) are also ontologically represented. Specifically, the GUI application allows the *User* to select such requirements on the basis of the existing *AiG ontology*, without needing to know it (see Sect. 9.4). The resulting ontology class expression, is passed from the GUI to the *LAgent*. The *LAgent* communicates with the *CIC* (passes the ontology fragment to the *CIC Agent*; see Sect. 9.5) to obtain a list of teams that satisfy the *User*-defined criteria. The *CIC* utilizes a reasoner to find individuals satisfying criteria from the received ontology class expression. These individuals represent potential partner teams (their *LMasters*), and are sent back to the *LAgent*. Next, the *LAgent* forwards the result to the GUI application and waits for the generated ontology fragment with *contract conditions* that the *User* specifies. Additionally, the *User* can limit the number of selected potential partner teams based, for instance, on trust verification. Note that, in a way similar to the selection of required resource characteristics, the specification of contract conditions is driven by the *AiG ontology* (its *contract ontology* part; see Sect. 9.6). Next, the *LAgent* communicates with the *LMasters* of selected teams, and they apply the *FIPA Iterated Contract-Net Protocol*[2] to negotiate the contract (SLA) (see Sect. 9.6, Wasielewska et al. 2011). All information exchanged during the negotiations is based on the *AiG ontology*. The *LAgent* sends a *Call-For-Proposal* message that contains contract conditions, represented in the form of a class expression, and obtains (from the *LMaster*s) contract offers represented as ontology individuals. If the *LAgent* finds an appropriate team, a Service Level Agreement is formed. If no such team is found, the *LAgent* informs the *User* and awaits further instructions. Let us stress that this process applies to both, the job execution scenario and the team joining scenario. The only difference is in the details of negotiations (e.g., content of exchanged messages) taking place in each case.

[2] www.fipa.org/specs/fipa00030/PC00030D.pdf

9.3 Ontologies in the System

As stated above, when designing the system, it was assumed that *all* data processed in it will be ontologically demarcated. Therefore, after a brief reflection, it was realized that what was needed was an ontology, covering: (a) computer hardware and software (Grid resources), (b) Grid structure, (c) concepts related to the SLA and contract definitions. After a comprehensive investigation of existing Grid-related ontologies (see Drozdowicz et al. 2009) it was decided to modify and extend the *Core Grid Ontology* (*CGO*[3]; Xing et al. 2005). While the *CGO* provided excellent base-terms concerning Grid resources and structure (parts (a) and (b)), there was a need to modify it slightly and to extend it to include the remaining concepts needed for the *AiG* system (concepts concerning part (c)). The complete description of the resulting ontology can be found in Drozdowicz et al. (2009, 2011). Here, let us briefly outline its main features. The extended *CGO* (the *AiG Ontology*) is structured into three layers (its core classes depicted in Fig. 9.2):

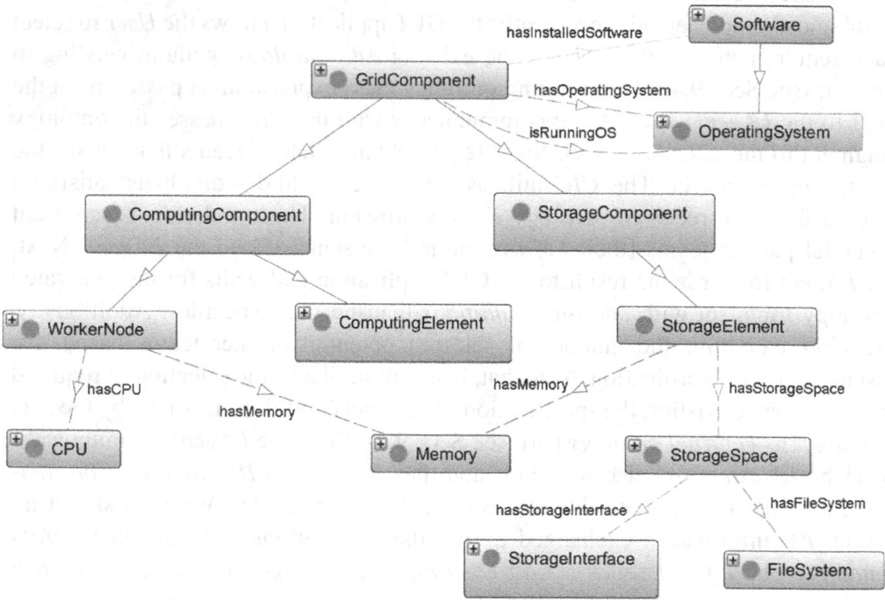

Fig. 9.2 Ontology diagram for *AiG* ontologies

[3]Unfortunately, the original CGO is not available online anymore and thus only the published work can be referenced.

1. *Grid Ontology*—directly extending the *CGO* concepts.
2. *Conditions Ontology*—includes classes required by the SLA negotiations (e.g., pricing, payment mechanisms, worker availability conditions, etc.); it imports the *Grid Ontology*, to use the terms related to the Grid structure and resources.
3. *Messaging Ontology*—contains definitions of messages exchanged by the agents, forming the communication protocols of the system (it uses the *Grid Ontology* and the *Conditions Ontology* to specify content of messages).

The crucial aspect of ontological modeling was the representation of constraints on ontology classes. For example, when a *User* is looking for a team to have a job executed, she needs to specify the necessary hardware (and possibly software) configuration. In this case, the common way of assigning values to class properties is not enough, as there is also a need to specify minimum, maximum, and range conditions. For instance, to execute her job, the *User* may need a processor that has at least four cores, but no more than eight cores (these restrictions could be based on the knowledge of characteristics of the problem/job; e.g., parallelization methods used when it was implemented, and its parallel performance profile). After considering several approaches, to solve this problem, designers of the *AiG* system have settled on class expressions. Here, requirements are defined as a new class that restricts the set of individuals to these satisfying conditions on class properties. It is thus possible to ask a reasoner to infer a list of individuals of the generated class and receive these fulfilling the constraints.

While it may be possible to question some specific decisions made when completing the "re-design" of the CoreGrid ontology[4]—and interested readers are invited to send comments and suggestions to the authors of this chapter—let us focus on issues that arise when it is to be used in an actual application. Specifically, when it is to be the core data representation form in an agent-based system, and used to facilitate agent negotiations leading to an SLA. Note that, for space limitations, the focus of this chapter is on the "job execution scenario". However, all issues and results presented in what follows apply directly to the "team joining scenario".

9.4 Front-End Design and Implementation

The front-end developed for the system was designed to help the user communicate her needs and/or preferences using terms familiar and convenient for her, and then to translate her requirements into appropriate ontology fragments, e.g., into classes of the *AiG ontology*. In other words, the front-end subsystem, while becoming a means to providing ontological data to the system (e.g., for the SLA negotiations), has to do this in a *User*-friendly way, without making assumptions about the user's knowledge

[4]Its current version can be found at http://gridagents.svn.sourceforge.net/viewvc/gridagents/trunk/ontology/AiGOntology/

concerning semantic technologies, and OWL in particular. After completing the requirements analysis, it was decided that, the front-end of the system has to consists of three main parts, allowing specification of requirements concerning:

1. *Scheduling job execution*—lets *User* specify hardware and software requirements that a team has to satisfy in order to be taken into consideration. In the second step of the scenario, the *User* creates a set of constraints on the contract for executing the job.
2. *Joining a team; Worker criteria*—specify information needed for negotiating joining a team, i.e., description of available resources. When an initial list of teams is found, the *User* also defines the restrictions on the contract between the *Worker* and the team.
3. *Joining a team; LMaster criteria*—also concerns worker joining a team. Here, the owner of the *LMaster* can specify conditions that must be met by any worker willing to join the team. These include, among others, hardware and software configuration of the Grid resource.

Note that, for brevity, material presented in this section is focused only on the first two sets of criteria (concerning direct *User*s of the system, rather than team managers). In this context, there exist two possible goals of the system. First, the system that would be 100 % autonomous, where all decisions would be made by software agents, without further *User* participation (except of the initial specification of requirements). Second, *User* participation would be also possible/required/expected in specific stages of SLA negotiations. For instance, it would be possible for the *User* to manually filter the initial list of teams received from the *CIC*. Here, this could be considered as means of letting the *User* restrict the executors of her tasks only to the entities that she trusts (see also Ganzha et al. 2007). While the first approach (total agent autonomy in representing *User*'s interests), can be seen as the "Holy Grail" of agent system design, it is the second approach that is more realistic (and has to be implementable; if not implemented). However, in the future, when reliance on autonomous software agents becomes a norm (e.g., when a complete system-wide trust management would be implemented), *User* involvement may not be needed (or, at least, considerably limited).

The design of the front-end of an agent system leads to a number of interesting problems. In the initial system prototype, the front-end was a desktop application with the *LAgent* running in the background (on the same machine). Advantages of that approach included simple architecture and ease of interactions between the client application and the *LAgent*. Note however, that in this approach, a copy of the *AiG ontology* had to be stored locally (at least this would be the most natural solution). As a result any change in this ontology would have to be propagated to *all LAgent*s residing on *all User*-machines. Furthermore, this approach also meant that: (1) the *LAgent* could only work while the front-end application was running, and (2) at least a part of the *User*'s data was stored on the local machine. Therefore, meaningful interactions with the *LAgent* from different machines would be difficult (if not impossible). At the very least they would require installing the front-end software (including the ontology), on any such device. Since, currently,

Specify requirements for the team:

ComputingElement
http://www.owl-ontologies.com/unnamed.owl#ComputingElement

hasStorageSpace | is constrained by | StorageSpace | remove

hasFileSystem | is equal to individual | winnt | remove

hasTotalSize | is greater than | 200

and

hasOperatingSystem | is equal to individual | vista_sp2

Update

and

The generated condition:


```
Response: <rdf:RDF xmlns:rdf="http://www.w3.org/1999/02/22-rdf-syntax-ns#" xmlns:owl="http://www.w3.org/2002/07/owl#"
xmlns:xsd="http://www.w3.org/2001/XMLSchema#" xmlns:rdfs="http://www.w3.org/2000/01/rdf-schema#"> <owl:Class
rdf:about="http://gridagents.sourceforge.net/TeamConditions#TeamCondition"> <owl:intersectionOf rdf:parseType="Collection">
<rdf:Description rdf:about="http://www.owl-ontologies.com/unnamed.owl#ComputingElement"/> <owl:Restriction>
<owl:someValuesFrom> <owl:Class> <owl:intersectionOf rdf:parseType="Collection"> <rdf:Description rdf:about="http://www.owl-
ontologies.com/unnamed.owl#StorageSpace"/> <owl:Restriction> <owl:hasValue rdf:resource="http://gridagents.sourceforge.net
/AiGGridOntology#winnt"/> <owl:onProperty rdf:resource="http://gridagents.sourceforge.net/AiGGridOntology#hasFileSystem"/>
</owl:Restriction> <owl:Restriction> <owl:hasValue>200</owl:hasValue> <owl:onProperty
rdf:resource="http://gridagents.sourceforge.net/AiGGridOntology#hasTotalSize"/> </owl:Restriction> </owl:intersectionOf>
</owl:Class> </owl:someValuesFrom> <owl:onProperty rdf:resource="http://gridagents.sourceforge.net
/AiGGridOntology#hasStorageSpace"/> </owl:Restriction> <owl:Restriction> <owl:hasValue
rdf:resource="http://gridagents.sourceforge.net/AiGGridOntology#vista_sp2"/> <owl:onProperty
rdf:resource="http://gridagents.sourceforge.net/AiGGridOntology#hasOperatingSystem"/> </owl:Restriction> </owl:intersectionOf>
</owl:Class> </rdf:RDF>
```


Fig. 9.3 A condition builder section

the possibility of accessing an application from *any* computer becomes highly desired (if not a necessity), it was decided to develop a web application that can be hosted in a "shared environment". Furthermore, such application, if properly designed, could help in solving the above mentioned problem of expected lack of *User* knowledge about ontologies. Finally, the proposed system could be friendly to potential ontology modifications. Therefore, it was decided to proceed with development of an ontology-driven front-end. Here, the vocabulary of specification of *User*-constraints would originate from the existing Grid ontology, hopefully simplifying tasks of *User*s of the system. Furthermore, the *AiG ontology* could be stored in a "single" place—with the application, considerably simplifying the ontology maintenance. Note that the most natural place for the location of the application would be the *CIC* component (see Fig. 9.1).

The core of the front-end is a condition builder—a set of condition boxes, each representing a description or constraint on a single class-property relationship (see Fig. 9.3 for screen-shots from the running front-end, representing the condition selection process, and the resulting OWL class). Depending on the selected class, the *User* may choose one of properties that the class is in the domain of. For instance, having selected the *WorkerNode* class, the expanded property box will contain properties such as *hasStorageSpace*, *hasMemory* or *hasCPU*.

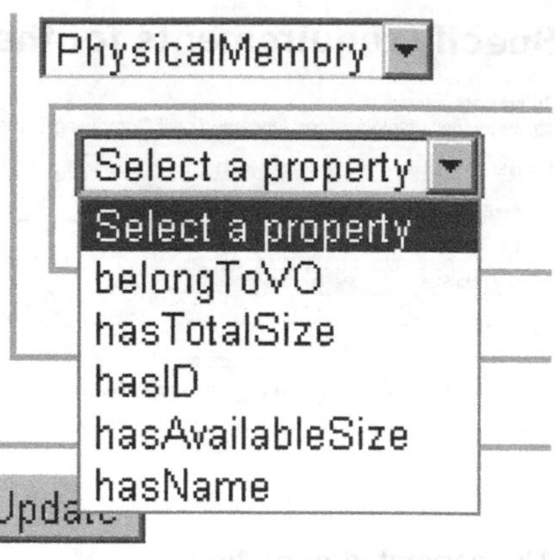

Fig. 9.4 Selecting a class property

Next, she can specify an *operator*, from the set of applicable ones, to the selected property. For example, for the datatype properties these may include: *equal to*, or *greater than*, *less than* whereas for object properties these would be *is equal to individual* and *is constrained by*. When an operator is selected, the system generates a "new" fragment of the user interface, used to specify value of the property. Again, controls depend on the selected operator—be it a simple text box, or a drop down list of applicable individuals. It is an important feature of this component that both: available properties, and possible class arguments, are inferred directly from the ontology using a reasoner, which means that the application fully supports class and property inheritance and other, more complex relations between the elements of the ontology.

To illustrate the relationship between the ontological metadata and the structure of user interface elements, let us look at the following examples. In Fig. 9.4 a drop-down list of properties that can be applied to the selected class—the *PhysicalMemory*—is presented. The elements of this list are generated from the ontology, the relevant part of which is contained in the following (RDF/XML) snippet.[5] Notice that these properties are actually defined in two different ontologies (listed in a single snippet, for clarity and brevity) and, furthermore, they do not specify the *PhysicalMemory* directly in their domain. This shows how the usage of a reasoner, when analyzing the metadata of the ontology, can help in making the system more robust and flexible.

```
ObjectProperty: belongToVO
 Domain: GridEntity
 Range: VO
ObjectProperty: hasID
 Domain: GridEntity
 Range: URI
DataProperty: hasTotalSize
 Characteristics: Functional
```

[5] All ontological snippets, cited in the text, shall be presented in the Manchester OWL Syntax with namespaces omitted for readability and space preservation.

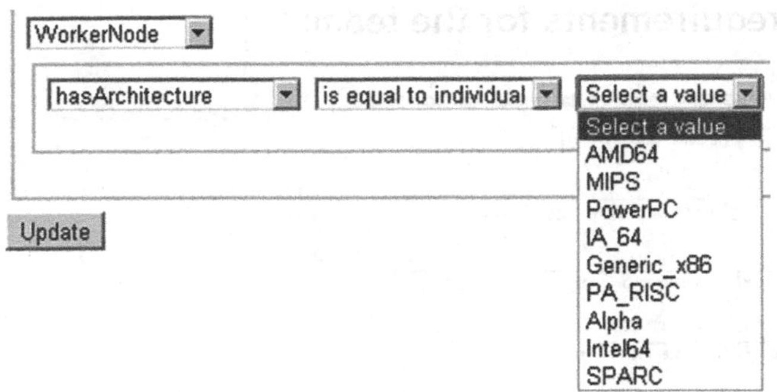

Fig. 9.5 Selecting an individual

```
 Domain: Memory or StorageSpace
 Range: int
DataProperty: hasAvailableSize
 Domain: Memory or StorageSpace
 Range: int
DataProperty: hasName
 Domain: GridApplication or GridEntity
 Range: string
```

In the next example, it is demonstrated how the *User* can specify that a property should be *equal to* a specific individual contained in the ontology. Figure 9.5 shows a list of individuals that can be used as a value of the property *hasArchitecture* for class *WorkerNode*. These reflect the following individuals from the ontology:

Turning our attention to more complex use cases, an interesting one is that of nested constraints. For object properties, when the *User* selects the operator *is constrained by*, for a class to be further specified, a new condition box is created within the existing one. It is used to describe the details, or requirements, regarding the value of the selected property. The front-end supports also setting constraints on multiple properties of the same class, using the *and* buttons, which add a new condition box at the same level as the previous one.

As an example let us consider a *User* specifying that the resource required for running her job should have a multi-core processor with clock speed greater than 1.4 GHz. This can be easily specified in the application as shown on Fig. 9.6. The *User* first specifies that the computing element should have the value of the *hasWN* set to an instance of the *WorkerNode* class. This instance is in turn constrained to an individual with an instance of the *CPU* class, as the value of the *hasCPU* class. Finally, the two conditions are set on the properties of the *CPU* class: the *hasCores* (greater than one) and the *hasClockSpeed* (greater than 1,400 MHz). The result of such specification, translated into the OWL by the server component is shown in the following listing.

```
Class: TeamCondition
 EquivalentTo: ComputingElement that hasWN some (WorkerNode that
hasCPU some (CPU that hasClockSpeed some integer[> 1400] and hasCores
some integer[> 1]))
```

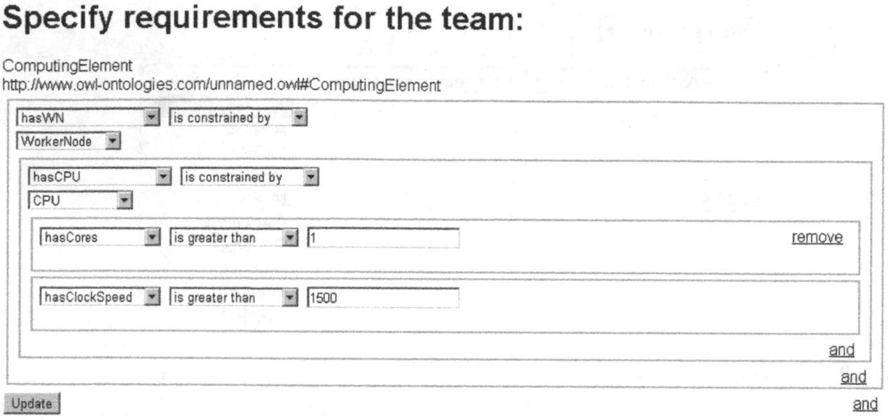

Specify requirements for the team:

ComputingElement
http://www.owl-ontologies.com/unnamed.owl#ComputingElement

hasWN | is constrained by
WorkerNode
hasCPU | is constrained by
CPU
hasCores | is greater than | 1 | remove
hasClockSpeed | is greater than | 1500
and
and
Update
and

Fig. 9.6 Example of a class constraint

When the *User* finishes specifying conditions and pushes the *update* button, the system parses the internal representation of the conditions, and transforms it into an OWL Class Expression. This OWL fragment is passed to the *JADE GatewayAgent*, which is responsible for passing information between the application server, and the *JADE* agent container. The *GatewayAgent* forwards the data to the *LAgent*, to handle it within the system.

Here, it is worth stressing (again) that in the front-end, all elements from which the *User* builds the ontological conditions and descriptions are generated dynamically, from the structure of the ontology. Therefore, all changes to the ontology can be applied automatically during the system runtime. This is extremely important, especially in the case of ontology matching and enriching, based on the information received from other agents. It also simplifies, in one more way, maintenance of changes in the ontology. For instance, if a new class of NVidia processors is introduced, the necessary changes in the ontology will almost automatically materialize in the front-end.

Furthermore, user interface elements are built dynamically, in response to *User* actions. For example, if the *User* wishes to specify a particular CPU architecture, individuals of the *CPUArchitecture* class will only be fetched from the ontology when the *User* selects an *equal to individual* condition on the *hasArchitecture* property. This allows the processing to be limited only to the needed parts of the ontology. Moreover, it allows displayed options to be based on the *User*'s previous choices. Observe that this could be the basis of developing a mechanism for providing automated assistance to the *User*, by suggesting the most useful or common options, or by filtering out inconsistent options.

The part of the user interface responsible for defining the concrete instances (e.g., the hardware and software configuration of a particular Grid resource), is built around the same condition builder components. Of course, here the available property operators are restricted to the *equal to* and the ontology elements generated by the OWL generator represent individuals instead of class expressions. Moreover, the

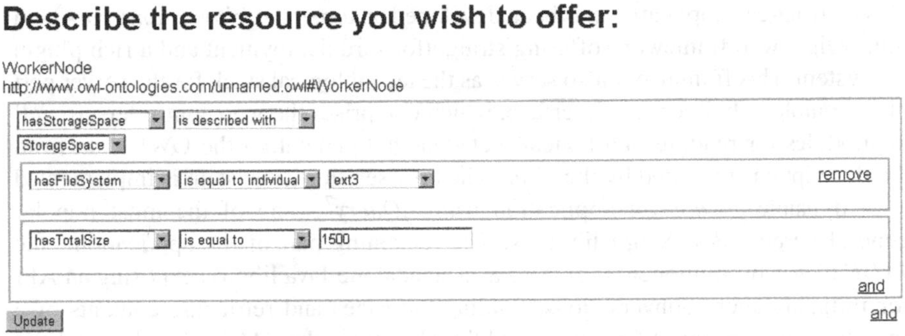

Describe the resource you wish to offer:

WorkerNode
http://www.owl-ontologies.com/unnamed.owl#WorkerNode

hasStorageSpace | is described with
StorageSpace
hasFileSystem | is equal to individual | ext3 | remove
hasTotalSize | is equal to | 1500
and
Update | and

Fig. 9.7 Example of a class constraint

class condition constraints have been modified slightly (for better *User* experience); the *is constrained by* operator has been replaced with the *is described with*. The functionality of specifying descriptions of individuals, instead of class expressions, is used, among others, when defining the hardware and software configuration of a resource that is offered to (join) a team.

The example, displayed in Fig. 9.7, illustrates a description of a *WorkerNode* having total size of 1,500 MB of storage space formatted using the *ext3* file system. The following snippet shows the rendering of the individual representing such resource as returned by the OWL generator.

```
Individual: WorkerDescription
 Types: WorkerNode
 Facts: hasStorageSpace _:storage
Individual: _:storage
 Types: StorageSpace
 Facts: hasFileSystem ext3, hasTotalSize 1500
```

Another interesting challenge that was encountered, while migrating the GUI from a desktop-based application towards a web-based one, was that of passing messages between the web controllers and the agents. Although the *JADE* agent environment contains special classes that provide valuable help in such scenarios (the *Gateway* and the *GatewayAgent* classes), and makes sending messages from a non-agent environment rather straightforward, handling requests coming from agents, within the user interface, is less trivial (for an interesting discussion and another possible solution, see Gawinecki et al. 2005; Gordon et al. 2002). This is mostly due to the fact that web applications are stateless by nature, and therefore it is not directly possible to implement an event-based system where a message coming from an agent triggers a particular action in the GUI. Instead, it is necessary to implement a queue of messages received by the *GatewayAgent*, representing the user interface, and some form of a polling mechanism that would check for new messages. In our implementation, the *GatewayAgent* is responsible for keeping a list of conversations containing messages. Through the use of the *Gateway* class, the web controllers are able to reach the message queue. Polling itself is achieved by using the client side *AJAX* requests.

The front-end application has been developed on top of the *Play! Framework*[6]—a lightweight web framework offering straightforward deployment and a rich plugin ecosystem. This framework also serves as the technological stack for the server part of the ontology builder user interface, which comprises the web controllers as well as modules for reading ontological metadata and generating the OWL data from the descriptions provided by the *User*. The browser-side subsystem is implemented as a dynamic *JavaScript* application using *jQuery*[7]—one of the most popular general purpose *JavaScript* libraries. The remaining part of the application—the *JADE Gateway* component is created as a standalone Java library, exposing an API for initiating agent conversations, sending messages and retrieving contents of a specific conversation. After some additional testing, the *JADE Gateway* and the ontology builder user interface are to be released as *Play!* modules, to be easily integrated into other *Play!* applications. Furthermore, the *JADE Gateway* will be released as a *JADE* add-on. It is worth noting that the *AJAX* functionality for listening on agent's responses has been developed as a *jQuery* plugin, enabling its easy embedding into any HTML page. Currently, the plugin is developed using a simple polling mechanism controlled on the browser-side with a request sent to the server every specific number of seconds. In the future versions of the software this mechanism will be replaced with a less server-consuming implementation based on the *Comet/Long polling mechanism*.[8]

9.5 Passing Ontological Information; Integrating Front-End and Back-End

Let us now assume that, as described above, the *User* requirements/constraints have been specified and transformed by the user interface into OWL class expressions/individuals and passed to the *LAgent* representing the *User*. Next, such information has to be passed further to various components of the system. For instance, it could be passed to the *CIC* infrastructure (the *CIC Agent*) to query for agent teams satisfying *User*'s needs. It can be also sent to the *LMaster* agents as a part of SLA negotiations. As noted, all these processes involve ontological matchmaking (which was introduced in Chaps. 7 and 8). In summary, communication in the *AiG* system relies on passing around, extracting information from, and manipulating instances of, ontologies. However, the issues raised here apply to any agent based system that is to use ontologies in practice and pass their "fragments" around for semantic data processing. Without flexible and robust support, use of ontologies in agent systems (e.g., as envisioned in the classic paper by J. Hendler (2001)) will be overly complex, thus reducing their uptake.

---

[6]http://www.playframework.org/

[7]http://www.jquery.com/

[8]Comet and Reverse Ajax: The Next-Generation Ajax 2.0, http://dl.acm.org/citation.cfm?id=1453096

Unfortunately, the default *JADE* ontological facilities are very limiting. In this framework, ontologies are stored in *static Java classes*. Those classes are not shared between agents (i.e., each agent needs to have a private copy) and, when used for communication purposes, may lead to misunderstandings between agents. The default *JADE* codecs for ontological communication can encode the Java classes into the FIPA SL (FIPA Semantic Language[9])—a language used to describe the context of any *JADE* ACL message. Using the FIPA SL in both context and content of the message is disadvantageous, as there is currently no good reasoner for this language. As a matter of fact, it seems that there is currently no publicly available FIPA SL reasoner. Moreover, the FIPA SL is not decidable, which may sometimes prevent an agent from "understanding" the content of the FIPA SL-encoded message. Using a non-decidable ontology language is simply not possible in the *AiG* system, because the problem domain requires introducing new, as well as changing the already existing data. Under such conditions it would be impossible to guarantee decidability of ontology at any time. Managing an ontology that is not decidable would require writing new reasoning algorithms capable of dealing with undecidability. Using an ontology language that is decidable is a much simpler and more feasible solution.

It should be stressed that having the ontology "constrained" within static classes means that there is no practical way to quickly add new class expressions, properties or constraints to the ontology. Any change in the ontology would require change in the Java files for *every* agent. New files would need to be sent to every agent and swapped with the old ones (possibly via dynamic class loading). In any case, updating *JADE* ontologies is extremely impractical and requires reloading, which in turn means that, for all practical purposes, the system would need to stop working during the ontology update process. The solution outlined in this chapter does not suffer from such penalties.

Observe also that, from the practical point of view, *JADE* ontologies are very hard to manage and do not offer many of the useful features that are present in OWL 2 (W3C OWL Working Group 2009). For instance, there is no multiple inheritance (which is also a property of Java itself), there are no cardinality restrictions, or datatype facets and reasoner support is missing. Using only the *JADE* ontologies, there is no way to, for example, define a team condition restricted to having exactly two computers with between four and eight processor cores. Creating such a class expression would require writing custom Java code to supplement the *JADE* classes. As a result it is not possible to create the team condition dynamically and contain its entire description within a *JADE* ontology class. One of the biggest downsides of *JADE* ontologies is also that they are hardly reusable. They cannot be used outside of a *JADE* agent system, which makes them rather unpopular. All these disadvantages of the *JADE* ontologies make them applicable only to very simple ontologies with basic vocabularies. Let us now present a solution that does not suffer from such problems.

[9] http://www.fipa.org/specs/fipa00008/SC00008I.html

As presented above, in the *AiG* system, it is essential to be able to transfer arbitrary fragments of OWL ontologies, including TBox definitions of classes, used for representing constraints and requirements. Previously, this problem has been discussed in Schiemann and Schreiber (2006), and resulted in creation of the *JadeOWL Codec* (Schiemann). Unfortunately, this plugin was extremely tightly integrated with the commercial RacerPro[10] reasoner, and its development seems to have stopped before the release of OWL 2 specification. Therefore, a *JADE* plugin called *JadeOWL* was developed, aimed at providing OWL support to the agent message processing. The *JadeOWL* uses the OWL API[11] interface and improves upon it by integrating it with *JADE* communication routines and adding other useful features.

A direct mapping of OWL 2 into any static object-oriented programming language is not possible; i.e., there is no way to represent OWL as Java classes while preserving its dynamic structure and properties (a partial solution to this problem can be found in Xin-yu and Juan-zi (2009)). Therefore, as opposed to the existing solutions, it was decided that any information instance, such as information about teams or negotiation deals, will be stored and accessed as OWL formatted text files. Thus, the plugin had to provide interface to files viewed both as a raw text, and as an OWL ontology; i.e., after passing a raw file, the plugin had to be able to probe the structure of the ontology, extract classes and instances, as well as their properties. In this way the plugin had to be able to serve as a high level interface to the structure and content of ontological messages, passed between *JADE* agents.

In communication scenarios considered here, data is prepared as a piece of the OWL ontology. The OWL content that is encoded in the message can contain any valid OWL entity including classes, instances, properties definitions, annotation properties, imports declarations and so on. The actual syntax can be any OWL expression supported by OWL 2. Currently the supported syntaxes include: Manchester, functional, RDF/XML, OWL/XML, and the Turtle syntax. Note that, as indicated above, the *AiG* ontologies are stored and communicated in the RDF/XML format. Using this format guarantees that the used ontologies can be read by any OWL 2 tool because the support for the RDF/XML in the OWL ontologies is a requirement set by the official OWL documents.

Although messages contain raw OWL data, their interpretation is done internally by the plugin, which separates the syntax from the semantics. In this way agents can access the information without the need to parse the text. This interpretation requires reasoning about the data. Therefore, an instance of a semantic reasoner had to be bundled with the communication plugin. *JadeOWL* currently supports: HermiT,[12] Pellet,[13] and FaCT++[14] reasoners. However, in the *AiG* implementation, the Pellet reasoner is used. Note that reasoners are used not only by the codec, but also provide

---

[10]http://www.racer-systems.com/

[11]http://owlapi.sourceforge.net/

[12]HermiT OWL Reasoner, http://hermit-reasoner.com/

[13]Pellet: OWL 2 Reasoner for Java, http://clarkparsia.com/pellet/

[14]OWL: FaCT++, http://owl.man.ac.uk/factplusplus/

the infrastructure for all agent reasoning. For instance, the *CIC* infrastructure uses it to match registered resource descriptions (teams, or worker candidate, profiles) against restrictions expressed with class expressions—for instance, in the two scenarios described in Sect. 9.2.

The design of the system requires agents to have shared (public) knowledge, as well as private knowledge. For example every agent in the Grid needs to understand basic concepts such as a computing node. This knowledge is considered to be shared by every agent and does not depend on its role in the system. On the other hand, detailed information about every team in the Grid is, by design, gathered in the *CIC* infrastructure. This information can be considered an example of the private knowledge of the *CIC*; i.e., it is up to the *CIC Agent* to decide how and with whom to share this knowledge. The separation of knowledge into public and private parts creates a need for a query language that would allow agents to ask specific questions about the private knowledge of other agents. This need is satisfied by the *JadeOWL* A-Box query language.

The *JadeOWL* query language provides a way to ask questions about the OWL ontologies using pieces of the OWL code. Any query can be answered locally or sent to another agent to be answered there. An answer to a query is a piece of data in the OWL format. To extract data (e.g., an OWL instance) from an ontology, a custom OWL class is created—a defined class called the "query class". The exact structure of this class depends on the data that needs to be extracted. For example, if the *CIC* is asked for agent teams with an IBM Linux machine, it sends information received from the *LAgent* to the *JadeOWL* plugin. The plugin creates an OWL class that extends the definition of the OWL class describing the team advertisements, but also contains an OWL property restrictions that forces any instance of this class to be a team with an IBM Linux computer. Other types of restrictions (like the cardinality restriction) supported by OWL 2[15] are also available.

Here, the reasoner performs consistency and satisfiability tests on the new class in the context of the ontology. If the tests fail, it means that either the class cannot have any instances or it contradicts other information in the ontology. In this case, an exception is thrown and the reasoner output is routed back to the creator of the instance, to provide information about the problem and, possibly, how to fix it. After passing the tests, the class prepared in this way is presented to the reasoner that finds all its instances. The prepared OWL instances are sent back to the *LAgent* that requested the information.

The *JadeOWL* is used in any communication routine required by the system. For example, advertising a team by the *LMaster* involves sending an instance of an OWL class (describing the team) to the *CIC*, which recognizes it as a team advertisement and stores it in an OWL file. When asked by the *LAgent*, it filters all stored instances, to satisfy the specified constraints.

To summarize, the *JadeOWL* plugin aids creation of OWL classes and instances by producing and structuring the actual OWL text, while the reasoner (that is internal to the plugin) performs the validity/consistency checks and filtering. The

[15]http://www.w3.org/TR/owl2-overview/

A-Box query system assists in finding teams or agents that fit the criteria defined by the *User* via the GUI. The *JadeOWL* also intermediates in the agent-to-agent communication, and makes full ontological communication available, while preserving constraints set upon ontologies in the OWL format. Finally, it makes it possible to exploit the dynamic nature of the OWL.

9.6 Negotiations in the System

Let us now assume that the preliminary processes (in the scenarios described in Sect. 9.2) have been completed and a group of team managers (*LMaster* agents) has been selected as potential job executors (see Fig. 9.8). In the next step, the SLA negotiations ensue. The SLA defines agreement reached by the parties, while negotiations are understood as a flow of messages between "parties" (in this case the *LAgents* and the *LMasters*). It should be obvious that, since in the *AiG* system, ontology fragments are passed as the message content (using the above described codec), all negotiation parameters and contract conditions are represented with respective class expressions and properties (from the *AiG ontology*). As stated in Wasielewska et al. (2011), the negotiation process is based on the *FIPA Iterated*

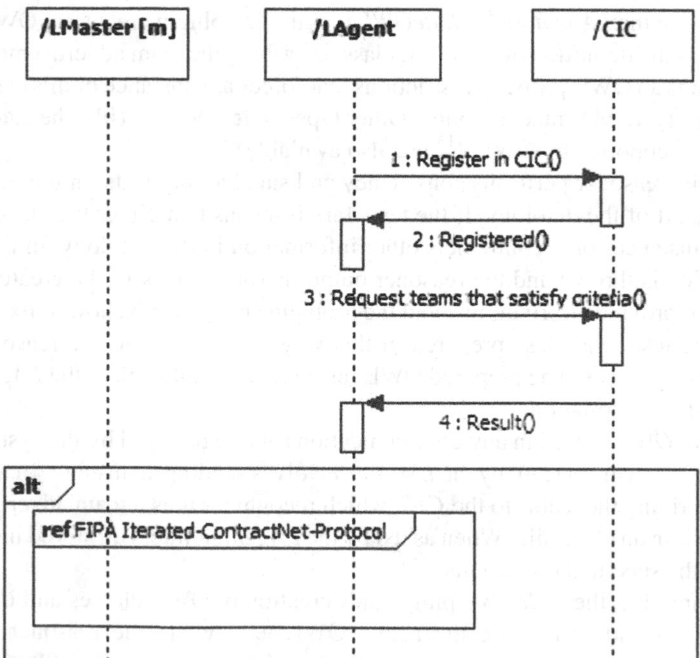

Fig. 9.8 Sequence diagram for job execution scenario

Contract-Net Protocol, and involves both *negotiable*, e.g., deadline penalty, job execution timeline, and *static* parameters, e.g., resource description specified by the *User* through the front-end (described in Sect. 9.4). Currently, a simplified version of the protocol, e.g., the *FIPA Contract-Net Protocol* is used, however, in the future its complete multi-round version of will be utilized.

After *User* specifies contract conditions and restrictions, an appropriate ontology with class expression is generated (by the GUI, see Sect. 9.4) and send to the *LAgent*, which constructs a *Call-For-Proposal* message with an OWL class expression representing restrictions on contract conditions (for either one of the negotiation scenarios) including also the required resource description—for the job execution scenario; or of a resource that the *User* wants to sell—for the team joining scenario. This message is sent to the selected *LMasters*, and those interested in the proposal reply with the OWL instances—individuals representing their offers. Before replying, each *LMaster* agent assesses received offers, based on its internal criteria, e.g., checking if any team member suitable to do a job is available. The *LAgent* verifies if received contract offers match its criteria and selects the best offer, in the case that one can be selected. In Fig. 9.9 the sequence of messages exchanged during the negotiation process based on the *FIPA Iterated Contract-Net Protocol* is depicted.

The following snippet shows a simple class expression with restrictions on the contract, where the deadline penalty should be less than 100, fixed resource utilization price should be less than 500, and the required resource should run Windows Vista SP2 operating system.

```
ObjectProperty: contractedResource
ObjectProperty: fixedUtilizationPrice
ObjectProperty: paymentConditions
ObjectProperty: isRunningOS
DataProperty: deadlinePenalty
DataProperty: peakTimePrice
Class: JobExecutionConditions
Class: PaymentConditions
Class: Pricing
Class: WorkerNode
Individual: vista_sp2
Class: JobExecutionConditions
 EquivalentTo: JobExecutionConditions that contractedResources some
(WorkerNode that isRunningOS value vista_sp2) and paymentConditions some
(PaymentConditions that fixedUnitizationPrice some (Pricing that
peakTimePrice some float[<= 500])) and deadlinePenalty some float[< 100]
```

In response to such a *CFP* message, the following snippet shows a potential offer (contract proposal) instance generated by the *LMaster* agent. Presented contract offer specifies the deadline penalty to be 91.56, and a fixed utilization price to be 450.0. Obviously, in both cases of the *CFP* and the contract proposal, the prices are represented in some imaginary currency.

```
Individual: Contract
 Types: JobExecutionConditions
 Facts: deadlinePenalty "91.56"^^xsd:float, paymentConditions
ContractPaymentConditions
Individual: ContractPaymentConditions
 Types: PaymentConditions
 Facts: fixedUtilizationPrice "450.0"^^xsd:float
```

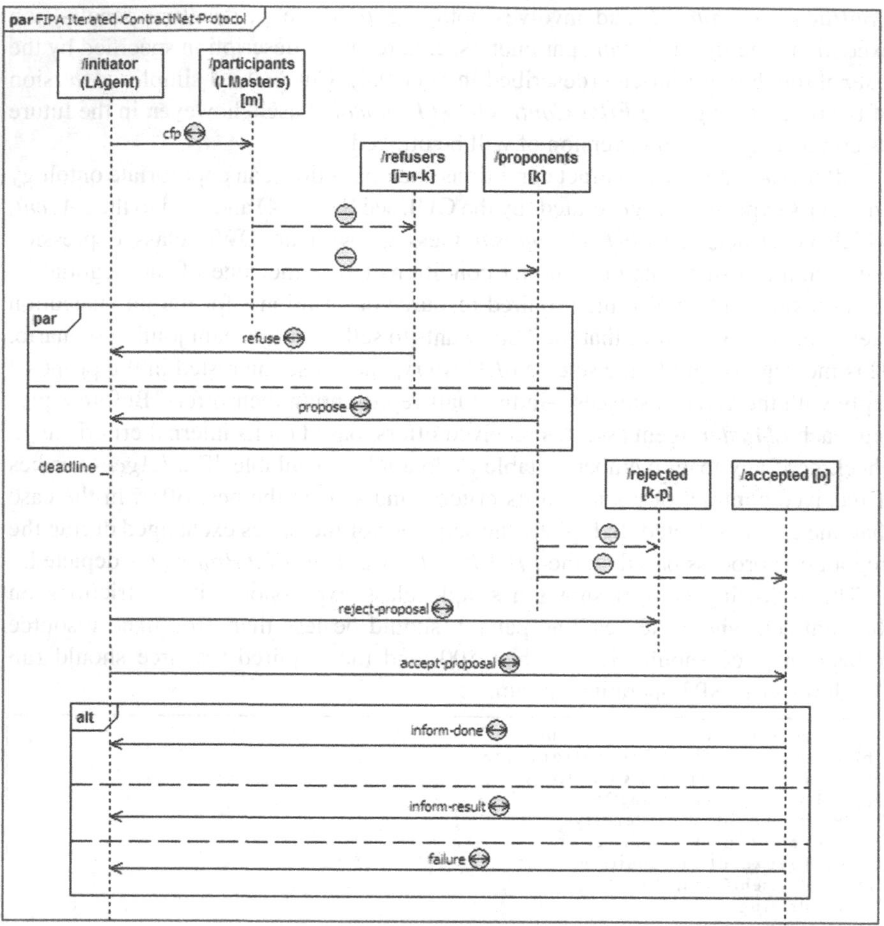

Fig. 9.9 Sequence diagram for contract negotiations

Note that, reasoning in the back-end part of the system is required for both negotiating parties, i.e., the *LAgent* and the *LMaster*s in order to select best offer, or respectively verify if an offer can be prepared (e.g., the contract conditions are acceptable). In the initial proof of concept application, the *LAgent* utilized a linear-additive model for three predefined criteria to select an offer (Kuranowski et al. 2008a). This model is a simple MCA model, in which criteria are treated and assessed independently. In the future, both parties shall use multicriterial analysis to evaluate received proposals and make offers that take into consideration their own ability to fulfill required conditions, as well as preferences. Additional criteria, that became available in the ontology (as compared to the proof of concept application) are also considered. Both negotiation parties should be able to handle arbitrary constraints from the *AiG ontology* based on the restricted property datatype and weight.

Upon receiving the offer from the *LMaster* agent, the *LAgent* uses the reasoner to verify if the received contract offer satisfies the criteria provided by the *User*. On the other hand, the *LMaster* agents may use reasoning and MCA to determine, for instance, the cost of job execution. Note that each resource needed for job execution, e.g., memory, I/O bandwidth, has a pricing property in the ontology. This property specifies the pricing type and the price. To evaluate the total price of the job execution, the *LMaster* combines prices for each required component. Reasoning is also used by the *LMasters* to verify if they are able to execute a given job, i.e., if there is an available member in the team that has resources required to execute a specific job. So far, team members resource descriptions have been stored in the *CIC* component, however, they will also be stored locally so that the *LMaster* can use the reasoner on its local ontological database.

9.7 Concluding Remarks

The aim of this chapter is to illustrate how ontologies and semantic data processing can be used in an actual application, to facilitate contract negotiations. It describes in detail the front-end, which permits the use of the application without knowledge of ontologies, the front-end back-end integration that allows agent systems to use ontologies without the need to turn them to Java classes, and the initial design of the negotiation mechanism. Since all the needed "front-end-tools" are in place, the focus of research will now shift to extending the existing simple SLA negotiations.

Acknowledgements The work of Maria Ganzha and Michał Drozdowicz was supported by the "Funds for Science" of the Polish Ministry for Science and Higher Education for years 2008–2011, as a research project (contract number N516 382434).

References

Dominiak, M., W. Kuranowski, M. Gawinecki, M. Ganzha, and M. Paprzycki. 2006. Utilizing agent teams in Grid resource management—preliminary considerations. In *Proceeding of the IEEE John Vincent Atanasoff conference*, 46–51. Los Alamitos: IEEE CS

Dominiak, M., M. Ganzha, M. Gawinecki, W. Kuranowski, M. Paprzycki, S. Margenov, and I. Lirkov. 2008. Utilizing agent teams in grid resource brokering. *International Transactions on Systems Science and Applications* 3(4): 296–306

Drozdowicz, M., M. Ganzha, M. Paprzycki, R. Olejnik, I. Lirkov, P. Telegin, and M. Senobari. 2009. Ontologies, agents and the grid: An overview. In *Parallel, distributed and grid computing for engineering*, ed. B. Topping and P. Iványi, 117–140. Stirlingshire: Saxe-Coburg

Drozdowicz, M., K. Wasielewska, M. Ganzha, M. Paprzycki, N. Attaui, I. Lirkov, R. Olejnik, D. Petcu, and C. Badica. 2011. Ontology for contract negotiations in agent-based grid resource management system. In *Trends in parallel, distributed, grid and cloud computing for engineering*, ed. P. Ivanyi and B. Topping. Stirlingshire: Saxe-Coburg

Foster, I., N. R. Jennings, and C. Kesselman. 2004. Brain meets brawn: Why grid and agents need each other. In *International joint conference on autonomous agents and multiagent systems*, vol. 1, 8–15. New York: ACM

Ganzha, M., M. Paprzycki, and I. Lirkov. 2007. Trust management in an agent-based grid resource brokering system—preliminary considerations. In: *Applications of mathematics in engineering and economics'33*. AIP Conference Proceeding, ed. M. Todorov, vol. 946, 35–46. College Park: American Institute of Physics

Gawinecki, M., M. Gordon, P. Kaczmarek, and M. Paprzycki. 2005. The problem of agent-client communication on the internet. In *Scalable computing: Practice and experience*, vol. 6, no. 1, 111–123. Poland: Warsaw School of Social Psychology

Gordon, M., M. Paprzycki, and V. Galant. 2002. Agent-client interaction in a Web-based E-commerce system. In *Proceedings of the international symposium on parallel and distributed computing*, 1–10. Iaşi: University of Iaşi Press

Hendler, J. 2001. Agents and the semantic web. *IEEE Intelligent Systems* 16(2): 30–37

Kuranowski, W., M. Ganzha, M. Gawinecki, M. Paprzycki, I. Lirkov, and S. Margenov. 2008a. Forming and managing agent teams acting as resource brokers in the grid—preliminary considerations. *International Journal of Computational Intelligence Research* 4(1): 9–16

Kuranowski, W., M. Ganzha, M. Paprzycki, and I. Lirkov. 2008b. Supervising agent team an agent-based grid resource brokering system initial solution. In *Proceedings of the conference on complex, intelligent and software intensive systems*, ed. F. Xhafa and L. Barolli, 321–326. Los Alamitos: IEEE CS

Schiemann, B. JADEOWL Codec. 2007. http://www8.informatik.uni-erlangen.de/inf8/en/demosdownloads.html

Schiemann, B., and U. Schreiber. 2006. OWL DL as a FIPA ACL content language. In *Proceedings of the workshop on formal ontology for communicating agents*, ed. R. Ferrario, N. Guarino, and L.P. Vot, pp. 73–80. University of Malaga

W3C OWL Working Group. 2009. OWL 2 Web Ontology Language Document Overview W3C Recommendation 27 October 2009. W3C Recommendation, World Wide Web Consortium (W3C). http://www.w3.org/TR/2009/REC-owl2-overview-20091027/

Wasielewska, K., M. Drozdowicz, M. Ganzha, M. Paprzycki, N. Attaui, D. Petcu, C. Badica, R. Olejnik, and I., Lirkov. 2011. Negotiations in an agent-based grid resource brokering systems. In *Trends in parallel, distributed, grid and cloud computing for engineering*, ed. P. Ivanyi and B. Topping. Stirlingshire: Saxe-Coburg

Xin-yu, Y., and L. Juan-zi. 2009. Research on mapping OWL ontology to software code model. *Computer Engineering* 35(3): 36–38

Xing, W., M.D. Dikaiakos, R. Sakellariou, S. Orlando, and D. Laforenza. 2005. Design and development of a core grid ontology. In *Proceedings of the CoreGRID workshop: Integrated research in grid computing*, ed. S. Gorlatch and M. Danelutto, pp. 21–31. Italy: Pisa

Part III
Norms

In the last decades norms have been an issue of growing concern in Multi Agent Systems and the importance of these mechanisms to regulate electronic institutions and electronic commerce and to deal with coordination and security issues has been largely recognized. The study of norms has been opened up to new approaches, such as cognitive science, behavioural and evolutionary economics, and has largely profited from the advent of computational and simulation-based social science. This interdisciplinary approach results in an innovative understanding of norms and their dynamics, both at the individual and social level. This part aims to provide an overview of current advances, approaches and problems related to the study of norms in the context of Multi-Agent Systems. Both formal and computational models of norms and normative systems are presented, including formal analysis of normative concepts and foundational models of norms; agent and systems architectures for implementing norms, and implemented systems. Finally the role of norms in combination with other agreement technologies, such as argumentation and trust, is discussed.

Chapter 10 gives us an overview of the fundamental issues and problems in the area of deontic logic. The authors focus on three main categories of problems. The first category is concerned with the nature of norms. The second category covers phenomena of conflict, violation and revision. The third category relates to deontic phenomena in the context of other logical structures. This first chapter introduces a set of concepts and notions that facilitate the understanding of the remaining contributions of this part of the book. Chapter 11 addresses several aspects of the treatment of norms, namely norm learning (or recognition), norm conflict, norm enforcement, and the measure of success of norms. In particular, the authors discuss how the merging of Agent Based Modelling and Multi Agent Systems appears as a promising direction to give strong, innovative impulse to the study of norms. Chapter 12 suggests a set of key ideas and perspectives connecting norms and games. In Chap. 13, the authors presents the main lines of inquiry of Artificial Intelligence and Law (AI and Law). It is argued that a rich picture of the law is emerging from the AI and Law research, which can complement and integrate not only research in law and legal theory, but also other attempts to provide formal and computational models of norms. Chapter 14 is aimed to understand how norms regulate agents' conduct and how norms impact on agents' reasoning and behavior. In particular, it focuses on the development of agents able to manage norms in some appropriate fashion. Chapter 15 is devoted to analyzing the complex relationship between norms and trust. Finally, in Chap. 16 an overview of the existing work in the field of argumentation and norms is presented. The authors identify various challenges for the domain and categorize them into two broad categories: how to argue about norms, and how norms influence the argumentation process.

Giulia Andrighetto and Cristiano Castelfranchi
Editors Part "Norms"

Chapter 10
Deontic Logic

Jan Broersen, Dov Gabbay, Andreas Herzig, Emiliano Lorini, John-Jules Meyer, Xavier Parent, and Leendert van der Torre

10.1 Introduction

The chapter is organized in ten sections, each of them presenting a fundamental issue or problem in the area of deontic logic. Section 10.2 is about the issue of norms and truth, i.e., whether norms should have truth value. It opposes deontic logic viewed as a logic of normative propositions to deontic logic viewed as a logic of imperatives. Section 10.3 deals with the problem of contrary-to-duty (CTD) reasoning while Sect. 10.4 is about the problem of normative conflicts, i.e., how a logic of norms can represent conflicting obligations both syntactically and semantically. Section 10.5 focuses on the issue of norm revision relating it to the problem of belief revision as studied in the classical approach of Alchourron, Gardenfors and Makinson (AGM). Sections 10.6 and 10.7 consider two fundamental problems in the logical representation of norms, namely the logical representation of the temporal aspects of norms and the logical representation of norms about

J. Broersen (✉) • J.-J. Meyer
Department of Information and Computing Sciences, Universiteit Utrecht, Utrecht, The Netherlands
e-mail: J.M.Broersen@uu.nl; jj@cs.uu.nl

D. Gabbay
Department of Computer Science, King's College London, London, UK
e-mail: dov.gabbay@kcl.ac.uk

A. Herzig • E. Lorini
Logic, Interaction, Language, and Computation Group, IRIT, Université Paul Sabatier, Toulouse, France
e-mail: herzig@irit.fr; Emiliano.Lorini@irit.fr

X. Parent • L. van der Torre
Individual and Collective Reasoning (ICR) group, University of Luxembourg, Walferdange, Luxembourg
e-mail: xavier.parent@uni.lu; leon.vandertorre@uni.lu

S. Ossowski (ed.), *Agreement Technologies*, Law, Governance and Technology Series 8, DOI 10.1007/978-94-007-5583-3_10,

actions (as opposed to norms about states of affairs). Section 10.8 touches on the issue of the relationship between norms and games and, in particular, the problem of the relationship between norms and agents' preferences and the problem of how norms are created through agreement. In Sect. 10.9 the problem of the representation of permissive norms is discussed, while Sect. 10.10 deals with the issue of the relationship between norms and mental attitudes such as beliefs, knowledge, preferences and intentions. Finally, Sect. 10.11 discusses the classical distinction between regulative rules and constitutive rules.

10.2 Norm Without Truth

The first problem is to reconstruct deontic logic in accordance with the idea that norms are neither true nor false. There are two approaches.

The mainstream approach is to reconstruct deontic logic as a logic of normative propositions. The idea is that, though norms are neither true nor false, one may state that (according to the norms), something ought to be done: the statement "John ought to leave the room" is, then, a true or false description of a normative situation. Such a statement is usually called a normative proposition, as distinguished from a norm. The Input/Output (I/O) framework of Makinson and van der Torre (2000), and the bi-modal system NOBL due to Åqvist (2008), are two different reconstructions of deontic logic as a logic of normative propositions, thus conceived.

The other approach consists of reconstructing deontic logic as a logic of imperatives. This approach is documented in Hansen (2005, 2008), to which the reader is referred for further details.

10.3 Reasoning About Norm Violation

The question of how to deal with violations and obligations resulting from violations is known as the problem of contrary-to-duty (CTD) reasoning (Chisholm 1963). It is of key importance to the analysis of multi-agent systems. Agents are supposed to be autonomous normative entities. So, they must be able to take into account the existence of social norms in their decisions (either to follow or violate the latter norms). Sanctions are also needed to increase the degree of predictibility of the system (Castelfranchi et al. 2000). Since SDL[1] was criticized for not being able to deal with CTD duties, the issue of CTD has not disappeared from the stage of deontic logic. New standards have been developed in order to make deontic logic suitable for application to the analysis of normative multi-agent systems.

[1] SDL stands for "Standard Deontic Logic". This is a misnomer, because it is no longer considered a standard.

These standards are documented in Hansson (1969), Loewer and Belzer (1983), Prakken and Sergot (1997), van der Torre and Tan (1997), Carmo and Jones (2002), Makinson and van der Torre (2001) and Parent (2003).

10.4 Normative Conflicts

There are two main questions here. The first one is: how can deontic logic accommodate possible conflicts between norms? The first systems of deontic logic precluded the possibility of any such conflict. This makes them unsuitable as a tool for analyzing normative reasoning. Different ways to accommodate normative conflicts have been studied over the last 15 years. A comparative study of them can be found in Goble (2007).

The second question is: how can the resolution of conflicts amongst norms be semantically modeled? An intuitively appealing modeling approach involves using a priority relation defined on norms. There have been several proposals to this effect, and the reader is referred to the discussions in Boella and van der Torre (2003), Hansen (2005, 2008), Horty (2007) and Parent (2010, 2011). An open question is whether tools developed for so-called non-monotonic reasoning are suitable for obligations and permissions.

10.5 Revision of a Set of Norms

Alchourrón and Makinson were the first to study the changes of a legal code (Alchourrón and Makinson 1981, 1982). The question is: how to revise a set of regulations or obligations? Does belief revision (as modelled by the so-called AGM model (Alchourrón et al. 1985)) offer a satisfactory framework for norms revision?

Some of the AGM axioms seem to be rational requirements in a legal context, whereas they have been criticized when imposed on belief change operators. An example is the *success* postulate, requiring that a new input must always be accepted in the belief set. It is reasonable to impose such a requirement when we wish to enforce a new norm or obligation. However, it gives rise to irrational behaviors when imposed to a belief set, as observed for instance in Gabbay et al. (2003).

On the other hand, when we turn to a proper representation of norms, like in the input/output logic framework, the AGM principles prove to be too general to deal with the revision of a normative system. For example, one difference between revising a set of propositions and revising a set of regulations (pointed out in Boella et al. 2009) is the following: when a new norm is added, coherence may be restored modifying some of the existing norms, not necessarily retracting any of them.

Another type of change that has been studied in deontic logic is the aggregation of regulations (Booth et al. 2006; Cholvy and Cuppens 1999; Grégoire 2004).

10.6 Time

Most formalisms do not have temporal operators in the object language, nor do they have, in their standard formulation, an interpretation in temporal models. Yet for several scenarios and decisions involving deontic reasoning, the temporal aspect of the reasoning seems crucial, and several researchers have sought to study logics for the interactions between temporal and deontic modalities. The research question is: what is the relation between deontic conditionals and temporal deontic modalities?

Two natural concepts to be considered are 'validity time' and 'reference time' of an obligation, prohibition or permission. The validity time is the point in time where a deontic modality is true (surpassing the issue of Sect. 10.2 here we simply assume normative modalities have truth values relative to some coherent body of norms that is left implicit) and the reference time is the point in time the obligation, prohibition or permission applies to. For instance, we can have the obligation now (validity time) to show up at the dentist's tomorrow (reference time).

Systems dealing with these temporal differences have been studied, for instance, in Åqvist and Hoepelman (1981) and Thomason (1981). Subtleties in expressing deontic temporal statements involving deontic deadlines have been studied in Broersen et al. (2004) and Broersen (2006).

10.7 Action

We often think of deontic modalities as applying to actions instead of states of affairs. The problems arising in this area are the following: how do we combine deontic modalities with action modalities? How do deontic and action modalities interact. Which action formalisms are best suited for a deontic extension?

Two approaches to deontic action logic prominent in the literature are dynamic deontic logic (Meyer 1988) and deontic *stit* logic (Horty 2001). In dynamic deontic logic normative modalities are reduced to dynamic logic action modalities by using violation constants. Prohibition, for instance, is modeled as the dynamic logic conditional assertion that if the action is executed, a violation will occur. In deontic *stit* logic, the perspective on action is different. Where in dynamic logic actions are objects that are given proper names in the object language, in *stit* logic actions derive their identity from the agent(s) executing them and the effect they achieve. This allows for a proper theory of agency, ability and joint ability. In Horty (2001) normativity is introduced in *stit* theory by means of a deontic ideality ordering. But the alternative of violation constants has also been used in the *stit* context (Bartha 1993; Broersen 2011). A perspective that is symmetric to violation constants is taken in Herzig et al. (2011a) where a dynamic logic is introduced that has special constants encoding an agent's permissions to perform actions (and these deontic abilities are opposed to constants encoding an agent's ontic or non-deontic abilities).

10.8 Norm Emergence and Games

To understand why a norm emerges in an agent society, one has to understand in what sense norms are related to the social preferences and abilities of coalitions of agents. This is the setting of game theory (see also Chap. 12). In deontic logic we distinguish between situations where norms are likely to be in-line with the individual preference, like in coordination problems, and situations where norms, once established, are likely to oppose the preferences of individuals.

Broersen et al. (2008) models the dependency of socially optimal norms on the underlying preferences, in the context of Coalition Logic (Pauly 2002). There it is assumed that the reachability of outcomes that are optimal for the whole group gives rise to a social norm saying that sub-groups should not pursue their own best interest if that conflicts with the group's interest. There are close connections with other work in deontic logic (Kooi and Tamminga 2008) that have to be explored. Open questions include the generalization to the fully strategic case (i.e., from normal game forms to extensive game forms), and the connection with logical models for the dynamics of preferences (Liu 2008).

Norm acceptance can also be considered a game played with other agents subject to the same norm. This idea is explored in Ågotnes et al. (2007). An open question is the complexity of deciding whether or not a normative system is a Nash-equilibrium (or 'Nash-implementation'), relative to a set of other normative systems.

Another interesting issue is how norms are created through agreement. Lorini and Longin (2008) and Lorini et al. (2009) have proposed a logical model of collective acceptance assuming that the existence and the dynamics of a norm depend on its acceptance by the members of an institution (e.g. the existence and dynamics of the rules of chess depend on their acceptance by chess players).

10.9 Permissive Norms

For a long time, it was naively assumed that permission can simply be taken as the dual of obligation, just as possibility is the dual of necessity in modal logic. Something is permitted if its negation is not forbidden. Nowadays in deontic logic a more fine-grained notion of permission is used. The notions of explicit permission, dynamic permission,[2] and permission as exception to a pre-existing obligation are also used. One main finding is that these normative concepts can all be given a well-defined semantics in terms of Input/Output logic (Boella and van der Torre 2008; Makinson and van der Torre 2003; Stolpe 1997, 2010). The main open problem concerns their proof-theory, which is still lacking.

[2] A dynamic permission is forward-looking and is like a constitutional right – it sets limits on what can be forbidden.

10.10 Knowledge and Intentions

For a complete logical picture of rational agency, we need to study the interactions of the deontic modalities with other motivational attitudes like desire and intention, and with epistemic attitudes like belief and knowledge.

The 'BOID' architecture (Broersen et al. 2002, 2005) studies the interplay between beliefs, obligations, intentions and desires in the formation of agent goals. One of the issues discussed in the context of BOID is that the interplay between 'internal' motivations and 'external' motivations (originating from norms of the agent's social context), enables one to distinguish between several agent types. For instance, a benevolent agent will give priority to norms, while an egocentric agent will not. The difference between benevolent agents and egocentric agents shows that the main issue here is 'norm acceptance'. Benevolent agents are more willing to internalize, or accept norms than egocentric ones.

In Broersen (2011) the relation between deontic modalities and epistemic modalities is studied in the context of formalizing different modes of acting. Different modes of acting are relevant in a deontic context, since the deontic status of an act depends, for instance, on whether it is performed knowingly, intentionally, deliberately, etc.

10.11 Constitutive Norms

In legal and social theory one encounters various types of norms. First of all there are the regulative norms describing obligations, prohibitions and permissions. But also there are so-called constitutive norms, which make possible basic 'institutional' actions such as the making of contracts, the issuing of fines, the decreeing of divorces. Basically they tell us what *counts as* what for a given institution. An example is that "cars count as vehicles" in a certain institution having to do with traffic. As pointed out in Boella and van der Torre (2006a), constitutive norms have been identified as the key mechanism to normative reasoning in dynamic and uncertain environments, for example to realize agent communication and electronic contracting.

Although the 'count-as' relation "X counts as Y in context C" was already introduced by Searle (1969), the paper by Jones and Sergot (1996) is often credited for having launched the area of logical investigation of constitutive norms. There, the counts-as relation is viewed as expressing the fact that a given action "is a sufficient condition to guarantee that the institution creates some (usually normative) state of affairs". A conditional connective $\Rightarrow_s$ is used to express the "counts-as" connection holding in the context of an institution s. In his thesis (2007) Grossi disentangles various notions of counts-as, such as classificatory, proper classificatory, and constitutive counts-as. He also treats their formal logical representations and axiomatisations (in modal logic), as well as their formal relations, and as such clarifies and improves upon the seminal work of Jones and Sergot mentioned above (also cf. Grossi et al. 2006).

When defining constitutive norms, the main issue is in defining their relation with regulative norms. To this end, Boella and van der Torre (2006b) use the notion of a logical architecture combining several logics into a more complex logical system, also called logical input/output nets (or lions). Grossi (2007, p. 104) argues that regulative norms may be viewed as a special case of constitutive norms by employing some kind of Anderson's reduction and putting Obligated(p) as "¬ p counts as V", where V stands for a violation atom. An approach combining a logic of action and deontic ability with a counts-as connective is in Herzig et al. (2011b).

It is expected that deontic logic, as a field of study, will increasingly attract the interest of researchers working in computer science, philosophy, legal theory and even cognitive science. Deontic logic is at the center of many new developments in computer science, motivated by the need to describe distributed interacting autonomous systems at higher levels of abstraction. In philosophy, theories of agency and action can only be seriously evaluated if normative aspects in the form of responsibility, blame and excuse are added to the picture. In legal theory there is a tendency towards formalization and automation and this cannot be achieved without input from deontic logic. Finally, in cognitive science, computational models of the mind might find inspiration in the models used to interpret systems of deontic logic, and vice versa.

References

Ågotnes, T., M. Wooldridge, and W. van der Hoek. 2007. Normative system games. In *Proceedings of the sixth international conference on autonomous agents and multiagent systems (AAMAS 2007), IFAMAAS (2007)*, Honolulu, ed. M. Huhns and O. Shehory, 876–883.

Alchourrón, C. E., and D. C. Makinson. 1981. Hierarchies of regulations and their logic. In *New studies in deontic logic*, ed. R. Hilpinen, 125–148. Dordrecht: D. Reidel.

Alchourrón, C. E., and D. C. Makinson. 1982. The logic of theory change: Contraction functions and their associated revision functions. *Theoria* 48: 14–37.

Alchourrón, C., P. Gärdenfors, and D. Makinson. 1985. On the logic of theory change: Partial meet contraction and revision functions. *Journal of Symbolic Logic* 50: 510–530.

Åqvist, L. 2008. Alchourrón and Bulygin on deontic logic and the logic of norm-propositions: Axiomatization and representability results. *Logique et Analyse* 51(203): 225–261.

Åqvist, L., and J. Hoepelman. 1981. Some theorems about a tree system of deontic tense logic. In *New studies in deontic logic*, ed. R. Hilpinen, 187–221. Dordrecht: D. Reidel.

Bartha, P. 1993. Conditional obligation, deontic paradoxes, and the logic of agency. *Annals of Mathematics and Artificial Intelligence* 9(1–2): 1–23.

Boella, G., and L. van der Torre. 2003. Permissions and obligations in hierarchical normative systems. In *Proceedings of the eighth international conference on artificial intelligence and law (ICAIL'03)*. Edimburgh, 109–118. ACM Press.

Boella, G., and L. van der Torre. 2006a. Constitutive norms in the design of normative multiagent systems. In *Computational logic in multi-agent systems, 6th international workshop, CLIMA VI*. LNCS, vol. 3900, 303–319. London: Springer.

Boella, G., and L. van der Torre. 2006b. A logical architecture of a normative system. In *Deontic logic and artificial normative systems. Proceedings of the 8th international workshop on deontic logic in computer scicence*, DEON 2006, Utrecht, ed. L. Goble and J. J. C. Meyer. Berlin: Springer.

Boella, G., and L. van der Torre. 2008. Institutions with a hierarchy of authorities in distributed dynamic environments. *Artificial Intelligence and Law* 16(1): 53–71.

Boella, G., G. Pigozzi, and L. van der Torre. 2009. Five guidelines for normative multiagent systems. In *JURIX*, Rotterdam, 21–30.

Booth, R., S. Kaci, and L. van der Torre. 2006. Merging rules: Preliminary version. In *Proceedings of the eleventh international workshop on non-monotonic reasoning (NMR'06)*, Lake District, UK, 2–5 June 2006.

Broersen, J. 2006. Strategic deontic temporal logic as a reduction to ATL, with an application to Chisholm's scenario. In *Proceedings 8th international workshop on deontic logic in computer science (DEON'06)*. Lecture Notes in Computer Science, vol. 4048, ed. L. Goble and J. J. Meyer, 53–68. Berlin: Springer.

Broersen, J. 2011. Deontic epistemic *stit* logic distinguishing modes of mens rea. *Journal of Applied Logic* 9(2): 127–152.

Broersen, J., M. Dastani, J. Hulstijn, and L. van der Torre. 2002. Goal generation in the BOID architecture. *Cognitive Science Quarterly Journal* 2(3–4): 428–447.

Broersen, J., F. Dignum, V. Dignum, and J. J. Meyer. 2004. Designing a deontic logic of deadlines. In *Proceedings 7th international workshop on deontic logic in computer science (DEON'06)*. Lecture Notes in Computer Science, vol. 3065, ed. A. Lomuscio and D. Nute, 43–56. Berlin: Springer.

Broersen, J., M. Dastani, and L. van der Torre. 2005. Beliefs, obligations, intentions and desires as components in an agent architecture. *International Journal of Intelligent Systems* 20(9): 893–920.

Broersen, J., R. Mastop, J. J. C. Meyer, and P. Turrini. 2008. A deontic logic for socially optimal norms. In *Proceedings 9th international workshop on deontic logic in computer science (DEON'08)*. Lecture Notes in Computer Science, vol. 5076, ed. L. v. d. Torre and R. v. d. Meyden, 218–232. Berlin: Springer.

Carmo, J., and A. Jones. 2002. Deontic logic and contrary-to-duties. In *Handbook of philosophical logic*, vol. 8, 2nd ed, ed. D. Gabbay and F. Guenthner, 265–344. Dordrecht: Kluwer Academic.

Castelfranchi, C., F. Dignum, C. M. Jonker, and J. Treur. 2000. Deliberative normative agents: Principles and architecture. In *6th international workshop on intelligent agents VI, agent theories, architectures, and languages (ATAL)*, 364–378. London: Springer.

Chisholm, R. 1963. Contrary-to-duty imperatives and deontic logic. *Analysis* 24(2): 33–36.

Cholvy, L., and F. Cuppens. 1999. Reasoning about norms provided by conflicting regulations. In *Norms, logics and information systems*, ed. P. McNamara and H. Prakken. Amsterdam: IOS.

Gabbay, D. M., G. Pigozzi, and J. Woods. 2003. Controlled revision – an algorithmic approach for belief revision. *Journal of Logic and Computation* 13(1): 3–22.

Goble, L. 2007. Prima facie norms, normative conflicts and dilemmas. In *Handbook of deontic logic and normative systems*, ed. D. Gabbay, J. Horty, R. van der Meyden, and L. van der Torre. London: College Publications.

Grégoire, E. 2004. Fusing legal knowledge. In *Proceedings of the 2004 IEEE international conference on information reuse and integration (IEEE-IRI'2004)*, Las Vegas, 522–529.

Grossi, D. 2007. Designing invisible handcuffs: Formal investigations in institutions and organizations for multi-agent systems. Ph.D. thesis, Utrecht University.

Grossi, D., J. J. C. Meyer, and F. Dignum. 2006. Classificatory aspects of counts-as: An analysis in modal logic. *Journal of Logic and Computation* 16(5): 613–643.

Hansen, J. 2005. Deontic logics for prioritized imperatives. *Artificial Intelligence and Law* 14: 1–34.

Hansen, J. 2008. Prioritized conditional imperatives: Problems and a new proposal. *Journal of Autonomous Agents and Multi-Agent Systems* 17(1): 11–35.

Hansson, B. 1969. An analysis of some deontic logics. *Noûs* 3: 373–398.

Herzig, A., E. Lorini, F. Moisan, and N. Troquard. 2011a. A dynamic logic of normative systems. In *Proceedings of the twenty-second international joint conference on artificial intelligence (IJCAI'11)*. Barcelona: IJCAI/AAAI.

Herzig, A., E. Lorini, and N. Troquard. 2011b. A dynamic logic of institutional actions (regular paper). In *Computational logic in multi-agent systems (CLIMA)*, LNC-S/LNAI, ed. J. Leite and P. Torroni. Berlin: Springer.

Horty, J. F. 2001. *Agency and deontic logic*. Oxford: Oxford University Press.

Horty, J. 2007. Defaults with priorities. *Journal of Philosophical Logic* 36: 367–413.

Jones, A., and M. Sergot. 1996. A formal characterisation of institutionalised power. *Journal of IGPL* 3: 427–443.

Kooi, B., and A. Tamminga. 2008. Moral conflicts between groups of agents. *Journal of Philosophical Logic* 37(1): 1–21.

Liu, F. 2008. Changing for the better: Preference dynamics and agent diversity. Ph.D. thesis. ILLC Dissertation Series, Amsterdam.

Loewer, B., and M. Belzer. 1983. Dyadic deontic detachment. *Synthese* 54(2): 295–318.

Lorini, E., and D. Longin. 2008. A logical account of institutions: From acceptances to norms via legislators. In *Proceedings of the international conference on principles of knowledge representation and reasoning (KR 2008)*, ed. G. Brewka and J. Lang, 38–48. Menlo Park: AAAI.

Lorini, E., D. Longin, B. Gaudou, and A. Herzig. 2009. The logic of acceptance: Grounding institutions on agents' attitudes. *Journal of Logic and Computation* 19(6): 901–940.

Makinson, D., and L. van der Torre. 2000. Input-output logics. *Journal of Philosophical Logic* 29(4): 383–408.

Makinson, D., and L. van der Torre. 2001. Constraints for input-output logics. *Journal of Philosophical Logic* 30(2): 155–185.

Makinson, D., and L. van der Torre. 2003. Permissions from an input-output perspective. *Journal of Philosophical Logic* 32(4): 391–416.

Meyer, J. J. C. 1988. A different approach to deontic logic: Deontic logic viewed as a variant of dynamic logic. *Notre Dame Journal of Formal Logic* 29: 109–136.

Parent, X. 2003. Remedial interchange, contrary-to-duty obligation and commutation. *Journal of Applied Non-Classical Logics* 13(3/4): 345–375.

Parent, X. 2010. Moral particularism and deontic logic. In *Proceedings of the 10th international workshop on deontic logic (DEON'10)*, pp. 84–96, ed. G. Governatori and G. Sartor. Berlin/Heidelberg: Springer.

Parent, X. 2011. Moral particularism in the light of deontic logic. *Artificial Intelligence and Law* 19: 75–98.

Pauly, M. 2002. A modal logic for coalitional power in games. *Journal of Logic and Computation* 12(1): 149–166.

Prakken, H., and M. Sergot. 1997. Dyadic deontic logic and contrary-to-duty obligation. In *Defeasible deontic logic*, ed. D. Nute, 223–262. Dordrecht: Kluwer Academic.

Searle, J. 1969. *Speech acts. An essay in the philosophy of language*. Cambridge: Cambridge University Press.

Stolpe, A. 1997. Relevance, derogation and permission. In *Defeasible deontic logic*, ed. D. Nute, 98–115. Dordrecht: Kluwer Academic.

Stolpe, A. 2010. A theory of permission based on the notion of derogation. *Journal of Applied Logic* 8(1): 97–113.

Thomason, R. H. 1981. Deontic logic as founded on tense logic. In *New studies in deontic logic*, ed. R. Hilpinen, 165–176. Dordrecht: D. Reidel.

van der Torre, L., and Y. H. Tan. 1997. The many faces of defeasibility in defeasible deontic logic. In *Defeasible deontic logic*, ed. D. Nute, 79–121. Dordrecht: Kluwer Academic.

Chapter 11
(Social) Norms and Agent-Based Simulation

Giulia Andrighetto, Stephen Cranefield, Rosaria Conte, Martin Purvis, Maryam Purvis, Bastin Tony Roy Savarimuthu, and Daniel Villatoro

11.1 Introduction

This chapter aims to identify the main relevant steps in the evolution of norms as well as some of the factors or determinants of such a process, and to discuss the most urgent scientific tasks to be fulfilled within a community of scientists committed to the study of norms. It is clearly the case that the scientific study of norms needs innovation and opening up to new instruments, new tools, new competencies, and especially new perspectives and approaches. In the last 50 years or so, the issue of norms has been of growing concern for moral and analytical philosophers and for several sub-communities within the social and behavioral sciences (see also Chap. 12). Our understanding of norms did not make significant progress until the advent of computational and simulation-based social science. The formal study of prosocial behavior accomplished within evolutionary game theory produced the most interesting results when scientists deducing macroscopic properties, such as norm-based societies, from properties at the microscopic level, started to look at the

G. Andrighetto (✉)
Institute of Cognitive Science and Technologies, CNR, Rome, Italy
e-mail: giulia.andrighetto@istc.cnr.it

S. Cranefield • M. Purvis • M. Purvis • B.T.R. Savarimuthu
Information Science Department, University of Otago, Dunedin, New Zealand
e-mail: scranefield@infoscience.otago.ac.nz; mpurvis@infoscience.otago.ac.nz; tehrany@infoscience.otago.ac.nz; TonyR@infoscience.otago.ac.nz

R. Conte
Institute of Cognitive Science and Technologies, CNR, Rome, Italy
e-mail: rosaria.conte@istc.cnr.it

D. Villatoro
IIIA – CSIC, Barcelona, Spain
e-mail: dvillatoro@iiia.csic.es

S. Ossowski (ed.), *Agreement Technologies*, Law, Governance and Technology Series 8, DOI 10.1007/978-94-007-5583-3_11,

conditions at which prosocial equilibria emerge. Rather than deducing equilibria from the bottom up, they inverted the methodological procedure: they started to wonder what minimal conditions are required for a certain effect to occur. This is not a cost-free procedure. It brought about a number of counterproductive effects, the most important being a certain degree of arbitrariness of the models developed (for a survey, see Conte and Paolucci 2002). The simulation-based study of the emergence of cooperation and norms started by Axelrod (1984) led to a myriad of agent-based models that are almost totally ad hoc. But interdisciplinarity helps. By the time the simulation-based study of social phenomena had become prominent, another computational field at the intersection between the social sciences and artificial intelligence had already come to the front stage of science, and that is (Multi) Agent Systems. This field is strongly indebted to the logic-based study of action, mental states, and social facts. Unlike game theory, this formal tradition is concerned with the mechanisms of agency at different levels of reality, more than its products. As argued in this chapter, the merging of Agent-Based Modelling (ABM) and Multi-Agent Systems (MAS) appears as a promising direction to give a strong, innovative boost to the study of norms.

11.2 Norm Learning

Research in Normative Multi-Agent Systems often assumes that norms are specified by the institution and all the agents in the society know about these norms ahead of time (Aldewereld et al. 2006; Shoham and Tennenholtz 1995). These works aim to study mechanisms for norm enforcement. On the other hand, researchers interested in the emergence of norms do not assume that agents know what the norms are a priori, but investigate how agents can derive norms from interactions. However, in studying how these norms emerge, most works model interactions based on simple cooperation or coordination games (Sen and Airiau 2007). Agents using these models can undertake few actions (e.g. cooperate and defect). Game-based interaction models do not capture rich interactions that take place in real life and also do not consider the large action-space of agents. So, there is a need for studying mechanisms that take into account the large number of actions that an agent is capable of performing. Some work in this direction has begun. For example, the work of Savarimuthu et al. makes use of a data-mining approach for the identification of norms (Savarimuthu et al. 2010a,b). However, the number of actions that are performed by agents in their work are small (e.g. four in Savarimuthu et al. 2010a, eight in Savarimuthu et al. 2010b). We believe this area has potential for further investigation. Additionally, how much domain knowledge an agent possesses and also its prior knowledge about norms may play a role in norm identification. These aspects can be explored further.

Another limitation of current simulation-based works on norms is the lack of consideration of all three aspects of active learning on the part of an agent (i.e. learning based on doing, observing and communicating). Most studies that investigate norm emergence using simulations employing simple games have only used learning based on doing (Sen and Airiau 2007; Walker and Wooldridge 1995). Some works have considered observation-based learning (Epstein 2001; Hoffmann 2003) and only a few have considered communication-based learning (Verhagen 2001; Walker and Wooldridge 1995). We believe there is a lot of scope for integrating these three types of learning wherever applicable. The EMIL framework (Andrighetto et al. 2007) and the framework for norm identification (Savarimuthu et al. 2010b) have considered all three aspects. However, several works have not considered combining these three aspects (Savarimuthu et al. 2011). We believe this is a good venue for future investigation. Additional problems that may arise such as the problem of lying in communication-based learning will need to be addressed.

An important aspect in the learning of norms is to endow agents with the ability to identify the presence of norms through sanctions and rewards. Thus, those actions that signal the presence of norms can be used as the starting point for learning norms. Some works have considered signalling as a starting point for norm identification (Savarimuthu et al. 2010a,b). More work in this area can be undertaken. For example, the question of *where do the motivations for these signals come from* can be investigated. The motivations could include the sanctioning agent's utility going below a certain threshold or that the sanctioning agent is altruistic and wants others to behave in a certain way. Additionally, in agent societies the action that is being sanctioned may not be known ahead of time and the sanctions/rewards may emerge dynamically and can also change during time. This can be investigated using simulation systems.

A potential area for the study of norms is to include humans in the simulation loop to seed norms where agents can learn from human agents and also investigate how software agents can recommend norms to humans who can then choose the norm that they believe to be most applicable in a given context.

11.3 Conflicting Norms in Agent Societies

The employment of norms in multi-agent societies parallels the way they are used in human societies. In both contexts, norms represent prescriptions spreading through a population, that are not rigidly encoded in law and that are not enforced by institutional authorities. Instead these normative rules evolve by mutual consent, and their use in society is encouraged in a distributed fashion by sanctioning on the part of the group members, themselves. The advantages of norms is that (a) their distributed enforcement makes them scalable with respect to the size of agent communities and (b) they can evolve according to changing social contexts.

However, the flexibility of agent norms (a strength) also leads to the likelihood of conflicting norms (a potential weakness): two norms may be invoked in a particular situation that dictate incompatible behaviour. Although conflicting norms have received considerable attention in the multi-agent research community (Oren et al. 2008; Vasconcelos et al. 2009), we believe that there are still many interesting issues to be addressed with respect to norm conflict.

A simple example is the case of a theater performance, where the norm usually prevails that the audience should be quiet. However, if someone in the audience were to become critically ill, then it would presumably be suitable for someone to cry out, "is there a doctor in the house". In this case a higher-level norm would be invoked that urges one to take extraordinary measures to save someone's life, and this norm would presumably override the conventional norm for audience silence. Similarly, we normally follow the norm of "first come, first served" while waiting in an airline ticket queue, but if there is a late-arriving passenger with an urgent need for immediate service, then that passenger might be allowed to jump the queue in order to service his or her emergency.

But norm conflict can be much more complicated than those above two examples, since norms may be conditioned by temporal, spatial, gender, cultural and social circumstances. An example of gender related norm is when normative behaviour associated with British royal society, was violated when Australian Prime Minister Paul Keating put his arm around Queen Elizabeth.

Some of the existing work has been confined to limited situations (Vasconcelos et al. 2009), where norm overlap has been considered only in the context of simple examples with two linear and measurable dimensions. There has been some interesting work using argumentation-based heuristics in order to maximize the compliancy among various norms and minimize the violations (conflicts) among them while trying to resolve conflicting norms (Giannikis and Daskalopulu 2011; Oren et al. 2008). For a complex scenario where different levels of norm may be involved, consider the case of a man who enrolls in a college class taught by a woman; here there are the overlapping norms (and potential conflicts) associated with normal classroom behavior (social circumstances) and also man-woman (gender) behaviour. But now consider further complications to this example. Suppose in this particular case that:

- The male student is a full professor and the woman is an assistant professor. Here the professor outranks the assistant professor, and there are norms associated with that hierarchical relationship.
- The male student is also the uncle or husband of the woman teacher. Now there are additional norms associated with that family relationship.
- The male student and the woman teacher come from different cultures, which may have conflicting norms associated with acceptable behavior.
- There may have been prior, special commitments made between the teacher and student, which invokes the norm that promises should be kept.

In general there may be some possible agreement concerning meta-norms associated with the resolution of norm conflict. Here are some examples:

- The principle that the least-restrictive imposition on behaviour should be chosen when norms conflict (or, alternatively, the most-restrictive interpretation may be preferred).
- The principle that the most recently installed norm of two conflicting norms is preferred, since it is presumably the most up-to-date.

- The principle that the more generally disadvantaged party in a social situation should be given the greatest consideration when it comes to norm conflict resolution.
- There may be a commonly accepted hierarchy of norms that can be invoked to resolve norm conflicts.

These meta-norms, of course, must be made public and achieve common consent for them to be effective. We believe that there would be interesting work that could be undertaken in this area that would make the use of norms in multi-agent social situation more practical and scalable in realistic open-system scenarios.

11.4 Norm Enforcement

Punishment is widely considered a viable tool for promoting and maintaining social order both in real and in virtual societies (Axelrod 1986; Fehr and Gachter 2000; Ostrom 1990). Several authors (Blanc et al. 2005; Boyd and Richerson 1992; Boyd et al. 2010; de Pinninck et al. 2007; Helbing 2010; Jaffe and Zaballa 2010) have tested the effect of punishment in regulating peer-to-peer simulated environments, showing that to solve free-riding problems a constant and stable punishment system is necessary. Other models have been designed to explain how to choose the most effective punishment to regulate (electronic) institutions (Grossi et al. 2007; Janssen et al. 2010; Rauhut and Junker 2009) (see also Chap. 15).

Although these studies have provided key insights to the understanding of punishment in artificial societies, they have largely looked at this mechanism from the classical economic perspective as a way of changing wrongdoers' conduct through the infliction of material costs (Becker 1968). This way of considering punishment is incomplete and not likely to maintain large-scale compliance at least with only a reasonable level of costs for the (artificial) social system. Instead, as suggested by Andrighetto et al. (2010b) and Villatoro et al. (2011), punishment is more effective in regulating agents' behaviour and promoting norm compliance when the economic incentive is combined with the communication of normative information about the prescribed conduct. If properly designed, punishment not only imposes a cost for the wrongdoing, but also informs violators (and the public) that the targeted behaviour is not approved of because it violates a social norm. Giardini et al. (2010) have referred to this mechanism as *sanction*, thus distinguishing it from mere *punishment*. Since sanction communicates the presence of norms and asks that they not be violated, it allows agents to learn of the existence of norms and that their violation is not condoned. As shown in Villatoro et al. (2011), sanction allows social norms to be activated and to spread more quickly in the population than if they were enforced only by mere punishment with the effect of increasing their compliance and substantially reducing the costs for achieving and maintaining social order.

Clearly, in real life situations there is often an overlap between these two mechanisms that makes it difficult to disentangle their relative effects. Therefore, agent-based simulation seems to be the ideal tool for virtually isolating punishment and sanction. In this way, it becomes possible to (a) explore the specific contribution of each in promoting and maintaining cooperation, (b) design actions aimed to highlight and exploit such contributions, and possibly (c) to perform what-if analyses that allow us to address policy design issues. To fully operationalize the difference between punishment and sanction requires a complex cognitive agent architecture and the EMIL architecture (EMIL-A) seems a good candidate for this undertaking (for an extended description of this architecture we refer to Andrighetto et al. (2010a), Conte et al. (forthcoming) and Conte and Andrighetto (2012)). Unlike the vast majority of simulation models in which heterogeneous agents interact according to simple local rules, e.g. imitation rules, all EMIL-A agents are endowed with a normative architecture, allowing them to: recognize norms; generate new normative representations and to act on them; and finally to infer the normative information (explicitly or implicitly) conveyed by different enforcing mechanisms, such as punishment and sanction.

11.5 Benchmark Problems

A recent discussion at the COIN@AAMAS 2011 workshop (COIN 2011) identified the lack of agreement on standard benchmark problems for normative multi-agent systems as a problem for this research community.[1] While there are some scenarios that are commonly addressed in simulation-based research, particularly those based on traffic intersection scenarios or simple abstracted coordination and social dilemma games from game theory, these are generally extended to multi-agent and repeated interaction settings in different ways by different researchers. Furthermore, it can be difficult to tease apart the aspects of a simulation scenario that are essential to the research problems being addressed from those that are specific to the mechanisms used to address those problems.

It would be beneficial for the normative multi-agent systems research community to develop a culture of sharing and reusing, as exists in, for example, the machine learning community (Frank and Asuncion 2010). Adopting such a culture would help to focus the community's effort on specific challenges, and would allow a more direct comparison of the benefits of different approaches to solving those challenges. However, sharing benchmark problems is not as straightforward in the area of normative multi-agent systems as it is in machine learning, where a benchmark problem typically consists of a data set, a well defined problem, and (for supervised machine learning tasks) the "ground truth" against which the results of an applied technique can be measured. In contrast, a scenario in a multi-agent system does not

[1]This section is inspired by and elaborates on some of the views expressed at that workshop, but is not intended to be a collectively agreed report of the discussion, which had a wider focus than simulation-based studies alone.

involve interpretation of a static data set; rather it involves agents interacting with each other and possibly an environment, and the object of study (from the point of view of normative MAS, at least) is the dynamics of the society. What, then, might benchmark problems for normative MAS look like? For simulation-based research it would be beneficial to have easily reusable simulation environments with well defined interfaces for agents to be 'plugged in'. These could be scenario-specific simulations or generic MAS simulation frameworks (Neville and Pitt 2009). Another possibility for constructing benchmark simulation environments is to make use of virtual world simulators such as Second Life[2] or World of Warcraft[3] and to share tools that ease the task of connecting agents to these environments (Dignum et al. 2009; Ranathunga et al. 2011). This approach would allow investigation into the challenges of reasoning with norms in complex environments with many observable events and possible behaviours.

However, developing reusable simulation frameworks for community use is time consuming and difficult to obtain funding for. A more realistic goal, therefore, would be to develop an online forum where researchers could propose, discuss and vote on simulation scenarios with a view to establishing a set of standard benchmarks. A crucial aspect of such a forum would be to classify the proposed scenarios in terms of the research problems that they highlight and elide, to identify the benefits that the employment of norms would be expected to bring to the scenario, and to establish measures of success for any proposed implementations of the scenarios. A valuable side effect would be the emergence of a better understanding of the differing research issues that are seen as important in the community.

References

Aldewereld, H., F. Dignum, A. García-Camino, P. Noriega, J. A. Rodríguez-Aguilar, and C. Sierra. 2006. Operationalisation of norms for usage in electronic institutions. In *Proceedings of the fifth international joint conference on autonomous agents and multiagent systems (AAMAS)*, 223–225. New York: ACM.

Andrighetto, G., M. Campennì, R. Conte, and M. Paolucci. 2007. On the immergence of norms: A normative agent architecture. In *Proceedings of AAAI symposium, social and organizational aspects of intelligence*, Washington, DC.

Andrighetto, G., M. Campennì, F. Cecconi, and R. Conte. 2010a. The complex loop of norm emergence: A simulation model. In *Simulating interacting agents and social phenomena*, Agent-based social systems, vol. 7, ed. H. Deguchi et al., 19–35. Tokyo: Springer.

Andrighetto, G., D. Villatoro, and R. Conte. 2010b. Norm internalization in artificial societies. *AI Communications* 23: 325–339.

Axelrod, R. M. 1984. *The evolution of cooperation*. New York: Basic Books.

Axelrod, R. 1986. An evolutionary approach to norms. *The American Political Science Review* 80(4): 1095–1111.

[2]http://secondlife.com/

[3]http://www.battle.net/wow/

Becker, G. S. 1968. Crime and punishment: An economic approach. *The Journal of Political Economy* 76(2): 169–217.
Blanc, A., Y. K. Liu, and A. Vahdat. 2005. Designing incentives for peer-to-peer routing. In *INFOCOM*, Miami, 374–385.
Boyd, R., and P. Richerson. 1992. Punishment allows the evolution of cooperation (or anything else) in sizable groups. *Ethology and Sociobiology* 13(3): 171–195.
Boyd, R., H. Gintis, and S. Bowles. 2010. Coordinated punishment of defectors sustains cooperation and can proliferate when rare. *Science* 328(5978): 617–620.
COIN. 2011. Web site of the international workshop series on coordination, organizations, institutions and norms in agent systems. http://www.pcs.usp.br/~coin/.
Conte, R., and G. Andrighetto. 2012. Cognitive dynamics of norm compliance: From norm adoption to flexible automated conformity. *Artificial Intelligence and Law*. DOI: 10.1007/s10506-012-9135-6.
Conte, R., and M. Paolucci. 2002. *Reputation in artificial societies: Social beliefs for social order*. Berlin: Springer.
Conte, R., G. Andrighetto, and M. Campenni (eds.). (forthcoming). *Minding norms. Mechanisms and dynamics of social order in agent societies*. Oxford Series on Cognitive Models and Architectures. USA: Oxford University Press.
de Pinninck, A. P., C. Sierra, and W. M. Schorlemmer. 2007. Friends no more: Norm enforcement in multi-agent systems. In *Proceedings of AAMAS 2007*, Honolulu, ed. M. Durfee and E. H. Yokoo, 640–642.
Dignum, F., J. Westra, W. A. van Doesburg, and M. Harbers. 2009. Games and agents: Designing intelligent gameplay. *International Journal of Computer Games Technology* 1–18.
Epstein, J. M. 2001. Learning to be thoughtless: Social norms and individual computation. *Computational Economics* 18(1): 9–24.
Fehr, E., and S. Gachter. 2000. Cooperation and punishment in public goods experiments. *American Economic Review* 90(4): 980–994.
Frank, A., and A. Asuncion. 2010. UCI machine learning repository. http://archive.ics.uci.edu/ml.
Giannikis, G. K., and A. Daskalopulu. 2011. Normative conflicts in electronic contracts. *Electronic Commerce Research and Applications* 10(2): 247–267.
Giardini, F., G. Andrighetto, and R. Conte. 2010. A cognitive model of punishment. In *Proceedings of the 32nd annual conference of the cognitive science society*, 11–14 Aug. 2010, 1282–1288. Austin: Cognitive Science Society.
Grossi, D., H. M. Aldewereld, and F. Dignum. 2007. Ubi lex, ibi poena: Designing norm enforcement in e-institutions. In *Coordination, organizations, institutions, and norms in agent systems II*, 101–114. Berlin: Springer.
Helbing, D., A. Szolnoki, M. Perc, and G. Szabo. 2010. Punish, but not too hard: How costly punishment spreads in the spatial public goods game. *New Journal of Physics* 12(8): 083,005.
Hoffmann, M. J. 2003. Entrepreneurs and Norm Dynamics: An Agent-Based Model of the Norm Life Cycle. Technical report, Department of Political Science and International Relations, University of Delaware.
Jaffe, K., and L. Zaballa. 2010. Co-operative punishment cements social cohesion. *Journal of Artificial Societies and Social Simulation* 13: 3. http://econpapers.repec.org/RePEc:jas:jasssj:2009-36-3.
Janssen, M. A., R. Holahan, A. Lee, and E. Ostrom. 2010. Lab experiments for the study of social-ecological systems. *Science* 328: 613–617.
Neville, B., and J. Pitt. 2009. PRESAGE: A programming environment for the simulation of agent societies. In *Programming multi-agent systems*. Lecture Notes in Artificial Intelligence, vol. 5442, ed. K. V. Hindriks, A. Pokahr, and S. Sardina, 88–103. Berlin: Springer.
Oren, N., M. Luck, S. Miles, and T. J. Norman. 2008. *An argumentation inspired heuristic for resolving normative conflict*. In *Proceedings of the fifth workshop on coordination, organizations, institutions, and norms in agent systems (COIN@AAMAS-08)*, 41–56.
Ostrom, E. 1990. *Governing the commons: The evolution of institutions for collective action*. New York: Cambridge University Press.

Ranathunga, S., S. Cranefield, and M. Purvis. 2011. Interfacing a cognitive agent platform with Second Life, Discussion Paper 2011-02, Department of Information Science, University of Otago. http://eprints.otago.ac.nz/1093/.

Rauhut, H., and M. Junker. 2009. Punishment deters crime because humans are bounded in their strategic decision-making. *Journal of Artificial Societies and Social Simulation* 12(3): 1. http://jasss.soc.surrey.ac.uk/12/3/1.html.

Savarimuthu, B. T. R., S. Cranefield, M. A. Purvis, and M. K. Purvis. 2010a. Norm identification in multi-agent societies. Discussion Paper 2010/03, Department of Information Science, University of Otago. http://eprints.otago.ac.nz/873/.

Savarimuthu, B. T. R., S. Cranefield, M. A. Purvis, and M. K. Purvis. 2010b. Obligation norm identification in agent societies. *Journal of Artificial Societies and Social Simulation* 13(4): 3. http://jasss.soc.surrey.ac.uk/13/4/3.html.

Savarimuthu, B. T. R. 2011. Norm learning in multi-agent societies. Discussion Paper 2011/05, Department of Information Science, University of Otago. http://otago.ourarchive.ac.nz/handle/10523/1690.

Sen, S., and S. Airiau. 2007. Emergence of norms through social learning. In *Proceedings of the twentieth international joint conference on artificial intelligence (IJCAI)*, 1507–1512. Menlo Park: AAAI Press.

Shoham, Y., and M. Tennenholtz. 1995. On social laws for artificial agent societies: Off-line design.*Artificial Intelligence* 73(1–2): 231–252.

Vasconcelos, W., M. Kollingbaum, and T. Norman. 2009. Normative conflict resolution in multi-agent systems. *Autonomous Agents and Multi-Agent Systems* 19: 124–152.

Verhagen, H. 2001. Simulation of the learning of norms. *Social Science Computer Review* 19(3): 296–306.

Villatoro, D., G. Andrighetto, R. Conte, and J. Sabater-Mir. 2011. *Dynamic sanctioning for robust and cost-efficient norm compliance*, 414–419. Barcelona: IJCAI/AAAI.

Walker, A., and M. Wooldridge. 1995. Understanding the emergence of conventions in multi-agent systems. In *Proceedings of the first international conference on multi-agent systems (ICMAS)*, ed. V. Lesser, 384–389. Menlo Park: AAAI.

Chapter 12
Norms in Game Theory

Davide Grossi, Luca Tummolini, and Paolo Turrini

12.1 Introduction

In this brief chapter we will overview several points of contact between games and norms. Since the following short exposition cannot be comprehensive, it aims to suggest a set of key ideas and perspectives connecting norms and games.

Generally speaking, the contributions in the literature at the interface between games and norms can be divided into two main branches: the first, mostly originating from economics and game theory (Coase 1960; Hurwicz 1996, 2008), exploits normative concepts, such as institutions or laws, as *mechanisms* that enforce desirable properties of strategic interactions; the second, that has its roots in social sciences and evolutionary game theory (Coleman 1990; Ulmann-Margalit 1977) views norms as *equilibria* that result from the interaction of rational individuals.

The chapter will reflect this division and be articulated in two parts. The first one—*norms as mechanisms*—will deal with those approaches within game theory (as well as related disciplines such as multi-agent systems (Shoham and Leyton-Brown 2008)) which study norms and institutions as components of games (e.g., mechanism design or implementation theory (Osborne and Rubinstein 1994,

D. Grossi (✉)
Department of Computer Science, University of Liverpool, Liverpool, UK
e-mail: d.grossi@liverpool.ac.uk

L. Tummolini
Institute of Cognitive Science and Technologies, CNR, Rome, Italy
e-mail: luca.tummolini@istc.cnr.it

P. Turrini
University of Luxembourg, Luxembourg City, Luxembourg
e-mail: paolo.turrini@uni.lu

S. Ossowski (ed.), *Agreement Technologies*, Law, Governance and Technology Series 8, DOI 10.1007/978-94-007-5583-3_12,

Chap. 10)). The second part—*norms as equilibria*—moves in the opposite direction reviewing approaches that use game-theoretic methods to explain and analyze norms, institutions[1] and their emergence.

12.2 Norms as Mechanisms

This section presents the view of norms as constraints that, imposed on players' behaviour, enforce desirable social outcomes in games. In this view, norms can be either seen as a way of engineering interactions from scratch, i.e., norms that dictate the 'legal' moves of a game, or as a way of transforming existing interactions, i.e., norms that modify the players' strategic possibilities in a game.

12.2.1 Norms as Rules of the Game: Mechanism Design

The view of norms as the rules of the game[2] is widespread within the so-called new institutional economics.[3] An interpretation of it from the standpoint of game theory is developed in Hurwicz (1996), which interprets the phrase literally in terms of the theory of mechanism design.

In brief, institutions are seen as collective procedures geared towards the achievement of some desirable social outcomes. An example of them are auctions, viz. mechanisms to allocate resources among self-interested players. In many auctions goods are not assigned to the bidder valuing them most as bidders might find it convenient to misrepresent their preferences. In such situations mechanism design can be used to enforce the desirable property of truth telling. For instance, when the bidders submit independently and anonymously and the winner pays an amount equivalent to the bid of the runner-up, truth telling is a dominant strategy.[4] In other words, in a second-price sealed bid auction, independently of the way they value the auctioned good, players cannot profitably deviate from telling the truth.

Viewing norms as mechanisms means considering them in the guise of auctions. Just like in auctions, they are supposed to make no assumptions on the preferences of the participating agents. They merely define the possible actions that participants can take, and their consequences. Slightly more technically, they are *game forms* (or mechanisms), viz. games without preferences.

[1] We will often use the terms "norm" and "institution" as synonyms.

[2] The phrase comes, as far as we know, from North (1990).

[3] New institutional economics has brought institutions and norms to the agenda of modern economics, viewing them as the social and legal frameworks of economic behavior. See Coase (1960) for a representative paper.

[4] This is the so-called Vickrey auction. See (Shoham and Leyton-Brown 2008, Chap. 11) for a neat exposition.

Two aspects of this view are particularly noteworthy. First, it clearly explains the rationale for norms and institutions: they are there in order to guarantee that socially desirable outcomes get realized (in jargon, *implemented*) as equilibria of the possible games that they support. Second, it presupposes some sort of infallible enforcement: implementation can be obtained only by assuming that players play within the space defined by the rules, which represents a strong idealization of the real workings of institutions.[5]

12.2.2 Norms as Game-Transformations

Norms can be conceptualized not only as the very framework of social interaction, like in the game-form conception above, but also as ways of *transforming* existing games in order to bring about outcomes that are more desirable from a welfaristic point of view. Game transformations include, for instance, appropriate restrictions of players' strategies or redistributions of such strategies among the agents.[6]

The game-transformation approach has been pioneered by Shoham and Tennenholtz (1995) in order to engineer laws which guarantee the successful coexistence of multiple programs. It has been further explored in the multi agent systems community to study temporal structures obeying systemic requirements, as in van der Hoek et al. (2007).

Sharing the same view of norms as game-transformations, the work of Grossi and Turrini (2010) investigates the role of interdependence in designing such norms. Instead of considering any arbitrary constraint on players' behavior, games are transformed respecting an underlying dependence structure among the players, i.e., taking into account what players would do if they could have a say on other players' actions. Inspired by previous work in social science (Castelfranchi et al. 1992), they also show formally how transforming games to implement desirable behavior is equivalent to enforcing a contract among the individuals involved, considering how players can mutually profit from one another.

12.3 Norms as Equilibria

Alternative to the view of institutions as 'rules of the game' is their conceptualization as equilibria, i.e., as stable behaviors, within games.[7] The difference might look subtle, but it is of a fundamental kind. Viewing institutions as game forms means viewing them as the 'hard constraints' defining the boundaries of possible

[5]This problematic assumption has been put under discussion extensively in Hurwicz (2008).

[6]See Parikh (2002) for an inspiring manifesto.

[7]This fundamental distinction has been emphasized, for instance, in Hurwicz (1996).

	C	D
C	2,2	0,3
D	3,0	1,1

	L	R
L	1,1	0,0
R	0,0	1, 1

Fig. 12.1 Prisoner's dilemma (with C = cooperate and D = defect) and Coordination game (with L = left and R = right)

interactions, while viewing them as equilibria means viewing them as some kind of 'softer' constraints from which it is possible, although 'irrational', to deviate.[8] Also, while the mechanism design view considers norms as an actual *component*—the game form—of the definition of a game, the equilibrium-based view considers norms as the result or *solution* of a game. So, in the former view norms define games, in the latter they are defined by games.

12.3.1 Social Norms

Starting from the classical problem of the spontaneous emergence of social order, the game-theoretic analysis of norms has focused in particular on informal norms enforced by a community of agents, i.e. *social* norms. From this perspective, the view of norms as Nash equilibria has been first suggested by Schelling (1966), Lewis (1969) and Ullmann-Margalit (1977). A Nash equilibrium is a combination of strategies, one for each individual, such that each player's strategy is a best reply to the strategies of the other players. Since each player's beliefs about the opponent's strategy are correct when part of an equilibrium, this view of norms highlights the facts that a norm is supported by self-fulling expectations.

However, not every Nash equilibrium seems like a plausible candidate for a norm. In the Prisoner Dilemma (see Fig. 12.1) mutual defection is a Nash equilibrium of the game without being plausibly considered a norm-based behavior. In fact, the view of norms as Nash equilibria has been refined by several scholars. Bicchieri (2006), for instance, has suggested that, in the case of norms conformity is always *conditional* upon expectations of what other players will do. Moreover, in this model, norms are different from mere conventions, in that norms are peculiar of mixed-motives games (e.g. the Prisoner Dilemma) and operate by transforming the original games into coordination ones.

Another influential view of norms characterizes them as devices that solve equilibrium selection problems. A comprehensive and concise articulation of this view can be found in Binmore (2007) which emphasizes two key features of norms.

[8]It might be worth stressing that the two views are not incompatible as institutions as equilibria can be thought of arising within games defined on institutions as game forms.

First, as equilibria, they determine self-enforcing patterns of collective behavior,[9] e.g., making cooperation an equilibrium of the (indefinitely iterated) prisoner's dilemma. Second, since repeated interaction can create a large number of efficient and inefficient equilibria, a norm is viewed as a device to select among them—a paradigmatic example of a game with multiple equilibria is the game on the right in Fig. 12.1, known as the coordination game.

Finally, it has been recently suggested that a norm is best captured as a correlating device that implements a correlated equilibrium of an original game in which all agents play strictly pure strategies (Gintis 2010). A correlated equilibrium is a generalization of the Nash equilibrium concept in which the assumption that the players' strategies are probabilistically independent is dropped. When playing their part on a correlated equilibrium the players condition their choice on the same randomizing device (Aumann 1987). Since the conditions under which a correlated equilibrium is played are less demanding than those characterizing Nash equilibria, the view of norms as a correlating device seems more plausible. Moreover, the correlating device is seen as a device that suggests separately to each player what she is supposed to do and thus seems to better characterize the prescriptive nature of norms (Conte and Castelfranchi 1995). On the other hand, the origins of such correlating devices is left unclear and are viewed as an emergent property of a complex social system.

Although an equilibrium-based analysis of norms might provide a rationale for compliance, it does not explain how such norms can possibly arise in strictly competitive situations—like the Prisoner's Dilemma. The next section discusses some approaches to this issue.

12.3.2 The Evolution of Norms

Axelrod (1986) studies norms starting from games in extensive forms with the following structure: the first player, *i*, chooses whether to comply or violate a (further unspecified) norm; if she violates it, a node is reached where nature chooses with what probability *i*'s violation is observed by some other agent *j*; in case *i*'s violation is observed, a choice node is reached where *j* has to decide whether to punish *i* or not; finally, the payoffs are the obvious ones for *i*, and *j* is assumed to incur costs when punishing *i*. In other words, the game provides a simple abstraction of norm compliance and defection, together with a basic enforcement mechanism. What Axelrod sets then out to do is to observe, by means of computer simulations,

[9] Self-enforcement is the type of phenomenon captured by the so-called *folk theorem*. The theorem roughly says that, given a game, any outcome which guarantees to each player a payoff at least as good as the one guaranteed by her minimax strategy is a Nash equilibrium in the indefinite iteration of the initial game (cf. Osborne and Rubinstein 1994, Chap. 8).

under what conditions[10] and how fast (i.e., after how many iterations of the game) compliance spreads among a population of players that randomly get to play role i and role j. In brief, the findings seem to show that, in order for compliance to arise, a meta-enforcement mechanism needs to be introduced, according to which j gets punished by other members of the population when not-punishing i.

A more analytical take on the evolution of norms can be found in Skyrms (1996), which uses techniques coming from the field of evolutionary game theory. The key idea behind this approach is to read games not as the interaction of players, but rather as the interaction of populations of strategies which are paired with each other; and payoffs not as utilities, but rather as the measures of fitness of the strategies that yield them. The higher the (average) fitness of a given strategy the larger will its population grow. The coordination game offers a very simple example: if the population of L (= drive left) strategies is more than half the whole population, it means that strategy L will have a higher average fitness than R, as R, under random pairing, will be more likely than L to end up in an uncoordinated outcome. Under this sort of evolutionary drive, the system will then stably reach the L,L equilibrium. As (Skyrms 1996) shows, this sort of analysis can be carried out to explain how equilibria are reached in all kinds of different games, and how even strictly dominated strategies (like cooperation in the Prisoner's dilemma) can be fixed into a stable evolutionary state.

References

Aumann, R. 1987. Correlated equilibrium as an expression of bayesian rationality. *Econometrica* 55: 1–18.

Axelrod, R. 1986. An evolutionary approach to norms. *The American Political Science Review* 80(4): 1095–1111.

Bicchieri, C. 2006. *The Grammar of Society: The Nature and Dynamics of Social Norms*. New York: Cambridge University Press.

Binmore, K. 2007. The origins of fair play. *Proceedings of the British Academy* 151: 151–193.

Castelfranchi, C., M. Miceli, and A. Cesta. 1992. Dependence relations among autonomous agents. In *Decentralized A.I.3*, pp. 215–227, ed. E. Werner and Y. Demazeau. Amsterdam: Elsevier.

Coase, R. 1960. The problem of social cost. *Journal of Law and Economics* 3: 1–44.

Coleman, J. 1990. *Foundations of social theory*. Cambridge, MA: Belknap Harvard.

Conte, R., and C. Castelfranchi. 1995. *Cognitive and social action*. London: UCL Press.

Gintis, H. 2010. *The bounds of reason*. Princenton: Princenton University Press.

Grossi, D., and P. Turrini. 2010. Dependence theory via game theory. In *Proceedings of the 9th international conference on autonomous agents and multiagent systems (AAMAS 2010)*, ed. W. van der Hoek and G. Kaminka, 1147–1154. Richland: IFAAMAS.

Hurwicz, L. 1996. Institutions as families of game forms. *Japanese Economic Review* 47(2): 113–132.

Hurwicz, L. 2008. But who will guard the guardians? *American Economic Review* 98(3): 577–585.

[10]The conditions considered are essentially three: how risk-seeking is i, what the probability of a violation to be detected is, and how prone is j to react upon a detection.

Lewis, D. 1969. *Convention: A philosophical study*. Cambridge, MA: Cambridge University Press.

North, D. C. 1990. *Institutions, institutional change and economic performance*. Cambridge, MA: Cambridge University Press.

Osborne, M. J., and A. Rubinstein. 1994. *A course in game theory*. Cambridge, MA: MIT.

Parikh, R. 2002. Social software. *Synthese* 132(3): 187–211.

Schelling, T. 1966. *The strategy of conflict*. London: Oxford University Press.

Shoham, Y., and M. Tennenholtz. 1995. Social laws for artificial agent societies: Off-line design. *Artificial Intelligence* 73(12): 231–252.

Shoham, Y., and K. Leyton-Brown. 2008. *Multiagent systems: algorithmic*. Game-Theoretic and Logical Foundations. Cambridge, MA: Cambridge University Press.

Skyrms, B. 1996. *Evolution of the social contract*. Cambridge/New York: Cambridge University Press.

Ulmann-Margalit, E. 1977. *The emergence of norms*. Oxford: Clarendon Press.

van der Hoek, W., M. Roberts, and M. Wooldridge. 2007. Social laws in alternating time: Effectiveness, feasibility, and synthesis. *Synthese* 156:1: 1–19.

Chapter 13
AI and Law

Giovanni Sartor and Antonino Rotolo

13.1 The Domain of AI and Law

Few disciplines may appear to be as far apart as law and artificial intelligence. The first can vaunt a tradition spanning millennia, while the second cannot go beyond 1950. The first is a cultural discipline, deeply enmeshed in the fabric of human life, while the second is a technological science, dealing with hardware and software artifacts. The first is usually conceived as a form of art (the art of the good and the right) which cannot be reduced to predetermined mechanical procedures, while the second focuses precisely on the problem of mechanisation. Besides those differences, however, there are also important points of convergence: both disciplines need to approach the complexities of the human mind and human action, both need to use and organise large quantities of information, both want to engage in flexible problem-solving activities in complex domains.

The combination of this challenging distance and this promising convergence between AI and law explains the reciprocal attraction between those disciplines, which has led to the establishment of an active research community and to the achievement of significant theoretical results as well as bearing fruit in many computer implementations. AI and Law research and results cover many different topics, such as

- Formal theories of norms and normative systems,
- Computational legal logic,

G. Sartor (✉)
EUI, Florence, Italy

CIRSFID – Faculty of Law, University of Bologna, Bologna, Italy
e-mail: giovanni.sartor@eui.eu

A. Rotolo
CIRSFID – Faculty of Law, University of Bologna, Bologna, Italy
e-mail: antonino.rotolo@unibo.it

S. Ossowski (ed.), *Agreement Technologies*, Law, Governance and Technology Series 8, DOI 10.1007/978-94-007-5583-3_13,

- Legal argumentation systems,
- Ontologies for the law,
- Game theory as applied to the law,
- Formal models of legal institutions and MAS,
- Simulations in legal and social norms,
- Rule-interchange languages for the legal domain,
- Legal e-discovery and information retrieval,
- NLP in the legal domain,
- Machine learning in the law.

Many AI researchers considered that the development of AI applications in the legal domain should make use, not only of legal sources, but should also interface with legal theory, legal doctrine, and philosophy. In this sense, AI and Law is indeed an interdisciplinary effort, combining methods and results also from deontic logic, norms and agent-based simulation, game theory and norms, normative agents, norms and organization, norms and trust, and norms and argumentation. In the remainder, we will shortly illustrate AI and Law research by revolving around some general key ideas in regard to how the law can be viewed from that research perspectives. The following outline should by no means be considered exhaustive and just considers some well-established research areas.

13.2 Law as a Deductive System or a Set of Rules

The first attempts to apply computational models to the law were inspired by the idea of the law as a deductive system, namely as a set of premises from which legal conclusions could be achieved through deductive inferences, a view that was inspired, e.g., by Allen (1957), Alchourrón and Bulygin (1971), Yoshino (1978) and Allen and Saxon (1991). Thus, according to this approach, given a set L of legal premises (a set of legal rules) and a set F of facts, through logical deduction (including predicate logic and possibly a deontic logic), one would achieve relevant legal consequences, namely, any (relevant) proposition p such that $L \cup F \vdash p$. This idea was implemented in knowledge-based systems. Over the last few years some systems have been developed and commercialised which correspond to these idea. In particular, I would mention the most successful of them, originally named Softlaw and developed in Australia by Peter Johnson, then managed as Ruleburst under the leadership of Surend Dayal and finally become Oracle's Policy automation system. This is a commercial product, which includes a set of tools for building knowledge-bases of regulations, for checking their correctness and consistency and for using them interactively.

A fundamental development of rule-based systems for the law has been investigating the connection with AI research on non-monotonic reasoning. In fact it appeared that various aspects of the law, such as the interaction between rules and exceptions, conflicts between norms, presumptions, temporal reasoning, the dynamics of legal systems, burdens of proof could at least partially be addressed through non-monotonic reasoning. This was starting with using Prolog and in particular negation by failure to model legal norms. Negation as failure can indeed be used to express that a rule is to be applied only as long as a negated element in the rule's antecedent cannot be derived from the knowledge base.

The seminal paper by Sergot et al. (1986) stimulated numerous attempts to use logic programming to build knowledge-based systems, as well as further theoretical inquiries into the use of logic programming for modelling legal reasoning and knowledge (McCarty 1988a,b). Modeling the law as a set of defeasible rules is thus a key idea in the AI and Law community: a recent overview of requirements for developing rule-based systems in the law can be found in Gordon et al. (2009). In fact, one may argue that legal reasoning is part of human cognition, which is defeasible (Pollock 1995a) or that is developed within argumentative settings where arguments and counter-arguments dialectically interact.

13.3 Law as an Argumentation Framework

Among the various approaches to non-monotonic reasoning, defeasible argumentation has been the most successful in the legal domain (see Chap. 16). Following this idea, the law L, in combination with facts F, appears as a multifaceted argumentation framework (including rules, assumptions, preferences, alternative interpretations, exclusions, values), from which multiple arguments can be constructed. What consequences follow (credulously or sceptically) from that argumentation framework depends on which arguments succeed in sustaining attacks over other arguments, so that such arguments (and their consequences) may be viewed as justified or at least defensible. While relying on general models of argument-based defeasible reasoning (such as Pollock (1995b) and Dung (1995)) researchers in AI and law have developed original models of defeasible argumentation (Bench-Capon and Prakken 2006; Dung and Thang 2008; Gordon 1995; Hage 1997; Prakken and Sartor 1996; Verheij 2003). A legal argumentation framework usually contains a logical layer, a dialectical layer, and a procedural layer of legal arguments: the first deals with the underlying formal language that is used to build legal arguments; the second studies when legal arguments conflict, how they can be compared and what legal arguments and conclusions can be justified; the third one considers the ways through which conclusions are dynamically reached in legal disputes.

The idea of the law as an argumentation framework has recently been enriched with the idea of argument schemes, an idea developed in particular by Douglas Walton (2005), Walton et al. (2008), Gordon et al. (2007) and Gordon and Walton (2009), though it can also be linked to Pollock (1995a). According to this idea rather than using in legal arguments a single kind of inference (defeasible rule-application) one would use multiple kind of inference schemes (witness testimony, expert testimony, practical syllogism, etc.), each one with its associated defeaters (or critical questions). This approach has being adopted in some argument graphing tools such as Araucaria (Reed and Rowe 2007), and more recently in the Carneades system (Gordon and Walton 2009).

A different development of work in legal argumentation consists in the development of dialogue systems. The focus here is the *process* of argumentation, rather than the analysis of the implications of a set of arguments (or a knowledge base offering material for a set of arguments). Thus arguments are seen as the content of speech acts by the agents taking part in an interaction, according to a certain protocol, i.e., a set of rules governing the allowed moves and their effects. Which arguments are successful crucially depends on the protocol, that establishes which arguments are admissible, at any stage of the dialectical interaction, and what impacts they have on its prosecution (Gordon 1995; Lodder 1999; Prakken 2001; Riveret et al. 2007; Verheij 2003; Walton and Krabbe 1995). Research on argumentation frameworks and on dialogue protocols can be integrated, since the impact of an argument on the state of the dialogue crucially depends on whether it sustains the attacks of previous or subsequent arguments (Prakken 2010).

13.4 Law as a Case-Based-Reasoning System

Legal argumentation frameworks can be developed on top of an underlying formal language, which is used to build arguments. Many formal methods for reasoning can be used for this purpose, among which legal case-based reasoning has been particularly investigated within the AI and Law community (Ashley 1990; Ashley and Rissland 1988; Branting 1994; Horty 1999; Prakken and Sartor 1998a). A key idea behind case-based reasoning in the law is to model reasoning about precedents: this is done by devising methods for generalizing from past cases in order to trace legal solutions for a current case or to evaluate such a case by comparing it to precedents. An important aspect of this research effort has been thus to embed legal case-based reasoning within argumentation frameworks, and so in terms of argument-based defeasible logics (Loui and Norman 1995; Loui et al. 1993; Prakken and Sartor 1998b).

In particular, significant works have attempted to reconstruct legal case-based reasoning in terms of theory-based defeasible reasoning, i.e., in systems where the evaluation and the choice of theories are introduced to explain and systematize the available legal input information (typically, a set of precedents): when a better theory becomes available, inferior theories are to be abandoned (Bench-Capon and Sartor 2003; Sartor 2002). The idea is that the parties in a case, given a shared legal background of past cases, develop alternative legal theories, and victory goes to the party who develops the better theory. This leads to the idea that legal debates consist in the dialectical exchange of competing theories, supporting opposed legal conclusions in the issue at stake. Theories can be compared according to different criteria, such as case-coverage (a better theory explains more precedents), factor-coverage (a better theory takes into account more features of those precedents), value-coverage (a better theory takes into account a larger set of values), analogical connectivity (a better theory includes more analogical connections between its components), non-arbitrariness (a better theory contains fewer ad-hoc statements, required neither for explaining the past evidence nor for implementing the shared assessment of value-priorities).

13.5 Law as a Set of Concepts: Legal Ontologies

Concepts play a key role in the law. Legal rules form a network where a legal effect (e.g., one's liability for violation of copyright) depends of qualifying a certain fact according to concepts provided by further rules (was there a violation of copyright, was there a damage?), which in its turn may depend on further facts (was there a protected work, was there an illegal use of it?), and so on. Moreover, the application of the law requires linking legal concepts to the common-sense and technical terms that are used to model the reality to which legal norms have to be applied.

Since the beginning of legal informatics, dictionaries and thesauri for the law have been developed. Researchers in AI and Law have been trying to provide a formal account of legal concepts and their relationships by using AI models for knowledge representation, from semantic networks, to frames, to ontologies (Breuker et al. 1997; Gangemi et al. 2005). In the framework of the semantic web the application of ontologies has been most studied (for a review, see Sartor et al. 2011).

13.6 Law as a Set of Deontic Concepts

The AI and Law research has also developed an interesting work at the interface of law and deontic logic (Allen and Saxon 1991; Hage 2011; Horty 2001; McCarty 1986; Sartor 2006) (see also Chap. 10). Besides importing well-known results from the deontic logic community, AI and Law scholars have for instance investigated Hohfeldian (1911) legal concepts, which correspond to typical effects of the application of legal norms, and of which these are the two main examples:

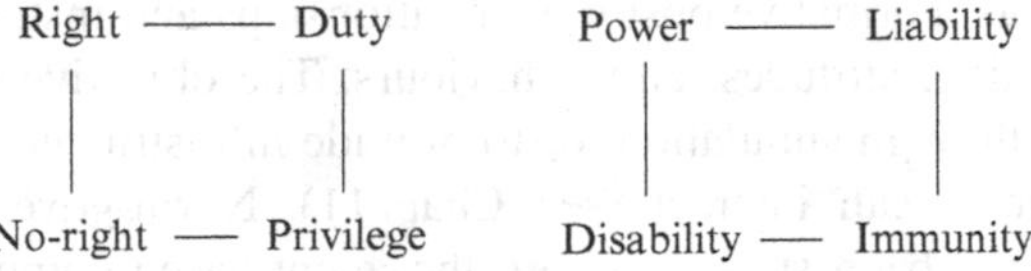

Right and duty are correlatives: if i (the bearer) has a right against j (the counterparty) that ϕ is brought about, then j has the obligation toward i to bring about ϕ. A privilege is the opposite of an obligation, e.g., j is not obliged toward i to bring about ϕ. Similarly no-right is the opposite of right and the correlative of privilege. These concepts are captured by the so-called *directed obligations*, i.e. obligations where bearers and counterparties are made explicit in a designed deontic logic (Herrestad and Krogh 1995).

A formal analysis of the second square appeared more problematic. Such an analysis was programmatically set by Jones and Sergot in 1996, a paper aiming at modeling the notion of institutionalized power. After then, this analysis has been applied and further developed within the AI and Law community (Gelati et al. 2004).

13.7 Further AI and Law Approaches to the Law

In the above sections we have presented what we view as mature and well-established approaches to modelling norms and normative reasoning developed within the AI and Law community. These approaches are not exhaustive of the applications of AI ideas to the law. Leaving aside the many uses of advanced techniques to the retrieval of legal texts (which fall beyond the scope of the present review) we need to mention in particular the use of neural networks and the development of hybrid approaches. In application of neural networks to the law, the basic model has consisted of identifying the factors which could influence a certain kind of decision, and then connecting those factors (as input nodes) to possible decisions (as output nodes), via one or more layers of intermediate nodes. The network is then trained with real and hypothetical cases until it provides the correct answers (Bench-Capon 1993; Bochereau et al. 1999; Philipps and Sartor 1999; Zeleznikow and Stranieri 1995). The application of neural networks to model legal decision-making has been subject to some criticisms, focusing in particular on the lack of explanations, which makes the use of networks very questionable in legal contexts. Connectionist approaches have also been considered for different purposes, e.g., measuring coherence in legal theories (Bench-Capon and Sartor 2001).

Finally, we need to mention approaches that address two or more of the above mentioned aspects of the law, in an integrated or hybrid way. So we had systems integrating cases and rules (Gardner 1987; Rissland and Skalak 1993), rules and neural networks (Zeleznikow and Stranieri 1995), rules and value-based teleological reasoning (Bench-Capon and Sartor 2000; Chorley and Bench-Capon 2003).

Agent-based models of normative behaviour also integrate different aspects of the law: rules, goals, normative positions, relationships and institutions as well as norm-based reasoning, attitudes, and behaviours. The objective may be studying human behaviour through simulation, or to provide infrastructures where artificial and/or human agents can interact (see Chap. 11). Norm-governed agent-based systems have mainly been studied within the agent-based community, but some proposals have also been developed in AI and Law (Artikis et al. 2002, 2003; Sartor et al. 2009).

References

Alchourrón, C. E., and E. Bulygin. 1971. *Normative systems*. Vienna: Springer.

Allen, L. E. 1957. Symbolic logic: A razor-edged tool for drafting and interpreting legal documents. *Yale Law Journal* 66: 833–879.

Allen, L. E., and C. S. Saxon. 1991. A-Hohfeld: A language for robust structural representation of knowledge in the legal domain to build interpretation-assistance expert systems. In *Proceedings of the first international workshop on deontic logic in computer science*, 52–71, ed. J. J. C. Meyer and R. J. Wieringa. Amsterdam: Vrjie Universiteit.

Artikis, A., M. J. Sergot, and J. Pitt. 2002. Animated specifications of computational societies. In *Proceeding AAMAS-2002*, 1053–1061. New York: ACM.

Artikis, A., M. J. Sergot, and J. Pitt. 2003. An executable specification of an argumentation protocol. In *Proceedings of the ninth international conference on artificial intelligence and law (ICAIL)*, 1–11. New York: ACM.

Ashley, K. D. 1990. *Modeling legal argument: Reasoning with cases and hypotheticals*. Cambridge MA: MIT.

Ashley, K. D., and E. L. Rissland. 1988. A case-based approach to modelling legal expertise. *IEEE Expert* 3: 70–77.

Bench-Capon, T. J. M. 1993. Neural networks and open texture. In *Proceedings of the fourth international conference on artificial intelligence and law*, 292–297. New York: ACM.

Bench-Capon, T. J. M., and H. Prakken. 2006. Justifying actions by accruing arguments. In *Computational models of argument. Proceedings of COMMA-06*, 247–258, ed. P. E. Dunne and T. J. M. Bench-Capon. Amsterdam: IOS.

Bench-Capon, T. J. M., and G. Sartor. 2000. Using values and theories to resolve disagreement in law. In *Proceedings of the thirteenth annual conference on legal knowledge and information systems (JURIX)*, 73–84, ed. J. Breuker, L. Ronald, and R. Winkels. Amsterdam: IOS.

Bench-Capon, T. J. M., and G. Sartor. 2001. A quantitative approach to theory coherence. In *Proceedings of the fourteenth annual conference on legal knowledge and information systems (JURIX)*, 53–62. Amsterdam: IOS.

Bench-Capon, T., and G. Sartor. 2003. A model of legal reasoning with cases incorporating theories and values. *Artificial Intelligence* 150: 97–143. doi:10.1016/S0004-3702(03)00108-5. http://portal.acm.org/citation.cfm?id=964763.964767.

Bochereau, L., D. Bourcier, and P. Bourgine. 1999. Extracting legal knowledge by means of a multilayered neural network: Application to municipal jurisprudence. In *Proceedings of the seventh international conference on artificial intelligence and law (ICAIL)*, 288–296. New York: ACM.

Branting, L. K. 1994. A computational model of ratio decidendi. *Artificial Intelligence and Law* 2: 1–31.

Breuker, J., A. Valente, and R. Winkels. 1997. Legal ontologes: A functional view. In *Proceedings of first international workshop on legal ontologies (LEGONT'97)*, 23–36, ed. P. R. S. Visser and R. G. F. Winkels. University of Melbourne, Law School, Melbourne, Australia.

Chorley, A., and T. J. M. Bench-Capon. 2003. Reasoning with legal cases as theory construction: Some experimental results. In *Proceedings of the seventeenth annual conference on legal knowledge and information systems (JURIX)*, 173–182, ed. D. Bourcier. Amsterdam: IOS.

Dung, P. M. 1995. On the acceptability of arguments and its fundamental role in nonmonotonic reasoning, logic programming, and *n*–person games. *Artificial Intelligence* 77: 321–357.

Dung, P. M., and Thang, P. M. 2008. Modular argumentation for modelling legal doctrines in common law of contract. In *Proceedings of JURIX 2008*, 108–117, ed. E. Francesconi, G. Sartor, and D. Tiscornia. Amsterdam: IOS (2008).

Gangemi, A., M. T. Sagri, and D. Tiscornia. 2005. A constructive framework for legal ontologies. In *Law and the semantic web*, 97–124, ed. V. R. Benjamins, P. Casanovas, J. Breuker, and A. Gangemi. Berlin: Springer.

Gardner, A. v. d. L. 1987. *An artificial intelligence approach to legal reasoning*. Cambridge, MA: MIT.

Gelati, J., A. Rotolo, G. Sartor, and G. Governatori. 2004. Normative autonomy and normative co-ordination: Declarative power, representation, and mandate. *Artificial Intelligence and Law* 12(1–2): 53–81.

Gordon, T. F. 1995. *The pleadings game. An artificial intelligence model of procedural justice*. Kluwer, Dordrecht.

Gordon, T. F., and D. N. Walton. 2009. Legal reasoning with argumentation schemes. In *Proceedings of the twelfth international conference on artificial intelligence and law (ICAIL 2009)*. New York: ACM.

Gordon, T. F., H. Prakken, and D. N. Walton. 2007. The Carneades model of argument and burden of proof. *Artificial Intelligence* 171: 875–896 (Forthcoming.)

Gordon, T. F., G. Governatori, and A. Rotolo. 2009. Rules and norms: Requirements for rule interchange languages in the legal domain. In *Rule Representation, Interchange and Reasoning on the Web*, LNCS, vol. 5858, 282–296, ed. G. Governatori, J. Hall, and A. Paschke. Berlin: Springer.

Hage, J. C. 1997. *Reasoning with rules: An essay on legal reasoning and its underlying logic*. Dordrecht: Kluwer.

Hage, J. C. 2011. A model of juridical acts: Part 2: The operation of juridical acts. *Artificial Intelligence and Law* 19: 49–73.

Herrestad, H., and C. Krogh. 1995. Obligations directed from bearers to counterparties. In *Proceedings of the 5th international conference on artificial intelligence and law (ICAIL'95)*, 210–218. New York: ACM Press.

Hohfeld, W. N. 1911. Some fundamental legal conceptions as applied in judicial reasoning. *Yale Law Journal* 23(16): 16–59.

Horty, J. F. 1999. Precedent, deontic logic and inheritance. In *Proceedings of the seventh international conference on artificial intelligence and law (ICAIL)*, 23–72. New York: ACM.

Horty, J. F. 2001. *Agency and deontic logic*. Oxford: Oxford University Press.

Jones, A. J. I., and M. Sergot. 1996. A formal characterization of institutionalised power. *Journal of the IGPL* 3: 427–443.

Lodder, A. R. 1999. *DiaLaw: On legal justification and dialogical models of argumentation*. Law and Philosophy Library. Dordrecht: Kluwer Academic.

Loui, R. P., and J. Norman. 1995. Rationales and argument moves. *Artificial Intelligence and Law*, 3: 159–189.

Loui, R. P., J. Norman, J. Olson, and A. Merrill. 1993. A design for reasoning with policies, precedents, and rationales. In *ICAIL*, 202–211.

McCarty, L. T. 1986. Permissions and obligations: An informal introduction. In *Automated analysis of legal texts*, ed. A. A. Martino and F. Socci, 307–337. Amsterdam: North Holland.

McCarty, L. T. 1988a. Clausal intuitionistic logic. i. fixed-point semantics. *Journal of Logic Programming* 5: 1–31.

McCarty, L. T. 1988b. Clausal intuitionistic logic ii – tableau proof procedures. *Journal of Logic Programming* 5: 93–132.

Philipps, L., and G. Sartor (eds.). 1999. Neural networks and fuzzy reasoning in the law. Special issue. *Artificial Intelligence and Law*, vol. 7.

Pollock, J. 1995a. *Cognitive carpentry*. Cambridge MA: MIT.

Pollock, J. L. 1995b. *Cognitive carpentry: A blueprint for how to build a person*. New York: MIT.

Prakken, H. 2001. Relating protocols for dynamic dispute with logics for defeasible argumentation. *Synthese* 127: 187–219.

Prakken, H. 2010. An abstract framework for argumentation with structured arguments. *Argument and Computation* 1: 93–124.

Prakken, H., and G. Sartor. 1996. Rules about rules: Assessing conflicting arguments in legal reasoning. *Artificial Intelligence and Law* 4: 331–368.

Prakken, H., and G. Sartor. 1998a. Modelling reasoning with precedents in a formal dialogue game. *Artificial Intelligence and Law* 6: 231–287.

Prakken, H., and G. Sartor. 1998b. Modelling reasoning with precedents in a formal dialogue game. *Artificial Intelligence and Law* 6(2–4): 231–287.

Reed, C., and G. Rowe. 2007. A pluralist approach to argument diagramming. *Law, Probability and Risk* 6: 59–85.

Rissland, E. L., and D. Skalak. 1993. Arguments and cases: An inevitable intertwining. *Artificial Intelligence and Law* 1: 3–44.

Riveret, R., N. Rotolo, G. Sartor, H. Prakken, and B. Roth. 2007. Success chances in argument games: A probabilistic approach to legal disputes. In *Proceeding of legal knowledge and information systems – JURIX 2007*, ed. A. R. Lodder, 99–108. Amsterdam: IOS.

Sartor, G. 2002. Teleological arguments and theory-based dialectics. *Artificial Intelligence and Law* 10: 95–112.

Sartor, G. 2006. Fundamental legal concepts: A formal and teleological characterisation. *Artificial Intelligence and Law* 21: 101–142.

Sergot, M. J., F. Sadri, R. A. Kowalski, F. Kriwaczek, P. Hammond, and H. Cory. 1986. The British Nationality Act as a logic program. *Communications of the ACM* 29, 370–386.

Sartor, G., M. Rudnianski, A. Rotolo, R. Riveret, and E. Mayor. 2009. Why lawyers are nice (or nasty): A game-theoretical argumentation exercise. In *Proceedings of the twelfth international conference on artificial intelligence and law*, 108–119. New York: ACM.

Sartor, G., P. Casanovas, M. Biasiotti, and M. Fernández-Barrera (eds.). 2011. *Approaches to legal ontologies*. New York: Springer.

Verheij, B. 2003. Artificial argument assistants for defeasible argumentation. *Artificial Intelligence* 150, 291–324.

Walton, D. N. 2005. *Argumentation methods for artificial intelligence in law*. Berlin: Springer.

Walton, D. N., and E. Krabbe. 1995. *Commitment in dialogue. Basic concepts of interpersonal reasoning*. Albany: State University of New York Press.

Walton, D. N., C. Reed, and F. Macagno. 2008. *Argumentation schemes*. Cambridge MA: Cambridge University Press.

Yoshino, H. 1978. Über die notwendigkeit einer besonderen normenlogik als methode der juristischen logik. In *Gesetzgebungstheorie, juristische Logik, Zivil, und Prozeßrecht*. Gedächtnisschrift für Jürgen Rödig, ed. U. Klug, T. Ramm, F. Rittner, and B. Schmiedel, 140–161. Berlin: Springer.

Zeleznikow, J., and A. Stranieri. 1995. The split-up system: Integrating neural networks and rule based reasoning in the legal domain. In *Proceedings of the fifth international conference on artificial intelligence and law (ICAIL)*, 185–194. New York: ACM.

Chapter 14
Normative Agents

Michael Luck, Samhar Mahmoud, Felipe Meneguzzi, Martin Kollingbaum, Timothy J. Norman, Natalia Criado, and Moser Silva Fagundes

14.1 Introduction

While there have been many efforts to consider norms in various different perspectives, from that of the logics and other formalisms used to represent them (see Chaps. 10 and 12) to their role in combination with argumentation and trust (see Chaps. 15 and 16), this chapter addresses work on the development of *normative agents*. In this sense, we focus on agent architectures in which action is determined by norms in a system or environment. More specifically, in open dynamic societies, agents are required to work with others that do not necessarily have the same set of objectives. If left unchecked, self-interested agents will try to accomplish their individual goals without regard for others. Norms provide a means to regulate agent behaviour, and this requires some consideration of the ways in which norms impact on agent reasoning and behaviour.

M. Luck (✉) • S. Mahmoud
Department of Informatics, King's College London, London, UK
e-mail: michael.luck@kcl.ac.uk; samhar.mahmoud@kcl.ac.uk

F. Meneguzzi
Faculdade de Informática, Pontifícia Universidade Católica do Rio Grande do Sul, Av. Ipiranga 6681, Prédio 32, 90619-900 Porto Alegre, Brazil
e-mail: felipe@meneguzzi.eu

M. Kollingbaum • T.J. Norman
Department of Computing Science, University of Aberdeen, Aberdeen, UK
e-mail: m.j.kollingbaum@abdn.ac.uk; t.j.norman@abdn.ac.uk

N. Criado
Departamento de Sistemas Informáticos y Computación, Universitat Politècnica de València, Camino de Vera s/n, 46022 Valencia, Spain
e-mail: ncriado@dsic.upv.es

M.S. Fagundes
CETINIA, University Rey Juan Carlos, c/ Tulipán s/n, 28933 Móstoles, Madrid, Spain
e-mail: moser.fagundes@urjc.es

S. Ossowski (ed.), *Agreement Technologies*, Law, Governance and Technology Series 8, DOI 10.1007/978-94-007-5583-3_14,

14.2 Normative Behaviour

It has been argued that, in many cases, autonomous agents can be assumed to obey standard protocols, and are thus predictable in some ways, implying a level of knowledge of the internal mechanisms of these agents (Dignum 1999). Here, predictability is the result of a set of hard-wired conventions, undermining agent autonomy and consequently an agent's ability to react to a dynamic environment. In this view, autonomous agents must be able to reason about the norms with which they should comply, and occasionally violate them if they are in conflict among themselves or with the agent's private goals. In this respect, Dignum (1999) distinguishes between three levels at which agent behaviour is influenced by such norms: the *conventions* level; the *contract* level; and the *private* level.

The conventions level covers obligations that constitute a default background against which agents interact. These are generally fixed on initialisation, and represent general rules for agents in a system to follow (termed *prima facie* norms), and it is assumed that agents follow the rules either due to a common sense benefit, or due to agents in charge of enforcing conventions. The contract level covers commitments between agents, in the form of either directed obligations or authorisations. Directed obligations express a commitment from one agent to another that either a world-state will hold or an action will be executed. Authorisations express the justification of an agent to perform an action involving another agent; for example, if an agent is to demand payment from another (implying that the latter agent is obliged to pay), it must be authorised to do so. The private level is used to translate the influences received from the other levels into something that directs an agent's future behaviour. For example, in a BDI setting, external influences and their conditions can be translated into conditional desires for an agent.

Following this view, López y López and Luck (2003) and López y López et al. (2004) provide a formal model of norms whose constructs are reasoned about by autonomous agents. In this model, norms are prescriptive in that they specify how agents should behave, and social as they are used in situations in which multiple agents might come into conflict. Moreover, given the possibility that norms might conflict with an agent's individual goals and that punishments are defined for non-compliance, norms also represent a form of social pressure upon the agent. Because norms in a given system are rarely isolated from each other, in López y López and Luck's model, systems of norms are created to ensure that agents comply with whole sets of norms rather than choosing individual norms with which to comply. Systems of norms can also be used to maintain consistency among constituent norms. The association of multiple norms can be attained by relating the activation of a given norm to the violation (or fulfilment) of another through activation triggers, whereby a *secondary* norm is activated to punish the non-compliant agent. Alternatively, agents can be encouraged to comply with certain norms if other norms are created to trigger rewards to compliant agents. These triggers may serve the purpose of either punishing norm violators or rewarding norm followers. In the case where a violator requires punishment for a transgression, an *enforcement* norm might be activated following the transgression (see also Chap. 11). Alternatively, achievement of a prescriptive goal might trigger a *reward* norm so that the compliant agent will be rewarded. Finally, norms may be used to provide for the evolution of the normative system itself. In this context, *legislation* norms are used to permit actions to issue new norms or abolish existing ones.

Since normative systems are maintained within the society employing them through delegation of punishment, reward and legislative goals, the effect of these systems upon prospective members of these societies can also be reasoned about by autonomous agents. When deciding whether to voluntarily join or leave a society regulated by norms, López y López et al. (2004) advocate that an autonomous agent must have an additional set of characteristics to include ways of reasoning about the advantages and disadvantages of complying with the norms, thus leading to the possibility of norm violation. Violation can occur for three main reasons: individual goals can conflict with society norms; norms might conflict among themselves; and agents might be members of more than one society. In light of the possibility of norm infringement and the need for autonomous agents to reason about normative societies, López y López et al. (2004) also define reasoning mechanisms over the effects of norm compliance and violation, as well as rewards and punishments. Their model proposes methods for evaluating the benefits of joining a society as well as methods for evaluating whether to stay in a society or to leave it. An agent is seen as staying in a society for two main reasons: due to unfulfilled goals within the society or social obligations. Here, a social obligation might be that of complying with agreed norms, to reciprocate or help a fellow agent, or even coercion from another member of the society. The autonomy advocated by this model also includes mechanisms for an agent to voluntarily adopt norms; that is, an agent recognises itself as an addressee and starts following the appropriate norms. This mechanism is important, for instance in situations in which societal laws change dynamically. Finally, the model defines processes through which an agent complies with the norms by adopting or refraining from adopting intentions to achieve normative goals.

All this suggests that agents must be endowed with abilities to be able to reason about, process and otherwise manage norms in some appropriate fashion. In short, it demands that agent architectures are considered in terms of their ability to address these concerns, and that suitable architectures are developed.

14.3 Normative Reasoning

Normative agents must be able to reason about their normative or social position within a society. Normative reasoning is an important concept for normative agents both: to congregate into social structures with other agents and establish agreements among them as the normative standard of their participation in concerted activities; and to reason about their actions in the context of these agreements. The social position of a normative agent is determined by the social pressures, which are in turn described by regulations, policies or *norms*, under which the agent operates. These regulatory concepts are external to the agent in its social context, but must be internalised as mental or normative attitudes (and represented as computational concepts in concrete implementations) in order to become effective in the agent's normative reasoning. The process of socialisation itself requires an agent to recognise the norms regulating the society and to adopt certain norms in the context of agreements. However, adopting new norms may lead to conflicts with norms already held by the agent or interfere with its goals (e.g., actions may be, at the same time, obliged and forbidden). The agent, therefore, has to resolve these conflicts in order to remain operational. We consider these issues below in more detail.

14.4 Norm Recognition

Norm recognition (Conte et al. 1999) refers to the ability of an agent to infer regulatory standards, conventions and norms of a society via observation and interaction with individuals. It also plays a role in monitoring norm-abiding behaviour and detecting deviations. According to Conte et al. (1999), new norms can be recognised as versions of existing norms if, for example, they are *instantiations* of existing norms or *interpretations* of them. Alternatively, an agent can accept a new norm if its *issuer* is known to be a normative authority that is allowed to issue norms. Finally, a new norm can be evaluated against the motivation of the issuer: if the norm was issued because of the issuer's self interest but has no utility for the society, then the agent may decide not to accept it.

14.5 Norm Adoption

Norm adoption is the process of an agent accepting new norms that will influence its practical reasoning. Conte et al. (1999) state that an agent accepts (adopts) a norm only if it believes that this norm helps in a direct or indirect way to achieve one of its goals. Adopting a norm does not mean that an agent will automatically comply with it (in fact, it may choose to violate norms). López y López et al. also point out that agents adopting a norm must actually be the individuals whose actions are regulated by this norm (the norm *addressee*). In addition, as argued in Kollingbaum and Norman (2003b), the adoption of new norms may cause conflicts with the norms already held by an agent and may render this agent unable to choose an action that is *norm-consistent*. For example, if an action required to fulfil an adopted obligation is already forbidden, an agent may not be able to remain norm-consistent in its behaviour, unless it finds another action that would equally fulfil the newly adopted obligation without being prohibited. Accordingly, as pointed out in Kollingbaum and Norman (2003b), so-called *consistency levels* for obligations can be introduced.

Strong consistency indicates that adopting a new obligation causes no conflicts, *weak consistency* indicates that among the set of candidate actions there is at least one that is prohibited, while *inconsistency* indicates that no actions are permitted to be deployed by the agent. If the agent adopts a new prohibition then this may impact on the consistency level of obligations already held and indicate a conflict within the set of norms. Conflict resolution strategies must thus be employed in order to resolve such situations.

14.6 Norm Compliance

Norm compliance is a critical phase of normative reasoning, as an agent decides within this phase if it is going to comply with a norm. Whatever the decision, this can bring a significant impact on agent behaviour. If an agent complies with a norm then some of its goals might conflict with this norm, causing the agent not to be able to achieve any of these goals. Conversely, if an agent refuses to conform to the norm then some punishments may be applied, which in turn can affect the achievement of some of goals. There have been few attempts to deal with the norm compliance decision. Most are concerned with decisions based on the existence of conflicts between different norms or between norms and goals. Existing proposals resolve these conflicts by using static procedures such as utility functions, preference ordering functions and so on. Thus, conflicts are the only cause of norm violations. However, Conte et al. (1999) argue that an agent decides to comply with a norm based on different criteria. It might refuse to comply with a norm if it conflicts with more important goals or with other norms that the agent has already decided to comply with. Conversely, an agent might decide to comply because of the *guilt* felt as a result of not complying or because of the consequence of not doing so. Kollingbaum and Norman (2003b) propose different strategies to resolve conflicts between different kinds of norm and determine which norm to comply with. For example, an agent can decide to comply with a norm that is issued by a source whose social power is higher, or to adopt a norm that has been activated more recently. In López y López et al. (2002) propose several strategies for allowing agents to make flexible decisions about norm compliance. These strategies are based on the impact of norms on agent's goals in terms of direct consequences and indirect consequences (i.e. sanctions and rewards) of norms.

14.7 Normative Agent Architectures

Normative agents require particular architectures for their implementation. While the Belief-Desire-Intention (BDI) model has been widely used to explain agent behaviour in terms of mental attitudes such as beliefs, desires and intentions, for a computational model of norm-governed agency, explicit representations of normative attitudes (as outlined in previous sections) are needed, with clarification of the reasons for these attitudes. Agents must recognise norms as social concepts, represent them as mental objects and act in the face of these norms (even if there are conflicts among them). Many proposals for a *normative* agent architectures take BDI as a starting point and extend it with norms. Classic implementations of BDI (such as PRS, the Procedural Reasoning System Georgeff and Lansky 1987) are based on reactive planning, with a set of pre-specified plan procedures as the behavioural repertoire of an agent and a deliberation process that selects a plan for action based on an agent's beliefs and goals. Many implementations of normative agent architectures thus take BDI and procedural reasoning as a starting point and introduce norms as an influencing factor into this deliberation process. Concerns, such as *norm-consistent* actions and resolution of conflicts between norms, further influence the design of these systems.

Early Approaches. Castelfranchi et al. (2000) propose a *generic* architecture for deliberative normative agents, which is able to recognise a norm in a society, adopt that norm, deliberatively follow it, and deliberatively violate it in an intelligent way. The work was one of the first efforts to incorporate norms into an agent architecture. Until then, experiments with normative agents sought to provide social simulations so as to compare selfish and altruistic behaviours hard-coded into agent specifications (such agents could not modify their behaviour over time). According to Castelfranchi et al. the precise knowledge by which goals are generated depends on the application addressed; their generic normative architecture only provides *elements* that can be used but does not commit to a specific approach to goal generation.

In another early effort, Dignum et al. (2000) present an approach to social reasoning that integrates prior work in norms and obligations (van der Torre and Tan 1999) with the BDI agent model of Rao and Georgeff (1995). Here, the agent has knowledge about norms and chooses whether or not to comply with norms, and how to assess the impact of punishment of violation. Norms are not hard-wired into agents: circumstances might change, making norms obsolete, and agents might interact with others that follow different norms, so explicit representation of norms and obligations can support more flexible and appropriate reasoning. In this model, an agent might not comply with an applicable norm automatically if the norm is in conflict with other norms, if the norm does not achieve its original intention, or if the norm is applicable but the agent has not adopted it. Choices between conflicting norms are made with predefined preference orderings.

Boella and Damiano (2002) propose a model of normative reasoning that allows an agent to react to norms in dynamically changing social contexts by forming norm-related intentions based on utility considerations. Here, utility of norm-compliant behaviour is evaluated with respect to the social environment in which the agent is situated: the agent decides whether a norm is worth compliance by comparing the utility difference from complying (thus avoiding a sanction) or violating it. The architecture relies on a *meta-deliberation* module to evaluate the need for intention revision. Deliberation is based on decision-theoretic notions: the agent is driven by the overall goal of maximising its utility based on a set of preferences encoded in a utility function. Every time an agent is obliged to comply with a norm, it forms a *normative goal* (exogenous goal) with reference to that norm.

BOID. The BOID architecture (Broersen et al. 2002) was introduced as a solution for BDI agents that act in a noisy environment, where the agent is overloaded with inputs. Its main problem is how an agent selects which obligation to comply with from a set of conflicting obligations, in addition to satisfying its own goals. BOID extends the BDI model by introducing obligations as a new component in addition to the main components of beliefs, desires and intentions, where goals are generated from the interaction between beliefs, obligations, intentions and desires, and biased by the type of agent: *realistic*, *stable*, *selfish* and *social*. The agent's candidate goals are selected based on a static priority function on the rules that govern the agent's behaviour, which also determine which inference steps must be made. As a consequence, some rules may be overridden by others, enabling the resolution of conflict between mental attitudes by different agent types. Thus, BOID agents always consider norms in the same manner; that is, they cannot decide to follow or violate a given norm according to their circumstances. These conflicts between mental attitudes can be classified into internal and external conflicts (Broersen et al. 2001). Internal conflicts are caused by information within the same component, such as the conflict between two beliefs or two obligations. For example, if an agent has an obligation to be polite and at the same time it has another obligation to be honest, this may cause a conflict as being honest sometimes implies impoliteness. External conflicts occur between information from two or more different components, such as a conflict between an intention and an obligation or between a desire and an obligation, for example a conflict between an obligation not to smoke in a non-smoking area and a desire to smoke in the office which is a non-smoking area. (See also the section on argumentation for more on practical reasoning with BOID in the presence of norms.)

EMIL-A. In the context of the EMIL-A architecture, Andrighetto et al. (2007, 2010) explain the main phases that norms undergo in order to evolve from the environment into the agent's internal state. These phases involve: recognising new norms and generating *normative beliefs*; deciding whether to adopt the norms, generating *normative goals*; determining whether to comply with them generating *normative intentions*; and, finally, generating plans that comply with the norms. In order to achieve the requisite behaviour, there is also an inventory containing a *normative board*, which is a set of existing norms and normative information available to an agent, and a repertoire of normative action plans (that consist of actions that comply with norms). The resulting behaviour of EMIL-A can be of two types: the agent can either comply with the norm or violate it. Violation may, however, trigger defence mechanisms that are used to spread the norms to other agents. Apart from the architecture design, Andrighetto's work also focuses on how EMIL-A allows a new norm to be perceived and established as an instance of an existing norm, as part of the norm recognition component. Moreover, EMIL-A agents are also capable of determining the pertinence of norms and their degree of activation; that is, the norm *salience* (Andrighetto et al. 2010; Villatoro et al. 2011). This norm salience is used as a criterion for accepting or rejecting norms, with the decision about norm compliance being determined by a utility function that calculates the expected utility that agents should obtain if they fulfill or violate the norm.

NoA. The NoA Normative Agent architecture (Kollingbaum and Norman 2003a) was one of the first practical agent architectures to support the implementation of norm-governed practical reasoning agents. NoA is based on classic BDI concepts with extensions that allow an agent to reason about norms; it is implemented as a reactive planning architecture. Here, obligations are the principal motivators for an agent to act, whereas prohibitions and permissions indicate which action choices would be allowed or forbidden. As NoA is based on reactive planning, the behavioural repertoire of an agent is described by a set of pre-specified plan procedures. NoA itself is characterised by two particular features: the distinction between an agent achieving a state of affairs or directly performing a particular action; and a specific form of deliberation, called *informed deliberation*. The NoA language (the semantics of which is implemented by the architecture) contains constructs for the specification of beliefs, goals, plans and norms. In line with the distinction between states and actions, norm specifications may regulate either the achievement of a particular state of affairs (e.g., an obligation demands an agent to employ whatever means are at its disposal to achieve a particular state of the world) or the performance of explicit actions (without consideration of the state that would be produced). This particular feature is reflected in the plan specifications, which are characterised by explicit declarations of effects, where an effect may become the reason for a plan to be selected as an action. The second aspect, informed deliberation, allows an agent to remain *norm-autonomous* in that options for actions (or plans) that are forbidden are not *excluded* but are instead labelled as forbidden and remain options if an agent chooses to act in violation of norms under special circumstances (e.g., to resolve conflicts between norms).

Normative AgentSpeak(L). Meneguzzi and Luck (2009) similarly provide a practical approach to norm management at the agent-level by extending the AgentSpeak(L) language with mechanisms for norm receipt and plan library modification to enforce compliance with norms. This extended interpreter, *Normative AgentSpeak(L)*, includes meta-level actions that allow an agent to scan its own plan library for plans that would violate a set of norms that an agent has previously accepted to comply. The plan library modification mechanism works exclusively with prohibitions and obligations. For prohibitions, violating plans are temporarily removed from the plan library while the prohibition is in effect. Conversely, for obligations, new plans are created using a planning mechanism (Meneguzzi and Luck 2008) so that an agent has plans that can accomplish such norms.

By using such a plan library modification and filtering mechanism that enforces compliance with norms, normative agents based on *Normative AgentSpeak(L)* achieve norm-compliant behaviour. Options for actions that are prohibited are removed from the plan library and are not available for the agent to be chosen during its deliberation. *Normative AgentSpeak(L)* therefore assumes that agents always seek to comply with norms. The framework is sufficiently generic that it can be extended into any traditional BDI style agent language. Importantly, the algorithms are reified in a concrete instantiation in Jason, enabling agents to generate new plans to comply with norms, and to remove plans when such norms are no longer relevant.

Recent Proposals. There are several further but less developed proposals for normative agents. To take just one example, the n-BDI architecture (Criado et al. 2010) consists in extending a multi-context graded BDI agent architecture with an explicit representation of norms. Thus, the n-BDI architecture brings agents the possibility of: identifying norms involving behaviour and inferring the content of these norms; making a decision about norm compliance; and generating motivations to comply with norms. Specifically, in Criado et al. (2011) this proposal was improved with a coherence-based reasoning mechanism (Joseph et al. 2010) that allows n-BDI agents to confront the norm compliance dilemma. Here, the coherence-based mechanism allows agents to address those conflicts that arise between norms and mental propositions. This process "computes a realistic preference ordering considering the constraints that exist among the cognitive elements of an agent" (Joseph et al. 2010).

In a rather different effort, Fagundes et al. (2010) put forward an architecture for normative rational self-interested agents inhabiting non-deterministic and dynamic environments governed by norms. This agent architecture uses the Markov Decision Process (MDP) framework to represent the agent's knowledge, norms and sanctions. To adapt to newly accepted norms, the architecture includes an *adaptive component* that represents these norms and their respective sanctions within the agent's MDP. In this model, an agent decides to violate a norm only if the expected utility obtained with the defection from this norm surpasses the expected utility obtained by being norm-compliant (*economical rationality*). The degree of impunity of the system is also taken into account through transition probabilities to sanctioned states of the world.

14.8 Challenges

Despite the increasing number of efforts devoted to developing and investigating different aspects of normative agents, as reviewed above, there are still very many open questions and challenges remaining. Boella et al. (2008) discuss ten challenges that arise in the *interactionist* perspective of normative multi-agent systems, when norms are not *legalistic* constraints imposed from above, but emerge through the interactions of individuals in a society. Among these challenges are those: to ensure that agents are able to recognise, explicitly represent and communicate norms as they emerge in a society; to ensure that agents are able to identify the redundancy of norms and remove them when they are no longer needed; to ensure that agents are provided with the means to dynamically impose, monitor and enforce norms, potentially through the creation and management of organisational structures; and to provide (some) agents with power to create, modify and remove norms from a society or from a single interaction.

In addition to these specific areas of functionality, to some of which we are beginning to see some efforts being addressed, there are other areas of more general concern. For example, as pointed out by Castelfranchi (2003), *autonomy* is a vital concept to preserve for agents even in the presence of norms and enforcement. In this view, norms must be understood as informal constructs or general directives that cannot cover all cases. However, existing work typically considers *conflict* to be the cause of norm violation (as a result of some a priori preference ordering or utility function), so that agents cannot adapt their norm compliance decisions to suit their circumstances. Here, autonomy can be seen to be removed from agents in situations in which compliance brings no benefit to the society, yet is established through mechanisms for monitoring and enforcement.

Similarly, work on the impact of norms on agent goals in order to decide which norms to comply with does not explain how this relates to norms that do not affect agent goals directly or indirectly (that is, by means of sanctions and rewards). Yet work from psychology (Elster 1989) suggests that there are other motivations for norm compliance, such as shame or pride, that have still not been considered in the context of computational normative agents.

An additional consideration of normative agents also suggests what may be considered a valuable side-effect. Until now, explicit normative reasoning has accounted for the possibility that an agent may choose to deliberatively defect from complying with a norm, as a consequence of conflicts between norms, or conflicts between norms and individual agent goals. However, the relation between norms and planning (means-end reasoning) has received less attention. In particular, the construction of plans with large state spaces is a resource-intensive process that impacts the response time of resource-bounded agents. There is thus a tradeoff between the improvement of plans for action and the consumption of computational resources. In this context, norms can provide the constraints that drive more efficient planning algorithms for finding near-optimal solutions. In this sense norms provide valuable constraints on aspects of an agent's reasoning process.

In summary, while there has been much progress on normative agents, providing a rich set of concepts, theories and tools, there is still much that can and should be done in this area. Indeed, the increasing move to open and dynamic computational systems of interacting entities in all walks of life suggests that this work will be vital if we are to ensure that our systems are effective and robust. In this sense, sophisticated normative agents are a necessity for us all.

References

Andrighetto, G., M. Campennì, R. Conte, and M. Paolucci. 2007. On the immergence of norms: A normative agent architecture. In *Proceedings of AAAI symposium, social and organizational aspects of intelligence*, Washington, DC.

Andrighetto, G., M. Campennì, F. Cecconi, and R. Conte. 2010. The complex loop of norm emergence: A simulation model. In *Simulating interacting agents and social phenomena*, Agent-based social systems, vol. 7, ed. H. Deguchi et al., 19–35. Tokyo: Springer.

Andrighetto, G., D. Villatoro, and R. Conte. 2010. Norm internalization in artificial societies. *AI Communications* 23: 325–339.

Boella, G., and R. Damiano. 2002. An architecture for normative reactive agents. In *Intelligent agents and multi-agent systems, 5th pacific rim international workshop on multi agents*, Lecture notes in computer science, vol. 2413, ed. K. Kuwabara and J. Lee, 1–17. Berlin: Springer.

Boella, G., L. van der Torre, and H. Verhagen. 2008. Ten challenges for normative multiagent systems. In *Programming multi-agent systems, no. 08361 in Dagstuhl seminar proceedings, schloss Dagstuhl – Leibniz-Zentrum fuer Informatik*, Dagstuhl, ed. R. Bordini, M. Dastani, J. Dix, and A.E. Fallah-Seghrouchni.

Broersen, J., M. Dastani, J. Hulstijn, Z. Huang, and L. van der Torre. 2001. The BOID architecture: Conflicts between beliefs, obligations, intentions and desires. In *Proceedings of the fifth international conference on autonomous agents*, 9–16. New York: ACM.

Broersen, J., M. Dastani, J. Hulstijn, and L. van der Torre. 2002. Goal generation in the BOID architecture. *Cognitive Science Quarterly Journal* 2(3–4): 428–447.

Castelfranchi, C. 2003. Formalising the informal. *Journal of Applied Logic* 1(1–2): 47–92.

Castelfranchi, C., F. Dignum, C.M. Jonker, and J. Treur. 2000. Deliberative normative agents: Principles and architecture. In *Intelligent agents VI: Proceedings of the sixth international workshop on agent theories architectures and languages*, Lecture notes in computer science, vol. 1757, ed. N.R. Jennings and Y. Lespérance, 364–378. Berlin: Springer.

Conte, R., C. Castelfranchi, and F. Dignum. 1999. Autonomous Norm Acceptance. In *Intelligent agents V: Proceedings of the fifth international workshop on agent theories architectures and languages*, Lecture notes in computer science, vol. 1555, ed. J.P. Müller, M.P. Singh, and A.S. Rao, 99–112. Berlin: Springer.

Criado, N., E. Argente, and V. Botti. 2010. Normative deliberation in graded BDI agents. In *Multiagent system technologies: Proceedings of the eighth german conference on multi-agent system technologies*, Lecture notes in artificial intelligence, vol. 6251, 52–63. Berlin: Springer.

Criado, N., E. Argente, V. Botti, and P. Noriega. 2011. Reasoning about norm compliance. In *Proceedings of the tenth international conference on autonomous agents and multiagent systems*, 1191–1192. Taipei: Taiwan.

Dignum, F. 1999. Autonomous agents with norms. *Artificial Intelligence and Law* 7(1): 69–79.

Dignum, F., D.N. Morley, L. Sonenberg, and L. Cavedon. 2000. Towards socially sophisticated BDI agents. In *Proceedings of the fourth international conference on multi-agent systems*, Boston, 111–118.

Elster, J. 1989. Social norms and economic theory. *Journal of Economic Perspectives* 3(4): 99–117.

Fagundes, M.S., H. Billhardt, and S. Ossowski. 2010. Reasoning about norm compliance with rational agents. In *Proceedings of the 19th European conference on artificial intelligence*, Frontiers in artificial intelligence and applications, vol. 215, ed. H. Coelho, R. Studer, and M. Wooldridge, 1027–1028. Amsterdam: IOS.

Georgeff, M., and A.L. Lansky. 1987. Reactive reasoning and planning. In *Proceedings of the 6th conference on AAAI*, Seattle, 677–682.

Joseph, S., C. Sierra, M. Schorlemmer, and P. Dellunde. 2010. Deductive coherence and norm adoption. *Logic Journal of the IGPL* 18(1): 118–156.

Kollingbaum, M.J., and T.J. Norman. 2003. NoA – A normative agent architecture. In *Proceedings of the eighteenth international joint conference on artificial intelligence*, ed. G. Gottlob and T. Walsh, 1465–1466. San Francisco: Morgan Kaufmann.

Kollingbaum, M.J., and T.J. Norman. 2003. Norm adoption in the NoA agent architecture. In *Proceedings of the second international joint conference on autonomous agents and multiAgent Systems*, 1038–1039. New York: ACM.

López y López, F., and M. Luck. 2003. Modelling norms for autonomous agents. In *Proceedings of the fourth Mexican international conference on computer science*, Tlaxcala, 238–245.

López y López, F., M. Luck, and M. d'Inverno. 2002. Constraining autonomy through norms. In *Proceedings of the first international joint conference on autonomous agents and multiagent systems*, 674–681. New York: ACM.

López y López, F., M. Luck, and M. d'Inverno. 2004. Normative agent reasoning in dynamic societies. In: *Proceedings of the third international joint conference on autonomous agents and multiagent systems*, pp. 732–739. New York: IEEE Computer Society (2004).

Meneguzzi, F., and M. Luck. 2008. Composing high-level plans for declarative agent programming. In *Declarative agent languages and technologies V, proceedings of the fifth international workshop*, Lecture notes in computer science, vol. 4897, ed. M. Baldoni, T.C. Son, M.B. van Riemsdijk, and M. Winikoff, 69–85. Berlin: Springer.

Meneguzzi, F., and M. Luck. 2009. Norm-based behaviour modification in BDI agents. In *Proceedings of the eighth international conference on autonomous agents and multiagent systems*, Budapest, 177–184.

Rao, A.S., and M.P. Georgeff. 1995. BDI agents: From theory to practice. In *Proceedings of the first international conference on multi-agent systems*, San Francisco, 312–319.

van der Torre, L.W.N., and Y.H. Tan. 1999. Contrary-to-duty reasoning with preference-based dyadic obligations. *Annals of Mathematics and Artificial Intelligence* 27(1–4): 49–78.

Villatoro, D., G. Andrighetto, R. Conte, and J. Sabater-Mir. 2011. *Dynamic sanctioning for robust and cost-efficient norm compliance*, 414–419. Barcelona: IJCAI/AAAI.

Chapter 15
Norms and Trust

Rino Falcone, Cristiano Castelfranchi, Henrique Lopes Cardoso, Andrew Jones, and Eugénio Oliveira

15.1 Introduction

In this chapter we would like to show how interesting and not at all trivial and obvious are the relationships between Norms and Trust. In fact, the relationship between Trust and Social and Legal Norms is rather complicated (for an analysis see also Part VI in this book). This has been object of several misunderstandings and controversies in the literature, and never clearly systematized in its various, well characterized aspects, on the basis of a principled and precise model, able to explain, not just to describe, those relationships.

In this chapter we will briefly introduce some different (and in part complementary) analyses and approaches to the study of this relationship. In Falcone and Castelfranchi's contribution (see Sect. 15.2), how we can consider Trust as based on Norms (on the norm-based behavior of other agents) is analized, and, at the same time, how we can consider Norms as based on Trust, on the fact that without Trust, Norms are in practice ineffective and superfluous. In Lopes Cardoso and Oliveira's contribution (see Sect. 15.3), starting from the fact that an agent's trustworthiness can be evaluated on its compliance with norms, the authors consider the different ways to comply with a norm and the relationships with this analysis and the trust models. In particular the feedback on the norm adaptation. In Jones'

R. Falcone (✉) • C. Castelfranchi
Institute of Cognitive Sciences and Technologies – National Research Council, Rome, Italy
e-mail: rino.falcone@istc.cnr.it; cristiano.castelfranchi@istc.cnr.it

H. Lopes Cardoso • E. Oliveira
LIACC/DEI, Faculdade de Engenharia, Universidade do Porto, Rua Dr. Roberto Frias, 4200-465 Porto, Portugal
e-mail: hlc@fe.up.pt, eco@fe.up.pt

A. Jones
Department of Informatics, King's College London, London, UK
e-mail: andrewji.jones@kcl.ac.uk

S. Ossowski (ed.), *Agreement Technologies*, Law, Governance and Technology Series 8, DOI 10.1007/978-94-007-5583-3_15,

contribution (see Sect. 15.4), there is an interesting analogy among Obligation, Role and Information Scenarios with respect to the "intimate connection" between trust and rules. Then the author evaluates the need to consider the volitional component in the trust concept. In this view, analyzing the epistemic and volitional components, he sees a close link with some types of emotions (regret, anxiety, hope).

15.2 Trust and Norms: A Complex Relationships

We will characterize and explain two main kinds of relationship between Trust and Norms:

- Trust is based on Norms;
- Norms are based on Trust.

15.2.1 Norms as a Base for Expectations

The existence of Norms in a given community usually (and correctly) is one of the bases for predicting agents behavior in that specific community. Even without previous experience and observation and some sort of "statistics" characterizing those behaviors, a foreigner, informed about the existence of that practice and (technical, social, legal) norm in the community, is entitled to expect certain behaviors by the agents, from simply assuming that they will respect the norm.

Except when X has specific reasons for assuming that Y doesn't know about the norm (N), or that Y has specific attitudes or habits against respecting norms or that kind of norm, or has specific contextual reasons for violating, X, by default, will assume and expect that Y will behave conforming to the norm N. In other terms, the awareness of N is taken as a basis for "predictions" about the behavior of Y, and thus as a basis for relying on it; that is as a basis for trust: X is confident that a given pedestrian will not cross with the red light, and on such a basis X will speed up and cross, risking killing the pedestrian, in the case of a wrong prediction.

Given this relevant role played by the Norms with respect to trust, can we say that predictions (and thus expectations, and thus trust) always are based on norms? Be they either statistical norms or deontic norms. We do not think so. There are many bases for predicting human behaviors: norm keeping or statistical distribution are just two of these bases (Castelfranchi et al. 2006). Other forms of reasoning can be responsible for a given prediction: For example, *plan and intention ascription or recognition*. Since X ascribes to Y a given intention or plan (on the basis of Y's declarations, or of Y's current action, or of Y's characters, values, etc.) he will expect that Y will perform a given action.

Another basis can be *case-based, analogical reasoning*. Just on the basis of another similar circumstance, of another case, X predicts that Y will make a given move. Another can be simulation, to identify oneself with the other: X imagines himself in Y's shoes and expects that Y will do as he would do in those circumstances. In sum, we deny that predictions and expectations always and necessarily build on norms of some kind (at least, preserving a sufficiently well defined meaning for the notion of "norm", if not covering everything).

We can attribute to the Norms two different meanings: the first more descriptive, relating a regularity in behavior; N allows us to know if a given behavior/phenomenon is more or less strange, deviating, unpredictable, or *regular*, *conform*, to the standards presented in N, and predictable on such a base. The second one is more prescriptive, aiming at establishing a regularity of behavior. This is established via communication. The prescription can be explicit (norm issuing) or implicit/tacit; the N impinges on a set of autonomous, goal-directed agents (N's addressees and subjects). It presupposes an authority deciding what constitutes desirable behavior, issuing N, monitoring and possibly sanctioning the subjects. N can be originated by and reinforce usual social practices and conventions, or can be explicitly negotiated by the participants (collective authorities), or can be decided by an official (institutional) authority endowed with such a power and role. N involves different attitudes and roles; it is multi-agent construct: the role of the issuer; the role of the addressee/subject (which should respect N, and obey N); the role of surveillance (about violation or conformity); the role of punishing. These roles can be played by the same agent; for example, an obedient subject tends to watch and blame the violators. In a social context norms of the first type tend to become norms of the second type (not only predictions but prescription); and norms of the second type tends to create norms of the first type (regularities in behavior).

In our model (Castelfranchi and Falcone 2010) Norms are one of the possible bases for trust, but neither necessary nor sufficient. Moreover, there is no incompatibility between trust and formal norms, controls, contacts, etc. This just means *that some forms of Trust* are insufficient (the merely interpersonal, either by default, or shared-value based, personal acquaintance-based forms of trust, or trust relying on goodwill, etc.), and that *other forms of Trust* are invoked. Without (specific forms of) trust norms, contacts, authorities, etc. are ineffective.

15.2.2 Trust is the Necessary Base for Norms and Institutions

An implicit or explicit form of trust, the development of some confidence, is a necessary step and basis for the evolution of spontaneous social conventions, based on tacit negotiation and agreements. In fact, there is a crucial and necessary transition in the formation of any convention and social norm, which is the very moment of the agent X having expectations about the behavior of the other agents, and basing his own (conforming) behavior on such an expectation. X's behavior is based on this expectation in two ways.

- On the one side, X adjusts his own behavior on the basis of the predicted behavior of the other for avoiding "collisions" (obstacles) and obtaining a profitable *coordination*. While doing so X is relying on the expected behavior of Y, and makes himself depending on Y as for the success of his own action and of the common coordination.
- On the other side, the expectation that the others (Y) will act accordingly, is also a *reason* and a *motive* for adopting the "prescribed/expected" behavior, for non-deviating from the social norm or convention. Since the others conform to (and pay their tribute) X decides to conform to as well, and gives his contribution to the collectivity and to its working and maintenance (Castelfranchi and Falcone 2010).

However, what eventually is such a *prediction*, *expectation* on the others' conformity and behavior, and the *decision to rely* on them? And what is this *confidence* in the behavior of the others while doing our part and share? It is clearly just "Trust". X trusts the others to act conformingly; and he acts so just because feels confident in this. No coordination, conventions or social norms might be established or maintained without this ground of trust: everybody trusting everybody to keep the convention and being predictable. X also trusts the others to understand his expectations, and to be in agreement, unless and until they do not explicitly manifest their disagreement. Without an explicit signal, X is entitled to believe and to trust them. In a sense, X also believes and wants the others to trust him based on conventional behavior. There is an implicit prescription of this: *you must trust me to be respectful, as I trust you.*

Trust in the systems, in the institution, in the authority, in the conventions, practices, and norms, is a fundamental basis for the functioning and maintenance of even the more formal and institutional norms and norm-related roles and acts. In fact, X is relying on the existence of a norm simply because he believes that there is some entitled, recognized, and respected authority issuing it, which is also monitoring possible violations, and is capable of sanctioning bad behavior; moreover, there are also legal procedures and places for defending, etc.

In fact, what actually "gives" a policeman power, for example, is the recognition of his role by the public, the fact that people act conformingly with this recognition, and consider the policeman's actions as special (count as) actions (for example, arresting or prescribing, prohibiting or issuing fines). While accepting this they in fact give him (and to the delegating institution) this power of performing those actions. Institutional actions and powers require (unconscious) compliance and cooperation by people. But they do so only because and while they believe that the policemen is acting as policeman, not for example for his own private interest or disregarding the law; and they respect the policeman (or worry about him) because they predict his behavior and rely on this. In other words, they trust the policeman and his actions in a specific way. To consider him as a policeman and to act accordingly, and trusting him (and rely on him) as a policeman, are just one and the same thing. Without this no use of norms (contracts, etc.) is possible. Nobody would trust this, and norms would become ineffective or superfluous.

15.2.3 *The Micro-Macro Loop*

What we have just claimed in the previous sections gives trust a primacy relative to norms: trust seems to be an evolutionary forerunner (regarding coordination, order, and safety) of norms, and also a presupposition for norm evolution, establishment, and functioning. But, it also gives rise to a loop between trust and norms; and this loop is also a micro-macro, top-down vs. bottom-up, circle (Conte and Castelfranchi 1995; Giddens 1991). In fact, trust (individual attitude, choice and behavior) provides a ground for the emergence of conventions, norms, laws, institutions, etc.; but there is also a feedback to the individuals (and their representations) Castelfranchi (2000): Norms and Institutions are the bases for new expectations about people, and are a new presupposition for trusting them, for depending and relying on them. Moreover, this circle is an evolutionary one: reliance based on norms and institutions allows more advanced forms of social coordination and cooperation that would be impossible at the merely interpersonal level; and those forms of cooperation allow new forms of trust based on new signals, on new grounds.

15.3 The Norms-Trust-Norms Loop

By describing how agents are expected to behave in particular situations, under social environments, norms can be an important source of information to assess the ability or willingness of agents to perform certain tasks. In particular, when norms are used as a regulatory mechanism to govern multi-agent activities, a norm monitoring facility may provide important information regarding the abidance of agents with their social commitments

A number of trust models (e.g. Urbano et al. 2010, Sabater and Sierra 2005 and Huynh et al. 2006) have been designed that include an aggregation engine combining a set of evidences for a particular agent, and providing as an output a trustworthiness assessment of that agent. When governed by appropriate norms prescribing what agents ought to do, past interactions can be monitored in order to serve as a source for evidences. The different ways in which an agent may respond to the norms it is subject to comprise different evidences that a trust mechanism may handle differently.

Once some notion of the trustworthiness of an agent regarding a particular situation is derived, we may work the other way around: to change or adapt the norms so that the agents raise their positive expectation of what they may get from another particular agent for which some trustworthiness assessment has been computed. Norm changes may include, e.g., different sanctions to be applied in case of lack of compliance, with the aim of influencing the agent's behavior.

Figure 15.1 shows this interplay that may be achieved between norms and their monitoring process, trust building, and trust exploitation by negotiating norms to govern further relationships.

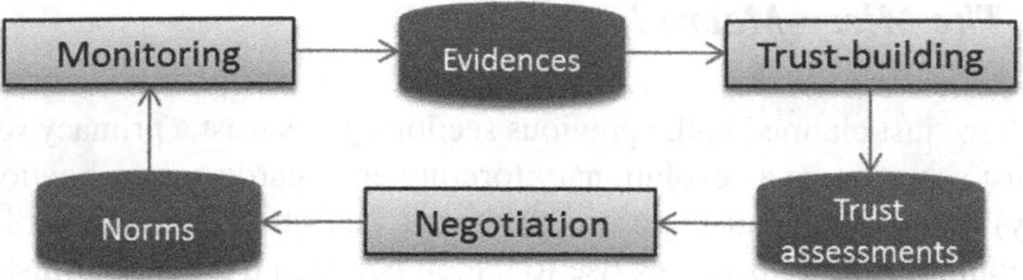

Fig. 15.1 Linking norms with trust with norms

15.3.1 Generating Evidence from Norm Monitoring

Different approaches to formalizing the notion of norms lead to different ways in which we might develop a mechanism for monitoring their compliance. Furthermore, in practical terms such compliance may be observed in a number of ways. The most simplistic one is to have a binary view and determine whether an agent either fulfills or violates a specific norm. This approach will, in turn, produce two kinds of evidences for trust building: either positive or negative. In some scenarios, however, we need to distinguish different cases in the "gray zone"; that is, cases where an agent has not fully complied with a norm but has nevertheless made an effort not to violate it. In this case we may have a number of different outcomes regarding the agents attitude towards the norm. And in turn, this means that we may have a richer set of inputs to feed a trust aggregation engine (Urbano et al. 2012).

For illustrative purposes, let us focus on a norm specification that prescribes a particular obligation of the form $Obl_{b,c}(l \prec f \prec d)$ Lopes Cardoso and Oliveira (2010): agent b is obliged towards agent c to bring about f between l (a lifeline) and d (a deadline). Different outcomes may be obtained from such an obligation. Let us distinguish those in which f is obtained from those where it is not. In the former case we may have (i) $f \prec l$, which denotes a lifeline violation; (ii) $l \prec f \prec d$, a perfect compliance; and (iii) $d \prec f$, denoting a deadline violation. Finally, (iv) where f is not the case we have a full obligation violation.

These different cases show disparate outcomes in the performance of an agent with regards to a norm it is subject to. The correct assessment of these outcomes is important when using such information to build trust, because each truster may evaluate differently the possible performances of a trustee (e.g., by giving more or less importance to delays). This approach also allows for richer trust models to be built, which take into account the context for which a trustworthiness assessment of an agent is needed (Urbano et al. 2012).

15.3.2 Using Trust for Norm Negotiation

Once we have some notion of the trustworthiness of agents for a particular situation, we may choose to avoid delegating any task to agents that fall below a certain threshold. Nevertheless, there will be cases when either we are short of alternatives or we need some extra confidence when delegating a task. This is when we can mix our trust in the other agent with some control mechanism (Castelfranchi and Falcone 2000; Das and Teng 1998; Tan and Thoen 2000) that allows us to influence his behavior.

One such mechanism will therefore be to propose a particular set of norms to govern an agent interaction. Norms are in this sense negotiated in order to promote the desired outcome in situations where agents do not trust each other enough. The prescriptive nature of norms makes them useful for specifying the consequences that will be obtained in situations where the involved agents do not fully comply with the commitments they establish.

15.3.3 Norm Enforcement as a Source for Trust

A normative environment is a common interaction infrastructure where agent behaviors are governed by norms. We can find at least two advantages of using such an environment. The first is related with having predefined norms that agents will be subject to Lopes Cardoso and Oliveira (2008). A normative environment will include a normative framework that accommodates the joint activities that are to be regulated. The second concerns monitoring and enforcement of norms. Enforcement means that the environment will do its best in applying any corrective measures regarding lack of compliance. The normative environment may also include adaptive policies, by changing at run-time the shape of its normative framework when addressing the agent population as a whole (as in the approach described in Lopes Cardoso and Oliveira 2011). In this perspective, trust is built in a collective sense. Trust is pointed towards the enforcement capabilities of the normative environment, rather than directly towards other agents.

15.3.4 Application Domains

The interconnection between different social aspects, such as norms and trust, is becoming increasingly important in diverse areas, especially where an open environment is the case. The vast amount of new applications exploiting the open nature of the Web are of particular relevance, including electronic contracting between both firms and individuals (where norms governing contractual relationships have a natural fit), and social networks that connect individuals whose acquaintance becomes at some stage questionable (where therefore trust issues are predominant). In any case, an appropriate balance between a regulative perspective on norms and inter-entity trust as complementary mechanisms seems to be the key to addressing open multi-agent scenarios.

15.4 Trust, Norms and Emotions

In Jones (2002) five different types of scenario were considered as illustrations of situations in which it would be true to say that some agent X trusts some other agent Y. In the interests of brevity, and because the current focus is on the relationship between norms and trust, here we rehearse just three of them:

- The obligation scenario (Oblig): X believes that Y is subject to a rule, or rules, requiring him (Y) to do Z (for, instance, to repay a debt) and that Y's behavior will in fact comply with this requirement.
- The role scenario (Role): X believes that Y occupies some particular role, and that Y will perform the tasks associated with that role in a competent and acceptable manner. (For instance, *X trusts his doctor, or X trusts his car mechanic*).
- The informing scenario (Inf): X believes that Y is transmitting some information, and that the content of Y's message, or signal, is reliable. (For instance, *X trusts what Y says*).

Regarding (Oblig) it was suggested that the two key features that comprise X's trusting attitude are X's belief that a rule applies to Y, and x's belief that this rule will be complied with. Accordingly, the core of trust in (Oblig) consists of *X's rule-belief* and *X's conformity-belief*, respectively.

It was further suggested that this same pattern of analysis of trust could also be applied to (Role), on the uncontroversial assumption that one of the key characteristics of any role is that the role-occupant is subject to particular rules requiring that certain standards of behaviour and competence are maintained. So X trusts his doctor Y in as much as X believes both that Y's behaviour, qua doctor, is governed by particular rules, and that Y will conduct himself in a manner that complies with those rules.

Regarding (Inf), it was assumed that Y's communicative act of informing, whether delivered as a non-verbal signal, or as a linguistic speech act, would be governed by some convention which itself indicated what the communicative act means. So, by convention, hoisting a particular sequence of coloured flags on board a ship conventionally means that the ship is carrying explosives; uttering the English sentence "The ship is carrying explosives" also conventionally means that the ship is carrying explosives. So Y's communicative act is made possible by the existence of a convention that stipulates what Y's act is supposed to indicate. It may be, of course, that Y flouts the convention (as he would if he were lying), but X trusts what Y says/signals to the extent that X believes, rightly or wrongly, that Y's behaviour will in fact conform to the convention, e.g., that Y signals that the ship is carrying explosives only if the ship is carrying explosives. In short, truster X believes that trustee Y is subject to a rule (here, the signaling convention), and x believes that the rule will be complied with. So the pattern of analysis applied to (Oblig) and (Role) applies to (Inf) too.[1]

This account of trust, in terms of rule-belief and conformity-belief, exploits quite deliberately the ambiguity of the term *rule*. In (Oblig) and (Role) the relevant rules are *directive norms* that specify obligations to which trustee Y is subject; whereas in (Inf) the rule concerned is of type *convention*, or *constitutive rule*, a rule that specifies what the signaling act counts as indicating. Accordingly, the account supposes that there is an intimate connection between trust and rule, and, for specific cases of the kind exhibited by (Oblig) and (Role), between trust and directive norm. As regards the attitude of the truster, the (Jones 2002) account focused exclusively on trusters' beliefs; it was admitted that a truster commonly *cares about* whether or not conformity-to-rule (by the trustee) is forthcoming, and that this is why *trust* is often associated with the notion of *risk*. But it was nevertheless maintained that one can make perfectly good sense of a trusting attitude even when it is coupled with indifference. (I trust that the bureaucrats in my local council office will follow slavishly the application of council rules and regulations, but for many of these rules I truly do not care whether they are complied with or not.)

But suppose that we put those somewhat eccentric cases to one side: how then should the (Jones 2002) account be supplemented in order to accommodate a volitional component, indicating that the conformity-to-rule that the truster believes will occur is also an outcome that he desires? This was the question raised, and to some extent addressed, in Jones and Pitt (2011), and it led in turn to the suggestion that there may be a very close connection between this more complex notion of trust and some fundamental types of emotions, and in particular the notion of hope.

The reader is referred to Jones and Pitt (2011) for details, but in barest outline that work starts from the modal-logical characterisation of emotions given in Pörn (1986), in which the guiding intuition is that basic types of emotions consist of two distinct components: an epistemic component describing what an agent believes he knows about what may or may not be the case, and a volitional component describing what the agent wants, or does not want, to be the case. For the former, Pörn combined normal modalities for knowledge and belief, and for the latter he employed an evaluative normative modality. (On the distinction between directive and evaluative norms, see Pörn 1977.) So, for instance, the formula

$$BKp \,\&\, D\neg p$$

says that the agent (subscript suppressed) believes that he knows that the state of affairs described by proposition p holds, and furthermore he desires that it is not the case that p: an instance of an emotion of type *regret*. Similarly for

$$BK\neg p \,\&\, Dp$$

[1]The convention-based account of communicative acts is developed in detail in Jones and Parent (2007).

As further cases, consider

$$B\neg Kp \,\&\, B\neg K\neg p \,\&\, Dp$$

$$B\neg Kp \,\&\, B\neg K\neg p \,\&\, D\neg p$$

both of which represent an emotion of type *anxiety*, because they describe a situation in which the agent is uncertain about whether what he desires to be the case is in fact the case. Finally, consider

$$B\neg Kp \,\&\, \neg BK\neg p \,\&\, \neg B\neg K\neg p \,\&\, D\neg p$$

and

$$B\neg K\neg p \,\&\, \neg BKp \,\&\, \neg B\neg Kp \,\&\, Dp$$

which may be understood to represent *hope*: although the agent is not certain that that which he desires is the case, he nevertheless believes that the realisation of his desire is compatible with all that he knows. Consider now that the scope formula p itself represents the situation that was core to the (Jones 2002) analysis: that a particular rule is in force and will be complied with. Jones and Pitt (2011) arrived at the following three modes of epistemic/volitional representation of *trust*:

$$TRUST1 \quad BKp \,\&\, Dp$$

$$TRUST2 \quad Bp \,\&\, B\neg Kp \,\&\, Dp$$

$$TRUST3 \quad Bp \,\&\, \neg BKp \,\&\, \neg B\neg Kp \,\&\, Dp$$

This way of viewing trust helps to place it more clearly in relation to its near neighbour *hope*. For while it may well be agreed that TRUST1 does fit intuitively with the concept of trust, it might well be suggested that TRUST2, given the uncertainty expressed by its second conjunct, is more akin to *hope*, with TRUST3 perhaps exhibiting a "strength" that falls somewhere between *trust* and *hope*.

In our opinion, what we have here is a good example of the analytical value of these formal tools, which perhaps also brings out the futility of trying to "force" the vague notion of trust into one particular mould. The analytical tools enable us to articulate the spectrum of concepts to which phenomena of type trust belong. No single point on that spectrum tells the whole story about trust. But when we have a clear, preferably formal-logical model[2] of that spectrum we can, in designing particular systems for particular applications, identify the points on the spectrum of most relevance to the requirements specifying the task at hand.

[2]We say "preferably formal-logical model" because of the obvious advantages such models bring in terms of testing for consistency and for relations of implication.

References

Castelfranchi, C. 2000. Through the agents' mind: Cognitive mediators of social action. *Mind and Society* 1: 109–140.

Castelfranchi, C., and R. Falcone. 2000. Trust and control: A dialectic link. *Applied Artificial Intelligence* 14(8): 799–823.

Castelfranchi, C., and R. Falcone. 2010. *Trust theory: A socio-cognitive and computational model*, Wiley series in agent technology. Chichester: Wiley.

Castelfranchi, C., R. Falcone, and M. Piunti. 2006. Agents with anticipatory behaviors: To be cautious in a risky environment. *Frontiers in Artificial Intelligence and Applications* 141: 693–694.

Conte, R., and C. Castelfranchi. 1995. *Cognitive and social action*. London: UCL Press.

Das, T., and B. Teng. 1998. Between trust and control: Developing confidence in partner cooperation in alliances. *Academy of Management Review* 23(3): 491–512.

Giddens, A. 1991. *Modernity and self-identity. Self and society in the late modern age*. Cambridge: Cambridge University Press.

Huynh, T., N. Jennings, and N. Shadbolt. 2006. An integrated trust and reputation model for open multi-agent systems. *Autonomous Agents and Multi-Agent Systems* 13(2): 119–154.

Jones, A.J.I. 2002. On the concept of trust. *Decision Support Systems* 33(3): 225–232.

Jones, A.J.I., and X. Parent. 2007. A convention-based approach to agent communication languages. *Group Decision and Negotiation* 16: 101–114.

Jones, A.J.I., and J. Pitt. 2011. On the classification of emotions and its relevance to the understanding of trust. In *Proceedings of the workshop on trust in agent societies, at the 10th international conference on autonomous agents and multi-agent systems (AAMAS 2011)*, Taipei, 69–82.

Lopes Cardoso, H., and E. Oliveira. 2008. Norm defeasibility in an institutional normative framework. In *Proceedings of The 18th European conference on artificial intelligence (ECAI 2008)*, ed. M. Ghallab, C. Spyropoulos, N. Fakotakis, and N.E. Avouris, 468–472. Amsterdam: IOS.

Lopes Cardoso, H., and E. Oliveira. 2010. Directed deadline obligations in agent-based business contracts. In *Coordination, organizations, institutions, and norms in agent systems V*, LNAI, vol. 6069, ed. J. Padget, A. Artikis, W. Vasconcelos, K. Stathis, V. Torresdasilva, E. Matson, and A. Polleres, 225–240. Berlin: Springer.

Lopes Cardoso, H., and E. Oliveira. 2011. Social control in a normative framework: An adaptive deterrence approach. *Web Intelligent and Agent Systems* 9: 363–375.

Pörn, I. 1977. *Action theory and social science: Some formal models*. Dordrecht: Reidel.

Pörn, I. 1986. On the nature of emotions. Changing Positions. *Philosophical Studies* 38: 205–214.

Sabater, J., and C. Sierra. 2005. Review on computational trust and reputation models. *Artificial Intelligence Review* 24: 33–60. http://portal.acm.org/citation.cfm?id=1057849.1057866.

Tan, Y., and W. Thoen. 2000. An outline of a trust model for electronic commerce. *Applied Artificial Intelligence* 14(8): 849–862.

Urbano, J., H. Lopes Cardoso, H. Oliveira, and E. Rocha. 2012. Normative and trust-based systems as enabler technologies for automated negotiation. In *Negotiation and argumentation in MAS*, ed. F. Lopes and H. Coelho. Bentham Science Publishers: Sharjah (United Arab Emirates).

Urbano, J., A. Rocha, and E. Oliveira. 2010. Trustworthiness tendency incremental extraction using information gain. In *Web intelligence and intelligent agent technology (WI-IAT)*, Toronto, 411–414.

Chapter 16
Norms and Argumentation

Nir Oren, Antonino Rotolo, Leendert van der Torre, and Serena Villata

16.1 Introduction

The study of norms and argument has become increasingly connected in recent times, particularly in domains such as law, knowledge representation, ethics, linguistics and, most recently, in various agreement technologies (see also Part V in this book). Here, norms are used to set the space of legal agreements (or commitments) and argumentation is used to choose among the possible agreements (Billhardt et al. 2011). Moreover, we may consider norms setting not only the scope of possible legal agreements, but also the way we can choose among these possible agreements.

In law, Bench-Capon et al. (2010) present how argumentation theory has been used in legal reasoning. For instance, legal disputes arise out of a disagreement between two parties and may be resolved by presenting arguments in favor of each party's position. These arguments are proposed to a judging entity, who will justify the choice of the arguments he accepts with an argument of his own, with the aim of convincing the public. The common conclusion shared by such works is that argumentation has the potential to become a useful "tool" for people working in the legal field. While legal practitioners typically believe that argumentation theory can

N. Oren (✉)
University of Aberdeen, Aberdeen, UK
e-mail: n.oren@abdn.ac.uk

A. Rotolo
CIRSFID – Faculty of Law, University of Bologna, Bologna, Italy
e-mail: antonino.rotolo@unibo.it

L. van der Torre
ICR Group, University of Luxembourg, Walferdange, Luxembourg
e-mail: leon.vandertorre@uni.lu

S. Villata
INRIA Sophia Antipolis, Sophia Antipolis, France
e-mail: serena.villata@inria.fr

S. Ossowski (ed.), *Agreement Technologies*, Law, Governance and Technology Series 8, DOI 10.1007/978-94-007-5583-3_16,

simply be used to deduce consequences from a set of facts and legal rules, or to detect conflicts within such sets, argumentation can offer much more. Following the example proposed by Bench-Capon et al. (2010), a case is not a mere set of facts, but can be seen as a story told by a client to their lawyer. The first thing the lawyer does is to interpret this story in a particular legal context. The lawyer can interpret the story in several different ways, and each interpretation will require further facts to be obtained. Then the lawyer has to select one of the possible interpretations, must provide arguments to persuade the judging entity of the client's position, and has to rebut any further objection. The major topics that emerge as relevant in norms and argumentation include, among others, case based reasoning (Ashley 1990; Rissland et al. 1993), arguing about conflicts and defeasibility in rule based systems (Prakken 1993; Prakken and Sartor 1996; Sergot et al. 1986), dialogues and dialectics (Gordon 1993), argument schemes (Bex et al. 2003; Gordon and Walton 2009), and arguing about the success of attacks (Farley and Freeman 1995; Prakken et al. 2005).

In this chapter, we highlight the future challenges in the research area of norms and argumentation. We show that existing work on norms and argumentation, some of which has been identified above, can be categorized into two different classes, namely (i) arguing about norms, and (ii) norms about argumentation. The former includes the greater part of existing work in the area of norms and argumentation, such as approaches which aim at resolving conflicts and dilemmas (in particular examining how norms interact with other norms), arguing about norm interpretation and dynamics, arguing about norm adoption, acceptance and generation, representing norm negotiation, and arguing about contracts. In spite of all the literature on these topics, several challenges still remain to be addressed and resolved. For instance, new frameworks where individuals can discuss the merits and effects of the norms to be adopted by a society, or the introduction of richer preference models to detect and reason about norm interactions still provide fertile ground for additional research. At the moment far less work exists dealing with norms about argumentation. This topic aims to address the challenges of dialogue and debate protocols, reasoning about epistemic norms, and enforcement models of the burden of proof. In this category of work, open questions remain regarding the introduction of new techniques to verify whether a virtual agent complies with an epistemic norm, and the development of tools able to support the judging entities and the lawyers in the enforcement of burden of proof. Finally, besides the norms about argumentation and arguing about norms, direct formal relations between deontic logic—in particular input/output logic—and abstract argumentation have been considered (Bochman 2003, 2005), leading to a number of additional challenges.

16.2 Arguing About Norms

In order to determine how argumentation can be useful when dealing with norms, we must first examine the concept of a norm in more detail as done in Part III. Searle (1997) distinguished between two types of norms, referred to as regulative and constitutive norms (Boella and Van der Torre 2004b). Such norms form a group or society's *normative system*, and directly or indirectly constrain the behaviour of the society. Regulative norms modify an individual society member's behaviour by *obliging, permitting* or *prohibiting* certain states of affairs from occurring. If such norms are *violated*, additional regulatory norms, referred to as *contrary-to-duty* norms, can come into effect, leading to sanctions against the violators.[1] Constitutive norms describe the society through a mapping from *brute facts* to societal or institutional facts via a *counts-as* relation (cf. the societal concept of marriage); by identifying societal power structures through notions such as roles, and by specifying how the normative system itself can be modified (e.g. by allowing an entity taking on some role to modify some of the norms).

While regulative and constitutive norms affect a society in very different ways, both types of norms must be recognized by the members of a society in order to affect the society. The question then immediately arises as to how norms can be created in such a way so as to be recognized by members of a society. One possibility involves the assumption of some underlying system of sanctions, rewards and existing norms that allow entities taking on the role of a legislator to simply insert new norms into the society, with these norms recognized by all members of a society (Artikis et al. 2009; Gelati et al. 2004; Oren et al. 2010). The injection of norms into a system by a system designer can be seen to fall into this category of norm creation. Another alternative, espoused by work such as (Boella and van der Torre 2004a) takes a game theoretic view of *norm emergence*; norms come into being and are accepted by the society when adhering to the norm results in a Nash equilibrium for the members of the society. The computational overheads of computing a Nash equilibrium can make the latter approach infeasible, while the former (effectively) assumes some dictatorial power in the system. An approach in which individuals within the society can debate the merits of a norm, discuss its effects, and persuade others as to the utility of its adoption could provide a level of societal modelling and control not found in existing systems. Such *argumentation based norm creation* could be used as both a modelling tool (e.g. to model how laws are generated), and as a technique to reason about the effectiveness of proposed norms.

Having briefly discussed the role of arguments in norm creation and recognition, we will now consider the advantages that an argumentation based approach can bring to various aspects of both constitutive and regulative norms.

16.2.1 Argumentation and Constitutive Norms

Constitutive norms capture two aspects of a society, namely an ontological aspect mapping brute facts (e.g. the recital of vows) to societal facts (e.g. a couple being viewed as married according to the society), and the power structures found in the

[1]This view of regulative norms encapsulates social norms, which impose requirements on behaviour with no explicit sanction.

society. Having discussed the latter aspect in the previous section, we now examine the contributions argumentation theory can make to the former.

While members of a society should agree on the definition of societal facts (i.e. share an ontology), this is not always the case. Even in human societies, legal cases often rest on the judge's interpretation of some definition. The question then arises as to how the ontology representing an individual's view of the societal facts can be aligned with those of all other member of the society. Most existing approaches to attacking this *ontology alignment problem* originate from the Semantic Web community, and are neither able to deal with conflicting perspectives on the meaning of terms, nor cater for non-Description Logic based knowledge representation schemes. Several argumentation based approaches have been proposed to tackle ontology alignment and matching. For example, dos Santos et al. (2009) represents the outcomes of several matching tools within an abstract argument framework; the extensions of this framework are then used to define the final ontology alignment process. Laera et al. (2007) takes a semantic approach, with agents exchanging arguments over the properties of the ontology in order to agree on a compromise. Evaluations of these argument based approaches have shown that they perform as well as the best standard ontology mapping techniques.

While promising, such techniques must overcome important restrictions before they are suitable for the alignment of constitutive norms. These include the assumption that only two agents are attempting to perform ontology alignment, and the requirement for a central ontology mapping repository.

16.2.2 Argumentation and Regulative Norms

Given some conditions, regulative norms impose obligations, permissions and prohibitions on members of a society. An individual must be able to recognise which norms should, according to the society, affect its behaviour. Since a single society can have multiple norm creators, there is no guarantee that the norms affecting the individual are consistent, and it must therefore be possible to detect *normative conflicts*. Now, one approach to dealing with such normative conflict involves ignoring all but one of the conflicting norms. However, an individual could ignore a norm for other reasons. For example, violating a norm could allow the individual to achieve an important goal. Therefore, rather than treating norms in isolation, normative reasoning must form part of practical reasoning.

The violation of a regulative norm typically carries with it the threat of a sanction. In order to make good on such a threat, a society must be able to monitor the compliance of an individual with regards to the norms affecting it. Argumentation has a role to play in addressing each of the aspects of regulative norms discussed so far. In the remainder of this section, we will examine each of these aspects in more detail, describe existing work dealing with the aspect, and identify how argumentation could be used to address remaining challenges.

16.2.2.1 Identifying Normative Constraints

Regulative norms most commonly impose conditional obligations on an individual or set of individuals. Such conditional obligations identify what state of affairs *should* hold when some situation occurs. Norms can also cause prohibitions to come into force. These are similar to obligations, but identify the state of affairs that *should not* hold. Finally, regulative norms can also instantiate permissions. Makinson and van der Torre (2003) identifies three separate types of permissions, namely weak, strong and dynamic permissions. Weak permissions—stating that what is obliged is permitted—exist implicitly within a normative system, and are not further discussed here. Strong permissions identify states of affairs which cannot be prohibited, while dynamic permissions are used to *derogate* obligations and prohibitions. The inclusion of the latter type of permission into a normative system therefore results in a defeasible system (Horty 1997); abstract argument frameworks can be used to represent such systems, with norms within an extension representing constraints upon the individual, and norms outside the extension being derogated.[2] Instantiations of such an abstract framework via a defeasible logic, in the vein of Governatori and Rotolo (2010), allows for complex normative reasoning to take place, incorporating concepts such as deadlines, norm violation, and norm fulfilment. The main direction of future work in this area involves further refining existing frameworks. Another possible area of investigation would make use of argument schemes to reason about why certain norms are, or are not in force, based on uncertain evidence from the domain. Preliminary work in this direction was discussed in Oren et al. (2008).

16.2.2.2 Detecting and Dealing with Normative Conflict

If complying with any norm will result in some other norm being violated, then the set of norms is in *normative conflict*. While some forms of normative conflict are easy to detect (e.g. an obligation to achieve a, and a prohibition on achieving a), others require explicit domain knowledge (such as mutual exclusivity between actions). Now permissions may *derogate* prohibitions and obligations, temporarily alleviating the conflict. Work such as (Governatori and Rotolo 2008) makes use of a defeasible framework to reason about such derogations.

Argumentation is designed to represent and reason about conflicts, for instance in Oren et al. (2008) an abstract argument based approach selecting which norms to violate in the presence of normative conflict was described. Possible enhancements to this argumentation based approach include richer preference models, as well as logics for reasoning about norm interactions in order to reason about, and detect, future potential norm conflicts.

---

[2]If such an abstract framework contains multiple extensions, then the potential exists for normative conflict to arise, as discussed later.

We have described how argumentation can be used to reason about normative conflict, allowing an agent to decide how to act in its presence. This reasoning process can be generalised further, namely by reasoning about how to act in the presence of conflicts between an agent's norms and its goals.

The BOID architecture (Broersen et al. 2001) utilised defeasible rules and a priority relation in order to perform practical reasoning in the presence of conflicts between obligations, intentions and desires. Work such as (Boella and van der Torre 2003) then investigated how argumentation could be used as the underlying reasoning mechanism within a BOID architecture. Advantages of argumentation in this context include the ability to include permissions as undercutting attacks, and naturally have agents influence each other's behaviour. Following this strand of work, Modgil and Luck (2009) makes use of extended argument frameworks to represent an agent's reasoning process when performing practical reasoning in the presence of conflicting desires and norms.

There are strong analogies between the practical reasoning problem and automated planning, and recent work (e.g. Toniolo et al. 2011) has proposed an argumentation based approach to planning in the presence of norms. Apart from its ability to handle conflict, the use of argumentation for practical reasoning enables easy integration of domain specific knowledge and inference (via argument schemes). The use of argumentation in this context offers the possibility of improved computational performance, potentially allowing for new reasoning heuristics. Preliminary work such as Medellin-Gasque et al. (2011) is now underway on encoding such domain specific argument schemes, and is possibly the most exciting area for future research.

16.2.2.3 Monitoring Norms

Until now, we have examined how an agent can reason about its norms in order to decide which norms should affect its behaviour, and how to act in the presence of these norms. Now if an agent violates a norm, then it can be sanctioned by other agents within the society. To this end, some mechanism is required to monitor the norm compliance (or lack thereof) of agents. Several such mechanisms, (e.g. DIO(DE)^2 van der Torre and Tan 1999) have been proposed to perform such monitoring. One important requirement for such a monitoring system is the ability to handle both conflicting and uncertain evidence; the former because agents with a vested interest in sanctioning the monitored agent could attempt to deceive the monitor, and the latter due to a lack of omniscience on the part of the monitor. This problem of norm monitoring is analogous to the problem of contract monitoring (Daskalopulu et al. 2002). In Oren et al. (2007, 2008), argumentation based approaches to reasoning about uncertain evidence were proposed. More generally, a large body of work exists regarding arguing in the presence of uncertainty (e.g. Haenni et al. 2001 and McBurney and Parsons 2000), and challenges here include identifying argument schemes which reason about uncertainty, how to weigh up conflicting uncertain evidence and so on.

16.2.2.4 Norm Dynamics

Obligations can change while the normative system remains the same. For example, due to change in the world or in the agents' knowledge and beliefs, new obligations can be detached from the norms, or an agent can delegate one of its obligations to another agent. This change of obligations and permissions over time is a relatively clear and well studied subject, investigated mostly in the 1970s and 1980s. Moreover, a code of regulations is itself not static either, but changes over time. For example, a legislative body may want to introduce new norms or to eliminate some existing ones. To study how norm change is different from how obligation change, and how these two are related, we have to address topics such as:

- Norm revision and contraction, e.g. change of legal code;
- Norm evolution, e.g. change of social norms;
- Merging normative systems, e.g. the merge of companies.

Note that we presuppose a distinction between norms and obligations, which is too often ignored. Norms, imperatives, promises, legal statutes, and moral standards are usually not viewed as being true or false. For example: "John, leave the room!" and "Mary, you may enter now" do not describe, but demand or allow a behaviour on the part of John and Mary. Lacking truth values, norms cannot be premise or conclusion in an inference, be termed consistent or contradictory, or be compounded by truth-functional operators. The usual way out is to say that "John is obliged to leave the room" describes the obligation which follows from the prescriptive "John, leave the room!" Makinson (1998) raises the question: How can deontic logic be reconstructed in accord with the philosophical position that norms are neither true nor false?

The derived problem is: How to formalize the relation between norm change and obligation change?

Little work exists on the logic of the revision of a set of norms. To the best of our knowledge, Alchourrón and Makinson were the first to study the changes of a legal code (Alchourrón and Makinson 1982). The addition of a new norm n causes an enlargement of the code, consisting of the new norm plus all the regulations that can be derived from n. Alchourrón and Makinson distinguish two other types of change. When the new norm is incoherent with the existing ones, we have an *amendment* of the code: in order to coherently add the new regulation, we need to reject those norms that conflict with n. Finally, *derogation* is the elimination of a norm n together with whatever part of G implies n.

Some of the AGM (Alchourrón et al. 1985) axioms seem to be rational requirements in a legal context, whereas they have been criticized when imposed on belief change operators. An example is the *success* postulate, requiring that a new input must always be accepted in the belief set. It is reasonable to impose such a requirement when we wish to enforce a new norm or obligation. However, it gives rise to irrational behaviors when imposed to a belief set, as observed for instance in Gabbay et al. (2003).

We now want to turn to another type of change, that is the aggregation of regulations. This problem has only recently been addressed in the literature and therefore the findings are still very partial. The aggregation of regulations can be addressed using argumentation techniques developed for merging argumentation frameworks.

The first noticeable thing is the lack of general agreement about where the norms that are to be aggregated originate. Some works focus on the merging of conflicting norms that belong to the same normative system, while other works assume that the regulations to be fused belong to different systems. The first situation seems to be more a matter of coherence of the whole system rather than a genuine problem of fusion of norms. However, such approaches have the merit of revealing the tight connections between fusion of norms, non-monotonic logics and defeasible deontic reasoning.

We have seen that the initial motivation for the study of belief revision was the ambition to model the revision of a set of regulations. On the contrary, the generalization of belief revision to *belief merging* is exclusively dictated by the goal to tackle the problem—arising in computer science—of combining information from different sources. The pieces of information are represented in a formal language and the aim is to merge them in an (ideally) unique knowledge base. Can the belief merging framework deal with the problem of merging sets of norms?

The AGM framework has the advantage of being very abstract but works with theories consisting of simple logical assertions. For this reason, it is perhaps suitable to capture the dynamics of obligations and permissions, not of legal norms. In fact, it is essential to distinguish norms from obligations and permissions (Boella et al. 2009; Governatori and Rotolo 2010): the latter ones are just possible effects of the application of norms and their dynamics do not necessarily require to remove or revise norms, but correspond in most cases to instances of the notion of *norm defeasibility* (Governatori and Rotolo 2010). Very recently, some research has been carried out to reframe AGM ideas within rule-based logical systems, which take this distinction into account (Stolpe 2010). However, also these attempts suffer from some drawbacks, as they fail to handle the following aspects of legal norm change:

1. The law usually regulate its own changes by setting specific norms whose peculiar objective is to change the system by stating what and how other existing norms should be modified;
2. Since legal modifications are derived from these peculiar norms, they can be in conflict and so are defeasible;
3. Legal norms are qualified by temporal properties, such as the time when the norm comes into existence and belongs to the legal system, the time when the norm is in force, the time when the norm produces legal effects, and the time when the normative effects hold.

Hence, legal dynamics can be hardly modeled without considering defeasibility and temporal reasoning. Some recent works (see, e.g., Governatori and Rotolo 2010) have attempted to address these research issues. All norms are qualified by the above mentioned different temporal parameters and the modifying norms are represented as defeasible meta-rules, i.e., rules where the conclusions are temporalized rules.

In this section we described how argumentation can be used with regards to several aspects of normative reasoning. Much of the future work in this area lies in making use of argumentation to extract, and utilize, the reasoning mechanisms specific to the normative domain. In the next section, we examine the dual of this approach. Namely, we examine how norms can be used to guide the process of argumentation.

16.3 Norms About Argumentation

In this section, we present and discuss some issues like debate protocols, and burden of proof where norms have the role of regulations on the argumentation process itself.

16.3.1 Dialogue and Debate Protocols

Norms about argumentation constitute what argumentation conceptually is and what it factually should be. Hence, such norms are supposed to provide a framework where the exchange of opinions makes sense, it rigorously takes place, looks acceptable and rational. This is done in argumentation theory by identifying, as mentioned in Chap. 13, formal requirements for at least three different layers: the logical layer, the dialectical layer, and a procedural layer (Prakken and Sartor 2002; Prakken and Vreeswijk 2002).

16.3.1.1 Logical Layer

The logical layer deals with the underlying language that is used to build arguments. Many languages and reasoning methods can be used for this purpose, such as deduction, induction, abduction, analogy, and case-based reasoning. If the underlying language refers to logic **L**, arguments can roughly correspond to proofs in **L** (Prakken and Sartor 2002). It may be argued that most argumentation systems are based on a *monotonic* consequence relation, since each single argument cannot be revised but can only be invalidated by *other* arguments (or better, counter-arguments) (Prakken and Vreeswijk 2002): it is the exchange of arguments and counter-arguments that makes the system non-monotonic. However, this is not strictly required: when the underlying logic is itself non-monotonic, an argumentation system can be simply seen as an alternative way to compute conclusions in that non-monotonic logic (Governatori et al. 2004).

Suppose we resort to a rule-based logical system where rules have the form $\phi_1, \ldots, \phi_n \Rightarrow \phi$ and represent defeasible norms. An argument for a normative conclusion ϕ can typically have a tree-structure, where nodes correspond to literals and arcs correspond to the rules used to obtain these literals; hence, the root corresponds to ϕ, the leaf nodes to the primitive premisses, and for every node corresponding to any literal ψ, if its children are $\psi_1, \ldots, \psi_n$, then there is a rule whose antecedents are these literals (Governatori et al. 2004).

Argumentation systems, however, do not need in general to specify the internal structure of their arguments (Dung 1995). In this perspective, any argumentation system $\mathscr{A}$ is a structure $(A, \rightsquigarrow)$, where A is a non-empty set of arguments and $\rightsquigarrow$ is binary attack relation on A: for any pair or arguments a and b in A, $a \rightsquigarrow b$ means that a attacks b. This leads us to discuss the dialectical layer.

16.3.1.2 Dialectical Layer

The dialectical layer addresses many interesting issues, such as when arguments conflict, how they can be compared and what arguments and conclusions can be justified.

Different types of attacks and defeat relations can apply to arguments. Pollock's (1995) original distinction between *rebutting* and *undercutting* is almost universally accepted in the argumentation literature (Prakken and Sartor 2002, 2004). An argument A_1 rebuts an argument A_2 when the conclusion of A_1 is equivalent to the negation of the conclusion of A_2. The rebutting relation is symmetric. For example, if arguments are built using rules representing norms (regulating, for example, smoking in public spaces), a conflict of this type at least corresponds to a clash between the conclusions obtained from two norms (for example, one prohibiting and another permitting smoking). The undercutting is when an argument challenges a rule of inference of another argument. This attack relation is not symmetric and occurs when an argument A_1 supporting the conclusion ϕ has some ground ψ but another argument A_2 states that ψ is not a proper ground for ϕ. To put it simply, if one builds an argument A_1 for ϕ using the rules $\Rightarrow \psi$ and $\psi \Rightarrow \phi$ but we contend that ψ is the case, then we undercut A_1.

16.3.1.3 Procedural Layer

The procedural layer considers the ways through which conclusions are dynamically reached by exchanging arguments between two or more players. Legal disputes, for instance, can be reconstructed in the form of dialogues, namely of players' dialectical moves (Gordon 1995; Prakken 2001). Disputes in turn are regulated by procedural rules stating what dialogue moves (claiming, challenging, conceding, etc.) are possible, when they are "legal", what effects the players get from them, and under what conditions a dispute terminates (Gordon 1995) (in general, see Walton and Krabbe 1995).

In this sense, the procedural layer is the place where the dimension of norms about argumentation and the one of argumentation about norms are strongly linked: complying with the norms that regulate, for example, deliberative processes or legal disputes is a guarantee of fairness and justice for those processes and disputes, but fairness and justice are supposed to be behind any legal, moral and social norms.

In general, different frameworks for the procedural layer can typically be thought in terms of defining different dialogue systems. In this perspective, Walton and Krabbe (1995) identified for example the following fundamental dialogue types: persuasion dialogue, negotiation, information seeking dialogue, deliberation, inquiry, and quarrel. Each of these types correspond to a different way through which the argumentation can dynamically take place.

An established method for characterizing dialogues specifies and regulates their dynamic development by the so called protocol, effect rules, and outcome rules (Barwise and Moss 1996; Prakken 2005). The protocol states what moves are allowed (the "legal" moves) at each point in a dialogue (turntaking and termination); the effect rules define, for each utterance, the consequences for the commitments of the players; the outcome rules state the outcome of a dialogue (for instance: in persuasion dialogues the outcome is establishing the winner and the loser, while in negotiations the outcome is some allocation of resources among the players).

A basic and fundamental question of the procedural layer regards how to govern and allocate the burden of proof (Prakken 2001). For example, basic legal dialogue protocols of 2-player in civil disputes are defined on account of the requirement that the plaintiff begins the dispute with his claim and has to propose, to win, at least one justified argument which supports such a claim. The burden of the defendant is not in principle the same, as it may be sufficient in most cases for her to oppose to the plaintiff argument moves that are only defensible counter-arguments. The concept of legal burden of proof is very complex and its logical treatment is difficult: the interested reader can refer to Prakken and Sartor (2008). Even more complex is to handle the interplay between the dialectical and the procedural layers (Prakken 2001).

16.3.1.4 Commitments

Norms about arguments are present also when we reason about commitments in dialogue (Brandom 1998). In particular, consider the case in which an individual is committed to a proposition. This means that she should only say things which she believes to be true. This is a norm about how to argue, and it poses constraints on the reasoning process. An individual is not permitted to first say that a proposition p holds, and later when she is questioned about the same assertion, simply to drop it. For instance, this kind of problems has been addressed by Boella et al. (2006). Future challenges in norms and argumentation applied to dialogues arise when we consider systems where more than one norm regulates the debate. How to detect the possible conflicts among these norms, and how to provide a mechanism such that conflicts are solved, are two open challenges for agreement technologies.

16.3.2 Epistemic Norms

Epistemic norms are norms that guide, regulate or control our epistemology (Fagin et al. 1995), that is, what should we know or believe, how should we acquire knowledge, and how should we know what we know? The well known AGM axioms of belief revision (Alchourrón et al. 1985) are thus epistemic norms, namely norms on how to change beliefs. For example, if you learn new information which you accept, then you should revise your knowledge in a minimal way to accommodate for this new information.

It is tempting to define epistemic norms as norms that involve an epistemic or doxastic operator, such as norms on what you should know, what you should believe, or what you are permitted to know. For example, in many legal systems there is a norm "you should know the law". Classically this was discussed by Åqvist (1967) in his paradox of knower, represented by the formula $OKp \rightarrow Op$ of traditional modal deontic logic: if you should know p, then p should be the case.

Castañeda (1988) developed the logic of epistemic obligation, Cuppens (1993) and Cuppens and Demolombe (1997) study obligations about knowledge in the context of computer security, and Aucher et al. (2010) further develop their logic and apply it to privacy regulations. Pacuit et al. (2006) study knowledge based obligations, such as the obligation of a doctor to help someone if he knows the patient is ill.

In the context of agreement technologies, and multiagent systems and computer science in general, epistemic norms lead to new challenges. We cannot look into the head of a human agent, and we therefore cannot verify whether a human knows or believes something. Consequently, we cannot verify whether a human agent complies with an epistemic norm that he is forbidden or permitted to know something. With artificial agents, we can often verify an agent program before it is accepted to a virtual organization, and we can verify that it conforms to the norms, or more generally complies with the epistemic policies. Likewise, we can let an artificial agent comply with epistemic norms by not making observations when the answer to the question might lead to a violation of an epistemic norm, or not ask another agent about some information in similar circumstances.

16.3.3 Enforcement Tools for the Burden of Proof

The notions of proof standards and burden of proof refer to argumentation as a dialogical process for making justified decisions. The process starts with an initial claim, and the aim of the whole process is to clarify the claim, and produce a justification of a decision. The process will return a set of claims together with the decision to accept or reject them. A fundamental part of the output process is the proof justifying the decision of each claim, to show how the decision is supported by the theory. As in legal reasoning, a proof in argumentation is a structure which demonstrates to an audience that a claim satisfies its applicable proof standard. A summary of proof standards and burden of proof is presented by Gordon and Walton (2010).

The proof standards and burden of proof provide a kind of norm applied to argumentation. While several burdens of proof have been theoretically defined in the literature, such as *burden of claiming* and *burden of questioning*, a future challenge is the development of tools to support the humans operating in the legal field. The idea is to start from systems like Carneades,[3] which already provide a tool for modeling legal dialogues, and improve them to support the interaction with humans. For instance, a judge can use such a tool to look at the argumentation framework which models the trial, and she will be able to detect the possible "irregularities" with respect to the burden of proof. Moreover, the tool should provide the judge with a summary of the argumentation framework representing the trial's arguments. The same tool can be used by the lawyers to detect the possible weak points of a deliberation. In this way, the lawyer will know precisely which weak point to appeal. The development of such kinds of tools based on burden of proof poses a challenge in the area of norms and argumentation.

16.3.4 Conclusions

In this section, we presented an overview of existing work in the field of argumentation and norms. The analysis of this work allows us to identify various challenges of the domain. These challenges fall into two broad categories: how to argue about norms, and how norms influence the argumentation process. In particular, we highlighted the following challenges:

- Arguing about norms:
  1. *Societal modelling and control*:
     - Individuals debate about the merits of norms and its effects;
     - Individuals persuade others about utility of norm adoption;
  2. *Constitutive norms*:
     - More than two agents performing ontology alignment;
     - Avoiding the central ontology mapping repository;
  3. *Regulative norms*: considering norms in practical reasoning;
  4. *Normative constraints*:
     - Complex normative reasoning for deadlines, norm violation, norm fulfillment;
     - Using argument schemes to reason about norms being or not in force;

[3] https://github.com/carneades/carneades

5. *Normative conflict*: developing richer preference models and logics for reasoning about norm interaction;
6. *Practical reasoning*:
   - Integration of domain specific knowledge and inference using argument schemes;
   - New reasoning heuristics;
7. *Monitoring norms*:
   - Identifying argument schemes which reason about uncertainty;
   - Weighting up conflicting uncertain evidence;

• Norms about argumentation:

1. *Dialogue*:
   - Interplay between dialectical and procedural norms;
   - Modelling dialogues where several norms regulate a dialogue;
2. *Burden of proof*: tools for supporting people in legal field to verify proof standards;

These future challenges should be addressed both from the theoretical and the design point of view. The former involves defining new innovative models which integrate argumentation theory and norms, while the latter involves the creation of tools which leverage, apply, and implement various aspects of existing theoretical work.

References

Alchourrón, C.E., and D.C. Makinson. 1982. The logic of theory change: Contraction functions and their associated revision functions. *Theoria* 48: 14–37.

Alchourrón, C., P. Gärdenfors, and D. Makinson. 1985. On the logic of theory change: Partial meet contraction and revision functions. *Journal of Symbolic Logic* 50(2): 510–530.

Åqvist, L. 1967. Good samaritans, contrary-to-duty imperatives, and epistemic obligations. *Nôus* 1: 361–379.

Artikis, A., M. Sergot, and J. Pitt. 2009. Specifying norm-governed computational societies. *ACM Transactions on Computational Logic* 10(1): 1–42.

Ashley, K.D. 1990. *Modeling legal argument – reasoning with cases and hypotheticals*, Artificial intelligence and legal reasoning. Cambridge: MIT.

Aucher, G., G. Boella, and L. van der Torre. 2010. Prescriptive and descriptive obligations in dynamic epistemic deontic logic. In *AI approaches to the complexity of legal systems (AICOL 2009)*, LNAI, vol. 6237, 150–161. Berlin: Springer.

Barwise, J., and L.S. Moss. 1996. *Vicious circles: On the mathematics of non-wellfounded phenomena*. Stanford: CSLI.

Bench-Capon, T., H. Prakken, and G. Sartor. 2010. *Argumentation in legal reasoning, argumentation in artificial intelligence*. Berlin: Springer.

Bex, F., H. Prakken, C. Reed, and D. Walton. 2003. Towards a formal account of reasoning about evidence: Argumentation schemes and generalisations. *Artificial Intelligence Law* 11(2–3): 125–165.

Billhardt, H., R. Centeno, C.E. Cuesta, A. Fernández, R. Hermoso, R. Ortiz, S. Ossowski, J.S. Pérez-Sotelo, and M. Vasirani. 2011. Organisational structures in next-generation distributed systems: Towards a technology of agreement. *Multiagent and Grid Systems* 7(2–3): 109–125.

Bochman, A. 2003. Collective argumentation and disjunctive logic programming. *Journal of Logic and Computation* 13(3): 405–428.

Bochman, A. 2005. Propositional argumentation and causal reasoning. In *Proceedings of the nineteenth international joint conference on artificial intelligence (IJCAI 2005)*, Edinburgh, 388–393.

Boella, G., and L. van der Torre. 2003. BDI and BOID argumentation. In *Proceedings of the third workshop on computational models of natural argument (CMNA 2003)*, Acapulco.

Boella, G., and L. van der Torre. 2004. The social delegation cycle. In *Proceedings of the 7th international workshop on deontic logic in computer science (DEON 2004)*, Madeira, 29–42.

Boella, G., and L. Van der Torre. 2004. Regulative and constitutive norms in normative multiagent systems. In *Proceedings of the ninth international conference on principles of knowledge representation and reasoning (KR 2004)*, Whistler, 255–266.

Boella, G., R. Damiano, J. Hulstijn, and L. van der Torre. 2006. ACL Semantics Between Social Commitments and Mental Attitudes. In *Agent communication II, international workshops on agent communication (AC 2005)*, Lecture notes in computer science, vol. 3859, 30–44. Berlin: Springer.

Boella, G., G. Pigozzi, and L. van der Torre. 2009. Normative framework for normative system change. In *Proceedings of the eighth international joint conference on autonomous agents and multiagent systems (AAMAS 2009)*, 169–176. New York: ACM.

Brandom, R. 1998. *Making it explicit: Reasoning, representing, and discursive commitment.* Cambridge: Harvard University Press.

Broersen, J., M. Dastani, J. Hulstijn, Z. Huang, and L. van der Torre. 2001. The BOID architecture: Conflicts between beliefs, obligations, intentions and desires. In *Proceedings of the fifth international conference on autonomous agents (AAMAS 2001)*, Ann Arbor, 9–16.

Castañeda, H.N. 1988. Knowledge and epistemic obligation. *Philosophical Perspectives* 2: 211–233.

Cuppens, F. 1993. A logical formalization of secrecy. In *IEEE computer security foundations workshop (CSFW 1993)*. Los Alamitos: IEEE Computer Society.

Cuppens, F., and R. Demolombe. 1997. A modal logical framework for security policies. In *Proceedings of the tenth international symposium on foundations of intelligent systems (ISMIS 1997)*, Charlotte, 579–589.

Daskalopulu, A., T. Dimitrakos, and T. Maibaum. 2002. Evidence-based electronic contract performance monitoring. *Group Decision and Negotiation* 11(6): 469–485.

dos Santos, C.T., P. Quaresma, R. Vieira, and A. Isaac. 2009. Comparing argumentation frameworks for composite ontology matching. In *Proceedings of the sixth international workshop on argumentation in multi-agent systems (ArgMAS 2009)*, Lecture notes in computer science, vol. 6057, 305–320. Berlin: Springer.

Dung, P.M. 1995. On the acceptability of arguments and its fundamental role in nonmonotonic reasoning, logic programming and n-person games. *Artificial Intelligence* 77(2): 321–357.

Fagin, R., J. Halpern, Y. Moses, and M. Vardi. 1995. *Reasoning about knowledge*. Cambridge: MIT.

Farley, A.M., and K. Freeman. 1995. Burden of proof in legal argumentation. In *Proceedings of the fifth international conference on artificial intelligence and law (ICAIL 1995)*, Edinburgh, 156–164.

Gabbay, D.M., G. Pigozzi, and J. Woods. 2003. Controlled revision – an algorithmic approach for belief revision. *Journal of Logic and Computation* 13(1): 3–22.

Gelati, J., G. Governatori, A. Rotolo, and G. Sartor. 2004. Normative autonomy and normative co-ordination: Declarative power, representation, and mandate. *Artificial Intelligence and Law* 12(1–2): 53–81.

Gordon, T.F. 1993. The pleadings game: Formalizing procedural justice. In *Proceedings of the fourth international conference on artificial intelligence and law (ICAIL 1993)*, Amsterdam, 10–19.

Gordon, T.F. 1995. *The pleadings game: An artificial intelligence model of procedural justice*. New York: Springer.

Gordon, T.F., and D. Walton. 2009. Legal reasoning with argumentation schemes. In *Proceedings of the twelfth international conference on artificial intelligence and law (ICAIL 2009)*, Barcelona, 137–146.

Gordon, T.F., and D. Walton. 2010. *Proof burdens and standards, argumentation in artificial intelligence*. Boston: Springer.

Governatori, G., and A. Rotolo. 2008. Changing Legal Systems: Abrogation and Annulment Part I: Revision of Defeasible Theories. In *Proceedings of the ninth international conference on deontic logic in computer science (DEON 2008)*, Lecture notes in computer science, vol. 5076, 3–18. Berlin: Springer.

Governatori, G., and A. Rotolo. 2010. Changing legal systems: Legal abrogations and annulments in defeasible logic. *The Logic Journal of IGPL* 18(1): 157–194.

Governatori, G., M. Maher, D. Billington, and G. Antoniou. 2004. Argumentation semantics for de-feasible logics. *Journal of Logic and Computation* 14(5): 675–702.

Haenni, R., B. Anrig, J. Kohlas, and N. Lehmann. 2001. A survey on probabilistic argumentation. In *Proceedings of the sixth European conference on symbolic and quantitative approaches to reasoning with uncertainty, workshop: Adventures in argumentation*, Boston, 19–25.

Horty, J. 1997. Nonmonotonic foundations for deontic logic. In *Defeasible deontic logic*, ed. D. Nute, 17–44. Dordrecht: Kluwer Academic.

Laera, L., I. Blacoe, V. Tamma, T.R. Payne, J. Euzenat, and T. Bench-Capon. 2007. Argumentation over Ontology Correspondences in MAS. In *Proceedings of the sixth international joint conference on autonomous agents and multiagent systems (AAMAS 2007)*, Honolulu, 228.

Makinson, D.C. 1998. On a fundamental problem of deontic logic. In *Norms, logics and information systems*, New studies in deontic logic and computer science, ed. H. Prakken and P. McNamara, 29–54. Amsterdam: IOS.

Makinson, D., and L. van der Torre. 2003. Permission from an input/output perspective. *Journal of Philosophical Logic* 32: 391–416.

McBurney, P., and S. Parsons. 2000. Risk agoras: Dialectical argumentation for scientific reasoning. In *Proceedings of the sixteenth conference on uncertainty in artificial intelligence (UAI 2000)*, Stanford, 371–379.

Medellin-Gasque, R., K. Atkinson, P. McBurney, and T. Bench-Capon. 2011. Arguments over co-operative plans. In *Proceedings of the first international workshop on the theory and applications of formal argumentation (TAFA 2011)*, Barcelona.

Modgil, S., and M. Luck. 2009. Argumentation in multi-agent systems. chap. *Argumentation based resolution of conflicts between desires and normative goals*, 19–36. Berlin: Springer.

Oren, N., T.J. Norman, and A. Preece. 2007. Subjective logic and arguing with evidence. *Artificial Intelligence Journal* 171(10–15): 838–854.

Oren, N., M. Luck, and T.J. Norman. 2008. Argumentation for normative reasoning. In *Proceedings of the symposium on behaviour regulation in multi-agent systems (BRMAS 2008) at AISB 2008*, Aberdeen, 55–60.

Oren, N., M. Luck, S. Miles, and T.J. Norman. 2008. An Argumentation Inspired Heuristic for Resolving Normative Conflict. In *Proceedings of the fifth workshop on coordination, organizations, institutions, and norms in agent systems (COIN@AAMAS-08)*, Toronto, 41–56.

Oren, N., M. Luck, and S. Miles. 2010. A model of normative power. In *Proceedings of the ninth international conference on autonomous agents and multiagent systems (AAMAS 2010)*, Toronto, 815–822. IFAAMAS.

Pacuit, E., R. Parikh, and E. Cogan. 2006. The logic of knowledge based obligation. *Synthese* 149(2): 311–341.

Pollock, J. 1995. *Cognitive carpentry*. Cambridge: MIT.

Prakken, H. 1993. A logical framework for modelling legal argument. In *Proceedings of the fourth international conference on artificial intelligence and law (ICAIL 1993)*, Amsterdam, 1–9.

Prakken, H. 2001. Relating protocols for dynamic dispute with logics for defeasible argumentation. *Syntese* 127: 187–219.

Prakken, H. 2005. AI & Law, logic and argument schemes. *Argumentation* 19(Special Issue on the Toulmin Model Today): 303–320.

Prakken, H., and G. Sartor. 1996. A dialectical model of assessing conflicting arguments in legal reasoning. *Artificial Intelligence Law* 4(3–4): 331–368.

Prakken, H., and G. Sartor. 2002. The role of logic in computational models of legal argument: A critical survey. In *Computational logic: Logic programming and beyond*, 342–381. Berlin: Springer.

Prakken, H., and G. Sartor. 2004. The three faces of defeasibility in the law. *Ratio Juris* 17: 118–139.

Prakken, H., and G. Sartor. 2008. A logical analysis of burdens of proof. In *Legal evidence and proof: Statistics, stories, logic*, ed. H. Kaptein. Aldershot: Ashgate.

Prakken, H., and G. Vreeswijk. 2002. Logics for defeasible argumentation. In *Handbook of philosophical logic*, vol. 4, 2nd ed, ed. D. Gabbay and F. Guenthner, 219–318. Dordrecht: Kluwer Academic.

Prakken, H., C. Reed, and D. Walton. 2005. Dialogues about the burden of proof. In *Proceedings of the tenth international conference on artificial intelligence and law (ICAIL 2005)*, Bologna, 115–124.

Rissland, E.L., D.B. Skalak, and M.T. Friedman. 1993. BankXX: A Program to Generate Argument Through Case-Base Research. In *Proceedings of the fourth international conference on artificial intelligence and law (ICAIL 1993)*, 117–124.

Searle, J.R. 1997. *The construction of social reality*. New York: Free Press.

Sergot, M.J., F. Sadri, R.A. Kowalski, F. Kriwaczek, P. Hammond, and H.T. Cory. 1986. The british nationality act as a logic program. *Communications of the ACM* 29(5): 370–386.

Stolpe, A. 2010. Norm-system revision: Theory and application. *Artificial Intelligence Law* 18(3): 247–283.

Toniolo, A., T.J. Norman, and K. Sycara. 2011. Argumentation schemes for policy-driven planning. In *Proceedings of the first international workshop on the theory and applications of formal argumentation (TAFA 2011)*, Barcelona.

van der Torre, L., and Y.H. Tan. 1999. Diagnosis and decision making in normative reasoning. *Artificial Intelligence and Law* 7: 51–67.

Walton, D., and E. Krabbe. 1995. *Commitment in dialogue: Basic concepts of interpersonal reasoning, SUNY series in logic and language*. Albany: State University of New York Press.

Part IV
Organisations and Institutions

Organisations and Institutions provide an interesting perspective for open Multi-Agent Systems and Agreement Technologies. For example, organisations can be employed to specify how to solve a complex task or problem by a number of agents in a declarative way; agents participating in an organisation can work together and form teams for the solution of a particular task that helps reach the global goals of the organisation; organisational structures can improve and accelerate co-ordination processes in open environments. Moreover, the notion of institution has been used within the agent community to model and implement a variety of socio-technical systems, enabling and regulating the interaction among autonomous agents in order to ensure norm compliance.

This part addresses how agent organisations and institutions can improve and accelerate coordination processes in open environments. A current state-of-the-art review of recent proposals for describing agent organisations is given in Chap. 17, relating the different methodologies and formal approaches for defining agent organisations in an explicit way. Moreover, a review and comparison of recent approaches of Artificial Institutions is provided in Chap. 18. Furthermore, there have been some recent approaches for developing agents capable of understanding the organisation structure and functionality and then being able for deciding whether to participate inside or even generate new structures for the organisation. A review of this kind of agents, known as organisation-aware agents, is provided in Chap. 19. Finally, an important question in open systems is how to endow an organisation with autonomic capabilities to yield a dynamical answer to changing circumstances. Thus, a review of methods for designing and/or implementing adaptive agent organisations is given in Chap. 20.

Estefanía Argente and Marco Colombetti
Editors Part "Organisations"

Chapter 17
Describing Agent Organisations

Estefanía Argente, Olivier Boissier, Sergio Esparcia, Jana Görmer, Kristi Kirikal, and Kuldar Taveter

17.1 Introduction

To cope with the openness, decentralisation and dynamicity of applications targeted by Multi-Agent technologies, an organisational perspective has been promoted in the domain these last few years. This perspective proposes that the joint activity inside Multi-Agent Systems should be explicitly regulated by a consistent body of norms, plans, mechanisms and/or structures formally specified to achieve some definite global purpose. Inspired by the metaphor of human organisations (Scott 1981), different organisational models have been proposed in the literature, for the engineering of such systems (e.g. Argente et al. 2011; da Silva et al. 2004; Dignum 2004; Esteva et al. 2001; Ferber et al. 2003; Horling and Lesser 2004; Hübner et al. 2002; Lesser et al. 2004; Parunak and Odell 2001; Tambe et al. 1999).

An organisational model consists of a conceptual framework and a syntax in which specifications for agent organisations can be written. We call this an Organisation Modelling Language (OML). From such specifications, called hereafter organisational specification, an organisation can be enacted on a traditional

E. Argente (✉) • S. Esparcia
Departamento de Sistemas Informáticos y Computación, Universitat Politècnica de València, Valencia, Spain
e-mail: eargente@dsic.upv.es; serparcia@dsic.upv.es

O. Boissier
ISCOD - LSTI ENS Mines Saint-Etienne, Saint-Etienne Cedex, France
e-mail: Olivier.Boissier@emse.fr

J. Görmer
Department of Informatics, TU Clausthal, Clausthal, Germany
e-mail: jana.goermer@tu-clausthal.de

K. Kirikal • K. Taveter
Tallinn University of Technology, Tallinn, Estonia
e-mail: kristi.kirikal@gmail.com; kuldar.taveter@ttu.ee

S. Ossowski (ed.), *Agreement Technologies*, Law, Governance and Technology Series 8, DOI 10.1007/978-94-007-5583-3_17,

multi-agent platform or, more realistically, by using some organisation management infrastructure (OMI) (Esteva et al. 2004; Gutknecht and Ferber 2001; Hübner et al. 2006, 2009). In general, these organisation management infrastructures take the organisational specifications as input, interpret them, and provide the agents with an organisation according to the given specification. In order to enter, to work inside or to leave the agent organisation, the agents are supposed to know how to access the services of the infrastructure and to make requests according to the available organisational specification. Equipped with such capabilities, agents develop what we call *Organisation Awareness* skills making them able to contemplate the organisation and decide whether or not to enter such a structure, to change it by setting in place a reorganisation process and finally whether or not to comply with the different rights and duties promoted by the organisation.

In this chapter, we will mainly focus on the Organisation Modelling Language. While there has been a strong emphasis on agent organisations, as shown by the number and diversity of proposed organisational models, some work is aimed at reviewing the proposals and assessing their modelling capabilities (Coutinho et al. 2009), at reviewing and comparing organisational paradigms (i.e., general types of organisational structures like hierarchies, teams, markets, matrix organisations, etc. Dignum and Dignum 2001; Horling and Lesser 2005), and at proposing taxonomies of organisation and social concepts for the engineering of agent organisations (Mao and Yu 2004).

As stated in Coutinho et al. (2009), Multi-Agent organisations exhibit basic traits, some of which can be found in the models proposed by the different approaches cited above. These basic traits that may be part of the organisational models are:

- System structure (resp. functions): elements that form the system and the relationships interconnecting these elements (resp. input/output relations coupling the system to the external environment)
- static (resp. kinetic) perspectives: time independent (resp. dependent) description of the system

In the sequel, we will also use the vocabulary introduced in Coutinho et al. (2009): *organisation models* may give birth to *organisation meta-models*, that is to say a model that represents the conceptualization behind a modelling language. Meta-models are used to produce and define organisation specifications. Organisation specifications are themselves used to implement organisations.

In the following, we will describe different approaches for Organisation Modelling Languages. More specifically, Sect. 17.2 details the $\mathcal{M}$oise organisation model (Hübner et al. 2002); whereas Sect. 17.3 details the VOM organisation model (Argente et al. 2009b).

Furthermore, in contemporary complex sociotechnical systems it is not feasible to possess all the information about the environment and to keep this information continuously updated. Agent-oriented modelling as advocated by Sterling and Taveter (2009) presents a holistic approach for analysing and designing organisations consisting of humans and technical components. We subsume both under the term of *agent*, which we define as an active entity that can act in the environment, perceive events, and reason (Sterling and Taveter 2009). We term organisations consisting of human and man-made agents as *sociotechnical systems*. In Sect. 17.4 we will explain how to apply agent-oriented modelling for describing such agent organisations.

Moreover, in Sect. 17.5, a conceptual metamodel and architecture for Groups in Organized Localities to facilitate the model-based development of agent organisations is briefly explained. Localities capture the idea of a restricted sphere of influence and environmental constraints in which semi-autonomous agents cooperate under the control of centralized regulation bodies, called institutions.

Finally, in Sect. 17.6, a comprehensive view of different Organisation Models is included, in which we compare different organisation models that have been proposed in the literature.

17.2 The $\mathscr{M}$oise Organisation Model

$\mathscr{M}$oise (Model of Organisation for multI-agent SystEms) (Hübner et al. 2002) is an organisational model that proposes an Organisation modelling language, an Organisation Management infrastructure and finally basic primitives to make possible the development of Organisation Aware Skills for the agents. We describe below first the $\mathscr{M}$oise OML.

17.2.1 $\mathscr{M}$oise Organisation Modelling Language

The $\mathscr{M}$oise OML explicitly distinguishes three aspects in the modelling of an organisation: the structural specification, the functional specification and the normative specification.

Structural Specification: The structural specification defines the agents' static relations through the notions of roles, role relations and groups. A role defines a set of constraints the agent has to accept to enter in a group. There are two kinds of constraints: structural and functional. Structural constraints are defined by means of links and compatibilities that a source role has in relation to a target role. The links are sub-divided in communication, acquaintance and authority links. The communication links enable message exchange between related roles. Acquaintance links enable agents playing one role to get information about agents playing another role. The authority links represent power relation between roles. All the links define constraints that an agent accepts when it enters a group and begins to play a role. In turn, the compatibility relation constrains the additional roles an agent can play given the roles it is already playing. A compatibility between a role A and a role B means that an agent playing role A is also permitted to play role B. In the structural specification, a group is defined by a group specification. A group specification consists of group roles (roles that can be played), sub-group specifications (group decomposition), links and compatibilities definitions, role cardinalities and sub-group cardinalities.

$\mathcal{M}$oise Functional Specification: The functional specification describes how an agent organisation usually achieves its global goals, i.e., how these goals are decomposed (by plans) and distributed to the agents (by missions). Global goals, plans and missions are specified by means of a social scheme. A social scheme can be seen as a goal decomposition tree, where the root is a global goal and the leaves are goals that can be achieved by an individual agent. In a social scheme, an internal node and its children represent a plan to achieve a sub-goal. The plan consists of performing the children's goals according to a given plan operator. There are three kinds of plan operators: sequence (to do the sub-goal in sequence), choice (to choose and do only one sub-goal) and parallel (to do all the sub-goals in parallel).

$\mathcal{M}$oise Normative Specification: The normative specification associates roles to missions by means of norms stating permissions and obligations. Norms can also have application-dependent conditions bearing on the organisation or environment state. For instance, norms may define sanction and reward strategies for violation and conformance of other norms. Note that a norm in $\mathcal{M}$oise is always an obligation or permission to commit to a mission. Goals are therefore indirectly linked to roles since a mission is a set of goals. Prohibitions are assumed 'by default' with respect to the specified missions: if the normative specification does not include a permission or obligation for a role-mission pair, it is assumed that the role does not grant the right to commit to the mission.

*17.2.2 $\mathcal{M}$*oise *Organisation Model: Other Components*

The $\mathcal{M}$oise organisation model is complemented by an organisation management infrastructure, *ora4mas*, and basic capabilities for making possible the development of organisation aware skills at the agent level.

Organisation Management Infrastructure: The Organisation Management In frastructure supporting this organisation model follows the Agent and Artifact model (Hübner et al. 2009; Omicini et al. 2008). In this approach, a set of organisational artifacts is available in the MAS environment providing operations and observable properties for the agents so that they can interact with the Organisation Management Infrastructure (OMI). For example, each scheme instance is managed by a "scheme artifact". A scheme artifact provides operations such as "commit to mission" and "goal *x* has been achieved" (whereby agents can act upon the scheme) and observable properties (whereby agents can perceive the current state of the scheme). The OMI can be effortlessly distributed by deploying as many artifacts as necessary for the application.

Following the ideas introduced in Hübner et al. (2010), each organisational artifact has within it an Normative Programming Language interpreter that is given as input: (i) the program automatically generated from the organisation specification for the type of the artifact (e.g. the artifact that will manage a social scheme will receive as input the corresponding program translated from that scheme specification), and (ii) dynamic facts representing the current state of (part of) the organisation (e.g. the scheme artifact itself will produce dynamic facts related to the current state of the scheme instance). The interpreter is then used to compute: (i) whether some operation will bring the organisation into an inconsistent state (where inconsistency is defined by means of the specified regimentations), and (ii) the current state of the obligations.

Agent Organisation Aware Mechanisms: Thanks to the *ora4mas* OMI, the set of organisational artifacts, available in the MAS environment, provides operations and observable properties for the agents so that they can interact with the organisation. These different concrete computational entities aimed at managing, outside the agents, the current state of the organisation in terms of groups, social schemes, and normative state encapsulate and enact the organisation behaviour as described by the organisation specifications.

Thanks to the A&A model (Omicini et al. 2008), Artifacts' operations and artifacts' observable properties and events are respectively mapped into agents' external actions and into agents' percepts (leading to beliefs and triggering events). This means that – at runtime – an agent can perform an action α if there is (at least) one artifact providing α as operation – if more than one such artifact exists, the agent may contextualise the action explicitly specifying the target artifact. On the perception side, a set of observable properties of the artifacts that an agent is observing are directly represented as (dynamic) beliefs in the agent's belief base – so as soon as their values change, new percepts are generated for the agent that are then processed automatically(within the agent reasoning cycle) and the belief base is updated. So programming an agent, it is possible to write down plans that directly react to changes in the observable state of an artifact or that are selected based on contextual conditions that include the observable state of possibly multiple artifacts. This mapping brings significant improvements to the action and perception model provided in general by agent programming languages.

Translating this to the organisation side, from an agent point of view, organisational artifacts provide the actions that can be used to proactively take part in an organisation (for example, to adopt and leave particular roles, to commit to missions, to signal to the organisation that some social goal has been achieved, etc.), and provide dynamically specific observable properties to make the state of an organisation perceivable along with its evolution. In addition, they provide actions that can be used by organisational agents to manage the organisation itself.

17.3 Modelling Virtual Organisations

The concept of Virtual Organisation (VO) firstly appeared in the business field. *BusinessDictionary.com* defines **Virtual Organisation** as "an organisation that does not have a physical (bricks and mortar) presence but exists electronically (virtually) on the Internet, or an organisation that is not constrained by the legal definition of a company, or an organisation formed in an informal manner as an alliance of independent legal entities".

DeSanctis and Monge (1998) define a virtual organisation as "a collection of geographically distributed, functionally and/or culturally diverse entities that are linked by electronic forms of communication and rely on lateral, dynamic relationships for coordination". Despite its diffuse nature, a common identity holds the organisation together in the minds of members, customers, or other constituents. The virtual organisation is often described as one that is replete with external ties (Coyle et al. 1995), managed via teams that are assembled and disassembled according to needs (Grenier and Metes 1995), and consisting of employees who are physically dispersed from one another (Clancy 1994). The result is a "company without walls" (Galbraith 1995) that acts as a "collaborative network of people" working together, regardless of location or who "owns" them (Grenier and Metes 1995).

Later the term Virtual Organisation was taken to be used in the research field of computer science. More precisely, in one of the most trending topics in distributed computation, Grid Computing. This field of distributed computation focuses on large-scale, high-performance and innovative systems. Foster and Kesselman (2001) define a VO as "a set of individuals and/or institutions defined by sharing computers, software, data, and other resources, as required by a range of collaborative problem-solving and resource-brokering strategies emerging in industry, science, and engineering".

The term Virtual Organisation was also used in Multi-Agent Systems, where this term tries to catch the essence of the concepts from business and grid computing. In this case, the "Virtual" concept of the Virtual Organisation term normally refers to its "virtuality", i.e. its software existence. Argente (2008) states that a Virtual Organisation is a social entity built by a set of agents that carry out different functionalities. They are structured as a set of communication patterns and a specific topology, following a set of norms, in order to achieve the global goals of the organisation. In fact, this last definition is the one that represents best our idea of Virtual Organisation.

Thus, a Virtual Organisation (VO) presents the following features:

- It is composed of agents, independently of their internal features and individual objectives.
- It follows a global goal, which is not dependent on the agents' individual objectives.
- Tasks to be executed by agents are divided by means of roles, which describe the activities and functionalities of the organisation.

- The system is distributed in groups or organisational units where interaction between agents takes place.
- Its bounds are clearly defined, determined by the environment of the organisation, the internal and external agents, as well as the functionality and services offered by the organisation.

This section presents two approaches for defining VOs: (i) an UML-based approach, named Virtual Organisation Model (VOM); and a formal approach, named Virtual Organisation Formalisation (VOF).

17.3.1 Virtual Organisation Model (VOM)

The Virtual Organisation Model (Argente et al. 2009b) is an Organisational Modelling Language, defined to describe an Organisation-Centred MAS by means of an UML-based language, identifying the elements that are relevant in an organisation. As most of the metamodels, VOM also gives support to a software development methodology by upholding the development of the Virtual Organisations defined in GORMAS methodology (Argente et al. 2009a). Systems defined by VOM are structured by means of the Organisational Dimensions (Criado et al. 2009), which are based on a specific method from the Organisation Theory to define human organisations. Thus, each of these dimensions (structural, functional, dynamical, en vironment, and normative) is represented by a model inside the Virtual Organisation Model. More specifically, the Organisational Dimensions describe:

- **Structural Dimension**. Describes the components of the system and their relationships. It defines the organisation, composed of agents and organisational units, roles, and their social relationships.
- **Functional Dimension**. Details the functionalities of the system based on services, tasks and objectives. It also describes the stakeholders that interact with the organisational units, the services offered by the organisation, and the resources used by the organisation.
- **Dynamical Dimension**. Defines interactions between agents, as well as the role enactment process, defining the roles that organisational units or agents are able to play.
- **Environment Dimension**. The environment of the organisation is defined by means of the workspaces that structure the environment and the artifacts (that are located inside of the environment). Thus, the organisation can make use of both: workspaces and artifacts.
- **Normative Dimension**. Describes normative restrictions to the action space of entities which populate the system, including organisational norms that agents must fulfil, with associated sanctions and rewards.

As an example, we depict here just a couple of these dimensions, the structural and environment ones, in order to give an overview on how these Organisational

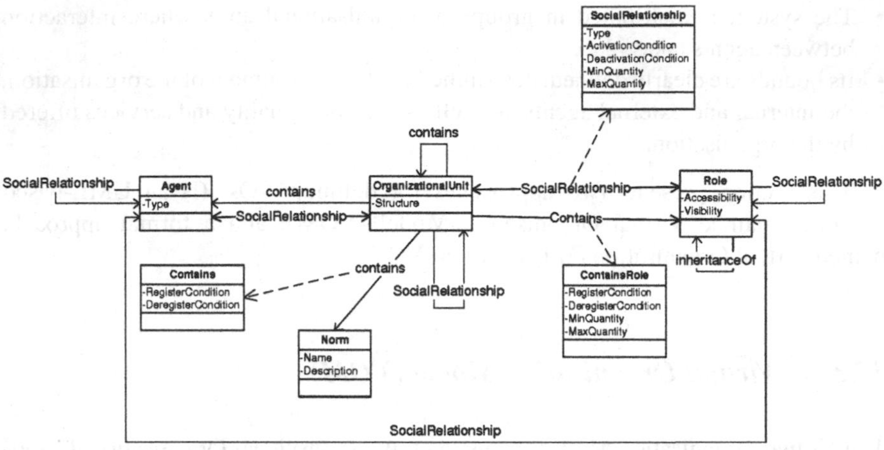

Fig. 17.1 Structural dimension (Argente et al. 2009b)

Dimensions are represented by means of VOM. A detailed description of all this model can be found in Argente et al. (2009b).

The *Structural Dimension* (Fig. 17.1) describes the system's components and their relationships. It allows defining the organisational elements that are independent from the entities that execute them. Specifically, it defines:

- *Organisational Units* (OUs) that build the system, which can also include other units in a recursive way, as well as agents.
- *Roles* defined inside OUs. A role defines the set of functionalities that an entity is able to carry out, and the set of goals and obligations associated to this role. The contains relationship allows to specify the cardinality of each role. A role hierarchy can be defined by means of relationships of inheritance between roles.
- The organisational *social relationships*. The kind of a social relationship between two units is related to their position in the organisational structure (i.e. information, monitoring, and supervision). These relationships allow us to describe how their roles are interrelated, making it possible for roles to exchange information, supervise how subordinated roles are developing their objectives, and to delegate their own tasks to subordinated roles.
- *Norms* that control the global behaviour of the members of the organisation.

The *Environment Dimension* (Fig. 17.2) of VOM defines the environment of a Virtual Organisation. It depicts how the environment is structured, adding a physical description, and which are the entities populating it, i.e. the resources that are available for the organisation to be used; or other organisations. This representation of the environment is based on the Agents and Artifacts conceptual framework (Omicini et al. 2008). The elements on the Environment Dimension are:

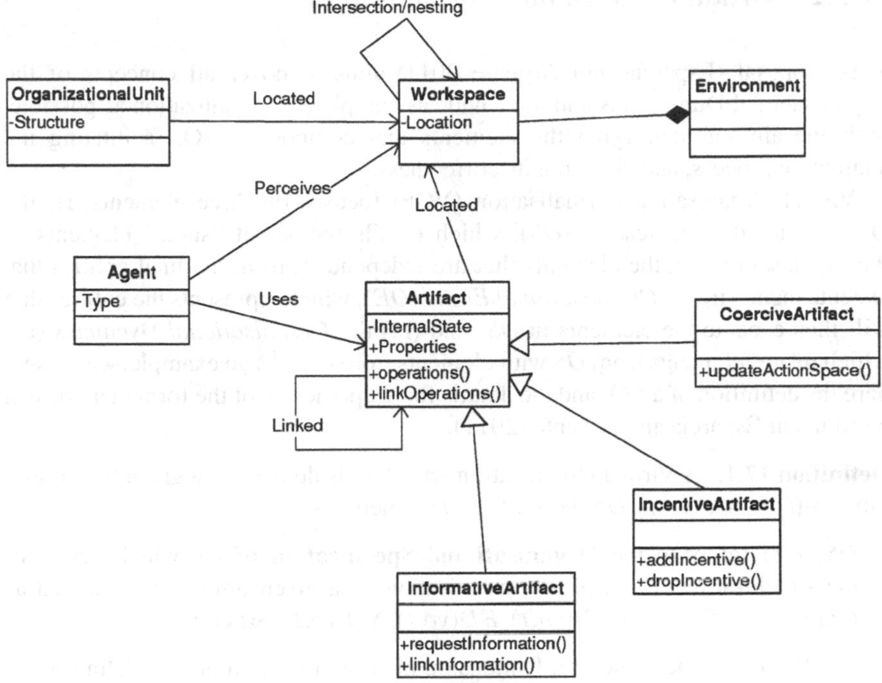

Fig. 17.2 Environment dimension (Argente et al. 2009b)

- *Workspaces* structure the environment in a similar way to how the physical world is structured. They are able to be intersected and nested between them, and organisations are located in one or some of them.
- *Artifacts*, which are reactive entities that agents use to achieve their objectives. Artifacts are located inside workspaces. Each type of artifact is represented in the metamodel by means of its particular operations and observable properties.
- *Agents*, proactive entities of the system (belonging to an organisation or not) that are able to perceive a set of workspaces of the environment and to use a set of artifacts.

The *artifact* entity has been refined into three inherited artifacts, i.e., the Artifacts for Organisational Mechanisms (Esparcia et al. 2010), which are a set of artifacts that present features from the Organisational Mechanisms (Centeno et al. 2009). Organisational Mechanisms enable regulating the behaviour of a MAS in both a macro and a micro perspective. The three types of artifacts defined in VOM are: (i) *Informative artifacts*, provided with operations that allow agents (and other artifacts) to request information; (ii) *incentive artifacts*, whose goal is to modify the reward system of the MAS, and are enhanced with operations for adding and deleting incentives from this reward system; and (iii) *coercive artifacts*, which are able to modify the action space of an agent by means of their particular operations.

17.3.2 Virtual Organisation Formalisation

This proposal (Esparcia and Argente 2011) aims to cover all concepts of the Organisational Dimensions and to provide as complete a formalization as possible, with the aim of identifying the elements that compose a VO, facilitating the adaptation process, and checking its correctness.

Virtual Organisation Formalisation (VOF) focuses on three elements: (i) the Organisational Specification (*OS*), which details the set of "static" elements of the organisation, i.e. the elements that are independent from the final entities that execute them; (ii) the *Organisational Entity* (*OE*), which represents the entities that will then execute the elements in *OS*; and (iii) the *Organisational Dynamics* (ϕ), which relates elements from *OS* with elements from *OE*. As an example, we present here the definition of a VO, and the details for deeper levels of the formalization can be found in Esparcia and Argente (2011).

Definition 17.1. A Virtual Organisation $vo \in \mathcal{VO}$ is defined, at a given time t, as a tuple $vo(t) = \langle OS(vo,t), OE(vo,t), \phi(vo,t)\rangle$ where:

- $OS(vo,t)$ refers to the **Organisational Specification** of *vo*, which describes the structural definition of the organisation, at a given time t. It is defined as $OS(vo,t) = \langle SD(vo,t), FD(vo,t), ED(vo,t), ND(vo,t)\rangle$ where:
  - $SD(vo,t)$ is the Structural Dimension of *vo* at a given time t. It defines roles and relations between them.
  - $FD(vo,t)$ is the Functional Dimension of *vo* at a given time t. It describes the functionalities of the system, including goals, services and tasks.
  - $ED(vo,t)$ is the Environment Dimension of *vo* at a given time t, which describes the environment of the organisation, including artifacts and workspaces.
  - $ND(vo,t)$ is the Normative Dimension of *vo* at a given time t, defining the norms that rule a VO.
- $OE(vo,t)$ refers to the **Organisational Entity** of *vo* at a given time t, which represents the entities populating the system, which can be agents or other VOs.
- $\phi(vo,t)$ refers to the **Organisational Dynamics** of *vo* at a given time t, allowing to relate $OS(vo,t)$ with $OE(vo,t)$. It has information about role allocation and active norms and services.

While VOM is able to define systems at design time, VOF is also able to represent different states that the system passes through its execution. This important feature, as well as its detailed and accurate description of the organisational elements will make it easier to identify different elements that change through time, provoking behaviour or structural changes in the organisation. Thus, VOF will become an excellent tool when dealing with organisational adaptation.

17.4 Agent-Oriented Modelling for Describing Agent Organisations

Agent-Oriented Modelling (AOM) as advocated by Sterling and Taveter (2009) presents a holistic approach for analysing and designing organisations consisting of humans and technical components. We subsume both under the term of *agent*, which we define as an active entity that can act in the environment, perceive events, and reason (Sterling and Taveter 2009). We term organisations consisting of human and man-made agents as *sociotechnical systems*.

The core of agent-oriented modelling lies in the viewpoint framework that can be populated with different kinds of models. Figure 17.3 depicts the viewpoint framework populated with a particular set of models by Sterling and Taveter (2009) that we are going to use in Sect. 20.6 for the case study of designing an adaptive socio-technical system for cell phone manufacturing. The viewpoint framework represented in Fig. 17.3 maps each model to the vertical viewpoint aspects of interaction, information, and behaviour and to the horizontal abstraction layers of analysis, design, and platform-specific design. Each cell in the table represents a specific viewpoint. Proceeding by viewpoints, we next give an overview of the types of models employed in Sect. 20.6.

From the viewpoint of *behaviour analysis*, a *goal model* can be considered as a container of three components: goals, quality goals, and roles (Sterling and Taveter 2009). A *goal* is a representation of a functional requirement of the sociotechnical system to be developed. A *quality goal*, as its name implies, is a non-functional or quality requirement of the system. Goals and quality goals can be further decomposed into smaller related subgoals and subquality goals. The hierarchical

	Viewpoint aspect		
Abstraction layer	Interaction	Information	Behaviour
Analysis	Role models and organization model	Domain model	Goal models and motivational scenarios
Design	Agent models, acquaintance model, and interaction models	Knowledge model	Scenarios and behaviour models
Platform-specific design	Platform-specific design models		

Fig. 17.3 The model types of agent-oriented modelling

Fig. 17.4 Notation for modelling goals and roles

Symbol	Meaning
(parallelogram)	Goal
(cloud)	Quality goal
(stick figure)	Role
(solid line)	Relationship between goals
(dashed line)	Relationship between goals and quality goals

structure is to show that the subcomponent is an aspect of the top-level component. Goal models also determine roles that are capacities or positions that agents playing the roles need to contribute to achieving the goals. Roles are modelled in detail in the viewpoint of interaction analysis. The notation for representing goals and roles is shown in Fig. 17.4. This notation is used in Sect. 20.6 in presenting requirements for the case study of an adaptive socio-technical system for cell phone manufacturing. Goal models go hand in hand with *motivational scenarios* that describe in an informal and loose narrative manner how goals are to be achieved by agents enacting the corresponding roles (Sterling and Taveter 2009).

From the viewpoint of *interaction analysis*, the properties of roles are expressed by role models. A *role model* describes the role in terms of the responsibilities and constraints pertaining to the agent(s) playing the role. *Organisation model* is a model that represents the relationships between the roles of the sociotechnical system, forming an organisation (Sterling and Taveter 2009). Organisation models are central in designing sociotechnical systems because organisational relationships between roles essentially determine interaction between roles in an organisation. Interactions will be addressed from the viewpoint of interaction design.

From the viewpoint of *information analysis*, *domain model* represents the knowledge to be handled by the sociotechnical system. A domain model consists of domain entities and relationships between them. A domain entity is a modular unit of knowledge handled by a sociotechnical system (Sterling and Taveter 2009).

From the viewpoint of *interaction design*, *agent models* transform the abstract constructs from the analysis stage, roles, to design constructs, *agent types*, which will be realized in the implementation process. The *acquaintance model* complements the agent models by outlining interaction pathways between the agents of the system. *Interaction models* represent interaction patterns between agents of the given types. They are based on responsibilities defined for the corresponding roles.

From the viewpoint of *information design*, the *knowledge model* describes the private and shared knowledge by agents of the Multi-Agent System to be designed.

Finally, from the perspective of *behaviour design*, *scenarios* and *behaviour models* describe the behaviours of agents in the system.

We described one possible way of populating the viewpoint framework with models. Agent-oriented modelling is a generic approach rather than another AOSE methodology. It means that rather than using particular types of models, the completeness of the design process matters. Design is complete when all the viewpoints corresponding to the cells of Fig. 17.3 are covered by models. For example, in Chap. 7 of Sterling and Taveter (2009) it is demonstrated how the viewpoint framework can be populated by (combinations of) models originating in the following AOSE methodologies: Gaia (Cernuzzi et al. 2004), MaSE (DeLoach and Kumar 2005), Tropos (Bresciani et al. 2004), Prometheus (Padgham and Winikoff 2004), ROADMAP (Juan et al. 2002), and RAP/AOR (Taveter and Wagner 2005). Agent-oriented modelling thus prescribes neither any specific agent-oriented software engineering methodology nor any agent-based software platform, but is compatible with most of them. Agent-oriented modelling instead proposes a conceptual framework that facilitates achieving the completeness of views and abstraction layers when designing a sociotechnical system, such as an information system or industrial automation system.

In Sect. 20.6 we will show how agent-oriented modelling can be applied to designing adaptive agent organisations. Our starting point is that adaptivity needs to be part of overall system design (Sterling and Adaptive 2011).

17.5 Describing Agent Organisations with Groups of Autonomous Agents in Organized Localities

Agent organisation systems are characterized by loosely coupled, software-controlled systems that cooperate to achieve joint goals. Each system operates semi-autonomously in order to pursue individual tasks, but it also obeys the current constraints within its local environment.

The assumption is that subsystems are developed independently due to their purposes and unifying requirements of an entire system. New control challenges arise from a shift from traditional hierarchical organisation to a Multi-Agent Systems organisation. But it also opens up ample new opportunities in terms of ad-hoc coordination and co-operation in order to maximize throughput and avoid breakdowns of agent organisations.

The integration of subsystems and the growing complexity of joint tasks, the need for "semantically rich abstract levels of description" (Heistracher et al. 2004) increases, specially social concepts like organisations, institutions and norms (Lopes Cardoso and Oliveira 2008; Vázquez-Salceda et al. 2005). Social concepts are a means of explicit representation of global objectives and constraints and of their relation to the level of interacting groups and even to individuals with their beliefs, desires, and intentions (BDI).

A conceptual metamodel and architecture is described for Groups in Organized Localities to facilitate the model-based development of agent organisations. Lo calities capture the idea of a restricted sphere of influence (Jennings 2000) and environmental constraints in which semi-autonomous agents cooperate under the control of centralized regulation bodies, called institutions.

Agent Organisations. They can be represented by the integration of four dimensions, introduced by Huhn et al. (2011) which consists of the interacting loop:

1. The *Environment* is represented as the *Locality* which is scanned by the agent and he performs action inside.
2. The *Agent* has an architecture with an *Execution Layer* where the agent is connected to the *Locality* and *LocalityRole* is allocated to the agent.
3. The *Organisation* is the connection between the *Agent* and the *MAS* where it is embedded together with *Institution*.
4. The *Institution* gives (structural, functional or deontic) rules and norms to the sphere of influence to the so-called *Locality*.

Representation of the Environment. To handle the environment's complexity the focus is just on the significant parts and to extract, collect, and pre-process important information about its state. Besides this filtering process the division of the global environment into smaller, well-defined local sections with specific properties and constraints, called **organized localities** is necessary. The locality is decomposed into several scenes and each scene is characterized by constraints which may take effect on different levels of the system.

An organized locality can be understood as a physical or virtual place offering a number of opportunities. It has a scope defining a boundary, so systems may enter, leave, and return later to the locality. Further a locality may provide organisations to foster coordination. It is associated with the concept of institutions to regulate the interaction of autonomous, heterogeneous agents beyond physical and technical constraints. They regulate the agent behaviour in order to balance between different interests and to establish and sustain certain notions of stability. Organisations structure the grouping and collaboration of agents within the locality.

In order to provide the structure of the localities, we need a representation of the environment, which enables a proper association between the specific regulation mechanisms and the localities. The institutions which are associated with a locality, provide regulation mechanisms within the scope of a specific scene. The division into scenes can be motivated by various tasks rules, processes, requirements, properties, constraints or resources (e.g. sensor properties, movement constrains or energy resources). Within these scenes, associated sets of norms are used to regulate the behaviour and interaction of the agents. According to this, the agents need an internal representation of the context which is relevant in the specific scope. The locality is defined as a virtual infrastructure to be used by the agents to achieve goals related to the subject of the locality. An approach towards adaptive IT-ecosystems is given in Rausch et al. (2012) and especially how to create an environment standard is specified in Behrens et al. (2011, 2012). Practical approaches are done in Görmer

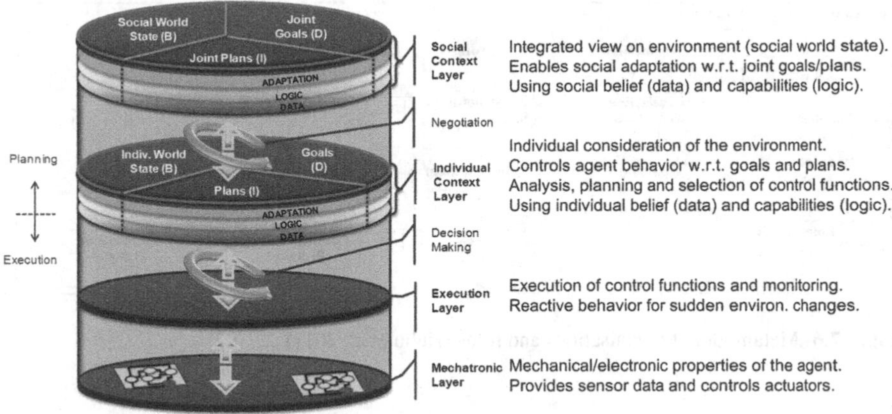

Fig. 17.5 AAOL agent architecture (Huhn et al. 2011)

et al. (2011b) for integrating also institutions, Chu et al. (2011) for combining tools for agent-based traffic behaviour which the novel traffic context for adaptive systems is described in Görmer et al. (2011a) and an application in Görmer and Mumme (2012) for cooperative traffic behaviour.

Representation of the Agents. Based on the design of intelligent agents of Müller (1996), also Huhn et al. (2011) propose an *agent architecture* with four layers: *Social Context Layer* (SCL), *Individual Context Layer* (ICL), *Execution Layer* (EL), and *Mechatronic Layer* (ML) (see Fig. 17.5). Agents perform predefined atomic or sequenced (plans) actions related to their goals. Goals and plans are potentially spread among multiple agents (joint goals/plans). Each layer has an authority. If multiple agents act in the same locality, joint tasks have to be coordinated in groups and resource conflicts need to be solved.

Relations of an agent in a metamodel are described according to Fischer (Hahn et al. 2009): an agent has accesses to a set of resources (information, knowledge, ontologies, etc.) from its environment, i.e., the locality. Furthermore, an agent has goals and is able to take on locality roles (to act in accordance to a plan) and behaviours, which are represented by the agents' capabilities. By acting the agent receives positive or negative rewards. Additionally Fischer uses the concept of *Instances* that can be considered as run-time objects of an agent that defines the corresponding type.

Representation of the Organisation. In the agent architecture described in Fig. 17.5 organisations are located in the *Social Context Layer* (SCL) and can be seen as computational methods inspired by concepts from economy and sociology that appear as one entity in the locality based upon social and functional distinctions and roles amongst individuals. Organisations can also be structured hierarchically e.g. by providing certain agents with more authority than others through role definitions. A peer-to-peer architecture is any distributed network composed of

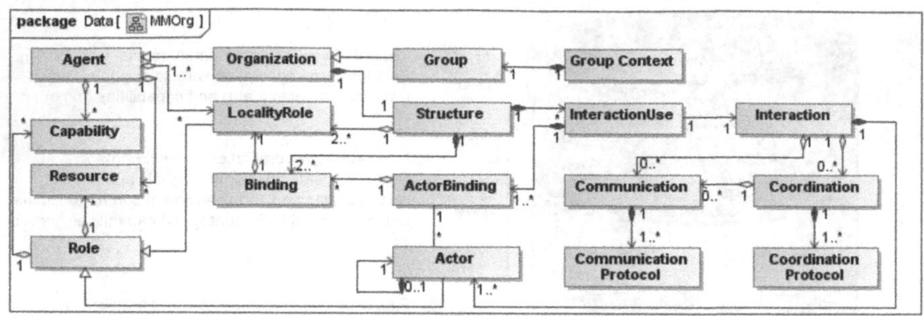

Fig. 17.6 Metamodel of organisations and roles (Huhn et al. 2011)

agents that make a portion of their resources directly available to other agents, without the need for central coordination instances. Peers are both suppliers and consumers of resources, in contrast to the traditional client-server model. The fully connected architecture has a general form of a chief director usually forming the single well-informed element, the so-called "voice" of an organisation to the outside, to sub-division managers and to the workers. A group can be seen as a specialized entity (or subsystem) of an organisation, usually consisting of only one leader and workers to reach a common goal or achieve a joint plan. For this, communication, negotiation and conflict resolution is connecting the individual with the social context layer. The connections between the agents with different roles imply interaction guaranteeing the service of the localities; this may lead to conflicts between agents which need to be handled like in Le et al. (2012).

Figure 17.6 is an extension of Hahn et al. (2009) and shows the metamodel of organisations. It includes the concept of an *Organisation* and its *Structure*, *Group* and its *Context*, *Institution* and *Norm*, *Binding*, *InteractionUse*, *ActorBinding*, *Interaction* and its *Protocols* for *Communication* and *Coordination*, *LocalityRole*, *Actor* and *Agent* as well as *Capability* and *Resource* (from the agent aspect). An organisation is derived from the agent perspective and it inherits characteristics of an agent (Hahn et al. 2009), i.e. capabilities which can be performed by its members. A *Group* is a special kind of an organisation that is bound by a *Group context*. The *Structure* defines the pattern of the organisation. It can bind agents or organisations to the *LocalityRole*. *Interaction* in an organisation has internal protocols that specify how its members communicate with each other and coordinate their activities. For interaction, *LocalityRole*s are bound to *Actor*s (by *ActorBinding*) that can be considered as representative entities within the corresponding interaction protocols. Thus, an actor can be seen as an agent (or organisation) with a *Role* and a task.

A role defines the behaviour of an agent in a given context (e.g., an organisation). Therefore it provides an agent with capabilities and a set of resources it has access to. An actor can be considered as a generic concept and either binds instances directly or through the concepts LocalityRole and Binding. The set of bound entities could be further specialized through the subactor (specialization of the superactor) reference that refers again to an actor.

Grouping allows an agent to extend its range of perception (RoP) by exchanging information with other members. Agents are coordinated at group level. Group-oriented coordination allows agents e.g. to form faster and slower agent groups like in Görmer and Müller (2012). In Sect. 20.8 a detailed description of group-oriented coordination is given.

Representation of the Institution. Institution is associated with a locality and provides normative regulations (norms) and mechanisms to establish or to ensure their compliance. It acts through an organisation that executes institutional tasks. The tasks contributing to norm compliance are:

1. An *information service* administers the identities of agents currently present in the locality and provides them with knowledge about the current norms,
2. *Norm monitors* monitor whether the agents behave according to the norms based on the information gathered from *observers*,
3. A *norm enforcement* guarantees that control is imposed on the agents participating in the locality in such a way that they will behave norm-compliant to assure vital global objectives and the safety of individuals.

Norms are an explicit description of the regulations that govern the agents' behaviour in the locality for the benefit of the community and itself as a member of it. In the approach of Huhn et al. (2011), norms are defined by the institution in a top-down manner and they consider that the agents are able to understand these norms.

Huhn et al. uses institutional agents (IAs), which act preemptively on agents only in case of obligations. At each step, the IAs compute a list of candidates of agents, for which an obligation applies. For each candidate, the IAs then identify forbidden actions, from the list of possible actions defined at design time. Only at this moment the IA acts and restricts the candidates from performing the forbidden actions. The other types of norms are handled by means of rewards and sanctions. A more detailed study is described in Klar and Huhn (2012) for interfaces and models.

A main benefit of the described approach based on Huhn et al. is that its concepts (localities, institutions, and norms) provide designers with instruments for flexible modelling of different control topologies of agent organisations, ranging from centralized and homogeneous to decentralized and heterogeneous settings. Further, the multi-agent based approach in conjunction with the localities concept supports well decentralised systems design scenarios, where the different parts evolve independently from each other while having to obey certain invariants or rules constraining the overall structural or behavioural development of agent organisations.

17.6 Conclusion and Discussion

In this chapter we have detailed four organisational models. Considering the synthesis presented in Coutinho et al. (2009), where the authors have analyzed existing organisation models (MOISE, AGR Ferber et al. 2003, TAEMS Decker 1996; Lesser et al. 2004, ISLANDER Esteva et al. 2001, OperA Dignum 2004, AGRE Ferber et al. 2005, MOISEInst Gâteau et al. 2005, ODML Horling and Lesser 2004, STEAM Tambe et al. 1999, AUML Parunak and Odell 2001, MAS-ML da Silva et al. 2004), different modelling dimensions have been exhibited (cf. Table 17.1).

It is shown that an organisational model may provide constructs to represent formal patterns in the structure and functions of an agent organisation, these patterns being either static or kinetic. This general analysis lead to posit four cohesive categories of modelling constructs in an organisational model:

- *Organisational Structure:* constructs to represent what aspects of the structure of the agent organisation have to be invariant through time;
- *Organisational Functions:* constructs that represent global goals and goal de compositions to be accomplished by the agent organisation;
- *Organisational Interactions:* constructs to represent time-dependent aspects of standardized actions and interactions involving the elements from the organisational structure and organisation function;
- *Organisational Norms:* constructs to further regulate and show how organisational structure (time-independent relations), organisational interaction (time-dependent functioning) and organisational functions are interrelated.

Beyond these dimensions that are mostly found in existing organisational models, other complementary traits of agent organisations have been found:

Table 17.1 Organisation modelling dimension in some organisational models

Model	Structure	Interaction	Function	Norms	Environment	Evolution	Evaluation	Ontology
AGR	+	+	−	−	−	−	−	−
TAEMS	−	−	+	−	+	−	+	−
ISLANDER	+	+	−	+	−	−	−	+
OperA	+	+	+	+	−	−	−	+
AGRE	+	+	−	−	+	−	−	−
MOISEInst	+	−	+	+	−	+	−	−
ODML	+	−	−	−	−	−	+	−
STEAM	+	−	+	−	−	−	−	−
AUML	+	+	+	−	+	−	−	−
MAS-ML	+	+	+	+	+	−	−	−
$\mathcal{M}$oise	+	−	+	+	−	+	−	−
VOM	+	+	+	+	+	−	−	+
Agent-oriented	+	+	+	+−	+	−	−	−
AAOL	+	+−	+−	+	+	+	+−	−

- *Organisational Environment:* constructs to represent a collection of resources in the space of the agent organisation formed by non-autonomous entities that can be perceived and acted upon (manipulated, consumed, produced, etc.) by the components agents;
- *Organisational Evolution:* constructs to model changes in the organisation (formal structure, norms and goals) at some points in the time in order to adapt the functioning of the agent organisation to new demands from the environment;
- *Organisational Evaluation:* constructs to measure the performance of the formal structure and norms of an agent organisation w.r.t. specific goals;
- *Organisational Ontologies:* constructs to build conceptualizations regarding the application domain of the agent organisation that must be consistently shared by the component agents. These global conceptualizations are important to maintain the coherence of the activity inside the agent organisation.

The models detailed in this chapter (VOM, Agent-Oriented Modelling and Autonomous Agents in Organized Localities (AAOL)), confirm the existence of these dimensions and the diversity of constructs proposed in the Multi-Agent literature to define organisation for agents to coordinate in decentralized and open systems. More specifically:

- Organisational Structure – in almost all models this is the primary modelling concern. The main modelling elements found were roles, groups, and relationships between them. The structure of roles and groups defines a system of possible positions where the agents should find a place to become a member of an agent organisation.
- Organisational Interactions – found mainly in ISLANDER and OperA. In this respect, the models provide constructs to express the dynamic of communicative interactions between the agents (positioned in the social structure). Some constructs are interaction protocols, scenes and scene structures. In AAOL it is found in Görmer et al. (2011b) to evaluate the system with an interaction level to combine the micro and macro level of a Multi-Agent System.
- Organisational Function – appeared with more emphasis in TAEMS, STEAM and MOISE+. In these models, (one of) the main concern is to provide means to specify procedures to achieve goals. In order to model this feature, we find in the models conceptual elements such as tasks or goals, missions and plans. In AAOL it is designed in its structure on the individual and global context layer.
- Organisational Norms – described in term of deontic norms (regulate the behaviour of social entities: what they are allowed to do –direct or indirectly–, what they are obliged to do, etc.). ISLANDER, OperA, MOISEInst and AAOL are representative examples of organisational models that provide mechanisms to specify normative structures.
- Organisational Environment – here the models provide means to describe elements lying in the topological space occupied by the agent organisation and the way agents (positioned in the social structure, performing some task and/or in the course of some dialogical interaction, respecting some norms) are related to these elements. AGRE, MAS-ML and AAOL are examples of organisational

models (modelling techniques) that provide constructs to represent organisation environment elements. MOISE+ and VOM define environment by means of the Agents and Artifacts (A&A) conceptual framework.

- Organisational Evolution – this is related to modelling the way organisations can change (their social, task decomposition, dialogical, and normative structures) in order to cope with changes in its purpose and/or environment. Among the organisational models reviewed, MOISE+ and its extension MOISEInst explicit address organisation evolution issues. AAOL has a big focus on adaptivity and controlling in order to achieve a system balance of an IT-ecosystem.
- Organisational Evaluation – in order to modify some organisation (re-organisation) it is important to know how well the present organisation is performing. Thus, some models have elements to specify means to assess some properties of an organisation. Among these we have found TAEMS and ODML. Partial evaluation is also done by AAOL.
- Organisational Ontology – here we find ontologies used to ground the elements of the other dimensions as can be seen in the organisational models ISLANDER and OperA, and to define mental states of the agents in VOM. In AAOL there exists also works for ontologies.

References

Argente, E. 2008. *GORMAS: Guias para el desarrollo de Sistemas multi-agente abiertos basados en organizaciones*. Ph.D. thesis, Universidad Politecnica de Valencia.

Argente, E., V. Botti, and V. Julian. 2009a. GORMAS: An organizational-oriented methodological guideline for open MAS. In *Proceedings of the agent-oriented software engineering*, Budapest, 85–96.

Argente, E., V. Julian, and V. Botti. 2009b. MAS modeling based on organizations. In *Post-proceedings 9th international workshop AOSE'08*, vol. 5386, 16–30. Berlin/Heidelberg: Springer.

Argente, E., V. Botti, C. Carrascosa, A. Giret, V. Julián, and M. Rebollo. 2011. An abstract architecture for virtual organizations: The THOMAS approach. *Knowledge and Information Systems* 29(2): 379–403.

Behrens, T.M., K.V. Hindriks, and J. Dix. 2011. Towards an environment interface standard for agent platforms. *Annals of Mathematics and Artificial Intelligence* 61(4): 261–295.

Behrens, T.M., K.V. Hindriks, R. Bordini, L. Braubach, M. Dastani, J. Dix, J. Hübner, and A. Pokahr. 2012. An interface for agent-environment interaction. In *Programming multi-agent systems*, Lecture notes in computer science, vol. 6599, ed. R. Collier, J. Dix and P. Novák, 139–158. Berlin/Heidelberg: Springer.

Bresciani, P., A. Perini, P. Giorgini, F. Giunchiglia, and J. Mylopoulos. 2004. Tropos: An agent-oriented software development methodology. *Autonomous Agents and Multiagent Systems* 8(3): 203–236.

Cernuzzi, L., T. Juan, L. Sterling, and F. Zambonelli. 2004. The GAIA methodology: Basic concepts and extensions, pp. 69–88. *Methodologies and software engineering for agent systems: The agent-oriented software engineering handbook*. Boston/London: Kluwer Publishing.

Centeno, R., H. Billhardt, R. Hermoso, and S. Ossowski. 2009. Organising MAS: A formal model based on organisational mechanisms. In *Proceedings of the 2009 ACM symposium on applied computing*, 740–746. New York: ACM.

Chu, V.H., J. Görmer, and J.P. Müller. 2011. Atsim: Combining aimsum and jade for agent-based traffic simulation. In *Avances en inteligencia artificial. Actas de CAEPIA '11*. vol. 1. San Cristóbal de La Laguna.

Clancy, T. 1994. The latest word from thoughtful executives. *Academy of Management Executive* 8(5): 8–10.

Coutinho, L.R., J.S. Sichman, and O. Boissier. 2009. *Handbook of research on multi-agent systems: Semantics and dynamics of organizational models*, Modelling dimensions for agent organizations, 18–50. Hershey: Information Science Reference.

Coyle, J., M. Coyle, and N. Schnarr. 1995. The soft-side challenges of the virtual corporation. *Human Resource Planning* 18: 41–42.

Criado, N., E. Argente, V. Julian, and V. Botti. 2009. Designing virtual organizations. In *Proceedings of the international conference on practical applications of agents and multi-agent systems*, 440–449. Berlin/Heidelberg: Springer.

da Silva, V.T., R. Choren, and C.J.P. de Lucena. 2004. A UML based approach for modeling and implementing multi-agent systems. In *Proceedings of the autonomous agents and multiagent systems, international joint conference on* 2, 914–921. Los Alamitos: IEEE Computer Society.

Decker, K.S. 1996. TÆMS: A framework for environment centered analysis and design of coordination mechanisms. In *Fundations of distributed artificial intelligence*, ed. G.M.P. O'Hare and N.R. Jennings, 429–447. New York: Wiley.

DeLoach, S.A., and M. Kumar. 2005. Multiagent systems engineering: An overview and case study. In *Agent-oriented methodologies*, 317–340. Hershey: Idea Group.

DeSanctis, G., and P. Monge. 1998. Communication processes for virtual organizations. *Journal of Computer-Mediated Communication* 3(4): 0–0.

Dignum, V. 2004. *A model for organizational interaction: Based on agents, founded in logic*. Ph.D. thesis, Universiteit Utrecht.

Dignum, V., and F. Dignum. 2001. Modelling agent societies: Co-ordination frameworks and institutions. In *Progress in artificial intelligence, 10th Portuguese international conference on artificial intelligence, EPIA'01*, LNAI, 191–204. Berlin: Springer.

Esparcia, S., and E. Argente. 2011. Formalizing virtual organizations. In *Proceedings of the 3rd international conference on agents and artificial intelligence (ICAART 2011)*, Rome, vol. 2, 84–93. SciTePress.

Esparcia, S., E. Argente, R. Centeno, and R. Hermoso. 2010. Enhancing MAS environments with organizational mechanisms. In *Proceedings of the 22nd IEEE international conference on Tools with artificial intelligence (ICTAI), 2010*, vol. 1, 457–464. Los Alamitos: IEEE.

Esteva, M., J.A. Padget, and C. Sierra. 2001. Formalizing a language for institutions and norms. In *Proceedings of the ATAL*, Lecture notes in computer science, vol. 2333, ed. J.J.C. Meyer and M. Tambe, pp. 348–366. Berlin/New York: Springer.

Esteva, M., J.A. Rodríguez-Aguilar, B. Rosell, and J.L. Arcos. 2004. AMELI: An agent-based middleware for electronic institutions. In *Proceedings of the third international joint conference on autonomous agents and multi-agent systems (AAMAS)*, ed. N.R. Jennings, C. Sierra, L. Sonenberg and M. Tambe, 236–243. New York: ACM.

Ferber, J., O. Gutknecht, and F. Michel. 2003. From agents to organizations: An organizational view of multi-agent systems. In *AOSE*, Lecture notes in computer science, vol. 2935, ed. P. Giorgini, J.P. Müller and J. Odell, 214–230. Berlin/New York: Springer.

Ferber, J., F. Michel, and J. Baez. 2005. AGRE: Integrating environments with organizations. In *Environments for Multi-agent Systems*, ed. D. Weyns, H. Van Dyke Parunak and F. Michel, 48–59. Berlin/Heidelberg: Springer.

Foster, I., and C. Kesselman. 2001. The anatomy of the grid: Enabling scalable virtual organizations. *The International Journal of Supercomputer Applications* 15: 200–222.

Galbraith, J. 1995. Designing organizations. San Francisco: Jossey-bass

Gâteau, B., O. Boissier, D. Khadraoui, and E. Dubois. 2005. Moiseinst: An organizational model for specifying rights and duties of autonomous agents. In *Third European workshop on multi-agent systems (EUMAS 2005)*, Brussels, 484–485.

Görmer, J., and J.P. Müller. 2012. Multiagent system architecture and method for group-oriented traffic coordination. In *Proceedings of IEEE DEST 2012*, Campione d'Italia. IEEE.

Görmer, J., and C. Mumme. 2012. Multiagentensysteme für das kooperative verkehrsmanagement. In *MMS 2012: Mobile und ubiquitäre informationssysteme*, ed. A. Back, M. Bick, M. Breunig, K. Pousttchi, and F. Thiesse, 138–142. Braunschweig: Ges. für Informatik.

Görmer, J., J.F. Ehmke, M. Fiosins, D. Schmidt, H. Schumacher, and H. Tchouankem. 2011a. Decision support for dynamic city traffic management using vehicular communication. In *Proceedings of the SIMULTECH*, Noordwijkerhout, 327–332.

Görmer, J., G. Homoceanu, C. Mumme, M. Huhn, and J.P. Müller. 2011b. Jrep: Extending repast simphony for jade agent behavior components. In *Proceedings fo the IAT*, Lyon, 149–154.

Grenier, R., and G. Metes. 1995. Going virtual: Moving your organization into the 21st century. Upper Saddle River: Prentice Hall PTR.

Gutknecht, O., and J. Ferber. 2001. The madkit agent platform architecture. In *Revised papers from the international workshop on infrastructure for multi-agent systems: Infrastructure for agents, multi-agent systems, and scalable multi-agent systems*, 48–55. London: Springer.

Hahn, C., C.M. Mora, and K. Fischer. 2009. A platform-independent metamodel for multiagent systems. *Autonomous Agents and Multi-Agent Systems* 18(2): 239–266.

Heistracher, T., T. Kurz, C. Masuch, P. Ferronata, M. Vidal, A. Corallo, G. Briscoe, and P. Dini. 2004. Pervasive service architecture for a digital ecosystem. In *Proceedings of the 1st workshop on coordination and adaptation techniques for software entities*, Oslo.

Horling, B., and V. Lesser. 2004. Quantitative organizational models for large-scale agent systems. In *MMAS*, Lecture notes in computer science, vol. 3446, ed. T. Ishida, L. Gasser and H. Nakashima, 121–135. Berlin/Heidelberg: Springer.

Horling, B., V. Lesser. 2005. A survey of multi-agent organizational paradigms. *The Knowledge Engineering Review* 19(04): 281–316.

Hübner, J.F., J. Sichman, and O. Boissier. 2002. A model for the structural, functional, and deontic specification of organizations in multiagent systems. In *Advances in artificial intelligence*, Lecture notes in computer science, vol. 2507, ed. G. Bittencourt, and G. Ramalho, 439–448. Berlin/Heidelberg: Springer.

Hübner, J.F., J.S. Sichman, O. Boissier. 2006. $\mathscr{S}$-$\mathscr{M}$oise^{+}: A middleware for developing organised multi-agent systems. In *Proceedings of the international workshop on organizations in multi-agent systems, from organizations to organization oriented programming in MAS (OOOP'2005)*, Utrecht, LNCS, vol. 3913, ed. O. Boissier, V. Dignum, E. Matson and J.S. Sichman. Springer.

Hübner, J.F., O. Boissier, R. Kitio, A. Ricci. 2009. Instrumenting multi-agent organisations with organisational artifacts and agents. *Journal of Autonomous Agents and Multi-Agent Systems*

Hübner, J.F., O. Boissier, and R.H. Bordini. 2010. From organisation specification to normative programming in multi-agent organisations. In *CLIMA XI*, 117–134.

Huhn, M., J. Müller, J. Görmer, G. Homoceanu, N.T. Le, L. Märtin, C. Mumme, C. Schulz, N. Pinkwart, and C. Müller-Schloer. 2011. Autonomous agents in organized localities regulated by institutions. In *Proceedings of the 5th IEEE international conference on digital ecosystems and technologies (IEEE DEST)*, 54–61. Piscataway: IEEE.

Jennings, N.R. 2000. On agent-based software engineering. *Artificial Intelligence* 177(2): 277–296.

Juan, T., A. Pearce, and L. Sterling. 2002. Roadmap: Extending the gaia methodology for complex open systems. In *Proceedings of the first international joint conference on autonomous agents and multiagent systems (AAMAS 2002)*, 3–10. Bologna: ACM.

Klar, D., and M. Huhn. 2012. Interfaces and models for the diagnosis of cyber-physical ecosystems. In *Proceedings of IEEE DEST 2012*, Campione d'Italia. IEEE.

Le, N.T., L. Märtin, C. Mumme, and N. Pinkwart. 2012. Communication-free detection of resource conflicts in multi-agent-based cyber-physical systems. In *Proceedings of IEEE DEST 2012*, Campione d'Italia. IEEE.

Lesser, V., K. Decker, T. Wagner, N. Carver, A. Garvey, B. Horling, D. Neiman, R. Podorozhny, M. NagendraPrasad, A. Raja, R. Vincent, P. Xuan, and X. Zhang. 2004. Evolution of the gpgp/taems domain-independent coordination framework. *Autonomous Agents and Multi-Agent Systems* 9(1): 87–143. Kluwer Academic Publishers.

Lopes Cardoso, H., and E. Oliveira. 2008. Electronic institutions for B2B: Dynamic normative environments. *Artificial Intelligence and Law* 16(1): 107–128.

Mao, X., and E. Yu. 2004. Organizational and social concepts in agent oriented software engineering. In *Proceedings of the AOSE*, Lecture notes in computer science, vol. 3382, ed. J. Odell, P. Giorgini and J.P. Müller, 1–15. Berlin/New York: Springer.

Müller, J.P. 1996. *The design of intelligent agents*, Lecture notes in artificial intelligence, vol. 1177. Berlin/New York: Springer.

Omicini, A., A. Ricci, and M. Viroli. 2008. Artifacts in the A&A meta-model for multi-agent systems. *Autonomous Agents and Multi-Agent Systems* 17(3): 432–456.

Padgham, L., and M. Winikoff. 2004. Developing intelligent agent systems: A practical guide. Chichester/Hoboken: Wiley.

Parunak, H.V.D., and J. Odell. 2001. Representing social structures in UML. In *Proceedings of the AOSE*, Lecture notes in computer science, vol. 2222, ed. M. Wooldridge, G. Weiß and P. Ciancarini, 1–16. Berlin/New York: Springer.

Rausch, A., J. Müller, U. Goltz, and D. Niebuhr. 2012. It ecosystems: A new paradigm for engineering complex adaptive software systems. In *Proceedings of IEEE DEST 2012*, Campione d'Italia. IEEE.

Scott, W.R. 1981. Organizations: Rational, natural, and open systems. Englewood Cliffs: Prentice Hall.

Sterling, L. 2011. Adaptive: A quality goal for agent-oriented models or a fundamental feature of agents? In *Proceedings of the 18th world congress of the international federation of automatic control (IFAC)*, Milano, Italy.

Sterling, L., and K. Taveter. 2009. *The art of agent-oriented modeling*. Cambridge/London: MIT.

Tambe, M., J. Adibi, Y. Alonaizon, A. Erdem, G.A. Kaminka, S. Marsella, and I. Muslea. 1999. Building agent teams using an explicit teamwork model and learning. *Artificial Intelligence* 110(2): 215–239.

Taveter, K., and G. Wagner. 2005. Towards radical agent-oriented software engineering processes based on AOR modelling. In *Agent-oriented methodologies*, ed. B. Henderson-Sellers and P. Giorgini, 277–316. Hershey: Idea Group.

Vázquez-Salceda, J., V. Dignum, and F. Dignum. 2005. Organizing multiagent systems. *Au tonomous Agents and Multi-Agent Systems* 11: 307–360.

Chapter 18
Modelling Agent Institutions

Nicoletta Fornara, Henrique Lopes Cardoso, Pablo Noriega, Eugénio Oliveira, Charalampos Tampitsikas, and Michael I. Schumacher

18.1 Introduction

In everyday language, the notion of "institution" is used in different contexts, for example when one talks about the "institution of marriage", when we say that a given university is an "institution of higher education", or when we say that a politician does not behave "institutionally". Those everyday uses and some typical institutions have been studied and formalized by economists, political scientists, legal theorists and philosophers (see Aoki 2001; Powell and Dimaggio 1991). There are three features that these conventional understandings have. The first is the distinction between "institutional" and "brute" (or actual, physical or real) facts (Jones and Sergot 1996; Searle 1995), and the correspondence between the two. Another key conceptual element is the separation between the institution itself and the

N. Fornara (✉)
Università della Svizzera italiana, Lugano, Switzerland
e-mail: nicoletta.fornara@usi.ch

H. Lopes Cardoso • E. Oliveira
LIACC/Departamento de Engenharia Informática, Faculdade de Engenharia, Universidade do Porto, Porto, Portugal
e-mail: hlc@fe.up.pt; eco@fe.up.pt

P. Noriega
IIIA – CSIC, Barcelona, Spain
e-mail: pablo@iiia.csic.es

C. Tampitsikas
Università della Svizzera italiana, Lugano, Switzerland

University of Applied Sciences Western Switzerland, Sierre, Switzerland
e-mail: charalampos.tampitsikas@usi.ch

M.I. Schumacher
University of Applied Sciences Western Switzerland, Sierre, Switzerland
e-mail: michael.schumacher@hevs.ch

S. Ossowski (ed.), *Agreement Technologies*, Law, Governance and Technology Series 8, DOI 10.1007/978-94-007-5583-3_18,

agents that participate in the collective endeavor that is the purpose of the institution. Finally, the assumption that institutions involve regulations, norms, conventions and therefore some mechanism of governance that make those components effective. In fact, most theoretical approaches to conventional institutions may be distinguished by the way this last assumption is made operational. In particular, while some approaches (for instance North 1990 and Ostrom 1986) take institutions to be the conventions themselves – and consequently draw a clear distinction between institutions (conventions) and organisations (the entities that put the conventions in practice) – others (like Simon 1996) take institutions to be organisations (with rules or norms, institutional objects and due processes or procedures) but still keep individuals out of the institution.

Borrowing from these everyday understandings, and influenced by their formalizations, the notion of institution has been used within the agents community to model and implement a variety of socio-technical systems that serve the same purposes that conventional institutions serve. Artificial, electronic, agent-mediated, agent-based or, simply, agent institutions are some of the terms that have been used to name such computational incarnations of conventional institutions in the agents community, and for the sake of economy we take them as synonymous in this introduction. Their main purpose is to *enable* and *regulate* the interaction among autonomous agents in order to achieve some collective endeavour.

These agent institutions, as agent-based organisations do, play a crucial role as *agreement technologies* because they allow to specify, implement and enact the conventions and the services that enable the establishment, execution, monitoring and enforcement of agreements among interacting agents.

Agent institutions have been implemented as multi-agent systems using different "frameworks" (conceptual models that have associated tools and a software architecture that allow implementation of particular institutions). However, these artificial institutions all hold three assumptions that mirror the three features of conventional institutions mentioned above:

1. Institution, on one hand, and agents, on the other, are taken as first-class entities. A particular institution is specified through a conceptual model, based on a metamodel, that may be more or less formalized, then it may be implemented on some type of institutional environment and enacted through interactions of some participating entities.
2. Institutions are open MAS, in the sense that: (i) it is neither known in advance what agents may participate in an enactment, nor when these agents may decide to enter or leave an enactment; (ii) the institution does not know what the particular goals of individual agents are; (iii) the institution has no control over the internal decision-making of agents (iv) agents may not necessarily comply with institutional conventions.
3. Institutions are regulated systems. Interactions in the agent institution must comply with some conventions, rules, and norms that apply to every participant agent and are somehow enforced. Regulations control interactions and are applicable to individual agents in virtue of the activities they perform and not because of who they are.

There are several ways that these assumptions lead to more precise notions of what constitutes an institution and how these may be implemented. This chapter discusses three frameworks that actually achieve that objective but before discussing those frameworks we would like to provide some background.

Institutions are Normative MAS. Institutions are a class of "normative multi-agent systems" (norMAS) (Boella et al. 2008, 2009):

> A *normative multi-agent system* is a multi-agent system organized by means of mechanisms to represent, communicate, distribute, detect, create, modify, and enforce norms, and mechanisms to deliberate about norms and detect norm violation and fulfilment.

The ground assumption in normative MAS is that norms are used to constrain undesired behaviour, on one hand, but they also create a space of interaction where successful social interactions take, which as we mentioned before is what agent institutions do by setting and enforcing the rules of the game, creating an institutional reality where these rules apply and are enforced. Not surprisingly, agent institutions do have mechanisms that are similar to the ones listed in the description above because institutions (by definition) create the space of opportunity and constrain interactions to better articulate towards the common endeavour. The class of normative MAS and agent institutions are not the same because the mapping between the ideal mechanisms and the way an agent institution framework captures the mechanism is not obvious and is seldom fully established. The following sections will give substance to this last claim but some three prior qualifications are due.

- It is usually assumed that norms ought to be expressed as deontic formulas with a standard proof-theoretic notion of consequence associated to them. This is useful for a declarative description of conventions that is easy to communicate, promulgate and perhaps reason about (at design time as well as at run time). However it is not absolutely necessary, this because there may be other convenient ways of expressing different types of norms. For example, an artificial institution may express conventions that constrain agent actions in procedural (non-declarative) form, for instance using commitment-based protocols and dialogical games, and still use, say, model-checking devices to prove normative properties of the protocol. Likewise, an electronic institution describes permissions, obligations and prohibitions through finite state machines whose transitions are in fact conditional statements in a first order language and paths and propagation take the function of the modal operator; and in these networks, colored Petri nets may provide appropriate semantics for on-line and off-line normative conflict detection, for example.
- It is usually understood that such deontic formulas are enough to fully specify and govern a multi-agent system. Not really. In addition to a collection of norms, a normative MAS requires several institutional constructs in order to legislate, apply, enforce and modify norms. Constitutive conventions for example may need extra-normative devices like bonds and identity certificates to provide entitlements to participating agents. Governance mechanisms may require the existence of institutional agents that perform norm-enforcement functions, etc.

- Normative notions are pertinent only if norms may be violated. The actual situation is richer. There are application contexts where governance may need to be fully regimented (in electronic markets, for instance) and others that may not (conflict resolution, for example). Hence, enforcement mechanisms in an agent institution may involve a variety of components dealing with observability of actions, institutional power, law enforcement roles, repair actions, etc.

Institutions vs. organisations. The notions of *institution* and *organisation* are closely related. The essential distinction, bluntly speaking, is that the institution is focused on what can be done, while organisations on who does it. Institutions, thus deal mainly with norms and governance, while organisations involve individuals, resources, goals. An institution creates a virtual environment, an organisation is an entity in the world (a crude physical reality). An organisation has boundaries that establish a clear differentiation: some rules apply inside, others apply outside; there are organisational staff, and there are customers and suppliers; there is a macroeconomic environment and there are objectives of the firm. On the other hand the organisation also has several institutional components: best practices, social structure and roles, decomposable activities, internal governance. Although the distinction exists and may be formally stated in a crisp way, when we treat agent institutions, we tend to bundle together the specification of the institution with the implementation of that specification, and where the distinction really becomes blurred we tend to identify the electronic institution (the virtual environment) with the running system that deals with actual transactions: that is, with the computational system *and* the firm that runs it.

Institutional Frameworks. In this chapter from Sects. 18.2–18.5 we will present three frameworks for agent-based institutions that illustrate how the previously mentioned ideas about institutions are made precise enough to model actual institutions and implement them as multi-agent systems. Those frameworks are: (i) ANTE, a model that considers electronic institutions as computational realizations of adaptive artificial environments for governing multi-agent interactions; (ii) OCeAN extended in MANET, a model for specifying Artificial Institutions (AIs), situated in agent environments, which can be used in the design and implementation of different open interaction systems; and (iii) a framework for Electronic Institutions (EIs), extended with the EIDE development environment, based on open, social, decomposable and dialogical interactions. In Sect. 18.6 we discuss and compare those three frameworks for agent-based institutions. Finally in Sect. 18.7 some open challenges in the field of specifications and use of institutions for the realization of real open multi-agent systems are discussed.

We should mention that in addition to these three frameworks, there are at least three other proposals that share the above principles. The first is the *OMNI* model (Dignum et al. 2004), which derives from the *OperA* and *HARMONIA* frameworks introduced in the dissertations of Dignum (2004) and of Vázquez-Salceda (2003) respectively. The *OMNI* model allows the description of MAS-based organisations where agent activities are organized as agent scripts (scenes) that are built around a collective goal. The admissible actions of each scene are regulated by a set of norms. The *OMNI* model contains three types of institutional component: normative, contextual and organisational; whose contents are specifiable in three levels of abstraction: descriptive, operational, implementation. Lately, they have developed the *OperettA* framework (Aldewereld and Dignum 2010), to support the implementation of real MAS. The second one is the *instAL* framework that puts together the research developed over many years in the University of Bath (Cliffe et al. 2007; Corapi et al. 2011). *InstAL* is a normative framework architecture and a formal mathematical model to specify, verify and reason about norms that are used to regulate an open MAS. Finally, the third one is the recent proposal by Pitt et al. (2011) that stems from Artikis et al. (2009) and draws on institutional notions proposed by Olstrom (2010).

18.2 The ANTE Framework: Electronic Institutions as Dynamic Normative Environments

In this section we will consider electronic institutions as computational realizations of adaptive artificial environments for governing multi-agent interactions.

The use of an *Electronic Institution* as an infrastructure that enables regulation in multi-agent systems presupposes the existence of a common environment where norms (see Part III) guide the way agents should behave. The role of an *institutional normative environment* (Lopes Cardoso 2010), besides providing a set of regulations under which agents' collective work is made possible, is twofold: to check whether agents are willing to follow the norms they commit to (through monitoring), and further to employ correction measures as a means of coercing agents to comply (through enforcement) (see also Chap. 11 on this).

Furthermore, when addressing open systems, the normative environment should enable the run-time establishment of new normative relationships, which are to be appropriately monitored and enforced. Hence, instead of having a predefined normative structure, the shape of the environment will evolve and adapt to the actual normative relationships that are established.

In order to make this feasible, we believe it is important to provide some infrastructure that facilitates the establishment of norm governed relationships. For that, we propose the provision, in an electronic institution platform, of a supportive and extensible *normative framework* (Lopes Cardoso and Oliveira 2008). Its main aim is to assist software agents in the task of negotiating and establishing electronic contracts.

Having in mind real-world domains such as agreements guided by electronic contracting, the normative environment will, while monitoring the compliance to norms that apply to specific contracts, record a mapping from the relevant interactions that take place (which concern electronic contracting exchanges). The connection between real-world interactions and the institutional environment is made through illocutions (speech acts) that empowered agents (Jones and Sergot 1996) perform with the intent of informing the institution that certain contract-related events have occurred. With an appropriate interface between the normative environment and the statements that agents make, we incrementally build a state of *institutional reality* (Searle 1995), which is an image of relevant real-world transactions that are, through this means, institutionally recognized (i.e., transactions are turned into *institutional facts* inside the normative environment).

Hierarchical normative framework. In order to facilitate the establishment of electronic contracts, the normative environment should provide a supportive and extensible normative framework. This framework may be inspired by notions coming from contract law theory, namely the use of "default rules" (Craswell 2000) – background norms to be applied in the absence of any explicit agreement to the contrary. We therefore propose that this normative structure is composed of a hierarchy of *contexts* (Lopes Cardoso and Oliveira 2009), within which norms are created that may apply to sub-contexts. The context hierarchy tries to mimic the fact that in business it is often the case that a B2B contractual agreement forms the business context for more specific contracts that may be created. Each contract establishes a new context for norm applicability.

A *norm defeasibility* approach (Lopes Cardoso and Oliveira 2008) is also proposed in order to determine whether a norm should be inherited, for a specific situation, from an upper context. This feature allows the normative framework to be adapted (to better fit a particular contract case) and extended (allowing new contract types to be defined). Furthermore, the rationale behind the possibility of overriding any norm is based on the assumption that "default rules" should be seen as facilitating rather than constraining contractual activity (Kaplow 2000) (see also Chap. 13 on defeasibility of rules in law).

Adaptive norm enforcement. Adaptive enforcement mechanisms are important in open environments, where the behaviour of an agent population cannot be directly controlled. When the normative specification of contracts includes flaws, namely by omitting normative consequences for some contract enactment outcomes, self-interested agents may try to exploit their potential advantage and intentionally violate contract clauses.

In general, an institution may employ two basic kinds of sanctions in order to incentive norm compliance. Direct *material sanctions* inflict immediate penalties, whereas indirect *social sanctions* have a more lasting effect, e.g. by affecting an agent's reputation. The effectiveness of these alternatives may differ according to the agents that interact within the institutional environment. If agents are not able to take advantage of reputation information, the use of material sanctions is probably a better alternative. Having in mind the deterrence effect of sanctions (i.e., their role in discouraging violations), an institution may use an adaptive sanction model to maintain order (by motivating agents to comply) and consequently trust in the system.

Economic approaches to law enforcement suggest analyzing sanctions by taking into account their effects on parties' activities. Based on this understanding, we have designed and experimentally evaluated a model for *adaptive deterrence sanctions* (Lopes Cardoso and Oliveira 2011) that tries to enforce norm compliance without excessively compromising agents' willingness to establish contracts. Raising deterrence sanctions has a side effect of increasing the risk associated with contracting activities.

We believe that our approach, which has been implemented as part of the ANTE framework (Lopes Cardoso et al. 2012), has the distinctive features of being both an open and a computationally feasible approach to the notion of artificial institution. In fact, an *institution* is grounded on some notion of regulation, which is materialized through rules and norms. While some researchers, mostly from fields other than computer science, take an abstract and immaterial perspective to institutions, we find it natural, when addressing electronic institutions, to follow a more proactive stance and ascribe to an electronic institution the role of putting its regulations into practice. These regulations are seen as evolving according to the commitments that agents, when interacting in an open environment, are willing to establish amongst themselves, relying on the institutional environment for monitoring and enforcement purposes. The guiding line for our approach has been the field of electronic contracting.

18.3 The OCeAN Metamodel for the Specification of Artificial Institutions

OCeAN (Ontology CommitmEnts Authorizations Norms) (Fornara and Colombetti 2009; Fornara et al. 2007) is a metamodel that can be used for specification of Artificial Institutions (AIs). Those institutions thanks to a process of contextualization in a specific application domain can be used and re-used in the design of different *open systems* thought for enabling the interaction of autonomous agents. The fundamental concepts that need to be specified in the design of artificial institutions are:

- An *ontology* for the definition of the concepts used in the communication and in the regulation of the interaction. With an application independent component with concepts and properties that are general enough (like the notion of time, action, event, obligation, and so on) and an application dependent part;
- The possible *events*, *actions*, *institutional actions and events* that may happen or can be used in the interaction among agents, this mainly in terms of preconditions that need to be satisfied for their successful performance and effects of their performance;
- The *roles* that the agents may play during an interaction and the rules for playing such roles;
- An *agent communication language (ACL)* for enabling a communication among agents, for example for promising, informing, requesting, agreeing and so on;

- the set of *institutional powers* for the actual performance of institutional actions;
- the set of *norms* for the definition of *obligations*, *prohibitions*, and *permissions*.

In our past works we have proposed a commitment-based semantics of an agent communication language (Fornara and Colombetti 2002) that is regulated by the basic institution of language (Fornara et al. 2007). We have formalized the concepts for the specification of AIs using different formalisms, and we have used them for specifying the institutions necessary for the design of different types of electronic auctions. In particular initially we specified our metamodel with a notation inspired by the UML metamodel and we used the Object Constraint Language (Object Management Group 2005) as notation for expressing constraints (Fornara et al. 2008). Subsequently, due to difficulties of efficiently matching the norms that regulate agents interaction with the actions performed by the agents and the need to perform automatic reasoning on the content of messages and norms, we decided to formally specify the basic concepts of our metamodel by using the Discrete Event Calculus (DEC), which is a version of the Event Calculus. The Event Calculus is a formalism that works well for the purpose of reasoning about action and change in time, for which it was introduced by Kowalski and Sergot in 1986. DEC has been introduced by Mueller (2006) to improve the efficiency of automated reasoning by limiting time to integers. This formalism has the advantage of making the simulation of the dynamic evolution of the state of the interaction easier, and making it possible to perform automated reasoning based on the knowledge of the state of the interaction. The main limits of this approach are that the DEC formalism is not widely known among software engineers and the performances of the prototype that we implemented for simulating a run of the English Auction did not scale well with the size of the concepts represented and the number of participating agents.

Consequently in 2009 we started to investigate the possibility of specifying our model using Semantic Web Technologies (Fornara 2011; Fornara and Colombetti 2010) (see also Part II). We proposed to specify the concepts (classes, properties, and axioms) of the OCeAN metamodel using OWL 2 DL: the Web Ontology Language recommended by W3C, which is a practical realization of a Description Logic system known as *SROIQ(D)*. We proposed an *upper level ontology* for the definition of the abstract concepts used in the specification of every type of artificial institution, like the concept of *event*, *action*, *time event*, *change event*, *temporal entity*, *instant of time* and so on. In particular for modelling time we used the standard OWL Time Ontology[1] enriched with some axioms useful for deducing information about instant of time and intervals. We specified the *OWL Obligation Ontology* (Fornara 2011) that can be used for the specification of the obligations that one agent has with respect to another agent to perform one action that belongs to a class of possible actions, within a given deadline, if certain activation conditions hold, and certain terminating conditions do not hold. Those obligations can be used to specify constrains on the behaviour of the interacting agents and to express

[1] http://www.w3.org/TR/owl-time/.

the semantics of conditional promises communicative acts (Fornara et al. 2012). The *OWL Obligation Ontology* together with some functionalities realized for performing closed-world reasoning about certain classes can be used for *monitoring* the evolution in time of the state of the obligations on the basis of the events and actions that happen during the interaction. In fact, reasoning in OWL is based on an *open-world assumption* but in our model, in order to be able to deduce that there is an obligation to perform an action, when the deadline is elapsed or violated, we need to implement closed-world reasoning and assume that in the interaction contexts where this model will be used, not being able to infer that action has been performed in the past is sufficient evidence that the action has not been performed. Regarding monitoring it is also important to solve the problem of finding an efficient and effective mechanism for mapping real agents' actions in element of the OWL ontology for being able to perform automated reasoning on them and deducing that an obligation to perform a given action is fulfilled or violated. Currently the OCeAN meta-model has not been completely specified using Semantic Web Technologies, we plan to do it in our future works.

The main advantage of the choice of using Semantic Web technologies is that they are increasingly becoming a standard for Internet applications, and given that the OWL logic language is decidable, it is supported by many reasoners (like Pellet and HermiT), tools for ontology editing (like Protégé) and library for automatic ontology management (like OWL-API and JENA). Moreover the specification of artificial institutions in OWL makes them easily reusable as data construct in many different applications in different domains.

18.4 Artificial Institutions Situated in Environment: The MANET Model

Thanks to the Agreement Technology COST Action in 2009 we started to investigate how to integrate the studies on the model of agent environments (Weyns et al. 2007), in particular the model presented in the GOLEM framework (Bromuri and Stathis 2009), with the OCeAN meta-model of AI. As first result of this work we proposed the MANET (Multi-Agent Normative EnvironmenTs) model where AI are situated in agent environments (Tampitsikas et al. 2012).

One of the most important tasks of an *environment* is to mediate the actions and events that happen, where *mediate* means that an environment is in charge of registering that an event has happened and of notifying this event to all agents registered to the template of this event (the agents that have a sensor for this type of events) (Bromuri and Stathis 2009). An environment is composed of *objects* and *physical spaces*, and is the place where *agents* interact. A physical space describes the infrastructure of the system and its infrastructural limitations to the agents behaviour in terms of physical rules.

Given that AIs are abstract description specified at design time, it is crucial to specify how certain AI can be concretely used at run-time for the definition and realization of open systems. Therefore we proposed to introduce in the model of environments the notion of *institutional space* that is used for having a first-class representation of AIs. In particular institutional spaces represent the boundaries of the effects of institutional events and actions performed by the agents, they may contain sub-spaces, and they enforce the norms of the system in response to the produced events.

Given that institutional spaces may contain sub-spaces, it is possible that the different AIs, used for the specification of different institutional spaces, may present some interdependencies. For example in a marketplace we can have many different auctions represented with sub-spaces created using different AIs. Given that agents may temporarily participate in more than one space, it may happen that the norms of one space, for example the marketplace, regulate also some events of its sub-spaces, for example by prohibiting an agent from making a bid in an auction represented in a sub-space if it has a specific role in the market-place. To solve this problem it is necessary to give to the designer of the system the possibility to define events that may be *observed* outside the boundaries of the space. Another problem may arise when the rules of a space (for example an auction) regulate for instance the participation of an agent to another space (another auction or a contract). In this case we need to introduce the possibility in the model for one space to *notify* another space about the fact that a specific event is happened.

The MANET model of artificial institutions situated in environment has been implemented in Prolog on top of GOLEM platform (Bromuri and Stathis 2009) and it was used for formalizing and running an e-energy marketplace (Tampitsikas et al. 2012) where agents representing different types of energy producers try to sell energy to potential consumers.

18.5 Electronic Institutions

The work we have been doing in the IIIA on electronic institutions (EIs, for short) may be observed from four complementary perspectives:

1. *The mimetic perspective:* EIs can be seen as computational environments that mimic the coordination support that conventional human institutions provide.
2. *The regulated MAS perspective* understands EIs as open multi-agent systems, that organise collective activities by establishing a restricted virtual environment where all interactions take place according to some established conventions.
3. *EIs as "artifacts" perspective* takes EIs to be the operational interface between the subjective decision-making processes of participants and the social task that is achieved through their interactions.
4. *The coordination support perspective:* EIs are a way of providing structure and governance to open multi-agent systems.

These four characterizations are supported by one single abstract model whose assumptions and core components we briefly discuss below. In turn, as we'll also see below, this abstract model is made operational through a set of software components that follow one particular computational architecture.

Over the past few years we have had the chance to build numerous examples of electronic institutions in a rather large variety of applications with those tools (d'Inverno et al. 2012)[2].

A conceptual core model for Electronic Institutions. Electronic institutions are grounded on the following basic assumptions about interactions:

- *Open.* Agents are black-boxes, heterogeneous, self-motivated and may enter and leave the institutional space on their own will.
- *Social.* Agents come together in pursuit of an endeavour that requires a collective participation; thus agents need to be aware of other agents and their roles and of the capabilities needed to achieve a particular goal in a collective activity.
- *Decomposable.* To contend with the possibility (due to openness) of large number of agents being involved in the social interaction we allow the collective endeavour to be decomposed into atomic activities (*scenes*) that achieve particular goals with the participation of fewer individuals. The decomposition requires that scenes be connected in a network in which the achievement of individual and collective goals correspond to paths in that network.
- *Replicable.* Simple activities may be either re-enacted by different groups of agents or enacted concurrently with different groups.
- *Co-incident.* An agent may be active, simultaneously, in more than a single activity[3].
- *Contextual.* Openness and decomposability limit the knowledge agents have of each other, thus interactions are naturally *local* within subgroups of agents that share a common "scene context", while as a dynamic virtual entity, the collectivity of agents is itself immersed in a larger "institutional context".
- *Dialogical.* Activities are achieved through interactions among agents composed of non-divisible units that happen at discrete points in time. Thus construable as point-to-point messages in a communication language, so that even physical actions may be thus wrapped[4].

[2]The IIIA model of Electronic Institutions is the result, mainly, of three dissertations (Esteva 2003; Noriega 1999; Rodriguez-Aguilar 2003).

[3]We will deal with to this ubiquity of a given agent as *agent processes* that stem from it, so that we have an objective ground for concurrency and control issues when implementing the institutional infrastructure.

[4]Messages make reference to an application domain and should be properly "anchored" (their meaning and pragmatics should be established and shared by participants), e.g. the term "pay" entails the real action of transferring funds in some agreed upon way; in a trial, the constant "exhibit A" corresponds to some object that is so labeled and available at the trial.

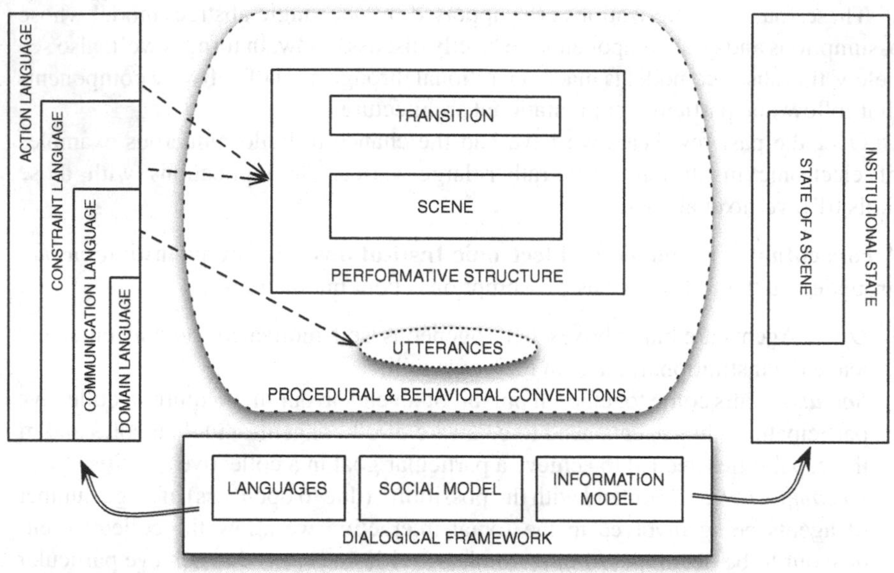

Fig. 18.1 Sketch of the electronic institutions conceptual model

These assumptions allow us to represent the conventions that will regulate agent interactions with the few constructs depicted in Fig. 18.1. The full detail of these constructs is presented in Arcos et al. (2005) but, broadly speaking, to specify an EI we need:

1. *A dialogical framework* that consists essentially of (i) a social model of roles and their relationships; (ii) a domain and a communication languages that will be used to express the institutional messages, plus a few other languages for expressing institutional constraints, and (iii) an information model to keep the *institutional state*, that is, the updated values of institutional variables.
2. *A performative structure* that captures the high level structure of the institutional interactions as a network of scenes connected by transitions.
3. *Procedural and behavioural constraints* that affect the contents of the performative structure; namely, (i) preconditions and postconditions of messages within scenes, (ii) constraints on the movement of roles between scenes and (iii) propagation of the effects of actions among scenes; for expressing all these constraints we make use of the tower of languages of the dialogical framework.

Our model has a straightforward operational semantics: institutional reality is changed through agent actions, but only those agent actions that comply with the institutional constraints have any institutional effect. More precisely, the institutional state is only altered through actions that comply with the procedural and behavioural constraints and in our model the only possible actions an agent can take are: to utter a message, to enter and leave the institution, and to move between

Table 18.1 Electronic institution operations

Operation	Called by	Effect on
Speak	Agent	Scene
RequestAccess	Agent	Electronic institution
JoinInstitution	Agent	Electronic institution, scene
LeaveInstitution	Agent	Electronic institution, scene
SelectNewTargets	Agent	Transition
RemoveOldTargets	Agent	Transition
StartElectronicInstitution	Infrastructure	Electronic institution
CreateSceneInstance	Infrastructure	Scene institution
CloseSceneInstance	Infrastructure	Scene
EnableAgentsToLeaveOrTransition	Infrastructure	Transition
EnableAgentsToLeaveAndTransition	Infrastructure	Transition
MovingFromSceneInstanceToTransitionInstance	Infrastructure	Scene, transition
MoveAgentFromTransitionToScene	Infrastructure	Scene, transition
RemoveClosedInstances	Infrastructure	Electronic institution
Timeout	Infrastructure	Scene

scenes. Figure 18.1, hides the fact that an *electronic* institution also constitutes the infrastructure that *enables* actual interactions. Thus, we need that our conceptual model includes all those operations that need to be supported by the infrastructure; namely, those operations triggered by the actions of an agent that we just mentioned, plus those operations that the infrastructure itself needs to accomplish so that the first ones are feasible. Table 18.1 summarizes all those operations, the last column indicates the constructs that the operation updates.

One computational architecture for Electronic Institutions. The model just presented may be implemented in different ways. We have chosen one particular architecture (see Esteva et al. 2004) where we build a centralized institutional infrastructure that is implemented as a separate "social milieu" that mediates all the agent interactions, as Fig. 18.2 shows.

- *Governor* All communications between a given agent and the institution are mediated by a corresponding infrastructure agent that is part of the institutional infrastructure called the *governor* (indicated as G in Fig. 18.2)[5]. The governor keeps a specification of the institution plus an updated copy of the institutional state, thus when its agent produces an utterance, that utterance is admitted by the governor if and only if it complies with the institutional conventions as they are instantiated at that particular state; only then, the utterance becomes an institutional action that changes the state. Likewise, the governor communicates to the agent those institutional facts that the agent is entitled to know, the moment

[5] Agents cannot interact directly with one another, they use an agent communication language (like JADE) to interact with their governors who mediate their interactions *inside* the electronic institution.

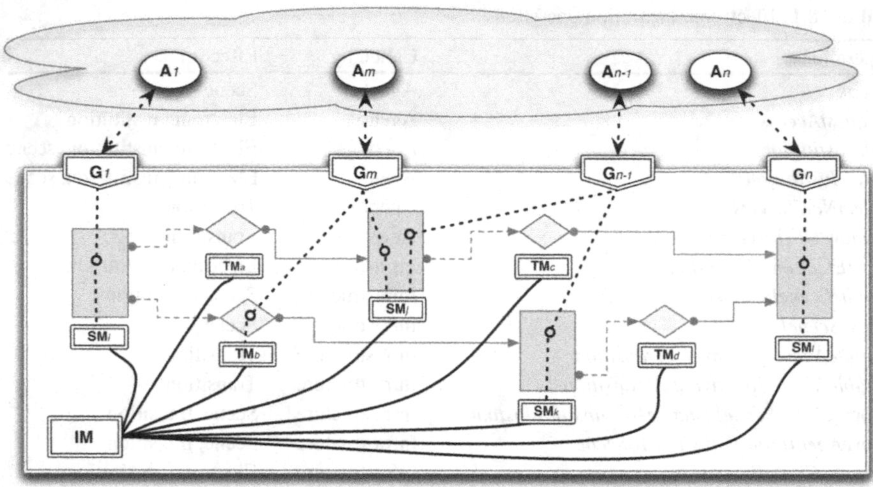

Fig. 18.2 An architecture for electronic institutions. Participating agents (*A*), communicate with (infrastructure) governor agents (*G*), which in turn coordinate with other infrastructure manager agents for each scene (*SM*) and each transition (*TM*) and with the institution manager agent (*IM*)

they happen. Additionally, the governor controls navigation of its agent between scenes, and the production of new instances of the agent itself (*agent processes*). It also keeps track of time for synchronization (time-outs) purposes. Note that in order to provide these services, a governor must coordinate with scene managers, transition managers, and the institution manager. In this realisation of the EI framework, therefore, governors are involved in the implementation of most of the operations in Table 18.1.

- *Institution Management* Each institution has one *institution manager* agent (IM), which activates (*StartElectronicInstituion* operation) and terminates the institution. It also controls the entry (*RequestAccess*, *JoinInstitution*) and exit (*LeaveInstitution*) of agents, together with the creation the closing of scenes (*CloseSceneInstance*, *RemoveClosedInstances*). Finally, it keeps track of the electronic institution state.
- *Transition management* Each transition has a *transition manager* (TM) that controls the transit of agents between scenes by checking that requested moves are allowed (*EnableAgentsToLeaveOrTransition, EnableAgentsToLeaveAndTransition*) and, if so, allowing agents to move (*MovingFromSceneInstanceToTransitionInstance, MoveAgentFromTransitionToScene*).
- *Scene management* Each scene has an associated infrastructure agent, the *scene manager* (SM), who is in charge of: starting and closing the scene (in coordination with the institution manager); keeping track of agents that enter and leave the scene; updating the state of the scene by processing utterances (*Speak*) and time-outs (*Timeout*); and coordinating with transition managers to

let agents in or out of a scene (*MovingFromSceneInstanceToTransitionInstance, MoveAgentFromTransitionToScene*).

Other architectures are feasible and we have, for instance, suggested a peer-to-peer variant of these ideas in Esteva et al. (2011).

A development environment based on that architecture. The computational model we just described, does not commit to any specific convention about the languages used in the specification of transitions and scenes, nor on the syntax and pragmatics of illocutions, nor on specific governance mechanisms. Those commitments come later when software tools to build actual electronic institutions become implemented. One way of implementing the computational model is the Electronic Institutions Development Environment (EIDE) (Esteva et al. 2008) which includes the following tools:

ISLANDER: a graphical specification language, with a graphic interface (Esteva et al. 2002). It allows the specification of any EI that complies with the conceptual model and produces an XML file that the AMELI middleware runs[6].

AMELI: a software middleware that implements the functions of the social layer at run-time (Esteva et al. 2004). It runs an enactment, with actual agents, of any ISLANDER-specified institution. Thus it activates infrastructure agents as needed; controls activation of scenes and transitions, access of agents, messages between agents and institution, and in general guarantees – in coordination with infrastructure agents – the correct evolution of scenes and the correct transitions of agents between scenes. AMELI may be understood as a two-layered middleware. One public layer formed by governors, the other private layer – not accessible to external agents – formed by the rest of the infrastructure agents. External agents are only required to establish communication channels with their governors.[7] Infrastructure agents use the institutional state and the conventions encoded in the specification to validate agent actions and evaluate their consequences.

SIMDEI: is a simple simulation tool used for debugging and dynamic verification. It is coupled with a *monitoring tool* that may be used to display the progress of

[6]ISLANDER allows static verification of a specification. It checks for *language integrity* (all roles and all terms used in illocutions, constraints and norms are properly specified in the dialogical framework), *liveness* (roles that participate in a given scene have entry and exit nodes that are connected and may be traversed), *protocol accessibility* (every state in the graph of a scene is accessible from the initial state and arcs are properly labeled), *norm compliance* (agents who establish "normative commitments" may reach the scenes where the commitments are due). ISLANDER may be extended to have a strictly declarative expression of scene conventions (Garcia-Camino et al. 2005).

[7]The current implementation of the infrastructure can either use JADE or a publish-subscribe event model as communication layer. When employing JADE, the execution of AMELI can be readily distributed among different machines, permitting the *scalability* of the infrastructure. Notice that the model is communication-neutral since agents are not affected by changes in the communication layer.

the enactment of an institution. It monitors every event that takes place and may display these events dynamically with views that correspond to events in scenes and transitions or events involving particular agents. Both tools may be used for dynamic verification.

aBUILDER: an agent development tool which, given an ISLANDER-specified institution, supports the generation of "dummy agents" that conform to the role specification and are able to navigate the performative structure, provided agent designers fill up their decision-making procedures[8].

Extensions of the framework. The EI framework has been used in many application domains (see d'Inverno et al. 2012 p. 87 for an enumeration). This experience as well as more theoretically minded research has motivated adaptations and extensions to it. These extensions are mainly due to (i) a normative understanding of electronic institutions (Garcia-Camino et al. 2005; Vasconcelos et al. 2012), (ii) the advantage of connecting the EI environment with other services (Arcos et al. 2007), (iii) to achieve peer-to-peer architecture in order to address scalability (Esteva et al. 2011) and (iv) institutions that evolve over time in order to adapt to changing conditions of the environment (Bou et al. 2007; Campos et al. 2010). A significant extension of the framework is that of the automatic generation of three dimensional immersive environments that represent the electronic institution. This work is described later in this book (Chap. 34).

18.6 Conclusions: A Comparison of the Described Institutional Models

In this section we compare the three proposed models of institutions, ANTE, OCeAN/MANET, and EI, discussing their crucial differences and analogies on a set of relevant aspects.

- *Institutional reality.*
  All three models adhere to the representation of institutional reality proposed by John Searle in 1995, in particular on the existence of an institutional reality that has a correspondence with the real or physical world, and on distinguishing between "institutional" facts and actions, on one side, and their possibly corresponding "brute" facts and actions, on the other.
- *Social model: roles and hierarchy of roles*
  - ANTE accommodates two types of roles within the institution. Agents providing core institutional services are seen as performing *institutional roles* that are under the control of the institution. Agents acting as delegates of

[8]Based on the same ideas, there is an extension of aBUILDER (Brito et al. 2009) that instead of code skeletons produces a simple human interface that complies with the ISLANDER specification and is displayed dynamically via a web browser at run-time.

external entities enact different roles that are normatively regulated by the institution, in the sense that they may be subject to norms and may further establish new normative relationships. Furthermore, some of these roles are empowered, through appropriate *constitutive rules*, by the institution to ascertain institutional reality (i.e. they act as trusted third parties from the institution's point of view).
  - OCeAN/MANET allows the definition of roles as labels defined by a given Artificial Institution (AI) and used in the AI to assign norms and institutional powers at design time to roles. This is necessary because at design time the name of the actual agents that will take part to the interaction is unknown. At run time AIs are realized in dynamically created institutional spaces, the agents in a space can start to play the roles defined in the space and coming from the AI. An agent can temporarily play more than one role. During an interaction an agent can start to play a role and subsequently stop playing it.
  - EI allows for specification of role subsumption and the specification of two forms of compatibility among roles: "dynamic" (each agent may perform different roles in different activities) and "static" no agent may perform both roles in an enactment of the institution. It also distinguishes between *internal* roles (played by agents whose behaviour is controlled by the institution), and *external* roles (the institution has no access to their decision-making capabilities) and this separation is static.

- *Atomic interactions*
  - ANTE, concerning its institutional component, assumes an open setting in which there are two kinds of interactions going on in the system. On one hand, agents are free to interact with any other agents, without the institution even noticing that such interactions have taken place. On the other hand, illocutionary actions performed by agents towards the normative environment are seen as attempts to obtain *institutional facts* that are used by the latter to maintain the normative state of the system.
  - OCeAN/MANET defines *institutional actions* that in order to be successfully performed needs to satisfy certain conditions. One of these conditions is that the actor of the action needs to have the power to perform the institutional action, otherwise the action is void. The model defines also *instrumental actions*, for example the exchange of messages that should be used to perform institutional actions. Finally in the model it is possible to represent actions performed in the real world and that are relevant for the artificial interaction, for example the payment of an amount of money or the delivery of a product.
  - EI: There are essentially only two types of institutional actions: *speech* acts (represented as illocutions) and the *movement* actions which are accomplished in two steps exiting from a scene to a transition and entering from a transition to a scene (in some contexts an agent may *stay-and-go*, i.e. remain active in the scene while at the same time becoming active in one or more different

scenes)[9]. Consequently, on one side, an agent can act only by uttering an illocution or notifying the institutional environment its intention to move in or out of a transition (possibly changing role); on the other side, the perception of any given agent is restricted to those illocutions that are uttered by another agent and have the given agent as part of the intended listeners of that illocution, and the indication of the institutional infrastructure that a movement has been achieved

- *Institutional state*
  - ANTE: The institutional normative state is composed of two sorts of so-called *institutional reality elements*. *Agent-originated events* are obtained as a consequence of agent actions, comprising essentially *institutional facts* that are obtained from the illocutions agents produce. These institutional facts map relevant real-world transactions that are through this means institutionally recognized. *Environment events*, on the other hand, occur as an outcome of the process of norm triggering and monitoring. Norms prescribe directed obligations with time windows, which when monitored may trigger different enactment states, namely temporal or actual violations, and fulfilments. All these elements are contextualized to the normative relationships that are established within the environment.
  - OCeAN/MANET: In the last version of the model the state of the interaction is represented using OWL 2 DL ontologies, one of the international standard language of the Semantic Web. Therefore the state of the interaction is represented using classes of concepts, individuals that belong to classes, object and data properties that connect two individuals or an individual to a literal (scalar values) respectively. The terminological box of the ontologies is also enriched with axioms, used to describe the knowledge on a given domain of application, and with SWRL rules, both are used by software reasoners to deduce new knowledge on the state of the interaction. Taking inspiration from the environment literature the state of objects, agents, events, and actions in a space are perceivable by the agents in that space.
  - EI: Only atomic interactions that comply with the institutional regimented conventions may be institutional actions and therefore change institutional facts. There is a data structure called the *institutional state* that contains all the institutional facts; that is, all the constants in the domain language plus the updated values of all those variables whose values may change through institutional actions. For each scene there exists a projection of that structure called the *state of the scene*. Additionally, there are some parameters whose default values are set by the institution and may be updated during an enactment. These are *institutional variables* (like the number of active scenes, the labels of active scenes and transitions), *scene variables* (like

[9]In fact, as indicated in Table 18.1 these movements are implemented with five operations, which include the two key actions of entering and leaving the electronic institution.

the number of participants, the list of items that remain to be auctioned, performance indicators such as the number of collisions or the rate of successful agreements) and *agent variables* (the list of external agents that have violated any discretional convention, the credit account of a trader). These parameters are not accessible to external agents although by design they may be accessible to some internal agents who may use the values of these variables in their individual decision-making.

- *Structure of the activities or compound interactions (contexts)*
  - ANTE: Interactions that need to be observed are executed through empowered agents, which will then inform the institutional environment of the actual real-world activities that are taking place. Such activities are segmented into different normative contexts, that is, they pertain to specific normative relationships that are established at run-time. Within each such context different empowered agents may need to act as intermediaries, since different kinds of actions may need to be accomplished in order to successfully enact the contract subsumed in the context.
  - OCeAN/MANET: The activities are realized into *institutional spaces* or *physical spaces* of interaction. Institutional spaces are used to realize AI at run-time, they may be entered and left by the agents starting from the root space. Physical spaces contains physical entities external with respect to the system, such as external resources, databases, external files, or web services, offering an abstraction that hide the low level details from the agents. Institutional spaces are in charge of representing and managing the social interaction of agents by realizing the concepts described in AIs and the services for norms monitoring and enforcement. Spaces are in charge of registering that an event has happened and represents the boundaries for the perception and of the effects of the events and actions.
  - EI: Activities are decomposable into *scenes* that are connected by *transitions* into a network of scenes called a *performative structure*.
    - Scenes are state transition graphs where edges are labeled by *illocutionary formulas* and nodes correspond to a scene-state. A new scene-state may only be attained with the utterance of an admissible illocution. An utterance is valid if and only if it complies with the regimented conventions that apply under the current state of the scene. At some scene-states agents may enter or leave or *stay-and-go* the scene. Every performative structure contains one "start" and one "finish" scene that have the merely instrumental purpose to delimit the structure for syntactic (in specification) and implementation purposes (for enactment of the electronic institution).
    - A transition is a device that is used for two main purposes, to control role flow and to control causal and temporal interdependence among scenes. In particular, (a) when an agent exits a scene, it exits with the role it was playing in that scene but inside the transition the agent may change that role to enter a new scene (provided some institutional conventions are satisfied)

(b) Moreover, when an agent enters a transition and depending on the type of transition it enters, that agent may join one, several or all the scenes that are connected to that transition. (c) Several agents, possibly performing different roles and coming possibly from different scenes, may enter the same transition and each has to decide on its own where to go from there and whether it changes role or not. (d) The transition coordinates flow by determining whether agents may proceed to their intended goal scene as soon as each agent arrives or wait until some condition holds in the state of the scene.

- *Hierarchical organisation of the structure of activities*
  - ANTE: Normative relationships established at run-time are organized as a hierarchy of contexts. Each context encompasses a group of agents in a specific regulated organisation, within which further sub-contexts may be created, allowing for norm inheritance to take place. An overall institutional normative layer is assumed to exist, of which every subsequently created context is a sub-context. Furthermore, each context may add its own norms, which may be used to inhibit norm inheritance or to enlarge the normative framework that will govern the context.
  - OCeAN/MANET: Spaces may contain other spaces generated dynamically at run-time, which become sub-spaces of the space where they are created. This hierarchy of spaces and the fact that one agent may be simultaneously in two spaces create interesting problems due to the interdependencies of spaces, this because the events of a space may be of interest to the father-space where this is contained or for a sibling space.
  - EI: All agent interactions within an electronic institution are organized, as we mentioned above, by what we call a performative structure which is a network of scenes and transitions between those scenes. Two aspects are worth stating: First, a performative structure may be be embedded into another as if it were a scene, thus forming nested performative structures of arbitrary depth. Second, a performative structure becomes instantiated at run-time, thus although it is defined *a priori*, so to speak, the actual scenes do not come into existence until appropriate conditions take place (if ever) and they disappear likewise. In particular, it is possible to specify conditions that empower an internal agent to spawn a particular scene or performative (sub)structure.
- *Procedural and functional conventions*
  - ANTE: The effects of institutional facts are expressed through norms and rules. When triggered, norms prescribe directed obligations that are due to specific agents within a normative context. Such obligations have attached time-windows that are conventionally understood as ideal time periods for obtaining the obliged state of affairs. Outside this window temporal violations are monitored which may lead to different outcomes depending on the will of the obligation's counterpart. This semantics is captured by a set of monitoring rules that maintain the normative state of the system. The

normative consequences of each obligation state is determined by the set of norms that shape the obligation's normative context, which may be established at run-time.

- OCeAN/MANET: Both are expressed through pre- and post-conditions of the actions defined by the institution. An important pre-condition for the performance of institutional actions (actions whose effects change institutional attributes that exist only thanks to the collective acceptance of the interacting agents) is the fact that the actor of the action should have the institutional power to perform the specific action.
- EI: Both are expressed as pre and post-conditions of the illocutionary formulas of the scene transition graphs and through the labeling of transitions between scenes (this labeling expresses conditions for accessing a scene or a group of scenes or a nested performative structure, synchronization, the change of roles, the creation of new scenes or activation of an existing scene). In the current EIDE implementation, there is also the possibility of explicitly expressing norms as production rules that are triggered whenever an illocution is uttered, thus allowing the specification and use of regimented and not-regimented conventions. Notice that although EI use illocutionary formulas to label actions, there are no social semantics of illocutionary particles involved. Thus scene protocols are not commitment-based protocols as is the case with Fornara and Colombetti (2002) or more generally, Colombetti (2000) and Chopra and Singh (2004).

• *Constitutive conventions*
  - ANTE: Obtaining institutional facts from brute facts (which are basically agent illocutions) is achieved through appropriate *constitutive rules*, which mainly describe empowerments of different trusted third parties. These constitutive rules, which can be easily extended and/or adapted, determine the ontology for brute and institutional facts that can be used in the institution. Furthermore, it is possible to define further constitutive rules within each context, in this case enriching the domain ontology by obtaining more refined institutional facts. As a basic implementation, three types of transactions are reportable to the normative environment, related with the flow of products, money and information.
  - OCeAN/MANET: In this model the content language used for communicative acts and norms is defined using domain ontologies written in OWL 2 DL or in RDF+RDF Schema. Those ontologies may be defined by the designer of the interaction system or may already exist as proposed standards on the Web, like the well known ontology FOAF[10] that may be used for describing agents. In many cases the link between the name of a resource (its URI)

[10]http://www.foaf-project.org/.

and the corresponding resource in the real world can be done using existing knowledge repositories[11].

 - EI: The EI framework does not include axioms or definition statements that establish basic institutional facts. Nevertheless, there is a *domain language* that is used for expressing illocutionary formulas and whose terms correspond with physical facts and actions (e.g a sculpture to be auctioned, pay 32 euros for the item that has just been adjudicated). The correspondence between language and real entities is established *ad-hoc* for the domain language. In practice, however, an electronic institution needs to have true constitutive conventions in order to establish the legal (actual) entitlements of intervening parties and the correspondence between institutional and brute facts and actions. Examples of constitutive conventions are the contracts that allow an old books dealer to offer a used book through Amazon.com and follow the process through from offer to book delivery.

• *Social Commitments*

 - ANTE: Social commitments, in a broad sense, are established as an outcome of a previous negotiation phase, the success of which obtains a new normative context within the institutional environment. Once a normative context is obtained, applicable norms dictate when (according to the normative state) and which commitment instantiations (directed obligations) are entailed.
 - OCeAN/MANET: A commitment-based Agent Communication Language (ACL) is used (Fornara and Colombetti 2002; Fornara et al. 2012). In particular communicative acts exchanged among agents have a meaning that is a combination of the meaning of the content of the messages and a meaning of the illocutionary force of the communicative acts (for example promise, query, assert).
 - EI: although, in EI, illocutionary formulas label actions, there is no social semantics of the illocutionary particles involved. Thus scene protocols are not commitment-based protocols properly speaking. However, commitments are hard-wired in scene specifications , and their evolution is captured in the evolving state of the institution. It should be noted, though, that in EI some commitments are expressed crudely but explicitly when a given admissible action (say winning a bidding round) has a postcondition that entails preconditions for future actions in other scenes.

• *Governance*

 - ANTE: The approach adopted in ANTE is to bear with the autonomy of agents, by allowing them to behave as they wish. From the institution's perspective, we assume it is in the best interest of agents to publicize their abidance with any standing obligations, by using the necessary means to obtain the corresponding institutional facts. Normative consequences of

[11] http://linkeddata.org/.

(non)fulfilment are assured by triggering applicable norms. Permissions and prohibitions are not handled explicitly in the system, i.e., not permitted actions simply have no effect within the normative environment. Entitlements are handled by defining norms triggered upon the occurrence of specific institutional facts. Any obligation outcomes – (temporal) violations and fulfilments – may also have further effects within the ANTE framework by reporting such events to a computational trust engine, which provides a mechanism of indirect social sanctioning.

- OCeAN/MANET: The openness of the interaction system realized using this model requires governance in order to create expectations on the actions of the participants agents. The model has to take into account the autonomy and heterogeneity of the interacting agents and avoid constraining their behaviour in rigid protocols. The main concepts introduced in the model related to governance are: *institutional power* (if an agent does not have the power to perform an action its effects are void), *permission* (if an agent does not have the permission to perform an action its effect take place but the agent incurs in a violation), *obligations* (the agent has to perform an action within a given deadline) and *prohibitions* (the agent cannot perform an action, if it does it will incur in a violation).
- EI: There are three different approaches for the implementation of governance in the EI model.

  1. In the standard model, all regimented conventions may be encoded in the performative structure as part of the specification of scenes and transitions and are therefore enforced in a strict and automatic fashion by the runtime implementation. Non-regimented conventions are encodable in the decision-making capabilities of internal agents and it is a matter of design whether some regimented ones may also be embedded in internal agents code. One may thus establish different types of (internal) norm-enforcement agents. Notice that although an internal agent may fail or decide not to enforce a violation, every violation is observed (registered) by the institution nonetheless.
  2. In the current implementation of EIDE one may choose to specify a collection of normative statements that are not part of the performative structure. This collection is coupled with an inference engine that takes hold of every utterance before it may be validated by the performative structure (see Garcia-Camino et al. 2005). The process is as follows (i) An illocution is first tested against the normative statements and if it is consistent, it is labeled as "admissible" or rejected otherwise. (ii) The admissible illocution is then added to the current collection and the engine is activated; (iii) If the illocution triggers a violation, the concomitant corrective actions are taken, otherwise control is given to the performative structure that deals with the illocution as in approach (1). This approach allows for dealing with discretional enforcement with more flexibility than approach (1) because in addition to all the mechanisms available in that

approach, this one allows for a declarative specification of norms, an explicit distinction between regimented and non-regimented norms, and a variety of contrary-to-duty devices encodable as corrective actions.

3. There is a proposed extension of the EI model that deals explicitly with norms and normative conflicts through the use a a "normative structure" that deals exclusively with norms and propagation of normative consequences between scenes (Gaertner et al. 2007; Vasconcelos et al. 2012).

- *Ubiquity and concurrent activities*
  - ANTE: Agents may freely establish new normative relationships, and hence many of them may be active at the same time. The institutional environment pro-actively monitors every active context. There is a strong distinction between the agent identity and the normative relationships in which it is engaged. There is no notion of "physical" displacement of the agents within the institution. Within the ANTE framework, several other activities may take place at the same time, such as negotiations and computational trust building, which is achieved by gathering relevant enactment data from the normative environment monitoring process.
  - OCeAN/MANET: An interaction system realized using one or more AIs consists of a root space that contains physical and institutional spaces. An agent situated in a given space can enter all its sub-spaces, therefore an agent can be in more than one space and it has a persistent identity.
  - EI: An electronic institution usually consists of multiple scenes that are active simultaneously. In many cases the number of active scenes changes during execution since new scenes are created, activated or closed as the enactment proceeds. A given agent may be simultaneously active in more than one scene but it has a persistent identity in the sense that the effects of its institutional actions are coherent (for example, in an electronic market where an agent may be closing deals in different negotiations, this agent has *one* variable that captures its credit so the value of that variable changes every time it commits to pay, in whatever scene they commit). The current EI framework does not include a "meta-environment" where multiple institutions co-exist, however the peer-to-peer architecture proposed in Esteva et al. (2011) would be suitable for the implementation of lightly-coupled (and uncoupled) institutions in a shared environment.

- *Performance Assessment*
  - ANTE: Agent performance is assessed and exploited from two different perspectives. The first one is based on computational trust: the enactment of contracts produces evidences that are fed into a computational trust engine, which then produces trustworthiness assessments of agents that can be used when entering into further negotiations. In the current prototype implementation, trust information may be used for pre-selection of negotiation peers or for proposal evaluation. Another assessment of performance is measured by the normative environment, which for the whole agent population is able

to determine the average enactment outcome for instances of stereotyped normative relationships (types of contracts).

- OCeAN/MANET: There are not yet available services for assessing system's or agent performance.
- EI: This model does not capture system goals explicitly, however scene and institutional variables may be used to specify some assessment of the performance of the institution with respect to whatever goals are defined. Internal agents may be designed to use such information in order to improve performance.

• *Formal properties*

- ANTE: No formal methods for analyzing normative relationships are employed – it is up to the system designer to ensure correctness. The normative environment does record on-line every possible event that is captured while monitoring norms, allowing for an off-line verification of correctness.
- OCeAN/MANET: For the moment there is not the possibility to check formal properties of AI at design-time. At run-time one crucial service is the monitoring of the state of the interaction, the detection of violations, and the enforcement of norms. Moreover in every instant of time it is possible to deduce the list of the actions that an agent is obliged, prohibited, permitted and empowered to perform, from this list and from an ontological definition of the terminology used to describe the actions it is possible to single out possible contradictions in the prescribed behaviour. At design time this check is harder because in this model all normative constrains are related to time.
- EI: There is off-line automatic syntactic checking of scene and transition behaviour. For example, in every scene: all roles have entry and exit states and these are reachable; every role has at least one path that takes it from start to finish; every term used in an illocution needs to be part of the domain ontology. On-line monitoring of all the activities: every utterance and attempted move produce a trace that may be displayed and captured for further use. The extensions mentioned in Vasconcelos et al. (2012) allow for some off-line and on-line formal and automated reasoning about an institution.

• *Institutional Dynamics*

- ANTE: The normative environment is assumed to be open and dynamic, in the sense that it encompasses an evolving normative space whose norms apply if and when agents commit to a norm-governed relationship. While providing an institutional normative framework, this infrastructure enjoys the properties of adaptability and extensibility, by providing support for norm inheritance and defeasibility. Normative contexts can therefore be created that adapt or extend a predefined normative scenario according to agents' needs.
- OCeAN/MANET: This model is based on the idea that a human designer specifies an AI and this AI may be used at run-time to dynamically create spaces of interaction. Similarly norms at design time are specified in terms of roles and have certain unspecified parameters, at run-time those norms

will be instantiated more than one time having as debtor different agents and different values for their parameters. In general this model does not include meta-operations for changing the model of AIs.
  - EI: With the current model internal agents may be given the capability to create new scenes from repositories of available scenes and even graft nested performative structures into a running institution. In a similar fashion internal agents may create new internal agents when needed (say for a newly grafted performative structure) by invoking a service that spawns new agents that is outside of the electronic institution proper but is available to the internal agent. This mechanism is also used to embed the EI environment into a simulation environment (Arcos et al. 2007). The current model includes no primitive meta-operations that would allow agents to change the specification of an institution beyond what was just said, however here have been proposals for other forms of autonomic adaptation (Bou et al. 2007; Campos et al. 2010).

- *Implementation architecture*
  - ANTE: The ANTE framework is realized as a Jade FIPA-compliant platform, where agents can make use of the available services (e.g. negotiation, contract monitoring, computational trust) through appropriate interaction protocols, such as FIPA-request and FIPA-subscribe. Using subscription mechanisms agents are notified of the normative state of the system in which their normative relationships are concerned. The normative environment has been implemented using the Jess rule-based inference engine.
  - OCeAN/MANET: The model of AI has been fully formalized in Event Calculus and we are currently formalizing it using Semantic Web Technologies. An AI for realizing a Dutch Auction has been also specified in PROLOG and tested in a prototype realized above the GOLEM environment framework (Tampitsikas et al. 2012). An implementation of a complete energy marketplace based on Semantic Web Technologies and the GOLEM framework is under development.
  - EI: The model has been fully detailed (d'Inverno et al. 2012) in the Z specification language (Spivey 1988) and deployed in the architecture sketched in Fig. 18.2. This architecture creates a sort of "social layer" that is independent of the communication layer used to exchange messages between an agent and the electronic institution. The normative engine extension is also implemented in the same architecture. A peer-to-peer architecture has been proposed (Esteva et al. 2011) and a prototype is now under construction.

- *Tools*
  - ANTE: The ANTE framework includes graphical user interfaces (GUI) that allow the user to inspect the outcomes of each provided service, including the evolution and outcome of a specific negotiation, the inspection of trustworthiness scores of the agents in the system, as well as the overall behaviour of the agent population in terms of norm fulfillment. The framework includes

also a complex API allowing for the specification of user agents, for which a set of predefined GUI are also available that enable the user to inspect the agent activity, namely its participation in negotiations and contracts. The API allows a programmer to easily encode agent behaviour models in response to several framework activities, such as negotiation and contract enactment, which makes it straightforward to run different kinds of experiments (although Jade has not been designed for simulation purposes).

– OCeAN/MANET: Thanks to the fact that we base our model on current standard semantic web technologies, it is possible to use the ontology editor Protègè for editing the ontologies used in the specification of the model of AI and spaces and to use one of the available reasoners (Pellet, HermiT, and so on) for checking their consistency. Our future goal is that once the model of a set of AIs is defined and a set of agents able to interact with a system getting its formal specification are developed, the interaction system can start to run and enable agents to interact using the available actions and constrained by the specified norms.
– EI: As mentioned in the previous section, EIDE includes a graphical specification language (ISLANDER), an agent middleware for electronic institutions (AMELI) that generates a runtime version of any ISLANDER compatible specification. EIDE also includes an automated syntactic checker, a simple simulator for on-line testing and debugging, a monitoring tool, and a software that generates agent skeletons that encode the navigational behaviour that is compatible with an ISLANDER specification.

• *Agents*

– ANTE: The framework is neutral in which user agents' internal architectures and implementation languages are concerned. It is assumed, however, that agents are able to communicate using FIPA ACL and the FIPA-based interaction protocols and ontologies interfacing each of the framework's services. It is also straightforward to allow human agents to participate, provided that appropriate user interfaces are developed.
– OCeAN/MANET: The model of the interaction system realized using the AI is independent on the agents' internal structure. Nevertheless it is assumed that the participating agents are able to interact using the available communicative acts whose content should be expressed using shared ontologies.
– EI: The model is agent-architecture independent. Agents are required only to comply with interface conventions that support institutional communication. Hence human agents may participate in an electronic institution enactment provided they have the appropriate interfaces. The tool HIHEREI (Brito et al. 2009) automatically generates such a human interface for any ISLANDER compatible specification of an electronic institution. In the current implementation, AMELI is communication-layer independent.

18.7 Challenges

There are many open challenges in the field of specification and use of institutions for the efficient realization of real open interaction systems in different fields of applications, going from e-commerce, e-government, supply-chain, management of virtual enterprise, and collaborative/social resource sharing systems.

One interesting challenge goes into the direction of using those formal and declarative models of *hybrid* open interaction systems involving both software and human agents. In this perspective one possibly important use of these technologies is for designing flexible open collaborative/social systems able to exploit the flexibility, the intelligence, and the autonomy of the interacting parties. This in order to improve existing business process automation systems where the flow of execution is completely fixed at design time or groupware where the work of defining the context and the rules of the interaction is left to the human interacting parties and no automatic monitoring of the completion of tasks is provided.

When considering the automation of e-contracting systems through autonomous agents, another important challenge is to endow agents with reasoning abilities that enable them to establish more adequate normative relationships. Infrastructural components need to be developed that ease this task, e.g. through normative frameworks that agents can exploit by relying on default norms that may nevertheless need to be overridden. A complementary challenge is how to ensure reliable behaviours when agents act as human or enterprise delegates, that is, how to simultaneously cope with expressivity and configurability through human interfaces and agents' autonomy in institutional normative environments. Another interesting challenge is to look at the Environment as a structured medium not only to facilitate agents' interaction but also as an active representative of the "society" in which agent relationships take place.

Acknowledgements This work was partially supported by the Hasler Foundation project n. 11115-KG, by the Swiss State Secretariat for Education and Research projects n. C08.0114 and "Open Interaction Frameworks, towards a Governing Environment", the Portuguese Fundação para a Ciência e a Tecnologia (FCT) under project PTDC/EIA-EIA/104420/2008, the Consolider AT project CSD2007-0022 INGENIO 2010 of the Spanish Ministry of Science and Innovation, as well as the Generalitat de Catalunya grant 2009-SGR-1434.

References

Aldewereld, H., and V. Dignum. 2010. Operetta: Organization-oriented development environment. In *LADS*, Lecture notes in computer science, vol. 6822, ed. M. Dastani, A.E. Fallah-Seghrouchni, J. Hübner, and J. Leite, 1–18. Heidelberg: Springer.

Aoki, M. 2001. *Toward a comparative institutional analysis*. Cambridge: MIT.

Arcos, J.L., M. Esteva, P. Noriega, J.A. Rodríguez-Aguilar, and C. Sierra. 2005. Engineering open environments with electronic institutions. *Engineering Applications of Artificial Intelligence* 18(2): 191–204.

Arcos, J.L., P. Noriega, J.A. Rodriguez-Aguilar, and C. Sierra. 2007. E4mas through electronic institutions. In *Environments for multi-agent systems III*, Lecture notes in computer science, vol. 4389, ed. D. Weyns, H. Parunak and F. Michel, 184–202. Berlin/Heidelberg: Springer.

Artikis, A., M. Sergot, and J. Pitt. 2009. Specifying norm-governed computational societies. *ACM Transactions on Computational Logic* 10(1): 1:1–1:42.

Boella, G., L. van der Torre, and H. Verhagen. 2008. Introduction to the special issue on normative multiagent systems. *Autonomous Agents and Multi-Agent Systems* 17(1): 1–10.

Boella, G., G. Pigozzi, and L. van der Torre. 2009. Five guidelines for normative multiagent systems. In *Legal knowledge and information systems: JURIX 2009*, ed. G. Governatore, 21–30. Amsterdam: IOS.

Bou, E., M. Lopez-Sanchez, and J.A. Rodriguez-Aguilar. 2007. Adaptation of autonomic electronic institutions through norms and institutional agents. In *Engineering societies in the agents world VII*, Lecture notes in computer science, vol. 4457, ed. G. O'Hare, A. Ricci, M. O'Grady and O. Dikenelli, 300–319. Berlin/Heidelberg: Springer.

Brito, I., I. Pinyol, D. Villatoro, and J. Sabater-Mir. 2009. HIHEREI: Human interaction within hybrid environments. In *Proceedings of the 8th international conference on autonomous agents and multiagent systems (AAMAS '09)*, Budapest, 1417–1418.

Bromuri, S., and K. Stathis. 2009. Distributed agent environments in the ambient event calculus. In *Proceedings of the third ACM international conference on distributed event-based systems, DEBS '09*, 12:1–12:12. New York: ACM.

Campos, J., M. Lopez-Sanchez, and M. Esteva. 2010. A case-based reasoning approach for norm adaptation. In *Proceedings of the 5th international conference on hybrid artificial intelligence systems (HAIS'10)*, San Sebastian, 23 June 2010, vol. 6077, ed. A.S.E. Corchado and M. Graña-Romay, 168–176. Berlin: Springer.

Chopra, A., and M. Singh. 2004. Nonmonotonic commitment machines. In *Advances in agent communication*, Lecture notes in computer science, vol. 2922, ed. F. Dignum, 1959–1959. Berlin/Heidelberg: Springer.

Cliffe, O., M. De Vos, and J. Padget. 2007. Specifying and reasoning about multiple institutions. In *Coordination, organization, institutions and norms in agent systems II – AAMAS 2006 and ECAI 2006 international workshops, COIN 2006, Hakodate, Japan, May 9, 2006 Riva del Garda, Italy, August 28, 2006*, Lecture notes in computer science, vol. 4386, ed. P. Noriega, J. Vázquez-Salceda, G. Boella, O. Boissier, V. Dignum, N. Fornara and E. Matson, 67–85. Berlin/Heidelberg: Springer.

Colombetti, M. 2000. A commitment-based approach to agent speech acts and conversations. In *Proceedings of the fourth international conference on autonomous agents, workshop on agent languages and conversation policies*, eds. M. Greaves, F. Dignum, J. Bradshaw, and B. Chaib-draa, 21–29. Barcelona: Spain.

Corapi, D., M. De Vos, J. Padget, A. Russo, and K. Satoh. 2011. Normative design using inductive learning. *Theory and Practice of Logic Programming* 11: 783–799.

Craswell, R. 2000. Contract law: General theories. In *Encyclopedia of law and economics*, The regulation of contracts, vol. III, ed. B. Bouckaert and G. De Geest, 1–24. Cheltenham: Edward Elgar.

Dignum, V. 2004. *A model for organizational interaction: Based on agents, founded in logic*. Ph.D. thesis, University Utrecht.

Dignum, V., J. Vázquez-Salceda, and F. Dignum. 2004. OMNI: Introducing social structure, norms and ontologies into agent organizations. In *Programming multi-agent systems, second international workshop ProMAS 2004, New York, NY, USA, July 20, 2004, Selected Revised and Invited Papers*. Lecture notes in computer science, vol. 3346, ed. R.H. Bordini, et al., 181–198. Berlin/Heidelberg: Springer.

d'Inverno, M., M. Luck, P. Noriega, J.A. Rodriguez-Aguilar, and C. Sierra. 2012. Communicating open systems. *Artificial Intelligence* 186(0): 38–94.

Esteva, M. 2003. *Electronic institutions: From specification to development*. Ph.D. thesis, Universitat Politècnica de Catalunya (UPC), 2003. Number 19 in IIIA Monograph Series. IIIA.

Esteva, M., D. de la Cruz, and C. Sierra. 2002. ISLANDER: An electronic institutions editor. In *Proceedings of the first international joint conference on autonomous agents and multiagent systems (AAMAS '02)*, 1045–1052. New York: ACM.

Esteva, M., J.A. Rodriguez-Aguilar, B. Rosell, and J.L. Arcos. 2004. AMELI: An agent-based middleware for electronic institutions. In *Proceedings of the 3rd international joint conference on autonomous agents and multi-agent systems (AAMAS '04)*, July 19–23 2004, vol. 1, ed. C. Sierra and L. Sonenberg, 236–246, IFAAMAS. New York: ACM.

Esteva, M., J.A. Rodriguez-Aguilar, J.L. Arcos, C. Sierra, P. Noriega, and B. Rosell. 2008. Electronic institutions development environment. In *Proceedings of the 7th international joint conference on autonomous agents and multiagent systems (AAMAS '08)*, Estoril, 12/05/2008, 1657–1658. Richland: International Foundation for Autonomous Agents and Multiagent Systems/ACM.

Esteva, M., J.A. Rodriguez-Aguilar, J.L. Arcos, and C. Sierra. 2011. Socially-aware lightweight coordination infrastructures. In *Proceedings of the AAMAS'11 12th international workshop on agent-oriented software engineering, May 2-6, 2011*, 117–128. Taipei: Taiwan.

Fornara, N. 2011. Specifying and monitoring obligations in open multiagent systems using semantic web technology. In *Semantic agent systems: Foundations and applications*, Studies in computational intelligence, vol. 344, ed. A. Elçi, M.T. Kone and M.A. Orgun, 25–46. Berlin: Springer.

Fornara, N., and M. Colombetti. 2002. Operational specification of a commitment-based agent communication language. In *Proceedings of the first international joint conference on autonomous agents & multiagent systems, AAMAS 2002*, July 15–19, 2002, Bologna, 536–542. New York: ACM.

Fornara, N., and M. Colombetti. 2009. Specifying artificial institutions in the event calculus. In *Handbook of research on multi-agent systems: semantics and dynamics of organizational models*, ed. V. Dignum, 335–366. Hershey: Information Science Reference/IGI Global.

Fornara, N., and M. Colombetti. 2010. Representation and monitoring of commitments and norms using OWL. *AI Communications - European Workshop on Multi-Agent Systems (EUMAS) 2009* 23(4): 341–356.

Fornara, N., F. Viganò, and M. Colombetti. 2007. Agent communication and artificial institutions. *Autonomous Agents and Multi-Agent Systems* 14(2): 121–142.

Fornara, N., F. Viganò, M. Verdicchio, and M. Colombetti. 2008. Artificial institutions: A model of institutional reality for open multiagent systems. *Artificial Intelligence and Law* 16(1): 89–105.

Fornara, N., D. Okouya, and M. Colombetti. 2012. Using OWL 2 DL for expressing ACL content and semantics. In *EUMAS 2011 selected and revised papers*, LNAI, vol. 7541, ed. M. Cossentino, M. Kaisers, K. Tuyls, and G. Weiss. 97–113. Berlin/Heidelberg: Springer.

Gaertner, D., A. Garcia-Camino, P. Noriega, J. A. Rodriguez-Aguilar, and W.W. Vasconcelos. 2007. Distributed norm management in regulated multi-agent systems. In *Proceedings of the 6th international joint conference on autonomous agents and multiagent systems (AAMAS '07)*, Honolulu, 624–631, 14/05/07. New York: ACM.

Garcia-Camino, A., P. Noriega, and J.A. Rodriguez-Aguilar. 2005. Implementing norms in electronic institutions. In *Proceedings of the 4th international joint conference on autonomous agents and multiagent systems (AAMAS '05)*, Utrecht, 667–673. New York: ACM.

Jones, A.J.I., and M.J. Sergot. 1996. A formal characterisation of institutionalised power. *Logic Journal of the IGPL* 4(3): 427–443.

Kaplow, L. 2000. General characteristics of rules. In *Encyclopedia of law and economics*, The economics of crime and litigation, vol. V, ed. B. Bouckaert and G. De Geest, 502–528. Cheltenham: Edward Elgar.

Kowalski, R.A. and M.J. Sergot. 1986. A logic-based calculus of events. *New Generation Computing* 4(1): 67–95.

Lopes Cardoso, H. 2010. *Electronic institutions with normative environments for agent-based E-contracting*. Ph.D. thesis, Universidade do Porto.

Lopes Cardoso, H., and E. Oliveira. 2008. Norm defeasibility in an institutional normative framework. In *Proceedings of the 18th European conference on artificial intelligence (ECAI 2008)*, Patras, ed. M. Ghallab, C. Spyropoulos, N. Fakotakis and N. Avouris, 468–472. Amsterdam: IOS.

Lopes Cardoso, H. and E. Oliveira. 2009. A context-based institutional normative environment. In *Coordination, organizations, institutions, and norms in agent systems IV*, LNAI, vol. 5428, ed. J. Hubner, E. Matson, O. Boissier and V. Dignum, 140–155. Berlin/Heidelberg: Springer.

Lopes Cardoso, H., and E. Oliveira. 2011. Social control in a normative framework: An adaptive deterrence approach. *Web Intelligence and Agent Systems* 9: 363–375.

Lopes Cardoso, H., J. Urbano, A. Rocha, A. Castro, and E. Oliveira. 2012. ANTE: Agreement negotiation in normative and trust-enabled environments. Chapter 32, in this volume, 549–564. Springer.

Mueller, E.T. 2006. *Commonsense reasoning*. San Francisco: Morgan Kaufmann.

Noriega, P. 1999. *Agent-mediated auctions: The fishmarket metaphor*. Ph.D. thesis Universitat Autònoma de Barcelona, 1997. Number 8 in IIIA monograph series. IIIA.

North, D.C. 1990. *Institutions, institutional change, and economic performance*. Cambridge: Cambridge University.

Object Management Group. 2005. UML 2.0 OCL specification. http://www.omg.org/.

Ostrom, E. 1986. An agenda for the study of institutions. *Public Choice* 48(1): 3–25.

Ostrom, E. 2010. Institutional analysis and development: Elements of the framework in historical perspective. In *Historical developments and theoretical approaches in sociology in encyclopedia of life support systems(EOLSS), developed under the auspices of the UNESCO*, ed. C. Crothers. Oxford: Eolss Publishers.

Pitt, J., J. Schaumeier, and A. Artikis. 2011. Coordination, conventions and the self-organisation of sustainable institutions. In *Proceedings of the 14th international conference on agents in principle, agents in practice, PRIMA'11*, 202–217. Berlin/Heidelberg: Springer.

Powell, W.W. and P.J. Dimaggio. 1991. *The new intitutionalism in organizational analyisis*. Chicago: University of Chicago.

Rodriguez-Aguilar, J.A. 2003. *On the design and construction of agent-mediated electronic institutions*, Ph.D. thesis, Universitat Autònoma de Barcelona, 2001. Number 14 in IIIA monograph series. IIIA.

Searle, J.R. 1995. *The construction of social reality*. New York: Free Press.

Simon, H.A. 1996. *The sciences of the artificial*, 3rd edn. Cambridge: MIT.

Spivey, J.M. 1988. *Understanding Z: A specification language and its formal semantics*. Cambridge/New York: Cambridge University.

Tampitsikas, C., S. Bromuri, N. Fornara, and M.I. Schumacher. 2012. Interdependent artificial institutions in agent environments. *Applied Artificial Intelligence* 26(4): 398–427.

Vasconcelos, W., A. García-Camino, D. Gaertner, J.A. Rodríguez-Aguilar, and P. Noriega. 2012. Distributed norm management for multi-agent systems. *Expert Systems with Applications* 39: 5990–5999.

Vázquez-Salceda, J. 2003. *The role of norms and electronic institutions in multi-agent systems applied to complex domains. The HARMONIA framework*. Ph.D. thesis, Universidad Politecnica de Catalunya.

Weyns, D., A. Omicini, and J. Odell. 2007. Environment as a first class abstraction in multiagent systems. *Autonomous Agents and Multi-Agent Systems* 14(1): 5–30.

Chapter 19
Organisational Reasoning Agents

Olivier Boissier and M. Birna van Riemsdijk

19.1 Introduction

In a MAS, agents are situated in a common environment, and are capable of flexible and autonomous behaviour. They make use of different cognitive elements and processes in order to control their behaviour (e.g. beliefs, desires, goals, capacities of situation assessment, of planning). Their autonomy is among the most important characteristics of the concept of agency. However, this autonomy can lead the overall system to exhibit undesired behaviour, since each agent may do what it wants. This problem may be solved by assigning an organisation to the system, as it is done in human societies. Roles, as they are defined in organisational models, are generally used to flag the participation of an agent to the organisation and to express what the expected behaviour is of that agent in the organisation. In the literature, more or less formal specifications of the requirements of a role exist (see for instance Boella et al. 2005 on the different notions of roles and Coutinho et al. 2009). Combined with the different dimensions that are expressed in the organisational models supporting the organisation specification, this leads to different sets of constraints that can be imposed on the agent's behaviour while participating in an organisation (constraints on beliefs, on goals, on the interaction protocols that it can use while cooperating with other agents, on the agents to communicate with, etc).

From this global picture at the macro level (i.e. organisation perspective), let's have a look at the micro level, i.e. agent perspective. Taking an agent's architecture perspective and analysing the reasoning capabilities with respect to organisation,

O. Boissier (✉)
FAYOL-EMSE, LSTI, Saint-Etienne, France
e-mail: Olivier.Boissier@emse.fr

M.B. van Riemsdijk
Electrical Engineering, Mathematics and Computer Science (EEMCS), Delft, The Netherlands
e-mail: m.b.vanriemsdijk@tudelft.nl

S. Ossowski (ed.), *Agreement Technologies*, Law, Governance and Technology Series 8, DOI 10.1007/978-94-007-5583-3_19,

different cases may be considered (Boissier 2001; Hübner 2003): first, agents may or may not have an explicit representation of the organisation, and second, they may or may not be able to reason about it. In this section, we mainly consider agents that, internally, have the capability to represent the organisation and that are able to reason about it. They could consider the organisation as an aid to deciding what to do (e.g., coalition formations Sichman et al. 1994), and/or as a set of constraints that aim to reduce their autonomy or, on the contrary may help them to gain certain powers.

From what precedes, one could ask why it would be worth having such kind of agents in a multi-agent organisation. From the analysis drawn in Boissier et al. (2005), mainly from human societies, it clearly appears that when an agent plays a role, its behaviour and its cognitive elements and processes change. Correspondingly, one may want to *recreate* these kinds of processes when artificial agents also play roles in artificial organisations.

Moreover, agents that are able to reason about organisations are needed in order to realize *open systems* (Boissier et al. 2007; Dignum et al. 2008). Increasingly, it is recognized that the Internet (including latest developments into sensor networks and the ‘Internet of things’) can form an open interaction space where many heterogeneous software agents co-exist and act on behalf of their users. Such open systems need to be regulated. However, such regulation is only effective if agents can understand the imposed regulations and adapt their behaviour accordingly, i.e., if agents are capable of organisational reasoning.

Finally, organisational reasoning agents facilitate engineering multi-agent systems adhering to the principle of *separation of concerns*. That is, when agents can reason about an organisation, the agents and the organisation can be developed separately. When the system designer changes parts of the organisation, e.g., norms that agent playing a certain role should adhere to, one does not need to change the agents as they will be able to adapt (within reasonable limits) to the changed organisation.

There are different ways in which an agent’s cognitive elements or behaviour can change because of the role it plays. It may adopt the role’s goals, desires or beliefs, it may acquire knowledge or new powers. It may also acquire or lose some powers and finally it may decide to do what’s best for the organisation, putting aside (for the moment) its own goals. Any agent playing a role is faced with the problem of integrating the cognitive elements of the role with its own. Moreover, when the internal motors of the agent change, its behaviour is likely to change too. An agent should also change its way of reasoning, to cope with the new dimensions of its behaviour, i.e., its mental processes are different when it plays a role. Besides the changes on the individual dimension of an agent, playing a role also affects the agent’s relationships with other agents: a change of the agent’s status by interpreting all of the agent’s physical actions, communications, beliefs, etc. as being the ones of its role, acquisition/loss of powers, dependence relationships with respect to other agents, trust relationship by being more (or less) trusted by others, etc.

After this brief introduction sketching the motivations for having organisation aware agents, we will first present in Sect. 19.2 some fundamental mechanisms for reasoning about organisations, identifying how and what kind of organisation-primitives agents may have. We will then present some approaches proposed by the literature that illustrate the use of reasoning about organisation. The adaptation of organisations being addressed in the following chapter (cf. Chap. 20), we focus here on the kind of reasoning that an agent should develop for the entry/exit in/of an organisation (cf. In Sect. 19.3) considering both the ability and desirability points of view.

19.2 Mechanisms for Reasoning About Organisations

In order to be able to develop reasoning behaviours on the organisation, an agent must be equipped with fundamental mechanisms as described in a very abstract way in Fig. 19.1 (van Riemsdijk et al. 2009). The agent must be equipped with a basic set of primitives to act on the organisation and, the dual aspect, the capabilities to acquire the organisation description and represent it internally. Then it should be able to reason with this representation, affecting the agent's cognitive reasoning (reasoning about how to achieve goals and react to events).

These capabilities must be included in an agent architecture for reasoning about the different constructs induced by the participation of the agent to an organisation. Different concrete architectures have been proposed (e.g. Castelfranchi et al. (2000), Broersen et al. (2001), Kollingbaum and Norman (2003) and Hübner et al. (2007)). Each of these allows agents to represent and reason about various treatments of norms and organisations.

19.2.1 Mechanisms for Making Agents Aware of the Organisation

Several proposals have been made in the literature, dealing with the way agents are connected to the organisation, i.e. how agents acquire the description of the organisation (either an abstract specification of it or a concrete one in terms of

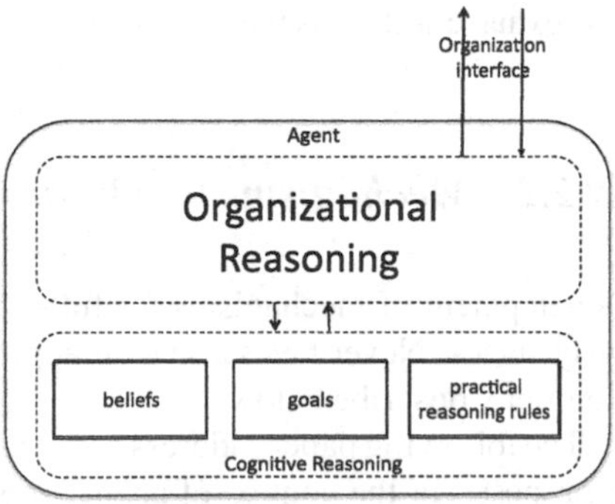

Fig. 19.1 Abstract Description of organisational reasoning agent architecture (van Riemsdijk et al. 2009)

which agent plays what, etc). To illustrate this more clearly, let's consider the $\mathcal{M}$oise organisational model (explained in Sect. 17.2 of this book) for which there is available an extension of the Jason language (Bordini et al. 2007) to develop reasoning plans and strategies on the organisation. This extension allows developers to use this high-level BDI language to program agents able to reason about the organisation, by making them able to acquire organisational descriptions, especially its changes (e.g., a new group is created, an agent has adopted a role), and to act upon it (e.g., create a group, adopt a role). In this model, the way it is done is strongly connected to the set of organisational artifacts (Hübner et al. 2010) that instruments the MAS environment to support the management of the organisations expressed with the $\mathcal{M}$oise organisation model.

These different concrete computational entities aimed at managing, outside the agents, the current state of the organisation in terms of groups, social schemes, and normative state encapsulate and enact the organisation behaviour as described by the organisation specifications.

From an agent point of view, such organisational artifacts provide the actions that can be used to proactively take part in an organisation (for example, to adopt and leave particular roles, to commit to missions, to signal to the organisation that some social goal has been achieved, etc.). They dynamically also provide specific observable properties to make the state of an organisation perceivable to the agents along with its evolution, directly mapped into agents' percepts (leading to beliefs and triggering events). So as soon as the observable properties values change, new percepts are generated for the agent that are then automatically processed (within the agent reasoning cycle) and the belief base updated. Besides, they provide actions that can be used by agents to manage the organisation itself (sanctioning, giving incentives, reorganising). They provide the operations and the observable properties for agents so that they can interact with the organisation. This means that, at runtime, an agent can perform an action α if there is (at least) one artifact providing α as operation – if more than one such artifact exist, the agent may contextualise the action explicitly specifying the target artifact. We refer the interested reader to Hübner et al. (2007, 2010) to have a look at the available repertoire of actions and observable properties.

So in programming an agent it is possible to write down plans that directly react to changes in the observable state of an artifact or that are selected based on contextual conditions that include the observable state of possibly multiple artifacts.

19.2.2 Mechanisms for Organisational Reasoning

Development of mechanisms for full-fledged organisational reasoning is still in its early stages. Nevertheless, several approaches have been proposed, some of which we briefly describe below.

The following papers address role enactment. In Dastani et al. (2003) an approach is proposed in the context of agent programming that defines when an agent and a role match or are conflicting. An agent can enact a role if they are not conflicting. Enactment is then, broadly speaking, specified as taking up the goals of the role, and defining a preference relation over the agent's own goals and the role's goals. In (Dastani et al. 2004) the authors propose programming constructs that allow an agent to enact and deact a role. The semantics of the constructs is defined by specifying how the agent's mental attitudes change when a role is enacted/deacted. In van Riemsdijk et al. (2011) it is investigated how agents can reason about their capabilities in order to determine whether they can play a role (see also Sect. 19.3.1). It is shown how reasoning about capabilities can be integrated in an agent programming language.

Once an agent enacts a role, it should take into account the norms and regulations that come with the role in its reasoning. In Meneguzzi and Luck (2009), an approach is proposed on how AgentSpeak(L) agents can adapt their behaviour to comply with norms. Algorithms are provided that allow an AgentSpeak(L) agent to adopt goals upon activation of obligations, or remove plans upon activation of prohibitions. Even if an agent participates in an organisation, it may still decide to violate some of the corresponding norms. In Meneguzzi et al. (2010) it is investigated how to extend plans with normative constraints that are used to customize plans in order to comply with norms. In Broersen et al. (2002) an approach based on prioritized default logic is proposed, that allows it to express whether an agent prioritizes obligations, desires or intentions. Based on this prioritization, the agent generates the goals that it will pursue. In Castelfranchi et al. (2000) an architecture is proposed by means of which norms can be communicated, adopted and used as meta-goals on the agent's own processes. As such they have impact on deliberation about goal generation, goal selection, plan generation and plan selection. The architecture allows agents to deliberatively follow or violate a norm, e.g., because it has a more important personal goal. Another proposal for deliberation about norms is put forward in Criado et al. (2010). It investigates the usage of coherence theory in order to determine what it means to follow or violate a norm according to the agent's mental state and making a decision about norm compliance. Moreover, consistency notions are used for updating agent mental state in response to these normative decisions. In Corkill et al. (2011), an extended BDI reasoning architecture is proposed for 'organisationally adept agents' that balances organisational, social, and agent-centric interests and that can adjust this balance when appropriate. Agent organisations specify guidelines that should influence individual agents to work together in the expected environment. However, if the environment deviates from expectations, such detailed organisational guidelines can mislead agents into counterproductive or even catastrophic behaviours. The proposed architecture allows agents to reason about organisational expectations, and adjust their behaviours when the nominal guidelines misalign with those expectations. In Panagiotidi and Vázquez-Salceda (2011) norms are taken into account during an agent's plan generation phase. Norms can be obligations or prohibitions which can be violated, and are accompanied by repair norms in case they are breached. Norm operational semantics is expressed as an extension/on top of STRIPS semantics, acting as a form of temporal restrictions over the trajectories (plans) computed by the planner.

19.3 Reasoning About the Participation in an Organisation

In this section we will see different approaches related to entering an organisation, playing a role in the organisation and leaving the organisation. Agents should be able to decide whether to enter an organisation, consider whether they are able to participate and whether they really desire to participate; and we will also analyse how roles affect agents, i.e., how playing a role affects directly an individual and how playing a role affects an individual's relationships with others.

19.3.1 Am I Able to Participate in an Organisation?

An important aspect that organisational reasoning agents should be able to reason about is whether they are able to play a role in an organisation, i.e., about whether it has the required *capabilities* (van Riemsdijk et al. 2011).

This is important as it allows an agent to decide, e.g., only to apply for roles for which it has (some of) the capabilities. Also, an agent may have to communicate the capabilities that it has. For example, consider organisations in which a dedicated agent (a *gatekeeper*) is responsible for admitting agents to the organisation. An example of an organisational modelling language in which such a gatekeeper is present, is OperA (Dignum 2004). The idea is then that the gatekeeper asks agents who want to join whether they have the necessary capabilities for playing the desired role in the organisation (similar to a job interview), and assigns roles to agents on the basis of this. In order to be able to answer the gatekeeper's questions, the agent needs to know what its capabilities are.

In order to develop general techniques that allow agents to determine what their capabilities are, it is important to make precise what kind of capabilities are considered. One may consider various capability types, like capabilities to execute *actions*, to *perceive* aspects of the environment in which the agents operate, to *communicate* information, questions or requests, and to achieve *goals* (van Riemsdijk et al. 2011).

Once it is precisely defined which capability types are considered, the agent should be endowed with mechanisms that allow it to *reflect on its own capabilities*. Reflection can in general be seen as an agent's introspective abilities. Reflection is also a technical term in programming. It allows a program to refer to itself at run-time (see, e.g., Java and Maude Clavel et al. 1996), which facilitates a modification of its run-time behaviour based on these reflections. Reflection in the latter sense can be a way to implement an agent's introspective abilities. In van Riemsdijk et al. (2011) it was proposed to allow an agent to derive beliefs about its capabilities, in this way integrating reflection in a natural way in its BDI reasoning mechanisms.

19.3.2 *Do I Desire to Participate in an Organisation?*

Besides being able to detect if it is able to play a role in an organisation, it is also necessary for an agent to detect if it is worth being part of an organisation.

For instance, in Carabelea et al. (2005), social commitments and social policies have been used to express what an agent is expected to do when entering an organisation. As in Vazquez-Salceda (2004) where playing a role is considered as a contract, it is considered that an agent playing a role in an organisation implies a set of commitments towards the organisation in which it plays this role. A role is thus defined by the social commitments it implies, but also by the resources put at the disposal in order to fulfil the social commitments that come with the role. We can classify the constraints imposed to an agent playing a role in an organisation into several categories:

- Goals to achieve: when it accepts to play a role, an agent accepts to try to achieve several goals, the role's goals.
- Authority relations: a role can have authority over another goal for something.
- Context-dependent obligations: when playing a role, an agent might have to fulfil several obligations towards the organisations.
- Permissions and prohibitions: when it accepts the playing a role, an agent receives permissions to perform some tasks and prohibitions to perform others.

From that understanding, the agent translated these commitments into power relations on which it was able to install social-power reasoning mechanisms that it used before deciding whether to adopt a role or not in order to assess the implications of this decision, i.e. what it will gain or lose by playing the role, what changes are likely to occur in his reasoning or behaviour.

This analysis and classification on the playing of a role may be conducted along two main directions: how playing a role directly affects an individual, how playing a role affects an individual's relationships with others.

19.3.2.1 How Playing a Role Directly Affects an Individual

There are different ways in which an agent's cognitive elements or behaviour change because of the role it plays. It may adopt the role's goals, desires or beliefs, it may acquire knowledge or new powers. It may also acquire or lose some powers and finally it may decide to do what's best for the organisation.

Adoption of the role's goals, desires, beliefs: Most related work in MAS focuses on the need for an agent to adopt the desires or goals of its role: most formal organisations divide the global goal of the organisation into subgoals delegated to its members, which are identified by the roles they play. Since the role's goals can facilitate or hinder the achievement of the agents' own set of goals (Dastani et al. 2003), agent adoption of the role's goals may depend on:

- Degree of autonomy, internal motivations. If there is no conflict between the role's and the agent's goals, then an agent will adopt its role's goals and will try to pursue them. If there is a conflict and the goals cannot be satisfied together, an agent should choose what to do: (i) it could either not adopt the role's goals, (ii) it could adopt them and discard its own contradicting goals, (iii) it could adopt all the goals and make a decision later which of its currently contradicting goals it will pursue
- Organisational incentives, etc.

Acquisition of knowledge, of new powers: In order to ensure that its members are able to achieve their roles' goals, an organisation usually: gives these members access to sources of information or knowledge, trains them to better perform their tasks, gives them physical resources (money, a house, a car, etc.) or permissions to access and use organisation's resources. Autonomous agents accept the taking of a role because of the acquisition of: knowledge, access to information, new powers (Castelfranchi 2002) (using the resources coming with role and associated permissions). However, agents might use knowledge/power for their own interest or they can take advantage of an information source (e.g., a library) or power to satisfy their own personal goals.

Losing powers: When an agent agrees to take a role in a group, it signs a more or less formal or explicit contract with the group: what powers will be given to the agent (resources, permissions) and lost by the agent (prohibitions, obligations), which of his powers an agent puts at the disposal of the group.

The role's prohibitions are one of the reasons for losing powers: If an agent was able to satisfy a goal, it will not be able anymore if there is a prohibition to pursue that goal or to execute a key action in the plan to achieve that goal. playing a role might imply the agent loses the physical access to a resource.

The role's obligations hinder an agent's powers in a more subtle way: by obliging the agent to consume resources needed for other goals.

Putting powers at the disposal of a group means that the agent's decision process is no longer autonomous: his decision process is influenced (or even controlled) by an external entity. He thus loses other powers because he is no longer free to decide to use them.

Desire the best for the group: Agents, even if self-interested, usually desire the best for the organisation they belong to: this is often implicit in an agent (especially in the case of MAS), but it is behind many decisions made by the agent when playing a role in that group. Therefore, it is important in multi-agent organisations to make explicit not only a role's goals and norms, but also this desire. Agent behaviour is affected in many ways when playing these roles, e.g. by using their personal powers for the best of the organisation enabling a functional violation of norms (i.e. to violate norms if it's in the organisation's best interest) (Castelfranchi 2005).

This desire to ensure the best of the group should be present in all roles and agents should adopt it when playing these roles. It might affect agents' behaviour in many ways, like using their personal powers for the best of the organisation, but also by enabling a functional violation of norms (Castelfranchi 2005). Agents could decide to disobey the norms imposed on their roles if they believe that by doing this they increase the well-being of the organisation. We believe that is important in multi-agent organisations to make explicit not only a role's goals and norms, but only this desire with its high importance, thus enabling agents to violate norms if it's in the organisation's best interest.

19.3.2.2 How Playing a Role Affects an Individual's Relationships with Others

Playing a role may impact the relationships an agent develops with other agents in different ways, in term of status, powers, dependence relationships and/or trust.

Count-as effect: playing a role changes the agent's status: all of its physical actions, communications, beliefs, etc. are interpreted as being the ones of its role, e.g. other agents interpret executed actions/communication as being the role that executed the action/communication, and not the agent (e.g. command has a different meaning coming from a role with authority or from a simple agent). Importance for agents to have a means to express whether their actions, communications, ... count as the actions, communications, ... of their role or not. Agents should be aware of this and act accordingly. This limits the ways they can behave.

Acquisition/losing powers: Roles in an organisation belong to a rich network of relationships that are inherited by the agents playing the roles. e.g. authority relationship: a "superior" role has authority over an "inferior" role for something, meaning that whenever an agent playing the superior role delegates a goal (or an action, etc.) to an agent playing an inferior role, the latter must adopt and achieve it. These relationships modify the powers of an agent playing a role: an agent playing a role with authority over another gains a power over the agent playing the inferior role, i.e. the first agent disposes whenever it wants of one of the powers of the second agent (the power for which it has authority). The first agent thus gains an indirect power, while the second agent loses its power, by losing the possibility of deciding about it. The higher the role of an agent in the role hierarchy, the more indirect powers it gains: however, due to the relative nature of authority, an agent could have power over others for something, while the others will have power over it for something else.

Dependence relationships: Even in a non-organisational context, when not playing any role, agents depend on each other for one power and not for another power (Sichman et al. 1994): lack of power of achieving goals, lack of the needed resources or know-how. Not only do agents have dependence networks, but also roles in organisations (Hannoun et al. 1998): agents playing the roles inherit these relationships and usually must use the role's dependence network instead of their own.

An agent should not solve only conflicts between his goals, beliefs, etc., and the ones of his role, but also conflicts between his personal dependences and those of his role. An interesting situation occurs when an agent takes several roles at the same time and combine and use several dependence networks, a situation from which an agent might benefit sometimes.

Being more (or less) trusted by others: Trust relationships (Sabater 2004) between agents change when they take roles (see Part VI). Institutional trust (Castelfranchi and Falcone 1998): An agent can be trusted by others simply because it plays a role in an institution. The others' trust in it comes from their beliefs in the characteristics of the role inherited by the agent. Another reason to trust an agent playing a role in a group more, is because the group acts as an enforcer: there are incentives for an agent to obey the role's specifications.

19.4 Conclusions

Organisations represent an effective mechanism for activity coordination, not only for humans but also for agents. Nowadays, the organisation concept has become a relevant issue in the multi-agent system area, as it enables the analysis and design of coordination and collaboration mechanisms in an easier way, especially for open systems. In this section we have presented some work aimed at endowing the agents with capabilities for reasoning about organisations. We have focused on the kind of reasoning that agents should develop about whether to enter an agent organisation or not. In the current landscape of agreement technologies this is an important issue in the sense that the systems that are considered are large scale and open systems. We can also add to this kind of reasoning, all the different reasoning methods developed for organisation adaptation (described in the next chapter), for norm compliance, given the fact that norms are often considered in the context of organisations (see Part III). Besides these different reasoning mechanisms, we have also described basic and fundamental mechanisms that make agents able to develop these different kinds of reasoning.

References

Boella, G., J. Odell, L. van der Torre, and H. Verhagen, H. 2005. *Roles, an interdisciplinary perspective, papers from the 2005 AAAI fall symposium*. Technical Report FS-05-08. Menlo Park: AAAI.

Boissier, O. 2001. Modèles et architectures d'agents. In *Principes et architectures des systèmes multi-agents*, ed. J.P. Briot and Y. Demazeau, 71–107. Paris: IC2, HERMES.

Boissier, O., C. Carabelea, C. Castelfranchi, J. Sabater-Mir, and L. Tummolini. 2005. The dialectics between an individual and his role. In *Roles, an interdisciplinary perspective, papers from the 2005 AAAI fall symposium*, vol. Technical report FS-05-08, ed. G. Boella, J. Odell, L. van der Torre, and H. Verhagen, 13–18. Menlo Park: AAAI.

Boissier, O., J.F. Hübner, and J.S.A. Sichman. 2007. Organization oriented programming: From closed to open organizations. In *Proceedings of the 7th international conference on engineering societies in the agents world VII. ESAW'06*, 86–105. Berlin/Heidelberg: Springer.

Bordini, R., J. Hübner, M. Wooldridge. 2007. *Programming multi-agent systems in agentSpeak using jason*. Chichester: John Wiley & Sons, Ltd.

Broersen, J., M. Dastani, J. Hulstijn, Z. Huang, and L.W.N. van der Torre. 2001. The BOID architecture: Conflicts between beliefs, obligations, intentions and desires. In *Proceedings of the fifth international conference on autonomous agents, AGENTS'01, Montreal, Quebec, Canada*, 9–16. ACM: New York, NY, USA.

Broersen, J., M. Dastani, J. Hulstijn, and L. van der Torre. 2002. Goal generation in the BOID architecture. *Cognitive Science Quarterly* 2(3–4): 428–447.

Carabelea, C., O. Boissier, and C. Castelfranchi. 2005. Using social power to enable agents to reason about being part of a group. In *Proceedings of 5th international workshop on engineering societies in the agents world (ESAW'04)*, LNCS, vol. 3451, 166–177. Berlin: Springer.

Castelfranchi, C. 2002. The social nature of information and the role of trust. *International Journal of Cooperative Information Systems* 11(3): 381.

Castelfranchi, C. 2005. Formalising the informal? *Nordic Journal of Philosophical Logic* 2: 1–46.

Castelfranchi, C., and R. Falcone. 1998. Principles of trust for MAS: Cognitive anatomy, social importance, and quantification. In *Proceedings of the third international conference on multiagent systems, ICMAS 1998, 3–7 July 1998*, IEEE Computer Society, ed. Y. Demazeau, 72–79. Paris: France.

Castelfranchi, C., F. Dignum, C.M. Jonker, and J. Treur. 2000. Deliberative normative agents: Principles and architecture. In *6th International workshop on intelligent agents VI, agent theories, architectures, and languages (ATAL'99)*, LNCS, vol. 1757, 364–378. Berlin: Springer.

Clavel, M., S. Eker, P. Lincloln, and J. Meseguer. 1996. Principles of maude. In *Proceedings first international workshop on rewriting logic and its applications. ENTC*, vol. 4, 65–89. Amsterdam: Elsevier.

Corkill, D., E. Durfee, V. Lesser, H. Zafar, and C. Zhang. 2011. Organizationally adept agents. In *12th international workshop on coordination, organization, institutions and norms in agent systems (COIN@AAMAS 2011)*, Taipei, 15–30.

Coutinho, L.R., J.S. Sichman, and O. Boissier. 2009. *Handbook of research on multi-agent systems: Semantics and dynamics of organizational models*, chap. Modelling dimensions for agent organizations, 18–50. Hershey: Information Science Reference Publisher.

Criado, N., E. Argente, P. Noriega, V.J. Botti. 2010. Towards a normative bdi architecture for norm compliance. In *Proceedings of 11th international workshop on coordination, organization, institutions and norms in multi-agent systems (COIN at MALLOW2010)*, Lyon.

Dastani, M., V. Dignum, and F. Dignum. 2003. Role-assignment in open agent societies. In *Proceedings of the second international conference on autonomous agents and multiagent systems (AAMAS'03)*. Melbourne: ACM.

Dastani, M., M.B.V. Riemsdijk, and J. Hulstijn. 2004. Enacting and deacting roles in agent programming. In *Proceedings of the 5th international workshop on agent-oriented software engineering (AOSE)*, vol. 3382, 189–204. New York: Springer.

Dignum, V. 2004. *A model for organizational interaction: Based on agents, founded in logic*. Ph.D. thesis, Universiteit Utrecht.

Dignum, F., V. Dignum, J. Thangarajah, L. Padgham, and M. Winikoff. 2008. Open agent systems? In *Proceedings of the 8th international workshop on agent-oriented software engineering (AOSE'07)*, LNCS, vol. 4951, 73–87. Berlin: Springer.

Hannoun, M., J.S. Sichman, O. Boissier, and C. Sayettat. 1998. Dependence relation between roles in a multi-agent system: Towards the detection of inconsistencies in organization. In *Proceedings of the first international workshop on multi-agent systems and agent-based simulation*, LNAI, vol. 1534, ed. J.s. Sichman, R. Conte, N. Gilbert 169–182. Berlin: Springer.

Hübner, J.F. 2003. *Um Modelo de Reorganizacao de Sistemas multiagentes*. Ph.D. thesis, Universidade de Sao Paulo, Escola Politecnica.

Hübner, J.F., J.S. Sichman, and O. Boissier. 2007. Developing organised multi-agent systems using the MOISE+ model: Programming issues at the system and agent levels. *Agent-Oriented Software Engineering* 1(3/4): 370–395.

Hübner, J.F., O. Boissier, R. Kitio, and A. Ricci. 2010. Instrumenting multi-agent organisations with organisational artifacts and agents: "giving the organisational power back to the agents". *Journal of Autonomous Agents and Multi-Agent Systems* 20(3): 369–400.

Kollingbaum, M.J., and T.J. Norman. 2003. Noa – a normative agent architecture. In *IJCAI*, ed. G. Gottlob and T. Walsh, pp. 1465–1466. San Francisco: Morgan Kaufmann.

Meneguzzi, F., and M. Luck. 2009. Norm-based behaviour modification in BDI agents. In *Proceedings of the eighth international joint conference on autonomous agents and multiagent systems (AAMAS'09)*, Budapest, 177–184.

Meneguzzi, F., N. Oren, and W. Vasconcelos. 2010. Using constraints for norm-aware BDI agents. In *The fourth annual conference of the international technology alliance*, London.

Panagiotidi, S., and J. Vázquez-Salceda. 2011. Norm-aware planning: Semantics and implementation. In *Proceedings of the 2011 IEEE/WIC/ACM international conferences on web intelligence and intelligent agent technology*, vol. 03, 33–36. Los Alamitos: IEEE.

Sabater, J. 2004. Evaluating the regret system. *Applied Artificial Intelligence* 18(9–10): 797–813.

Sichman, J.S., R. Conte, C. Castelfranchi, and Y. Demazeau. 1994. A social reasoning mechanism based on dependence networks. In: *ECAI*, Amsterdam, 188–192.

van Riemsdijk, M.B., V. Dignum, C.M. Jonker, and H. Aldewereld. 2011. Programming role enactment through reflection. In: *2011 IEEE/WIC/ACM international conference on web intelligence and intelligent agent technology (WI-IAT'11)*, vol. 2, 133–140. Los Alamitos: IEEE.

van Riemsdijk, M.B., K.V. Hindriks, and C.M. Jonker. 2009. Programming organization-aware agents: A research agenda. In *Proceedings of the tenth international workshop on engineering societies in the agents' world (ESAW'09)*, LNAI, vol. 5881, 98–112. Berlin: Springer.

Vazquez-Salceda, J. 2004. *The role of norms and electronic institutions in multi-agent systems.* Whitestein Series in Software Agent Technology, Birkh-user Verlag AG, Switzerland.

Chapter 20
Adaptive Agent Organisations

Estefanía Argente, Holger Billhardt, Carlos E. Cuesta, Sergio Esparcia, Jana Görmer, Ramón Hermoso, Kristi Kirikal, Marin Lujak, José-Santiago Pérez-Sotelo, and Kuldar Taveter

20.1 Introduction

It is well known that the growing complexity of software is emphasizing the need for systems that have autonomy, robustness and adaptability among their most important features. Nowadays it is also accepted that MAS have been developed in artificial intelligence area as a generic approach to solve complex problems. However, in order to fulfil their promise of generality and extensibility, they should also reach self-adaptivity, i.e. the capability of autonomous adaption to changing conditions. This feature requires agents to be able to alter their own configuration, and even their own composition and typing. Therefore, their reorganisation can be seen as the first necessary steps to reach actual self-adaptation.

E. Argente (✉) • S. Esparcia
Departamento de Sistemas Informáticos y Computación, Universitat Politècnica de València, Valencia, Spain
e-mail: eargente@dsic.upv.es; serparcia@dsic.upv.es

H. Billhardt • R. Hermoso • M. Lujak • J.-S. Pérez-Sotelo
CETINIA, University Rey Juan Carlos, Madrid, Spain
e-mail: holger.billhardt@urjc.es; ramon.hermoso@urjc.es; lujak@ia.urjc.es; josesantiago.perez@urjc.es

C.E. Cuesta
ETSII, University Rey Juan Carlos, Madrid, Spain
e-mail: carlos.cuesta@urjc.es

J. Görmer
Department of Informatics, TU Clausthal, Clausthal, Germany
e-mail: jana.goermer@tu-clausthal.de

K. Kirikal • K. Taveter
Tallinn University of Technology, Tallinn, Estonia
e-mail: kristi.kirikal@gmail.com; kuldar.taveter@ttu.ee

S. Ossowski (ed.), *Agreement Technologies*, Law, Governance and Technology Series 8, DOI 10.1007/978-94-007-5583-3_20,

In this chapter, first we present some basic concepts about agent adaption that have been broadly used. Next, in Sect. 20.3, we present an approach to deal with adaptation in Virtual Organisations, in which we propose several guidelines for identifying internal and external forces that motivate organisational change, studied in depth in Organisation Theory (Gazendam and Simons 1998). Thus, in Sect. 20.3 we describe how to define an Adaptive Virtual Organisation using an Organisational Theory approach.

In Sect. 20.4, we detail a framework for Adaptive Agent Organisation that provides an architectural solution to tackle the dynamism of organisations. This framework implies an evolving architectural structure based on combining pre-defined controls and protocols, handled in the context of a service-oriented, agent-based and organisation-centric framework.

As explained in Sect. 17.4, software-intensive systems can be seen as so ciotechnical systems that consist of interacting agents. The methods for designing adaptive sociotechnical systems can be borrowed from social sciences. In Sect. 20.5, we analyse the differences between social and technical systems and we introduce requirements which should be considered while designing sociotechnical systems. A case study of adaptive and iterative development is then introduced and explained in Sect. 20.6.

A particularly difficult task for an agent is deciding with whom to interact when participating inside an Open Multi-Agent System. In Sect. 20.7 we present a mechanism that enables agents to take more informed decisions regarding their partner selection. This mechanism monitors the interactions in the Open Multi-Agent System, evolves role taxonomy and assigns agents to roles based on their observed performance in different types of interactions. So then this information can be used by agents to estimate better the expected behaviour of potential counterparts in future interactions.

Dealing with groups of autonomous agents the IT-ecosystem can balance on one hand its adaptability and on the other hand its controllability. In Sect. 20.8 we present group-oriented coordination, in which we explain how this kind of cooperation and coordination mechanisms finds an equilibrium for global and individual objectives. We apply the group oriented coordination on a simple example allowing agents to form faster and slower groups.

Finally, we also consider the problem of coordinating multiple mobile agents which collaborate to achieve a common goal in an environment with variable communication constraints. In Sect. 20.9 we present a task assignment model for cooperative MAS, in which a team of mobile agents has to accomplish a certain mission under different inter-agent communication conditions.

20.2 Concepts on Adaptive Agent Organisations

Adaptive organisations is a key research topic inside the MAS domain. In this section we will present and discuss relevant concepts and definitions for adaptive agent organisations, mainly focusing on adaptive Organisation-Centred MAS (OCMAS).

Aldewereld et al. (2008) define adaptive software systems as "those that must have the ability to cope with changes of stakeholders' needs, changes in the operational environment, and resource variability". DeLoach et al. (2008) define adaptive organisations as distributed systems that can autonomously adapt to their environment. The system must be provided with organisational knowledge, by which it can specify its own organisation, based on the current goals and its current capabilities.

Picard et al. (2009) describe that an OCMAS is adaptive when it changes whenever its organisation is not adequate, i.e. the social purpose is not being achieved and/or its structure is not adapted to the environment. This situation occurs when the environment or the MAS purposes have changed, the performance requirements are not satisfied, the agents are not capable of playing their roles in a suitable way or a new task arrives and the current organisation cannot face it. In this case, adaptation implies modifying both organisation specification (modifying tasks, goals, structure) and role allocation.

Dignum and Dignum (2006) state that in order to remain effective, organisations must maintain a good fit with the environment. Changes in the environment lead to alterations on the effectiveness of the organisation and therefore in a need to reorganize, or at least, the need to consider the consequences of the change to the organisation's effectiveness and, possibly, efficiency. On the other hand, organisations are active entities, capable not only of adapting to the environment but also of changing that environment.

In summary, an Adaptive Organisation in MAS presents the following properties:

- The organisation changes if its environment forces it to do so.
- Changes in goals, internal requirements, etc. of the organisation could also force a change.
- The organisation is considered to be an open system since the environment might change and external agents may join the organisation.
- The organisation is populated by agents playing different roles, some of them being responsible for deciding about change.

Based on these previous works, a definition for *Adaptive Virtual Organisation* is proposed in Esparcia and Argente (2012): An Adaptive Virtual Organisation is a virtual organisation that is able to modify both its structural (topology, norms, roles, etc.) and functional (services, tasks, objectives, etc.) dimensions in order to respond or to be ahead of changes produced in its environment, or by internal requirements, i.e. if it detects that its organisational goals are not being achieved in a satisfactory way.

When executing an adaptation process in an OCMAS, two types of change can be distinguished: dynamical (behavioural) and structural (Dignum 2009). *Dynamical changes* are those in which the structure of the system remains fixed, while agents and aspects like role enactment are modified. *Structural changes* are produced in structural elements of the system, like roles, topology or norms.

Regarding dynamical changes, there are three types that must be considered:

- A new agent joins the system. It is necessary to reach an agreement to join the organisation, playing a particular role that indicates the rights and duties of the agent that plays that role.
- An agent leaves the system. It is necessary to determine if this operation is possible, taking into account certain imposed conditions by the MAS management. Sometimes, it could not be appropriate to allow an agent playing a specific role to leave the system. In other moments, it may be convenient to reassign that role as soon as the agent leaves the system.
- Instantiation of the interaction pattern. A change of this kind consists of two agents that carry out a certain interaction pattern and reach an agreement to follow a protocol adjusted to this interaction pattern. In this kind of changes there are included, for example, changes related to the role enactment process, changes in the agents that are providing a service or in the set of active norms, etc. These changes force agents to modify their interaction pattern.

Regarding structural changes, there are two ways to carry out a structural change in an organisation:

- Self-organisation: implies the emergence of changes, appearing because of the interaction between agents in a local level, that generates global level changes in the organisation.
- Reorganisation: designed societies are adapted to modifications in the environment by adding, deleting or modifying their structural elements (roles, dependencies, norms, ontologies, communication primitives, etc.).

Self-organisation changes are bottom-up, where an adaptation in the individual behaviour of the agents will lead to a change in the organisation in an emergent way. Thus, self-organisation is an endogenous process (carried out by the agents). Agents are not aware of the organisation as a whole, they only work with local-level information to adapt the system to environmental pressures by indirectly modifying the organisation. Therefore, agents, using local interactions and propagation, modify the configuration of the system (topology, neighbours, influences, differentiation).

There are some proposals about MAS self-adaptation, and here we present some of them as an example. Gardelli et al. (2008) use artifacts as a tool to introduce self-organisation inside a MAS. In the work by Kota et al. (2009) a pair of agents estimate the utility of changing their relation and take the appropriate action accordingly. ADELFE (2002) is a methodology that proposes the design of agents that are able to modify their interactions in an autonomous and local way in order to react to the changes that are produced in their environment. MACODO (Haesevoets et al. 2009) is a middleware that offers the life-cycle management of dynamic organisations as a reusable service separated from the agents.

Regarding reorganisation, it is a top-down approach, so that a modification in an organisational aspect will produce changes in agents composing the organisation. Reorganisation can be both an endogenous or an exogenous process (controlled by the user or by an external system), referred to systems where the organisation is explicitly modified through specifications, restrictions or other methods, in order to ensure a suitable global behaviour when the organisation is not appropriate. Agents are aware of the state of the organisation and its structure, being able to manipulate primitives to modify their social environment. This process can be initialized by an external entity or by the agents, directly reasoning over the organisation (roles, organisational specification), and the cooperation patterns (dependencies, commitments, powers).

The OCMAS community of researches has presented different proposals to deal with adaptive organisations, one of each using their own point of view. Three of these works (the ones from ALIVE (Aldewereld et al. 2008), Dignum and Dignum (Dignum et al. 2005), and Hoogendorn (Hoogendoorn et al. 2007)) state that they based their knowledge about organisational change on the human Organisation Theory. Also, both human and agent organisations have many elements in common. These three proposals conceive organisational change as an endogenous process, where agents populating the organisation will be responsible for organisational adaptation. These agents could be all the agents populating the organisation, or just only a set of agents (typically playing a management role) that are organisation aware, and are provided with all the knowledge they need to understand modifications and to perform changes inside the organisation.

Nevertheless, the approach followed by MOISE (2004) is different. In this case, MOISE was not initially conceived to give support to adaptation, but it was later adapted to provide support to reorganisation. Roles inside MOISE are distributed in different groups, so as to give support to adaptation, a new group, external to the organisation, was added. This makes the process of change to be exogenous, making a difference with respect to the rest of proposals. However, this process still preserves the common steps for reorganisation, including monitoring, design and implementation of change.

It must be noticed that these proposals follow a formal approach to define change. Dignum and Dignum have an interesting background in formal and logic languages, with proposals like OperA (Dignum 2003) or LAO (Dignum and Dignum 2007). ALIVE also takes inspiration from previous proposals by Dignum and Dignum, since it is a joint project of some European universities, including the Universities from Delft and Utrecht, where Dignum and Dignum develop their work. Therefore, their proposals are very similar. Hoogendoorn also works with a formal logic language, TTL, that makes easier to check the correctness of the definition of a system and its adaptation process.

The next sections of this chapter present proposals for designing and developing adaptive agent organisations and other related elements. These proposals are mixed, since some of them follow a reorganisation, top-down approach to define organisations, and some others define a self-organisation, bottom-up development.

20.3 Adaptive Virtual Organisations Using an Organisational Theory Approach

As presented in Sect. 17.3 of this book, the Virtual Organisation concept is based on human organisations. Therefore, changing factors in a human organisation can also be considered as changing factors in a Virtual Organisation. In the domain of the Organisation Theory (Gazendam and Simons 1998) these factors are known as *forces* that lead to organisational change. Those forces can be *internal* or *external*, depending on where their source is located. Usually, a change in the environment is the main external cause, while a change in the requirements or goals of the organisation is the most common internal reason for change. Obviously, these changes are generic, and specific changing factors must be defined depending on the domain of each system.

In the following, we present the most common forces, both internal and external, and we also depict our proposal for dealing with these forces, thus turning a Virtual Organisation into an Adaptive Virtual Organisation (Esparcia and Argente 2012).

Forces that drive organisational change. An organisational change is produced by one or some forces that can be differentiated by their nature. Some organisations are more vulnerable than others due to the pressure of change, such as organisations with diffuse objectives, uncertain support, unstable values and those that face a declining market for their products and services.

The ***external forces*** are those that promote changes inside an organisation due to changes in its environment. Thus, the external forces are referred to the environment where the organisation is located. They are due to elements such as other organisations that populate the same environment (and some of them suppose competence) or different heterogeneous agents in the same environment. Among external forces, the following forces can be found: (a) *Obtaining resources*: if a failure occurs in an organisation while obtaining resources, it leads to an organisational change to guarantee organisational survival (Aldrich 1999). Therefore, it could be necessary for organisational survival to improve the way in which resources are obtained; (b) *Market forces*: Requirements of products and services of an organisation by internal and external agents may change through time, so the number of requests for a product or a service that an organisation is offering is not constant. Therefore, organisations that offer services or products that nobody is requiring have no reason to exist, so they will disappear if they do not decide to change in order to offer new products and services that are currently being demanded (Aldrich 2007); (c) *Generalisation*: some organisations that are unable to acquire enough resources by specializing themselves in a limited range of products or services manage to survive by becoming generalists, i.e. by offering a set of products and services that are oriented to a more general purpose, thus increasing their number of potential customers; (d) *Decay and deterioration*: An organisation can be affected by environmental changes that will make its objectives obsolete or they could lose their sense (Aldrich 2007); (e) *Technological changes*: An organisation can adopt new technology in order to improve its productivity inside the market where it is developing its activities (Barnett and Carroll 1995); (f) *Competence*: One of the reasons for the organisational change is the existence of organisations with a similar purpose, turning into competence for them (Barnett and Carroll 1995); (g) *Demographical features*: Since organisations are open systems, agents populating them and their environment are heterogeneous. An organisation must control this diversity in an effective way, paying attention to the different needs of these agents, but trying to avoid malicious and/or self-interested behaviours by them (McShane et al.); (h) *Laws and regulations*: There can be external laws that could affect the environment of an organisation or its neighbours organisations (Barnett and Carroll 1995); and (i) *Globalisation*: Globalisation refers to the increasing unification of the world's economic order through reduction of such barriers to international trade as tariffs, export fees, and import quotas (Robertson 1992). The goal is to increase material wealth, goods, and services through an international division of labour by efficiencies catalysed by international relations, specialisation and competition.

The ***internal forces*** of an organisation are signals produced inside an organisation, indicating that a change is necessary. Thus, it is important to clearly define these forces, in order to monitor them and to achieve the change in the most appropriate form and moment. The internal forces are: (a) *Growth*: When an organisation grows in both members or budget, it is necessary to change its structure to a more hierarchical organisation, with higher levels of bureaucratisation and differentiation among its members (Aldrich 2007); (b) *Power and political factors*: The most powerful members of an organisation may have different objectives to agents in a lower hierarchical level, which can differ even from the organisational objectives. The organisation may assure (for instance, by means of observers) that manager agents do not impose their objectives above organisational objectives (Aldrich 2007); (c) *Goal succession*: There are certain organisations that disappear after reaching their goals. However, some other organisations look for new goals to achieve. Therefore, these organisations will continue with their existence; (d) *Life-cycle*: Some existing organisations follow the classic life-cycle model. Thus, they appear, grow, change, and disappear, to give way to other organisations (Barnett and Carroll 1995); (e) *Human resources*: Managers of the organisation must control that their agents are committed with the organisation, present an adequate behaviour and their performance is acceptable; (f) *Decisions and managers behaviour*: Industrial disputes between agents and their supervisors inside organisations are an important force for change. If a subordinated agent disagrees with his/her supervisor, he/she could ask for new tasks to develop inside the organisation. If the management approves his/her petition, an action must be carried out; (g) *Economical restrictions*: Organisations want to maximize their performance. Therefore, they will try to obtain maximum benefits using the least possible amount of resources. If it is considered that too many resources are being consumed, a change can be necessary; (h) *Merging and acquisitions of organisations*: One of the internal forces that will drive organisational change is the merging of two or more organisations, or the acquisition of one organisation by another, leading to bigger organisations where their structure and members should be reorganized. Merging will allow the

Table 20.1 Guideline for detecting a force that drives organisational change

Guideline for detecting a driving force	
Field	Description
Name	Name of the force which is able to be detected by following this guideline
Description	Describes how this force acts over an organisation
Type	*Internal* or *external*, depending on whether this force comes from the own organisation or its environment
Factors	
Name	The name of the factor that helps identifying the force
Description	The description of this factor
Type	The type of the factor (e.g. behaviour of agent/role, goal achievement, etc.)
Value	The value that this element must reach/not reach in order to be considered as a factor for change
Triggers	Specifies whether this factor triggers the force by itself, of other factors are required in order for a force to start acting over an organisation

organization to compete against other organizations from a better position; and (i) *Crisis*: If an organisation is in a crisis due to a sudden drop of its efficiency, a possible solution is a deep organisational change, modifying structural and/or functional elements, depending on the specific needs of the organisation.

How to identify an acting force. A key issue when dealing with adaptation is that forces that drive organisational change should be correctly detected. We have defined a guideline (Table 20.1) (Esparcia and Argente 2012) for detecting when a force is acting over the organisation. For each common force that leads to organisational change, a guideline has been completed. On each of these guidelines, there are represented the different factors that should be monitored in order to detect that a force is acting. It must be noted that not all factors are required to be detected in order to state that a specific force is acting over an organisation, but just a subset of these factors could be able to trigger a force. It is possible for each factor to come from different sources, such as from the behaviour of an agent, or the level of fulfilment of set of goals.

Solution for preventing damage or taking advantage from a force. We have also defined a guideline (Table 20.2) (Esparcia and Argente 2012) for identifying the different organisational actions that should be carried out in the organisation in order to take advantage or to prevent damage from a specific force.

Each solution is described by its name, its description, the force (or forces) that are intended to take advantage of or trying to reduce its damaging effects over the organisation. Also, this guideline points out the factors for detecting a force that must appear along with the force in order to be possible to apply this solution, as well as the specific roles that will carry out this solution.

The organisational actions are those actions that will produce a change in the organisational definition when they are executed. Taking the Virtual Organisation Formalisation (built by the *OS* referring to the Organisational Specification, *OE* to

Table 20.2 Guideline for applying a solution

Solution for preventing damage or taking advantage of a force	
Field	Description
Name	Name of the solution
Description	Text describing this solution
Force	The force that must be acting to apply this solution
Factor	The set of factors that must be detected in order to be able to apply this solution
Actions	The set of actions that must be carried out to apply this solution
Roles	The responsible roles for applying this solution

the Organisational Entity, and ϕ to the Organisational Dynamics, as explained in Sect. 17.3) as reference, the execution of an organisational action *oa* in a virtual organisation vo_i implies that the time increases ($t \to t+1$). An organisational action is defined as:

$$\frac{vo_i \quad \to_{oa} \quad vo_i'}{\langle OS, OE, \phi \rangle \to \langle OS', OE', \phi' \rangle}$$

This expression states that a virtual organisation vo_i, at a given time t, carries out an organisational action *oa* that causes a change in the organisational state, being vo_i' the new state of the organisation, at a time $t+1$. Notice that it is not mandatory for an organisation to change every component in order to change its state, i.e. $(OS = OS' \vee OE = OE' \vee \phi = \phi')$.

The two proposed guidelines have been applied, as an example, to the description of the external force "Obtaining resources" (Table 20.3), which is explained as follows:

Obtaining resources (External force). Resources are commonly used as raw materials to produce the results of the services of an organisation. Therefore, if a service is called, and it has a precondition that specifies that a resource is needed to execute a service, but the resource cannot be obtained using the current organisational structure, it is necessary to look for a solution. In this case, the most appropriate solution could be to move any of the entities to a workspace where this resource is available (i.e. place the entity inside the population of this workspace).

The solution to this force (Table 20.4) is to move an entity of the organisation to a workspace where this resource is available. In our approach, that means to execute the organisational action 'move entity' to a workspace of the organisation $vo_1 \in \mathcal{VO}$ at a given time t.

A different solution is to negotiate with another organisation, in order to be able to go inside this organisation to get resources or to allow an external agent which is able to get these resources to join the organisation. Notice that this solution is appropriate only in case where the organisation is not able to find the required resource among its perceived workspaces. So, it must look for it outside the organisation.

Table 20.3 Example of the guideline for detecting a force that drives organisational change

Detecting "obtaining resources" external force	
Field	Description
Name	Obtaining resource
Description	A resource is not able to be accessed by an organisation
Type	External
Factors	
Name	Successful calls to a service
Description	If the rate for successfully executing a service is lower than a given threshold, it means that this force is acting
Type	Service providing rate
Value	Threshold
Triggers	This factor itself triggers the force

Table 20.4 Example of the guideline for applying a solution

Solution for "obtaining resources" external force	
Field	Description
Name	Move entity to a workspace
Description	An entity of the organisation is placed in a workspace where the artifact is located
Force	Obtaining resource
Factor	Threshold of successfully executing a service
Actions	Move entity to a workspace
Roles	The responsible roles for applying this solution

20.4 A Framework for Adaptive Agent Organisations

It is well known that the growing complexity of software is emphasizing the need for systems that have autonomy, robustness and adaptability among their most important features. It is also accepted nowadays that MAS have been developed in artificial intelligence area as a generic approach to solve complex problems. However, in order to fulfil their promise of generality and extensibility, they should also reach self-adaptivity, i.e. the capability of autonomously adapting to changing conditions. This feature requires them to be able to alter their own configuration, and even their own composition and type. Their reorganisations can be seen, therefore, as the first necessary steps to reach actual self-adaptivity.

This section proposes an architectural solution to tackle the dynamism, which will be supported by an emergent agreement – an evolving architectural structure based on combining predefined controls and protocols. These are handled in the context of a service-oriented, agent-based and organisation-centric framework (Pérez-Sotelo et al. 2009). Next, we will discuss not only the architectural framework but also the mechanisms to change their composition patterns and element types, which are necessary to achieve real self-adaptivity.

The Basic Framework for Adaptive Organisations. As the proposed approach is based on service-oriented concepts, the main idea is to export the agent system as a system of services, and the environment must be truly adaptive and dynamic, it requires the use of rich semantic and highly technological capabilities. Therefore, it is considered a wise use of *agents* in a broader context, with an upper layer of services added to provide, in particular, the interoperability feature. It is easy to conceive of a service to present the operational capabilities of an agent or, even better, of a collection of agents as an organisation, which in turn provides services. Using agents allows the explicit treatment of semantics, a structured coordination, the use of a methodology to service development, to structure them into organisations, and the use of their learning capacity, among others features.

Implicit in the definition of MAS is the need to *register* agents in the system, to separate those ones who belong to the architecture from those who do not. The same approach will be used to identify services. To allow their external access, they will be explicitly registered and grouped as part of a service.

The current research, which is included as part of the OVAMAH project (OVAMAH 2010), is extending the objectives of the original platform THOMAS (Argente et al. 2011). Besides providing the necessary technology for the development of virtual organisations in open environments, it will allow to facilitate dynamic answers for changing situations by means of the adaptation and/or evolution of the organisations. For example, agents forming an organisational unit could create (or remove) another unit, affecting the groups of the system; decide the moment to add or delete norms; the social relationship between roles could change at runtime, the conditions to activate/deactivate, as well as the cardinality of roles; the system topology (given by the relationships) could be changed also at runtime and then validate the changes with objectives and organisational type; the services could be matched to new roles; etc.

The framework is evolving (currently adapting to OSGi (2009) specification) and the applications are modularizing into smaller entities called bundles. These entities can be installed, updated or removed on the fly and dynamically, provide the ability to change the system behaviour without ever having to disrupt its operation. Among the services provided by this standard, the Service Tracker appears as particularly relevant, in the light of the proposed approach. This service makes it possible to track other registered services on the platform. It is used to ensure that the services to be provided are still available or not.

In summary, the evolution of the agreement-based approach, including the concepts and constructs that it describes, has already shown its relevance. The main concern now, beyond performance issues, is the essential dynamism and the adaptive functionality required by the underlying architecture.

Adaptive Organisations based on *Initiatives*. A group of individuals can be arranged into certain structures, depending on concrete goals, and they can be formed by using two different kinds of mechanisms: *controls* and *protocols*, which are both based on limiting the range of available actions. The former can be seen as elements that either enforce or forbid specific interactions (or architectural connections).

Self-adaptive structures, being typically centralized (Andersson et al. 2009), show many classic examples of this kind: most of them manifest explicit control loops, inspired in regulators of classic control theory. On the other hand, protocols, which either enable or channel behaviour, are based on consensus and agreements. They can be described generically as the way to control decentralized (even distributed) structures (Galloway 2004). Basically, when protocols are present, every agent knows the way to interact with the rest; it is necessary to comply with them to be able to communicate, but at the same time they are also regulating the development of the interacting structure itself.

These two mechanisms define a wide spectrum of regulation, in which agent organisations and their architectures are simultaneously harnessed by atomic, unary controls (norms, limits, locks, control loops or constraints) and multiple, connective protocols (hubs, bridges, channels, or spaces). It is important to note that the purpose of these mechanisms is to "discover" a suitable structure of controls and protocols so that a global structure can emerge. These elements make it possible to define the main inner structures in order to obtain agreement-based organisations. Once a primary structure can be defined, an elemental group emerges as a preliminary organisation, which will be referred as an *initiative*: not yet fully established, but still evolving.

Nevertheless, the *initiative* can continue growing and mutating because of its adaptive nature, but when it has some "stable" structure, it can be called organisation. This "stable" structure is achieved when all the participants can afford the necessary agreement in order to gain the objective. This process can be thought as the system moving to a new state, in which the structure of the "past" is supplanted by a "new" emergent structure. Obviously, this novel structure admits new elements because of the dynamic environment, but now one of its goals is to reinforce its nature.

An *initiative* can be generated from patterns, named *adaptation patterns*, where the term is used in an architectural sense. They are pre-designed from the required services of an *initiative* and the corresponding semantic refining. Some of them have been already identified, and receive such names as Façade, Mediator, or Surveyor, among others (see Fig. 20.1). The patterns represent a fragment of a static structure, leading to a dynamic one, the *initiative*, reaching a "stable" form, the organisation.

Adaptation Patterns. As already noted, the adaptation patterns are pre-designed from the required services of an *initiative* and for the corresponding semantic refinement. Particularly, these are not classic object-oriented patterns, because they are defined in a different context: they are architectural patterns.

According to Ramirez and Cheng (2010) it is possible to classify the architectural design patterns as follows: monitoring (M), decision-making (DM), or reconfiguration (R) based on their objective. M and DM patterns can also be classified as either creational (C) or structural (S), as defined in Gamma et al. (1994). Likewise, R patterns can also be classified as behavioural (B) and structural (S) since they specify how to physically restructure an architecture. Several of these patterns have been already identified for the proposed approach. In Fig. 20.1, for instance, three of them are described: Façade, Mediator, and Surveyor.

Name	Category	Description
Façade	M, S	To be able to easily interact with an organisation, which still lacks a defined structure, some agent has to represent the organization itself in terms of interaction. This agent redirects any incoming communication.
Mediator	R, B	During the emergence process, the organization is not yet established, and data services are probably not working. Some agent must act as a *mediator*, which makes possible to access to data sources, although indirectly, and also to perform the necessary (*semantic*) translations.
Surveyor	R, S	During the emergence process, at least one agent must monitor the growing of the initiative itself, both to decide when new elements are inserted, and also when the initiative forms a "stable" organization. It has access to the pattern library and decides when a certain pattern must be triggered.

Fig. 20.1 Adaptation patterns: architectural design patterns

Obviously, there are more patterns and not all of them describe only roles. For instance, the Surveyor Election defines the protocol (one among many) to decide the next surveyor; and Surveyor Change describes a protocol to demote the current surveyor and forward its knowledge to a new one.

All these pre-figured changes are applied to organisations that have reached a quiescent or safe state for adaptation (Kramer and Magee 2007). In this case, namely pure adaptation, the importance lies in the way that an existing organisation has to adapt to a new behaviour. First, it has to realize that a change has occurred, i.e. a change can emerge in an intrinsic way (Prokopenko et al. 2008), and then it has to adapt itself.

There are several scenarios to develop this adaptive behaviour, reaching ultimately a "stable" configuration for an *initiative* which therefore becomes an organisation. For example, in an emergency situation, some police cars can arrive at the crisis area but no one is the leader of the group. They follow a previous internal protocol to choose a leader (even hierarchy is a protocol), and this agreement generates a preliminary organisation. This is what it is called a *generative protocol.* When the individuals follow this kind of protocols, they define implicit structural patterns.

Lifecycle of Self-Organizing Structures. As we already noted, depending on concrete goals, any group of individuals can be arranged into certain structures by using controls and protocols. These elements will make possible to define the main inner structures in order to obtain agreement-based organisations. Once a primary structure is defined, an "elemental" group emerges as a preliminary entity: the *initiative*. It will grow with the environmental dynamics until become into a "stable" organisation.

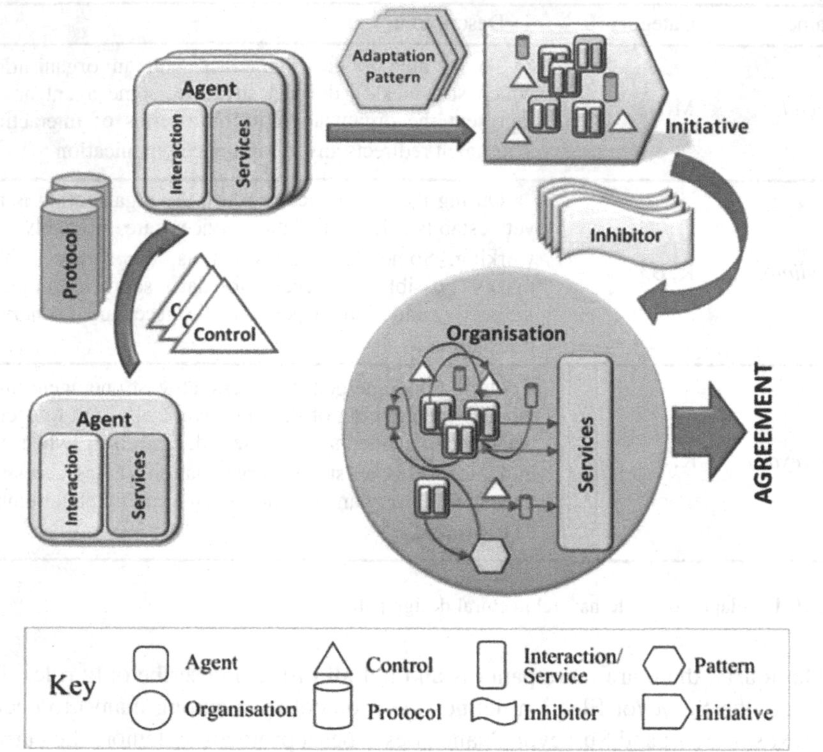

Fig. 20.2 Lifecycle of a self-organizing structure (From Cuesta et al. (2011))

Figure 20.2 summarizes briefly the lifecycle of our self-organizing structures (Cuesta et al. 2011). This cycle can begin with a single agent, which is able to perform certain interactions and has the potential to export some services. Initially, it does not belong to any organisation when reaches the system. However, it complies with a number of predefined controls and protocols, which "guide" the agent's interaction and enable it to maintain structured conversations with others, composing informal groups of agents.

When an external change occurs, the system must react with an adaptive behaviour, and this is the functionality that must trigger the formation of the self-organizing structures (organisations). The system is provided with a number of adaptation patterns in order to achieve some desired reaction. These patterns are partial definitions of elements and relationships, which include enough information for an agent to learn how to perform some behaviour. Therefore, under the guidance of an adaptation pattern, certain agents within the group acquire specific functions, and begin to form an actual structure: this is the *initiative*. Of course, these organisations are able to evolve themselves, and to participate in larger agreements (Cuesta et al. 2011).

As already noted, the system is ultimately conceived as a service-oriented architecture; so methodologically, the first stable organisations must be considered as the providers for certain high-level services. Then, these services must be proposed as the starting point for the functional definition of those first organisations.

20.5 Adaptive Agent Organisations with Sociotechnical Systems

The challenges in creating software for modern complex and distributed computing environments are described by Sterling and Taveter (2009). They are time-sensitivity, uncertainty, unpredictability, and openness. It is a problem how to design systems that work effectively in the modern environment, where computing is pervasive, people interact with technology existing in a variety of networks, and under a range of policies and constraints imposed by the institutions and social structures that we live in. The key concepts that Sterling and Taveter (2009) use for designing open, adaptive, distributed, and self-managing systems are *agents* and *sociotechnical systems*. An *agent* is suitable as a central modelling abstraction for representing distributed interconnected nodes of the modern world. A *sociotechnical system* encompasses a combination of people and computers, hardware and software.

The novelty of the approach to be presented in this section is that it shows how treating software-intensive systems as sociotechnical systems that consist of interacting agents facilitates the design of such systems. We claim that the methods for designing adaptive sociotechnical systems should be borrowed from social sciences rather than from exact sciences. We show how it can be done.

To start with, it is crucial to understand how social and technical systems differentiate each other. Only when this understanding is achieved will it become possible to form the foundations for designing systems. On this grounding, in this section we first analyse differences between social and technical systems. Then we introduce requirements which should be considered while designing sociotechnical systems. Finally a case study of adaptive and iterative development will be introduced and explained.

Social Systems. Sociotechnical systems are more complex than merely technical systems. Methods of exact sciences are not applicable to social systems. As Prigogine (1997) pointed out, the world is a complex system which develops in irreversible time. It is impossible to re-create the same situation in a social environment because social experiments are not conducted in a laboratory. Social experiments have an impact on society and therefore initial conditions will also change. A social system can be viewed as having two kinds of statuses. These modes are "is" and "is not" or "agree" and "disagree", depending on the situation. The action of choosing a status by an agent triggers some event.

Popper states that no scientific predictor – whether a human scientist or a calculating machine – can possibly predict, by scientific methods, its own future (Popper 1964). Luhmann (1995, p. 177) claims that establishing and maintaining the difference between system and environment becomes the problem, because for each system the environment is more complex than the system itself. Allert and Richter (2008) lead this thought to its conclusion by saying that "the difference system/environment is not ontological but an epistemological – it is continuously constructed by the observer, based on his actual motive".

Technical Systems. In contrast to social systems, technical systems can be studied by applying the methods of exact sciences. The experiments conducted with technical systems in a laboratory are repeatable and the same outcome is expected from them. For example, the results from chemical experiments should be identical when the same experiment is repeated under the same initial conditions.

Also in software development time does not have an effect on the system when the system is not intentionally changed. This means that while testing the system, the same test case should end with the same results. A software system is considered to be of a high quality when it functions as expected.

In technical systems, the difference between system and environment is drawn from early on. For example, use cases of UML pressure the modeller to decide the system boundary already at the beginning of requirements engineering. We can conclude this section by stating that important features of technical systems are predictability and clear system/environment difference.

Considerations for Designing Sociotechnical Multi-Agent Systems. In the previous section we pointed out that social systems are essentially different from technical systems. Here, we supplement this reasoning by elaborating considerations for designing sociotechnical systems. The most important point that we argue is that *sociotechnical systems should be designed by following principles of behavioural and social sciences*. The rationale for this is that behavioural and social sciences are more complex and therefore their characteristics should be used when designing sociotechnical systems. Only then can social and technical systems be merged.

First of all, we need proper abstractions for engineering sociotechnical systems. Central among such abstractions is that of an *agent*, which we term as an active entity, such as person, software agent, or robot. It is worth pointing out here that people are also agents. People live and act in the world and interact with each other. Viewing people as agents helps to conceptualize systems in terms of agents.

Because of continuous time, sociotechnical systems are *here-and-now* systems or run-time systems where agents should adapt to changes in the environment gradually at run-time. It is important that no agent in the system needs to know everything. It is sufficient when an agent knows enough to achieve his/her own goals. If the information required is not available in the current situation, the agent will use the information that is available or will try again after a while. However, that will be another *here-and-now* situation.

Sociotechnical systems should be gradually extendable. In other words, sociotechnical systems do not require that all of their constituent agents should be implemented at once. For example, a human agent can create a one-person company. When one person cannot any more manage with all of the tasks and there are enough resources to hire another person, the organisation can be extended.

In order to develop good-quality sociotechnical systems, the goals of the *system* should be known, usually by human agents. Designing a self-organizing agent system without a known outcome is of no value because the outcome can be order as well as chaos. What is not predictable is how exactly the goals of the system are achieved. As time is irreversible, normally there are several options for achieving the same goal. Therefore adaptive and flexible systems which can keep up with changes occurring at run-time should be designed.

In sociotechnical systems, storing history is not the main priority. Rather it is important for each agent of the system to know from where to obtain information and how to utilize it. More important than having a lot of data in the system is having agents that can interpret data for realizing their goals.

Sociotechnical systems should follow patterns of social systems. In a society, each person is an autonomous agent. No one knows information about the society as a whole but everyone knows the information necessary to fulfil its objectives. Moreover, no one, not even the President, knows all the information about a reasonably large organisation such as Tallinn University of Technology. However, society as a complex system works reasonably well, despite the fact that each member of a society knows only a very small part of the whole system. We are convinced that this approach is also applicable to engineering sociotechnical systems.

Based on the preceding arguments, when designing sociotechnical systems, there is no need to describe their environments as accurately as possible (and as was indicated in the *Social Systems* paragraph, it is not even possible). What matters is that each constituent agent of the system knows enough about its specific objectives and about the means of achieving them.

System design for complex sociotechnical systems requires new approaches. In next Sect. 20.6 we propose a solution for adaptive development of flexible sociotechnical systems in such a way that an environment does not have to be analysed in its entire complexity and the system can be developed adaptively and iteratively to match a continuously changing world.

20.6 Adaptive and Iterative Development

In this section we propose an approach for iterative bottom-up development of sociotechnical systems based on agent-oriented modelling. We claim that this approach is applicable to the systems consisting of human and/or man-made agents. Another claim is that if sociotechnical systems are developed this way, they can be easily adapted to the changing conditions.

Agent 1.1 ⟵⟶ Agent 1.2

Fig. 20.3 Acquaintance model for agents of the first level

The rationale for this approach is that contemporary complex systems can have no agents who know all the information. It is not even necessary to have such agents. Instead, it is important for each agent to know its objectives and the means of achieving them. In our view, sociotechnical systems should be developed in iterative phases. A system in its any phase should include at least one agent who is aware of the goal which should be achieved by the system as a whole, i.e. the system's purpose. As we do not yet live in the world described by Isaac Asimov (1950), where man-made agents can create themselves, at the beginning of adaptive development the agent who is aware of the system goal is a human agent. When an agent knows the system goal, a complex system environment does not have to be described in detail. Each agent knows its objectives and this is sufficient to achieve the system's goal.

Our approach is rooted in agent-oriented modelling proposed by Sterling and Taveter (2009), which was overviewed in Sect. 17.4. However, instead of using agent-oriented modelling for just *top-down* development of sociotechnical systems, as proposed by Sterling and Taveter (2009), we propose applying agent-oriented modelling also to iterative *bottom-up* development of sociotechnical systems. We have chosen agent-oriented modelling because it supports the openness of sociotechnical systems well by postponing deciding the system/environment boundary until platform-independent design.

In our approach, agents belong to different abstraction levels. First-level agents are always used because they do the actual work, such as assembling cars or cell phones on a production line. Therefore agents of the first-level are created before agents of other levels. Figure 20.3 represents two first-level agents who know each other. If the goals to be achieved by these agents are straightforward, the agents can coordinate their activities just between themselves. The coordination may lie in passing the product that is being assembled from one industrial robot to another in a timely manner. This kind of situation is depicted in Fig. 20.3.

Let us suppose that the requirements of a sociotechnical system are represented in the form of a goal model of agent-oriented modelling (Sterling and Taveter 2009) that was overviewed in Sect. 17.4. Examples of goal models are depicted in Figs. 20.6 and 20.8. If new goals and/or roles are added to the goal tree, more agents may need to be created at the same level and/or at higher levels. In particular, agents of a higher level have to be created if agents of lower level(s) need more coordination to achieve their objectives. In Fig. 20.4, an agent of the second level – manager – has been added who interacts with agents of the first level. If a manager is added, agents of the next lower level need to become aware of it because the manager knows a higher-level goal. Another reason for adding a higher level agent may be that in certain situations lower-level agents cannot anymore manage the task at hand and need advice from a higher-level agent. For example, if lower-level agents

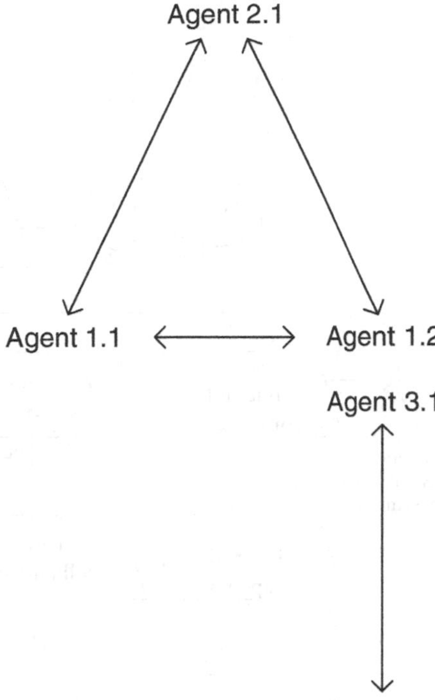

Fig. 20.4 Acquaintance model for an agent of the second level

Fig. 20.5 Acquaintance model for an agent of the third level

in a sociotechnical system are man-made agents like robots or software agents and the higher-level agent is a human, lower-level agents might ask for his/her advice through a graphical user interface built for this purpose. In this kind of situation all lower-level agents have to be aware of the higher-level agent.

An agent of a higher level might not be aware of (all) the agents at the levels below it. This is illustrated by Fig. 20.5, according to which an agent of the third level is aware of just one agent of the second level, who is probably the manager of the second-level agents. Agents of different levels can be added to a sociotechnical system separately and adaptively when system requirements change or goals develop.

Case study of adaptive and iterative development. We illustrate our considerations by introducing an example from the problem domain of assembling cell phones by a sociotechnical industrial automation system consisting of autonomous robots and humans. The robots are equipped with sensors and actuators and are capable of reasoning and interactions.

We describe the requirements for the sociotechnical system in the form of a goal model. Figure 20.6 shows that for achieving the purpose of the system – Assembling cell phone – several subgoals need to be achieved. Just one agent – an agent playing the Manager role – is aware of the system purpose: Assemble cell phone. For achieving the subgoals, agents playing the six other roles depicted in Fig. 20.6

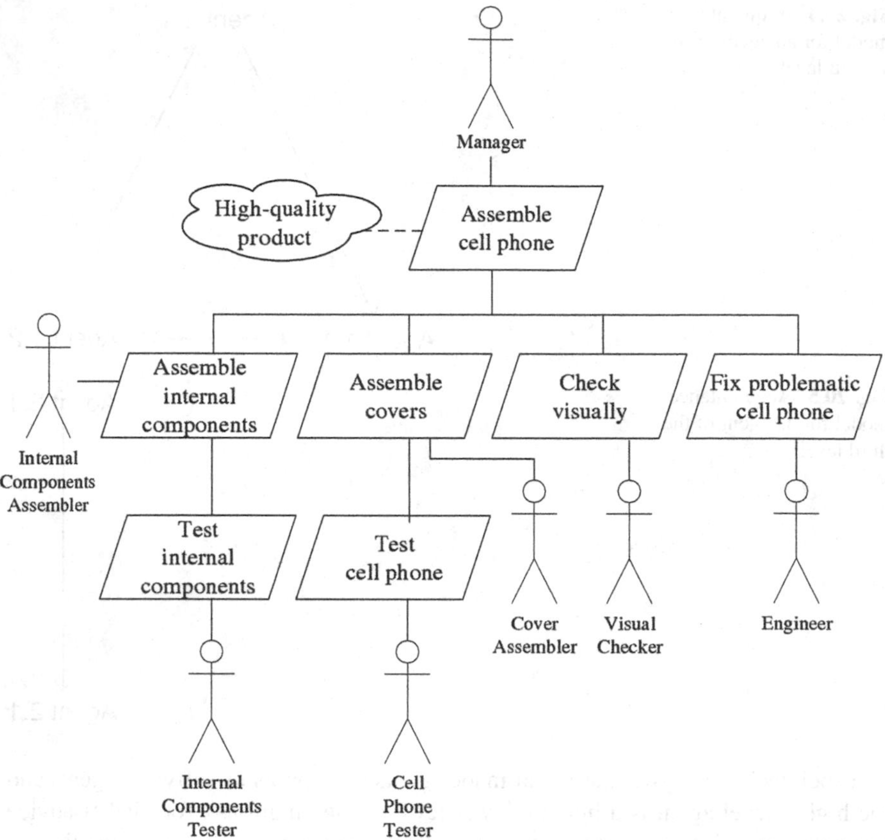

Fig. 20.6 Goal model of assembling cell phones

are required. First, an agent playing the Internal Components Assembler role puts together internal components of a cell phone. After that it passes the intermediate product to an Internal Components Tester. If the intermediate product does not pass the tests, an Engineer will fix it and return the product to an Internal Components Tester for an additional iteration of the same tests. After the tests have been passed, an Internal Components Tester sends the intermediate product to a Cover Assembler who equips the cell phone with display and covers. Thereafter it passes the final product to a Cell Phone Tester for ultimate testing. As previously, if a cell phone does not pass the tests, an Engineer will identify and fix the problem. If a cell phone has passed all the tests, it will be forwarded to a Visual Checker for final visual checking. Most of the roles explained can be performed by either human or man-made agents, such as industrial robots. Please note also that goal models, such as the one represented in Fig. 20.6, do not prescribe any temporary sequence of achieving subgoals.

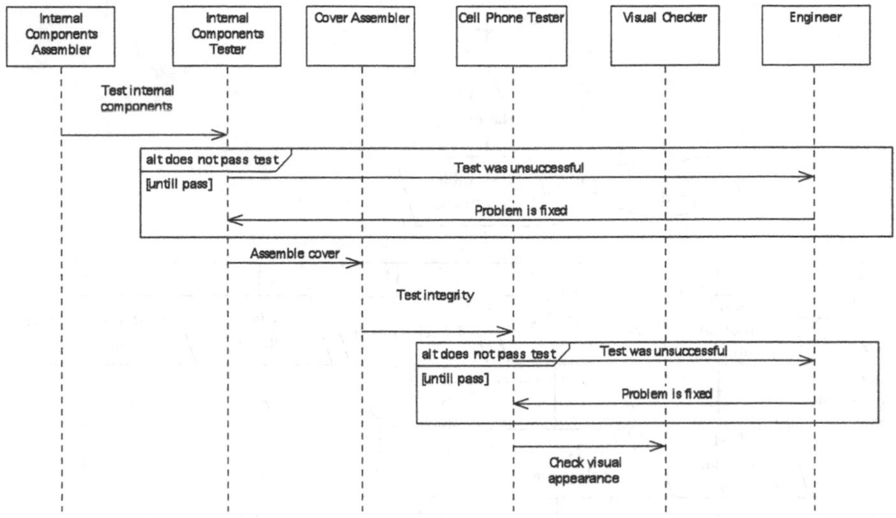

Fig. 20.7 Interaction protocol of assembling cell phones

Temporary sequence is present in *design models*, such as the interaction protocol represented in Fig. 20.7. Another difference between analysis and design models is that design models represent interactions, behaviours, and knowledge of *agents* of specific types playing the roles of the system. The interaction diagram depicted in Fig. 20.7 represents that the production process begins with placing internal components of a cell phone onto the printed circuit board. This task is performed by a robot playing the role Internal Components Assembler. After the internal components have been placed onto the circuit board, a human agent playing the role Internal Components Tester tests the internal components. If the internal components pass the tests, the Internal Components Tester will pass the circuit board to the robot performing the role Cover Assembler. If the internal components fail one or more tests, the Internal Components Tester will pass the circuit board to a human agent playing the role Engineer. In Fig. 20.7 this case is represented by the first alternative box "does not pass test". The box includes the condition which models that the Internal Components Tester keeps sending the circuit board to the Engineer until the circuit board passes the tests. Thereafter the circuit board is forwarded to the robot playing the role Cover Assembler. The robot shields the circuit board and all the other components according to the model specification by the front and back cover and passes the resulting cell phone to the human agent playing the role Cell Phone Tester. The integrity of the cell phone as a whole is tested next. If everything is working properly, the cell phone will be sent to another human agent playing the role Visual Checker who makes sure that the appearance of a cell phone has not been damaged during the assembling process. In case the Cover Assembler has failed to produce a high-quality cell phone and the Cell Phone Tester discovers a problem with it, the newly assembled cell phone will be sent to the Engineer. The Engineer

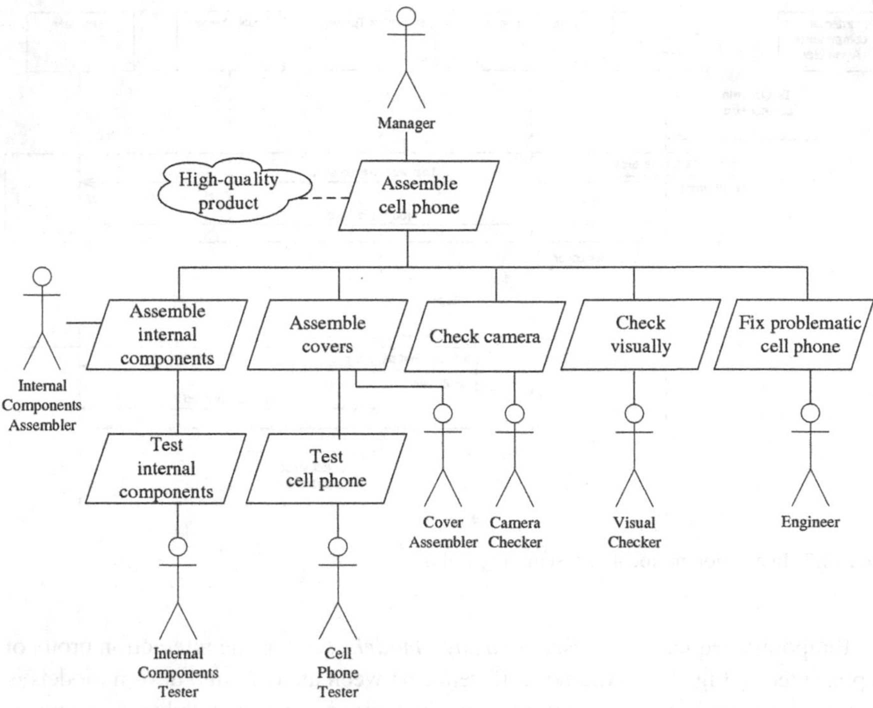

Fig. 20.8 Goal model of assembling cell phones with cameras

finds and fixes the problem and returns the phone to the Cell Phone Tester. This process continues until the cell phone passes the tests, after which it is again sent to the Visual Checker.

Let us now suppose that the cell phone industry has new requirements for new cell phones with cameras. A sociotechnical system has to be as flexible as possible to adjust to new processes and incorporate new goals and roles if needed. The production process of cell phones with cameras needs more attention as compared to the production process of "ordinary" cell phones. In the new requirements described as a goal model in Fig. 20.8, this is reflected by the new goal of checking a camera and the new Camera Checker role attached to it. As a result of this change in the requirements, an agent playing the Camera Checker role joins the sociotechnical system. After this, the sociotechnical system continues to function as the production line described in the previous paragraph. The only difference is that an agent playing the Camera Checker role checks cameras before the ultimate visual checking activity is performed. If this new agent can inform the other agents of the system about its capabilities, the interactions, behaviours, and knowledge of just the *affected agents* in the supply chain will change accordingly. There is no need for all the agents of the system to become aware of a new agent playing the Visual Checker role. The whole system functions perfectly well when the new agent knows what to do and who to interact with and only some agents are aware of the new agent. In a

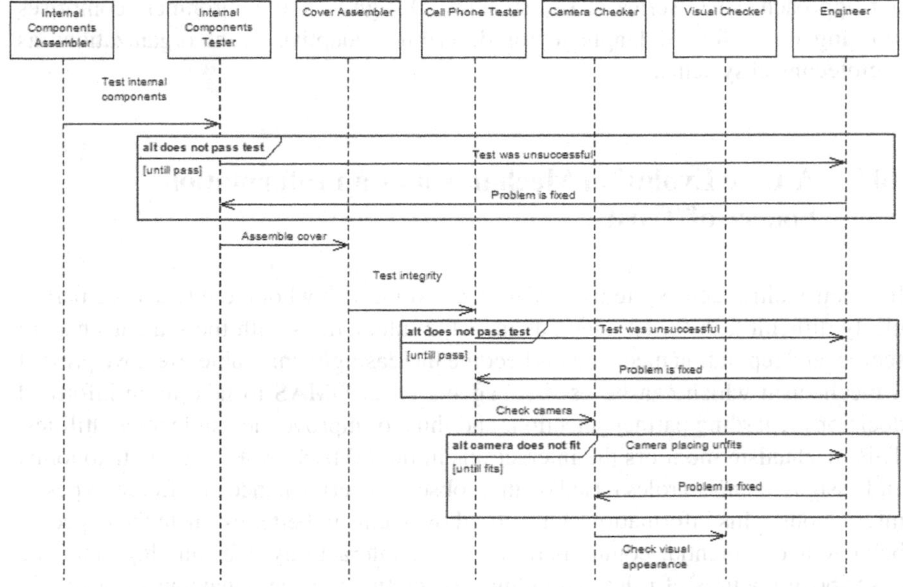

Fig. 20.9 Interaction protocol of assembling cell phones with cameras

similar way, all agents do not have to be aware of the overall goal of the system. For example, a Visual Checker does not have to know that the purpose of the system is to assemble cell phones. The system operates very well when a Visual Checker only knows how to control cameras and who to interact with.

Figure 20.9 depicts the interaction model of assembling cell phones with cameras. In comparison with the interaction diagram represented in Fig. 20.7, it includes another alternative box entitled "camera does not fit". The box models that if the camera is improperly placed or contains dust, a human agent playing the role Camera Checker will send it to the Engineer. This alternative process is repeated until the Engineer has fixed all the problems with the camera that have been detected.

Bottom-up iterative design organized in the way described in this section results in *evolutionary* sociotechnical systems. In such systems, all the agents do not have to know what each of them knows. A sociotechnical system functions properly when each agent is aware of its own objectives as a minimum and about the means of achieving them.

In contemporary complex sociotechnical systems it is not feasible to possess all the information about the environment and to keep this information continuously updated. To reflect this, we proposed in Sects. 20.5 and 20.6 of this Chapter an iterative bottom-up development approach of sociotechnical systems. Such iterative development is flexible and adaptive. Therefore it is easy to adapt to a rapidly changing environment. In the near future, we plan to complement goal models by role and domain models, and interaction models by agent behaviour and knowledge models and to design and implement an environment that would enable to try our approach out in series of experiments. Designing the environment comprises working out a formal language for describing adaptive agent organizations as sociotechnical systems.

20.7 A Role Evolution Mechanism as an Information Source of Trust

In Open Multi-Agent Systems (OMAS), deciding with whom to interact is a particularly difficult task for an agent, as repeated interactions with the same agents are scarce, and reputation mechanisms become increasingly unreliable. Here we present a mechanism which can be used by agents in an OMAS to take more informed decisions regarding partner selection, and thus to improve their individual utilities. This mechanism monitors the interactions in the OMAS, evolves a role taxonomy, and assigns agents to roles based on their observed performance in different types of interactions. This information can be used by agents to better estimate the expected behaviour of potential counterparts in future interactions. We thus highlight the descriptive features of roles, providing expectations of the behaviour of agents in certain types of interactions, rather than their normative facets.

In decision making (DM) processes for selecting partners agents may make their choice supported on three different types of information, namely: (i) past own experience; (ii) opinions from neighbours (reputation); and (iii) other "organisational" information sources. The first two types have already been widely studied in many works (Huynh et al. 2004; Teacy et al. 2006). Some other works (Hermoso et al. 2007) have studied how organisational information influences agents' selections, especially when no direct experiences – or not reliable enough – have been collected before.

We deal here with this third type of information aforementioned, namely how agents can use organisational structures to better determine "good" partners to interact with, especially if no valuable direct experiences are available to reason about. We show that agents cannot only exploit existing organisational structures, in particular, role taxonomies, to determine trustworthy candidates to interact with, but we also put forward a mechanism that makes use of the information managed by the agents' trust models so as to create and evolve role taxonomies. We claim that this taxonomy evolution provides agents with more precise information, helping them to make better decisions such as to decide which other agents to interact with. Thus, in Centeno et al. (2010) it is proposed an adaptive mechanism that evolves role taxonomies by using a multidimensional clustering algorithm to capture behavioural patterns among agents.

Organisational Structures for Agents DM. The environment we use to describe the mechanism presented in this work is based on Task-oriented Multi-Agent Systems (T-MAS) which can be specified as follows:

Definition 20.1. A *T-MAS* is a tuple TM=$\langle \mathscr{A}_g, \mathscr{X}, \mathscr{T}, \mathscr{U} \rangle$, where:

- $\mathscr{A}_g$ is a set of agents participating in the MAS; we assume each agent $a \in \mathscr{A}_g$ has an utility function $\mathscr{U}_a : \mathscr{A}g \times \mathscr{T} \rightarrow R$, where $\mathscr{A}g$ is the delegated agent that performs the task $\mathscr{T}$;
- $\mathscr{X}$ is the environmental state space;
- $\mathscr{T}$ is a set of tasks that can be performed by agents;
- $\mathscr{U} : \mathscr{X} \rightarrow R$ is the system utility function;

The functioning of a T-MAS is as follows (at each time step): (i) a task is assigned to each agent $a_1 \in \mathscr{A}_g$; (ii) if an agent a_1 cannot perform the task by itself it reassigns (delegates) the tasks to another agent $a_2 \in \mathscr{A}_g$; and (iii) agents a_2 performs the task and a_1 obtains a utility from the performance. Furthermore, we assume that the utility obtained by an agent at a certain time step is equivalent to the agent's perception on the fulfilment of the delegated task to another agent. Note that this definition of individual utility allows for *subjective* utility functions. In this sense, $\mathscr{U}_a(b,t)$ represents the subjective perception of agent a on how well agent b performs task t. Notice that an agent may delegate a task to itself if considers that it is the more qualified agent to carry it out.

Organisational Information. The mechanism presented in Centeno et al. (2010) is based on the use of the concepts *role* and *role specialisation taxonomy*. We conceive roles from the point of view of an observer, i.e. as a set of *expectations* regarding the behaviour of agents performing certain actions. This means that a role generates by itself some public expectations over certain actions that agents playing it should accomplish.

A *role* in a T-MAS is a pair $\langle r, \mathscr{E} \rangle$ so that the agents playing the role r are qualified to perform the tasks in the set $\mathscr{E}$ in the sense that they are "skillful" for those tasks.

A role specialisation taxonomy structures the roles by establishing a specialisation relation $\triangleright_r$ based on the skills of the agents playing those roles; that is, given two different roles $r_1, r_2 \in R$ then $r_1 \triangleright_r r_2$ iff. there is a subset of tasks from r_2 on which agents playing role r_1 perform better, on average, than agents playing role r_2. The hierarchy contains a top role – the root of the taxonomy $\langle r_{root}, \mathscr{E}_{root} \rangle$ – which contains all tasks and is not a specialisation of any other role. This is consistent with the assumption that every agent can perform every task. We can assume that every agent in a T-MAS plays at least the top role.

A Trust Model for Agent's DM. A trust model is usually used to endow agents with an internal representation of information about others in order to better choose partners to interact with in any DM process. In the context of a T-MAS, we use the notion of trust model as a mechanism that drives the agent to choose the most trustworthy agent to which it can delegate a given task. Trust models aim to calculate expectations on other agents on particular situations, by either using past information gathered over time – based on past interactions – or inferring using opinions from third party using their own previous assessments.

The main contribution of the work is twofold: (i) building role taxonomies containing on the expectations that the agents participating in the T-MAS are currently calculating during their execution in the T-MAS; and, (ii) agents may make use of the created role taxonomies in order to tune up their own expectations on different situations. These two processes are executed in parallel and continuously repeat during the T-MAS lifetime.

Next, the algorithm describes how an agent a uses the information provided by a role specialisation taxonomy $\mathscr{RT}$ together with its own experience about previously delegated tasks in order to select an appropriate agent to which it can delegate a given task t.

1. $r = mostSpecializedRolesForTask(t)$
2. $\mathscr{A}_x = agentsPlayingRoles(r)$
3. $bestAgent = localTrustEvaluation(\mathscr{A}_x, r, t)$
4. $delegate(t, bestAgent)$

For the calculation of trust values $t_{a \rightarrow \langle a_i, r_k \rangle} \in [0..1]$, we assume that agents store their past experiences in their internal structure in form of confidence values $c_{a \rightarrow \langle a_i, r_k \rangle}$, denoting the recompiled confidence an agent a has in agent a_i playing role r_k.

Evolution of Role Taxonomies. Creation of new roles is be based on trust that other agents have on a specific role – that is similar to say "on the agents playing that role in the system". Trust is a subjective measure, since not all agents have to either share the same preferences in the system or use the same trust model. The mechanism defined in Centeno et al. (2010) tries to build a source of information – role taxonomy – from subjective individual assessments of trust.

This mechanism employs clustering methods to capture behavioural patterns of agents performing tasks. The idea is to identify groups of agents that perform a set of tasks better than others and to reflect such cases in form of a new role. In order to do this it is assumed that agents store confidence values $c_{a \rightarrow \langle a_i, t \rangle}$, representing agent a's recompiled experience on how well agent a_i performs a task t (from its particular point of view). The confidence values stored by agents provide a means to represent agents as a point in the n-dimensional vector space formed by all possible tasks $t \in \mathscr{T}$ in the T-MAS where n is the number of tasks in $\mathscr{T}$. In particular, each agent a_i can be represented as a tuple $\widehat{a} = (c_1, c_2, \ldots, c_n)$ where c_k is defined as follows:

$$c_k = \frac{\sum\limits_{a \in \mathscr{A}_g} c_{a \rightarrow \langle a_i, t_k \rangle}}{|\mathscr{A}_g|}$$

The set of vector representations of agents – e.g., the trust space formed by agents – is denoted by $TS = \{\widehat{a} = (c_1, c_2, \ldots, c_n) | a \in \mathscr{A}_g\}$. In a similar way, given a role $r_k \in \mathscr{R}$, a trust space for the agents that have ever played that role is defined as: $TS_{r_k} = \{\widehat{a} = (c_1, c_2, \ldots, c_n) | a \in \mathscr{A}_g \, and \, a \, enacts \, r_k\}$.

Trust-based Multidimensional K-Means. To specialize roles – create new roles in the role taxonomy – the *K-means* clustering algorithm can be applied, where k represents the number of clusters to be created in each execution. Let TM be a T-MAS with a set of roles R and a role specialisation taxonomy $\mathscr{RT} = (R, \triangleright_r)$. In order to evolve the role taxonomy, the clustering algorithm is applied to each set TS_{r_j} with $r_j \in R$ and r_j being a leaf in the taxonomy $\mathscr{RT}$. On each execution, the algorithm returns a set of k clusters. A cluster centroid represents the expected behaviour of all the agents belonging to it and the whole cluster represents a pattern of behaviour for all the agents included.

The possible clusters returned by the algorithm are candidates for the creation of new roles. We process the clusters and only convert it into a new role r_x if the agents enacting r_x provide a better performance (on average) on at least one of the tasks of the role it extends. Furthermore, when deciding whether a cluster should form a new role or not, the mechanism applies two additional criteria: (a) we do not create roles with "bad" behaviours. We apply a threshold θ such that a new role is only created if the tasks it specializes have at least an expected value of θ; (b) in most of the cases we would want to create new roles if, in fact, they may have a "long" life. That is, most of the times there is no much sense on creating roles when only an agent may play it. Would make sense to create role *Surgeon* if only one agent in the world could play it? For that reason, we include another threshold, called Υ that determines the minimum number of agents that a cluster must include to have the possibility of converting the cluster into a new role.

20.8 Group-Oriented Coordination

Adaptive Agent Organisation can focus on different perspectives: the macro-level for analysing and coordinating the overall performance of an IT-ecosystem, and the micro-view for observing and manipulating the autonomous agents and an interaction layer for interlinking both. Taking global and individual objectives into account, the metaphor of groups can combine them to improve their utilities and benefits. Cooperation and coordination mechanisms need to find an equilibrium for global and individual objectives. We apply the group-oriented coordination on a simple example allowing agents to form faster and slower groups, described more in detail in Görmer and Müller (2012). As previously explained in Sect. 17.5, *Grouping* allows an agent to extend its range of perception (RoP) by exchanging information with other members. Agents are coordinated at group level. Group-oriented coordination allows agents e.g. to form faster and slower agent groups. Each group has an agent group leader. In case fast groups are blocked by other slow groups, the group leaders will communicate with each other to arrange plans for each group (called group plans). The group plans are known to all group members. Acting based on group plans, quick agents can avoid being blocked by other slow agents and vice versa. Informally, the three main elements of group-oriented coordination can be described as follows:

1. **Decentralised dynamic agent grouping**: Agents autonomously form groups desiring the same goal. An agent group contains a group leader and members. The group leader is responsible for the coordination of the group's members to avoid detected *conflict situations* with other groups or agents. Since agent organisations usually are situated in dynamic environments, agent groups are dynamically created and maintained. This means, the number of agent groups and the number of members of a group change constantly over time.
2. **Conflict detection and global coordination**: The second element of group-oriented cooperation is to coordinate members in case of conflict between agent groups. A conflict situation can be detected by group leader or members. Each agent of a group will scan in its range of perception (RoP) for other groups, which potentially will block its group (conflict group detection). Once a conflict situation between two or more groups is detected, it will be communicated to group leaders. A group leader coordinates its members by defining an appropriate group plan. The choice of group plans is a negotiating process between leaders of groups, which are in conflict situation. The group plans have a warranty that members are not blocked by members of other groups. Communication limitations only allow an agent to communicate with other agents when they are in a fixed RoP. This means, a leader cannot exchange message with another leader of a conflict group if the two are out of communication range. However, we assume that members of an agent group can forward messages of their leaders to receivers in a multihop fashion.
3. **Coordination strategy of an individual agent**: At this step agents decide their plan of actions for the next time period. Reaching and maintaining desired goal is the original goal of each agent. An agent chooses its plans, which allows it to reach its goal as soon as possible. However a member agent should (sometimes) obey the coordination of its group leader to avoid conflict situations. Thus, an agent should always decide whether to choose its own plan based on the coordination of leader or to choose it based on its local goal.

20.9 Organisational Perspective of a Task Assignment Model for Cooperative MAS

The problem of coordination of multiple mobile agents which collaborate to achieve a common goal in an environment with variable communication constraints arises in numerous man-made systems. In order to analyze such systems, the design of coordination and agreement strategies and mechanisms with specific inter-agent information exchange principles, and limited communication, together with their influence to the emergent behaviour of the system must be addressed.

In Giordani et al. (2010) we address a cooperative control problem in which a team of mobile agents under different inter-agent communication conditions has to accomplish certain mission. Generating the individual agent trajectories and associated actions that accomplish this objective can be viewed as the dynamic assignment of each agent to certain subset of spatially distributed tasks in some chronological order.

To efficiently assign agents to tasks, we are interested in finding a maximum matching (i.e., a one-to-one assignment of agents to tasks) which minimizes some multi-agent system's (MAS) collective cost function. The value of the latter is assumed to be the sum of the individual costs associated with each agent-task pair matching in each assignment run, depending on some factor (e.g., time, energy, etc.) that it takes every agent to travel to and complete its assigned task. This kind of problem is equivalent to the minimum weight maximum matching problem in a bipartite graph or assignment problem in the operational research field; the latter can be written as an integer linear program and optimal solutions can be computed in polynomial time. Many centralized algorithms of polynomial complexity exist to solve it, e.g., primal simplex methods, Hungarian, dual simplex (see, e.g., Nash and Sofer 1996) and relaxation methods (see, e.g., Hung and Rom 1980).

However, in the case of decentralized cooperative MAS where there is no centralized decision-maker and each agent keeps potentially different local information, the centralized algorithms for task assignment are inadequate. Since, generally, agents are placed on different positions and possibly with different utility functions, the benefit and the costs of getting assigned to a particular task will be different. Assuming that agents are capable of communication, and that each agent may have information that is local and not known globally throughout the team, agents will have to exchange relevant information and negotiate in order to find the sufficiently good assignment for all. Such MAS scenarios require decentralized coordination mechanisms and rules which will assign tasks to appropriate agents in order to obtain a mutually acceptable and efficient outcome. In Giordani et al. (2010), a distributed coordination model for task assignment is proposed, which is based on two coordination mechanisms which are complementing one another based on the shape of the communication graph among agents: a distributed version of the Hungarian method (Giordani et al. 2010) which calculates an optimal solution to the task assignment problem, and the dynamic iterative auction (Lujak and Giordani 2011) inspired by Bertseka's auction algorithm. Agents select the task assignment mechanism based on the connectivity of their communication graph, and when selected, the mechanism defines a set of roles and the strategies for these roles that by mutual interaction find the multiple task assignment that maximizes the global system's utility. It is clear that the shape of the communication graph is directly influenced by the choice of the agents' transmitting range, i.e., the larger the range, the less likely it is that the communication network becomes disconnected.

The proposed task-assignment model integrates two mechanisms for efficient task assignment: distributed algorithm based on the Hungarian method (Giordani et al. 2010) in the case of complete communication graph and the distributed iterative auction algorithm (Lujak and Giordani 2011) inspired by Bertsekas auction algorithm (Bertsekas 1988) in the case of a disconnected communication graph among agents. They are integrated in this way because the former is less computationally expensive and together with the latter, it gives the optimal assignment solution in the case of completely connected communication network. The latter can function also in the case of disconnected communication network, resulting in the sub-optimal result where the performance is bounded in the worst case (Giordani et al. 2010; Lujak and Giordani 2011).

These two coordination mechanisms promote desirable social behaviour in terms of efficient optimal or close to optimal task assignment solutions for collaborative organisation-based multi-agent systems (MAS) with variable inter-agent communication range. These two mechanisms complement each other depending on the momentary communication range among agents.

The result is a joint plan that is optimal, or sub-optimal regarding the global utility of a MAS. The mechanisms are stable, informational decentralized and efficient in respect to the information exchange in the sense that agents communicate small amounts of relevant information in each round of the performance instead of completely specifying their preferences over the entire space of future actions and possible events. The distributed Hungarian method is much less computationally expensive than the auction algorithm which, in contrary can be used also when the communication graph among agents is not fully connected. The lack of information in unconnected communication graph results in an inferior but still acceptable assignment result. We applied the model in the organisation-based ambulance management of patient emergencies. In this scenario, ambulances act as a team that has the objective to reach each appearing emergency patient in the shortest time possible. Obviously, patients might appear in different times and places. Then, the task of the ambulance team is to organize its operation by reaching an agreement on ambulance-patient assignment. In the scope of our model, patients are seen as tasks. We assume a decentralized scenario since ambulances are intrinsically decentralized resources, i.e., each ambulance crew can control only its local behaviour and can only exchange information by communication with other agents in the emergency management system. It is assumed that each ambulance agent has an information regarding its position and can receive the information regarding the position of all patients in the environment through the coordinates on a map of the environment. If the number of patients is small, a patient assignment problem can be solved by a centralized emergency manager. If the latter is missing, then the ambulance agents, by mutual communication and information exchange, find an optimal assignment solution through the distributed Hungarian method algorithm. When the connectivity of the communication graph is not complete, the agents can follow the dynamic iterative auction algorithm with mobility to get assigned and manage the emergency patient cases in a decentralized manner. More details of the application of distributed task-assignment model presented here can be found in the Part on Applications of Agreement Technologies in this book.

20.10 Conclusions

Organisations represent an effective mechanism for activity coordination, not only for humans but also for agents. Nowadays, the organisation concept has become a relevant issue in the multi-agent system area, as it enables the analysis and design of coordination and collaboration mechanisms in an easier way, especially for open systems.

In this chapter, we have presented different approaches for adaptive agent organisations, including methods for designing and/or implementing these kinds of systems. In all these sections we have emphasized the proposals developed within the COST action IC0801.

References

Aldewereld, H., L. Penserini, F. Dignum, and V. Dignum. 2008. Regulating organizations: The ALIVE approach. In *Proceedings of ReMoD*, Montpellier.

Aldrich, H. 1999. *Organizations evolving*. London: Sage.

Aldrich, H. 2007. *Organizations and environments*. Stanford: Stanford Business Books.

Allert, H., and C. Richter. 2008. Practices, systems, and context working as core concepts in modeling socio-technical systems. In *Proceedings of the fifth international workshop on philosophy and informatics, WSPI 2008*, Kaiserslautern.

Andersson, J., R. de Lemos, S. Malek, and D. Weyns. 2009. Modeling dimensions of self-adaptive software systems. In *Software engineering for self-adaptive systems*, Lecture Notes in Computer Science, vol. 5525, 27–47. Heidelberg: Springer.

Argente, E., V.J. Botti, C. Carrascosa, A. Giret, V. Julián, and M. Rebollo. 2011. An abstract architecture for virtual organizations: The THOMAS approach. *Knowledge and Information Systems* 29(2): 379–403.

Asimov, I. 1950. *I, Robot*. New York: Gnome Press.

Barnett, W., and G. Carroll. 1995. Modeling internal organizational change. *Annual Review of Sociology* 21: 217–236.

Bernon, C., M.P. Gleizes, S. Peyruqueou, and G. Picard. 2002. ADELFE, a methodology for adaptive multi-agent systems engineering. In *ESAW'02*, Madrid.

Bertsekas, D. 1988. The auction algorithm: A distributed relaxation method for the assignment problem. *Annals of Operations Research* 14: 105–123.

Centeno, R., R. Hermoso, V.T. da Silva. 2010. Role evolution in open multi-agent systems as an information source for trust. In *Proceedings of the 9th international conference on autonomous agents and multiagent systems (AAMAS 2010)*. Toronto: ACM.

Cuesta, C.E., J.S. Pérez-Sotelo, and S. Ossowski. 2011. Self-organising adaptive structures: The Shifter experience. *ERCIM News* 85: 35–36.

DeLoach, S., W. Oyenan, and E. Matson. 2008. A capabilities-based theory of artificial organizations. *Journal of Autonomous Agents and Multiagent Systems* 16: 13–56.

Dignum, V. 2003. A model for organizational interaction: Based on agents, founded in logic. Ph.D. thesis, Utrecht University.

Dignum, V. 2009. *Handbook of research on multi-agent systems: Semantics and dynamics of organizational models*. Hershey: Information Science Reference.

Dignum, V., and F. Dignum. 2006. Towards formal semantics for reorganization. Technical report, UU-CS.

Dignum, V., and F. Dignum. 2007. A logic for agent organizations. In *Proceedings of the 3rd workshop on formal approaches to multi-agent systems (FAMAS)*. Logic Jnl IGPL, vol. 20(1), 283–316. Durham: Oxford University Press.

Dignum, V., F. Dignum, V. Furtado, A. Melo, and L. Sonenberg. 2005. Towards a simulation tool for evaluating dynamic reorganization of agents societies. In *Proceedings of socially inspired computing*, AISB Convention, vol. 230. Hatfield.

Esparcia, S., and E. Argente. 2012. Forces that drive organizational change in an adaptive virtual organization. In *Proceedings of CISIS-2012 conference*, Palermo.

Galloway, A. 2004. *Protocol: How control exists after decentralization*. Cambridge: MIT.

Gamma, E., R. Helm, R. Johnson, and J. Vlissides. 1994. *Design patterns: Elements of reusable object-oriented software*. Reading: Addison-Wesley.

Gardelli, L., M. Viroli, M. Casadei, and A. Omicini. 2008. Designing self-organising environments with agents and artefacts: A simulation-driven approach. *International Journal of Agent-Oriented Software Engineering* 2(2): 171–195.

Gazendam, H., and J. Simons. 1998. An analysis of the concept of equilibrium in organization theory. In *Proceedings of the computational and mathematical organization theory workshop*. Montreal.

Giordani, S., M. Lujak, and F. Martinelli. 2010. A distributed algorithm for the multi-robot task allocation problem. In *Trends in applied intelligent systems: Proceedings of the 23rd international conference on industrial engineering and other applications of applied intelligent systems*, Lecture notes in artificial intelligence, 721–730. Berlin/Heidelberg: Springer.

Görmer, J., and J.P. Müller. 2012. Multiagent system architecture and method for group-oriented traffic coordination. In *Proceedings of IEEE DEST 2012*. Washington, DC: IEEE, Campione.

Haesevoets, R., D. Weyns, T. Holvoet, and W. Joosen. 2009. *A formal model for self-adaptive and self-healing organizations*. Software Engineering for Adaptive and Self-Managing Systems. In *ICSE Workshop on SEAMS'09*, 116–125. Vancouver.

Hermoso, R., H. Billhardt, R. Centeno, and S. Ossowski. 2007. Effective use of organisational abstractions for confidence models. In *ESAW*, Lecture Notes in Artificial Intelligence, vol. 4457, 368–383. Berlin/Heidelberg: Springer.

Hoogendoorn, M., C.M. Jonker, M.C. Schut, and J. Treur. 2007. Modeling centralized organization of organizational change. *Computational and Mathematical Organization Theory* 13(2): 147–184.

Hubner, J., J. Sichman, and O. Boissier. 2004. Using the moise+ for a cooperative framework of MAS reorganisation. In *Advances in artificial intelligence–SBIA 2004*, LNAI, vol. 3171, 506–515. Berlin/New York: Springer

Hung, M., and W. Rom. 1980. Solving the assignment problem by relaxation. *Operations Research* 28: 969–982.

Huynh, T.D., N.R. Jennings, and N.R. Shadbolt. 2004. Fire: An integrated trust and reputation model for open multi-agent systems. In *Proceedings of the 16th european conference on artificial intelligence (ECAI)*, Valencia.

Kota, R., N. Gibbins, and N.R. Jennings. 2009. Self-organising agent organisations. In *Proceedings of The 8th international conference on autonomous agents and multiagent systems*, vol. 2, 797–804. International Foundation for Autonomous Agents and Multiagent Systems. Budapest.

Kramer, J., and J. Magee. 2007. Self-managed systems: An architectural challenge. In *Future of software engineering (FOSE@ ICSE2007)*, 259–268. IEEE, Los Alamitos: Mineapolis.

Luhmann, N. 1995. *Social systems*. Stanford: Stanford University Press.

Lujak, M., and S. Giordani. 2011. On the communication range in auction-based multi-agent target assignment. In *IWSOS11: Proceedings of the 5th international conference on self-organizing systems*, Lecture Notes in Computer Science, vol. 6557, 32–43. Berlin/Heidelberg: Springer.

McShane, S., T. Travaglione, M. Bazley, P. Hancock, C. Hill, J. Berk, P. DeMarzo, R. Stone, N. Tichy, and W. Bennis, et al. *Organisational behaviour on the pacific rim+ E book*, Prentice hall international series in industrial and systems engineering. Nedlands.

Nash, S., and A. Sofer. 1996. *Linear and nonlinear programming*, vol. 692. New York: McGraw-Hill.

OSGi Alliance. OSGi service platform service compendium. Technical report, Release 4, Version 4.2. http://www.osgi.org/. Accessed August 2010.

OVAMAH: Ovamah – organizaciones virtuales adaptativas: Técnicas y mecanismos de descripción y adaptación. http://ovamah.gti-ia.dsic.upv.es/. Accessed 2010.

Pérez-Sotelo, J.S., C.E. Cuesta, and S. Ossowski. 2009. The agreement as an adaptive architecture for open multi-agent systems. In *II taller de sistemas autonomos y adaptativos (WASELF 2009)*, vol. 3, 62–76. San Sebastian: SISTEDES.

Picard, G., J.F. Hubner, O. Boissier, and M.P. Gleizes. 2009. Reorganisation and self-organisation in multi-agent systems. In *1st international workshop on organizational modeling*, 66. Paris.

Popper, K. 1964. *The poverty of historicism*. New York: Harper and Row.

Prigogine, I. 1997. *The end of certainty. Time, chaos and the new laws of nature*. New York: Free Press.

Prokopenko, M., F. Boschetti, and A. Ryan. 2008. An information-theoretic primer on complexity, self-organization, and emergence. *Complexity* 15: 11–28.

Ramirez, A.J., and B. Cheng. 2010. Design patterns for developing dynamically adaptive systems. In: *ICSE2010-SEAMS*, Cape Town, 49–58.

Robertson, R. 1992. *Globalization: Social theory and global culture*, vol. 16. London: Sage.

Sterling, L., and K. Taveter. 2009. *The art of agent-oriented modeling*. Cambridge/London: MIT.

Teacy, W.L., J. Patel, N.R. Jennings, and M. Luck. 2006. Travos: Trust and reputation in the context of inaccurate information sources. *Autonomous Agents and Multi-Agent Systems* 12(2): 183–198.

Part V
Argumentation and Negotiation

Argumentation, initially studied in philosophy and law, has been researched extensively in computing in the last decade, especially for inference, decision making and decision support, dialogue, and negotiation. Simply stated, argumentation focuses on interactions where parties plead for and against some conclusion. It provides a powerful mechanism for dealing with incomplete, possibly inconsistent information. It is also fundamental for the resolution of conflicts and differences of opinion amongst different parties. Further, it is useful for explaining outcomes generated automatically. As a consequence, argumentation is a useful mechanism to reach agreement.

Agreement also benefits from negotiation, especially when autonomous agents have conflicting interests/desires but may benefit from cooperation in order to achieve them. In particular, this cooperation may amount to a change of goals (e.g. as in conflict-resolution) and/or to the introduction of new goals (e.g. for an agent to provide a certain resource to another, even though it may not have originally planned to do so). Typically negotiation involves (fair) compromise.

In this part, we provide an overview of some of the contributions in the literature incorporating argumentation to add value to applications and methods. We also briefly review key concepts of multi-attribute negotiation and an approach to complex negotiations in situations where unanimous agreement is not possible or simply not desired, in negotiations involving complex, non-monotonic utility spaces.

Francesca Toni and Sanjay Modgil
Editors Part "Argumentation and Negotiation"

Chapter 21
The Added Value of Argumentation

Sanjay Modgil, Francesca Toni, Floris Bex, Ivan Bratko, Carlos I. Chesñevar, Wolfgang Dvořák, Marcelo A. Falappa, Xiuyi Fan, Sarah Alice Gaggl, Alejandro J. García, María P. González, Thomas F. Gordon, João Leite, Martin Možina, Chris Reed, Guillermo R. Simari, Stefan Szeider, Paolo Torroni, and Stefan Woltran

21.1 Introduction

21.1.1 An Overview of Argumentation

The theory of argumentation is a rich, interdisciplinary area of research straddling philosophy, communication studies, linguistics, psychology and artificial intelligence. Traditionally, the focus has been on 'informal' studies of argumentation and its role in natural human reasoning and dialogue. More recently, formal logical accounts of argumentation have come to be increasingly central as a core

S. Modgil (✉)
Kings' College London, London, UK
e-mail: sanjay.modgil@kcl.ac.uk

F. Toni • X. Fan
Imperial College London, London, UK
e-mail: ft@imperial.ac.uk; x.fan11@imperial.ac.uk

F. Bex • C. Reed
University of Dundee, Dundee, UK
e-mail: florisbex@computing.dundee.ac.uk; chris@computing.dundee.ac.uk

I. Bratko • M. Možina
University of Ljubljana, Ljubljana, Slovenia
e-mail: bratko@fri.uni-lj.si; martin.mozina@fri.uni-lj.si

C.I. Chesñevar • M.A. Falappa • A.J. García • M.P. González • G.R. Simari
Universidad Nacional del Sur, Bahía Blanca, Buenos Aires, Argentina
e-mail: cic@cs.uns.edu.ar; mfalappa@cs.uns.edu.ar; ajg@cs.uns.edu.ar; mpg@cs.uns.edu.ar; grs@cs.uns.edu.ar

W. Dvořák • S.A. Gaggl • S. Szeider • S. Woltran
Vienna University of Technology, Vienna, Austria
e-mail: dvorak@dbai.tuwien.ac.at; gaggl@dbai.tuwien.ac.at; stefan@szeider.net; woltran@dbai.tuwien.ac.at

S. Ossowski (ed.), *Agreement Technologies*, Law, Governance and Technology Series 8, DOI 10.1007/978-94-007-5583-3_21,

study within Artificial Intelligence (Bench-Capon and Dunne 2007), providing a promising paradigm for modelling reasoning in the presence of conflict and uncertainty, and for communication between reasoning entities.[1] In these works, an argument consists of premises and a claim expressed in some logical language $\mathcal{L}$, where the premises support the claim according to some localised notion of proof. For example, the claim that 'Information about Tony should be published' is supported (via application of modus ponens) by the premises: 'Tony has political responsibilities'; 'the information about Tony is in the national interest'; 'if a person has political responsibilities and information about that person is in the national interest then that information should be published'. The arguments thus constructed are then evaluated in the light of their interactions with other arguments. For example, the preceding argument $A1$ is 'attacked' by the argument $A2$ claiming 'Tony does not have political responsibilities', supported by (because) 'Tony resigned from parliament' and 'if a person resigns from parliament then that person no longer has political responsibilities'. $A1$ therefore loses out at the expense of the winning argument $A2$. Consider the following counter-argument to $A2$: $A3$ = 'Tony does have political responsibilities because Tony is now middle east envoy and if a person is a middle east envoy then that person has political responsibilities'. $A3$ attacks $A2$ by contradicting $A2$'s claim, and $A2$ attacks $A1$ by contradicting a premise in $A1$. The winning arguments can then be evaluated. $A1$ is attacked by $A2$, but since $A2$ is itself attacked by $A3$, and the latter is not attacked, we obtain that $A1$ and $A3$ are the winning arguments.

This example illustrates the modular nature of argumentation that most formal theories (models) of argumentation adopt: (1) arguments are constructed in some underlying logic that manipulates statements about the world; (2) interactions between arguments are defined; (3) given the network of interacting arguments, the winning arguments are evaluated. The appeal of the argumentation paradigm resides in this intuitive modular characterisation that is akin to human modes of reasoning. Also, recent work in AI, and the computer science community at

T.F. Gordon
Fraunhofer FOKUS, Berlin, Germany
email: thomas.gordon@fokus.fraunhofer.de

J. Leite
Universidade Nova de Lisboa, Lisbon, Portugal
email: jleite@fct.unl.pt

P. Torroni
University of Bologna, Bologna, Italy
email: p.torroni@unibo.it

[1]As witnessed by the recently inaugurated series of international conferences and workshops (www.comma-conf.org, www.mit.edu/~irahwan/argmas/argmas11, www.csd.abdn.ac.uk/~niroren/TAFA-11) and major European research projects (ARGUGRID: www.argugrid.eu, ASPIC: www.cossac.org/projects/aspic, IMPACT: www.policy-impact.eu)

large, has illustrated the potential for tractable implementations of logical models of argumentation, and the wide range of application of these implementations in software systems. Furthermore, the inherently dialectical nature of argumentation models provide principled ways in which to structure exchange of, and reasoning about, justifications/arguments for proposals and or statements between human and/or automated reasoning entities (agents).

Consider the above example where, instead of a single agent engaging in its own internal argumentation to arrive at a conclusion, we now have two agents, Greg and Alistair, involved in a dialogue. Greg proposes $A1$, Alistair $A2$, and then Greg counters with $A3$. This represents a dialogue where each participant has the goal of persuading the other to adopt a belief through the process of exchanging arguments that must interact and be evaluated according to the underlying model of argumentation.

Of course, dialogues introduce an added dimension, in the sense that realistic dialogues often involve more than simply the exchange of arguments. For example, Alistair might challenge a premise in argument $A1$, by asking why the information about Tony is in the national interest. The burden of proof is on Greg to provide an argument as to why this information is in the national interest. Otherwise, Alistair can be legitimately be said to be 'winning' the argument or dialogue. The formal study of dialogue models therefore accounts for a broader range of statements or 'locutions' than simply those involving submission of arguments, as well as the strategic behaviour of interlocutors.

The construction, evaluation and exchange of arguments and related locutions, has great potential for application in the general area of agreement technologies. Arguably, any non-trivial process resulting in an agreement presupposes some kind of conflict and the need to resolve the conflict. Such conflicts may arise between the positions or preferences held by parties involved in negotiating over some kind of resource, or between the beliefs of parties engaged in debate and dialogue, where the purpose is to arrive at some settled (agreed) view. More generally, conflicts will arise whenever alternative outcomes present themselves, independently of whether the parties involved adhere to them or not, for example when parties deliberate over an appropriate course of action from amongst a number of alternatives. In such cases, the alternatives are simply those that present themselves, independently of whether any given party has a particular interest in pursuing a given alternative.

In these dialogues, the reasons or arguments for offers, stated beliefs, or proposed actions can be usefully used to further the goal of the dialogue. The goal of the dialogue may determine a specific set of statements or allowed locutions, as well as rules for making locutions at any point in the dialogue, and rules for determining the outcome of the dialogue. These rules are encoded in a dialogue's protocol. Consider for example the following negotiation dialogue between a buyer and seller of cars in which locutions also involve making, accepting and rejecting offers:

Seller – Offer: Renault
Buyer – Reject: Renault

Buyer – Argue: Because Renault is a French make of car, and French cars are unsafe
Seller – Argue: Renaults are not unsafe as Renaults have been given the award of safest car in Europe by the European Union
Buyer – Accept: Renault

The above example illustrates the utility of argumentation-based models of reasoning and their application to dialogues. Online negotiations involving automated software agents are a key area of research and development. In a handshaking protocol, a seller would simply successively make offers and have these either rejected or accepted. The exchange of arguments provides for agreements that would not be reached in simple handshaking protocols. In the above example, it is by eliciting the reason for the rejection, and successfully countering this reason, that the seller is then able to convince the buyer to buy the car.

The above introduction to argumentation articulates some general reasons for why argumentation may be of value in agreement technologies. In what follows, we more precisely articulate the added value that argumentation brings, above and beyond existing non-monotonic approaches to reasoning in the presence of uncertainty and conflict more generally.

21.1.2 Bridging Between Machine and Human Reasoning

Many theoretical and practical developments in argumentation build on Dung's seminal abstract theory of argumentation (Dung 1995). A Dung *argumentation framework* (*AF*) consists of a conflict-based binary *attack* relation $\mathscr{C}$ over a set of arguments $\mathscr{A}$. The justified arguments are then evaluated based on subsets of $\mathscr{A}$ that are referred to as *extensions*, and that are defined under a range of semantics. Irrespective of the chosen semantics, the arguments contained in an extension are required to not attack each other (the extensions are *conflict free*), and attack any argument that in turn attacks an argument in the extension (extensions *defend* their contained arguments). Dung's theory has been developed in a number of directions. These include argument game proof theories (Modgil and Caminada 2009) in which an argument X is shown to belong to an extension under a given semantics, if the player moving X can defend against attacking arguments moved by the player's opponent. Also, several works augment *AF*s with preferences or values (Amgoud and Cayrol 2002; Bench-Capon 2003; Prakken 2010), attacks on attacks (Baroni et al. 2011; Modgil 2009), support relations (e.g., Amgoud et al. 2008), collective attacks (e.g., Bochman 2003), those that accommodate numerical information (e.g., Dunne et al. 2011), and other extensions.

The continuing development and widespread application of Dung's work can in part be attributed to its level of abstraction. *AF*s are simply directed graphs that can be instantiated by a wide range of logical formalisms; one is free to choose a logical language $\mathscr{L}$ and define what constitutes an argument and attack between arguments defined by a theory. The theory's inferences can then be defined in terms of the claims of the theory's justified arguments, so that the above mentioned argument games can be seen as providing proof theories for the logical formalism. Furthermore, the inference relations of existing logics (with their own proof theories) can be given an argumentation-based characterisation. Thus, as shown in Bondarenko et al. (1997), Dung (1993), Dung (1995) and Governatori and Maher (2000), the inferences defined by theories in logic programming and non-monotonic logics (e.g. default, auto-epistemic and defeasible logic), can be defined in terms of the claims of the justified arguments of *AF*s instantiated by arguments and attacks defined by theories in these logics. Dung's theory can therefore be understood as a dialectical semantics for these logics, and the argument games can be viewed as alternative dialectical proof theories for these logics.

The fact that reasoning in existing non-monotonic logics can thus be characterised, testifies to the generality of the principle whereby one argument defends another from attack; a principle that is also both intuitive and familiar in human modes of reasoning, debate and dialogue. Indeed, recent, empirically validated work in cognitive science and psychology supports the latter claim, by proposing that the cognitive capacity for human reasoning evolved primarily in order to assess and counter the claims and arguments of interlocutors in social settings (Mercier and Sperber 2011).

Argumentation theory thus provides a *language independent* characterisation of both human and logic-based reasoning in the presence of uncertainty and conflict, through the abstract dialectical modelling of the *process* whereby arguments can be moved to attack and defend other arguments. The theory's value can therefore in large part be attributed to its explanatory potential for making non-monotonic reasoning processes inspectable and readily understandable for human users, and it's underpinning of dialogical and more general communicative interactions involving reasoning in the presence of uncertainty and conflict, where such interactions may be between heterogeneous agents (i.e., machine and human). Thus, through such interactions, the reasoning processes of machines can be augmented by intuitive modular argumentation-based characterisations of human reasoning and interaction, and the reasoning processes of humans can be augmented by intuitive modular argumentation-based characterisations of machine reasoning. Indeed, one might argue that the integration of human and machine reasoning is a key requirement for logic-based reasoning techniques to be usefully deployed in practical applications.

It is this value proposition that will be explored in the remainder of this chapter. In Sect. 21.2 we review some applications and research projects in which human provided arguments, and argumentation-based characterisations of human interactions, are or have been used to inform machine reasoning. In Sect. 21.3 we review some applications and research projects in which formal models of argumentation are or have or been used to inform human reasoning.[2] Section 21.4 then points towards the need for benchmark libraries for evaluating tools developed

[2]Our reviews in these sections are by no means comprehensive; rather, selected examples are chosen to illustrate the salient points.

for processing Dung frameworks: a key requirement if the value proposition of argumentation is to be realised. Section 21.5 finally concludes.[3]

21.2 Argumentation Informing Machine Reasoning

In this section we review some applications and research projects in which human provided arguments, and argumentative characterisations of human interactions are or have been used to inform machine reasoning. Specifically, these applications incorporate forms of argumentation within:

1. Machine learning (in the form of the rule induction CN2 method Clark and Boswell 1991)
2. Dempster-Shafer belief functions (Shafer 1985)

Both approaches use very simple models of argumentation. The first approach uses two types of arguments (attached to examples during the learning phase): positive (to explain/argue why an example is classified as it is) and negative (to explain/argue why an example should not be classified in a certain manner). The second approach uses very simple abstract argumentation frameworks (Dung 1995) with less than ten arguments. Despite the simplicity of the underlying argumentation, both approaches give improved performances. We outline these two approaches below.

21.2.1 Argumentation and Machine Learning

21.2.1.1 Overview of Argumentation Based Machine Learning

Machine learning is concerned with the development of algorithms that enable computer programs to learn and improve from experience (Mitchell 1997). The most common type of machine learning (ML) is learning from labeled examples,

[3] Different parts of this chapter have been written/edited by different authors, as follows:

- this Sect. 21.1 has been written by Sanjay Modgil;
- Section 21.2 has been edited by Francesca Toni, with Sect. 21.2.1 written by Ivan Bratko and Martin Možina and Sect. 21.2.2 written by Francesca Toni;
- Section 21.3 has been edited by Sanjay Modgil, with Sect. 21.3.1.1 written by Sanjay Modgil, Sect. 21.3.1.2 written by Carlos Chesñevar, Sect. 21.3.1.3 written by Francesca Toni, QUI Sect. 21.3.2.1 written by Sanjay Modgil, Sect. 21.3.2.2 written by Thomas Gordon, Sect. 21.3.2.3 written by Francesca Toni, Sect. 21.3.2.4 written by Xiuyi Fan and Francesca Toni, Sect. 21.3.3 written by Floris Bex, Chris Reed and Sanjay Modgil, and Sect. 21.3.4 written by Joao Leite and Paolo Torroni;
- Section 21.4 has been written by Wolfgang Dvořák, Sarah Alice Gaggl, Stefan Szeider and Stefan Woltran;
- Section 21.5 has been written by Sanjay Modgil and Francesca Toni.

called also supervised inductive learning. Each example is described by a set of descriptive attributes (inputs), and a class variable (output). The task is to formulate a hypothesis that can infer outputs of examples given inputs. The hypothesis can be used to predict outcomes of new cases, where the true values are unknown.

Machine learning has been shown to be useful in many areas. One of its possible applications is automatic knowledge acquisition to address the bottleneck in building expert systems (Feigenbaum 2003). While it was shown that it can be successful in building knowledge bases (Langley and Simon 1995), the major problem is that automatically induced models rarely express the knowledge in the way an expert wants. Models that are incomprehensible have less chance to be trusted by experts and other users.

A common view is that a combination of a domain expert and machine learning would be best to address this problem (Webb et al. 1999). Most of the applications in the literature combine machine learning and the experts' knowledge in one of the following ways: (a) experts validate induced models after machine learning was applied, (b) experts provide constraints on induced models in the form of background knowledge, and (c) the system enables iterative improvements of the model, where experts and machine learning algorithm improve the model in turns. The last approach is often the most effective; however, it requires considerable effort on the part of the expert. This calls for a method that allows the expert to express his or her knowledge in a most convenient way and combines this knowledge with knowledge extracted from data. In this contribution we discuss argumentation about specific examples as an effective such method. It is commonly accepted that knowledge elicitation based on argumentation, where experts argue about a specific case instead of being asked to articulate general knowledge, is considerably simpler due to the following:

- When providing their knowledge, domain experts have to focus on a specific problem only and do not need to be concerned whether their provided knowledge given for this problem is generally accepted for all possible problems. Counter-arguments will take care of exceptions.
- Disagreements between domain experts do not pose a problem; all provided arguments (for and against) can be imported in the knowledge base and it is left to the reasoner to select which of them are acceptable.

The idea of argument-based machine learning (ABML) (Možina et al. 2007), a combination of machine learning and argumentation, is to induce a hypothesis that is consistent with learning data and provided arguments. The motivation for using arguments in machine learning lies in two expected advantages:

1. Arguments impose constraints over the space of possible hypotheses, thus reducing overfitting and guiding learning algorithms to induce better hypotheses.
2. An induced theory should make more sense to experts as it has to be consistent with the given arguments provided by the experts.

With respect to advantage 1, by using arguments, the computational complexity associated with search in the hypothesis space can be reduced considerably, and enable faster and more efficient induction of theories. The second advantage is crucial for building knowledge bases. From the perspective of a machine learning method, there are several possible hypotheses that explain the given examples sufficiently well with respect to predictive accuracy; however, some of those hypotheses can be incomprehensible to experts. Using arguments should lead to hypotheses that explain given examples in similar terms to those used by the expert.

During the process of interactive knowledge acquisition with experts and machine learning, it is not rare that provided arguments contradict the data. In such cases, the experts need to either: (a) revise their knowledge about the domain, or (b) make amendments to the data. Whatever option they decide to choose, both are useful for them. In the first case, they learn something new about the domain, while in the latter, the corrections result in more accurate data.

In ABML, arguments are provided by human experts, where each argument is attached to a single learning example only, while one example can have several arguments. There are two types of arguments; positive arguments are used to explain (or argue) why a certain learning example is in the class as given, and negative arguments are used to explain why it should not be in the class as given. Examples with attached arguments are called *argumented examples*.[4]

An ABML method is required to induce a theory that uses given arguments to explain the examples. If an ABML method is used on normal examples only (without arguments), then it should act the same as a normal machine learning method. We developed the ABCN2 (Možina et al. 2007) method, which was used in all case-studies described in the following section. ABCN2 is an argument-based extension of the well known method CN2 (Clark and Boswell 1991), that learns a set of unordered probabilistic rules from argumented examples. In ABCN2, the theory (a set of rules) is said to explain the examples using given arguments, when there exists at least one rule for each argumented example that is consistent with at least one positive argument (contains argumentative in its condition part) and is not consistent with any negative argument.

21.2.1.2 Interaction Between an Expert and ABML

It is not feasible for an expert to provide arguments for all the examples. Therefore, we use the following loop to pick out the *critical examples* that should be explained by the expert. The loop resembles an argument-based dialogue between a computer and an expert.

1. Learn a hypothesis with ABML using given data.
2. Find the most critical example and present it to the expert. If a critical example can not be found, stop the procedure.

[4]Due to space limitations, we will only roughly describe ABML (see Možina et al. 2007 for precise details).

3. The expert explains the example; the explanation is encoded in arguments and attached to the learning example.
4. Return to step 1.

A critical example (step 2) is an example the current hypothesis can not explain very well. The hypothesis assigned a wrong class value to this example, and therefore asks the expert to argue why he or she believes this example should be in a different class. Using expert's arguments, ABML will sometimes be able to explain the critical example, while sometimes this will still not be entirely possible. In such cases, we need additional information. The whole procedure for one-step knowledge acquisition (step 3) is described with the next 5 steps:

Step 1: Explaining critical example. The experts are asked the following question: "Why is this example in the class as given?" Then, the experts provide a set of arguments $A_1, \ldots, A_k$ all confirming the example's class value.

Step 2: Adding arguments to example. Arguments A_i are given in natural language and need to be translated into domain description language (attributes). Each argument supports its claim with a number of reasons. When reasons are some attribute values of the example, then the argument can be directly added to the example. On the other hand, if reasons mention other concepts, not currently present in the domain, these concepts need to be included in the domain.

Step 3: Discovering counter examples. Counter examples are used to spot whether the availabe arguments suffice to successfully explain the critical example or not. If ABML fails to explain the example, then the counter examples will show where the problem is. A counter example has the opposite class of the critical example, however arguments given for the critical example apply also for the counter example.

Step 4: Improving arguments. The expert needs to revise the initial arguments with respect to the counter example. This step is similar to steps 1 and 2 with one essential difference; the expert is now asked "Why is critical example in one class and why counter example in the other?" The answer is added to the initial argument.

Step 5: Return to step 3 if counter example found.

21.2.1.3 Examples Applications of ABML

We above outlined ABML, a generic method for integrating argumentation and machine learning. We now give some example scenarios where ABML has been applied.

Construction of Sophisticated Chess Concepts

For the purposes of a chess tutoring application developed by Sadikov et al. (2006), we used ABML to acquire knowledge for two sophisticated chess concepts: *bad bishop* and *attack on king*. In this section, we will shortly discuss the process of knowledge acquisition in both cases and give an overview of the results (Možina et al. 2008 and Možina et al. 2010 give a more elaborate description of case-studies).

In the bad bishop case, 200 chess positions were selected. For each of them, the experts gave a qualitative assessment whether the bishop in the position was strategically bad or not. We furthermore described the positions with 100 positional features, which served as attributes. These features are commonly used by strong chess programs and suffice for playing chess on a strong level. We used the ABCN2 method to induce a set of rules with the following structure:

IF conjunction of some features THEN *bishop* = *bad*.

The ABML based knowledge acquisition process discovered eight critical examples and experts explained them with arguments. During the argumentation, experts used five concepts that were not included among 100 default attributes. These five concepts were encoded as five new attributes. Surprisingly, the final rules considered only these five attributes and dropped others that are otherwise very useful for computer play. This demonstrates, on the one hand, how chess players think differently from computers and, on the other hand, suggests that without knowledge introduced through arguments, learned rules would be incomprehensible to experts.

The final model, after all iterations, was evaluated on the test dataset. The improvement of the model was evident: from the initial 72 % classification accuracy (Brier score 0.39, AUC 0.80), the final 95 % accuracy (Brier score 0.11, AUC 0.97) was achieved.

Our domain experts (a chess master and a woman grandmaster) clearly preferred the ABML approach to manual knowledge acquisition. They tried to formalize the concept of bad bishop without ABML, however it turned out to be beyond their practical ability. They described the process as time consuming and hard, mainly because it is difficult to consider all relevant elements. However, with ABML and by considering only critical examples, the time of experts' involvement decreased, making the whole process much less time consuming.

In the second experiment, involving conceptualization of *attack on king* concept, the process took much longer: 38 iterations. This probably happened because the concept itself is considerably more complicated. The process itself was similar to the one with bishops, with one important difference, the expert changed the class value of positions in 10 out of 38 iterations. In all of those cases they decided to change the class value, as they were unable to argue why they assigned the original class in the first place.

After the ABML process, special care was given to examine the interpretability of rules. The experts compared rules obtained with and without arguments. In the case without arguments, they identified three rules (out of 12) that contained counter-intuitive terms for a chess expert. It is not uncommon for ML to produce such seemingly nonsensical explanations as an artefact of the data. On the other hand, ABML produced 16 rules, and none of them included any illogical terms as deemed by the experts. As our goal is to use this model in a chess tutoring application, such terms could be very harmful. A teacher using illogical argumentation (even of a correct decision) is never a good idea. And it is surprising how harmful are the three rules with illogical terms in our case. With a statistical experiment, we showed that in 85 % of the cases, where the model correctly predicted the class value, it used the wrong argumentation to explain its decision.

Acquisition of Neurological Knowledge

In the following, we will briefly describe the process of knowledge acquisition for a neurological decision support system (Groznik et al. 2011). Our goal was to learn a rule-based model that would help the neurologists differentiate between three types of tremors: Parkinsonian, essential, and mixed tremor (co-morbidity). The system is intended to act as a second opinion for the neurologists. Our data set consisted of 67 patients diagnosed and treated at the Department of Neurology, University Medical Centre Ljubljana.

Due to a small number of cases, we shall focus only on a qualitative evaluation. Although the final model (after argumentation) had a better accuracy, the small number of available cases limits us from drawing any statistically significant conclusions. For a qualitative evaluation, the domain expert was asked to evaluate each rule according to its consistency with his domain knowledge. We found a significant difference between the evaluation of initial and final rules. All the rules in the final model were consistent with domain knowledge, while three of the starting rules were not. Furthermore, five of the final rules were marked as *strong rules* meaning that they are sufficient for making a diagnosis. In the initial set, the machine learning algorithm identified only one such rule. Moreover, the relevance of the argumentation process involving ABML and expert (with critical and counter examples) was also reflected by the fact that they assisted the expert to spot 2 mistakes in the initial diagnosis. Therefore, such a tool could be a useful addition to their usual practice.

21.2.1.4 Discussion: Open Issues and Challenges

The above experiments demonstrate the benefits that argumentation brings to machine learning. From the perspective of argumentation, there are two sets of open questions that could further improve the synergy between machine learning and argumentation. The first set concerns the type of arguments applicable in ABML. At the moment, we consider only arguments that directly argue about the outcome of the example: positive arguments and negative arguments rebut each other. The question is, could we also use arguments that undermine (rebut on the *premises* of) other arguments? An extension of the basic ABML theory considering other types of arguments is given in Možina (2009), however, it still needs to be evaluated on practical examples. Furthermore, would it be possible to exploit the structure of argument-based reasoning in ABML? In other words, is it possible to use an attack graph (i.e., Dung framework) of arguments instead of just single arguments? These are some of the ideas that could further increase the added value of argumentation in machine learning.

The second set of questions is related to how the output of ABML methods could help argumentation. Could an ABML method be used to facilitate the construction of a knowledge base for an argumentation-based expert system? Such a method would try to discover rules that would together with an argumentation reasoning mechanism (e.g. Dung 1995) infer correct classes for all learning examples. It is unlikely that we are able to learn such rules with ABCN2, as ABCN2 is specialized in learning classification rules. A possible direction would be to interface the ABILP algorithm (Bratko et al. 2009), an argument-based version of induction logic programming (ILP), with argumentation reasoning. Such an ILP algorithm would, instead of classical monotonic reasoning, use non-monotonic reasoning to evaluate candidate hypotheses.

21.2.2 Argumentation and Dempster-Shafer Belief Functions

21.2.2.1 Overview of Integration

Dempster-Shafer belief functions (Shafer 1985) provide a generalization of the Bayesian theory of subjective probability based on two core concepts: that degrees of belief for one question can be obtained from subjective probabilities for a related question, and a rule for combining these degrees of belief when they are based on independent items of evidence. Yu and Singh (Yu and Singh 2002) deploy Dempster-Shafer belief functions to answer the question of whether a given agent (the evaluator) should trust another (the target), given statistical information concerning the past behaviour of the target. Matt et al. (2010) integrate argumentation into this method, by proposing a method for constructing Dempster-Shafer belief functions modeling the trust of the evaluator in the target by combining statistical information concerning the past behaviour of the target and arguments concerning the target's expected behaviour. For concretely evaluating these method, the arguments are built from current and past contracts between evaluator and target (see Sect. 21.2.2.2 below). Here, we briefly review how argumentation can contribute to defining Dempster-Shafer belief functions to reason about trust.

In general, a belief functions $Bel : 2^{\Omega} \rightarrow [0,1]$, where Ω is a given universe, need to be defined via some evidence mass function, $m : 2^{\Omega} \rightarrow [0,1]$, which needs to be positive, normalised and such that $m(\emptyset) = 0$. Given such m, for every subset $E \subseteq \Omega$, $Bel(E) = \Sigma_{X \subseteq E} m(X)$. Yu and Singh (2002) use a (Dempster-Shafer) belief function as a mathematical model of trust, where $\Omega = \{T, \neg T\}$ is a simple universe with T ($\neg T$) representing that the evaluator considers the target to be trustworthy (untrustworthy, respectively). In their approach, the evidence mass function may be derived either from the knowledge of the evaluator's own past interactions with the target (local trust rating), or by combination of belief functions representing testimonies from other entities concerning the target (belief combination). Matt et al. (2010) focus only on local trust rating. In this case, the evidence mass function is defined in terms of the history of past interactions between the evaluator and the target (assuming that this is sufficiently long), classified as *oor*, *satisfying*, or *inappreciable*. Given that the total number of past interactions is $N = N^- + N^+ + N_?$ with N^-, N^+, $N_?$ the number of times the quality of the interaction was poor, satisfying and inappreciable, respectively, the evidence mass function m is given by

$$m(\emptyset) = 0 \quad m(\{T\}) = \frac{N^+}{N} \quad m(\{\neg T\}) = \frac{N^-}{N} \quad m(\Omega) = \frac{N_?}{N}$$

The evaluator can use the belief function obtained from this evidence mass function to decide whether to interact with the target if and only if its trust in the target (i.e. $Bel(\{T\})$) exceeds its distrust (i.e. $Bel(\{\neg T\})$) by a threshold value $\rho \in [0,1]$ that represents how *cautious* the evaluator is.

Matt et al. define a new (Dempster-Shafer) belief function Bel_a taking into account, in addition to the statistical information (N^-, N^+, $N_?$), also an abstract argumentation framework F including, amongst its arguments, a set A of arguments each supporting one of T (in favour of trusting the target) or $\neg T$ (against trusting the target). They use F and A to define $\hat{p}_A : 2^\Omega \to [0,1]$, the *argumentation-based prior* as

$$\hat{p}_A(E) = \frac{1}{I}\left[\hat{p}(E) + V_A \sum_{a \in A} s_F(a)\hat{p}(E|\{X_a\})\right]$$

where (see Matt et al. 2010 for details):

- $\hat{p}(E)$ is the statistical prior, determined from N^- and N^+
- I and V_A are suitably defined parameters, informally representing the total amount of information available (I) and the information contributed by arguments in A (V_A), namely how much arguments for or against trust count in determining trustworthiness, in relation to statistical information
- $\hat{p}(E|\{X_a\})$ is the conditional probability of E given the conclusion X_a of argument $a \in A$
- $s_F(a)$ gives the strength of argument $a \in A$; this strength is measured taking into account all arguments in F (and not solely those in A within F) as well as the attack relation amongst arguments

Then, Bel_a is obtained, according to the standard Dempster-Shafer theory, from the *argumentation-based evidence mass function* $m_A : 2^\Omega \to [0,1]$ given by

$$\begin{aligned} m_A(\emptyset) &= 0 & m_A(\{T\}) &= (1-\varepsilon_A)\,\hat{p}_A(\{T\}) \\ m_A(\Omega) &= \varepsilon_A & m_A(\{\neg T\}) &= (1-\varepsilon_A)\,\hat{p}_A(\{\neg T\}) \end{aligned}$$

with ε_A a parameter giving a measure of the uncertainty of the evaluator given the past interactions with the target (see Matt et al. 2010 for details).

Although defined in the context of trust computing, this method for combining argumentation and statistics is generic, in that $\hat{p}_A$ (and thus Bel_a) can be obtained for any given argumentation framework F with special arguments A (for answering a question) given a prior $\hat{p}$.

From an argumentation perspective, this method requires a way to compute the (numerical) strength of arguments in an abstract argumentation framework. This could be defined as 1 for "acceptable" arguments according to some argumentation semantics (e.g. admissibility as in Dung (1995)) and 0 otherwise, or according to some quantitative notion, e.g. presented in one of Besnard and Hunter (2000), Cayrol and Lagasquie-Schiex (2005) and Matt and Toni (2008). In the experimental evaluation of this model for trust, discussed later on in Sect. 21.2.2.2, the quantitative, game-theoretic notion of strength of Matt and Toni (2008) is considered. Furthermore, in Sect. 21.2.2.3, we outline some open issues for deploying argumentation-based belief functions for trust and in general.

21.2.2.2 Arguments from Contracts for Trust Computing

The above described method integrating abstract argumentation and (Demptster-Shafer) belief functions has been applied in the context of assessing trust in contract-regulated interactions in general Matt et al. (2010), but with emphasis on interactions amongst service providers and service requestors in service-oriented architectures, with contracts represented by SLAs (Service Level Agreements). In this setting, the argumentation framework F consists of arguments for or against trust (A), based upon the existence or lack (respectively) of contract clauses providing evidence for one of four dimensions or service provision (namely availability, security, privacy and reliability). In addition, F may also contain up to four arguments (in $F \setminus A$) attacking an argument for trust along a dimension on the ground that the target has in the past "most often" violated existing contract clauses concerning that dimension.

Matt et al evaluate their method experimentally, in this service-oriented setting, against the method of Yu and Singh (2002), relying upon statistical information only (see Sect. 21.2.2). The two methods have identical predictive performance when the evaluator is highly "cautious", but the use of arguments built from contracts gives a significant increase when the evaluator is not or is only moderately "cautious". Moreover, target agents are more motivated to honour contracts when evaluated using the argumentation-based model of trust than when trust is computed on a purely statistical basis.

21.2.2.3 Summary and Open Issues

In conclusion, the method integrating abstract argumentation and (Demptster-Shafer) belief functions has been applied in the context of assessing trust in contract-regulated interactions, and in particular in the setting of service-oriented architectures. However there a number of open challenges. Firstly, the experimental setting makes use of a limited set of arguments (based upon the existence or lack of contracts and the tendency of target agents to default their contractual commitments); it would be interesting to consider a broader set of arguments, e.g. taking into account opinions by other agents. Secondly, the method has been experimented with in a simulated environment, whereas it would be interesting to apply it in a real setting. Finally, although defined in the context of trust computing, the method for combining argumentation and statistics is generic, as discussed earlier; it would be interesting to study further applications of this method, to see how useful and effective it is.

21.3 Argumentation Informing Human Reasoning

In this section we review a number of applications and research projects in which formal models of argumentation are or have been used to inform human understanding, reasoning and debate. Specifically, these applications utilise one or more of the following:

1. Models structuring the contents of individual arguments, and the way in which these contents are related, have been used in explaining the reasoning of machines.
2. Models of the dialectical relationships between arguments have been used to guide authoring and mapping of arguments by individuals and in debates and opinion gathering forums, and evaluate the status of arguments.
3. Formal dialogical models have been used to mediate the rational exchange of arguments between humans and/or automated agents.

In Sect. 21.3.1 we briefly review the use of models of argument for structuring explanations in medical decision making tools, and then go on to discuss more recent uses of argumentation in decision making. Section 21.3.2 then considers the use of argumentation in distributed decision making, in which participants exchange arguments for and against proposals for action. Specifically, we review previous and current European Union funded research on development of tools for facilitating distributed decision making. Some of these make use of the schemes and critical questions approach to structuring arguments and their interactions (Walton 1996) that is key to facilitating the use of argumentation in guiding rational and focussed deliberation. We also review, in Sect. 21.3.2.4, some recent work on argumentation-based dialogues, that can be used to support deliberation as well as several other forms of exchanges in distributed settings. Finally, the plethora of existing argument visualisation and mapping tools (Kirschner et al. 2003) (e.g., Berg et al. 2009 and Reed and Rowe 2004) testifies to the enabling function of argumentation models in guiding rational human reasoning and debate. A number of these tools are available online suggesting the notion of an *argument web* in which authored arguments can be exchanged and reused. It is in the context of this envisaged *argument web* that

Sect. 21.3.3 reviews recent work on tools for argument mapping and authoring. Section 21.3.4 then suggests how argumentation can enhance interaction in the *social web*.

21.3.1 Argumentation-Based Decision Making

21.3.1.1 Medical Decision Making

Amongst the earliest works that utilise formal model of argument, are the medical expert systems developed by researchers at Cancer Research UK (see Fox et al. 2007 and www.cossac.org/projects/archive). A key feature of these applications is that knowledge resources, augmented by human entered data, are used in making some recommendation. The reasoning by which these recommendations are made, are presented in the form of arguments for and against the recommendations. For example, the *REACT* system (Glasspool et al. 2007) supports a doctor's consultation with a patient at risk from ovarian or breast cancer. The system visually shows how risk levels are affected by combinations of various medical interventions and other planned patient decisions (e.g., having a baby), where these changes in risk are evaluated using rules encoded in the system. A key explanatory function of the system is the presentation of arguments for and against a given intervention, where these arguments (justifying a reduction/increase in risk) are constructed based on the aforementioned rules, and are augmented by other arguments relevant to the well being of the patient. A key feature is that the structuring of individual arguments is based on the Toulmin model of argument structure (Toulmin 1958), whereby an argument consists of a claim (e.g., remove ovaries) justified by given data (the patient is over 40 and a BRCA2 gene carrier) and a warrant linking the data to the claim (patients over 40 who are BRCA2 gene carrier are reasons to remove ovaries for prevention of cancer), supported by a *backing* (the clinical studies that support the warrant) and with some qualifier indicating the strength of the claim (the degree of risk reduction).

21.3.1.2 Dialectical Explanation for Decision Making

Recent work by Argentinean researchers in argumentation has led to formalizing and implementing several aspects of argumentation for decision making. In García et al. (2009) the concept of *dialectical explanation* was introduced and can be applied for decision making domains. The purpose of a dialectical explanation is to transfer the understanding of how the warrant status of a particular argument can be obtained from a given argumentation framework. When applying this framework in a decision making domain, the dialectical explanation can provide, as formulated in Girle et al. (2003), an advice that can be presented in a form which can be readily understood by the decision maker; and since that explanation reflects the argumentative analysis that was carried out, it provides access to both the information and the reasoning that underpins the given advice. In Ferretti et al. (2008) a model for *defeasible* decision making was introducing by combining *defeasible* decision rules and arguments. The principles stated in that work were exemplified in a robotic domain, where a robot should make decisions about which box must be transported next. In that decision framework, the agent's decision policy can be changed in a flexible way, with minor changes in the criteria that influence the agent's preferences and the comparison of arguments. The proposal includes a simple methodology for developing the decision components of the agent.

Providing a full-fledged model for characterizing explanation in decision making involves a number of open issues and challenges. Significant research has been dedicated to the enhancement of the explanation capabilities of knowledge-based systems and decision support systems, particularly in *user support systems*. Recent investigations have shown how to enhance them using argumentation techniques (Chesñevar et al. 2009) for providing rational recommendations supported by a procedure explicitly justified. An open issue is the integration of quantitative and qualitative information when providing explanations, so that the systems can perceived as more reliable and user-friendly. The strength of an explanation can also be affected by the existence of several arguments supporting a given conclusion (i.e., argument accrual). New argument-based inference procedures for the accrual of arguments have been developed (Lucero et al. 2009), but their deployment in actual *Argument-based Decision Support Systems* (ArgDSS) requires further investigation.

Another interesting aspect for decision making concerns the development of so called *Argument Assistance Systems* (AAS) (Verheij 2003) and *Hybrid Argument Systems* (HAS) (González et al. 2011). While AAS focus on graphical-oriented functionalities for graphically representing an argumentation process (providing facilities for creating and analyzing arguments and their interrelationships), HAS aim to combine such facilities with an automatic inference procedure for evaluating the argumentation semantics under consideration. Following these ideas, some ArgDSS implementations have explicitly considered usability (González et al. 2010). However, there are no standard adopted model and criteria for assessing the usability of ArgDSS within the argumentation community, mainly due to the necessity of developing interfaces of a novel kind in an area where there is still much to be learnt about the way arguments can be sensibly and clearly presented to the users (Verheij 2003). It is necessary to further explore alternative usability-oriented evaluations to validate and improve the usability-oriented design guidelines currently identified, as well as the corresponding usability principles in play. In particular, the datamining technique presented in González and Lorés (2008) for detecting and charaterizing common usability problems of particular contexts of usage (such as ArgDSS) is under consideration. For the particular case of the DeLP (Defeasible Logic Programming) Client that interacts with a DeLP Server (García et al. 2007) which provides a reasoning service, an incremental iterative usability-oriented development process is being performed. In the near future, direct manipulation of arguments has to be considered, leading to a novel interaction style for ArgDSS as well as the revision of the questions associated with every design guideline to cover it.

A key challenge for development of argumentation based decision support systems, concerns a key concept mentioned by Girle et al. (2003), which refers to the detailed analysis of the epistemic state of the decision maker, providing a suitable model for considering or obtaining those salient features ("unusual details" in their words) that might led to alternative decisions. Such details can be introduced as triggers of changes in the beliefs to adapt the agent's epistemic state when considering the acceptance of a new piece of information as part of that state.

Argumentation research impacts belief revision research by introducing consideration of the support of each belief in the epistemic state; this support has the form of arguments that can be constructed from that state. Each belief takes the role of the claim of an argument built from a set of premises, and the decision of accepting the belief is made after considering the status of all the arguments in favor of and against the argument supporting the claim.

Investigating the multifaceted relationship between Belief Revision and Argumentation requires considering cross-links between different aspects on either side while also considering their place in the higher context of reasoning. There has been recent work trying to define change operations on argumentation frameworks (Falappa et al. 2011, 2009). Among them, we may group those defining revision operators and those defining contraction operators. For instance, in Rotstein et al. (2008), Moguillansky et al. (2008) and Moguillansky et al. (2010) revision operators are defined in order to warrant some (new) claim, and in García et al. (2011) different contraction operators are defined in order to retract some inferences from the original knowledge base.

Further steps exploring the relation between argumentation and the dynamics of beliefs are necessary. An interesting area to explore is the one dedicated to decision support systems dedicated to diagnosis. For instance, if I is a query such as "If element α is supplied, will effect β be produced?", whatever the element α and the effect β are, reasoning will become hypothetical to answer the *what-if* query; this type of query will require the consideration of alternative hypothetical epistemic states, a complex task whose outcome could be improved combining belief revision and argumentation.

21.3.1.3 Decision Making in ARGUGRID

The ARGUGRID project (funded by the EC, 2006–2009)[5] developed a platform populated by rational decision-making agents associated with service requestors, service providers and users (Toni et al. 2008), to be used in the context of grid and service-oriented applications. Within agents, argumentation as envisaged in the Assumption-Based Argumentation (ABA) framework (Bondarenko et al. 1997; Dung et al. 2006, 2007, 2009) is used to support decision making, taking into account (and despite) the often conflicting information that these agents have, as

[5] www.argugrid.eu

well as the preferences of users, service requestors and providers (Dung et al. 2008; Matt et al. 2008, 2009). Here, argumentation is used to compute "optimal" decisions, in ways that have a direct correspondence in standard, *normative* decision theory. For example, the method in Matt et al. (2009) computes dominant decisions, and the method in Dung et al. (2008) deploys the minimax principle. The use of argumentation, however, also provides a *descriptive* explanatory counter-part to the optimal decisions. An overview of the decision-making methods deployed in ARGUGRID can be found in Toni (2010).

The ARGUGRID approach to decision making has been validated by way of industrial application scenarios in e-procurement and earth observation (Matt et al. 2008, 2009; Toni et al. 2008) (as described later in Sect. 21.3.2.3).

21.3.2 Argumentation-Based Agreement

In Sect. 21.1 we described how theories of argumentation have provided a basis for development of dialogical models supporting the exchange of information in order to arrive at an agreement. In particular, there have been proposals for generalising argumentation-based decision making to cases where multiple (human and or automated) agents deliberate to agree on a preferred course of action. To illustrate, we briefly review the *CARREL* system (Tolchinsky et al. 2006a,b, 2012), developed as part of the European Union *ASPIC* project on argumentation models and technologies[6] to support the exchange of arguments across several agents, the approach to deliberative democracy taken in the current IMPACT project[7] and the approach to inter-agent negotiation developed within the ARGUGRID project.[8] Finally, we overview a generic form of argumentation-based dialogue to support agreement by means of various forms of dialogues, ranging from information-seeking to deliberation.

21.3.2.1 CARREL

The CARREL system developed a dialogue manager that mediated the exchange of arguments between geographically distributed human agents deliberating over whether a given available organ was viable for transplantation to a given recipient. The aim of the system was to increase the likelihood that an organ would be transplanted, in cases where the medical guidelines suggested the organ was unsuitable, but a well argued case for deviating from the guidelines could be made. One of the main challenges in developing the system was to realise the key aim

[6] www.cossac.org/projects/aspic

[7] www.policy-impact.eu

[8] www.argugrid.eu

of using argumentation-based models to facilitate rational reasoning and debate. To this end, CARREL made extensive use of the schemes and critical questions (*ScCQ*) approach (Walton 1996; Walton et al. 2008). For the moment we digress from our description of of CARREL to explain how *ScCQ* can be used to bridge between formal models and human argumentation.

Argument schemes identify generic patterns of reasoning that can be represented as rules in formal logic or as natural language templates. These generic argument schemes (upwards of 60 have been identified) are then associated with critical questions that identify the presumptions that any specific instantiation of the scheme (i.e., an argument) makes, and thus the potential points of attack by counter-arguments that may themselves be instances of argument schemes with their own critical questions. For example, consider Atkinson's (2005) argument scheme – *SA* – for action:

> In circumstances *S*, action *A* achieves goal *G* which promotes value *V*, and so action *A* should be done.

The variables in this scheme can be instantiated by a human or logic based agent *Ag*1 (in which case the scheme would be represented as a defeasible implication) to construct a specific argument *Arg*1, where *S* = 'Saddam has weapons of mass destruction (wmd)', *A* = 'invade Iraq', *G* = 'remove wmd' and *V* = 'world peace'. Critical questions for the scheme *SA* include, 'Is *S* the case?', 'Does *G* promote *V*?', 'Are there alternative actions for realising *G*', etc. Each of these questions can then be addressed by an agent *Ag*2 as a question in its own right, so placing the burden of proof on *Ag*1 to justify the questioned presumption with a supporting argument that might itself be an instance of a scheme. A question can also be addressed as a counter-argument instantiating a scheme. For example, consider the scheme – *SE* – from expert opinion:

> *E* is an expert in domain *D*, *E* asserts that *A* is known to be true, *A* is in domain *D*, and so *A* is true.

*Ag*2 might instantiate this scheme with *E* = 'Hans Blick', *A* = 'Saddam does not have wmd', *D* = 'weapons inspection', yielding an argument *Arg*2, which instead of *questioning* the premise 'Saddam has wmd' in *Arg*1, *attacks Arg*1 on this premise. *SE* has its own critical questions (e.g., 'is *E* an expert in domain *D*?), and so *Arg*2 can be attacked by arguments (instantiating schemes) addressing these critical questions, and so on. In general then, one can see that schemes and critical questions can be used to guide rational exploration through a space of possible argumentation, providing for human and machine authoring of arguments, and identification of relevant counter-arguments.

In employing the *ScCQ* approach, the developers of CARREL realised the need for schemes and critical questions that were more tailored to the domain of organ transplantation, in order to effectively guide argument-based deliberation over the viability of organs. The development of this tailored set of *ScCQ* was undertaken in consultation with domain experts. The implemented CARREL dialogue manager was then deployed to animate these specialised *ScCQ*, presenting arguments to agents, together with their associated critical questions, and the schemes that could be used to address these questions as attacking arguments. The arguments exchanged during the course of a deliberation, were then organised into a Dung argumentation framework, and together with sources of knowledge providing information about the relative strengths of (preferences over) arguments, the frameworks were evaluated to determine whether an argument assigning an organ to a recipient was winning (see Sect. 21.1.2).

21.3.2.2 IMPACT

CARREL was intended primarily for use by human (medical) experts. On the other hand, the current *IMPACT* project intends to engage both experts and lay members in policy deliberation. IMPACT is a 3 year European Union project[9] that began in 2010, and aims to develop and integrate formal, computational models of policy and arguments about policy, to facilitate deliberations about policy at a conceptual, language-independent level.

The basic idea of deliberative democracy is to empower citizens with the means to participate in a more direct way in the development and evaluation of policy alternatives. However, the current state-of-the-art in eParticipation technology, in which arguments are exchanged in natural language using discussion forums, weblogs and other social software, cannot scale up to handle large-scale policy deliberations, as it requires too much manual translation, moderation and mediation to be practical. As the number of participants increases, it becomes more and more difficult for participants to follow the discussion and keep track of the issues and arguments which have been made, even when they are fluent in the language, not to mention messages in foreign languages. The signal-to-noise level in discussion forums can be very low, due to repetition of points which have already been made, personal attacks and other ad hominem arguments, by persons who are more interested in provoking others or attracting attention to themselves than in constructively contributing to a rational debate.

The IMPACT project thus aims to apply state-of-the-art argumentation technology to facilitate more rational, focussed, deliberative forms of democracy. Specifically, the phases of a policy cycle can be sequenced as: (1) agenda setting, (2) policy analysis, (3) lawmaking, (4) administration and implementation, and (5) monitoring. IMPACT is focusing on the second policy analysis phase. The project aims to:

1. Develop argument schemes and critical questions specifically orientated towards deliberation and debate about policy, and to use these *ScCQ* to automatically generate online surveys that invite lay members of the public to submit their opinions. The guidance provided by the *ScCQ* will overcome many of the problematic issues highlighted above.

---

[9]www.policy-impact.eu

2. Leverage the explanatory capabilities of argumentation-based structuring of knowledge. IMPACT is using methods from the field of Artificial Intelligence and Law to model policies as context-dependent rules or principals which may conflict with one another or be subject to exceptions and to simulate the effects of these policies on a range of cases, using an inference engine based on a computational model of argumentation. The policy models built with these tools will improve the ability of citizens and government to predict the impact of policy measures on both specific cases and on an aggregated set of benchmark cases as a whole. For example, models of social benefits or tax policy of this kind would enable citizens to predict the impact of proposed policy changes on their entitlements or tax burden, respectively.
3. Provide tools for experts to mine arguments from natural language text so enabling the huge amounts of information publicly available on the Internet (for example in web sites, online newspapers, blogs and discussion forums) to be intelligently harvested to gather stakeholders' interests, values, issues, positions and arguments about policy issues. More specifically, such tools would enable the vast amount of information available on public sector resources on the Internet to be optimally used and reused in policy deliberations.
4. Develop dialogical models and software methods and tools for constructing, evaluating, and visualizing arguments to meet the challenges of large-scale public deliberations on the Internet.

21.3.2.3 Negotiation in ARGUGRID

In the ARGUGRID platform (Toni et al. 2008), argumentation is used, in a grid/service-oriented architecture setting, to support the negotiation between agents (Dung et al. 2008; Hussain and Toni 2008) on behalf of service requestors/provider-s/users, as well as to support decision making (as described in Sect. 21.3.1.3). This negotiation takes place within dynamically formed virtual organisations (McGinnis et al. 2011). The agreed combination of services, amongst the argumentative agents, can be seen as a complex service within a service-oriented architecture (Toni 2008).

The need for negotiation arises when agents have conflicting goals/desires but need or may benefit from cooperation in order to achieve them. In particular, this cooperation may amount to a change of goals (e.g. towards less preferable, but socially acceptable goals) and/or to the introduction of new goals (e.g. for an agent to provide a certain resource to another, even though it may not have originally planned to do so).

Argumentation-based negotiation is a particular class of negotiation, whereby agents can provide arguments and justifications as part of the negotiation process (Jennings et al. 2001). It is widely believed that the use of argumentation during negotiation increases the likelihood and/or speed of agreements being reached (Rahwan et al. 2004). In ARGUGRID, argumentation, in the form of ABA (Bondarenko et al. 1997; Dung et al. 2006, 2007, 2009), was used to support negotiation between a buyer and a seller (e.g. of services) and resulting in (specific forms of) contracts, taking into account contractual properties and preferences that buyer and seller have (Dung et al. 2008). Here, negotiation is seen as a two-step process, with a first step where ABA is used to support decision making (see Sect. 21.3.1.3), and then a second step uses a *minimal concession strategy* (Dung et al. 2008) that is proven to be in symmetric Nash equilibrium. Adopting this strategy, agents may concede and adopt a less-preferred goal to the one they currently hold for the sake of reaching agreement. This strategy can also incorporate rewards during negotiation (Dung and Hung 2009), where rewards can be seen as arguments in favour of agreement.

ABA is also used to support negotiation in Hussain and Toni (2008), for improved effectiveness, in particular concerning the number of dialogues and dialogue moves that need to be performed during negotiation without affecting the quality of solutions reached, in more general resource reallocation settings. This work complements studies on protocols for argumentation-based negotiation (e.g. van Veenen and Prakken 2006) and argumentation-based decision making during negotiation as discussed earlier for (Dung et al. 2008), by integrating argumentation-based decision making with the exchange of arguments to benefit the outcome of negotiation. In this work, agents engage in dialogues with other agents in order to obtain resources they need but do not have. Dialogues are regulated by simple communication policies that allow agents to provide reasons (arguments) for their refusals to give away resources; agents use ABA in order to deploy these policies. The benefits of providing these reasons are assessed both informally and experimentally: by providing reasons, agents are more effective in identifying a reallocation of resources if one exists and failing if none exists.

We conclude by listing three main scenarios in which ARGUGRID applied argumentation-based methods for decision making, negotiation and trust computing (see Toni et al. 2008 and www.argugrid.eu for details):

- e-procurement (Matt et al. 2008), in particular for an e-ordering system, where service providers sell e-procurement products and service requestors are users needed a combination of these products to fulfil their goals;
- Earth observation (Matt et al. 2009), in particular for checking oil-spills, where service providers return or manipulate images (e.g. from satellites) and service-requestors are users need (processed) images to fulfil their goals;
- e-business migration (Dung and Hung 2009), investigating the development of formal frameworks for modelling contracts, contract negotiation and conflict resolution that are essential in the business process for outsourcing activities, focusing on a migration of computer assembly activities setting.

21.3.2.4 Argumentation-Based Dialogues

Argumentation-based dialogue systems have attracted substantial research interest in recent years. In Prakken (2005), Prakken has presented a brief summary of the development of dialogue systems. The modern study of formal dialogue systems for argumentation starts from Charles Hamblin's work (Hamblin 1971). The topic was initially studied within philosophical logic and argumentation theory (Mackenzie 1990; Walton and Krabbe 1995). Subsequently, researchers from the field of artificial intelligence and law (Gordon 1995; Prakken 2001) and multi-agent systems (Amgoud 2000; Wooldridge 2003) have looked into dialogues systems as well.

Two major questions need to be addressed in a study of dialogue models. Firstly, how to construct "coherent" dialogues? Secondly, how to construct dialogues with specific goals? The first question is addressed by introducing *dialogue protocols*; and the second question is addressed by studying *dialogue strategies*.

A more recent effort in formalising two-agent dialogues can be seen in Fan and Toni (2011). In this work, Fan and Toni define a dialogue protocol for generic dialogues. They have used Assumption-based Argumentation (ABA) (Dung et al. 2009) as the underlying representation, as ABA is a general-purpose, widely used argumentation framework. In their model, a dialogue is composed of a sequence of utterances of the form

$$\langle From, To, Target, Content, ID \rangle,$$

where $From$ and To are agents; $Target$ and ID are identifiers; and $Content$ is either a topic, a rule, an assumption, a contrary,[10] or pass. A dialogue starts with an agent posing a topic and completes when both agents utter pass.

To ensure the integrity of a dialogue, Fan and Toni have introduced a set of *legal-move* and *outcome* functions. Legal-move functions are mappings from dialogues to utterances. Hence, given an (incomplete) dialogue, a legal-move function returns a set of allowed utterances that extend the dialogue. Legal-move functions can also be viewed as functions that specify dialogue constraints. For instance, the *related legal-move* function requires that a latter utterance must be related to some earlier utterance; and the *flat legal-move* function requires that if a sentence has been uttered as the head of a rule, then it is not uttered again as an assumption. Outcome functions are mappings from dialogues to *true/false*. Given a dialogue, an outcome function returns true if a certain property holds within that dialogue. For instance, the *last-word outcome* function returns true if the fictitious proponent agent answers all attacks made by the fictitious opponent agent.

Through dialogues, the participating agents construct a "joint knowledge base" by pooling all information disclosed in the dialogue to form the *ABA framework drawn from a dialogue*, $\mathscr{F}_\delta$. Since a $\mathscr{F}_\delta$ contains all information that the two agents have uttered in the dialogue, it gives the context of examining the acceptability of the claim of the dialogue. Conceptually, a dialogue is "successful" if its claim is acceptable in $\mathscr{F}_\delta$. This soundness result is obtained by mapping the *debate tree* generated from a dialogue to an *abstract dispute tree* (Dung et al. 2006) that has been developed to prove acceptability results for arguments for various argumentation semantics. This result can be used to prove that certain kinds of these dialogues

[10]Rules, assumptions, and contraries are components of ABA.

are successful in resolving conflicts and thus supporting deliberation (Fan and Toni 2012b).

Some of the earlier study on dialogue systems have categorised dialogues into six types: *persuasion, negotiation, inquiry, deliberation, information-seeking* and *eristics* (Walton and Krabbe 1995). It is easy to imagine that each of these types of dialogues has its own goals; and agents participating in different types of dialogue have different interests. Hence different types of dialogues call for different dialogue strategies.

Building upon the aforementioned dialogue protocol, dialogue strategies can be formulated via *strategy-move* functions (Fan and Toni 2012a,c). These are mappings from dialogues and legal-move functions to utterances. Hence, given a dialogue and a legal-move function, the legal-move function returns a set of utterances that are compatible with the dialogue protocol; and a strategy-move function selects a subset from these allowed utterances such that utterances within this subset advance the dialogue towards its specific goal.

For instance, in an information-seeking dialogue, where a questioner agent poses a topic and an answerer agent puts forward information that is related to the topic. The behaviours of the questioner and the answerer can be captured in two strategy-move functions: the *pass* and the *non-attack* strategy-move functions, respectively (Fan and Toni 2012a). Agents (questioners) that use the pass strategy-move function put forward the claim and no any other utterance in a dialogue; agents (answerers) that use the non-attack strategy-move function only utter rules and assumptions, but not contraries.

Similarly, in an inquiry dialogue, both agents are interested in investigating the acceptability of a given topic. Hence, both agents should be honest and utter all information that each of them knows about the topic. This behaviour can be captured in *truthful* and *thorough* strategy-move functions (Fan and Toni 2012a), where the truthful strategy-move function selects utterances from one agent's own knowledge base and the thorough strategy-move functions does not select pass if there is any other possible utterances for the agent to make.

In order to support persuasion dialogues, *proponent* and *opponent* strategy-move functions can be used to guarantee that agents are truthful (Fan and Toni 2012c).

21.3.3 The Argument Web

The plethora of argument visualisation and mapping tools (Kirschner et al. 2003) testifies to the enabling function of argumentation-based models for human clarification and understanding, and for promoting rational reasoning and debate. The proliferation of opinion gathering resources and discussion forums on the web, and their lack of support for checking the relevance and rationality of online discussion and debate, has led to increased focus on developing online versions of the aforementioned tools. The advent of such tools in turn raises the possibility of re-use of *ready made* arguments authored online (one of the key issues highlighted

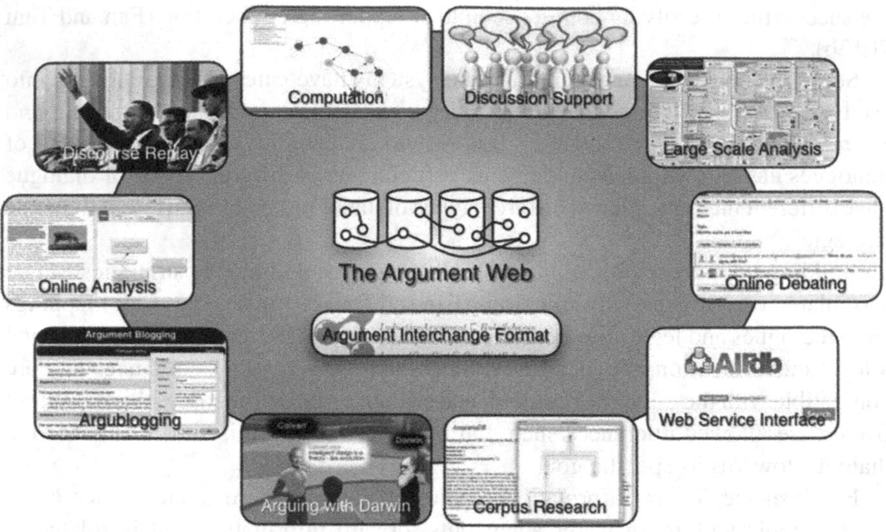

Fig. 21.1 The Argument Web

by IMPACT is the mining of arguments from online resources). To facilitate both the development of such tools and the reuse of authored arguments, researchers have proposed a need for engineering new systems and standards into the heart of the Internet, to encourage debate, to facilitate good argument, and to promote a new online critical literacy. This is the vision of the *Argument Web* (Rahwan et al. 2007). The Argument Web serves as a common platform that brings together applications in different domains (e.g. broadcasting, mediation, education and healthcare) and interaction styles (e.g. online argument analysis, real-time online debate, blogging). Online infrastructure for argument is combined with software tools that make interacting with the argument web easy and intuitive for various audiences. The infrastructure is built on a putative standard for argument representation, the Argument Interchange Format or *AIF* (Chesñevar et al. 2006; Rahwan et al. 2007). The software tools allow for interactions with the structures represented by the AIF that naturally allow people to express their opinions and link them to those of others, and to use debate as a way of navigating complex issues. The main idea of the Argument Web is visualised in Fig. 21.1. In what follows, we provide a number of examples of specific interactions with the Argument Web, illustrating with prototype tools developed at the School of Computing, University of Dundee.

Arvina

Direct and real-time discussions between two or more people on the web takes place not just via email and instant messaging but also on forums and message boards. These technologies offer only the most basic of structural tools: the discussion is

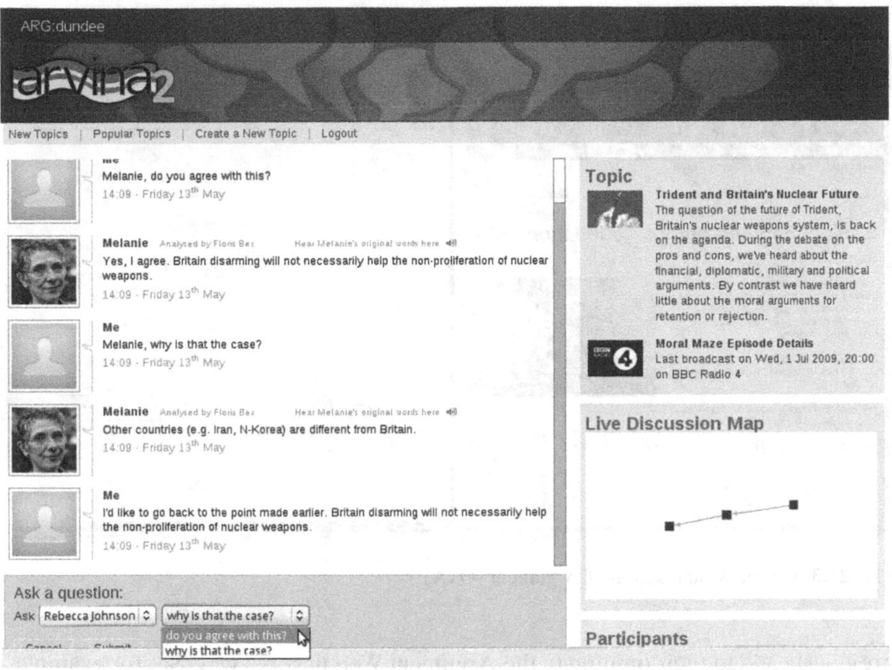

Fig. 21.2 The Arvina 2 debate interface

rendered in a linear way and most structure is often brought in by the participants themselves, e.g. by putting "@Chris" in front of their message when they reply to a point made by Chris. The structure of the arguments that are formed in a discussion is thus easily lost.

Our web-based discussion software Arvina (Snaith et al. 2010) allows participants to debate a range of topics in real-time in a way that is structured but at the same time unobtrusive. Arvina uses dialogue protocols to structure the discussion between participants. Such protocols determine which types of moves can be made (e.g. questioning, claiming) and when these moves can be made (e.g. a dialogue starts with a claim, questions can only be moved after a claim has been made). Protocols facilitate a good and rational debate because they, for example, ensure that each participant's opinion is fairly represented and they provide structure to the dialogue itself as well as to the opinions expressed in this dialogue (Reed et al. 2010). Figure 21.2 shows the debate interface. Notice that a (small) part of the Argument Web is displayed as a live discussion map on the right. The argumentative "moves" the user can make in this particular dialogue are represented in the drop-down menu at the bottom.

In Arvina, reasons for and against opinions are linked to the already available arguments on the Argument Web. Furthermore, Arvina can also use the arguments already on the Argument Web in real-time debate. Arvina takes a multi-agent system populated by agents representing (the arguments of) specific authors who have

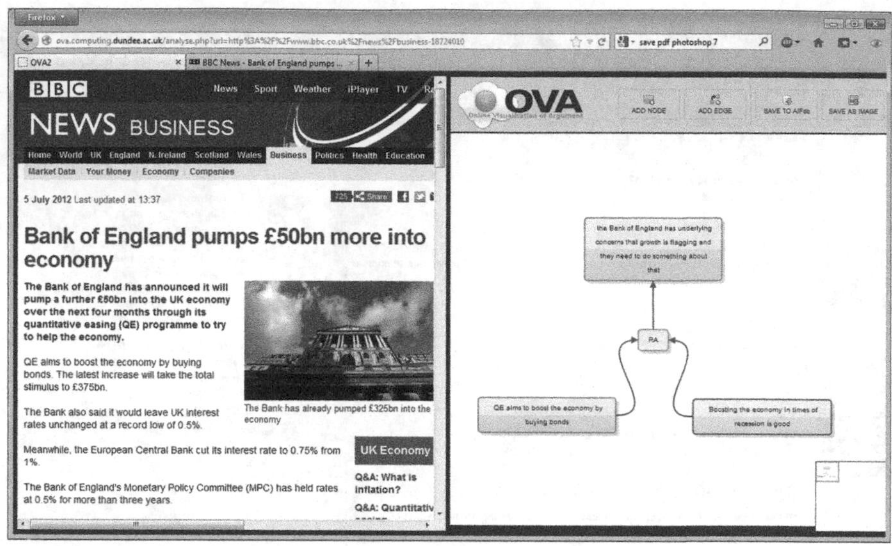

Fig. 21.3 Online Visualisation of Argument (OVA)

previously added their opinion to the Argument Web in some way. So, for example, say that Floris has constructed a complex, multi-layered argument using OVA (see below), concerning the use of nuclear weapons. An agent representing Floris can then be added to an Arvina discussion and questioned about these opinions and the agent will answer by giving Floris' opinions. Thus, Arvina cannot just be used to express arguments but also to explore them and to use arguments made by others in one's own reasoning.

OVA

Argument visualisation tools help a user make sense out of a specific complex problem by allowing him to visually structure and analyse arguments. In our opinion, there exists a significant niche market for a lightweight tool which is easily accessible in a browser and makes full use of the functionality provided by the Argument Web. OVA (Online Visualisation of Argument, Fig. 21.3)[11] is a tool for analysing and mapping arguments online. It is similar in principle to other argument analysis tools (being based on Araucaria (Reed and Rowe 2004)), but is different in that it is accessible from a web browser. This web-based access has allowed for built-in support for direct analysis of web pages, while also maintaining the ability to analyse standard text files.

[11] ova.computing.dundee.ac.uk

OVA is fully linked to the Argument Web and can be used to explore and express arguments in this Argument Web in an intuitive visual manner. One significant advantage that OVA provides over offline packages is that a team of analysts can work together on a problem. Argument analysis is a cognitively intensive and time-consuming task; using OVA, individual analysts can each work on a small part of a complex argument, letting the infrastructure of the Argument Web take care of linking these small subarguments into one complete argument.

Argument Blogging

Our third and final example of how argumentation technologies based on the Argument Web can facilitate online debate concerns the popular activity of blogging. As with message boards, the current structure of the Internet only allows for simple dialogue and argument structures: if one wants to reply to an opinion presented somewhere on the web in one's blog, for example, one can provide a simple hyperlink to the article in which this opinion is expressed. The resulting structure of supporting and competing opinions is then easily lost. Furthermore, because each new claim is expressed on its own page (i.e. someone's blog page) and there is no overview of the dialogue between the various authors and bloggers.

In order to improve rational debate that uses the popular blogging format, we have built a very simple tool for Argument Blogging (Wells et al. 2009) which allows opinions in blogs and other web pages to be easily linked using the underlying infrastructure of the Argument Web. The tool is essentially an addition to the context-menu in a web browser (the "right-click" menu): when selecting some text on a webpage, the user can opt to either agree or disagree with this text and type in their reasons for (dis)agreement. These reasons are then automatically posted to the user's blog, with a link (URI) to the original text. More importantly, the "agree" or "disagree" argument moves and their resulting claims are all aggregated on the Argument Web. A discussion, which may be the result of multiple subsequent uses of the tool, can then be explored using any other tool for the Argument Web, such as Arvina or OVA.

Linking Computational Models of Argument to Human Authored Arguments

Formal models of argumentation enable the structuring of individual arguments and the dialogical exchange of argument in offline and online tools for argumentation-based human reasoning and debate. Thus far, there has been little work on organising human authored arguments into Dung argumentation frameworks, and evaluating the status of these under Dung's various semantics (see Sect. 21.1.2). The provision of this evaluative functionality would: (1) ensure that the assessment of arguments is formally and rationally grounded; (2) enable humans to track the status of arguments so that they can be guided in which arguments to respond to; (3) enable 'mixed' argumentation integrating both machine and human authored arguments.

We briefly report on recent work aiming at providing this functionality. Earlier we referred to the Argument Interchange Format (AIF) (Chesñevar et al. 2006 and Rahwan et al. 2007) that has been proposed as a standardised format for representation of argumentation knowledge. The idea is that the AIF can serve as a common representation language for human authored arguments and arguments constructed in logic, so that (for example) human authored arguments can be translated to a formal logic representation for evaluation under Dungs semantics. This idea is explored in Bex et al. (2012), in which two-way translations between the AIF and the recent $ASPIC^+$ framework (Modgil and Prakken 2012; Prakken 2010) are defined. $ASPIC^+$ is a general framework that provides a structured (rather than fully abstract) account of argumentation. The idea is that one can define a range of logic-based instantiations of this structured framework such that the defined arguments and their defeats (attacks that succeed with respect to preferences over arguments) can be evaluated under Dung's semantics, while ensuring that rationality postulates for argumentation (Caminada and Amgoud 2007) are satisfied. One can then take AIF representations of arguments and their interactions defined in the above mentioned tools, and translate these to instantiations of the $ASPIC^+$ framework, so enabling evaluation under Dung's semantics. This is explored in Bex et al. (2012), in which arguments and their interactions authored in the *Rationale* tool (Berg et al. 2009) are translated to the AIF and then to $ASPIC^+$ representations.

21.3.4 Argumentation and the Social Web

In the Social Web, users connect with each other and share knowledge and experiences of all types, in interactions that often resemble debates with exchange of arguments (e.g. in comments on blogs). Nevertheless, the argumentative structure is implicit (Schneider et al. 2010), arguments need to be inferred (Toni et al. 2012), debates are unstructured, often chaotic (Leite and Martins 2011), not to mention the disruption caused by the Trolls and their inflammatory, extraneous, or off-topic participation (Torroni et al. 2010).

Whereas the use of argumentation in the Social Web context has been advocated by many authors Torroni et al. (2009), Torroni et al. (2010), Schneider et al. (2010), Leite and Martins (2011) and Toni et al. (2012) as a channel by means of which argumentation can inform human reasoning, the realisation of such a vision is yet to come.

Most existing work considering online systems and argumentation (some of which discussed is elsewhere in this chapter) focuses on extracting argumentation frameworks, of one form or another, manually or semi-automatically from user exchanges, e.g. through the use of argument schemes as a way to understand the contributions in these exchanges (Heras et al. 2010), or by mapping these contributions onto the AIF format, again using argument schemes as well as semantic web technology for editing and querying arguments (Rahwan et al. 2007). These works implicitly assume that the extraction of argumentation frameworks is down to "argumentation engineers", fluent in (one form or another of) computational argumentation. This prevents these systems to scale and be widely adopted in the Social Web.

Recently, some steps that do not assume the existence of such argumentation engineers have been taken, two of which we outline next, one using Abstract Argumentation and the other Assumption Based Argumentation.

21.3.4.1 Social Abstract Argumentation

In Leite and Martins (2011), Leite and Martins introduce the notion of *Social Abstract Argumentation Frameworks*, an extension of Dung's AAF with the possibility to associate votes to arguments.

Social Abstract Argumentation Frameworks are meant to provide formal support to self-managing online debating systems capable of accommodating two archetypal levels of participation. On the one hand, experts, or enthusiasts, will be provided with simple mechanisms to specify their arguments and also a way to specify which arguments attack which other arguments. To promote participation, arguments can be anything such as a textual description of the argument, a link to some source, a picture, or any other piece of information these users deem fit. On the other hand, less expert users who prefer to take a more observational role will be provided with simple mechanisms to vote on individual arguments, and even on the specified attacks. The system will then be able to autonomously determine outcomes of debates – the social value of arguments – taking into account the structure of the argumentation graph consisting of arguments and attacks, and the crowd's opinion expressed by the votes. These will be fed to a GUI, which will display arguments and attacks with shades or sizes proportional to their strengths, while adapting as new arguments, attacks and votes are added, thus enabling users to observe the current state of the debate.

In Leite and Martins (2011), the authors define a class of semantics for Social Abstract Argumentation Frameworks where the social value assigned to arguments goes beyond the usual accepted/defeated and can take values from any arbitrary set of values. Some of the proposed semantics exhibit several formal properties which can be mapped to desirable features of the online debating system, related to democracy, universality, etc. According to Leite and Martins, the use of abstract argumentation allow great flexibility in the process of specifying arguments, thus fostering participation by allowing users with different levels of expertise to be able to easily express their arguments.

We illustrate some possible novel uses of argumentation in a Social Web context:

Participatory journalism

Let us consider the following (fictitious) scenario. User Bob is reading an online newspaper. He just finished reading a controversial article on *Do Androids Dream of Electric Sheep?* and he wants to share his thoughts on the matter. But there are already 1,357 user comments! The two comments at the top of the page seem quite interesting. Next to the first comment Bob reads 45 people like this. 32 people like the second one. Then there are some adverts. After that, there are a couple of recently added comments, followed by an older and quite long thread of insults, directed to readers, androids, and sheep alike. Now Bob's problems are:

- Gosh, there is so much noise in this discussion - what do people think about this article? does anyone feel like me about it? I don't want to read 1,364 user comments[12]
- If I write something that has already been said, are people going to insult me?
- I don't know any of these people writing their comments here – is there anyone who knows what he is talking about?
- What did I want to write? I forgot
- What was the article about?

If we think of it, the management of debates in current Social Web sites is very primitive. There are no solutions that can solve Bob's problems. The more people give their contribution, the less their contribution is usable, because there is too much noise. This is because these technologies do not have debate-oriented concepts. Argumentation can provide these concepts.

We envisage the possibility of a new participatory journalism web site (let us call it ArguingtonPost.com) empowered with argumentation and voting technologies. It provides many innovative debate-oriented features such as: visualizing comments in a more usable way, e.g. by clustering comments that agree with each other; maintaining collateral user information, such as the user's authority on specific subjects, as emerged from previous discussion, or its positive/negative contribution to discussion; filtering out comments posted by trolls and grievers; promoting connections between users who agree on similar positions.:

Sentiment-Aware Search Engines

Modern search engines represent, for a large share of Internauts, the "Portal" to the World Wide Web. If you want to know what is a "gridiron," or how "George Benson" looks like, or where to go "out for dinner in Kowloon", or "how to prepare tiramisù" you just type a couple of keywords in Google or Yahoo and get the answer. Well, let's say you get a number of possible links, ranked by very smart algorithms, and a bunch of related adverts. In many cases, you are lucky and the first or second link is what you need.

This was true until just recently. Now the way people access the Web is changing. Instead of typing your queries in a search engine, you can change your status in Facebook or Twitter, saying for example you're preparing a tiramisù for your darling, and some of your friends will probably give you tips and links with tested

[12] Meanwhile, some more insults appeared, which increased the comments counter.

receipts.[13] A possible reason of this change in the Internauts' life style is that your Facebook friends will actually give you better information, and pester less with useless spam. Indeed, search engines are interested in opinion mining and sentiment analysis (Godbole et al. 2007; Pang and Lee 2008) and we expect this hot research area to produce very interesting results in the near future.

We envisage a sentiment-aware search engine (let us call it Arguugle.com) that mines large online discussion boards that use technologies such as the aforementioned ArguingtonPost.com. In this way, Arguugle.com can offer some innovative features, including advanced clustering of result based on user agreement/sentiment, and guessing of user intention and display of additional, not-asked-for information such as positions "in favour" or "against", tips and advice.

Advanced ranking

Suppose that I never read any novel by Stephen King. I want to start with a good one. I type "Wiki Stephen King's novels" on Google. The first hit is Stephen King's Wikipedia main article. The second one is Wikipedia's article about the novel *It*. The third hit is Stephen King's bibliography's Wikipedia main article (obviously what I was looking for). The fourth hit is Listverse's "Top 15 Stephen King Books."

Listverse is a "Top 10 List" web site. That particular ranking is made by a user called Mon. At the time of writing, that ranking has 535 comments of users who agree or disagree with Mon's list. The Web is full of web sites like Listverse: Rankopedia, Squidoo, lists by newspapers such as the Guardian, the Times or USA Today, bookseller lists like Amazon and Barnes & Noble, etc. Ranking and recommendation are everywhere, because they can help us every time we must make a decision about things that require expertise we don't have. Where shall I stop in my Andalucia tour? Which optic is best for my camera? Who's the best catcher of all times?

Recommendation web sites can be very simple: just a numerical ranking, as a result of voting. Or they can require some expert to write their opinion and people to comment. Some popular recommendation services for trip organization, typically associated with online hotel booking services, divide comments into positive and negative ones. That helps. But in general, as a lazy user, I don't want to read too much text, and at the same time I am not impressed by crude rankings because I want to know *what* people give value to when they say "this hotel if fabulous" or "that book is boring".

[13] A 2010 survey illustrates Facebook overtaking Google's popularity among US Internet users. See "Facebook becomes bigger hit than Google" by By Chris Nuttall and David Gelles on Financial Times, online March 17, 2010 www.ft.com/cms/s/2/67e89ae8-30f7-11df-b057-00144feabdc0.html#axzz1MSvZe0pb. Recently Facebook is investing on a "social web search" project in order to better exploit its social data. See "Facebook Delves Deeper Into Search" By Douglas MacMillan and Brad Stone on Bloomberg Business Week, online March 29, 2012 www.businessweek.com/articles/2012-03-28/facebook-delves-deeper-into-search.

We envisage an argumentation-empowered recommendation web site (let us call it Argubest.com) that uses argumentation technologies and is able to:

- Use numerical rating together with user comments and relations between comments when computing the ranking, thus providing a very convincing ranking
- Organize feedback and opinions in a simple and intuitive way for the user to browse them
- Understand which comments seem to be misleading or of little use, and filter them out
- Understand which users seem to be more reliable and give more importance to their ratings

21.3.4.2 Bottom-Up Argumentation

In Toni et al. (2012), Toni and Torroni propose the use of Assumption-Based Argumentation to assess the dialectical validity of the positions debated in, or emerging from the exchanges in online social platforms.

They envisage a system where active participants in the exchange are annotating the exchanges, where annotations indicate that pieces of text in natural language are either comments or opinions, and links can be drawn to indicate source, support or objection. Users will add comments, opinions and links dynamically, in the same way as exchanges grow over time in existing online systems. These annotations are then mapped to an existing computational argumentation framework, Assumption-Based Argumentation (ABA), paving the way to the automatic computation of the dialectical validity of comments, opinions, and links, and thus topics that these encompass.

According to Toni and Torroni, the use of ABA as the underlying computational argumentation framework is justified by the fact that it is equipped with a variety of well-defined semantics and computational counterparts for assessing dialectical validity, its ability to distinguish arguments, support as well as attack amongst them, and its capability of dealing with defeasibility of information, important as the system evolves over time.

Whereas both Social Abstract Argumentation and ABA based Bottom-Up Argumentation both share the view that users, instead of specialised "argumentation engineers", share the burden of defining the structure of the argumentation framework, some features set them apart. In Social Abstract Argumentation, users are allowed to vote on arguments and attack relations, and the votes dynamically reflect on the gradual value of arguments – implementing a more subjective view on argumentation which is perhaps closer to real interactions in the Social Web where consensus hardly ever exists. In ABA based Bottom-Up Argumentation, there is no counterpart to voting and the underlying semantics sticks to the classical accepted/defeated assignment. Then, in contrast to Social Abstract Argumentation, ABA based Bottom-Up Argumentation permits the specification of a support relation which is a common feature of most interactions in the Social Web. Perhaps a combination of both is the best approach to better reflect what goes on in the Social Web, adopting the votes and gradual values from Social Abstract Argumentation and the support relation from ABA based Bottom-Up Argumentation.

21.3.4.3 Discussion: Open Issues and Challenges

We discuss here several challenges that lay ahead for a full integration of argumentation in a Social Web context.

Firstly, the use of Argumentation in Social Computing requires the development of a suitable underlying knowledge representation framework that accommodates all the information provided by the users, together with a semantics that combines an argumentation framework with the community feedback to assign a value to each argument. We need to understand and formalize new concepts such as "social support", "social acceptability", to describe the positions of the community with respect to the matter under discussion. Such semantics should exhibit several desirable properties, to ensure acceptance of the outcomes and promote appropriate user behaviour.

There are many suitable candidates for the basic argumentation framework: Abstract Argumentation Frameworks (Dung 1995), Value-based Argumentation Frameworks (Bench-Capon 2002), Assumption-based Argumentation Frameworks (Dung et al. 2009), Meta-level Argumentation Frameworks (Modgil and Bench-Capon 2011). Recently, Leite and Martins (Leite and Martins 2011) introduced Social Abstract Argumentation Framework which allows to attach votes to abstract arguments and exhibits several desirable semantical properties for using it in Social Computing.

Secondly, successful Social Computing services are based on few mechanisms, which are already known to the user, or easy to be learned. In many applications, information and social exchange has an entertainment component. The use of argumentation in social computing introduces an additional level of structure in interactions which will bring additional challenges in the development of interfaces. This new class of interfaces should be simple enough to be engaging, but at the same time allowing for richer interactions, accommodating the participation of users with various degrees of expertise and motivation.

The interface must provide, for all kinds of users, the right level of abstraction that allows them to interact at the desired level of detail by adding content, identifying relations between claims, navigating through the debate, etc., or simply by voting. As a debate proceeds, the interface will perhaps resort to colors, fonts, geometries or other visual artifacts to highlight a prevailing opinion, and emphasize agreements, supporting arguments, attacks and contradictions. Existing visualization tools (Kirschner et al. 2003) could be used to enhance clarity of presentation and promote user acceptance.

Thirdly, a key challenge is the development of efficient algorithms that can effectively support argumentation and voting together at run time and at a large scale (comments, users). Such algorithms will have to rapidly propagate the effect of changes in a debate, be it a new argument or simply a new vote.

Finally, automated text extraction is one of the most challenging problems in any application that involves knowledge intensive interaction between man and machine. Techniques that automatically identify claims from human-generated text would enable automating tasks such as establishing relations between claims, checking for consistency, etc. Recent advances in automated text extraction and, specifically, on Web dispute identification (Ennals et al. 2010), lead us to believe that soon the technology will be ripe to identify claims in discussion forums effectively and automatically, or at least semi-automatically (e.g. with the help of the social community). An increase in the efficiency of automated text extraction and claim identification will be accompanied with a significant increase in the potential for use of argumentation in the Social Web.

21.4 Benchmark Libraries for Argumentation

For formal models of argumentation to inform human and machine reasoning, argumentation needs to be supported by computational systems and tools. The argumentation community has been very active in the last decade in delivering argumentation engines. Several dedicated engines have been released, such as, for instance, DeLP[14] for the argumentation framework of (García and Simari 2004), the CaSAPI system[15] for the Assumption-Based Argumentation (ABA) framework of (Bondarenko et al. 1997; Dung et al. 2006, 2007, 2009), CARNEADES[16] for the argumentation framework of (Gordon and Walton 2006), the ASPIC system,[17] for the argumentation framework of (Prakken 2010), as well as an increasing number of implementations for computing extensions in abstract argumentation (Dung 1995). Well-known representatives of this latter class of systems are Verheij's system[18] (Verheij 2007), ArguLab[19] (Podlaszewski et al. 2011), and ASPARTIX[20] (Egly et al. 2010).

While the former two are based on tailored algorithms for abstract argumentation, ASPARTIX follows a reduction approach where the actual computation is delegated to an ASP-engine.[21] A number of other approaches using ASP have also been proposed (see Toni and Sergot 2011 for a survey). A similar approach has been followed in Bistarelli and Santini (2010), suggesting to use CSP solvers for the

[14]http://lidia.cs.uns.edu.ar/delp_client/

[15]http://www.doc.ic.ac.uk/~ft/CaSAPI/

[16]http://carneades.berlios.de/

[17]http://www.arg.dundee.ac.uk/toast/

[18]http://www.ai.rug.nl/~verheij/comparg/

[19]http://heen.webfactional.com/

[20]http://rull.dbai.tuwien.ac.at:8080/ASPARTIX

[21]Answer-Set Programming (ASP) (Niemelä 1999) is a declarative programming paradigm which allows for succinct representation of combinatorial problems.

main computations. Another option would be to employ SAT-solvers, as discussed by Besnard and Doutre (2004), or QSAT-solvers, as discussed by Egly and Woltran (2006) (however implemented systems of these two kinds are not available yet). Recent work demonstrates that other methods are also applicable to abstract argumentation, in particular dynamic algorithms based on tree decompositions (Dvořák et al. 2012b) or computations based on backdoor sets (Dvořák et al. 2012a). All of the mentioned systems or proposals cover a certain range of abstract argumentation semantics (see e.g. Baroni and Giacomin 2009 for an overview), but nearly all of them include Dung's standard semantics, such as preferred, stable, or complete extensions (Dung 1995).

Considering the number of proposed argumentation systems, we believe that a benchmark library is indispensable for a systematic comparison and evaluation thereof, with an eye towards application scenarios and deployment in applications. We shall highlight here some main requirements for such a library, have a look at similar such collections in other areas, and raise some questions which the argumentation community should consider and agree upon. We will focus on abstract argumentation systems and consider the following issues:

- How to compare the performance of the different systems for abstract argumentation?
- How to verify the correctness of the systems?
- To which level of problem size do current approaches scale well?
- How can data between different applications and solvers be exchanged?
- How can we - in the long term - measure the progress the community makes in terms of practical systems?

We will advocate the importance of a benchmark library as a way to address these issues. We will also discuss general issues like suitable input formats. Taking the wide variety of extensions of abstract argumentation into account, such a format should be extendable in the sense that, for example, value-based argumentation frameworks (VAFs) (Bench-Capon 2002) and argumentation frameworks with recursive attacks (AFRAs) (Baroni et al. 2011; Modgil 2009) can be captured as well.

It is worth mentioning at this point that abstract argumentation itself is not the only framework available and may not be suitable for all applications (see e.g. Caminada and Amgoud 2007) and abstract argumentation systems are only some of the available engines, as our earlier discussion shows. Nonetheless, efficient systems for abstract argumentation deserve attention as they are an important step towards handling problems of real-world size in order to prolong the success-story of argumentation within the AI community.

Finally, we will raise concrete questions about how a benchmark library for argumentation should be set up and also have a look at how other communities dealt with this kind of service.

21.4.1 *The Value of a Benchmark Library*

The following thesis was proposed by Toby Walsh in his talk at the 2009 AAAI Spring Symposium.[22]

> Every mature field has a benchmark library.

We would like to subscribe to this thesis and paraphrase some of the general benefits of a benchmark library as pointed out by Walsh.

With a growing and well-maintained benchmark library for argumentation, researchers can test their ideas and concepts on instances from a wide range of applications. If the library includes instances of different size, from a few dozens to thousands of arguments, one can use it to evaluate how well an algorithm or reasoning method scales, to which kind of instances it applies best, and to which kind of instances it does not. In order to establish and maintain a useful library, the research community should therefore be encouraged to contribute benchmark instances. Instances should be from various categories, including random instances, hand-crafted instances, and instances that arise from real-world instantiations of argumentation.

A benchmark library will bring various benefits to the field of argumentation as it will support the implementation of new theoretical ideas, as well as their testing and comparison with the state of the art. It will also reward efforts put into the engineering part of the implementation, and so support the combination of theoretical and practical contributions. A benchmark library will highlight some low level aspects that are easily overlooked by a purely abstract theoretical treatment.

For instance, research on propositional satisfiability (SAT) has enormously benefited from a large and diverse benchmark library (see Hoos and Stützle 2000 and respectively http://www.satlib.org/). By means of a benchmark library one can witness the progress over the years. For SAT, the size of solvable instances increased by an order of magnitude every 10 years since the 1980s (see, e.g. Berre and Simon 2006 or http://www.satcompetition.org for the more recent progress).

A well-maintained benchmark library is a necessary prerequisite for a solver competition. There can be a benchmark library without a competition, but no competition without a benchmark library. Maybe in a couple of years argumentation will be ready for such a competition.

21.4.2 *Towards a Benchmark Library*

Following Toby Walsh a benchmark library should be located on the web and easy to find. We would suggest to use http://www.arglib.org (following the naming

[22] Benchmarking of Qualitative Spatial and Temporal Reasoning Systems, Stanford University, CA, USA, March 23–25, 2009

convention from other related areas, e.g. http://www.csplib.org and http://www.satlib.org) and we have already reserved it for this purpose. In what follows, we thus use arglib as a shorthand for the library we have in mind.

To set up arglib, an important issue is to find an appropriate format to represent instances. The following points can be made:

- It has to be decided whether a hi-tech format like XML or a lo-tech format like DIMACS, which is successfully used in SATLib (Hoos and Stützle 2000), shall be used.
- The format should be non-proprietary and widely accepted by the community.
- On the one hand we would like a simple representation of abstract argumentation frameworks. On the other hand, the format should be able to capture extensions of Dung's abstract frameworks like the aforementioned VAFs, AFRAs, and many others. In addition, the format should allow to represent information about the internal structure of arguments in case they are obtained from an instantiation process. As the argumentation community is widespread and frequently comes up with new formal systems, it is very unlikely that one can provide a format capturing all relevant ideas. Hence we seek for a format that is both *simple* and *easily extendable*.

  A potential role model could be the *UAI file format* used for benchmarking probabilistic reasoning problems.[23] For probabilistic reasoning, one takes as input a graphical model of a probability distribution which consists of a graph whose nodes are annotated with numerical values or tables. The UAI file format uses for that purpose a simple ASCII text file. The first part of the file represents the *graph structure* of the graphical model, the second part represents the *annotations*. A similar approach might be useful for argumentation, where one could use the first part to represent the basic attack relation, the second part to represent additional information such as preferences, weights, etc. The first part would remain the same for exchanging data for a wide range of argumentation systems, whereas the second part could provide some flexibility for special application or extensions of basic abstract argumentation frameworks.

We believe that the existing argument interchange format (Rahwan and Reed 2009), AIF for short, is not well suited for arglib. In particular, this format was introduced with a different motivation, namely to have a common ontology supporting interchange between different argumentation approaches and systems. Thus its facilities go far beyond the purely abstract formalisms we consider here. Although AIF provides a rich framework to specify graphs (via its so-called upper ontology), we believe that for the purpose of a benchmark library for abstract argumentation systems a simple format is the better choice. Once translations between a simple format and AIF are established, there might be also the opportunity to extract benchmarks directly from AIF specifications.

[23] www.cs.huji.ac.il/project/UAI10/fileFormat.php

21.4.3 *Instances*

It is obvious that arglib should offer a broad range of instances.

- There should be small (maybe hand-crafted) instances as well as huge instances. This allows to test and compare how different solvers scale.
- A simple way of generating instances is to use a random generator. Such random instances have the advantage that one can produce a wide range of instances with increasing size and gradual changes in density. However, random instances have the disadvantage that they lack the typical structure that is present in real-world instances, hence using them alone for measuring the performance of a solver can produce misleading results, and optimizing a solver solely on random instances is not useful for its performance in practise.
- Real-world instances should be obtained from various applications and different kind of instantiations to avoid that arglib becomes biased.
- For solved instances, the solutions should be available as well. This would allow to empirically verify new solvers.

We conclude by mentioning that a successful library needs the support of the community. Who should maintain arglib: a consortium, a research group, or even just a single person? To build a representative library it is important that researchers submit benchmarks. So inevitably the question arises as to how to motivate the community to submit their examples to arglib?

There are several related research areas close to argumentation that already have widely accepted benchmark libraries. Hence it might be a good idea to learn from them. A joint workshop with organisers from other areas such as SAT, CSP, or ASP (Denecker et al. 2009) might be a starting point.

21.5 Conclusions

We have provided an overview of a number of approaches relying upon argumentation to either support humans or machines towards reaching agreement. Examples of argumentation-augmented machine reasoning include methods for machine learning and trust computing. Examples of argumentation in support of human reasoning include several forms of (individual and collaborative) decision-making and methods in the context of the Web and Social Networks. We have also discussed some open issues, in the context of the individual approaches surveyed as well as in general, for argumentation to strengthen its potential and further demonstrate the added value it brings to applications. Concretely, we have identified the need for benchmark libraries as an important open challenge.

The approaches we have overviewed witness the added value of argumentation in a number of settings. Recent work in cognitive science and psychology (Mercier and Sperber 2011) gives an argumentation-based account of how human capacity to reason evolved. This theory further suggests the use of argumentation in supporting humans to arrive at better outcomes when engaged in the interactive process of arriving at agreements.

Acknowledgements Many thanks to Jordi Sabater-Mir and Vicente Botti for useful suggestions and comments on an earlier version of this chapter.

References

Amgoud, L. 2000. Modeling dialogues using argumentation. In *ICMAS '00: Proceedings of the fourth international conference on multiAgent systems*, 31. Washington: IEEE Computer Society.

Amgoud, L., and C. Cayrol. 2002. A reasoning model based on the production of acceptable arguments. *Annals of Mathematics and Artificial Intelligence* 34(1–3): 197–215.

Amgoud, L., C. Cayrol, M. Lagasquie-Schiex, and P. Livet. 2008. On bipolarity in argumentation frameworks. *International Journal of Intelligent Systems* 23(10): 1062–1093.

Atkinson, K. 2009. *What should we do?:computational representation of persuasive argument in practical reasoning*. Ph.D. thesis, Department of Computer Science, University of Liverpool.

Baroni, P., and M. Giacomin. 2009. Semantics of abstract argument systems. In *Argumentation in artificial intelligence*, ed. I. Rahwan and G. Simari, 25–44. New York: Springer.

Baroni, P., F. Cerutti, M. Giacomin, and G. Guida. 2011. AFRA: Argumentation framework with recursive attacks. *International Journal of Approximate Reasoning* 52(1): 19–37.

Bench-Capon, T.J.M. 2002. Value-based argumentation frameworks. In *Proceedings of the 10th international workshop on non-monotonic reasoning (NMR'02)*, Whistler, 443–454.

Bench-Capon, T.J.M. 2003. Persuasion in practical argument using value-based argumentation frameworks. *Journal of Logic and Computation* 13(3): 429–448.

Bench-Capon, T.J.M., and P.E. Dunne. 2007. Argumentation in artificial intelligence. *Artificial Intelligence* 171: 10–15.

Berg, T., T. van Gelder, F. Patterson, and S. Teppema. 2009. *Critical thinking: Reasoning and communicating with rationale*. Amsterdam: Pearson Education Benelux.

Berre, D.L., and L. Simon. 2006. Preface. Journal on Satisfiability, Boolean Modeling and Computation 2(1–4): 103–143.

Besnard, P., and A. Hunter. 2000. A logic-based theory of deductive arguments. *Artificial Intelligence* 128(1–2): 203–235.

Besnard, P., and S. Doutre. 2004. Checking the acceptability of a set of arguments. In *Proceedings of the 10th international workshop on non-monotonic reasoning (NMR'02)*, Whistler, 59–64.

Bex, F., S. Modgil, H. Prakken, and C. Reed. 2012. On logical reifications of the argument interchange format. *Journal of Logic and Computation*. doi: 10.1093/logcom/exs033.

Bistarelli, S., and F. Santini. 2010. A common computational framework for semiring-based argumentation systems. In *Proceedings of the 19th European conference on artificial intelligence (ECAI'10)*, Frontiers in artificial intelligence and applications, vol. 215, ed. H. Coelho, R. Studer, and M. Wooldridge, 131–136. Amsterdam: IOS.

Bochman, A. 2003. Collective argumentation and disjunctive programming. *Journal of Logic and Computation* 13(3): 405–428.

Bondarenko, A., P. Dung, R. Kowalski, and F. Toni. 1997. An abstract, argumentation-theoretic approach to default reasoning. *Artificial Intelligence* 93(1–2): 63–101.

Bratko, I., J. Žabkar, and M. MoŽabkarina. 2009. Argument based machine learning. In *Argumentation in artificial intelligence*, ed. I. Rahwan and G. Simari, 463–482. New York: Springer.

Caminada, M., and L. Amgoud. 2007. On the evaluation of argumentation formalisms. *Artificial Intelligence* 171(5–6): 286–310.

Cayrol, C., and M.C. Lagasquie-Schiex. 2005. Graduality in argumentation. *Journal of Artificial Intelligence Research* 23: 245–297.

Chesñevar, C., J. McGinnis, S. Modgil, I. Rahwan, C. Reed, G. Simari, M. South, G. Vreeswijk, and S. Willmott. 2006. Towards an argument interchange format. *The Knowledge Engineering Review* 21: 293–316.

Chesñevar, C., A. Maguitman, and M.P. González. 2009. Empowering recommendation technologies through argumentation. In *Argumentation in artificial intelligence*, ed. I. Rahwan and G. Simari, 403–422. New York: Springer.

Clark, P., and R. Boswell. 1991. Rule induction with CN2: Some recent improvements. In *Machine learning – Proceeding of the fifth Europen conference (EWSL-91)*, Berlin, 151–163.

Denecker, M., J. Vennekens, S. Bond, M. Gebser, and M. Truszczynski. 2009. The second answer set programming competition. In *Proceedings of the 10th international conference on logic programming and nonmonotonic reasoning (LPNMR 2009)*, LNCS, vol. 5753, ed. E. Erdem, F. Lin, and T. Schaub, 637–654. Berlin: Springer.

Dung, P.M. 1993. An argumentation semantics for logic programming with explicit negation. In *Proceedings of the tenth logic programming conference*, 616–630. Cambridge: MIT.

Dung, P., R. Kowalski, and F. Toni. 2006. Dialectic proof procedures for assumption-based, admissible argumentation. *Artificial Intelligence* 170: 114–159.

Dung, P., P. Mancarella, and F. Toni. 2007. Computing ideal sceptical argumentation. *Artificial Intelligence* 171(10–15): 642–674. Special issue on argumentation in artificial intelligence.

Dung, P., R. Kowalski, and F. Toni. 2009. Assumption-based argumentation. In *Argumentation in Artificial Intelligence*, ed. I. Rahwan and G. Simari, 199–218. Berlin: Springer.

Dung, P.M., P.M., Thang, and F. Toni. 2008. Towards argumentation-based contract negotiation. In *Proceedings of the 1st international conference on computational models of argument (COMMA'08)*. Amsterdam: IOS.

Dung, P.M. 1995. On the acceptability of arguments and its fundamental role in nonmonotonic reasoning, logic programming and n-person games. *Artificial Intelligence* 77(2): 321–358.

Dung, P.M., P.M. Thang, and N.D. Hung. 2009. Argument-based decision making and negotiation in e-business: Contracting a land lease for a computer assembly plant. In *Proceedings of the 9th international workshop on computational logic in multi-agent systems (CLIMA IX)*, Lecture notes in computer science, vol. 5405, ed. M. Fisher, F. Sadri, and M. Thielscher, 154–172. Berlin: Springer.

Dunne, P.E., T. Hunter, P. McBurney, S. Parsons, and M. Wooldridge. 2011. Weighted argument systems: Basic definitions, algorithms, and complexity results. *Artificial Intelligence* 175: 457–486.

Dvořák, W., S. Ordyniak, and S. Szeider. 2012a. Augmenting tractable fragments of abstract argumentation. *Artificial Intelligence* 186: 157–173.

Dvořák, W., Pichler, and S. Woltran. 2012b. Towards fixed-parameter tractable algorithms for abstract argumentation. *Artificial Intelligence* 186: 1–37.

Egly, U., and S. Woltran. 2006. Reasoning in argumentation frameworks using quantified boolean formulas. In *Proceedings of the 1st international conference on computational models of argument (COMMA'06)*, Frontiers in Artificial Intelligence and Applications, vol. 144, ed. P.E. Dunne and T.J.M. Bench-Capon, 133–144. Amsterdam: IOS.

Egly, U., S.A. Gaggl, and S. Woltran. 2010. Answer-set programming encodings for argumentation frameworks. *Argument and Computation* 1(2): 147–177.

Ennals, R., B. Trushkowsky, J.M. Agosta. 2010. Highlighting disputed claims on the web. In *Proceedings of the 19th WWW*, 341–350. New York: ACM.

Falappa, M., A. García, G. Kern-Isberner, and G. Simari. 2011. On the evolving relation between belief revision and argumentation. *Knowledge Engineering Review* 26(1): 35–43.

Falappa, M., G. Kern-Isberner, and G.R. Simari. 2009. *Argumentation in artificial intelligence*, chap. Belief revision and argumentation Theory, ed. I. Rahwan, G.R. Simari, 341–360. New York: Springer.

Fan, X., and F. Toni. 2011. Assumption-based argumentation dialogues. In *Proceedings of the IJCAI 2011*, Pasadena.

Fan, X., and F. Toni. 2012a. Agent strategies for aba-based information-seeking and inquiry dialogues. In *Proceedings of the ECAI 2012)*, Montpellier.

Fan, X., and F. Toni. 2012b. Argumentation dialogues for two-agent conflict resolution. In *Proceedings of the 4th international conference on computational models of argument (COMMA12)*, Amsterdam: IOS.

Fan, X., and F. Toni. 2012c. Mechanism design for argumentation-based persuasion dialogues. In *Proceedings of the 4th international conference on computational models of argument (COMMA12)*, Amsterdam: IOS.

Feigenbaum, E.A. 2003. Some challenges and grand challenges for computational intelligence. *Source Journal of the ACM* 50(1): 32–40.

Ferretti, E., M. Errecalde, A. García, and G.R. Simari. 2008. Decision rules and arguments in defeasible decision making. In *Proceedings of the 2nd international conference on computational models of arguments (COMMA)*, Frontiers in artificial intelligence and applications, vol. 172, ed. P. Besnard et al., 171–182. Amsterdam: IOS.

Fox, J., D. Glasspool, D. Grecu, S. Modgil, M. South, V. Patkar. 2007. Argumentation-based inference and decision making–a medical perspective. *IEEE Intelligent Systems* 22(6): 34–41. doi:10.1109/MIS.2007.102. http://dx.doi.org/10.1109/MIS.2007.102.

García, A., and G. Simari. 2004. Defeasible logic programming: An argumentative approach. *Theory and Practice of Logic Programming* 4(1): 95–138.

García, A., N. Rotstein, M. Tucat, and G.R. Simari. 2007. An argumentative reasoning service for deliberative agents. In *KSEM 2007*, LNAI, vol. 4798, 128–139. Berlin: Springer.

García, A.J., Rotstein, N., Chesñevar, C., Simari, G.R.: Explaining why something is warranted in defeasible logic programming. In *ExaCt*, Copenhagen, ed. T.R.B. et al., 25–36.

García, D., S. Gottifredi, P. Krümpelmann, M. Thimm, G. Kern-Isberner, M. Falappa, and A. García. 2011. On influence and contractions in defeasible logic programming. In *LPNMR*, Lecture notes in computer science, vol. 6645, ed. J.P. Delgrande and W. Faber, 199–204. Berlin: Springer.

Girle, R., D. Hitchcock, P. McBurney, and B. Verheij. 2003. *Argumentation machines. New frontiers in argument and computation*, chap. Decision support for practical reasoning: A theoretical and computational perspective, 55–84. Dordrecht: Kluwer Academic.

Glasspool, D., A. Oettinger, J. Smith-Spark, F. Castillo, V. Monaghan, and J. Fox. 2007. Supporting medical planning by mitigating cognitive load. *Methods of Information in Medicine* 46: 636–640.

Godbole, N., M. Srinivasaiah, and S. Skiena. 2007. Large-scale sentiment analysis for news and blogs. In *Proceedings of the international Conference on weblogs and social media (ICWSM)*, Salt Lake City.

González, M., J. Lorés, and T. Granollers. 2008. Enhancing usability testing through datamining techniques: A novel approach to detecting usability problem patterns for a context of use. *Information and Software Technology* 50(6): 547–568.

González, M., C. Chesñevar, N. Pinwart, M. Gomez Lucero. Developing argument assistant systems from usability viewpoint. In *Proceedings of the international conference on knowledge management and information sharing*, Valencia, 157–163. INSTICC.

González, M.P., S. Gottifredi, A.J. García, and G.R. Simari. 2011. Towards argument representational tools for hybrid argumentation systems. In *HCI (12)*, Lecture notes in computer science, vol. 6772, ed. G. Salvendy and M.J. Smith, 236–245. Berlin: Springer.

Gordon, T.F. 1995. *The pleadings game. An artificial intelligence model of procedural justice*. Dordrecht/Boston/London: Kluwer Academic.

Gordon, T.F., and D. Walton. 2006. The Carneades argumentation framework – using presumptions and exceptions to model critical questions. In *Proceedings of the 1st international conference on computational models of argument (COMMA'06)*, Frontiers in artificial intelligence and applications, vol. 144, ed. P.E. Dunne and T.J.M. Bench-Capon, 195–207. Amsterdam: IOS.

Governatori, G., and M.J. Maher. 2000. An argumentation-theoretic characterization of defeasible logic. In *Proceedings of the fourteenth European conference on artificial intelligence*, Berlin, 469–473.

Groznik, V., M. Guid, A. Sadikov, M. Možina, D. Georgijev, V. Kragelj, S. Ribarič, Z. Pirtošek, and I. Bratko. 2011. Elicitation of neurological knowledge with ABML. In *Proceedings of the 13th conference on artificial intelligence in medicine (AIME'11)*, Bled, July 2–6, 2011.
Hamblin, C.L. 1971. Mathematical models of dialogue. *Theoria* 37: 130–155.
Heras, S., K. Atkinson, V.J. Botti, F. Grasso, V. Julian, and P. McBurney. 2010. How argumentation can enhance dialogues in social networks. In *Proceedings of the 3rd international conference on computational models of argument (COMMA'10)*, Desenzano del Garda, September 8–10, 2010, Frontiers in Artificial Intelligence and Applications, vol. 216, ed. P. Baroni, F. Cerutti, M. Giacomin, and G.R. Simari, 267–274. Amsterdam: IOS.
Hoos, H.H., and T. Stützle. 2000. SATLIB: An online resource for research on SAT. In *Proceedings of the SAT 2000*, 283–292. Amsterdam: IOS.
Hussain, A., and F. Toni. 2008. On the benefits of argumentation for negotiation – preliminary version. In *Proceedings of 6th European workshop on multi-agent systems (EUMAS-2008)*, Bath.
Jennings, N.R., P. Faratin, A.R. Lomuscio, S. Parsons, C. Sierra, and M. Wooldridge. 2001. Automated negotiation: Prospects, methods and challenges. *Group Decision and Negotiation* 10(2): 199–215.
Kirschner, P.A., S.J. Buckingham Shum, and C.S. Carr (eds.). 2003. *Visualizing argumentation: Software tools for collaborative and educational sense-making*. Springer, London. http://oro.open.ac.uk/12107/.
Langley, P., and H.A. Simon. 1995. Applications of machine learning and rule induction. *Communications of the ACM* 38(11): 54–64. doi:http://doi.acm.org/10.1145/219717.219768.
Leite, J., and J. Martins. 2011. Social abstract argumentation. In *IJCAI 2011, Proceedings of the 22nd international joint conference on artificial intelligence*, Barcelona, Catalonia, July 16–22, 2011, pp. 2287–2292. IJCAI/AAAI.
Lucero, M.G., C. Chesñevar, and Simari, G.R. 2009. On the accrual of arguments in defeasible logic programming. In *IJCAI*, Pasadena, ed. C. Boutilier, 804–809.
Mackenzie, J. 1990. Four dialogue systems. *Studia Logica* 49(4): 567–583.
Matt, P.A., and Toni, F. 2008. A game-theoretic measure of argument strength for abstract argumentation. In *11th European conference on logics in artificial intelligence*, Dresden.
Matt, P.A., F. Toni, T. Stournaras, D. Dimitrelos. 2008. Argumentation-based agents for eprocurement. In *Proceedings of the 7th international conference on autonomous agents and multiagent systems (AAMAS 2008) – Industry and applications track*, Estoril, ed. M. Berger, B. Burg, and S. Nishiyama, 71–74.
Matt, P.A., F. Toni, and J. Vaccari. 2009. Dominant decisions by argumentation agents, argumentation in multi-agent systems. In *ArgMAS 2009*, Budapest, ed. P. McBurney, S. Parson, I. Rawan, and N. Maudet.
Matt, P.A., M. Morge, and F. Toni. 2010. Combining statistics and arguments to compute trust. In *Proceedings of the 9th international conference on autonomous agents and multiagent systems (AAMAS 2010)*, Toronto, ed. W. van der Hoek and G.A. Kaminka.
McGinnis, J., K. Stathis, and F. Toni. 2011. A formal model of agent-oriented virtual organisations and their formation. *Multiagent and Grid Systems* 7(6): 291–310.
Mercier, H., and Sperber, D. 2011. Why do humans reason? Arguments for an argumentative theory. *Behavioral and Brain Sciences* 34(2): 57–74.
Mitchell, T. 1997. *Machine learning*. McGraw-Hill Education (ISE Editions). http://www.amazon.ca/exec/obidos/redirect?tag=citeulike09-20&path=ASIN/0071154671.
Modgil, S. 2009. Reasoning about preferences in argumentation frameworks. *Artificial Intelligence* 173(9–10): 901–934.
Modgil, S., and T. Bench-Capon. 2011. Metalevel argumentation. *Journal of Logic and Computation* 21: 959–1003.
Modgil, S., and M. Caminada. 2009. Proof theories and algorithms for abstract argumentation frameworks. In *Argumentation in Artificial Intelligence*, ed. I. Rahwan and G. Simari, 105–129. Springer.

Modgil, S., and H. Prakken. 2012. A general account of argumentation and preferences. *Artificial Intelligence*. http://dx.doi.org/10.1016/j.artint.2012.10.008, 2012.

Moguillansky, M., N. Rotstein, M. Falappa, A. García, and G.R. Simari. 2008. Argument theory change: Revision upon warrant. In *Proceedings of the twenty-third conference on artificial intelligence, AAAI 2008*, Chicago, 132–137.

Moguillansky, M., N. Rotstein, M. Falappa, A. García, and G.R. Simari. 2010. Argument theory change through defeater activation. In *Proceedings of the 3rd international conference on computational models of argument (COMMA'10)*, Frontiers in artificial intelligence and applications, vol. 216, ed. P. Baroni, F. Cerutti, M. Giacomin, and G.R. Simari, 359–366. Amsterdam: IOS.

Možina, M. 2009. *Argument based machine learning*. Ph.D. thesis, University of Ljubljana: Faculty of Computer and Information Science, Ljubljana.

Možina, M., M. Guid, J. Krivec, A. Sadikov, and I. Bratko. 2008. Fighting knowledge acquisition bottleneck with argument based machine learning. In *The 18th European conference on artificial intelligence (ECAI)*, Patras, 234–238.

Možina, M., M. Guid, J. Krivec, A. Sadikov, and I. Bratko. 2010. Learning to explain with ABML. In *Proceedings of the 5th international workshop on explanation-aware computing (ExaCt'2010)*, Lisbon, pp. 37–49, ISNN 1613–0073. CEUR-WS.org.

Možina, M., J. Žabkar, and I. Bratko. 2007. Argument based machine learning. *Artificial Intelligence* 171(10/15): 922–937.

Niemelä, I. 1999. Logic programming with stable model semantics as a constraint programming paradigm. *Annals of Mathematics and Artificial Intelligence* 25(3–4): 241–273.

Pang, B., and L. Lee. 2008. Opinion mining and sentiment analysis. *Foundations and Trends in Information Retrieval* 2(1–2): 1–135.

Podlaszewski, M., M. Caminada, and G. Pigozzi. 2011. An implementation of basic argumentation components (demonstration). In *Proceedings AAMAS 2011*, Taipei, 1307–1308.

Prakken, H. 2001. Modelling reasoning about evidence in legal procedure. In *Proceedings of the eighth international conference on artificial intelligence and law (ICAIL-01)*, 119–128. New York: ACM Press.

Prakken, H. 2005. Coherence and flexibility in dialogue games for argumentation. *Journal of Logic and Computation* 15(6): 1009–1040.

Prakken, H. 2010. An abstract framework for argumentation with structured arguments. *Argument and Computation* 1(2): 93–124.

Rahwan, I., S.D. Ramchurn, N.R. Jennings, P. McBurney, S. Parsons, and L. Sonenberg. 2004. Argumentation-based negotiation. *The Knowledge Engineering Review* 18(4): 343–375.

Rahwan, I., and C. Reed. 2009. The argument interchange format. In *Argumentation in artificial intelligence*, ed. I. Rahwan and G. Simari, 383–402. New York: Springer.

Rahwan, I., F. Zablith, and C. Reed. 2007. Laying the foundations for a world wide argument web. *Artificial Intelligence* 171: 897–921.

Reed, C., and G. Rowe. 2004. Araucaria: Software for argument analysis. Diagramming and representation. *International Journal of AI Tools* 13(4): 961–980.

Reed, C., S. Wells, K. Budzynska, J. Devereux. 2010. Building arguments with argumentation: The role of illocutionary force in computational models of argument. In *Proceedings of the 3rd international conference on computational models of argument (COMMA'10)*, Desenzano del Garda. Amsterdam: IOS.

Rotstein, N., M. Moguillansky, M. Falappa, A. García, and G.R. Simari. 2008. Argument theory change: Revision upon Warrant. In *Proceedings of the international conference on computational models of argument (COMMA'08)*, Toulouse, 336–347. Amsterdam: IOS.

Sadikov, A., M. Možina, M. Guid, J. Krivec, and I. Bratko. 2006. Automated chess tutor. In *Proceedings of the 5th international conference on computers and games*, Turin.

Schneider, J., A. Passant, T. Groza, and J.G. Breslin. 2010. Argumentation 3.0: How semantic web technologies can improve argumentation modeling in web 2.0 environments. In *Proceedings of the international conference on computational models of argument (COMMA'10)*, Desenzano del Garda, September 8–10, 2010, Frontiers in artificial intelligence and applications, vol. 216, ed. P. Baroni, F. Cerutti, M. Giacomin, and G.R. Simari, 439–446. Amsterdam: IOS.

Shafer, G. 1985. Probability judgment in artificial intelligence. In *Proceedings of the first annual conference on uncertainty in artificial intelligence (UAI'85)*, Los Angeles, ed. L.N. Kanal and J.F. Lemmer, 127–136. Elsevier.

Snaith, M., J. Lawrence, and C. Reed. 2010. Mixed initiative argument in public deliberation. In ed. F. De Cindio et al., *From e-Participation to online deliberation, proceedings of OD2010*, Leeds.

Tolchinsky, P., U. Cortés, S. Modgil, F. Caballero, and A. Lopez-Navidad. 2006a. Increasing the availability of human organs for transplantation through argumentation based deliberation among agents. *IEEE Special Issue on Intelligent Agents in Healthcare* 21(6): 30–37.

Tolchinsky, P., S. Modgil, U. Cortés, M. Sánchez-Marré. 2006b. Cbr and argument schemes for collaborative decision making. In *Proceedings of the 1st international conference on computational models of argument*, pp. 71–82. Liverpool: IOS.

Tolchinsky, P., S. Modgil, K. Atkinson, P. McBurney, U. Cortes. 2012. Deliberation dialogues for reasoning about safety critical actions. *Journal of Autonomous Agents and Multi-Agent Systems (JAAMAS)* 25: 209–259.

Toni, F. 2008. Argumentative KGP agents for service composition. In *Proceedings of the AITA08, architectures for intelligent theory-based Agents, AAAI spring symposium*, Stanford University, ed. M. Balduccini and C. Baral.

Toni, F. 2010. Argumentative agents. In *Proceedings of the international multiconference on computer science and information technology*, 223–229. Piscataway: IEEE.

Toni, F., and M. Sergot. 2011. Argumentation and ASP. In *LP, KR, and NMR: Essays in honor of michael gelfond*. Berlin: Springer.

Toni, F., and P. Torroni. 2012. Bottom-up argumentation. In *First international workshop on theory and application, TAFA 2011*, Barcelona, July 16–17, 2011, Revised selected papers, Lecture notes in computer science, vol. 7132, ed. S. Modgil, N. Oren, and F. Toni, 249–262. Berlin: Springer.

Toni, F., M. Grammatikou, S. Kafetzoglou, L. Lymberopoulos, S. Papavassileiou, D. Gaertner, M. Morge, S. Bromuri, J. McGinnis, K. Stathis, V. Curcin, M. Ghanem, and L. Guo. 2008. The ArguGRID platform: An overview. In *Proceedings of grid economics and business models, 5th international workshop (GECON 2008)*, Lecture notes in computer science, vol. 5206, ed. J. Altmann, D. Neumann, and T. Fahringer, 217–225. Berlin: Springer.

Torroni, P., M. Gavanelli, and F. Chesani. 2009. Arguing on the semantic grid. In *Argumentation in Artificial Intelligence*, ed. I. Rahwan and G. Simari, 423–441. Springer. doi:10.1007/978-0-387-98197-0_21.

Torroni, P., M. Prandini, M. Ramilli, J. Leite, and J. Martins. 2010. Arguments against the troll. In *Proceedings of the eleventh AI*IA symposium on artificial Intelligence*, Brescia, Arti Grafiche Apollonio, 232–235.

Toulmin, S. 1958. The Uses of Argument. Cambridge: Cambridge University Press.

van Veenen, J., and H. Prakken. 2006. A protocol for arguing about rejections in negotiation. In *Proceedings of the 2nd international workshop on argumentation in multi-agent systems (ArgMAS 2005), affiliated to AAMAS 2005*, Lecture notes in computer science, vol. 4049, ed. S. Parsons, N. Maudet, P. Moraitis, and I. Rahwan, 138–153. Berlin: Springer.

Verheij, B. 2003. Artificial argument assistants for defeasible argumentation. *Artificial intelligence* 150(1–2): 291–324.

Verheij, B. 2007. A labeling approach to the computation of credulous acceptance in argumentation. In *Proceedings of the 20th international joint conference on artificial intelligence (IJCAI 2007)*, Hyderabad, ed. M.M. Veloso, 623–628.

Walton, D.N. 1996. *Argument schemes for presumptive reasoning*. Mahwah: Lawrence Erlbaum Associates.

Walton, D.N., and E.C.W. Krabbe. 1995. *Commitment in dialogue: Basic concepts of interpersonal reasoning*. SUNY series in logic and language. Albany: State University of New York.

Walton, D.N., C. Reed, and F. Macagno. 2008.*Argumentation schemes*. Cambridge: Cambridge University.

Webb, G.I., J. Wells, and Z. Zheng. 1999. An experimental evaluation of integrating machine learning with knowledge acquisition. *Machine Learning* 35(1): 5–23. doi:http://dx.doi.org/10.1023/A:1007504102006.

Wells, S., C. Gourlay, and C. Reed. 2009. Argument blogging. In *9th international workshop on computational models of natural argument*, Pasadena.

Wooldridge, M. 2003. Properties and complexity of some formal inter-agent dialogues. *Journal of Logic and Computation* 13: 347–376.

Yu, B., and M.P. Singh. 2002. Distributed reputation management for electronic commerce. *Computational Intelligence* 18(4): 535–549.

Chapter 22
Trends in Multiagent Negotiation: From Bilateral Bargaining to Consensus Policies

Enrique de la Hoz, Miguel A. López-Carmona, and Iván Marsá-Maestre

22.1 Introduction

Negotiating contracts with multiple interdependent issues, which may yield non-monotonic, highly uncorrelated preference spaces for the participating agents, is specially challenging because its complexity makes traditional negotiation mechanisms not applicable (López-Carmona et al. 2012). In this chapter, we will review key concepts about multi-attribute negotiation and the most relevant works in the field, and then we focus on the main recent research lines addressing complex negotiations in uncorrelated utility spaces. Finally, we describe CPMF (de la Hoz et al. 2011), a *Consensus Policy Based Mediation Framework* for multi-agent negotiation which allows to search for agreements following predefined consensus policies, which may take the form of linguistic expressions.

22.2 Multi-attribute Negotiation

Multi-attribute negotiation may be seen as an interaction between two or more agents with the goal of reaching an agreement about a range of issues which usually involves solving a conflict of interest between the agents. This kind of interaction has been widely studied in different research areas, such as game theory (Rosenschein and Zlotkin 1994), distributed artificial intelligence (Faratin et al. 1998) and economics.

Multi-attribute negotiation is seen as an important challenge for the multi-agent system research community (Lai et al. 2004), and there is a great variety

E. de la Hoz (✉) • M.A. López-Carmona • I. Marsá-Maestre
Computer Engineering Department, Universidad de Alcalá, Escuela Politécnica, 28871 Alcalá de Henares (Madrid), Spain
e-mail: enrique.delahoz@uah.es; miguelangel.lopez@uah.es; ivan.marsa@uah.es

S. Ossowski (ed.), *Agreement Technologies*, Law, Governance and Technology Series 8, DOI 10.1007/978-94-007-5583-3_22,

of negotiation models and protocols intended to address different parts of this challenge. These models may be classified according to different criteria (Buttner 2006), such as their structure, the dynamics of the negotiation process, or the different constraints imposed on the problem (e.g. deadlines, information availability…). According to the theoretical foundations of the negotiation models, we can find approaches based on game theory, heuristic approaches (Gatti and Amigoni 2005; Ito et al. 2008; Klein et al. 2003; Lai et al. 2006; Ros and Sierra 2006) and argumentation-based approaches (Amgoud et al. 2000; Jennings et al. 1998; Rahwan et al. 2003, 2007).

Regardless of the theoretical approach involved, different authors agree that there are three key components in a negotiation model (Fatima et al. 2006; Jennings et al. 2001; Kraus 2001b):

- An *interaction protocol*, which defines the rules of encounter among the negotiating agents, including what kind of offer exchange is allowed and what kind of deals may be reached and how they are established.
- The *preference* sets of the different agents, which allow them to assess the different solutions in terms of gain or utility and to compare them.
- A set of *decision mechanisms* and *strategies*, which govern agents' decision making, allowing them to determine which action will be the next one under a given negotiation state.

The most-widespread interaction protocol for negotiation is based on the exchange of offers and counter offers, which are expressed as an assignment of values to the different attributes. This kind of negotiation protocols are known as positional bargaining. A particular protocol family for multi-lateral negotiations are *auction-based protocols*, where negotiating agents send their offers (also called *bids*) to a mediator, which then decides the winning deal (Teich et al. 1999). Auction-based protocols allow one-to-many and many-to-many negotiations to be dealt with efficiently. Another important division regarding interaction protocols is between *one-shot* protocols and *iterative* protocols. In one-shot protocols, there is a single interaction step between the agents. In iterative protocols, on the other hand, agents have the opportunity to refine their positions in successive protocol iterations (Osborne and Rubinstein 1990).

Preference sets express the absolute or relative satisfaction for an agent about a particular choice among different options (Keeny and Raiffa 1976). Cardinal preference structures are probably the most widely used in complex negotiations. In particular, it is usual to define agent preferences by means of utility functions. The most basic form to represent a utility function is to make an enumeration of the points in the solution space which yield a non-zero utility value. It is easy to see that, although this representation for utility functions is fully expressive, its cardinality may grow greatly with the number of issues or with the cardinality of each issue's domain. Because of this, more succinct representations for utility functions are used in most cases. Examples of such representations which are widely used in the negotiation literature are *linear-additive* utility functions (Faratin et al. 2002) or *k-additive* utility functions (Grabisch 1997).

Another widely used way to represent preferences and utility functions is the use of constraints over the values of the attributes: either hard, soft, probabilistic or fuzzy constraints (Ito et al. 2008; Lin 2004; Luo et al. 2003b). A particular case of constraint-based utility representation which has been used to model complex utility spaces for negotiation are *weighted constraints*. There is a utility value for each constraint, and the total utility is defined as the sum of the utilities of all satisfied constraints. This kind of utility functions produces nonlinear utility spaces, with high points where many constraints are satisfied, and lower regions where few or no constraints are satisfied.

Finally, the main challenge in an automated negotiation scenario is to design *rational* agents, able to choose an adequate negotiation strategy. In negotiations among selfish agents, negotiation mechanisms should motivate the agents to act in an adequate way, since if a rational, selfish agent may benefit from taking a strategy which is different to the one expected by the protocol, it will do so. This problem is closely related to the notion of *equilibrium* and *strategic stability* defined in game theory. In an equilibrium, each player of the game has adopted a strategy that they have no rational incentive to change (because it is the best alternative, given the circumstances). There are different equilibrium conditions which can be defined, like dominant strategies (Kraus 2001a), Nash equilibrium or Bayes-Nash equilibrium (Harsanyi 2004).

A potential threat to mechanism stability is strategic revelation of information. In incomplete information scenarios (Jonker et al. 2007), since the agents' beliefs about the preferences of a given agent may influence the decision mechanisms they use, an agent may use as a strategy to lie about its own preferences in order to manipulate the decision mechanisms of the rest of the agents to its own benefit. It would be desirable to design protocols which are not prone to be manipulated through insincere revelation of information. *Incentive-compatibility* is defined as the property of a negotiation mechanism which makes telling the truth the best strategy for any agent, assuming the rest of the agents also tell the truth. An example of an incentive-compatible protocol is the Clarke tax method (Clarke 1971).

22.3 Related Research on Automated Negotiation in Complex Utility Spaces

Klein et al. (2003) presented, as far as we are aware, the first negotiation protocols specific for complex preference spaces. They propose a simulated annealing-based approach, a refined version based on a parity-maintaining annealing mediator, and an unmediated version of the negotiation protocol. Of great interest in this work are the positive results about the use of simulated annealing as a way to regulate agent decision making, along with the use of agent expressiveness to allow the mediator to improve its proposals. However, this expressiveness is somewhat limited, with only four possible valuations which allow the mediator to decide which contract to use as a parent for mutation, but not in which direction to mutate it. On the other hand, the performed experiments only consider the bilateral negotiation scenario, though the authors claim that the multiparty generalization is simple. Finally, the family of negotiation protocols they propose are specific for binary issues and binary dependencies. Higher-order dependencies and continuous-valued issues, common in many real-world contexts, are known to generate more challenging utility landscapes which are not considered in their work.

Luo et al. (2003a) propose a fuzzy constraint based framework for multi-attribute negotiations. In this framework a buyer agent defines a set of fuzzy constraints to describe its preferences. The proposals of the buyer agent are a set of hard constraints which are extracted from the set of fuzzy constraints. The seller agent responds with an offer or with a relaxation request. The buyer then decides whether to accept or reject an offer, or to relax some constraints by priority from the lowest to highest. In Lopez-Carmona and Velasco (2006) and Lopez-Carmona et al. (2007) an improvement to Luo's model is presented. They devise an expressive negotiation protocol where proposals include a valuation of the different constraints, and the seller's responses may contain explicit relaxation requests. This means that a seller agent may suggest the specific relaxation of one or more constraints. The relaxation suggested by a seller agent is based on utility and viability criteria, which improves the negotiation process.

Another interesting approach to solve the computational cost and complexity of negotiating interdependent issues is to simplify the negotiation space. Hindriks et al. (2006) propose a weighted approximation technique to simplify the utility space. They show that for smooth utility functions the application of this technique results in an outcome that closely matches the outcome based on the original interdependent utility structure. The method is evaluated for a number of randomly generated utility spaces with interdependent issues. Experiments show that this approach can achieve reasonably good outcomes for utility spaces with simple dependencies. However, an approximation error that deviates negotiation outcomes from the optimal solutions cannot be avoided, and this error may become larger when the approximated utility functions become more complex. The authors acknowledge as necessary future work the study of which kind of functions can be approximated accurately enough using this mechanism. Another limitation of this approach is that it is necessary to estimate a region of utility space where the actual outcome is expected to be (i.e. it is assumed that the region is known a priori by the agents).

In Robu et al. (2005) utility graphs are used to model issue interdependencies for binary-valued issues. Utility graphs are inspired by graph theory and probabilistic influence networks to derive efficient heuristics for non-mediated bilateral negotiations about multiple issues. The idea is to decompose highly non-linear utility functions in sub-utilities of clusters of inter-related items. They show how utility graphs can be used to model an opponent's preferences. In this approach agents need prior information about the maximal structure of the utility space to be explored. The authors argue that this prior information could be obtained through a history of past negotiations or the input of domain experts.

There are several proposals which employ genetic algorithms to learn the opponent's preferences, according to the history of the counter-offers, based upon stochastic approximation. In Choi et al. (2001) a system based on genetic algorithms for electronic business is proposed. Lau et al. (2004) have also reported a negotiation mechanism for non-mediated automated negotiations based on genetic algorithms. The fitness function relies on three aspects: an agent's own preference, the distance of a candidate offer to the previous opponent's offer, and time pressure. In this work, the agents' preferences are quantified by a linear aggregation of the issue valuations. However, non-monotonic and discontinuous preference spaces are not explored.

In Yager (2007) a mediated negotiation framework for multi-agent negotiation is presented. This framework involves a mediation step in which the individual preference functions are aggregated to obtain a group preference function. The main interest is focused on the implementation of the mediation rule where they allow a linguistic description of the rule using fuzzy logic. A notable feature of their approach is the inclusion of a mechanism rewarding the agents for being open to alternatives other than simply their most preferred. The negotiation space and utility values are assumed to be arbitrary (i.e. preferences can be non-monotonic). However, the set of possible solutions is defined a priori and is fixed. Moreover, the preference function needs to be provided to the mediation step in the negotiation process, and pareto-optimality is not considered. Instead, the stopping rule is considered, which determines when the rounds of mediation stop.

Fatima et al. (2009) analyze bilateral multi-issue negotiation involving nonlinear utility functions. They consider the case where issues are divisible and there are time constraints in the form of deadlines and discounts. They show that it is possible to reach Pareto-optimal agreements by negotiating all the issues together, and that finding an equilibrium is not computationally easy if the agents' utility functions are nonlinear. In order to overcome this complexity they investigate two possible solutions: approximating nonlinear utilities with linear ones; and using a simultaneous procedure where the issues are discussed in parallel but independently of each other. This study shows that the equilibrium can be computed in polynomial time. An important part of this work is the complexity analysis and estimated approximation error analysis performed over the proposed approximated equilibrium strategies. Heuristic approaches have generally the drawback of the lack of a solid mathematical structure which guarantees their viability. This raises the need of an exhaustive experimental evaluation. An adequate complexity analysis and establishing a bound over the approximation error contribute in giving the heuristic approaches part of the technical soundness they usually lack. We also point out that this work is focused on symmetric agents where the preferences are distributed identically, and the utility functions are separable in nonlinear polynomials of a single variable. This somewhat limits the complexity of the preference space.

Finally, combinatorial auctions (Giovannucci et al. 2010; Xia et al. 2005) can enable large-scale collective decision making in nonlinear domains, but only of a very limited type (i.e. negotiations consisting solely of resource allocation decisions). Multi-attribute auctions, wherein buyers advertise their utility functions, and sellers compete to offer the highest-utility bid (Parkes and Kalagnanam 2005; Teich et al. 2006) are also aimed at a fundamentally limited problem (a purchase negotiation with a single buyer) and require full revelation of preference information.

In summary, in the existing research nearly all the models which assume issue interdependency rely on monotonic utility spaces, binary valued issues, low-order dependencies, or a fixed set of a priori defined solutions. Simplification of the negotiation space has also been reported as a valid approach for simple utility functions, but it cannot be used with higher-order issue dependencies, which generate highly uncorrelated utility spaces. Therefore, new approaches are needed if automated negotiation is to be applied to settings involving non-monotonic and highly uncorrelated preference spaces.

22.4 New Directions on Multiparty Negotiation Protocols: Consensus Policy Based Negotiation Framework

Most research in multiparty automated negotiation has been focused on building efficient mechanisms and protocols to reach unanimous agreements, which optimize some kind of social welfare measurement like the sum or product of utilities (Klein et al. 2003; Lai and Sycara 2009). They normally avoid considering situations where unanimous agreements are neither possible nor desired. We believe that the type of consensus employed to reach an agreement should be taken into consideration as an integral part when building multiparty negotiation protocols. We describe here CPMF (de la Hoz et al. 2011), a *Consensus Policy Based Mediation Framework* for multi-agent negotiation. This framework allows the search for agreements following predefined consensus policies (which may take the form of linguistic expressions) in order to satisfy system requirements or to circumvent situations where unanimous agreements are not possible or not desirable.

The basic protocol of the proposed negotiation process in an scenario with n agents and m issues under negotiation is as follows:

1. The mediator proposes a set of points (mesh) around an initial random contract $x(1)$ using a step-length parameter Δ_1. The points are generated according to the expression $x^+(k) = x(k) \pm \Delta_k e_j, j \in \{1,\ldots,m\}$, where e_j is the jth standard basis vector in the m-dimensional space. We will use the notation $x^{+o}(k)$ to designate the mesh at round k including the current point $x(k)$ (Fig. 22.1).

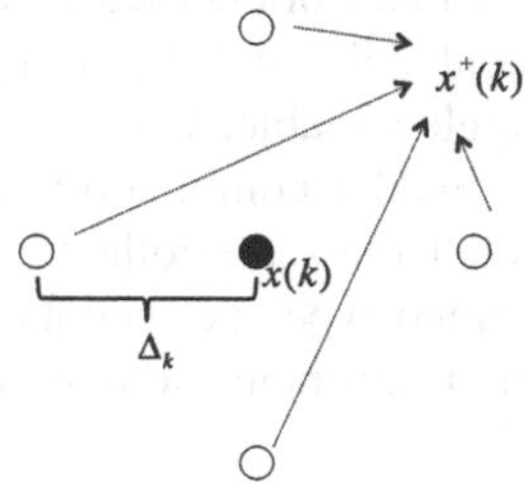

Fig. 22.1 Set of points or mesh for a two-dimensional preference space

2. Each agent provides the mediator their preferences for each on of the contracts in the current mesh x^{+o}, in terms of a mapping $S_i : X \rightarrow [0,1]$ such that for example $S_i(x^{e_j}(k))$ indicates agent i's support for the alternative $x^{e_j}(k)$. An agent does not know the other agents' support for the contracts.
3. For every point in the mesh, the mediator computes an aggregation of the individual agents' preferences. Each aggregation represents the group preference for the corresponding contract in the mesh. We shall refer to this as the *aggregation of preferences* step.
4. The mediator decides which is the *preferred contract* in the mesh according to the group preferences for the different contracts.
5. Based on the *preferred contract*, the mediator decides to generate a new set of points to evaluate, either *expanding* or *contracting* the mesh using the procedure outlined in step 1 but using a new step-length parameter $\triangle_2$. Should a contraction make $\triangle_k$ small enough, the negotiation ends, otherwise mediator goes to step 2.

We assume that the negotiation process is such that a solution from X is always obtained. At each stage of the process an agent provides a support measure determined by its underlying payoff function and any information available about the previous stages of the negotiation.

One of the key points in the protocol is the process that the mediator uses to aggregate the individual support for the contracts in the mesh at round k. We assume each agent has provided at round k her preference $S_i(x^{+o}(k))$ over the set of points under evaluation $(x^{+o}(k))$ such that it indicates the degree to which each agent A_i supports each contract. The mediator objective in this mediation step is to obtain a group preference function $G : x^{+o} \rightarrow [0,1]$ which associates with each alternative $x^{e_j}(k) \in x^{+o}(k)$ a value $G(x^{e_j}(k)) = M(S_1(x^{e_j}(k)),\ldots,S_n(x^{e_j}(k)))$.

Here M is the *mediation rule* and describes the process of combining the individual preferences. The form of M can be used to reflect a desired mediation imperative or *consensus policy* for aggregating the preferences of the individual agents to get the mesh group preferences. M will guide the mediator in the expansion-contraction decisions in order to meet the desired type of agreements for the negotiation process. The aggregation takes the form of a OWA operator (Yager and Kacprzyk 1997). OWA operators provide a parametrized class of mean type aggregation operators. In the OWA aggregation the weights are not directly associated with a particular argument but with the ordered position of the argument. If *ind* is an index function such that $ind(t)$ is the index of the tth largest argument, then we can express using OWA as $M(S_1 \ldots, S_n) = \sum_{t=1}^{n} w_t S_{ind(t)}$. Examples of OWA operators are the max operator, which, in our case would give us the aggregation $Max_i[S_i]$, the min operator, which would give us the aggregation $min_i[S_i]$ or the *avg* operator, which would give us the average $\frac{1}{n}\sum_{i=1}^{n} S_i$.

The final objective is to define consensus policies in the form of a linguistic agenda. For example, the mediator could make decisions following mediation rules like "*Most* agents must be satisfied by the contract". These statements are examples of *quantifier guided aggregations*. Under the quantifier guided mediation approach a group mediation protocol is expressed in terms of a linguistic quantifier

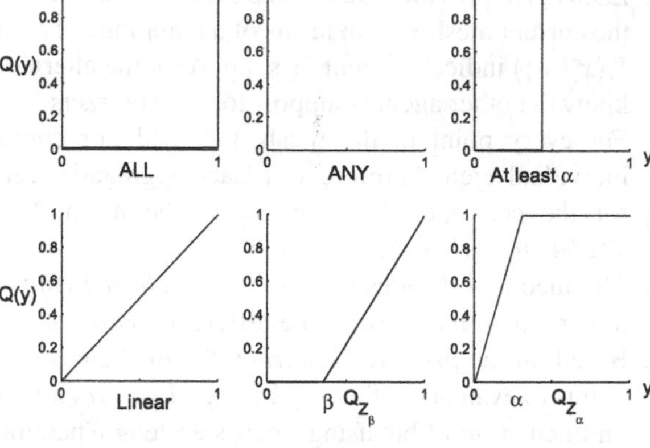

Fig. 22.2 Functional form of typical quantifiers: all, any, at least, linear, piecewise linear Q_{Z_β} and piecewise linear Q_{Z_α}

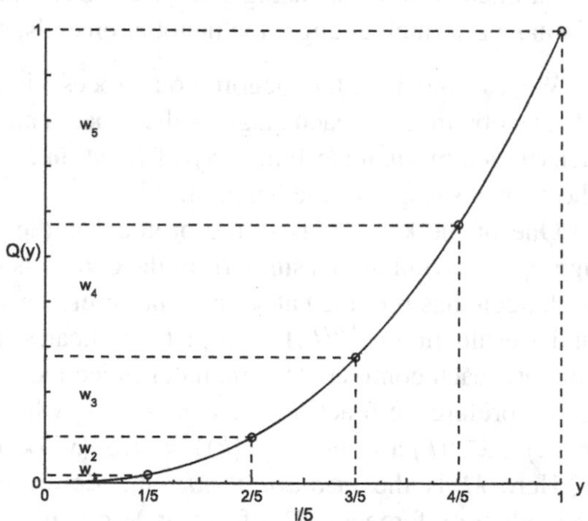

Fig. 22.3 Example of how to obtain the weights from a quantifier for $n = 5$ agents

Q indicating the proportion of agents whose agreement is necessary for a solution to be acceptable. The quantifiers *all*, *any* and *at least* α shown at Fig. 22.2 are examples of this. First, we will express the mediation rule using Q and then we will derive the OWA weights from Q de la Hoz et al. (2011). Figure 22.3 shows an example. Finally, let us describe the search process used by the mediator to decide whether to generate a new mesh in order to continue with a new negotiation round, or to finish the negotiation process. This process starts just after any aggregation of preferences process, when the mediator has determined the group preferred contract $x^{e_*}(k)$. The mediator generates a new mesh in order to continue the search process. If the preferred contract is the previous mesh centre ($x(k)$), the step-length $\triangle_{k+1}$ used to generate the new mesh is halved. Otherwise, the step-length $\triangle_{k+1}$ is doubled.

In order to avoid getting stuck in local optima, we use a probabilistic process in the search procedure. The principle of this approach is analogous to the simulated annealing technique (Klein et al. 2003) without reannealing.

22.5 Conclusions

Automated negotiation can be seen from a general perspective as a paradigm to solve coordination and cooperation problems in complex systems, providing a mechanism for autonomous agents to reach agreements on, e.g., task allocation, resource sharing, or surplus division. Although a variety of negotiation models have been proposed according to the many different parameters which may characterize a negotiation scenario, the consensus type by which an agreement meets in some specific manner the concerns of all the negotiators is not usually taken into account. Most of the works focus only on unanimous agreements. Such solutions do not fit well on every environment. We believe that the consensus type should be considered as an integral part of multiparty negotiation protocols. We propose a multiagent negotiation protocol where the mediation rules at the mediator may take the form of a linguistic description of the type of consensus needed using OWA operators and quantifier guided aggregation. This protocol performs a distributed exploration of the contract space in a process governed by the mediator that aggregates agent preferences in each negotiation round applying the type of consensus desired. This negotiation framework opens the door to a new set of negotiation algorithms where consensus criteria will play an important role. A possible scenario for this algorithms is consortium building in brokerage events where the linguistic expressed mediation rules could be of great utility for guiding the set partitioning process and the identification of high-valued consortia.

References

Amgoud, L., S. Parsons, and N. Maudet. 2000. Arguments, dialogue and negotiation. In *Proceedings of the European conference on artificial intelligence (ECAI-2000)*, Amsterdam, 338–342.

Buttner, R. 2006. A classification structure for automated negotiations. In *WI-IATW '06: Proceedings of the 2006 IEEE/WIC/ACM international conference on web intelligence and intelligent agent technology*, Washington, DC, 523–530.

Choi, S.P.M., J. Liu, and S.-P. Chan. 2001. A genetic agent-based negotiation system. *Computer Networks* 37(2): 195–204. Electronic Business Systems.

Clarke, E.H. 1971. Multipart pricing of public goods. *Public Choice* 11(1): 17–33.

de la Hoz, E., M. Lopez-Carmona, M. Klein, and I. Marsa-Maestre. 2011. Consensus policy based multi-agent negotiation. In *Agents in principle, agents in practice*, Lecture notes in computer science, vol. 7047, ed. D. Kinny, J. Hsu, G. Governatori, and A. Ghose, 159–173. Berlin/Heidelberg: Springer.

Faratin, P., C. Sierra, and N.R. Jennings. 1998. Negotiation decision functions for autonomous agents. *Robotics and Autonomous Systems* 24(3–4): 159–182.

Faratin, P., C. Sierra, and N.R. Jennings. 2002. Using similarity criteria to make issue trade-offs in automated negotiations. *Artificial Intelligence* 142(2): 205–237.

Fatima, S., M. Wooldridge, and N.R. Jennings. 2006. Multi-issue negotiation with deadlines. *Journal of Artificial Intelligence Research* 27: 381–417.

Fatima, S., M. Wooldridge, and N.R. Jennings. 2009. An analysis of feasible solutions for multi-issue negotiation involving nonlinear utility functions. In *AAMAS '09: Proceedings of The 8th international conference on autonomous agents and multiagent systems*, Richland, 1041–1048. International Foundation for Autonomous Agents and Multiagent Systems.

Gatti, N., and F. Amigoni. 2005. An approximate pareto optimal cooperative negotiation model for multiple. In *IAT '05: Proceedings of the IEEE/WIC/ACM international conference on intelligent agent technology*, 565–571. Washington, DC: IEEE Computer Society.

Giovannucci, A., J. Cerquides, U. Endriss, and J. Rodríguez-Aguilar. 2010. A graphical formalism for mixed multi-unit combinatorial auctions. *Autonomous Agents and Multi-Agent Systems* 20: 342–368. doi:10.1007/s10458-009-9085-x.

Grabisch, M. 1997. k-order additive discrete fuzzy measures and their representation. *Fuzzy Sets Systems* 92(2): 167–189.

Harsanyi, J.C. 2004. Games with incomplete information played by bayesian players. *Management Science* 50(12 Supplement): 1804–1817.

Hindriks, K., C. Jonker, and D. Tykhonov. 2006. Eliminating interdependencies between issues for multi-issue negotiation. In *Cooperative information agents X*, Lecture notes in computer science, vol. 4149, 301–316. Berlin: Springer.

Ito, T., M. Klein, and H. Hattori. 2008. A multi-issue negotiation protocol among agents with nonlinear utility functions. *Journal of Multiagent and Grid Systems* 4(1): 67–83.

Jennings, N.R., S. Parsons, P. Noriega, and C. Sierra. 1998. On argumentation-based negotiation. In *Proceedings of international workshop on multi-agent systems (IWMAS-1998)*, Dedham, 1–7.

Jennings, N.R., P. Faratin, A.R. Lomuscio, S. Parsons, C. Sierra, and M. Wooldridge. 2001. Automated negotiation: Prospects, methods and challenges. *International Journal of Group Decision and Negotiation* 10(2): 199–215.

Jonker, C., V. Robu, and J. Treur. 2007. An agent architecture for multi-attribute negotiation using incomplete preference information. *Autonomous Agents and Multi-Agent Systems* 15: 221–252. doi:10.1007/s10458-006-9009-y.

Keeney, R.L., and H. Raiffa. 1993. *Decisions with multiple objectives-preferences and value tradeoffs*. Cambridge University Press: Cambridge & New York, 569 pages, ISBN 0-521-44185-4 (hardback).

Klein, M., P. Faratin, H. Sayama, and Y. Bar-Yam. 2003. Protocols for negotiating complex contracts. *IEEE Intelligent Systems* 18(6): 32–38.

Kraus, S. 2001. Automated negotiation and decision making in multiagent environments. In *Mutliagents systems and applications*, 150–172. New York: Springer.

Kraus, S. 2001. *Strategic negotiation in multiagent environments*. Cambridge: MIT.

Lai, G., and K. Sycara. 2009. A generic framework for automated multi-attribute negotiation. *Group Decision and Negotiation* 18: 169–187.

Lai, G., C. Li, K. Sycara, and J. Giampapa. 2004. *Literature review on multiattribute negotiations*. Technical report CMU-RI-TR-04-66, Robotics Institute, Carnegie Mellon University, Pittsburgh.

Lai, G., C. Li, and K. Sycara. 2006. Efficient multi-attribute negotiation with incomplete information. *Group Decision and Negotiation* 15(5): 511–528.

Lau, R.Y., M. Tang, and O. Wong. 2004. Towards genetically optimised responsive negotiation agents. In *Proceedings of the IEEE/WIC/ACM international conference on intelligent agent technology (IAT'04)*, Beijing, ed. I.C. Society, 295–301, September 20–24 2004. Los Alamitos: IEEE Computer Society.

Lin, M.-W. 2004. Modeling agent negotiation via fuzzy constraints in e-business. *Computational Intelligence* 20: 624–642.

López-Carmona, M.A., and J.R. Velasco. 2006. An expressive approach to fuzzy constraint based agent purchase negotiation. In *Proceedings of the international joint conference on autonomous agents and multi-agent systems (AAMAS-2006)*, 429–431, Hakodate.

López-Carmona, M.A., J.R. Velasco, and I. Marsa-Maestre. 2007. The agents' attitudes in fuzzy constraint based automated purchase negotiations. In *Multi-agent systems and applications V*, Lecture Notes in artificial intelligence, vol. 4696, 246–255. Berlin: Springer.

López-Carmona, M.A., I. Marsá-Maestre, M. Klein, and T. Ito. 2012. Addressing stability issues in mediated complex contract negotiations for constraint-based, non-monotonic utility spaces. *Autonomous Agents and Multi-Agent Systems* 24(3): 485–535.

Luo, X., N.R. Jennings, N. Shadbolt, Ho-Fung-Leung, and J.H.M. Lee. 2003. A fuzzy constraint based model for bilateral, multi-issue negotiations in semi-competitive environments. *Artificial Intelligence* 148(1–2): 53–102.

Luo, X., J.H. Lee, H.F. Leung, and N.R. Jennings. 2003. Prioritised fuzzy constraint satisfaction problems: Axioms, instantiation and validation. *Fuzzy Sets and Systems* 136(2):151–188.

Osborne, M., and A. Rubinstein. 1990. *Bargaining and markets*. San Diego: Academic.

Parkes, D.C. and J. Kalagnanam. 2005. Models for iterative multiattribute procurement auctions. *Management Science* 51(3): 435–451.

Rahwan, I., S.D. Ramchurn, N.R. Jennings, P. Mcburney, S. Parsons, and L. Sonenberg. 2003. Argumentation-based negotiation. *The Knowledge Engineering Review* 18(4): 343–375.

Rahwan, I., L. Sonenberg, N.R. Jennings, and P. McBurney. 2007. Stratum: A methodology for designing heuristic agent negotiation strategies. *Applied Artificial Intelligence* 21(6): 489–527.

Robu, V., D.J.A. Somefun, and J.A. La Poutré. 2005. Modeling complex multi-issue negotiations using utility graphs. In *AAMAS '05: Proceedings of the fourth international joint conference on Autonomous agents and multiagent systems*, 280–287. New York: ACM.

Ros, R., and C. Sierra. 2006. A negotiation meta strategy combining trade-off and concession moves. *Autonomous Agents and Multi-Agent Systems* 12(2): 63–181.

Rosenschein, J.S., and G. Zlotkin. 1994. *Rules of encounter*. Cambridge: MIT.

Teich, J.E., H. Wallenius, J. Wallenius, and A. Zaitsev. 1999. A multiple unit auction algorithm: Some theory and a web implementation. *Electronic Markets* 9(3): 199–205.

Teich, J.E., H. Wallenius, J. Wallenius, and A. Zaitsev. 2006. A multi-attribute e-auction mechanism for procurement: Theoretical foundations. *European Journal of Operational Research* 175(1): 90–100.

Xia, M., J. Stallaert, A.B. Whinston. 2005. Solving the combinatorial double auction problem. *European Journal of Operational Research* 164(1): 239–251.

Yager, R. 2007. Multi-agent negotiation using linguistically expressed mediation rules. *Group Decision and Negotiation* 16(1): 1–23.

Yager, R., and Kacprzyk, J. 1997. *The ordered weighted averaging operators: Theory and applications*. Boston: Kluwer Academic.

Part VI
Trust and Reputation

The study of computational trust and reputation mechanisms has a relatively long history and nowadays we can say it has reached certain maturity. Since the appearance of the multiagent systems paradigm, the importance of these social mechanisms to regulate e-societies became clear, as they are used in human societies. Recently however there has been an evolution in the kind of topics explored by researchers in this area.

After several years of concentrating efforts on the design of better models (better forms of aggregation, the use of new sources of information to feed the models, the use of different mathematical tools to represent and manipulate social evaluations, etc.) researchers have realized it is the right time to start thinking more broadly. Trust and reputation models can no longer be considered black boxes isolated from any other process performed by the agent. It is time to start putting together different parts and processes that, until now, were studied independently from one another. Specifically, computational trust and reputation mechanisms will not be fully understood and operative if they are not considered together with the other parts of the agent in the context of the different processes that revolve around the notion of interaction. At the same time, agents are situated, so the environment is also relevant when talking about trust and reputation.

This chapter aims to be a sample of how computational trust and reputation models can be studied from the point of view of (or together with) other agreement technologies. Chapter 23 is devoted to introducing the related concepts, putting special emphasis in the interplay between trust and reputation. Chapter 24 focuses on how trust can be modeled in a human-centric way. The next Chap. 25 gives us an overview of how argumentation can be used in trust and reputation models and vice versa. The chapter on ontologies, semantics and reputation (Chap. 26) presents several approaches to the problem of how agents can talk about trust and reputation among themselves. The chapter on attacks and vulnerabilities (Chap. 27) reviews the attacks that trust and reputation models can suffer and presents some current solutions when they are available. In Chap. 28 the authors analyze how reputation can influence different dimensions of an organization as it does for an agent's behavior. Finally, Chap. 29 is devoted to the description of a trust model that has been designed by looking at the concept of trust from the broader perspective of a relationship. It serves as an example for the approach to trust and reputation models as an integrated mechanism that is part of a more general process, and not an isolated element.

Jordi Sabater-Mir and Carles Sierra
Editors Part "Trust and Reputation"

Chapter 23
A Socio-cognitive Perspective of Trust

Joana Urbano, Ana Paula Rocha, and Eugénio Oliveira

23.1 Introduction

Trust is a social construct that is present in the day-to-day routine of humans. In fact, every time a person (hereafter named *truster*[1]) needs to interact with, delegate to or rely on the intension of another individual, group or thing (hereafter named *trustee*), a decision about trust is made. Intension is here considered as "choice with commitment" as defined by Cohen and Levesque (1990) and may, or may not, lead to an action. However, it always denotes an agent (trustee) behavior that may interfere with the truster own goals.

Hence, due to the vital role that trust plays in society, it is of no surprise that it receives attention from academics in several areas of research, including sociology, social psychology, philosophy, economics, management, and political science (e.g. Castelfranchi and Falcone 2010; Cvetkovich et al. 2002; Dasgupta 2000; Elangovan and Shapiro 1998; Finkel et al. 2002; Fitness 2001; Hardin 2001; Heimer 2001; Ireland and Webb 2007; Kiyonari et al. 2006; Rotter 1967; Sako 2002; Schoorman et al. 2007; Wathne and Heide 2000; Williamson 1979). More recently, trust and reputation started receiving growing attention from the computer science community, particularly from multiagent systems academics. The underlying idea is to confer to intelligent agents the ability to estimate the trustworthiness of interacting partners, in order to improve their social interactions (Sabater-Mir and Paolucci 2007). We say then that agents use *computational trust models* based on trust theories to assist their trust-based decisions.

---

[1]Some authors use instead the word *trustor*, and some others even *trustier*.

J. Urbano (✉) • A.P. Rocha • E. Oliveira
LIACC/DEI, Faculdade de Engenharia, Universidade do Porto, Rua Dr. Roberto Frias, 4200-465 Porto, Portugal
e-mail: joana.urbano@fe.up.pt; arocha@fe.up.pt; eco@fe.up.pt

S. Ossowski (ed.), *Agreement Technologies*, Law, Governance and Technology Series 8, DOI 10.1007/978-94-007-5583-3_23,

Trust theory suffers from a diversity of notions and concepts that reveals a "degree of confusion and ambiguity that plagues current definitions of trust" (Castelfranchi and Falcone 2010). This by no means eases the work of computer scientists when they attempt to formalize models of computational trust for assisting the decision making of artificial entities.

A frequent misconception in trust literature concerns the distinction between trust and trustworthiness, and the way they relate. This issue is addressed in Sect. 23.2. Sections 23.3–23.5 overview different perspectives of trust, including its main dimensions, nature, and dynamics. In Sect. 23.6, two distinct hypothesis concerning the relation between trust and reputation are provided. Finally, Sect. 23.7 briefly refers some of the most representative models of computational trust, and the main conclusions are presented in Sect. 23.8.

23.2 Trust and Trustworthiness

Trust and *trustworthiness* are two related concepts that must be distinguished. In fact, trust is a property of the truster in relation to the trusted entity, while trustworthiness is a characteristic of the latter. It is expected that a trustworthy entity presents high values of competence, integrity, benevolence, and predictability in the situation in assessment. Also, the trustworthiness of the trustee concerning the truster (and a given situation) is objective, but trusting agents deal with the *perceived* or evaluated trustworthiness, which is subjective (Castelfranchi and Falcone 2010; Marsh 1994).

Besides trustworthiness, some authors consider that trust must account for other factors, such as the truster's propensity and disposition to trust (Castelfranchi and Falcone 2010; Mayer et al. 1995). The propensity to trust is commonly viewed as a personality trait of the truster that is stable across situations, a kind of generalized trust of others that highly influences the trust for a trustee *prior* to data on that trustee being available (Mayer et al. 1995; Schoorman et al. 2007). Some authors consider, however, that propensity is situational (cf. Cvetkovich et al. 2002 for a study of propensity in the realm of nuclear power industry). In contrast, Hardin (2002) assumes that the explanation of trusting in some context is "simply an epistemological, evidentiary matter (…)[and] not a motivational problem". He considers that trustworthiness, and not trust, can be explained as dependent of motivation, and disposition to trust should not be understood as different from learning how to judge trustworthiness.

Other studies suggest that stereotyping, categorization and in-group situations must also be accounted for in trust assessment (Foddy et al. 2009; Hardin 2001; Venanzi et al. 2011). Castelfranchi and Falcone (2010) refer that unknown agents can be put in different categories according to the characteristics or signs they exhibit – the *manifesta* –, and that these can be used to infer the internal factors of these agents (including moods and emotions), i.e., their *kripta*.[2] At the end, trust is inferred from kripta. Following this idea, Venanzi et al. (2011) propose that *categorial reasoning*, which allows to infer hidden information from observable features, is considered a source of information for trust. In the same vein, Foddy et al. (2009) observe that a trustee is more worthy of the confidence of trusting entities if both entities belong to the same group and if the trusting part acknowledges that the trustee is aware of their group membership. That is, trusting agents have the *expectation* of "altruistic and fair behavior toward fellow in-group members".

It can then be concluded that there are different sources of evidence that can be used to judge the trustworthiness of trustees:

- Direct Contact, or *image* (Conte and Paolucci 2002). This is the most valuable of the information sources. By interacting directly with the trustee, the truster has a frank perception of the different dimensions of the trustee's trustworthiness. However, the effectiveness of this normally requires multiple and repeated interactions with the same party (Venanzi et al. 2011), which normally is not plausible in social environments characterized by high openness and dynamicity.
- Reputation. Another important source of evidence is *reputation*, which can be defined as the outcome of the social process of transmission of beliefs about the trustee; it is about social evaluations that circulate and are represented as *reported evaluations* (Sabater-Mir et al. 2006). Reputation is characterized by being highly available,[3] but also by its low credibility, due to the bias introduced by partial reporters (Venanzi et al. 2011) and to the noise inherent in multiple transmissions. Also, the agents that spread the reputation information do not necessarily believe its content.
- Other sources. Other sources of information include opinions and information from trusted third parties (e.g. certificates Huynh 2006; Pavlou et al. 2003 and contracts Urbano et al. 2010). The former is subjective and the latter is normally safe and objective. In both of them, availability and affordability are issues to take into consideration. *Indirect evidence*, including categorization, stereotyping, in-group situations, and organizational roles (Castelfranchi et al. 2003; Hermoso et al. 2009), can also be considered.

23.3 Factors and Dimensions of Trust

When assessing the trustworthiness of a trustee, it is important to distinguish between its different dimensions. One of such dimensions is *competence* (also named *ability*), which relates to the potential and abstract ability of the evaluated

[2]The authors recover the idea of kripta and manifesta from Bacharach and Gambetta (2010).

[3]Sometimes it can be the only source of information available to predict the trustworthiness of trustees.

entity to perform a given task (Castelfranchi and Falcone 2010; Mayer et al. 1995). Ability translates into a set of qualities that makes the trustee able to perform the task, such as skills, know-how, expert knowledge, self-esteem and self-confidence (Castelfranchi and Falcone 2010). Other qualities (depending on the situation) are common language, common vision, discretion (Levin et al. 2004), experience and maturity (Hardin 2002).

Besides competence/ability, Mayer et al. (1995) consider *benevolence* and *integrity* as key dimensions of trust. These authors define benevolence as "the extent to which a trustee is believed to want to do good to the trustor, aside from an egocentric profit motive". In a similar vein, Elangovan and Shapiro relate benevolence to "a feeling of goodwill toward the trustor" (Elangovan and Shapiro 1998). In turn, integrity is commonly referred to as a commitment to the principles acceptable by the truster (Elangovan and Shapiro 1998; Mayer et al. 1995). Individuals at higher levels of moral development tend not to trivialize trust violations and are less likely to switch to a different set of principles due to external reasons, thus scoring higher values for the integrity dimension (Elangovan and Shapiro 1998).

Some trust academics also consider the *predictability* (Castelfranchi and Falcone 2010; Straker 2008) dimension, which relates to the ability and the willingness of the trustee in performing the assigned task.

23.4 The Nature of Trust

Some authors consider that trust is just a decision and not an act (Hardin 2001), where others consider that trust is a multi-layer concept that includes disposition, decision and act (Castelfranchi and Falcone 2010). In a different perspective, trust is not necessarily mutual or reciprocal (Kiyonari et al. 2006; Schoorman et al. 2007). Another important characteristic is the *degree of trust* (Bhattacharya et al. 1998; Castelfranchi and Falcone 2010; Hardin 2001). As mentioned by Castelfranchi and Falcone, "only a trust decision eventually is a yes/no choice, and clearly needs some threshold" (Castelfranchi and Falcone 2010, p. 49). In the same way, the *strength* of trust (i.e., the confidence that the truster has on his trust) serves as basis to the degree of trust (Bhattacharya et al. 1998; Castelfranchi and Falcone 2010; Huynh 2006; Patel 2006).

Finally, trust is by nature *contextual*: A trusts B to do X (Hardin 2001). Mayer et al. (1995) consider that trust varies across domains as trustees have different abilities in different domains. Dimitrakos provides a somewhat broader conception of situational trust by defining trust as a measurable belief that the truster has on the competence of the trustee in behaving in a dependably way, in a given period of time, within a given context and relative to a specific task (Dimitrakos 2001). In turn, in one of the earliest research on computational trust, Marsh (1994) considers trust as situational, and provides this clarifying example: "I may trust my brother to drive me to the airport, I most certainly would not trust him to fly the plane".

23.5 Trust Dynamics

Social interactions are traditionally secured by both ongoing relationships and governance mechanisms such as contracts, incentives, and institutions. Legalistic remedies are usually costly and not always effective (Williamson 1979), but there are situations where the risk of loss justifies the expense of using them (Hardin 2001). In opposition, the establishment of long-term relationships is cost effective and is widely used in one-to-one relationships and in commercial relationships.

However, the reality of present days indicates the urge for new forms of relationships, mainly in business and in social networks, where relationships are formed more quickly and, increasingly, with anonymous others, or strangers. There, the truster cannot ground his trust in the partners through ongoing relationships, and the use of institutional back-up may be inadequate. Therefore, in order to construct robust computational trust models, it is essential to understand how trust forms and evolves, both for allowing intelligent agents to promote their own trustworthiness, and to allow them to correctly predict others' trustworthiness even in case of new partnerships.

Next, different aspects that may alter the dynamics of trust formation and maintenance, namely, long-term relationships, betrayal of trust, formation of trust, asymmetry, and perseverance in trust building, are analyzed.

23.5.1 Long-Term Relationships

Long and stable relations with others usually provide the conditions, and the incentives, for trustworthiness and trust (Hardin 2001). In fact, there are several benefits associated with trust maintenance in a relationship, including the open exchange of ideas and information above normal levels (Elangovan and Shapiro 1998), a certain flexibility concerning the fulfillment of contractual obligations, the easy resolution of short-term inequities (Elangovan and Shapiro 1998), and mutual benchmarking with partners, improving the quality processes of the organizations (Schoorman et al. 2007).

Long-term relationships are initiated when one or more parties to the relationship demonstrate benevolence toward the interacting partners, initiating *norms of reciprocity* that, when established, lead to *goodwill trust* between the interacting partners (Ireland and Webb 2007; Sako 2002). In long-term relations, it is expected that actors show high levels of benevolence and integrity. Also, they would do their best to tune hard and soft skills, in order to increase their competence dimension to the level agreed with the interacting partners, thus increasing their predicatibility.

23.5.2 Betrayal

Betrayal is often associated with the *breach of trust*. It is distinct from other negative incidents because it involves the *voluntarily* violation of known pivotal expectations and rules that govern interaction, causing harm to the victim (Elangovan and Shapiro 1998; Finkel et al. 2002). Also, the consequences of betrayal can be devastating (Cvetkovich et al. 2002; Fitness 2001; Poortinga and Pidgeon 2004). If the relation can ever be repaired, it will imply that the victim forgives the betrayer. *Forgiveness* will depend on the severity of the betrayal (Fitness 2001), the emotions and cognitions that accompany the act, but also on personal values and long-term goals of the victim of betrayal (Finkel et al. 2002).

Elangovan and Shapiro (1998) present a general model of opportunistic betrayal in organizations. They propose that there are certain conditions (e.g. a financial crisis, unfulfilled needs or traits of the trustee) that prompt the trustee to assess the situation at present, taking into consideration: (i) the benefits associated with betraying the truster; (ii) the relationship with the truster; and (iii) the principles involved in the betrayal decision. If the present situation is ranked poorly, the trustee is motivated to betray. However, the actual decision to betray is influenced by the trustee's perceived likelihood of suffering severe penalties due to betrayal.

23.5.3 Building Trust from Scratch

In practically all kinds of social relationships, the best way to create trust is to be trustworthy. And in this field, it is known that acts of benevolence increase the trustworthiness of the actor. Schoorman et al. refer that acts of benevolence from partners in inter-firm relationships (e.g. in joint ventures) helps to build trust (Schoorman et al. 2007). A second form to give incentives to trustworthiness is through the reliance on societal and institutional devices (Hardin 2002; Williamson 1979).

23.5.4 Asymmetry and Perseverance

Slovic (1993) introduced the concept of *asymmetry principle* in a study in the realm of nuclear power plants, where he analyzed the effect that distinct information about positive and negative events had on participants of the study. From the results, he formulated that negative events tend to have a stronger impact on decreasing trust than positive events on increasing trust.

Subsequent studies (Cvetkovich et al. 2002) confirmed Slovic's asymmetry principle and showed that "existing attributions of trust persevere because they affect the interpretation and meanings of new information" (*confirmatory bias*), and that individuals at a trusting stage tend to maintain or increase trust as they acknowledge positive events while individuals at a distrusting stage tend to maintain or increase distrust as they learn negative events. In turn, contradictory evidence lead to a discount of information. The asymmetry principle was also confirmed in general terms in a study concerning genetically modified food (Poortinga and Pidgeon 2004). It was observed that participants with clear positive or negative beliefs tend to interpret new information in line with their prior attitudes, *ambivalent* participants find information about negative events more informative than positive events (*negativity bias*), and *indifferent* participants suffer the least impact from positive and negative information.

23.6 Trust and Reputation

In Sect. 23.2, reputation was referred to as a source or antecedent of trust, especially relevant in open and dynamic environments, where other types of information about the trustee can be either inexistent or costly. However, reputation is, per se, a social phenomenon as complex as trust, and the interrelation between trust and reputation is a subject of, at least, as much ambiguity as the notion of trust itself.

We hypothesize that the relationship between trust and reputation can be understood at two different levels. On the one hand, reputation is an antecedent of trust, and it may or may not influence the trust put by the truster on the trustee, depending on the existence and relevance of other types of evidence. As put by Jøsang, Ismail, and Boyd, "I trust you because of your good reputation" and "I trust you despite your bad reputation" are both plausible (Jøsang et al. 2007). On the other hand, the process of reputation building is subject to specific social influences that are not present in the process of building trust, such as badmouthing and win-lose games. In this perspective, it is possible to envision trust and reputation as isolated constructs, where both contribute (in conjunction with other factors, such as risk and utility) to the final desideratum of decision making. Therefore, in this vision, reputation *does not* influence trust.

23.7 Computational Models

In the last few years, several computational trust models have been proposed in the distributed artificial intelligence (DAI) literature in order to allow intelligent agents to make trust-based decisions. Computational trust academics have been busy in formalizing, implementing and evaluating models of trust that rely on trust theory, which in part was covered in previous sections.

Until now, most of the existing computational trust models have focused on the aggregation of past evidence about the agent under evaluation in order to estimate its trustworthiness. Several different algorithms have been proposed to this end. Some of them compute the trustee's trustworthiness by averaging the past experiences of the trustee and weighting them by their recency (Huynh 2006; Sabater and Sierra 2001), others are based on beta models (Jøsang and Ismail 2002; Patel 2006), fuzzy cognitive maps (Venanzi et al. 2011), and other mathematical techniques or heuristics. More recent models try to cope with specific properties of trust and its dynamics, such as context (Rehak et al. 2006; Tavakolifard 2009; Urbano et al. 2010) and asymmetry (Jonker and Treur 1999; Melaye and Demazeau 2005; Urbano et al. 2009).

However, there is still a long path to run in computational trust. As an example, only a few computational models (Marsh 1994; Venanzi et al. 2011) deal with the inclusion of the truster's disposition in the trust equation, or consider some kind of categorization (Hermoso et al. 2009; Venanzi et al. 2011). In the same way, we have shown in a recent study (Urbano et al. 2011) that traditional computational trust models fail to capture the evolution of the relationship between different agents (e.g. relations that evolve due to the establishment of goodwill trust or to the change of the power relationship between the interacting partners), and thus are not able to model the effect that the *relationship* has on trust. Indeed, we think that these last issues – as well as the introduction of emotions and affects into the trust loop – are critical points for the success and wide acceptance of credible computational trust models to be widely and safely used, for example in business and industry.

Although the field of *computational reputation* has its own set of research questions and challenges, different academics have proposed models of computational trust and reputation that integrate both social concepts, assuming the perspective of reputation as an antecedent of trust (e.g., Huynh 2006; Jøsang and Ismail 2002; Jurca and Faltings 2003; Patel 2006; Sabater-Mir et al. 2006; Yu and Singh 2002).

The interplay between trust and reputation raises different challenges. On the one hand, computation trust models that use reputation need to estimate the credibility of both the transmitted information and the agent(s) reporting the information, in order to weight the received information accordingly. On the other hand, computational reputation systems must provide adequate incentives for referrals to provide reputational information; also, they must be able to tackle the problem of the heterogeneity (both syntactic and semantic) of the different images that constitute the reputation score being transmitted. Other challenges include discrimination and change in the quality of opinions of information providers (Jøsang et al. 2007).

23.8 Conclusions

This section gave a brief overview of trust, a social construct that is present in all human interactions (be it with other humans, institutions or things), and that is viewed by several academics as a kind of fuel of society. The section started by distinguishing between trust and trustworthiness. Then, it focused on different perspectives of trust, including its factors, nature, and dynamics. It was referred to that most of the existing computational models of trust fail to capture these distinct perspectives.

Finally, its was hypothesized that the interplay between reputation and trust can be understood at two different levels: either reputation is an antecedent of trust, *or* both contribute to the ultimate decision making as isolate components, where trust is not influenced by reputation. In either view, the study of trust would be enriched if we had a deep understanding of reputation, in the same way that it is not possible to understand reputation without having a thorough knowledge of the trust phenomenon. In conjunction, trust and reputation constitute an extremely important dyadic mechanism of social order and a very cost-effective governance tool for all types of social interactions. As such, they are considered vital agreement technologies.

References

Bhattacharya, R., T. M. Devinney, and M. M. Pillutla. 1998. A formal model of trust based on outcomes. *The Academy of Management Review* 23(3): 459–472.

Castelfranchi, C., and R. Falcone. 2010. *Trust theory: A socio-cognitive and computational model*. Wiley Series in Agent Technology. Chichester: Wiley.

Castelfranchi, C., R. Falcone, and G. Pezzulo. 2003. Trust in information sources as a source for trust: A fuzzy approach. In *Proceedings of the second international joint conference on autonomous agents and multiagent systems, AAMAS '03*, 89–96. New York: ACM. doi:http://doi.acm.org/10.1145/860575.860590.

Cohen, P. R., and H. J. Levesque. 1990. Intention is choice with commitment. *Artificial Intelligence* 42(2–3): 213–261. doi:10.1016/0004-3702(90)90055-5. http://www.sciencedirect.com/science/article/pii/0004370290900555.

Conte, R., and M. Paolucci. 2002. *Reputation in artificial societies: Social beliefs for social order*. Norwell: Kluwer Academic.

Cvetkovich, G., M. Siegrist, R. Murray, and S. Tragesser. 2002. New information and social trust: Asymmetry and perseverance of attributions about hazard managers. *Risk Analysis* 22(2): 359–367.

Dasgupta, P. 2000. Trust as a commodity. In *Trust: Making and breaking cooperative relations*, ed. D. Gambetta, 49–72. Department of Sociology, University of Oxford: Oxford.

Dimitrakos, T. 2001. System models, e-risks and e-trust. In *Proceedings of the IFIP conference on towards the E-society: E-Commerce, E-Business, E-Government, I3E '01*, 45–58. Deventer: Kluwer.

Elangovan, A. R., and D. L. Shapiro. 1998. Betrayal of trust in organizations. *The Academy of Management Review* 23(3), 547–566.

Finkel, E. J., C. E. Rusbult, M. Kumashiro, and P. A. Hannon. 2002. Dealing with betrayal in close relationships: Does commitment promote forgiveness? *Journal of Personality and Social Psychology* 82(6): 956–974.

Fitness, J. 2001. Betrayal, rejection, revenge, and forgiveness: An interpersonal script approach. In *Interpersonal rejection*, ed. M. Leary, 73–103. New York: Oxford University Press.

Foddy, M., M. J. Platow, and T. Yamagishi. 2009. Group-based trust in strangers. *Psychological Science* 20(4): 419–422. doi:10.1111/j.1467-9280.2009.02312.x. http://pss.sagepub.com/content/20/4/419.abstract.

Hardin, R. 2001. Conceptions and explanations of trust. In *Trust in society*, vol. 2, ed. K. S. Cook, 3–39. Russell Sage Foundation Series on Trust. New York: Russell Sage Foundation.

Hardin, R. 2002. *Trust and trustworthiness*. The Russell Sage Foundation Series on trust. New York: Russell Sage Foundation.

Heimer, C. 2001. Solving the problem of trust. In *Trust in society*, 40–88. Russell Sage Foundation Series on Trust, ed. K. S. Cook. New York: Russell Sage Foundation.

Hermoso, R., H. Billhardt, and S. Ossowski. 2009. Dynamic evolution of role taxonomies through multidimensional clustering in multiagent organizations. In *Principles of practice in multi-agent systems*. Lecture Notes in Computer Science, ed. J.-J. Yang, M. Yokoo, T. Ito, Z. Jin, P. Scerri, vol. 5925, 587–594. Berlin/Heidelberg: Springer.

Huynh, T. D., N. R. Jennings, and N. R. Shadbolt. 2006. An integrated trust and reputation model for open multi-agent systems. *Autonomous Agents and Multi-Agent Systems* 13: 119–154.

Ireland, R. D., and J. W. Webb. 2007. A multi-theoretic perspective on trust and power in strategic supply chains. *Journal of Operations Management* 25(2): 482–497. doi:10.1016/j.jom.2006.05.004. Special Issue Evolution of the Field of Operations Management SI/Special Issue Organisation Theory and Supply Chain Management.

Jonker, C. M., and J. Treur. 1999. Formal analysis of models for the dynamics of trust based on experiences. In *MultiAgent system engineering*. Lecture Notes in Computer Science, ed. F. Garijo, M. Boman, vol. 1647, 221–231. Berlin/Heidelberg: Springer.

Jøsang, A., and R. Ismail. 2002. The beta reputation system. In *Proceedings of the 15th bled electronic commerce conference*, Bled Slovenia, 17–19 June 2002.

Jøsang, A., R. Ismail, and C. Boyd. 2007. A survey of trust and reputation systems for online service provision. *Decision Support Systems* 43(2): 618–644. doi:10.1016/j.dss.2005.05.019.

Jurca, R., and B. Faltings. 2003. An incentive compatible reputation mechanism. In *Proceedings of the second international joint conference on autonomous agents and multiagent systems, AAMAS '03*, 1026–1027. New York: ACM.

Kiyonari, T., T. Yamagishi, K. S. Cook, and C. Cheshire. 2006. Does trust beget trustworthiness? trust and trustworthiness in two games and two cultures: A research note. *Social Psychology Quarterly* **69**(3): 270–283. doi:10.1177/019027250606900304.

Levin, D. Z., R. Cross, L. C. Abrams, and E. L. Lesser. Trust and knowledge sharing: A critical combination. In *Creating value with knowledge: Insights from the IBM institutue for business value, 36–43*, ed. E. Lesser and L. Prusak. Oxford: Oxford University (2004).

Marsh, S. 1994. Formalising trust as a computational concept. Ph.D. thesis, University of Stirling.

Mayer, R. C., J. H. Davis, and F. D. Schoorman. 1995. An integrative model of organizational trust. *The Academy of Management Review* 20(3): 709–734.

Melaye, D., and Y. Demazeau. 2005. Bayesian dynamic trust model. In *Multi-agent systems and applications IV*. Lecture Notes in Computer Science, vol. 3690, ed. M. Pechoucek, P. Petta, L. Varga, 480–489. Berlin/Heidelberg: Springer.

Patel, J. 2006. A trust and reputation model for agent-based virtual organisations. Ph.D. thesis, University of Southampton.

Pavlou, P. A., Y. H. Tan, and D. Gefen. 2003. The transitional role of institutional trust in online interorganizational relationships. *Hawaii International Conference on System Sciences* 7: 215–224. doi:http://doi.ieeecomputersociety.org/10.1109/HICSS.2003.1174574.

Poortinga, W., and N. F. Pidgeon. 2004. Trust, the asymmetry principle, and the role of prior beliefs. *Risk Analysis* 24(6): 1475–1486.

Rehak, M., M. Gregor, and M. Pechoucek. 2006. Multidimensional context representations for situational trust. In *Proceedings of the IEEE workshop on distributed intelligent systems: Collective intelligence and its applications, DIS '06*, Washington, DC, USA, 315–320. IEEE Computer Society.

Rotter, J. B. 1967. A new scale for the measurement of interpersonal trust. *Journal of Personality* 35(4): 651–665.

Sabater, J., and C. Sierra. 2001. REGRET: Reputation in gregarious societies. In *Proceedings of the fifth international conference on autonomous agents, AGENTS '01*, 194–195. New York: ACM. doi:http://doi.acm.org/10.1145/375735.376110. http://doi.acm.org/10.1145/375735.376110.

Sabater-Mir, J., and M. Paolucci. 2007. On Representation and aggregation of social evaluations in computational trust and reputation models. *International Journal of Approximate Reasoning* 46(3), 458–483.

Sabater-Mir, J., M. Paolucci, and R. Conte. 2006. Repage: Reputation and image among limited autonomous partners. *Journal of Artificial Societies and Social Simulation* 9(2): 3. http://jasss.soc.surrey.ac.uk/9/2/3.html.

Sako, M. 2002. Does trust improve business performance? http://hdl.handle.net/1721.1/1462.

Schoorman, F. D., R. C. Mayer, and J. H. Davis. 2007. An integrative model of organizational trust: Past, present, and future. *Academy of Management Review* 32(2): 344–354.

Slovic, P. 1993. Perceived risk, trust, and democracy. *Risk Analysis* 13(6): 675–682.

Straker, D. 2008. *Changing minds: In detail.* Crowthorne: Syque.

Tavakolifard, M. 2009. Situation-aware trust management. In *Proceedings of the 2009 ACM conference on recommender systems, RecSys 2009*, 413–416. New York: ACM.

Urbano, J., H. Lopes Cardoso, and E. Oliveira. 2010. Making electronic contracting operational and trustworthy. In *12th Ibero-American conference on artificial intelligence, IBERAMIA-2010*, 264–273. Bahia Blanca: Springer.

Urbano, J., A. P. Rocha, and E. Oliveira. 2009. Computing confidence values: Does trust dynamics matter? In *Proceedings of the 14th Portuguese conference on artificial intelligence: Progress in artificial intelligence, EPIA '09*, 520–531. Berlin/Heidelberg: Springer.

Urbano, J., A. Rocha, and E. Oliveira. 2010. Trustworthiness tendency incremental extraction using information gain. In *IEEE/WIC/ACM international conference on web intelligence and intelligent agent technology (WI-IAT), 2010*, vol. 2, 411–414. doi:10.1109/WI-IAT.2010.151.

Urbano, J., A. P. Rocha, and E. Oliveira. 2011. A dynamic agents' behavior model for computational trust. In *Proceedings of the 15th Portugese conference on progress in artificial intelligence, EPIA'11*, 536–550. Berlin/Heidelberg: Springer. http://dl.acm.org/citation.cfm?id=2051115.2051164.

Venanzi, M., M. Piunti, R. Falcone, and C. Castelfranchi. 2011. Facing openness with socio-cognitive trust and categories. In *IJCAI 2011, proceedings of the 22nd international joint conference on artificial intelligence*, ed. T. Walsh, 400–405. IJCAI/AAAI. Barcelona: Spain.

Wathne, K. H., and J. B. Heide. 2000. Opportunism in interfirm relationships: Forms, outcomes, and solutions. *The Journal of Marketing* 64(4): 36–51.

Williamson, O. E. 1979. Transaction-cost economics: The governance of contractual relations. *Journal of Law and Economics* 22: 233–261.

Yu, B., and M. P. Singh. 2002. An evidential model of distributed reputation management. In *Proceedings of the first international joint conference on autonomous agents and multiagent systems: part 1, AAMAS '02*, 294–301. New York: ACM.

Chapter 24
Qualitative Assessment Dynamics: QAD

Denis Trček

24.1 Introduction

As presented so far, there exist nowadays many trust management solutions for agent environments. The main common property of these solutions is the deployment of various established and proven artificial intelligence (AI) methodologies. However, there exist some gaps in this area, because artificial worlds have to be interfaced with the human domain for many reasons. Most notably, for multi and interdisciplinary research it is desirable that agent technologies could be deployed in a manner where they would model human behavior when it comes to trust. Furthermore, human-focused metrics should exist that would enable mapping between the AI domain and humans domain – while the first kind of metrices are typically quantitative, the latter are typically qualitative. And this is exactly where Qualitative Assessment Dynamics (QAD) comes in.

QAD is based on linguistic grounds, more precisely, it is based on language expressions that are related to trust and which are used in various cultural settings. This makes QAD principles understandable to a large number of users, while at the same time enabling simulations of trust with which to study the dynamics in human structures (communities, organizations, etc.). Put another way, QAD is based on operators and operands that are aligned with human reasoning, and have therefore appropriate counterparts in the majority of languages.

In order to better grasp the main foundations behind QAD, two typical trust management methodologies from the AI domain will be elaborated in the next section. Then, a section follows that focuses on a definition of trust that will be suitable for QAD purposes. Afterward, QAD is presented in more detail with an application example. The chapter ends with conclusions.

D. Trček (✉)
Faculty of Computer and Information Science, University of Ljubljana,
Tržaška cesta 25, 1000 Ljubljana, Slovenia
e-mail: denis.trcek@fri.uni-lj.si

S. Ossowski (ed.), *Agreement Technologies*, Law, Governance
and Technology Series 8, DOI 10.1007/978-94-007-5583-3_24,

24.2 Traditional Approaches

An important stream of traditional trust management methodologies is rooted in Bayes theorem and its generalization, the Dempster Shafer Theory of Evidence, or ToE. They are described in the following sub-subsections. This stream encompasses a large part of the approaches to trust management in agent communities, but is certainly not exhaustive. Other important streams include those based on, e.g., game theory, but focusing on that above-mentioned stream gives sufficient grounds to properly position and understand the intention and potential of QAD.

24.2.1 Naive Trust Management

These kinds of trust management methodologies is based on pure Bayesian probability. A typical example of this kind of implementation is in peer-to-peer networks, where various files are shared (Wang and Vassileva 2003). To achieve the goal of "computing trust", all agents build their own Bayesian networks for each file provider that they have been interacting with. The root is about trust (more precisely, about trustworthiness in other agent's competence), while leafs cover aspects related to trustworthiness (in our case file type, file quality, and file download speed). The evaluation of other agent's trustworthiness T (in terms of probability in its competence) in relation to the provided file, its quality, and its download speed can be depicted as follows (Table 24.1).

So the root of the network is assigned 1, when interaction is as expected, and 0 when this is not the case. Probability $p(\mathrm{T}=1)$ for satisfying interactions is obtained by dividing m with n, $p(\mathrm{T}=1)=m/n$, while for unsatisfying interactions it is obtained as $p(\mathrm{T}=0)=(n-m)/n$ (in both cases m stands for the number of satisfying, and n for the number of all interactions). After evaluating this value, an agent may (or may not) decide to initiate interaction. In case of interaction, values for m and n are updated accordingly to the experience (of course, the initial interaction cannot be supported by this methodology directly, but through, e.g., existing calculations of other agents). This whole procedure is analogously performed for file quality and file download speed. The computation of the above network values is given in the following Table 24.2.

Having the above values and using the extended Bayes formula

$$p(H|D_1,D_2)=\frac{p(H,D_1,D)}{p(D_1,D_2)}=\ldots=p(D_1|H,D_2)*\frac{p(H|D_2)}{p(D_1|D_2)},$$

Table 24.1 A network for file exchange trust evaluations

Trust in competence		
File type	File quality	Download speed

Table 24.2 Probabilities calculation for trustworthiness derivation of other agent's (related to provide file type)

	T=1	T=0
Music	p(FT=music I T=1)	p(FT=music I T=0)
Video	p(FT=video I T=1)	p(FT=video I T=0)
Book	p(FT=book I T=1)	p(FT=book I T=0)
Image	p(FT=image I T=1)	p(FT=image I T=0)
Software	p(FT=software I T=1)	p(FT=software I T=0)
...	...	...

an agent can calculate probabilities for realistic questions related to trust. For example, which agent is most trustworthy when it comes to exchanging an image files and that this file is of a high quality? Translating this into Bayesian domain gives the following equation: $p(T = 1|FT = image, FQ = high)$, where FT stands for file type and FQ for file quality.

To sum up, as can be seen in the above example, the strength of such methodologies is well established and widely understood basic, i.e. Bayesian statistics, which also enables effective implementations. On the other hand, its major weakness is treating trust (and related cognitive processes) as being equal to the notion of probability.

24.2.2 *Theory of Evidence and Subjective Algebra*

Generalization of Bayesian statistics leads to Dempster-Shafer Theory of Evidence, ToE (Shafer 1976). ToE starts with a set of possible (atomic) states, called a frame of discernment Θ, where exactly one state is assumed to be true at any time. Based on this frame of discernments, basic probability assignment, or BPA (also called belief mass) function is defined as

$$m : 2^{\Theta} \rightarrow [0,1],$$

where m{ } = 0, and $\Sigma_{A \subseteq 2^{\Theta}} m(A) = 1$. Now belief function $b(X)$ is introduced and defined as the sum of the beliefs committed to possibilities Y that are being observed at the level of X. By adding disbelief d and uncertainty u functions, a triplet $\omega = (b, d, u)$ is obtained that forms the basis of subjective algebra (Jøsang 1999, 2001):

$$b(X) = \sum_{Y \subseteq X} m(Y),\; d(X) = \sum_{Y \cap X = \emptyset} m(Y),\; u(X) = 1 - b(X) - d(X),$$

$$\omega = (b, d, u)$$

Having defined the above triplet, it is possible now to model trust manifestations by introducing operators like recommendation and consensus. To define the first operator, let A and B be two agents where $\omega_B^A = (b_p^{AB}, d_p^{AB}, u_p^{AB})$ is A's opinion about B's recommendations, and p a binary statement where $\omega_p^B = (b_p^B, d_p^B, u_p^B)$ is B's opinion about p expressed in a recommendation to A. Then A's opinion about p as the result of the recommendation from B is calculated as

$$\omega_p^{AB} = \omega_B^A \otimes \omega_p^B = (b_p^{AB}, d_p^{AB}, u_p^{AB}),$$

where

$$b_p^{AB} = b_B^A b_p^B,\ d_p^{AB} = d_B^A + d_p^B,\ u_p^{AB} = d_B^A + u_B^A + b_B^A u_p^B.$$

Now to define the consensus, let $\omega_p^A = (b_p^A, d_p^A, u_p^A)$and $\omega_p^B = (b_p^B, d_p^B, u_p^B)$ be opinions held by agents A and B about a binary statement p. Then the consensus is calculated as

$$\omega_p^{AB} = \omega_B^A \oplus \omega_p^B = (b_p^{AB}, d_p^{AB}, u_p^{AB}),$$

where

$$\begin{aligned} b_p^{AB} &= (b_p^A u_p^B + b_p^B u_p^A)/(u_p^A + u_p^B - u_p^A u_p^B), \\ d_p^{AB} &= (d_p^A u_p^B + d_p^B u_p^A)/(u_p^A + u_p^B - u_p^A u_p^B), \\ u_p^{AB} &= (u_p^A u_p^B)/(u_p^A + u_p^B - u_p^A u_p^B) \end{aligned}$$

The strength of subjective algebra is its formal basis, which also addresses so-called "uncertain probabilities" that in certain contexts can be effectively applied to deal with humans estimates. The weak point is that trust is treated as being equal to the above defined triplet of functions.

24.3 Defining Trust for QAD

Having addressed some basic principles behind the major trust management methodologies, the question now is what trust is. More precisely – how can trust be formally defined? The notion of trust was a matter of definition efforts for decades, especially in the social sciences, where this phenomenon was initially addressed. However, most of these definitions are implicit, and where this is not the case, they are too informal for computational use. Nevertheless, some of them provide important bases and they are briefly discussed here. In these kind of definitions it is often at least implicitly assumed that trust is required (and exists) only in situations that contain a probability of an adverse outcome. Therefore it is claimed that its basic function is to enable coping with uncertain situations (Mayer et al. 1995). Further, trust is also considered to be related to decreased judgment complexity by reducing the number of options that an agent has to consider (Lewis and Weigert 1985). Related to definition of trust, proper understanding of its forms is important, where authors distinguish between cognitive, i.e., rational, and affective, i.e., emotional trust (McAllister 1995).

Getting to explicit definitions, the following one, proposed by Giddens, should be mentioned first: Trust is a form of faith, in which the confidence vested in probable outcomes expresses a commitment to something rather than just a cognitive understanding (Giddens 1991). Further, in relation to methodologies discussed above, we have observed that some authors treat trust as being equal to objective probability (Wang and Vassileva 2003), while others (implicitly) treat it as being equal to (uncertain) subjective probability derived on the basis of Dempster Shafer Theory of evidence (Jøsang 1999). Another explicit definition from one definite source, Merriam-Webster dictionary, goes as follows: Trust is assured reliance on the character, ability, strength, or truth of someone or something. However, trust cannot be treated in isolation, and its social dimension is crucial, as expressed in the definition given by D.E. Denning: Trust is not a property of an entity or a system, but is an assessment. Such assessment is driven by experience, it is shared through a network of people interactions and it is continually remade each time the system is used (Denning 1993). This last definition is concise enough to enable formal treatment in computerized environments, which is also the case with QAD, where trust is defined as follows (Trček 2009): Trust is a qualitatively weighted relation between entities, where these entities can be atomic or compound.

24.4 Qualitative Assessment Dynamics

The advantages of the above presented (traditional) approaches are supposed to be obvious to a reader. They deploy established and widely accepted AI methodologies. By focusing on the gap that exists in linking traditional trust management methodologies to humans domain, and to enable human-centric modeling of agents' operators and operands, the following important issues should be mentioned (agents in this case and the rest of the paper should be understood as human agents):

- Agents are not (always) rational (this is the problem with all above mentioned trust methodologies).
- If they are rational they (may) have problems with the basic notion of probability (this is crucial for Bayesian, as well as for TOE based methodologies).
- Even if agents do not have problems with the basic notion of probability, they will likely not understand sophisticated mathematics (this especially applies to ToE and subjective algebra).
- In case of trust they may have no preferences. But if they have preferences, these may not be transitive (this is crucial for game-theory based trust management methodologies).

Qualitative Assessment Dynamics, QAD, is a trust management methodology that is complementary to those described earlier. Its main goal is to model trust phenomenon in agents systems as closely to human trust as possible. Therefore its basis is formed through experiments (so far with questionnaire research batteries, while other experiments are being designed and will be applied in the near future).

The goal of these experiments is straightforward: to determine the operands and operators that would model human trust and its dynamics as close as possible.

Now to address the above issues and define appropriate operands and operators, experiments are supporting the following claims that form the basis of QAD Trček (2011) and Trček (2009):

1. Users would choose qualitative assessment for evaluating (describing) trust.
2. Users would choose five levels ordinal scale for trust assessments.
3. Users have problems with conforming to the basic definition of probability when it comes to trust.
4. To users trust is not a reflexive relation, neither is it symmetric, nor transitive.
5. When users belong to a certain group their assessment may generally differ from that of the group.
6. When users assess a certain group as a whole their assessment equals to the assessment of the majority of the members of this group.
7. Users may occasionally change trust assessment on a non-identifiable basis.
8. Users trust may be initialized on a non-identifiable basis.
9. Users would choose direct trust management.

Questions 1 and 2 serve for identification of operands, questions 3–8 for identification of trust (dynamics) operators, while the last question serves to address one basic dilemma: Would users be willing to completely leave computerized systems to decide on their behalf when it comes to trust or not?

For the above claims we have selected a threshold of 30% of users' population supporting the claim (so one should actually read the above claims as "More than 30% of users would choose qualitative assessment of trust", etc.). The logic behind this threshold is that QAD is supposed to be at least the second major player in the field of trust management solutions. Based on statistical data for the core three solutions/services in IT sector (operating systems, web browsers and search engines) it has turned out that the necessary threshold can be as low as 8%, but in the most optimistic scenario it does not exceed 30%. These thresholds are based on market research analysis carried out in 2011 and referenced in Trček (2011).

The results of two piloting studies and one full-blown study support the above claims, with the only exception being the claim that more than 30% of users are likely to violate the basic definition of probability when it comes to trust. On this basis, trust in QAD is defined as a qualitatively weightily relation between agents A and B that is denoted by $\alpha_{A,B}$, which means agent's A assessment of agent B. Having defined trust as a relation, it is possible to represent trust assessment in a certain society by qualitatively weighted graph or (equivalently) by corresponding matrix (see Fig. 24.1).

In the above matrix the symbol "–" denotes unknown (unexpressed) or unexisting assessment (for example, when one agent is not aware of the other one). This shows that QAD enables also treatment of dumb agents (in the above case, agent one could be such agent providing e.g. virtual storage, because it is not able to express its assessments no arcs are started from this node). The structure developed so far can now be completed by adding operators that model trust dynamics. In Fig. 24.2 some most often used operators defined so far are given (Trček 2011).

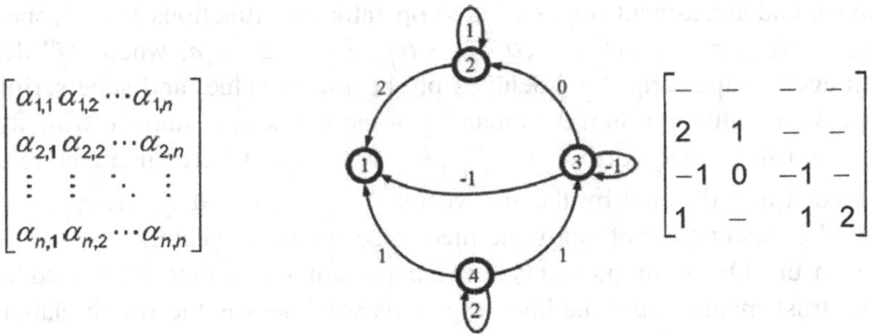

Fig. 24.1 QAD general matrix (*left*) and an example society (*middle*) with the corresponding assessment matrix (*right*)

a $\alpha^{-}_{j,i} \neq -$:

- $\Uparrow_j$: $$max(\alpha^{-}_{1,i}, \alpha^{-}_{2,i}, \alpha^{-}_{3,i}, \ldots, \alpha^{-}_{j,i}, \ldots, \alpha^{-}_{n,i}) \rightarrow \alpha^{+}_{j,i} \qquad i = 1,2,\ldots,n$$
- $\Downarrow_j$: $$min(\alpha^{-}_{1,i}, \alpha^{-}_{2,i}, \alpha^{-}_{3,i}, \ldots, \alpha^{-}_{j,i}, \ldots, \alpha^{-}_{n,i}) \rightarrow \alpha^{+}_{j,i} \qquad i = 1,2,\ldots,n$$
- $\uparrow_j$: $$\begin{cases} \alpha^{-}_{j,i} \rightarrow \alpha^{+}_{j,i} & if\ \frac{1}{n_1}\sum_{i=1}^{n_1} \alpha^{-}_{i,k} \leq \alpha^{-}_{j,i} \\ \lfloor \alpha^{-}_{j,i} + 1 \rfloor \rightarrow \alpha^{+}_{j,i} & otherwise \end{cases}$$
- $\downarrow_j$: $$\begin{cases} \alpha^{-}_{j,i} \rightarrow \alpha^{+}_{j,i} & if\ \frac{1}{n_1}\sum_{i=1}^{n_1} \alpha^{-}_{i,k} \geq \alpha^{-}_{j,i} \\ \lceil \alpha^{-}_{j,i} - 1 \rceil \rightarrow \alpha^{+}_{j,i} & otherwise \end{cases}$$
- $\rightsquigarrow_j$: $$\begin{cases} \left\lceil \frac{1}{n_1}\sum_{i=1}^{n_1} \alpha^{-}_{i,k} \right\rceil \rightarrow \alpha^{+}_{j,i} & if\ \frac{1}{n_1}\sum_{i=1}^{n_1} \alpha^{-}_{i,k} < 0 \\ \left\lfloor \frac{1}{n_1}\sum_{i=1}^{n_1} \alpha^{-}_{i,k} \right\rfloor \rightarrow \alpha^{+}_{j,i} & otherwise \end{cases}$$
- $\leftrightarrow_j$: $$\begin{cases} \left\lceil \frac{1}{n_1}\sum_{i=1}^{n_1} \alpha^{-}_{i,k} \right\rceil \rightarrow \alpha^{+}_{j,i} & if\ \frac{1}{n_1}\sum_{i=1}^{n_1} \alpha^{-}_{i,k} > 0 \\ \left\lfloor \frac{1}{n_1}\sum_{i=1}^{n_1} \alpha^{-}_{i,k} \right\rfloor \rightarrow \alpha^{+}_{j,i} & otherwise \end{cases}$$
- $\odot_j$: $$\alpha^{-}_{j,i} \rightarrow \alpha^{+}_{j,i} \qquad i = 1,2,\ldots,n$$
- $\updownarrow_j$: $$rand(-2,-1,0,1,2) \rightarrow \alpha^{+}_{j,i} \qquad i = 1,2,\ldots,n$$

b $\alpha^{-}_{j,i} = -$:

$$- \rightarrow \alpha^{+}_{j,i} \qquad i = 1,2,\ldots,n$$

Fig. 24.2 The definitions of QAD operators

Operators are elements of the set $\Psi = \{\Uparrow, \Downarrow, \uparrow, \downarrow, \rightsquigarrow, \leftrightarrow, \odot, \updownarrow\}$, and they are referred to as extreme optimistic assessment, extreme pessimistic assessment, moderate optimistic assessment, moderate pessimistic assessment, centralist consensus seeker assessment, non-centralist consensus-seeker assessment, self-confident assessment and assessment-hoping. These operators are functions $f_j \in \Psi$, such that $f_j : A_{n,i} = (\alpha^-_{1,i}, \alpha^-_{2,i}, \ldots, \alpha^-_{j,i}, \ldots, \alpha^-_{n,i}) \rightarrow \alpha^+_{j,i}$, $j = 1,2,\ldots,n$, where "j" denotes the j-th agent, superscript "−" denotes pre-operation value, and superscript "+" post-operation value. Further, the meaning of the index n_1 is derived from agent's k trust vector $A_{k,n} = (\alpha^-_{k,1}, \alpha^-_{k,2}, \ldots, \alpha^-_{k,n})$, $k = 1,2,\ldots,n$, where undefined relations are excluded and denoted by the sub-vector $\underline{A}_{n_1,k} = (\alpha^-_{1,k}, \alpha^-_{2,k}, \ldots, \alpha^-_{n_1,k})$, where index n_1 denotes number of non-undefined values in a trust vector.

To sum up, QAD complements some important views that are not addressed by other trust management methodologies. Its weakness is the rough elaboration of existing operators that needs further refinement and support of more realistic scenarios (weighting of other agents' opinions, etc.). Research that is addressing these issues is currently underway.

24.5 Conclusions

This chapter presented a trust management methodology called Qualitative Assessment Dynamics, QAD, which complements traditional (mostly AI based) trust management methodologies. It takes into account human specifics when it comes to trust. QAD rests on a premise that language expressions related to trust actually reflect the corresponding mental processes and thus defines operators and operands that have clear counterparts in many languages. By doing so it extends possibilities to use agents technologies for purposes like human structures modeling (e.g., communities, organizations, states) and studying their dynamics through computer simulations.

Last but not least, it should be emphasized that when compared to traditional trust management methodologies in various contest settings, QAD may perform worse in terms of detecting cheating agents, etc. But one should note that this does not render QAD useless. On the contrary, QAD is about human-like agents, so it is aimed at reflecting human reality. But one thing remains certain – the work presented here is just a basis, so further refinement of operands and operators will have to be a subject of future research.

References

Denning, D. E. 1993. A new paradigm for trusted systems. In *Proceedings on the 1992–1993 workshop on new security paradigms, NSPW '92–93*, 36–41. New York: ACM. doi:10.1145/283751.283772.

Giddens, A. 1991. *The consequences of modernity*. Stanford: Stanford University Press.

Jøsang, A. 1999. An algebra for assessing trust in certification chains. In *Proceedings of the network and distributed system security symposium, NDSS '99*, 618–644. Reston: The Internet Society.

Jøsang, A. 2001. A logic for uncertain probabilities. *International Journal of Uncertainty, Fuzziness and Knowledge-Based Systems* 9(3): 279–311.

Lewis, J. D., and A. Weigert. 1985. Trust as a social reality. *Social Forces* 63(4): 967–985. doi:10.2307/2578601.

Mayer, R. C., J. H. Davis, and F. D. Schoorman. 1995. An integrative model of organizational trust. *The Academy of Management Review* 20(3): 709–734. doi:10.2307/258792.

McAllister, D. J. 1995. Affect- and cognition-based trust as foundations for interpersonal cooperation in organizations. *The Academy of Management Journal* 38(1): 24–59. doi:10.2307/256727.

Shafer, G. 1976. A mathematical theory of evidence. Princeton: Princeton University Press.

Trček, D. 2009. A formal apparatus for modeling trust in computing environments. *Mathematical and Computer Modelling* 49(1–2): 226–233.

Trček, D. 2011. Trust management methodologies for the web. In *Proceedings of the 7th international conference on reasoning web: Semantic technologies for the web of data, RW'11*, 445–459. Berlin/Heidelberg: Springer.

Wang, Y., and J. Vassileva. 2003. Trust and reputation model in peer-to-peer networks. *IEEE International Conference on Peer-to-Peer Computing* 0: 150. doi:http://doi.ieeecomputersociety.org/10.1109/PTP.2003.1231515

Chapter 25
Argumentation and Trust

Andrew Koster, Jordi Sabater-Mir, and Marco Schorlemmer

25.1 Introduction

Trust is a technique for dealing with uncertainty regarding other agents' actions and communications. As such, it is a necessary aspect of a reasoning agent in a multiagent system. Such an agent must coordinate and communicate with the other agents in the system. Trust plays a role in deciding with whom to cooperate and which information sources are reliable. However, it is not the only factor in such decisions. Recently work has been done to combine trust in agents' reasoning systems, specifically systems that use argumentation, in a number of different manners. The first is by using the trustworthiness of a source of information within an argument to decide whether it is acceptable or not, which we discuss in Sect. 25.2. The second, discussed in Sect. 25.3 is to incorporate information from the argumentation into the computation of that same trustworthiness. Finally, argumentation has been used as a method for communicating more accurately about trust, and we describe this in Sect. 25.4.

25.2 Trusted Arguments

One of the problems encountered in a multiagent society is that agents use information from a variety of sources in their reasoning process. Such sources may be more, or less, reliable. Argumentation frameworks (Rahwan and Simari 2009) provide a way of reasoning using such information, by giving a formal method for dealing with conflicting information, often with degrees of uncertainty.

A. Koster (✉) • J. Sabater-Mir • M. Schorlemmer
IIIA – CSIC, Barcelona, Spain
e-mail: andrew@iiia.csic.es; jsabater@iiia.csic.es; marco@iiia.csic.es

S. Ossowski (ed.), *Agreement Technologies*, Law, Governance and Technology Series 8, DOI 10.1007/978-94-007-5583-3_25,

When considering the sources' trustworthiness as a measure of confidence in the information they provide the link between argumentation and trust is obvious. This is precisely the approach taken by Tang et al. (2010). Their work uses the trustworthiness of the information sources as a measure of the probability that information is true.

Parsons et al. abstract from this work and give a formal account of the properties of an argumentation framework when considering different ways of calculating trust and combining arguments (Parsons et al. 2011). Specifically they try to satisfy the condition:

> If an agent has two arguments A_1 and A_2 where the supports have corresponding sets of agents Ag_1 and Ag_2 then A_1 is stronger than A_2 only if the agent considers A_1 to be more trustworthy than A_2 (Parsons et al. 2011).

This condition states that arguments grounded in information from less trustworthy sources will not be able to defeat arguments with grounds from more trustworthy sources. The work then describes some computational methods for treating trust and argumentation that satisfy this condition. Unfortunately these methods have very strict properties, the most troublesome is the assumption that trust is transitive, while current sociological research indicates that this is only true in very specific situations (Castelfranchi and Falcone 2010). Despite this, the work lays a solid theoretical foundation for incorporating trust into argumentation.

Another approach to incorporating trust into argumentation is taken by Villata et al. (2011). Their work takes a similar approach to Tang et al.'s work and explicitly represents the sources providing the different arguments. The major contribution is in allowing argumentation about the trustworthiness of sources. It allows meta-arguments to support, and attack, statements about the trustworthiness of sources. The effect of this argumentation is to change the confidence agents have in the sources providing different arguments, which, in turn, changes the strength of the various arguments. This is thus a combination of two different forms of combining trust and argumentation. In meta-argumentation arguments are used to evaluate the trustworthiness of agents. In turn this trustworthiness is used as the strength of another set of arguments. This combination seems very powerful, but in relying purely on argumentation for evaluating the trustworthiness, a very coarse concept of trustworthiness is used. As they themselves state:

> Trust is represented *by default* as the absence of an attack towards the sources, or towards the information items and as the presence of evidence in favour of pieces of information (Villata et al. 2011).

However, trust is a far more complex relationship than this. Trust is a decision, based on, often conflicting, pieces of information, which is why contemporary trust models do not use a binary value for trustworthiness, but rather use a more fine-grained approach, such as a probability that the target will act in a trustworthy manner, or even a probability distribution over the possible outcomes. In the next section we discuss some methods for incorporating argumentation into a statistical model of trust.

25.3 Argument-Supported Trust

Prade's model (2007) was, insofar as we know, the first model to incorporate argumentation into a trust model. In this work, trust is considered along a variety of dimensions. Specifically, trust is split into trust categories, which represent different behavioural aspects of the target. Each behavioural aspect may be qualified as good, or not good, for a target agent. The trust model consists principally of a rule-base in which levels of trust are related to the target's behaviours. The trust model then uses the target's actual behaviour to perform abduction and find the range in which the trust evaluations must fall. This range is the trust evaluation of a target.

The arguments in Prade's work thus constitute the trust model itself. By performing the abduction with the rules in the trust model, the agent constructs arguments for its observations. The arguments are thus not part of the input of the trust model, but an inherent part of the calculation process. Matt et al. do consider arguments as a separate source of information for calculating the trustworthiness of a target (Matt et al. 2010).

Matt et al. propose a method for combining justified claims about a target with statistical evidence for that target's behaviour. These justified claims provide context-specific information about an agent's behaviour. The basis for their trust model is Yu and Singh's model (2002), which uses a Dempster-Shafer belief function to provide an estimate of whether an agent will fulfill its obligations, given some evidence about that agent's past behaviour. Matt et al. propose to extend this model with a method for evaluating arguments drawn from contracts, in which an agent's obligations are fixed and guarantees are provided about the quality of interactions. Specifically these contracts specify the requirements along a number of dimensions. These dimensions are aspects of an interaction, such as availability, security or reliability. For each dimension an agent wishes to take into account when evaluating trust, it can construct an argument forecasting the target's behaviour with regards to that dimension, given the specification of a contract. For each dimension d, Matt et al. can construct the following arguments:

- An argument forecasting untrustworthy behaviour, based on the fact that the contract does not provide any guarantee regarding d.
- An argument forecasting trustworthy behaviour, based on the fact that there is a contract guaranteeing a suitable quality of service along dimension d.
- An argument that mitigates a forecasting argument of the second type, on the grounds that the target has, in the past, "most often" violated its contract clauses concerning d.

They then integrate these arguments into Yu and Singh's trust model, by providing new argumentation-based belief functions that combine the information from forecast arguments with evidence. By incorporating more information, the agent should be able to obtain more accurate trust evaluations and Matt et al. show this empirically.

All the methods discussed so far highlight the different aspects of argumentation and trust for dealing with uncertain information; either by applying trust to argumentation in order to get more accurate arguments, or by applying argumentation to trust to obtain more accurate trust evaluations. However there is another useful way to combine trust and argumentation that has not been discussed so far. Evaluating trust often requires communication, but this communication may be unreliable, simply because trust is a subjective concept. By having agents argue about the trust evaluations themselves, an agent may discover whether the other's communicated trust evaluation is useful to it, or whether its interpretation of the various criteria for evaluating trustworthiness are too different from its own criteria (Pinyol and Sabater-Mir 2009). Furthermore, this communication can be used to adapt its own trust model in order to accept more information. Both of these methods are discussed in the next section.

25.4 Arguments About Trust

Trust is a relationship in which, given a certain context, an agent trusts a target to perform a task, resulting in a specific goal being achieved. This context is represented by an agent's beliefs about the environment and the goal is something the trustor wishes to achieve. Therefore trust is an agent's personal and subjective evaluation of a target. When communicating such a subjective evaluation it is often unclear how useful this evaluation is to the receiving agent: it needs to discover whether the context in which the communicated evaluation was made similar to the context in which the receiver needs to evaluate the target. Pinyol proposes a framework to argue about trust evaluations and decide whether another agent's communicated evaluations can be accepted or not (Pinyol 2011).

Pinyol starts by modeling the trust model as an inference relation between sentences in $\mathscr{L}_{Rep}$, a first-order language about trust and reputation (Pinyol and Sabater-Mir 2007). This language is defined by a taxonomy of terms used for describing the process of computing trust, which is discussed in more detail in Chap. 26, Sect. 26.4.2 of this book. A trust model is considered as a computational process: given a finite set of inputs, such as beliefs about direct experiences or reputation, it calculates a trust evaluation for a target. The semantics of a computational process can be given by the application of a set of inference rules (Jones 1997). Following Koster et al.'s formalization of trust models in a similar manner (Koster et al. 2012a), we define this as follows:

Definition 25.1 (Semantics of a trust model). We say that a set of inference rules $\mathscr{I}$ is a specification of a trust model if, given input Δ and the resulting trust computation δ, we have that $\Delta \vdash_T \delta$, i.e., there exists a finite number of applications of inference rules $\iota \in \mathscr{I}$ by which we may infer δ from Δ.

The inference rules themselves depend on the specifics of the computational process and thus the actual trust model being used, but for any computational trust model, such an inference relation exists. For instance, a trust model might have a rule:

$$\frac{img(T,X), rep(T,Y)}{trust(T, \frac{X+Y}{2})}$$

With *img*, *rep* and *trust* predicate symbols in $\mathscr{L}_{Rep}$. For a specific target *Jim*, an agent knows $\{img(Jim,3),\ rep(Jim,5)\}$. It can thus infer $trust(Jim,4)$ using the rule above. For a full example of representing a trust model in inference rules, we refer to Pinyol and Sabater-Mir (2009).

25.4.1 Reasons for Having a Trust Evaluation

Arguments are sentences in the $\mathscr{L}_{Arg}$ language. This language is defined over $\mathscr{L}_{Rep}$. A sentence in $\mathscr{L}_{Arg}$ is a formula $(\Phi : \alpha)$ with $\alpha \in \mathscr{L}_{Rep}$ and $\Phi \subseteq \mathscr{L}_{Rep}$. This definition is based on the framework for defeasible reasoning through argumentation, given by Chesñevar and Simari (2007). Intuitively Φ is the defeasible knowledge required to deduce α. Defeasible knowledge is the knowledge that is rationally compelling, but not deductively valid. The meaning here, is that using the defeasible knowledge Φ and a number of deduction rules, we can deduce α. The defeasible knowledge is introduced in a set of elementary argumentative formulas. These are called *basic declarative units*.

Definition 25.2 (Basic Declarative Units). A basic declarative unit (bdu) is a formula $(\{\alpha\} : \alpha) \in \mathscr{L}_{Arg}$. Additionally, we define an argumentative theory as being a finite set of bdus.

Arguments are constructed using an argumentative theory Γ and the inference relation $\vdash_{Arg}$, characterized by the deduction rules *Intro-BDU, Intro-AND* and *Elim-IMP* from Chesñevar and Simari (2007):

Definition 25.3 (Deduction rules of $\mathscr{L}_{Arg}$).

$$\text{Intro-BDU:} \quad \frac{}{(\{\alpha\} : \alpha)}$$

$$\text{Intro-AND:} \quad \frac{(\Phi_1 : \alpha_1), \ldots, (\Phi_n : \alpha_n)}{(\bigcup_{i=1}^{n} \Phi_i : \alpha_1 \wedge \cdots \wedge \alpha_n)}$$

$$\text{Elim-IMP:} \quad \frac{(\Phi_1 : \alpha_1 \wedge \cdots \wedge \alpha_n \rightarrow \beta), (\Phi_2 : \alpha_1 \wedge \cdots \wedge \alpha_n)}{(\Phi_1 \cup \Phi_2 : \beta)}$$

An argument $(\Phi : \alpha)$ is valid on the basis of an argumentative theory Γ iff $\Gamma \vdash_{Arg} (\Phi : \alpha)$. Because the deduction rules, and thus $\vdash_{Arg}$, are the same for all agents, they can all agree on the validity of such a deduction, however each agent builds its own argumentative theory, using its own trust model. Let $\mathscr{I}$ be the set of inference rules that specify an agent's trust model. Its bdus are generated from a set of $\mathscr{L}_{Rep}$ sentences Δ as follows:

- For any ground element α in Δ, there is a corresponding bdu $(\{\alpha\} : \alpha)$ in $\mathscr{L}_{Arg}$.
- For all $\alpha_1, \ldots, \alpha_n$ such that $\Delta \vdash_T \alpha_k$ for all $k \in [1,n]$, if there exists an application of an inference rule $\iota \in \mathscr{I}$, such that $\frac{\alpha_1, \ldots, \alpha_n}{\beta}$, then there is a bdu:

$$(\{\alpha_1 \wedge \cdots \wedge \alpha_n \rightarrow \beta\} : \alpha_1 \wedge \cdots \wedge \alpha_n \rightarrow \beta)$$

i.e., there is a bdu for every instantiated inference rule for the trust model specified by $\mathscr{I}$.

Continuing the example from above, our agent might have bdus:

$$(\{img(Jim,3)\} : img(Jim,3)),$$
$$(\{rep(Jim,5)\} : rep(Jim,5))\text{and}$$
$$(\{img(Jim,3) \wedge rep(Jim,5) \rightarrow trust(Jim,4)\} :$$
$$img(Jim,3) \wedge rep(Jim,5) \rightarrow trust(Jim,4)).$$

These bdus constitute an argumentative theory, from which $(\Phi : trust(Jim,4))$ can be inferred, with Φ the union of the defeasible knowledge of the argumentative theory. Similarly, working backwards, an agent can build a valid argument supporting a trust evaluation it believes. Moreover, it can communicate this argument. The other agent, upon receiving such an argument can decide whether or not to accept the trust evaluation. By doing so, the agent effectively filters out communicated trust evaluations that do not coincide with its own frame of reference. However, in a complex domain where trust evaluations can be based on many different criteria, agents might reach the point where they filter out too much information. To reduce the amount of information discarded, agents, when sending a trust evaluation, could personalize their trust evaluations to the receiver.

25.4.2 Personalized Trust Recommendations

Koster et al. present a framework for personalized trust recommendations (Koster et al. 2012a) that builds upon the argumentation framework presented by Pinyol, which we described above. This extension of the argumentation allows agents to communicate about more than just the trust evaluations: it allows agents to connect these trust evaluations to their beliefs and goals. The sender can then tailor its trust model to give a trust recommendation tailored to the receiver's goal, or the two agents can argue about their beliefs about the environment. In this manner agents can personalize their trust recommendations to each other.

For this argumentation framework, it is necessary for agents to be able to justify their trust evaluations using their goals and beliefs. In order to do this, Koster et al. rely on AdapTrust (2012b), an extension of the BDI agent model (Rao and Georgeff 1991), that specifies a method for connecting the parameters in a computational trust model to the beliefs and goals an agent has. Before discussing how the argumentation framework allows agents to personalize their trust evaluations to one another's needs, we briefly summarize AdapTrust.

25.4.3 AdapTrust

AdapTrust (Koster et al. 2012b) provides an abstract method for specifying how a trust model is dependent on an agent's goals and beliefs. It is an extension of the Beliefs-Desires-Intentions framework for intelligent agents (Rao and Georgeff 1991).

Computational trust models are, fundamentally, methods of aggregation: they combine and merge data from several different sources into a single value, the trustworthiness of a target. However, trust is a subjective concept: it is dependent on the beliefs an agent has about its environment and the goal it is trying to achieve by selecting a partner, for which it requires the trust evaluation. Luckily most computational trust models come equipped with a way of implementing this dependency: they have parameters that can be used to adjust the behaviour of the trust model. The aim of AdapTrust is not to present another trust model, but to incorporate existing trust models into an intelligent agent. This can be used to deal with the multi-faceted aspects of trust or, as we discuss in this chapter, adapt the trust model to improve communication about trust.

In any computational trust model, there are parameters that represent criteria for evaluating trustworthiness. For instance, many trust models use a parameter to give less importance to old information than new. This is useful if old information can become outdated and thus new information is more accurate than old. However, in a largely static environment this is not the case. The value of this parameter should be adjusted to the dynamicity of the environment. In general, the parameters of the trust model should be influenced by an agent's changing criteria for evaluating trustworthiness in a changing environment.

25.4.3.1 Priority System

The parameters of a trust model describe the importance of the different criteria for evaluating trustworthiness. However, it is more useful to consider this the other way round: the relative importance between the different criteria define a set of parameters for the trust model. These criteria are directly under an intelligent agent's control, and thus an agent is able to adapt its trust model. AdapTrust describes the specific techniques necessary to do this. The first of these is $\mathscr{L}_{PL}$, a language to describe the relative importance of any two criteria that influence a parameter of the trust model. AdapTrust uses a subset of first-order logic with a family of predicates to define this importance relation, also called a priority ordering. For each parameter p of the trust model, the binary predicates $\succ_p$ and $=_p$ are defined with the expected properties of strict ordering and equality, respectively. The terms of the language are a set of elements representing the criteria that influence how the trust model should work. A Priority System is defined as a satisfiable theory in this language. For instance, consider an eCommerce environment. If an agent uses a weight w to calculate its evaluation of a sale and it finds the price of an item to be more important than its delivery time, it can have the priority $price \succ_w delivery\_time$ in its Priority System.

25.4.3.2 Priority Rules

The second technique of AdapTrust is to create the link between, on the one hand, an agent's beliefs and goals and, on the other hand, the priority between the different criteria for evaluating trust. This link makes explicit the adaptive process: a change in an agent's beliefs or goals effects a change in the priorities over the criteria, which changes the parameters of the trust model. The connection between the beliefs or goals and the priorities is made through *priority rules*. The priority rules are specified using another first-order language, $\mathscr{L}_{Rules}$, with predicates $\rightsquigarrow_{Belief}$ and $\rightsquigarrow_{Goal}$ specifying how a set of beliefs, or a goal, respectively, leads to a specific priority relation between two criteria. By using these rules, the priorities are changed when the belief base changes. Additionally this is how the multi-faceted aspect of trust is emphasized: the goal the agent is trying to achieve influences the priority system and thus the trust model. For instance, in the eCommerce example above, our agent might need to buy a bicycle urgently. It then has the goal $buy\_urgent(bicycle)$. For this goal, delivery time is more important than the price, so it has the priority rule $buy\_urgent(bicycle) \rightsquigarrow_{Goal} (delivery\_time \succ_w price)$ and therewith *adapts* its trust model to the requirements of the goal.

We do not go into detail on how these priority rules come to be. They can be programmed by a designer, or generated dynamically by a machine learning algorithm. In this chapter we focus specifically on another method, namely that they can be incorporated through communication with another agent.

25.4.4 Adapting a Trust Recommendation

The argumentation framework by Pinyol et al. that we described earlier in this section does not allow us to completely address the question of what criteria play a role in computing a trust evaluation, let alone connect these to underlying beliefs and goals. AdapTrust can answer this, but does not provide a language in which to do so. In Koster et al. (2012a), Pinyol et al.'s argumentation framework is extended with concepts from AdapTrust and we summarize that work here.

The priorities that define the trust model's parameters can be incorporated into the argumentative theory. For this, the dependency of the trust model on the beliefs and goal of an agent must be represented in $\mathscr{L}_{Arg}$. In $\mathscr{L}_{Rep}$, the inference rules $\mathscr{I}$ specify a trust model algorithm. However, in AdapTrust this algorithm has parameters that depend on the agent's beliefs and goal. The inference rules should reflect this. The proposed extension of the language is therefore quite straightforward. Rather than using $\mathscr{L}_{Rep}$ as the single language on which the argumentation framework is built, the agent can argue about concepts in $\mathscr{L}_{KR} = \mathscr{L}_{Rep} \cup \mathscr{L}_{PL} \cup \mathscr{L}_{Rules} \cup \mathscr{L}_{Bel} \cup \mathscr{L}_{Goal}$, where $\mathscr{L}_{PL}$ and $\mathscr{L}_{Rules}$ are the languages of the priorities and priority rules, respectively, in AdapTrust, $\mathscr{L}_{Bel}$ the language of the agent's beliefs and $\mathscr{L}_{Goal}$ that of the agent's goals. Let $\Delta \subseteq \mathscr{L}_{Rep}$ and $\delta \in \mathscr{L}_{Rep}$, such that $\Delta \vdash_T \delta$. From Definition 25.1 we know there is a proof applying a finite number of inference rules $\iota \in \mathscr{I}$ for deducing δ from Δ. However, this deduction in AdapTrust depends on a set of the parameters, which we denote *Params*. Therefore, the inference rules must also depend on these parameters. For each $\iota \in \mathscr{I}$, we have $Params_\iota \subseteq Params$, the (possibly empty) subset of parameters corresponding to the inference rule. Let the beliefs Ψ and goal γ determine the values for all these parameters. We denote this as $\Delta \vdash_T^{\Psi,\gamma} \delta$, which states that the trust model infers δ from Δ, given beliefs Ψ and goal γ. Similarly we have $\iota^{\Psi,\gamma} \in \mathscr{I}^{\Psi,\gamma}$ to denote a specific instantiation of the parameters $Params_\iota$ using beliefs Ψ and goal γ.

This allows us to redefine the set of bdus and thus the argumentative theory in such a way that the argumentation supporting a trust evaluation can be followed all the way down to the agent's beliefs and goal. The deduction rules are the same as in Pinyol et al.'s framework, but the bdus for $\mathscr{L}_{Arg}$ are defined as follows in Koster et al. (2012a):

Definition 25.4 (Basic Declarative Units for $\mathscr{L}_{Arg}$). Let $\delta \in \mathscr{L}_{Rep}$ be an agent's trust evaluation based on inference rules $\mathscr{I}^{\Psi,\gamma}$, such that $\Delta \vdash_T^{\Psi,\gamma} \delta$ with $\Delta \subseteq \mathscr{L}_{Rep}$, $\Psi \subseteq \mathscr{L}_{Bel}$ and $\gamma \in \mathscr{L}_{Goal}$. For each $\iota \in \mathscr{I}^{\Psi,\gamma}$, let $Params_\iota$ be the corresponding sets of parameters. Let labels be a function that, given a set of parameters, returns a set of constants in $\mathscr{L}_{PL}$, the language of the priority system. Additionally let $\Xi \subseteq \mathscr{L}_{Rules}$ be the agent's set of trust priority rules and $\Pi \subseteq \mathscr{L}_{PL}$ be its priority system based on Ψ and γ, then:

1. For any sentence $\psi \in \Psi$, there is a corresponding bdu $(\{\psi\} : \psi)$ in $\mathscr{L}_{Arg}$.
2. The goal γ has a corresponding bdu $(\{\gamma\} : \gamma)$ in $\mathscr{L}_{Arg}$
3. For all priorities $\pi \in \Pi$ and all the rules $\xi \in \Xi$ the following bdus are generated:
   - If ξ has the form $\Phi \rightsquigarrow_{Belief} \pi$ and $\Phi \subseteq \Psi$ then $(\{(\bigwedge_{\varphi \in \Phi} \varphi) \rightarrow \pi\} : (\bigwedge_{\varphi \in \Phi} \varphi) \rightarrow \pi)$ is a bdu in $\mathscr{L}_{Arg}$
   - If ξ has the form $\gamma \rightsquigarrow_{Goal} \pi$ then $(\{\gamma \rightarrow \pi\} : \gamma \rightarrow \pi)$ is a bdu in $\mathscr{L}_{Arg}$
4. For all $\alpha_1, \ldots, \alpha_n$ such that $\Delta \vdash_T^{\Phi,\gamma} \alpha_k$ for all $k \in [1,n]$, if there exists an application of an inference rule $\iota^{\Psi,\gamma} \in \mathscr{I}^{\Psi,\gamma}$, such that $\frac{\alpha_1,\ldots,\alpha_n}{\beta}$ and $\mathsf{labels}(Params_{\iota^{\Psi,\gamma}}) = L$ then $(\{(\bigwedge_{\pi \in \Pi_L} \pi) \rightarrow (\alpha_1 \wedge \cdots \wedge \alpha_n \rightarrow \beta)\} : (\bigwedge_{\pi \in \Pi_L} \pi) \rightarrow (\alpha_1 \wedge \cdots \wedge \alpha_n \rightarrow \beta))$ is a bdu of $\mathscr{L}_{Arg}$. With $\Pi_L \subseteq \Pi$ the set of priorities corresponding to labels L.

In items 1 and 2 the relevant elements of the agent's reasoning are added to the argumentation language. In items 3 and 4 the implements for reasoning about trust are added: in 3 the trust priority rules and in 4 the rules of the trust model. The bdus added in 4 contain a double implication: they state that if an agent has the priorities in Π_L then a *trust rule* (which was a bdu in Pinyol's argumentative theory) holds. In practice what this accomplishes, is to allow the argumentation to go a level deeper: agents can now argue about *why* a trust rule, representing an application of a deduction rule in the trust model, holds. An argument for a trust evaluation can be represented in a tree. At each level, a node can be deduced by using the deduction rules of $\mathscr{L}_{Arg}$ with as preconditions the node's children. A leaf in the tree is a bdu. Each agent can construct its own argumentation tree for a trust evaluation and used in a dialogue to communicate personalized trust evaluations. The dialogue starts as an information-seeking dialogue, but if the agents discover their priorities are incompatible, they can discover whether this is due to a lack of information of either agent, or whether their world views are simply incompatible. If either agent is lacking information or the agents think they can reach an agreement on beliefs, they can enter a persuasion dialogue to achieve an agreement on the beliefs and trust priority rules. If this succeeds, they can restart the dialogue and see if they now agree on trust evaluations. In this way the argument serves to allow cooperative agents to converge on a similar model of trust and supply each other with personalized trust recommendations.

25.5 Conclusions

In this section we have given an overview of the ways in which argumentation is used in trust and reputation models and vice versa. We have discussed the application of trust metrics in argumentation frameworks for evaluating the strength of an argument, using the trustworthiness of its information sources. Similarly we have seen how arguments can support trust in various manners. Argumentation about contracts can supply valuable information about an agent's behaviour. Villata et al. (2011) combine both types and allow arguments to support trust evaluations in a meta-argument, which in turn decides the strength of an argument at the normal level of argumentation. Finally we discuss two ways in which argumentation can be used in the communication of trust evaluations. The first is a method for deciding whether a communicated trust evaluation is an acceptable source of information. The second aims to adapt agents' trust models in order for more sources of information to be acceptable. There is no shortage of productive manners for combining trust and argumentation that is only recently gaining popularity. It is the authors' opinion that both fields can benefit greatly from the tools proposed in the other and we look forward to seeing how the area will develop.

References

Castelfranchi, C., and R. Falcone. 2010. *Trust theory: A socio-cognitive and computational model*. Chichester: Wiley.

Chesñevar, C., and G. Simari. 2007. Modelling inference in argumentation through labelled deduction: Formalization and logical properties. *Logica Universalis* 1(1): 93–124.

Jones, N. D. 1997. *Computability and complexity: From a programming perspective*. Foundations of Computing. Cambridge, MA: MIT.

Koster, A., J. Sabater-Mir, and M. Schorlemmer. 2012a. Personalizing communication about trust. In *Proceedings of the eleventh international conference on autonomous agents and multiagent systems (AAMAS'12)*, ed. V. Conitzer, M. Winikoff, W. van der Hoek, and L. Padgham, 517–524. Valencia: IFAAMAS.

Koster, A., M. Schorlemmer, and J. Sabater-Mir. 2012b. Opening the black box of trust: Reasoning about trust models in a BDI agent. *Journal of Logic and Computation* (Forthcoming). doi:10.1093/logcom/EXS003.

Matt, P. A., M. Morge, and F. Toni. 2010. Combining statistics and arguments to compute trust. In *Ninth international joint conference on autonomous agents and multiagent systems (AAMAS'10)*, 209–216. Toronto: IFAAMAS.

Parsons, S., Y. Tang, E. Sklar, P. McBurney, and K. Cai. 2011. Argumentation-basded reasoning in agents with varying degrees of trust. In *Proceedings of AAMAS'11*, 879–886. Taipei, Taiwan: IFAAMAS.

Pinyol, I. 2011. *Milking the reputation Cow: Argumentation, reasoning and cognitive agents*. Monografies de l'Institut d'Investigació en Intel·ligencia Artificial, vol. 44. Bellaterra, Barcelona: Consell Superior d'Investigacions Científiques.

Pinyol, I., and J. Sabater-Mir. 2007. Arguing about reputation. the LRep language. In *Engineering societies in the agents world VIII: 8th international workshop, ESAW 2007*. LNAI, vol. 4995, ed. A. Artikis, G. O'Hare, K. Stathis, and G. Vouros, 284–299. Berlin: Springer.

Pinyol, I., and J. Sabater-Mir. 2009. Towards the definition of an argumentation framework using reputation information. In *Proceedings of the 12th workshop on trust in agent societies (TRUST@AAMAS'09)*, 92–103.

Prade, H. 2007. A qualitative bipolar argumentative view of trust. In *International conference on scalable uncertainty management (SUM 2007)*. LNAI, vol. 4772, ed. V. Subrahmnanian and H. Prade, 268–276. Berlin/New York: Springer.

Rahwan, I., and G. Simari. 2009. *Argumentation in artificial intelligence*. Dordrecht/New York: Springer.

Rao, A. S., and Georgeff, M. P. 1991. Modeling rational agents within a BDI-architecture. In *Proceedings of KR'91*, 473–484. San Mateo, CA: Morgan Kaufmann.

Tang, Y., K. Cai, P. McBurney, and S. Parsons. 2010. A system of argumentation for reasoning about trust. In *Proceedings of EUMAS'10*, Paris, France.

Villata, S., G. Boella, D. Gabbay, and L. van der Torre. 2011. Arguing about the trustworthiness of information sources. In *Symbolic and quantitative approaches to reasoning with uncertainty*. LNCS, vol. 6717, 74–85. Heidelberg: Springer.

Yu, B., and M. P. Singh. 2002. An evidential model of distributed reputation management. In *AAMAS '02: Proceedings of the first international joint conference on Autonomous agents and multiagent systems*, 294–301. New York: ACM. doi:http://doi.acm.org/10.1145/544741.544809.

Chapter 26
Ontology, Semantics and Reputation

Andrew Koster and Jeff Z. Pan

26.1 Introduction

This section presents an overview of ontologies for reputation. Ontology is a term borrowed from philosophy that refers to the science of describing the kinds of entities in the world and how they are related. In computer science, ontology is, in general, a model of (some parts of) the world, which not only identifies important vocabulary (including classes and properties) but also specifies their meaning with a formal logic. An ontology of reputation is thus a description of the types and causes of reputation, as well as a description of all entities involved with reputation.

Ontologies are widely used to represent the *shared* understanding of a domain and, in the case of reputation, thus represent a shared meaning of reputation between individuals. This allows these individuals to freely exchange evaluations of other agents in the system, thereby propagating trust, warning against irreputable, and recommending reputable agents. In Sect. 26.4 we describe some ontologies for reputation. While they enable the exchange of reputative evaluations, ontologies have difficulty providing a shared notion of trust. Trust is more of a subjective notion than reputation and, therefore, agents are less likely to agree on the meaning and causes of a trust evaluation. In Sect. 26.5 we discuss several methods that allow agents to communicate subjective notions of trust in a meaningful manner.

We start this section with a more general discussion of ontologies. We give a brief overview of OWL, the most widely used language for defining ontologies, in Sect. 26.2. Moreover, if different agents have different ontologies, then it is

A. Koster (✉)
IIIA – CSIC, Barcelona, Spain
e-mail: andrew@iiia.csic.es

J.Z. Pan
University of Aberdeen, King's College, Aberdeen, UK
e-mail: jeff.z.pan@abdn.ac.uk

S. Ossowski (ed.), *Agreement Technologies*, Law, Governance and Technology Series 8, DOI 10.1007/978-94-007-5583-3_26,

necessary to perform some form of agreement management among these ontologies. In this case, argumentation (cf. Sect. 26.3) may help work out a shared understanding and, at the same time, identify the disagreements.

26.2 Ontology and OWL

The most well known ontology language is the Web ontology language OWL, standardised by the World Wide Web Consortium. The more updated version of OWL is OWL 2.[1] The formal underpinning for OWL 2 is Description Logics (Baader et al. 2002). OWL is considered as one of the key foundations of the Semantic Web (Pan 2004).

OWL 2 provides the constructors for building complex class and property descriptions from atomic ones. For example, 'elephants with their ages greater than 20' can be described by the following OWL class description:[2]

$$Elephant \sqcap \exists age. >_{20},$$

where Elephant is an atomic class, age is an atomic datatype property, $>_{20}$ is a data range, and $\sqcap$, $\exists$ are class constructors. Class and property descriptions can be used in axioms in an OWL ontology. For example, we can define the class AdultElephant with the following OWL axiom:

$$AdultElephant \equiv Elephant \sqcap \exists age. >_{20};$$

we can represent the constraint 'Elephant are a kind of Animal':

$$Elephant \sqsubseteq Animal;$$

we can also assert that the individual elephant Ganesh is an instance of the class description 'Elephants who are older than 25 years old':

$$Ganesh : (Elephant \sqcap \exists age. >_{25}).$$

Reasoning plays an important role in ontologies, as it could make implicit connections explicit (Hogan et al. 2010) and help detect inconsistency and incoherency (Du et al. 2011; Flouris et al. 2006; Meyer et al. 2006). For example, in the above elephant ontology, we could infer that Ganesh is an AdultElephant.

OWL 2 provides two levels of ontology languages: the expressive and decidable language OWL 2 DL (Horrocks et al. 2006), and three tractable sub-languages

[1] http://www.w3.org/TR/owl-overview/

[2] To save space, we use DL syntax (Baader et al. 2002) rather than RDF/XML syntax.

OWL 2 EL (Baader et al. 2005), OWL 2 QL (Calvanese et al. 2005) and OWL 2 RL. Accordingly, OWL 2 provides three level of reasoning services:

- Sound and complete reasoning for OWL 2 DL: this allows modellers to have more expressive power for their ontologies but there is no guarantee for efficient reasoning services, due to the high computational complexity for OWL 2 DL. Available reasoners include, e.g., HermiT, Pellet, FaCT++ and RacerPro.
- Sound and complete reasoning for tractable languages (EL, QL and RL): this allows modellers to enjoy the efficient reasoning services but the available expressive power is limited. Available reasoners include, e.g., CEL, QuOnto, and TrOWL.
- Approximate reasoning services for OWL 2 DL (based on the tractable sub-languages): this allows the modellers to have more expressive power for their ontologies and enjoy the efficient reasoning services; however, theoretically the reasoning could be incomplete. A typical reasoner of this kind is TrOWL,[3] which implements, e.g., a faithful approximate reasoning approach (Ren et al. 2010) that has been shown to be complete for the classification service on e.g. the evaluation ontologies in the HermiT Benchmark.[4]

26.3 Ontology and Argumentation

Ontology reasoning services can be used to help manage agreements and disagreements among different ontologies from different domain experts. Before reaching agreements, argumentation support (Black et al. 2009) is needed.

1. To detect disagreements between two expert ontologies, one could merge the two ontologies and check if the merge ontology is inconsistent or incoherent (Flouris et al. 2006). If so, disagreements exist.
2. To identify the agreed subsets, one could compute the maximally consistent (coherent) sub-ontologies of the inconsistent (incoherent) one (Meyer et al. 2006).
3. To resolve the disagreement, one could debug the ontology (Du et al. 2011) and remove the problematic parts from the inconsistent (incoherent) ontology.

In the above Steps 2 and 3, argumentation support is needed. An argument is a pair (S, c), where c is a claim and S is the support of the claim. In the case of ontology argumentation, c is an axiom in or an entailment of the given ontology, S is a justification (Horridge et al. 2010) of c in the given ontology. For detailed discussions on ontology argumentation, we refer the reader to the part in this book on ontologies and semantics.

[3]http://trowl.eu/

[4]http://hermit-reasoner.com/2009/JAIRbenchmarks/

26.4 Ontologies for Reputation

Insofar as we know two ontologies have been proposed for the communication of reputation. The first is FORe, described by Casare and Sichman (2005) and the second is $\mathscr{L}_{Rep}$, introduced by Pinyol and Sabater (2007). The second ontology was briefly discussed in Chap. 25 but we discuss it in more detail below.

26.4.1 FORe

The Functional Ontology of Reputation (FORe) considers a dual definition of reputation. Reputation as a *social product* is the agreement of opinion about some target and reputation as a *social process* is the transmission of opinions through a social network to form such an agreement. FORe defines the concepts used to specify reputation in both its forms. To do this, they base their ontology on Valente's Functional Ontology of Law (1995), because they claim that "the concepts of the legal world can be used to model the social world, through the extension of the concept of legal rule to social norm".

The reason the ontology is a *functional* ontology is because it models the products of reputation in terms of the function they have in the social process of reputation. The main classes of the ontology are *Reputative Knowledge*, *Responsibility Knowledge*, *Normative Knowledge* and *World Knowledge*.

Reputative Knowledge represents reputation in its understanding as a product, or evaluation. An instance of reputative knowledge models the specifics of an evaluation using a number of properties, the most important of which are the role of the agents involved (whether they are targets, first-hand evaluators, propagators of information or recipients of information) and the type of the reputative information (for instance, direct reputation or propagated reputation). For a full overview of the properties, we refer to (Casare and Sichman 2005).

World Knowledge represents the knowledge about the environment.

Normative Knowledge represents the social norms in this environment.

Responsibility Knowledge represents the knowledge an agent has regarding the responsibility the various agents have with regards to behaviour and norms.

Altogether the ontology allows for the modeling of the processing of reputation: the World Knowledge allows for the modeling of behaviour of agents and the Normative Knowledge contains the information of whether such behaviour is acceptable or not. Using Responsibility Knowledge an evaluator can decide that an agent is responsible for its behaviour and thus the evaluator's Reputative Knowledge regarding that agent is affected. This reputation can be propagated, creating new instances of Reputative Knowledge for other agents in the environment.

Casare and Sichman give a short example of how this works by considering how a trust evaluation is formed, step by step, from world knowledge: the agent observes someone smoking in a closed space. This world knowledge is combined with the normative knowledge that it is forbidden to smoke in closed spaces to identify a norm violation. Further responsibility knowledge is needed to know whether the smoker is responsible for this norm violation, and the agent ascribes responsibility to the smoker for his actions. This is evaluated into a reputative evaluation and combined with other sources of knowledge about the same person. This results in an evaluation that can be communicated to other agents in the system.

FORe thus provides an ontological description of how reputation models work: it allows for the communication of the input (using the world knowledge and normative knowledge) of a reputation model and the output (an instance of reputative knowledge). However, it does not detail what happens if two agents, using the same input, obtain different output. In this case, communication might be problematic. An attempt to deal with this is given by Nardin et al. (2008), who present an ontology alignment service to promote interoperability between reputation models. As a proof-of-concept they show how FORe can be used as a shared ontology and how the concepts from two different trust models can be translated in and out of FORe. However, they encountered concepts in both trust models that could not be properly translated into FORe. Furthermore, they do not present a method for automatically mapping a trust model into FORe and an agent designer must provide such a mapping manually. This limits the applicability of FORe for representing and communicating reputation.

26.4.2 $\mathscr{L}_{Rep}$

An entirely different approach is taken by Pinyol et al., who propose the $\mathscr{L}_{Rep}$ language for communicating about reputation (Pinyol et al. 2007). Section 25.4 describes how this language is used in argumentation about trust, but it could be used as a shared language for describing trust without argumentation as well. This language is based on a comprehensive ontology for discussing concepts of trust and reputation. The ontology defines a *social evaluation* with three compulsory elements: a *target*, a *context* and a *value*. The *context* is specified using a second language $\mathscr{L}_{Context}$, which is a first-order dynamic language (Harel 1979) for describing the domain. The target is the agent under evaluation and the value describes the quantification of the social evaluation. We will not go into details of this quantification, but the original description of the $\mathscr{L}_{Rep}$ language gives different alternatives for the representation of this quantification, encompassing most, if not all, representations used in modern computational trust and reputation models (Pinyol et al. 2007).

The taxonomy of social evaluations is given in Fig. 26.1. Here we see how social evaluations are split into the different types of evaluations related to trust and reputation. This taxonomy is based on a sociological model of trust and reputation (Conte and Paolucci 2002), which splits trust into a direct component, *image*, and a generalized concept of what the society thinks, *reputation*. These, in turn, are

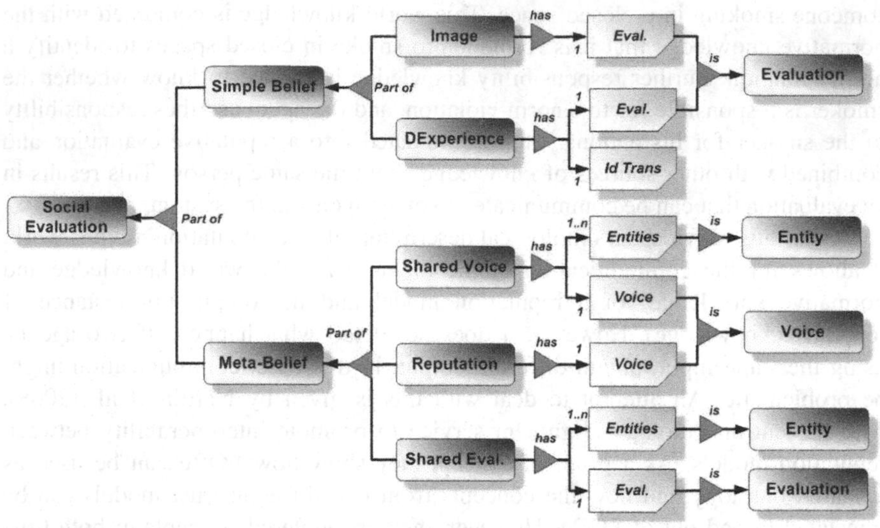

Fig. 26.1 Taxonomy of social evaluations in the $\mathscr{L}_{Rep}$ ontology for talking about trust (Copied from Pinyol (2011))

aggregations of direct experiences, shared voices and shared evaluations. In this way the ontology allows for the discussion of not just the final trust evaluation, but also the intermediate evaluations that are used in its calculation. The $\mathscr{L}_{Rep}$ language is a first-order language with the vocabulary from the ontology described above and operators $\wedge, \neg$ and $\rightarrow$. A special subset of sentences in $\mathscr{L}_{Rep}$ are ground atoms with either the predicate symbol *DExperience* or *Comm*. These are the basic elements in the ontology that are evaluations of experiences the agent has had, or communications it has received.

Pinyol et al. thus do not aim to model reputation as a process, but only the reputation (and trust) evaluations. These evaluations are modeled in detail and the language allows agents to communicate them. They acknowledge, however, that there may be subjective differences between the way different agents compute and interpret the evaluations and, for effective communication Pinyol proposes an argumentation framework for obtaining all the information about an evaluation in $\mathscr{L}_{Rep}$ and allowing the agent to decide whether or not a communicated evaluation is acceptable (Pinyol 2011).

26.5 Subjectivity of Reputation

A large problem with using an ontology for trust and reputation is that trust is an inherently subjective concept. Despite the fact that reputation seems to escape this problem, because it is, per definition, “what is said about an individual by a social entity", the question then remains of how the individual subjective trust evaluations of the members of such a social entity are combined to form this consensual reputation. Despite sharing a language, for discussing, comparing, or aggregating individuals' subjective trust evaluations, the agents need to discuss their underlying preferences, or at the very least, an extensive description of the context in which a trust evaluation was formed.

Staab and Engel discuss this problem (2008). Rather than presenting a new trust model, they review the various problems that computational trust models encounter. One of these is the exchange of witness-information, or communicating trust evaluations directly. Their approach divides a computational trust model into three different stages and they discuss the communication at each of these. In a trust model, the first step is to monitor a target's behaviour. This results in observations, which can be analyzed and, as the second step in their approach, interpreted as positive or negative experiences. The third step is to perform some computation, which is effectively an aggregation of the experiences with a target, resulting in a trust evaluation. At each of these steps communication can take place to augment the next process. Agents can communicate about observations, about experiences or about trust evaluations, although at each subsequent stage the level of subjectivity increases.

26.5.1 Communication at the Level of Observations

Communicating at the level of observations has the advantage of being a direct communication about the agent's observations of the environment and thus being the nearest to an objective description of an interaction. Şensoy et al. use this approach to communicate witness information and incorporate it into the trust model directly (Şensoy and Yolum 2007). They provide a trust model for evaluating web services and to communicate, they propose a dual ontology for communicating agents' interactions with service providers. The first ontology is the base ontology, which captures the fundamental concepts that all web services have in common and a second domain ontology for describing the particular service the agents are discussing. When communicating, an agent can communicate all its observations of an interaction using these ontologies and the receiving agent can then evaluate these as if it had the interaction itself. However, there are two problems with this approach. The first is the assumption that an agent's observations of an interaction can be objectively described. The ontology that Şensoy et al. propose includes properties like "quality" and "isAsDescribed" in the domain ontology, which they assume can be assessed in an objective manner by each agent. This seems to contradict their own assertion that any rating is always subjective, however it also begs the question of whether any domain exists in which an interaction, that can serve to support a trust evaluation, can be satisfactorily described using only objective facts. The second problem with such an approach is more straightforward: for a receiving agent to be able to interpret an interaction as if it has observed it itself, the entire interaction must be faithfully recorded and communicated. An agent, in order to be a useful information source, must thus record details of interactions that it itself might consider trivial and never use. Furthermore, the shared ontology must include all properties all agents consider relevant for evaluating and, on top of that, it ignores possible privacy issues. While agents may be willing to communicate whether an interaction succeeded or failed, they may not be willing to communicate the exact details of that interaction. Especially if that contains sensitive information, such as, for instance, financial data.

A solution could be to allow agents to communicate partial observations of an interaction, however this leads to problems for the receiver. It has to use partial observations to evaluate the trust of a target. If the receiver needs to perform some kind of processing of the information in any case, it might be possible to use some of the more subjective information from the higher stages of trust models.

26.5.2 Communicating Experiences and Evaluations

The reason a shared ontology for trust is infeasible is because of what Euzenat calls pragmatic heterogeneity (Euzenat and Shvaiko 2007). He discusses three different levels at which ontological heterogeneity might appear. The first level is that of syntactic heterogeneity, which is quite straightforward: two agents use a different syntax to describe the same domain. An example in the real world would be a Chinese and an English speaking agent trying to communicate. At the second, or semantic, level the problem of syntax is presumed solved, but two agents use a different semantic for the same words. For instance, two agents who are discussing a minivan. One categorizes a minivan as a small bus, while the other categorizes it as a large car, so the meaning they assign to the word minivan is slightly different. This is the level at which most research into ontology alignment falls. The last level is that of pragmatics. At this level two agents agree on the syntax and the conceptual meaning of the word, however there is heterogeneity in how the word is used: this is almost always the problem when two agents try to talk about subjective concepts, such as “taste”, but also trust.

However, it is only recently that heterogeneity of trust has been considered as a problem of pragmatic heterogeneity. One of the contributing factors has been an attempt to solve the problem of heterogeneous trust concepts through techniques of ontology alignment (Nardin et al. 2008). As briefly mentioned in Sect. 26.4.1, Nardin et al. recognized the problem of heterogeneous trust evaluations and that ontologies did not properly capture different models’ concepts. A particular problem for attempts to use ontology alignment for trust is that most trust models focus on how outcomes, that Staab and Engel call experiences, are aggregated, possibly together with other information, in order to compute the trust evaluations. The trust models therefore already incorporate a large part of the subjectivity of trust at their lowest level. It is unclear how these outcomes can be mapped into a shared ontology.

An entirely different approach is that taken by Teacy et al. in their TRAVOS model (2006) and Şensoy et al. with POYRAZ (2009). These models deal principally with liars, but their method may work equally well with trust evaluations from witnesses with too different a viewpoint. Both models learn how to filter out communicated evaluations from witnesses they mark as liars: the learning algorithm learns to distinguish liars by analyzing past experiences and consistently finding a difference between the witness' communicated evaluation and the actual evaluation after interacting. In other words, the algorithms use past experiences, together with witnesses' recommendations, to classify witnesses as either liars, or truthful agents. The main difference between TRAVOS and POYRAZ is that POYRAZ takes the context into account, in the form of an ontology for describing interactions. In fact, they use the same ontology as in Şensoy and Yolum (2007), but rather than just communicating about the interaction, they include trust evaluations based upon the interaction. The reason this method works for detecting more than liars, is because, given a specific context, the method calculates the difference between a received evaluation and an evaluation based on personal experience. The latter is thus based on the agent's own subjective criteria, while the former is based on the witness' criteria. If these are too dissimilar too often for a single witness, this witness is considered a liar. The advantage is that this allows an agent to filter out information from agents that are too dissimilar to itself. One of the disadvantages is that it marks such agents as liars. This is problematic, because there is often a negative action attached to discovering a lying agent, such as the notification of the community that the agent is a liar. In the case of miscommunication based on subjectivity, this may lead to many agents incorrectly being marked as liars, with all its repercussions. Even if this is not the case, the filtering methods have another disadvantage: if there are many different possible criteria for calculating a trust evaluation, algorithms that learn to filter out evaluations, may very well filter out too much information for them to be viable.

An alternative is what Koster et al. (2011) call trust alignment. This provides a translation, similar to the one proposed by Nardin et al., but taking the domain level information into account and, rather than attempting to translate to a central, shared ontology, attempt to learn an individualized translation between two agents' trust models.

26.5.3 Trust Alignment

There are a number of methods that can be considered trust alignment mechanisms. The first is described by Abdul-Rahman and Hailes' trust model (2000). This work describes a trust model that evaluates a trustee with an integer between 1 and 4, where 1 stands for *very untrustworthy* and 4 for *very trustworthy*. The alignment process uses the recommendations from another agent about *known* trustees to calculate four separate biases: one for each possible trust value. First the alignment method calculates the own trust evaluations of the corresponding trustee for each incoming recommendation. The *semantic distance* between the own and other's trust is simply the numerical difference between the values of the trust evaluations. The semantic distances are then grouped by the value of the corresponding received trust value, resulting in four separate groups. Finally the bias for each group is calculated by taking the mode of the semantic distances in the group, resulting in four integers between -3 and 3, which can be used when the agent receives recommendations about unknown trustees. Simply subtract the corresponding bias from the incoming trust evaluation to translate the message.

This is a very simple approach to translating another agent's trust evaluation: it simply learns a vector of numerical biases and uses this, but, as shown in (Koster et al. 2011), this actually works remarkably well. However, methods that take the context into account work better. One of these is BLADE (Regan et al. 2006). This model uses a conjunction of propositions to represent the context and a Bayesian network to learn the relation between the own trust evaluation and the other's trust evaluation given a certain context. While this works well, their representation of the context is very limited. For instance, the ontology of Şensoy and Yolum (2007) requires a more expressive language, as does any other OWL, or even OWL Lite ontology (OWL web ontology language overview 2009). In order to learn a context-based translation in a more expressive language, Koster et al. (2012) propose to use Inductive Logic Programming. This approach learns a conjunction of Horn clauses that generalizes from a set of examples, with each example constituting the own trust evaluation, the other's trust evaluation and a description of the interaction in a first-order language. The algorithm performs regression, or if the trust evaluations are not numeric, then classification can be used, to find a translation. An approach like this, taking the context into account, is able to obtain more accurate estimates of a target's trustworthiness, as is shown in Koster et al. (2011). Furthermore, these methods are able to deal with a limited amount of lying, by substituting inconsistent trust evaluations with descriptions of the context and thus learn the context in which the witness' trust evaluations are inconsistent, or, if the context is specific enough, even learn a translation of a message regardless of whether the trust evaluation is a lie or not.

All these alignment methods attempt to deal with the problem of the pragmatic heterogeneity of trust by learning a specific alignment between two agents' based not on a conceptual representation of trust, but based on how an agent calculates and uses the trust evaluations. The latter two approaches do this by, additionally, taking the context into account and recognize that a trust evaluation of a target may change significantly in different contexts and thus any translation must do this too. This resolves two of the issues we discussed earlier: by using a machine learning approach, they do not require manual mappings of agents' models into a shared ontology and they do not filter out information, but instead translate it. This translation comes with an additional reliability measure, so, if the reliability is low, an agent may still make the choice to filter it out. Furthermore, it resolves some of the issues with communicating only at the lowest level that Staab and Engel (2008) identify, because by using the subjective evaluations and learning a translation, the agent does not need to know all the specifics of the underlying interaction.

These advantages come at a cost. Because both BLADE (Regan et al. 2006) and Koster et al.'s approach (2012) use quite complex machine learning algorithms, they need a large set of training data to learn an accurate translation. The training data consists of interactions that are shared between the requesting agent and the witness supplying information. The alignment is thus quite intensive, both from a communication and computation perspective. It also requires a domain in which it is likely that two agents can have a large number of similar interactions. However, if the conditions are met, these algorithms solve many of the issues with communicating trust and their application seems promising in a number of domains, including P2P routing, eCommerce and grid computing, although they have so far not been tested in such, realistic, application domains.

26.6 Conclusions

Communication with other agents is an important source of information for finding trustworthy interaction partners, however this communication is not straightforward. In this section we discuss a number of ways in which such communication can be established. The first is through a shared ontology. If the application provides an ontology for communicating trust, such as the $\mathscr{L}_{Rep}$ or FORe ontologies that we discuss in Sect. 26.4, then the communication should not be problematic. The problem, however, is that such a fixed definition of trust does not allow agents to use trust as a personal and subjective evaluation: their use of trust is fixed by the shared ontology. Trust Alignment provides a solution for this, by allowing agents to learn a translation based on some shared set of evidence for each agent's trust evaluation. This allows each agent to communicate its own personal trust evaluations, which are translated by the receiving agent. A disadvantage of such methods is that a large number of shared interactions are required to learn this alignment. Another approach to communicating about trust can be found in Chap. 25 of this same book.

References

Abdul-Rahman, A., and S. Hailes. 2000. Supporting trust in virtual communities. In *Proceedings of the 33rd Hawaii international conference on system sciences*, vol. 6, 4–7. Maui: IEEE.

Baader, F., S. Brandt, and C. Lutz. 2005. Pushing the $\mathscr{EL}$ envelope. In *Proceedings of IJCAI-05*, 364–369. Edinburgh: Professional Book Center.

Baader, F., C. Lutz, H. Sturm, and F. Wolter. 2002. Fusions of description logics and abstract description systems. *Journal of Artificial Intelligence Research (JAIR)* 16: 1–58.

Black, E., A. Hunter, and J. Z. Pan. 2009. An argument-based approach to using multiple ontologies. In *Proceeding of the 3rd international conference on scalable uncertainty management (SUM 2009)*, LNAI, vol. 5785, ed. L. Godo and A. Pugliese, 68–79. Washington, DC: Springer.

Calvanese, D., G. D. Giacomo, D. Lembo, M. Lenzerini, and R. Rosati. 2005. DL-Lite: Tractable description logics for ontologies. In *Proceedings of AAAI 2005*.

Casare, S., and J. Sichman. 2005. Towards a functional ontology of reputation. In *AAMAS '05: Proceedings of the fourth international joint conference on autonomous agents and multiagent systems*, 505–511. Utrecht: ACM. doi:http://doi.acm.org/10.1145/1082473.1082550.

Conte, R., and M. Paolucci. 2002. *Reputation in artificial societies: Social beliefs for social order*. Boston: Kluwer Academic.

Şensoy, M., and P. Yolum. 2007. Ontology-based service representation and selection. *IEEE Transactions on Knowledge and Data Engineering* 19(8): 1102–1115.

Şensoy, M., J. Zhang, P. Yolum, and R. Cohen. 2009. Context-aware service selection under deception. *Computational Intelligence* 25(4): 335–366.

Du, J., G. Qi, J. Z. Pan, and Y.-D. Shen. 2011. A decomposition-based approach to OWL DL ontology diagnosis. In *Proceeding of the 23rd IEEE international conference on tools with artificial intelligence (ICTAI 2011)*, 659–664. Boca Raton, FL.

Euzenat, J., and P. Shvaiko. 2007. *Ontology matching*. Heidelberg: Springer.

Flouris, G., Z. Huang, J. Z. Pan, D. Plexousakis, and H. Wache. 2006. Inconsistencies, negations and changes in ontologies. In *Proceedings of AAAI2006*, 1295–1300.

Harel, D. 1979. *First-order dynamic logic*. Lecture Notes in Computer Science. Springer. http://books.google.es/books?id=mp4pAQAAIAAJ.

Hogan, A., J. Z. Pan, A. Polleres, and S. Decker. 2010. SAOR: Template rule optimisations for distributed reasoning over 1 Billion linked data triples. In *Proceedings of the 9th international semantic web conference (ISWC2010)*, LNCS, vol. 6496, ed. P. Patel-Schneider, Y. Pan, P. Hitzler, P. Mika, L. Zhang, J. Z. Pan, I. Horrocks and B. Glimm, 337–353. Berlin: Springer.

Horridge, M., B. Parsia, and U. Sattler. 2010. Justification oriented proofs in owl. In *International semantic web conference (1)*. Lecture Notes in Computer Science, ed. P. F. Patel-Schneider, Y. Pan, P. Hitzler, P. Mika, L. Zhang, J. Z. Pan, I. Horrocks, and B. Glimm, 354–369. Berlin: Springer.

Horrocks, I., O. Kutz, and U. Sattler. 2006. The even more irresistible SROIQ. In *Proceedings of KR 2006*, 57–67. AAAI Press.

Koster, A., J. Sabater-Mir, and M. Schorlemmer. 2011. Trust alignment: A sine qua non of open multi-agent systems. In *Proceedings of on the move to meaningful internet systems (OTM 2011, Part I)*. LNCS, vol. 7044, ed. R. Meersman, T. Dillon, and P. Herrero, 182–191. Hersonissos: Springer.

Koster, A., M. Schorlemmer, and J. Sabater-Mir. 2012. Engineering trust alignment: Theory, method and experimentation. *Journal of Human-Computer Studies* 70(6): 450–473. doi:10.1016/j.ijhcs.2012.02.007.

Meyer, T., K. Lee, R. Booth., and J. Z. Pan. 2006. Maximally satisfiable terminologies for the description logic ALC. In *Proceedings of AAAI '06*, 269–274. Boston, MA: AAAI Press.

Nardin, L. G., A. A. F. Brandão, G. Muller, and J. S. Sichman. 2008. SOARI: A service-oriented architecture to support agent reputation models interoperability. In *Trust in agent societies – 11th international workshop, TRUST 2008*. LNAI, vol. 5396, ed. R. Falcone, S. K. Barber, J. Sabater-Mir, and M. P. Singh, 292–307. Estoril: Springer.

OWL web ontology language overview. 2009. http://www.w3.org/TR/owl-features, 12 Nov. 2009.

Pan, J. Z. 2004. Description logics: Reasoning support for the semantic web. Ph.D. thesis, School of Computer Science, The University of Manchester.

Pinyol, I. 2011. *Milking the reputation Cow: Argumentation, reasoning and cognitive agents*. Monografies de l'Institut d'Investigació en Intel·ligencia Artificial, vol. 44. Bellaterra, Barcelona: Consell Superior d'Investigacions Científiques.

Pinyol, I., and J. Sabater-Mir. 2007. Arguing about reputation. the lrep language. In *Engineering societies in the agents world VIII: 8th international workshop, ESAW 2007*. LNAI, vol. 4995, ed. A. Artikis, G. O'Hare, K. Stathis, and G. Vouros, 284–299. Berlin/Heidelberg/New York: Springer.

Pinyol, I., J. Sabater-Mir, and G. Cuni. 2007. How to talk about reputation using a common ontology: From definition to implementation. In *Proceedings of tenth workshop "Trust in Agent Societies" at AAMAS '07*, Honolulu, Hawaii, USA, 90–102.

Regan, K., P. Poupart, and R. Cohen. 2006. Bayesian reputation modeling in e-marketplaces sensitive to subjectivity, deception and change. In *Proceedings of the 21st national conference on artificial intelligence (AAAI)*, 1206–1212. Boston: AAAI.

Ren, Y., J. Z. Pan, and Y. Zhao. 2010. Soundness preserving approximation for TBox reasoning. In *Proceedings of the 25th AAAI conference (AAAI-2010)*, 351–356. Atlanta, GA: AAAI Press.

Staab, E., and T. Engel. 2008. Combining cognitive with computational trust reasoning. In *TRUST 2008*. LNAI, vol. 5396, ed. R. Falcone, K. Barber, J. Sabater-Mir, and M. P. Singh, 99–111. Berlin: Springer.

Teacy, W. T. L., J. Patel, N. R. Jennings, and M. Luck. 2006. Travos: Trust and reputation in the context of inaccurate information sources. *Journal of Autonomous Agents and Multi-Agent Systems* 12(2): 183–198.

Valente, A. 1995. *Legal knowledge engineering – A modeling approach*. Amsterdam: IOS.

Chapter 27
Attacks and Vulnerabilities of Trust and Reputation Models

Jose M. Such

27.1 Introduction

As explained throughout this part, trust and reputation play a crucial role in the Agreement Technologies. This is because agents usually need to assess either the trustworthiness or the reputation of other agents in a given system. Trust and reputation are even more important in open systems, in which previously unknown parties may interact. For instance, if a buyer agent enters an e-marketplace for the first time, it will need to choose among all of the available seller agents. As the buyer agent has no previous interactions with the seller agent, the reputation of the seller agent in the e-marketplace can play a crucial role for the buyer agent to choose a specific seller agent.

The agent community has developed a vast number of trust and reputation models (Pinyol and Sabater-Mir 2011; Sabater and Sierra 2005). However, most of them suffer from some common vulnerabilities. This means that malicious agents may be able to perform attacks that exploit these vulnerabilities. Therefore, malicious agents may be able to modify the expected behavior of these models at will. As a result, these models may even become completely useless. For instance, in our previous example, a seller agent may be able to cheat the reputation model used by the buyer agent. Thus, the buyer agent may end up interacting with a malicious agent instead of what it believes a reputable agent. This has the potential to cause much harm such as monetary losses. Therefore, these vulnerabilities have the potential to place the whole system in jeopardy.

In this chapter, we detail some of the most important vulnerabilities of current trust and reputation models. We also detail examples of attacks that take advantage

J.M. Such (✉)
Departamento de Sistemas Informáticos y Computación, Universitat Politècnica de València, Valencia, Spain
e-mail: jsuch@dsic.upv.es

S. Ossowski (ed.), *Agreement Technologies*, Law, Governance and Technology Series 8, DOI 10.1007/978-94-007-5583-3_27,

of these vulnerabilities in order to achieve strategic manipulation of trust and reputation models. Moreover, we review in this chapter works that partially/fully address these vulnerabilities, and thus, prevent possible attacks from being successful. We particularly focus on two general kinds of vulnerabilities that have received much attention from the agent community because of their fatal consequences: identity-related vulnerabilities and collusion. We firstly detail identity-related vulnerabilities and available solutions (Sect. 27.2). Secondly, we explain how reputation can be manipulated by means of collusion and how this can be partially addressed (Sect. 27.3). Then, we briefly outline other possible attacks and vulnerabilities of trust and reputation models (Sect. 27.4). Finally, we present some concluding remarks (Sect. 27.5).

27.2 Identity-Related Vulnerabilities

Current trust and reputation models are based on the assumption that identities are long-lived, so that ratings about a particular agent from the past are related to the same agent in the future. However, when such systems are actually used in real domains this assumption is no longer valid. For instance, an agent that has a low reputation due to its cheating behavior may be really interested in changing its identity and restarting its reputation from scratch. This is what (Jøsang et al. 2007) called the *change of identities* problem. This problem has also been identified by other researchers under different names (e.g. *whitewashing* Carrara and Hogben (2007)).

The work of Kerr and Cohen (2009) shows that trust and reputation models exhibit multiple vulnerabilities that can be exploited by attacks performed by cheating agents. Among these vulnerabilities, the *re-enter* vulnerability exactly matches the *change of identities* problem exposed by Jøsang et al. They propose a simple attack that takes advantage of this vulnerability: An agent opens an account (identity) in a marketplace, uses her account to cheat for a period, then abandons it to open another.

Kerr and Cohen (2009) also point out the fact that entities could create new accounts (identity in the system) at will, not only after abandoning their previous identity but also holding multiple identities at once. This is known as the *sybil* attack (Jøsang and Golbeck 2009). An example of this attack could be an agent that holds multiple identities in a marketplace and attempts to sell the same product through each of them, increasing the probability of being chosen by a potential buyer.

It is worth mentioning that this is not an authenticity problem. Interactions among entities are assured,[1] i.e, an agent holding an identity is sure of being able to interact with the agent that holds the other identity. However, there is nothing

[1] We assume that agents are running on top of a secure Agent Platform that provides authentication to the agents running on top of them, such as Such et al. (2011a).

which could have prevented the agent behind that identity from holding another identity previously or holding multiple identities at once. For instance, let us take a buyer agent and a seller agent in an e-marketplace. The buyer has an identity in the e-marketplace under the name of *buy1* and the seller two identities in the e-marketplace *seller1* and *seller2*. Authentication in this case means that if *buy1* is interacting with *seller1*, *buy1* is sure that it is interacting with the agent it intended to. However, *buy1* has no idea that *seller1* and *seller2* are, indeed, the very same agent.

These vulnerabilities can be more or less harmful depending on the final domain of the application. However, these vulnerabilities should be, at least, considered in domains in which trust and reputation play a crucial role. For instance, in e-marketplaces these vulnerabilities can cause users to be seriously negatively affected through losing money. This is because a seller agent could cheat on a buyer agent, e.g., a seller may not deliver the product purchased by the buyer agent. If the seller agent repeats this over a number of transactions with other buyer agents, it could gain a very bad reputation. The point is that when the seller agent gets a very bad reputation because it does not deliver purchased products, it could simply change its identity and keep on performing the same practices, causing buyer agents to lose money.

Another example can be a social network like Last.fm[2] in which users can recommend music to each other. A user who always fails to recommend good music to other users may gain a very bad reputation. If this user creates a new account in Last.fm (a new identity in Last.fm) her reputation starts from scratch, and she is able to keep on recommending bad music. Users may be really bothered by such recommendations and move to other social networks. In this case it is the social network itself which is seriously damaged through losing users.

27.2.1 Problem Formulation

Such et al. (2011b) formulated the problem that is behind these vulnerabilities. To this aim, they used the concept of partial identity (Pfitzmann and Hansen 2010): a set of attributes[3] that identify an entity in a given context. For instance, a partial identity can be a pseudonym and a number of attributes attached to it.

They also used the concept of unlinkability (Pfitzmann and Hansen 2010): "Unlinkability of two or more items of interest (e.g., subjects, messages, actions, ...)

[2]Last.fm http://www.last.fm

[3]Identity attributes can describe a great range of topics (Rannenberg et al. 2009). For instance, entity names, biological characteristics (only for human beings), location (permanent address, geo-location at a given time), competences (diploma, skills), social characteristics (affiliation to groups, friends), and even behaviors (personality or mood).

from an attacker's perspective means that within the system (comprising these and possibly other items), the attacker cannot sufficiently distinguish whether these IOIs are related or not".

Definition 27.1. The *partial identity unlinkability* problem (PIUP) states the impossibility that an agent, which takes part in a system, is able to sufficiently distinguish whether two partial identities in that system are related or not.

This problem is what causes identity-related vulnerabilities of reputation models. It is easily observed that the *change of identities* problem is an instantiation of PIUP. For instance, an agent with an identity by which she is known to have a bad reputation, acquires another identity. From then on, other agents are unable to relate the former identity to the new acquired one. Therefore, this agent starts a fresh new reputation.

Regarding multiple identities, a similar instantiation can be made, so that an entity holds several identities and has different reputations with each of them. Thus, another entity is unable to relate the different reputations that the entity has because it is unaware that all of these identities are related to each other and to the very same entity.

27.2.2 Existing Solutions

There are many works that try to address the identity-related vulnerabilities of trust and reputation models. We now describe some of them based on the approaches that they follow:

Based on Identity Infrastructures: A possible solution for these vulnerabilities is the use of *once-in-a-lifetime* partial identities (Friedman and Resnick 1998). A model for agent identity management based on this has been proposed in Such et al. (2011b) and has been integrated into an agent platform as described in Such et al. (2012b). This model considers two kinds of partial identities: permanent and regular. Agents can only hold one permanent partial identity in a given system. Regular partial identities do not pose any limitation. Although both kinds of partial identities enable trust and reputation, only permanent partial identities guarantee that identity-related vulnerabilities are avoided. Then, agents that want to avoid identity-related vulnerabilities will only consider reputation when it is attached to a permanent partial identity. This model needs the existence of trusted third parties called Identity Providers to issue and verify partial identities. This may not be a difficulty in networks such as the Internet. However, this may not be appropriate in environments with very scarce resources such as sensor networks in which an identity infrastructure cannot be assumed.

Based on Cost: When an identity infrastructure cannot be assumed, there are other approaches such as adding monetary cost for entering a given system (Friedman and Resnick 1998). Thus, a potentially malicious agent would have a sufficient incentive (if the fee is high enough compared to the benefit expected) not to re-enter the system with a new identity. The main problem of this approach is that if the cost for entering the particular system is too high, even potentially benevolent agents may choose not to enter the system because of the high cost associated with it.

Based on Social Networks: There are also other solutions for identity-related vulnerabilities of trust and reputation models that can be used when trusted third parties (such as an identity infrastructure or an entity that imposes monetary costs for entering a system) cannot be assumed (Hoffman et al. 2009). Yu et al. (2006) present an approach based on social networks represented as a graph in which nodes represent pseudonyms and edges represent human-established trust relationships among them in the real world. They claim that malicious users can create many pseudonyms but few trust relationships. They exploit this property to bound the number of pseudonyms to be considered for trust and reputation. However, this approach is not appropriate for open Multiagent Systems in which agents act on behalf of principals that may not be known in the real world.

Based on Mathematical Properties: There is another approach that consists of reputation models specifically designed to meet some mathematical properties that are proved to avoid identity-related vulnerabilities. For instance, Cheng et al. (2005) have demonstrated several conditions using graph theory that must be satisfied when calculating reputation in order for reputation models to be resilient to sybil attacks. The only drawback of these kinds of approaches is that they usually need a particular and specific way to calculate reputation ratings about an individual. Thus, this approach cannot be applied to reputation models that follow other approaches for managing reputation ratings.

27.3 Collusion

Collusion means that a group of agents coordinate themselves to finally achieve the manipulation of either their reputation or the reputation of other agents from outside these group. Therefore, colluding agents are able to change reputation ratings at will based on attacks that exploit this vulnerability. There are two attacks that base on collusion: *ballot stuffing* and *bad mouthing* (Carrara and Hogben 2007; Jøsang et al. 2007). These attacks mainly differ in the final objective of manipulating the reputation model. The first one attempts to gain the target agent a good reputation while the second one attempts to gain the target agent a bad reputation. They achieve this by means of providing false positive/negative ratings about the target agent. These two attacks are now described with further detail.

In ballot stuffing, a number of agents agree to spread positive ratings about a specific agent. Thus, this specific agent may quickly gain a very good reputation without deserving it. For instance, a number of buyer agents in an e-marketplace may spread positive ratings about fictitious transactions with a seller agent. Thus, this seller agent may gain a very good reputation. As a result, this seller agent can cheat other buyer agents that choose it because of its good reputation.

In bad mouthing, a number of agents agree to spread negative ratings about a specific agent, which is the victim in this case. Therefore, a reputable agent may quickly gain a bad reputation without deserving it. For instance, a number of buyer agents in an e-marketplace may spread negative untrue ratings about a seller agent. Thus, this seller agent may gain a very bad reputation so that other buyer agents will not be willing to interact with this seller agent.

There are some existing solutions to avoid collusion. All of these solutions try to avoid ballot stuffing and bad mouthing based on different approaches:

Based on Discounting Unfair Ratings: One of the approaches to avoid collusion is the discount of presumable unfair ratings. There are two main approaches to do this. According to Jøsang et al. (2007) there are approaches that provide what they call *endogenous* discounting of unfair ratings and others that provide what they call *exogenous* discounting of unfair ratings.

Endogenous approaches attempt to identify unfair ratings by considering the statistical properties of the reported ratings. This is why they are called endogenous, because they identify unfair ratings based on analyzing and comparing the rating values themselves. For instance, Dellarocas (2000) presents an approach based on clustering that divides ratings into fair ratings and unfair ratings, Whitby et al. (2004) proposes a statistical filtering algorithm for excluding unfair ratings, and (Chen and Singh 2001) propose the use of collaborative filtering for grouping raters according to the ratings they give to the same objects. Although all of these approaches provide quite accurate results, they usually assume that unfair ratings are in a minority. If this assumption does not hold, these approaches are less effective and even counterproductive (Whitby et al. 2004).

Exogenous approaches attempt to identify unfair ratings by considering other information such as the reputation of the agent that provides the rating and the relationship of the rating agent to the rated agent. For instance, Buchegger and Boudec (2003) present an approach for classifying raters as trustworthy and not trustworthy based on a Bayesian reputation engine and a deviation test. Yu and Singh (2003) propose a variant of the Weighted Majority Algorithm (Littlestone and Warmuth 1994) to determine the weights given to each rater. Teacy et al. (2006) present TRAVOS, a trust and reputation model. This model considers an initially conservative estimate of the reputation accuracy. Through repeated interactions with individual raters, this model learns to distinguish reliable from unreliable raters.

Based on Anonymity: Another possible approach is to use *controlled anonymity* (Dellarocas 2000). This approach is based on the anonymity of buyer agents and seller agents. This can potentially minimize bad mouthing because it could be very difficult (if not impossible) for colluding agents to identify the victim. However, this may not be enough to avoid ballot stuffing. This is because the seller agent may still be able to give some hidden indications of its identity to its colluding agents. For instance, the seller agent might signal its colluding agents by pricing its products at a price having a specific decimal point.

Based on Monetary Incentives: There is another approach to avoid collusion that is based on monetary incentives. In particular, monetary incentives are given to agents so that they find more profit providing real ratings rather than providing unfair ratings. For instance, the reputation model presented by Rasmusson and Jansson (1996) uses incentives to ensure that paid agents tell the truth when providing ratings. A similar mechanism is proposed by Jurca et al. (2007) for discouraging collusion among the agents that spread ratings. They focus on payment schemes for ratings that makes the strategy of not colluding and providing true ratings rational. Therefore, agents cannot spread false ratings without suffering monetary losses. Other very similar approaches have been provided in the existing literature. For instance, the authors of Bhattacharjee and Goel (2005) and Kerr and Cohen (2010) focus on discouraging ballot stuffing by means of transaction costs (e.g. commissions) that are larger than the expected gain from colluding.

27.4 Other Attacks and Vulnerabilities

27.4.1 Discrimination

Discrimination means that an agent provides services with a given quality to one group of agents, and services with another quality to another group of agents (Jøsang and Golbeck 2009). Discrimination can be either positive or negative (Dellarocas 2000; Fasli 2007). On the one hand, negative discrimination is when an agent provides high quality services to almost every other agent except a few specific agents that it does not like. The problem is that if the number of agents being discriminated upon is relatively small, the reputation of the seller will remain good so that this agent is known to provide high quality services. On the other hand, positive discrimination is when an agent provides exceptionally high quality services to only a few agents and average services to the rest of the agents. If the number of buyers being favored is sufficiently large, their high ratings will inflate the reputation of the agent. Note that discrimination is different from unfair ratings because raters are providing their true/real/fair ratings about an agent. The point is that this agent behaves differently based on the specific agent it interacts with. However, some of the solutions that are used for preventing collusion can also be applied to avoiding discrimination. For instance, the controlled anonymity and the cluster filtering approaches presented by Dellarocas (2000) can be used to avoid negative discrimination and positive discrimination respectively.

27.4.2 Value Imbalance

In e-commerce environments, ratings do not usually reflect the value of the transaction that is being rated. This is what is known as *value imbalance*

(Jøsang and Golbeck 2009; Kerr and Cohen 2009). An attack that can exploit this is the following. A seller agent in an e-marketplace can perform honestly on small sales. Thus, this seller agent can get a very good reputation on that e-marketplace at a very low cost. Then, this seller agent could use the reputation gained to cheat on large sales and significantly increase its benefits. Kerr and Cohen (2010) present a trust and reputation model called Commodity Trunits. This model avoids the exploitation of value imbalance because it explicitly considers the value of transactions.

27.4.3 Reputation Lag

There is usually a time lag between a sale and the corresponding rating's effect on the agent's reputation (Jøsang and Golbeck 2009; Kerr and Cohen 2009). A seller agent could potentially exploit this vulnerability by providing a large number of low quality sales over a short period just before suffering the expected reputation degradation. Commodity Trunits (Kerr and Cohen 2010) provides an approach to solving this based on limiting the rate at which transactions can occur.

27.4.4 Privacy

Enhancing privacy is by itself of crucial importance in computer applications (Such et al. 2012a). Moreover, for the case of applications in which trust and reputation are fundamental, privacy is required in order for the raters to provide honest ratings on sensitive topics (Carrara and Hogben 2007). If not, this could be the cause of some well-known problems. For instance, the eBay reputation system is not anonymous (i.e., the rater's identity is known) which leads to an average 99% of positive ratings (Resnick and Zeckhauser 2002). This could be due to the fact that entities in eBay do not negatively rate other entities for fear of retaliations which could damage their own reputation and welfare.

Pavlov et al. (2004) introduce several privacy-preserving schemes for computing reputation in a distributed scenario. They focus on reputation systems in which the reputation computation is very simple (e.g. the summation of reputation scores). Following a similar approach, Gudes et al. (2009) propose several methods for computing the trust and reputation while preserving privacy. In this case, they propose three different methods to carry out the computations of the Knots model (Gal-Oz et al. 2008). Two of them make use of a third party while the third one is based on one of the schemes proposed by Pavlov et al. (2004). Both approaches (that of Pavlov et al. and that of Gudes et al.) present works which are only suitable for a reduced subset of trust and reputation models because they assume a particular way of calculating trust and reputation scores.

There are also some works that focus on enhancing privacy in centralized reputation systems (Androulaki et al. 2008; Schiffner and Clau 2009; Voss 2004). In these systems, information about the performance of a given participant is collected by a central authority which derives a reputation score for every participant, and makes all scores publicly available. These works focus on providing raters with anonymity. They do not modify the computation of reputation measures but the protocols followed to carry out the computations. These protocols are based on anonymous payment systems (such as Chaum et al. (1990)).

27.5 Conclusions

Over the course of this chapter, some of the most important vulnerabilities of current trust and reputation models as well as existing works on different approaches to solving them have been detailed. While some of the works presented offer solutions to some of the aforementioned vulnerabilities which are suitable under certain conditions, further research is still needed in order to completely address them. For instance, the problem of identity-related vulnerabilities in environments in which an identity infrastructure cannot be assumed remains open.

References

Androulaki, E., S. G. Choi, S. M. Bellovin, and T. Malkin. 2008. Reputation systems for anonymous networks. In *PETS '08: Proceedings of the 8th international symposium on privacy enhancing technologies*, 202–218. Berlin/Heidelberg: Springer

Bhattacharjee, R., and A. Goel. 2005. Avoiding ballot stuffing in ebay-like reputation systems. In *Proceedings of the 2005 ACM SIGCOMM workshop on economics of peer-to-peer systems, P2PECON '05*, 133–137. New York: ACM

Buchegger, S., and J. Y. L. Boudec. 2003. A robust reputation system for mobile ad-hoc networks. Techincal Report IC/2003/50, EPFL-IC-LCA

Carrara, E., and G. Hogben. 2007. Reputation-based systems: a security analysis. ENISA Position Paper. Heraklion, Crete: Greece

Chaum, D., A. Fiat, and M. Naor. 1990. Untraceable electronic cash. In *CRYPTO '88: Proceedings on advances in cryptology*, 319–327. New York: Springer

Chen, M., and J. P. Singh. 2001. Computing and using reputations for internet ratings. In *Proceedings of the 3rd ACM conference on electronic Commerce, EC '01*, 154–162. New York: ACM. doi:http://doi.acm.org/10.1145/501158.501175. http://doi.acm.org/10.1145/501158.501175

Cheng, A., and E. Friedman. 2005. Sybilproof reputation mechanisms. In *Proceedings of the 2005 ACM SIGCOMM workshop on economics of peer-to-peer systems, P2PECON '05*, 128–132. New York: ACM. doi:http://doi.acm.org/10.1145/1080192.1080202. http://doi.acm.org/10.1145/1080192.1080202

Dellarocas, C. 2000. Immunizing online reputation reporting systems against unfair ratings and discriminatory behavior. In *Proceedings of the 2nd ACM conference on Electronic commerce, EC '00*, 150–157. New York: ACM

Fasli, M. 2007. *Agent technology For E-Commerce*. Hoboken: Wiley

Friedman, E. J., and P. Resnick. 1998. The social cost of cheap pseudonyms. *Journal of Economics and Management Strategy* 10: 173–199

Gal-Oz, N., E. Gudes, and D. Hendler. 2008. A robust and knots-aware trust-based reputation model. In *Proceedings of the 2nd joint iTrust and PST conferences on privacy, trust management and security (IFIPTM'08)*, 167–182. Springer

Gudes, E., N. Gal-Oz, and A. Grubshtein. 2009. Methods for computing trust and reputation while preserving privacy. In *Proceedings of the 23rd annual IFIP WG 11.3 working conference on data and applications security XXIII*, 291–298. Berlin/Heidelberg: Springer

Hoffman, K., D. Zage, and C. Nita-Rotaru. 2009. A survey of attack and defense techniques for reputation systems. ACM Comput. Surv. 42: 1:1–1:31. doi:10.1145/1592451.1592452. http://doi.acm.org/10.1145/1592451.1592452

Jøsang, A., R. Ismail, and C. Boyd. 2007. A survey of trust and reputation systems for online service provision. *Decision Support Systems* 43(2): 618–644

Jøsang, A., and J. Golbeck. 2009. Challenges for Robust trust and reputation systems. In *Proceedings of the 5th international workshop on security and trust management (STM)*, 1–12. Springer

Jurca, R., and B. Faltings. 2007. Collusion-resistant, incentive-compatible feedback payments. In *Proceedings of the 8th ACM conference on electronic commerce, EC '07*, 200–209. New York: ACM

Kerr, R., and R. Cohen. 2009. Smart cheaters do prosper: defeating trust and reputation systems. In *Proceedings of The 8th international conference on autonomous agents and multiagent systems (AAMAS)*, 993–1000. Richland: IFAAMAS

Kerr, R., and R. Cohen. 2010. Trust as a tradable commodity: A foundation for safe electronic marketplaces. *Computational Intelligence* 26(2): 160–182

Littlestone, N., and M. Warmuth. 1994. The weighted majority algorithm. *Information and Computation* 108: 212–261

Pavlov, E., J. S. Rosenschein, and Z. Topol. 2004. Supporting privacy in decentralized additive reputation systems. In *iTrust*, 108–119

Pfitzmann, A., and M. Hansen. 2010. A terminology for talking about privacy by data minimization: Anonymity, unlinkability, undetectability, unobservability, pseudonymity, and identity management. http://dud.inf.tu-dresden.de/Anon_Terminology.shtml. V0.34

Pinyol, I., and J. Sabater-Mir. 2011. Computational trust and reputation models for open multi-agent systems: a review. *Artificial Intelligence Review* (In press). doi:10.1007/s10, 462–011–9277–z

Rannenberg, K., D. Royer, and A. Deuker (eds.). 2009. *The future of identity in the information society: Challenges and opportunities*. Berlin/New York: Springer

Rasmusson, L., and S. Jansson. 1996. Simulated social control for secure internet commerce. In *NSPW '96: Proceedings of the 1996 workshop on new security paradigms*, 18–25. New York: ACM. doi:http://doi.acm.org/10.1145/304851.304857

Resnick, P., and R. Zeckhauser. 2002. Trust among strangers in Internet transactions: Empirical analysis of eBay's reputation system. In *The economics of the Internet and E-Commerce*. Advances in Applied Microeconomics, vol. 11, ed. M. R. Baye, 127–157. Emerald Group Publishing Limited, Bingley, United Kingdom

Sabater, J., and C. Sierra. 2005. Review on computational trust and reputation models. *Artificial Intelligence Review* 24: 33–60

Schiffner, S., S. Clauβ, and S. Steinbrecher. 2009. Privacy and liveness for reputation systems. In *EuroPKI*. Springer

Such, J. M., J. M. Alberola, A. Espinosa, and A. García-Fornes. 2011a. A group-oriented secure multiagent platform. *Software: Practice and Experience* 41(11): 1289–1302

Such, J. M., A. Espinosa, A. García-Fornes, and V. Botti. 2011b. Partial identities as a foundation for trust and reputation. *Engineering Applications of Artificial Intelligence* 24(7): 1128–1136

Such, J. M., A. Espinosa, and A. García-Fornes. 2012a. A survey of privacy in multi-agent systems. *Knowledge Engineering Review* (In press). http://dx.doi.org/10.1016/j.engappai.2012.06.009

Such, J. M., A. García-Fornes, A. Espinosa, and J. Bellver. 2012. Magentix2: A privacy-enhancing agent platform. *Engineering Applications of Artificial Intelligence* (In press). doi:http://dx.doi.org/10.1016/j.engappai.2012.06.009

Teacy, W., J. Patel, N. Jennings, and M. Luck. 2006b. Travos: Trust and reputation in the context of inaccurate information sources. *Autonomous Agents and Multi-Agent Systems* 12(2): 183–198

Voss, M. 2004. Privacy preserving online reputation systems. In *International information security workshops*, 245–260. Springer

Whitby, A., A. Jøsang, and J. Indulska. 2004. Filtering out unfair ratings in bayesian reputation systems. In *Proceedings of the 7th international workshop on trust in agent societies*, New York, NY, USA

Yu, B., and M. P. Singh. 2003. Detecting deception in reputation management. In *Proceedings of the second international joint conference on autonomous agents and multiagent systems, AAMAS '03*, 73–80. New York: ACM

Yu, H., M. Kaminsky, P. B. Gibbons, and A. Flaxman. 2006. Sybilguard: defending against sybil attacks via social networks. In *Proceedings of the conference on applications, technologies, architectures, and protocols for computer communications (SIGCOMM)*, 267–278. New York: ACM

Chapter 28
Reputation and Organisations

Olivier Boissier, Jomi Fred Hübner, and Laurent Vercouter

28.1 Introduction

An important role of reputation in the context of organisations is to implement mechanisms for norm enforcement and incentives so that agents behave as expected by the organisation they belong to. However, an organisation also provides other useful elements to compute reputation for that issue. As a collective phenomenon, reputation is better thought of as embodied in an organisation.

Before going further into the analysis of reputation in organisations, we define what is meant by organisation in this chapter. Although, there is no unique and general definition of organisation in MAS (a detailed study about organisations and related concepts in MAS is provided by Part IV), we can consider it as the expression of cooperation patterns to achieve some global purpose. Cooperation patterns may take different forms. In general, different dimensions may be used to describe them: structural, functional, normative, dialogic, etc. (Coutinho et al. 2007). Two main complementary approaches have been adopted to deal with these cooperation patterns: agent-centered and organisation-centered. According to an agent-centered view, an organisation has no particular explicit and global representation. It is a set of social relations that result from the interaction between the different agents based on their local behaviour. The cooperation patterns that may describe their interactions are in the eye of the observer or of different agents. According to

O. Boissier (✉)
FAYOL-EMSE, LSTI, F-42023 Saint-Etienne, France
e-mail: Olivier.Boissier@emse.fr

J.F. Hübner
Federal University of Santa Catarina, PO Box 476, Florianópolis, SC 88040-900 Brazil
e-mail: jomi@das.ufsc.br

L. Vercouter
INSA de Rouen, avenue de l'université BP 8, 76801 Saint-Etienne du Rouvray, France
e-mail: laurent.vercouter@insa-rouen.fr

S. Ossowski (ed.), *Agreement Technologies*, Law, Governance and Technology Series 8, DOI 10.1007/978-94-007-5583-3_28,

an organisation-centered view, on the contrary, the organisation is explicitly and globally represented, building a formal organisation specification. This specification is defined/adapted either by the designer of the system or by the agents themselves. The organisation is used to help the agents to coordinate with each other and to regulate and control their behaviour while participating in the different cooperations that it proposes. In this chapter both approaches are considered.

Section 28.2 analyses how reputation can bear on different dimensions of an organisation as it does for agent's behaviour. From this first statement, an opposite view is adopted in order to show how organisation provides different inputs for computing reputation in a multiagent system (Sect. 28.3). Having identified the sources and trustees of reputation within a multiagent organisation, in Sect. 28.4 we focus on the reputation building process within an organisation, i.e. what are the different possible cooperation schemes that underlie the building of the reputation in an MAS.

28.2 Organisational Trustees of Reputation

Reputation has been defined as "the outcome of the social process of transmission of beliefs about the trustee". It is usually considered that the trustee is an agent that is evaluated from the observation of its behaviours. However, it may be interesting to extend this definition to other kinds of trustees in order to maintain finer and more precise evaluations of the parts of a multiagent system influencing its global efficiency. We are especially interested in this chapter in the concepts related to multiagent organisations. Reputation may thus be ascribed to organisational concepts going from the more specific to the more general ones. For instance in sentences like "The reputation of professors from this University is very good", some level of reputation is ascribed to a role (an organisational concept) and not to an agent. In this example, by assigning a reputation to a role we are indeed assigning a reputation to every agent while playing the role. This kind of reputation assignment can be used in an even more general context like in the sentence "This University has a good reputation". In this latter example, however, the reputation cannot be implied for the members of the University. Both cases however have in common the fact that a reputation is assigned to an organisational concept. In this area there are a myriad of such concepts as defined by several organisation models.

Most of the organisational models provide a structure defining what agents should do by the attribution of *goals*. A first assessment of an agent's behaviour in an organisation is to evaluate how efficient it is when trying to achieve its organisational goals. As it is often done with trust models, attaching reputation values to pairs (agent, goal) allows the expression of different evaluations for a same agent depending on the corresponding organisational goal. For example, in the ForTrust model (Herzig et al. 2010) the reputation is defined as a five-argument predicate $reputation(I,j,\alpha,\phi,\kappa)$ to be read "j has reputation in group I to do the action α with respect to goal ϕ in circumstances κ".

The concept of goal is widely used in multiagent systems and not specifically dedicated to organisations. Indeed, goals are sometimes linked to the organisational concepts aiming at their achievement. Agent's *roles* or *missions* are various ways to represent how an agent should behave to achieve a goal. Attaching social evaluations such as reputation to roles or missions is again a finer representation of agents' efficiency. For instance, it may express that an agent is good at achieving a given goal while fulfilling a given role, but not with another role that should achieve this same goal. One of the main tasks expected when using multiagent organisations is to provide descriptive elements or mechanisms facilitating the coordination of several agents involved together in a collective task. Depending on the organisational model, such a coordinated activity is implemented by the concepts of *coalition* (Sichman 1998), *teams* (Decker 1996; Pynadath and Tambe 2003), or *group* (Ferber and Gutknecht 1998; Hübner et al. 2002).

It is then possible to use reputation at two different levels:

- Reputation as a social evaluation *within* a group. This corresponds to the definition of Conte and Paolucci (2002) who consider that the concept of reputation integrates the way evaluations are shared inside a social entity. The trustee of the reputation is an agent but it is attached to a given group (or to a similar social entity concept) and an agent can have different reputations in different groups of agents.
- Reputation *of* a group. In this case, the trustee of the social evaluation is not a single agent, but a collective of several agents as well as the group's coordination structure. There can be different meanings attached to the reputation of a group. It can be an evaluation of the abstract definition of the group (i.e. its structure), or of the specific set of agents belonging to the group, or even of both by considering the set of agents as well as the way they are structured.

These two views are not incompatible. One can imagine building reputations of a group shared inside another group.

At last, the most general concept is *organisation*. Reputation can be ascribed to a given organisation especially in multiagent systems where several organisations co-exist. Here also, it is possible to distinguish two levels: an agent reputation within an organisation or the reputation of an organisation.

28.3 Organisational Sources for Reputation

Social evaluations that circulate in a society and represent agent's reputations are built from several sources. When reputation is related to organisational concepts, it is natural to consider that these sources provide views or testimonies about agents as part of an organisation. An intuitive example is the feedback on the agents' efficiency while performing tasks for the organisation.

A direct way to obtain such feedback is to collect feedbacks from agents sharing the same group as the one which is evaluated. SocialRegret (Sabater and Sierra 2002) is an example of a multiagent reputation model using feedbacks from agents of the trustee group. This reputation is called *neighbourhood reputation* and it assumes that agents sharing a group will interact more than if they were in different groups. Neighbourhood reputation is built locally by agents from the feedback they perceived from agents in the trustee group. It is then a subjective social evaluation and two different agents can have different representations of a neighbourhood reputation if they perceived different feedbacks or if their aggregation function is different.

Centralised repositories (see Dellarocas (2003) for a global description of centralized reputation systems) are sometimes used to gather all the feedbacks in order to increase the amount of data upon which reputation is calculated. Of course, a prerequisite of this approach is that the centralisation of data and/or calculation processes is possible. The hybrid reputation model of Torres da Silva et al. (2009) proposes a dual mechanism combining centralised and decentralised process. Decentralisation occurs when each agent computes evaluations about the others. The local computation is based on perceived situations in which the trustee satisfies or violates norms. Both individual and organisational norms are considered here, but in the case of organisational norms, the perceived situation is sent to a centralised data store. Each agent may then send queries to the centralised data store to get reputation information coming from others.

A similar approach has been proposed by the implementation of the *reputation artefacts* (Hübner et al. 2008). This proposal relies on the $\mathcal{M}$oise organisational model. Following the A&A paradigm (Omicini et al. 2008), an artefact is defined to store records about the agents' performance in the organisation. Reputation is here represented as a set of three values: (i) *obedience* (how well an agent achieves its obligations); (ii) *pro-activeness* (how many goals an agent achieves without being obliged to); (iii) *results* (how many successful global plans – schemes in $\mathcal{M}$oise model – the agent has been involved into). In this work, the feedbacks should come from any entity in charge of monitoring the execution of the organisation, typically an agent or an institution.

28.4 Organizational Processes for Reputation Building

While the previous sections have presented how organisational concepts can be used as trustees or sources of the reputation relationship, this section focuses on the *process* of building reputation *within* an organisation. It represents how the organisation ascribes reputation to agents based on their behaviour as members of the organisation.

This process is viewed according to two approaches in the community (briefly listed in Table 28.1). Most of the reputation processes have as input evaluations provided by the agents that belong to the organisation, while few models consider

Table 28.1 Classification of reputation processes inside organisations

Approach	Information source	Kind of input	Output
Agent based	Agent	Opinion	Aggregation of opinions
Organisation based	Organisation	Measurements	Aggregation of measurements

organisation internal evaluation as input. For instance, in the proposal of Silva et al. (2009) and Hermoso et al. (2007), agents participating in the organisation send to the organisation their own images about other agents in the context of their roles. However, in proposals like Hübner et al. (2008), the organisation has its own mechanisms to measure the participants as role players. The evaluation regarding the norm compliance, for example, in the former is performed by the agents and in the latter performed by monitoring mechanisms installed in the organisation platform. While the former approach better supports the idea of *shared voices* as an important component of the reputation formation (being the organisation just a repository of agent's voices), the latter has the advantage of independence of agent's opinion and its inherent subjectivity. The problem of agents lying about others or not being good evaluators is thus avoided. In the latter, the output of the process is better seen as the image or evaluation of an agent based on the eyes of the organisation instead of its reputation. However, even in the former approach, the output of the process perhaps cannot be strictly seen as reputation in the sense of Conte and Paolucci (2002). The output is the aggregation of agent's opinion carried out by the organisation using organisational parameters in that process. This output may be different of that resulting from the same set of agents sharing their opinions instead of being intermediated by the organisation. Of course, this "organisational image" can be used in the formation of the reputation of some agent.

Based on the input given either by agents or by measurements mechanisms, the service the organisation provides by this process is essentially the aggregation of evaluations. This aggregation will then be used by the agents forming the reputation of the agents in the context of some organisation.

28.5 Conclusions

In this chapter some approaches to integrating reputation and organisation have been briefly shown. The potential for application of reputation on multiagent organisation and organisation on reputation mechanisms is wide and not fully explored yet.

Several questions deserve further investigation in the future. In the following we list some of them:

- What kind of support is provided by the organisation when confronted with the proposal of reputation built from shared voices (Conte and Paolucci 2002)?
- How can reputation be used in the processes of entry/exit of agents in open systems (Kitio 2011)?

- How can reputation be used in reorganisation processes?
- Are there new attacks or new protections against existing attacks on reputation models brought by the introduction of organisational concepts?

References

Conte, R., and M. Paolucci. 2002. *Reputation in artificial societies: Social beliefs for social order*. Dordrecht: Kluwer.

Coutinho, L., J. Sichman, and O. Boissier. 2007. Organizational modeling dimensions in multiagent systems. In *Proceedings of workshop agent organizations: Models and simulations (AOMS@IJCAI 07)*, ed. V. Dignum, F. Dignum, and E. Matson.

Decker, K. S. 1996. TÆMS: A framework for environment centered analysis and design of coordination mechanisms. In *Fundations of distributed artificial intelligence, chap. 16*, ed. G. M. P. O'Hare and N. R. Jennings, 429–447. New York: Wiley.

Dellarocas, C. 2003. The digitization of word-of-mouth: Promise and challenges of online reputation systems. *Management Science* 49(10): 1407–1424.

Ferber, J., and O. Gutknecht. 1998. A meta-model for the analysis and design of organizations in multi-agents systems. In *Proceedings of the 3rd international conference on multi-agent systems, ICMAS 1998, 3–7 July 1998*, ed. Y. Demazeau, 128–135. IEEE Computer Society. Paris: France.

Hermoso, R., H. Billhardt, and S. Ossowski. 2007. Integrating trust in virtual organisations. In *Coordination, organizations, institutions, and norms in agent systems II*. LNAI, vol. 4386, ed. P. Noriega, J. Vázquez-Salceda, G. Boella, O. Boissier, V. Dignum, N. Fornara, and E. Matson, 19–31. Berlin/New York: Springer. Revised Selected Papers.

Herzig, A., E. Lorini, J. F. Hübner, and L. Vercouter. 2010. A logic of trust and reputation. *Logic Journal of the IGPL, Normative Multiagent Systems* 18(1): 214–244.

Hübner, J. F., J. S. Sichman, and O. Boissier. 2002. A model for the structural, functional, and deontic specification of organizations in multiagent systems. In *Proceedings of the 16th Brazilian symposium on artificial intelligence (SBIA'02)*, 118–128, Porto de Galinhas, PE, Brazil.

Hübner, J. F., L. Vercouter, and O. Boissier. 2008. Instrumenting multi-agent organisations with reputation artifacts. In *Proceedings of coordination, organizations, institutions and norms (COIN@AAAI), held with AAAI 2008*, Chicago, EUA, ed. V. Dignum and E. Matson, 17–24. AAAI. http://www.das.ufsc.br/~jomi/pubs/2008/hbv-coin08.pdf.

Kitio, R. 2011. Managing openness within multi-agent organizations. Ph.D. thesis, ENS Mines Saint-Etienne, France (in french).

Omicini, A., A. Ricci, and M. Viroli. 2008. Artifacts in the A&A meta-model for multi-agent systems. *Journal of Autonomous Agents and Multi-Agent Systems* 17(3): 432–456.

Pynadath, D. V., and M. Tambe. 2003. An automated teamwork infrastructure for heterogeneous software agents and humans. *Autonomous Agents and Multi-Agent Systems* 7(1–2): 71–100.

Sabater, J., and C. Sierra. 2002. Reputation and social network analysis in multi-agent systems. In *The first international joint conference on autonomous agents & multiagent systems (AAMAS 2002), July 15–19, ACM 2002*, 475–482. Bologna: Italy

Sichman, J. S. 1998. DEPINT: Dependence-based coalition formation in an open multi-agent scenario. *Journal of Artificial Societies and Social Simulation* 1(2): (1998). http://jasss.soc.surrey.ac.uk/1/2/3.html.

Silva, V.T., Hermoso, R., and Centeno, R. 2009. A hybrid reputation model based on the use of organization. *Coordination, organizations, institutions and norms in agent systems IV*. Lecture Notes in Computer Science, vol. 5428, ed. J. F. Hübner, E. Matson, O. Boissier, and V. Dignum, 111–125. Berlin/Heidelberg: Springer.

Chapter 29
Building Relationships with Trust

Carles Sierra and John Debenham

29.1 Introduction

In this chapter trust is presented as the foundation for a rich sense of friendship between agents in a multiagent system. When agents interact their growing history of illocutionary dialogues is their *relationship*. An agent understands its relationships using various measures that summarise its dialogue history. These summary measures, of which trust is fundamental, enable relationships to be understood in the context of a multifaceted continuum rather than the simplistic cooperative/competitive divide. On the basis of this understanding an agent may choose: to form speculative beliefs concerning the future behaviour of other agents, to decide who to interact with under given circumstances, and to determine how to interact with them. This opens the way for an agent to proactively influence its dialogues with the aim of shaping its relationships so that they provide some degree of protection against future unknowns in an uncertain world.

Section 29.2 introduces the framework within which the work is developed; in particular, the term trust is defined in the context of the signing, enactment and evaluation of contracts. Section 29.3 describes the components of the trust model: the ontology, the core trust mechanism, the representation of prior knowledge, and the context. Then in Sect. 29.4 the relationship model is introduced—this models the relationships between agents. Section 29.5 draws the previous ideas together by discussing negotiation.

C. Sierra (✉)
IIIA – CSIC, Barcelona, Spain
e-mail: sierra@iiia.csic.es

J. Debenham
QCIS, University of Technology, Sydney, NSW, Australia
e-mail: john.debenham@uts.edu.au

S. Ossowski (ed.), *Agreement Technologies*, Law, Governance and Technology Series 8, DOI 10.1007/978-94-007-5583-3_29,

29.2 Trust

The informal meaning of the statement "agent α trusts agent β" is that α expects β to act in a way that is somehow preferred by α. Human agents seldom trust another for *any* action that they may take—it is more usual to develop a trusted expectation with respect to a particular set of actions. For example, "I trust John to deliver fresh vegetables" whilst the quality of John's advice on investments may be terrible. This section describes trust when the set of actions is restricted to negotiating, signing and enacting contracts that are expressed using some particular ontology.

A multiagent system $\{\alpha, \beta_1, \ldots, \beta_o, \xi, \theta_1, \ldots, \theta_t\}$, contains an agent α that interacts with negotiating agents, $\mathscr{X} = \{\beta_i\}$, information providing agents, $\mathscr{I} = \{\theta_j\}$, and an *institutional agent*, ξ, that represents the institution where the interactions are assumed to happen (Arcos et al. 2005). Institutions give a normative context to interactions that simplify matters (e.g. an agent can't make an offer, have it accepted, and then renege on it). The institutional agent ξ may form opinions on the actors and activities in the institution and may publish reputation estimates on behalf of the institution. The agent ξ also fulfils a vital role to compensate for any lack of sensory ability in the other agents by promptly and accurately reporting observations as events occur. For example, without such reporting an agent may have no way of knowing whether it is a fine day or not.

Our agents are information-based (Sierra and Debenham 2007), they are endowed with machinery for valuing the information that they have, and that they receive. They were inspired by the observation that "everything an agent says gives away information", even if the utterances are not truthful. They model how much they know about other agents, how much they believe other agents know about them, and the extent to which they believe other agents are telling the truth. Everything in their world, including their information, is uncertain; their only means of reducing uncertainty is acquiring fresh information. To model this uncertainty, their world model, $\mathscr{M}^t$, consists of random variables each representing a point of interest in the world. Distributions are then derived for these variables on the basis of information received. Over time agents acquire large amounts of information that are distilled into convenient measures including trust. By classifying private information into functional classes, and by drawing on the structure of the ontology, information-based agents develop other measures including a map of the 'intimacy' (Sierra and Debenham 2007) of their relationships with other agents.

In this section agent interaction is limited to dealing with contracts. The scenario is: two agents α and β negotiate with the intention of leading to a *signed contract* that is a pair of commitments, (a, b), where a is α's and b is β's. A contract is signed by both agents at some particular time t. At some later time, t', both agents will have enacted their commitments[1] in some way, as say (a', b'). At some later time again,

[1] For convenience it is assumed that both agents are presumed to have completed their enactments by the same time, t'.

Fig. 29.1 Contract signing, execution and evaluation

Action	Sign	Enact	Evaluate
Object	(a,b)	(a',b')	b'
Time	t	t'	t''

t'', α will consume b' and will then be in a position to evaluate the extent to which β's enactment of (a,b), b', was in α's interests. See Fig. 29.1.

α's trust of agent β is expressed as an expectation of β's future actions. We consider how α forms these expectations, how α will compare those expectations with observations, and how α then determines whether β's actions are preferred to α's expectations of them.

α forms expectations of β's future actions on the basis of all that it has: its full interaction history $H_\alpha \in \mathcal{H}_\alpha$ where $\mathcal{H}_\alpha$ is the set of all possible interaction histories that may be expressed in α's ontology.[2] H_α is a record of all interactions with each negotiating agent in $\mathcal{X}$ and with each information providing agent in $\mathcal{I}$. Let $\mathcal{B} = (b_1, b_2, \ldots)$ denote that space of all enactments that β may make and $\mathcal{A}$ the space of α's enactments. α's expectations of β's behaviour will be represented as probability distributions over $\mathcal{B}$. Assuming that the space of contracts and enactments are the same, the space of all contracts and enactments is: $\mathcal{C} = \mathcal{A} \times \mathcal{B}$.

This raises the strategic question of given an expectation of some particular future requirements how should α strategically shape its interaction history to enable it to build a reliable expectation of β's future actions concerning the satisfaction of those particular requirements. At time t'' α compares b' with α's expectations of β's actions, β having committed at time t to enact b at time t'. That is:

$$\text{compare}^{t''}_{\alpha}(\mathbb{E}^t_\alpha(\text{Enact}^{t'}_\beta(b)|\text{sign}^t_{\alpha,\beta}((a,b)), H^t_\alpha), b')$$

where $\text{sign}^t_{\alpha,\beta}((a,b))$ is a predicate meaning that the joint action by α and β of signing the contract (a,b) was performed at time t, and $\text{Enact}^{t'}_\beta(b)$ is a random variable over $\mathcal{B}$ representing α's expectations over β's enactment action at time t', $\mathbb{E}^t_\alpha(\cdot)$ is α's expectation, and $\text{compare}(\cdot,\cdot)$ somehow describes the result of the comparison.

Expectations over β's enactment actions:

$$\mathbb{E}^t_\alpha(\text{Enact}^{t'}_\beta(b)|\text{sign}^t_{\alpha,\beta}((a,b)), H^t_\alpha)$$

could form the basis for trust. In practice, developing a sense on expectation over β's actions is tricky except possibly in the case that there is a history of contracts with a high degree of similarly to (a,b). Given such an expectation an agent may be prepared to use the structure of the ontology to propagate these expectations. For example, if α has a history of observing β's 'trusted' executions of orders for

[2]The ontology is not made explicit to avoid overburdening the notation.

cow's cheese then it may be prepared to partially propagate this expectation to goat's cheese—perhaps on the basis that cow's cheese and goat's cheese are semantically close concepts in the ontology.

The discussion above is based on expectations of *what action* β will do. It makes more practical sense to develop a sense of expectation over *the evaluation of* β's actions. Let $\mathcal{V} = (v_1, v_2, \ldots, v_V)$ be the valuation space. Then α's expectation of the evaluation of a particular action that β may make is represented as a probability distribution over $\mathcal{V}$: $(f_1, f_2, \ldots, f_V)$. For example, a simple valuation space could be (good, ok, bad). The sequence $\mathcal{V}$ will generally be smaller than the sequence $\mathcal{B}$, and so developing a sense of expectation for the value of β's actions should be easier than for the actions themselves. That is, it is simpler to form the expectation:

$$\mathbb{E}^t_\alpha(\text{Value}^{t''}_\beta(b) | \text{sign}^t_{\alpha,\beta}((a,b)), H^t_\alpha)$$

where $\text{Value}^{t''}(b)$ is a random variable over $\mathcal{V}$ representing α's expectations of the value of β's enactment action given that he signed (a,b) and given H^t_α. At time t'' it then remains to compare expectation, $\mathbb{E}^t_\alpha(\text{Value}^{t''}_\beta(b) | \text{sign}^t_{\alpha,\beta}((a,b)), H^t_\alpha)$, with observation, $\text{val}_\alpha(b')$, where $\text{val}(\cdot)$ represents α's preferences—i.e. it is α's utility function.[3]

We are now in a position to define 'trust'. *Trust*, $\tau_{\alpha\beta}(b)$, is a computable[4] estimate of the distribution: $\mathbb{E}^t_\alpha(\text{Value}^{t''}_\beta(b) | \text{sign}^t_{\alpha,\beta}((a,b)), H^t_\alpha)$. τ is a summarising function that distils the trust-related aspects of the (probably very large) set H_α into a probability distribution that may be computed. $\tau_{\alpha\beta}(b)$ summarises the large set H_α. The set of contracts $\mathcal{C}$ is also large. It is practically unfeasible to estimate trust for each individual contract. The structure of the ontology is used to deal with this problem by aggregating estimates into suitable classes such as John's trustworthiness in supplying Australian red wine.

In real world situations the interaction history may not reliably predict future action, in which case the notion of trust is fragile. No matter how trust is defined trusted relationships are expected to develop slowly over time. On the other hand they can be destroyed quickly by an agent whose actions unexpectedly fall below expectation. This highlights the importance of being able to foreshadow the possibility of untrustworthy behaviour.

$\tau_{\alpha\beta}(b)$ is predicated on α's ability to form an expectation of the value of β's future actions. This is related to the famous question posed by Laplace "what is the probability that the sun will rise tomorrow?". Assume that it has always previously been observed to do so and that there have been n prior observations. Then if the observer is in complete ignorance of the process he will assume that the probability distribution of a random variable representing the prior probability that the sun will

[3]It is arguably more correct to consider: $\text{Value}((a,b)) = \text{Value}(b) - \text{Value}(a)$, as β's actions may be influenced by his expectations of α's enactment of a—this additional complication is ignored.

[4]*Computable* in the sense that it is finitely computable, and hopefully not computationally complex.

rise tomorrow is the maximum entropy, uniform distribution on $[0,1]$. Further, using Bayes' theorem he will derive the posterior estimate $\frac{n+1}{n+2}$; the key assumption is that the observer is "in complete ignorance of the process". There may be many reasons why the sun may not rise such as the existence of a large comet on a collision trajectory with earth. These all important reasons are the *context* of the problem.

Laplace's naïve analysis above forms the basis of a very crude measure of trust. Suppose that the valuation space is: $\mathscr{V} = (\text{bad}, \text{good})$, and that α is considering signing contract (a,b) with β. Let the random variable B denote the value of β's next action. Then assume that nothing is known about the contract or about β except that this contract has been enacted by β on n prior occasions and that the valuation was "good" on s of those occasions. Using the maximum entropy prior distribution for B, $[0.5, 0.5]$, Bayes' theorem gives us a posterior distribution $[\frac{n-s+1}{n+2}, \frac{s+1}{n+2}]$. If at time t α signs the contract under consideration then the expected probability of a "good" valuation at time t'' is: $\frac{s+1}{n+2}$. This crude measure has little practical value although it readily extends to general discrete valuation spaces, and to continuous valuation spaces. The zero-information, maximum entropy distribution is the *trivial trust measure*. The crude Laplacian trust measure is in a sense the simplest non-trivial measure.

The weaknesses of the crude trust measure above show the way to building a reliable measure of trust. A reliable trust measure will include:

Prior knowledge. The use of the maximum entropy prior[5] is justified when there is absolutely no prior knowledge or belief of an agent's behaviour. In practical scenarios prior observations, reputation measures or the opinions of other agents are expected to be available and to be reflected in the prior.

Time. There is no representation of time. In the crude trust measure all prior observations have the same significance, and so an agent that used to perform well and is deteriorating may have the same trust measure as one that used to perform badly and is now performing well.

Context. There is no model of general events in the world or of *how* those events may affect an agent's behaviour. This includes modelling causality, namely *why* an agent might behave as it does.

29.3 Trust Model

The previous section defines trust as an optimistic[6] estimator of the expected value of future enactments, and concluded with three features of a reliable measure of trust. This section describes such a measure that uses the computational methods of information-based agents (Sierra and Debenham 2007) particularly their

[5]The maximum entropy prior expresses total uncertainty about what the prior distribution is.

[6]*Optimistic* in the sense that the estimation can be performed on the basis of the agent's interaction history.

information evaluation, acquisition and revelation strategies that ideally suits them to this purpose. Section 29.2 also described the fundamental role that the structure of the ontology plays in the trust model. This is described next followed by the core trust mechanism and then a reliable measure of trust.

29.3.1 Ontology

The structure of the ontology plays a central role in maintaining the trust model. Observations are propagated across the model moderated by their "semantic distance" from the concepts in the observation to nearby concepts.

Our agent communication language, U, is founded on three fundamental primitives: Commit(α,β,φ) to represent, in φ, the world that α aims at bringing about and that β has the right to verify, complain about or claim compensation for any deviations from, Observe(α,φ) to represent that a certain state of the world, φ, is observed, and Done(u) to represent the event that a certain action u[7] has taken place. In our language, norms, contracts, and information chunks are represented as instances of Commit$(\cdot)$ where α and β can be individual agents or institutions, U is the set of expressions. $u \in U$ is defined as:

$$
\begin{aligned}
u &::= illoc(\alpha,\beta,\varphi,t) \mid u;u \mid \textbf{Let } context \textbf{ In } u \textbf{ End}\\
\varphi &::= term \mid \text{Done}(u) \mid \text{Commit}(\alpha,\beta,\varphi) \mid \text{Observe}(\alpha,\varphi) \mid \varphi \wedge \varphi \mid\\
&\quad\ \varphi \vee \varphi \mid \neg\varphi \mid \forall v.\varphi_v \mid \exists v.\varphi_v\\
context &::= \varphi \mid id = \varphi \mid prolog\_clause \mid context;context
\end{aligned}
$$

where φ_v is a formula with free variable v, *illoc* is a predicate defining any appropriate set of illocutionary particles, ';' means sequencing, and *context* represents either previous agreements, previous illocutions, or code that aligns the ontological differences between the speakers needed to interpret an action u, and *term* represents logical predicates. t represents a point in time.[8] We denote by Φ the set of expressions φ used as the propositional content of illocutions.

For example, the following offer: "If you spend a total of more than €100 in my shop during October then I will give you a 10% discount on all goods in November", is represented as:

$$
\begin{aligned}
&\text{Offer}(\alpha, \beta, \texttt{spent}(\beta, \alpha, \texttt{October}, \text{X}) \wedge \text{X} \geq €100 \rightarrow\\
&\quad \forall\, \text{y. Done}(\text{Inform}(\xi, \alpha, \text{pay}(\beta, \alpha, \text{y}), \text{November})) \rightarrow\\
&\qquad \text{Commit}(\alpha, \beta, \text{discount}(\text{y}, 10\%)))
\end{aligned}
$$

[7] All actions are assumed to be dialogical.

[8] Usually omitted to simplify notation.

or, "If I tell you who I buy my tomatoes from then would you keep that information confidential?" as:

$$\text{Offer}(\alpha, \beta, \exists\delta.\ (\text{Commit}(\alpha,\beta,\text{Done}(\text{Inform}(\alpha,\beta,\text{provider}(\delta,\alpha,\text{tomato})))) \wedge \forall\gamma.\ \forall\, t.\ \text{Commit}(\beta,\alpha,\neg\text{Done}(\text{Inform}(\beta,\gamma,\text{provider}(\delta,\alpha,\text{tomato}), t))))$$

In order to define the *terms* of the language introduced above (e.g. pay(β,α,y) or discount$(y, 10\%)$) an ontology is required that includes a (minimum) repertoire of elements: a set of *concepts* (e.g. quantity, quality, material) organised in a is-a hierarchy (e.g. platypus is a mammal, australian-dollar is a currency), and a set of relations over these concepts (e.g. price(beer,AUD)).[9]

We model ontologies following an algebraic approach (Kalfoglou and Schorlemmer 2003) as: an *ontology* is a tuple $\mathcal{O} = (C, R, \leq, \sigma)$ where:

1. C is a finite set of *concept symbols* (including basic data types);
2. R is a finite set of *relation symbols*;
3. $\leq$ is a reflexive, transitive and anti-symmetric relation on C (a partial order)
4. $\sigma : R \to C^+$ is the function assigning to each relation symbol its arity

where $\leq$ is a traditional *is-a* hierarchy, and R contains relations between the concepts in the hierarchy.

The semantic distance between concepts plays a fundamental role in the estimation of trust. The concepts within an ontology are closer, semantically speaking, depending on how far away they are in the structure defined by the $\leq$ relation. Semantic distance plays a fundamental role in strategies for information-based agency. How signed contracts, Commit$(\cdot)$ about objects in a particular semantic region, and their execution Observe$(\cdot)$, *affect* our decision making process about signing future contracts on nearby semantic regions is crucial to modelling the common sense that human beings apply in managing trading relationships.

A measure (Li et al. 2003) bases the *semantic similarity* between two concepts on the path length induced by $\leq$ (more distance in the $\leq$ graph means less semantic similarity), and the *depth* of the subsumer concept (common ancestor) in the shortest path between the two concepts (the deeper in the hierarchy, the closer the meaning of the concepts). Li et al. (2003) defines semantic similarity as:

$$\text{Sim}(c,c') = e^{-\kappa_1 l} \cdot \frac{e^{\kappa_2 h} - e^{-\kappa_2 h}}{e^{\kappa_2 h} + e^{-\kappa_2 h}}$$

where e is Euler's number (≈ 2.71828), l is the length (i.e. number of hops) of the shortest path between the concepts, h is the depth of the deepest concept subsuming both concepts, and κ_1 and κ_2 are parameters scaling the contribution of shortest path length and depth respectively. If $l = h = 0$ then $\text{Sim}(c,c') = 1$; in general $\text{Sim}(c,c') \in [0,1]$.

[9]Usually, a set of axioms defined over the concepts and relations is also required. We will omit this here.

29.3.2 The Core Trust Mechanism

Section 29.2 ends with three essential components of a reliable trust model. Those three components will be dealt with in due course. This section describes the core trust estimation mechanism. In subsequent sections the core is enhanced with the three essential components. The final component, context, is unresolved as it relies on the solution to hard problems, such as modelling rare but significant contextual events, that are beyond the scope of this discussion.

The general idea is that whenever α evaluates $\text{val}_{\alpha}^{t''}(b')$ for the enactment (a',b') of some previously signed contract (a,b) the trust estimates are updated. The contract space is typically very large and so estimates are not maintained for individual contracts; instead they are maintained for selected abstractions based on the ontology. Abstractions are denoted by the 'hat' symbol: e.g. $\hat{a}$. For example, "red wine orders for more that 24 bottles" or "supply of locally produced cheese". Whenever an evaluation $\text{val}_{\alpha}^{t''}(b')$ is performed the trust estimates, $\tau_{\alpha\beta}(\hat{b})$, for certain selected nearby abstractions, $\hat{b}$, are updated.

In the absence of incoming information the integrity of an information-based agent's beliefs decays in time. In the case of the agent's beliefs concerning trust, incoming information is in the form of valuation observations $\text{val}_{\alpha}^{t''}(b')$ for each enacted contract. If there are no such observations in an area of the ontology then the integrity of the estimate for that area should decay.

In the absence of valuation observations in the region of $\hat{b}$, $\tau_{\alpha\beta}(\hat{b})$ decays to a *decay limit distribution* $\overline{\tau_{\alpha\beta}(\hat{b})}$ (denoted throughout this section by 'overline'). The decay limit distribution is the zero-data distribution, but not the zero-information distribution because it takes account of reputation estimates and the opinions of other agents (Sierra and Debenham 2009). We assume that the decay limit distribution is known for each abstraction $\hat{b}$. At time s, given a distribution for random variable $\tau_{\alpha\beta}(\hat{b})^s$, and a decay limit distribution, $\overline{\tau_{\alpha\beta}(\hat{b})^s}$, $\tau_{\alpha\beta}(\hat{b})$ decays by:

$$\tau_{\alpha\beta}(\hat{b})^{s+1} = \Delta(\overline{\tau_{\alpha\beta}(\hat{b})^s}, \tau_{\alpha\beta}(\hat{b})^s)$$

where s is time and Δ is the *decay function* for the X satisfying the property that $\lim_{s\to\infty} \tau_{\alpha\beta}(\hat{b})^s = \overline{\tau_{\alpha\beta}(\hat{b})}$. For example, Δ could be linear:

$$\tau_{\alpha\beta}(\hat{b})^{s+1} = (1-\mu)\times\overline{\tau_{\alpha\beta}(\hat{b})^s} + \mu\times\tau_{\alpha\beta}(\hat{b})^s$$

where $0<\mu<1$ is the decay rate.

We now consider what happens when valuation observations are made. Suppose that at time s, α evaluates β's enactment b' of commitment b, $\text{val}_{\alpha}^{s}(b') = v_k \in \mathcal{V}$. The update procedure updates the probability distributions for $\tau_{\alpha\beta}(\hat{b})^s$ for each $\hat{b}$ that is "moderately close to" b. Given such a $\hat{b}$, let $\mathbb{P}^s(\tau_{\alpha\beta}(\hat{b}) = v_k)$ denote the prior probability that v_k would be observed. The update procedure is in two steps. First, estimate the posterior probability that v_k would be observed, $\mathbb{P}^{s+1}(\tau_{\alpha\beta}(\hat{b}) = v_k)$ for the particular value v_k. Second, update the entire posterior distribution for $\tau_{\alpha\beta}(\hat{b})$ to accommodate this revised value.

Given a $\hat{b}$, to revise the probability that v_k would be observed three things are used: the observation: $\mathrm{val}^s_\alpha(b')$, the prior: $\mathbb{P}^s(\tau_{\alpha\beta}(\hat{b}) = v_k)$, and the decay limit value: $\overline{\mathbb{P}^s(\tau_{\alpha\beta}(\hat{b}) = v_k)}$. The observation $\mathrm{val}^s_\alpha(b')$ may be represented as a probability distribution with a '1' in the k'th place and zero elsewhere, $\mathbf{u}_k$. To combine it with the prior its significance is discounted for two reasons:

- b may not be semantically close to $\hat{b}$, and
- $\mathrm{val}^s_\alpha(b') = v_k$ is a single observation whereas the prior distribution represents the accumulated history of previous observations.

to discount the significance of the observation $\mathrm{val}^s_\alpha(b') = v_k$ a value is determined in the range between '1' and the zero-data, decay limit value $\overline{\mathbb{P}^s(\tau_{\alpha\beta}(\hat{b}) = v_k)}$ by:

$$\delta = \mathrm{Sim}(b,\hat{b}) \times \kappa + (1 - \mathrm{Sim}(b,\hat{b}) \times \kappa) \times \overline{\mathbb{P}^s(\tau_{\alpha\beta}(\hat{b}) = v_k)}$$

where $0 < \kappa < 1$ is the learning rate, and $\mathrm{Sim}(\cdot,\cdot)$ is a semantic similarity function such as that shown in Eq. 29.3.1. Then the posterior estimate $\mathbb{P}^{s+1}(\tau_{\alpha\beta}(\hat{b}) = v_k)$ is given by:

$$\mathbb{P}^{s+1}(\tau_{\alpha\beta}(\hat{b}) = v_k) = \frac{\rho\delta(1-\omega)}{\rho\delta(1-\omega) + (1-\rho)(1-\delta)\omega} = \nu$$

where $\rho = \mathbb{P}^s(\tau_{\alpha\beta}(\hat{b}) = v_k)$ is the prior value, and $\omega = \overline{\mathbb{P}^s(\tau_{\alpha\beta}(\hat{b}) = v_k)}$ is the decay limit value.

It remains to update the entire posterior distribution for $\tau_{\alpha\beta}(\hat{b})$ to accommodate the constraint $\mathbb{P}^{s+1}(\tau_{\alpha\beta}(\hat{b}) = v_k) = \nu$. Information-based agents (Sierra and Debenham 2007) employ a standard procedure for updating distributions, $\mathbb{P}^t(X = x)$ subject to a set of linear constraints on X, $c(X)$, using:

$$\mathbb{P}^{t+1}(X = x|c(X)) = \mathrm{MRE}(\mathbb{P}^t(X = x), c(X))$$

where the function MRE is defined by: $\mathrm{MRE}(\mathbf{q},\mathbf{g}) = \arg\min_{\mathbf{r}} \sum_j r_j \log \frac{r_j}{q_j}$ such that $\mathbf{r}$ satisfies $\mathbf{g}$, $\mathbf{q}$ is a probability distribution, and $\mathbf{g}$ is a set of n linear constraints $\mathbf{g} = \{g_j(\mathbf{p}) = \mathbf{a_j} \cdot \mathbf{p} - c_j = 0\}, j = 1,\ldots,n$ (including the constraint $\sum_i p_i - 1 = 0$). The resulting $\mathbf{r}$ is the *minimum relative entropy distribution*[10] MacKay (2003). Applying this procedure to $\tau_{\alpha\beta}(\hat{b})$:

---

[10]This may be calculated by introducing Lagrange multipliers λ: $L(\mathbf{p},\lambda) = \sum_j p_j \log \frac{p_j}{q_j} + \lambda \cdot \mathbf{g}$. Minimising L, $\{\frac{\partial L}{\partial \lambda_j} = g_j(\mathbf{p}) = 0\}, j = 1,\ldots,n$ is the set of given constraints $\mathbf{g}$, and a solution to $\frac{\partial L}{\partial p_i} = 0, i = 1,\ldots,I$ leads eventually to $\mathbf{p}$.

$$\mathbb{P}^{s+1}(\tau_{\alpha\beta}(\hat{b}) = v) = \text{MRE}(\mathbb{P}^s(\tau_{\alpha\beta}(\hat{b}) = v), \mathbb{P}^{s+1}(\tau_{\alpha\beta}(\hat{b}) = v_k) = v)$$

where v is the value given by Eq. 29.3.2.

Whenever α evaluates an enactment $\text{val}^s_\alpha(b')$ of some commitment b, the above procedure is applied to update the distributions for $\mathbb{P}(\tau_{\alpha\beta}(\hat{b}) = v)$. It makes sense to limit the use of this procedure to those distributions for which $\text{Sim}(b, \hat{b}) > y$ for some threshold value y.

29.3.3 Prior Knowledge

The decay-limit distribution plays a key role in the estimation of trust. It is not directly based on any observations and in that sense it is a "zero data" trust estimate. It is however not "zero information" as it takes account of opinions and reputations communicated by other agents (Sierra and Debenham 2009). The starting point for constructing the decay-limit distribution is the maximum entropy (zero-data, zero-information) distribution. This gives a two layer structure to the estimation of trust: opinions and reputations shape the decay-limit distribution that in turn plays a role in forming the trust estimate that takes account of observed data. Communications from other agents may not be reliable. α needs a means of estimating the reliability of other agents before they can be incorporated into the decay-limit distribution—reliability is discussed at the end of this section.

Reputation is the opinion (more technically, a social evaluation) of a group about something. So a group's reputation about a thing will be related in some way to the opinions that the individual group members hold towards that thing. An *opinion* is an assessment, judgement or evaluation of something. Opinions are represented in this section as probability distributions on a suitable ontology that for convenience is identified with the *evaluation space* $\mathcal{V}$. That is, opinions communicated by β concerning another agent's trustworthiness are assumed to be expressed as predicates using the same valuation space as $\mathcal{V}$ over which α represents its trust estimates.

An opinion is an evaluation of an *aspect* of a thing. A rainy day may be evaluated as being "bad" from the aspect of being suitable for a picnic, and "good" from the aspect of watering the plants in the garden. An aspect is the "point of view" that an agent has when forming his opinion. An opinion is evaluated in context. The *context* is everything that the thing is being, explicitly or implicitly, evaluated with or against. The set of valuations of all things in the context calibrates the valuation space; for example, "this is the best paper in the conference". The context can be vague: "of all the presents you could have given me, this is the best". If agents are to discuss opinions then they must have some understanding of each other's context.

Summarising the above, an *opinion* is an agent's evaluation of a particular aspect of a thing in context. A representation of an opinion will contain: the thing, its aspect, its context, and a distribution on $\mathcal{V}$ representing the evaluation of the thing.

α acquires opinions and reputations through communication with other agents. α estimates the reliability of those communicating agents before incorporating that information into the decay-limit distributions. The basic process is the same for opinions and reputations; the following describes the incorporation of opinions only.

Suppose agent β' informs agent α of his opinion of the trustworthiness of another agent β using an utterance of the form: $u = \texttt{inform}(\beta', \alpha, \tau_{\beta'\beta}(b))$, where conveniently b is in α's ontology. This information may not be useful to α for at least two reasons: β' may not be telling the truth, or β' may have a utility function that differs from α's. We will shortly estimate β''s "reliability", $R^t_\alpha(\beta')$ that measures the extent to which β' is telling the truth and that α and β' "are on the same page" or "think alike".[11] Precisely, $0 < R^t_\alpha(\beta') < 1$; its value is used to moderate the effect of the utterance on α's decay-limit distributions. The estimation of $R^t_\alpha(\beta')$ is described below.

Suppose that α maintains the decay limit distribution $\overline{\tau_{\alpha\beta}(\hat{b})^s}$ for a chosen $\hat{b}$. In the absence of utterances informing opinions of trustworthiness, $\overline{\tau_{\alpha\beta}(\hat{b})^s}$ decays to the distribution with maximum entropy. As previously this decay could be linear:

$$\overline{\tau_{\alpha\beta}(\hat{b})^{s+1}} = (1-\mu) \times \text{MAX} + \mu \times \overline{\tau_{\alpha\beta}(\hat{b})^s}$$

where $\mu < 1$ is the decay rate, and MAX is the maximum entropy, uniform distribution.

When α receives an utterance of the form u above, the decay limit distribution is updated by:

$$\begin{aligned}\overline{\tau_{\alpha\beta}(\hat{b})^{s+1}} \mid \texttt{inform}(\beta', \alpha, \tau_{\beta'\beta}(b)) = \\ \left(1 - \kappa \times \text{Sim}(\hat{b}, b) \times R^s_\alpha(\beta')\right) \times \overline{\tau_{\alpha\beta}(\hat{b})^s} \\ + \kappa \times \text{Sim}(\hat{b}, b) \times R^s_\alpha(\beta') \times \tau_{\beta'\beta}(b)\end{aligned}$$

where $0 < \kappa < 1$ is the learning rate and $R^s_\alpha(\beta')$ is α estimate of β''s reliability. It remains to estimate $R^s_\alpha(\beta')$.

Estimating $R^s_\alpha(\beta')$ is complicated by its time dependency. First, in the absence of input of the form described following, $R^s_\alpha(\beta')$ decays to zero by: $R^{s+1}_\alpha(\beta') = \mu \times R^s_\alpha(\beta')$. Second, describe how $R^s_\alpha(\beta')$ is increased by comparing the efficacy of $\overline{\tau_{\alpha\beta}(\hat{b})^s}$ and $\tau_{\beta'\beta}(b)^s$ in the following interaction scenario. Suppose at a time s, α is considering signing the contract (a, b) with β. α requests β''s opinion of β with respect to b, to which β may respond $\texttt{inform}(\beta', \alpha, \tau_{\beta'\beta}(b))$. α now has two estimates of β's trustworthiness: $\overline{\tau_{\alpha\beta}(\hat{b})^s}$ and $\tau_{\beta'\beta}(b)^s$; $\overline{\tau_{\alpha\beta}(\hat{b})^s}$ and $\tau_{\beta'\beta}(b)^s$ are both probability distributions that each provide an estimate of $\mathbb{P}^s(\text{Value}_\beta(b) = v_i)$

[11] The reliability estimate should perhaps also be a function of the commitment, $R^t_\alpha(\beta', b)$, but that complication is ignored.

for each valuation v_i. α increases its reliability estimate of β if the trust estimate in β's `inform` is 'better' than α's current decay limit value. Suppose that α signs the contract (a,b) at time t, and at some later time t'' evaluates β's enactment $\text{val}_{\alpha}^{t''}(b') = v_k$, say. Then:

$$\mathbb{P}(\tau_{\beta'\beta}(b)^s = v_k) > \mathbb{P}(\overline{\tau_{\alpha\beta}(\hat{b})^s = v_k})$$

and β''s trust estimate is better than α's; α increases $R^s_{\alpha}(\beta')$ using:

$$R^{s+1}_{\alpha}(\beta') = \kappa + (1-\kappa) \times R^s_{\alpha}(\beta')$$

where $0 < \kappa < 1$ is the learning rate.

29.3.4 Time

The core trust mechanism and the prior knowledge both give greater weight to recent observations than to historic data. This may be a reasonable default assumption but has no general validity. Trust, $\tau_{\alpha\beta}(\hat{b})^s$, estimates *how* β is expected to act. If an agent is considering repeated interaction with β then he may also be interested in how β's actions are expected to *change* in time.

The way in which the trust estimate is evolving is significant in understanding which agents to interact with. For example, an agent for whom $\tau^s_{\alpha\beta}(\hat{b})$ is fairly constant in time may be of less interest than an agent who is slightly less trustworthy but whose trust is consistently improving. To capture this information something like the finite derivative is required: $\frac{\delta}{\delta s}\tau^s_{\alpha\beta}(\hat{b})$. The sum of the elements in such a vector will be zero, and in the absence of any data it will decay to the zero vector.

Estimating the rate of change of $\tau^s_{\alpha\beta}(\hat{b})$ is complicated by the way it evolves that combines continual integrity decay with periodic updates. Evolution due to decay tells us nothing about the rate of change of an agent's behaviour. Evolution caused by an update is performed following a period of prior decay, and may result in compensating for it. Further, update effects will be very slight in the case that the commitment b is semantically distant from $\hat{b}$. In other words, the evolution of $\tau^s_{\alpha\beta}(\hat{b})$ itself is not directly suited to capturing the rate of change of agent behaviour.

The idea for an indirect way to estimate how β's actions are evolving comes from the observation that $\tau_{\alpha\beta}(\hat{b})^s$ is influenced more strongly by more recent observations, and the extent to which this is so depends on the decay rate. For example. if the decay rate is zero then $\tau_{\alpha\beta}(\hat{b})^s$ is a time-weighted "average" of prior observations. Suppose that $\tau_{\alpha\beta}(\hat{b})^s$ has been evaluated. We perform a parallel evaluation using a lower decay rate to obtain $\tau^-_{\alpha\beta}(\hat{b})^s$, then $\tau_{\alpha\beta}(\hat{b})^s - \tau^-_{\alpha\beta}(\hat{b})^s$ is a vector the sum of whose elements is zero, and in which a positive element indicates a value that is presently "on the increase" compared to the historic average.

The preceding method for estimating change effectively does so by calculating a first difference. If another first difference is calculated using an even lower decay rate then calculate a second difference to estimate the *rate of* change. This may be stretching the idea too far!

29.3.5 Trust in Context

The informal meaning of context is information concerning everything in the environment that could affect decision making *together with* rules that link that information to the deliberative process. That is, *context* consists of facts about the environment, including rare but significant events, *and* rules that link those facts to the agent's reasoning. Those rules typically rely on common sense reasoning. Dealing with context is a hard problem for intelligent agents generally and for their management of trust estimates in particular.

From an artificial intelligence point of view, artificial agents lack the skills of their human counterparts for dealing with context. Humans then rely on common sense and experience to learn how to key contextual information to their deliberation, and to identify incompleteness in their knowledge. For artificial agents; identifying and dealing with inconsistency and incompleteness is a hard problem, and so is keying general information to their own deliberative apparatus.

Even if 'trust in context' is narrowed to just one issue "is there any reason to distrust our trust estimate due to a *change* in context?" the problems remain hard. Supposing that α is considering signing a contract (a,b) at time t, to address this issue the following are required:

1. Knowledge of the context of previous observations of behaviour. Their *context* is the state of each of the observables in the environment and of the states of the other agents when those previous observations of behaviour were made.
2. Founded beliefs concerning the context that will pertain at the future time of the evaluation of the presumed future behaviour—i.e. at time t'' in Fig. 29.1.
3. Some reasoning apparatus that enables us to decide whether *differences* between the believed future context and the observed previous contexts cause us to modify our experience-based trust estimate.

The information-based architecture makes a modest contribution to trust in context in the following sense. An agent builds up a sense of trust on the basis of its own past experience and statements of opinion and reputation from other agents. In a sense those statements of opinions and reputation are contextual information for the business of estimating trust. It also moderates its trust estimates through the persistent decay of contextual information integrity by Eq. 29.3.2. Beyond that no 'magic bullet' solutions are given to the contextual problems described above and the discussion is left as a pointer to the work that is required to increase the reliability of trust estimation in dynamic environments.

29.4 Relationship Model

The trust model described in Sect. 29.3 is a summary of the history of interaction between α and β, $H_{\alpha\beta}$, augmented by reputation estimates. Reputation estimates *per se* are outside the α's direct experience and are therefore part of the *context* of α's trust. Trust is not the only way in which the interaction history may be usefully summarised. The *relationship model* contains summary estimates that include trust. Before describing these measures human relationships are examined particularly ways in which they are summarised. This leads to a discussion of the formal representation of relationships using the LOGIC framework.

29.4.1 Relationships

A *relationship* between two human or artificial agents is their *interaction history* that is a complete record of their interactions evaluated *in context*. There is evidence from psychological studies that humans seek a *balance* in their negotiation relationships. The classical view (Adams 1965) is that people perceive resource allocations as being distributively fair (i.e. well balanced) if they are proportional to inputs or contributions (i.e. equitable). However, more recent studies (Sondak et al. 1995; Valley et al. 1995) show that humans follow a richer set of norms of distributive justice depending on their *intimacy* level: equity, equality, and need. Here *equity* is allocation proportionally to the effort (e.g. the profit of a company goes to the stock holders proportional to their investment), *equality* being the allocation in equal amounts (e.g. two friends eat the same amount of a cake cooked by one of them), and *need* being the allocation proportional to the need for the resource (e.g. in case of food scarcity, a mother gives all food to her baby).

We believe that the perception of balance in dialogues, especially in negotiation, is grounded on social relationships, and that every dimension of an interaction between humans can be correlated to the social closeness, or *intimacy*, between the parties involved. The more intimacy the more the *need* norm is used, and the less intimacy the more the *equity* norm is used. This might be part of our social evolution. There is ample evidence that when human societies evolved from a hunter-gatherer structure[12] to a shelter-based one[13] the probability of survival increased (Sondak et al. 1995).

---

[12]In its purest form, individuals in these societies collect food and consume it when and where it is found. This is a pure equity sharing of the resources, the gain is proportional to the effort.

[13]In these societies there are family units, around a shelter, that represent the basic food sharing structure. Usually, food is accumulated at the shelter for future use. Then the food intake depends more on the need of the members.

In this context, for example, families exchange not only goods but also information and knowledge based on need, and that few families would consider their relationships as being unbalanced, and thus unfair, when there is a strong asymmetry in the exchanges. For example, a mother does not expect reciprocity when explaining everything to her children, or buying toys for them. In the case of partners there is some evidence (Bazerman et al. 1992) that the allocations of goods and burdens (i.e. positive and negative utilities) are perceived as fair, or in balance, based on equity for burdens and equality for goods.

The perceived balance in a negotiation dialogue allows negotiators to infer information about their opponent, about its stance, and to compare their relationships with all negotiators. For instance, if every time requested information is provided, and that no significant questions are returned, or no complaints about not receiving information are given, then that probably means that our opponent perceives our social relationship to be very close. Alternatively, issues that are causing a burden to our opponent can be identified by observing an imbalance in their information or utilitarian utterances on that issue.

We assume that the interactions between agents can be organised into dialogues, where a *dialogue* is a set of related utterances. This section is concerned with *commitment dialogues* that contain at least one commitment, where a commitment may simply be the truth of a statement or may be a contractual commitment. We assume that all commitment dialogues take place in some or all of the following five stages:

1. The *prelude* during which agents prepare for the interaction
2. The *negotiation* that may lead to
3. *Signing* a contract at time t
4. The *enactment* of the commitments in the contract at time t'
5. The *evaluation* at time t'' of the complete interaction process that is made when the goods or services acquired by enactment of the contract have been consumed

The notation of a commitment dialogue is broad in that a dialogue that does not contain any sort of commitment is arguably of little interest.

A major issue in building models of dialogues and relationships is dealing with the reliability of the utterances made. For an information-based agent the *reliability* of an utterance is an epistemic probability estimate of the utterance's veracity. For example, if the utterance is an `inform` containing a proposition then its reliability is an estimate of the probability that the proposition is correct. If the utterance is an `opinion` then its reliability is an estimate of the probability that the `opinion` will in time be judged to be sound. The difficulty with estimating reliability is that it may take months or years for an agent to be able to say: "Ah, that was good advice". Reliability is a measure attached to an utterance, and integrity is a measure attached to a complete dialogue. A blanket estimation of the reliability of an agent was described in Sect. 29.3.3.

29.4.2 The LOGIC Framework

The LOGIC illocutionary framework for classifying argumentative interactions was first described in Sierra and Debenham (2007) where it was used to help agents to prepare for a negotiation in the *prelude stage* of an interaction as described above. This section generalises that framework and uses it to define one of the two dimensions of the relationship model described below, the second dimension is provided by the structure of the ontology as specified by a partial order $\leq$ defined by the is-a hierarchy, and a distance measure between concepts such as Eq. 29.3.1. The five LOGIC categories for information are quite general:

- *Legitimacy* contains *information* that may be part of, relevant to or in justification of contracts that have been, or may be, signed.
- *Options* contains information about *contracts* that an agent may be prepared to sign.
- *Goals* contains information about the *objectives* of the agents.
- *Independence* contains information about the agent's *outside options*—i.e. the set of agents that are capable of satisfying each of the agent's needs.
- *Commitments* contains information about the *commitments* that an agent has.

and are used here to categorise all incoming communication that feeds into the agent's relationship model. This categorisation is not a one-to-one mapping and some illocutions fall into multiple categories. These categories are designed to provide a model of the agents' information as it is relevant to their relationships. They are *not* intended to be a universal categorising framework for all utterances.

Taking a more formal view, the LOGIC framework categorises information in an utterance by its relationship to:

L $= \{B(\alpha, \varphi)\}$, that is a set of *beliefs*, communicated by: `inform`.
O $= \{\text{Accept}(\beta, \alpha, c)\}$, that is a set of *acceptable contracts*, communicated by: `offer`, `reject` and `accept`.
G $= \{D(\alpha, \varphi)\}$, that is a set of *needs* or *desires*, communicated by: `Ineed`.
I $= \{\text{Can}(\alpha, \text{Do}(p))\}$, that is a set of *capabilities*, communicated by: `canDo`.
C $= \{I(\alpha, \text{Do}(p))\} \cup \{\text{Commit}(\alpha, \text{Do}(p))\}$, that is a set of *commitments* and *intentions*, communicated by: `commit` (for future commitments), and `intend` (commitments being enacted).

Four predicates L, O, G, I and C recognise the category of an utterance. Information in an `inform` utterance is categorised as Goals, Independence and Commitments if the `inform` contains the illocutions listed above: `Ineed`, `canDo`, `commit` and `intend`. Otherwise it is categorised as Legitimacy.

Given a need ν and an agent β the variables $L^t_{\nu\beta}$, $O^t_{\nu\beta}$, $G^t_{\nu\beta}$, $I^t_{\nu\beta}$ and $C^t_{\nu\beta}$ are aggregated from observations of how forthcoming β was during prior dialogues. They are then used to form α's expectation of β's future readiness to reveal private information across the five LOGIC categories. They are updated at the end of each dialogue[14] using a linear form that is consistent with (Behrens et al. 2007) for the human brain in a volatile environment.

In the following a dialogue Γ commences at time $t-s$ and terminates at time t when the five variables are updated. $t-d$ denotes the time at which these variables were previously updated. For convenience assume that $d \geq s$. Γ aims to satisfy need ν. All the estimates given below are for the effect of Γ on variables for a nearby need ν' for which $\eta' = \eta \times \text{Sim}(\nu, \nu')$, η is the learning rate, and μ the decay rate.

$L^t_{\nu\beta}$ measures the amount of information in β's Legitimacy `inform` utterances. The procedure by which `inform` utterances update $\mathcal{M}^t$ is described in Sierra and Debenham (2007). The Shannon information in a single `inform` statement, u, is: $\mathbb{I}(u) = \mathbb{H}(\mathcal{M}^{t-1}) - \mathbb{H}(\mathcal{M}^t|u)$. It is defined in terms of the contents of $\mathcal{M}^t$, and so the valuation is restricted to 'just those things of interest' to α. During Γ observe: $l = \sum_{u \in \Gamma, \mathsf{L}(u)} \mathbb{I}(u)$. Then update $L^t_{\nu'\beta}$ with:

$$L^t_{\nu'\beta} = \eta' \sum_{u \in \Gamma, \mathsf{L}(u)} \mathbb{I}(u) + (1-\eta')\mu^d L^{t-d}_{\nu'\beta}$$

$O^t_{\nu\beta}$ measures the amount of information β reveals about the deals he will accept. β's limit contracts were modelled on the basis of observed behaviour in Sierra and Debenham (2007). Let random variable Y over contract space $\mathscr{C}$ denote α's beliefs that a contract is a limit contract for β. The information gain in Y during Γ is: $\mathbb{H}^{t-s}(Y) - \mathbb{H}^t(Y)$, and $O^t_{\nu'\beta}$ is updated by:

$$O^t_{\nu'\beta} = \eta' \left(\mathbb{H}^{t-s}(Y) - \mathbb{H}^t(Y)\right) + (1-\eta')\mu^d O^{t-d}_{\nu\beta}$$

$G^t_{\nu\beta}$ measures the information β reveals about his goals, and $I^t_{\nu\beta}$ about his suggested capabilities. $G^t_{\nu\beta}$ and $I^t_{\nu\beta}$ are similar in that both `Ineed` and `canDo` preempt the terms of a contract. Suppose β informs α that: `Ineed`(ν) and `canDo`(δ). If β is being forthcoming then this suggests that he has in mind an eventual contract (a,b) in which $a \leq \nu$ and $b \leq \delta$ (using $\leq$ from the ontology). Suppose that Γ leads to the signing of the contract (a,b) then observe: $g = \text{Sim}(a, \nu)$ and $i = \max_\delta \text{Sim}(b, \delta)$; $\max_\delta$ is in case β utters more than one `canDo`. $G^t_{\nu'\beta}$ is aggregated by:

$$G^t_{\nu'\beta} = \eta' \text{Sim}(a, \nu) + (1-\eta')\mu^d G^{t-d}_{\nu'\beta}$$

Similarly: $I^t_{\nu'\beta} = \eta' \max_\delta \text{Sim}(b, \delta) + (1-\eta')\mu^d I^{t-d}_{\nu'\beta}$.

$C^t_{\nu\beta}$ measures the amount of information β reveals about his commitments and intentions. These are measured just as for $L^t_{\nu\beta}$ by aggregating the observation: $c = \sum_{u \in \Gamma, \mathsf{C}(u)} \mathbb{I}(u)$, and $C^t_{\nu'\beta}$ is updated by:

[14] This is for efficiency. Updating the model following each utterance could expend resources to little effect.

$$C^t_{\nu'\beta} = \eta' \sum_{u \in \Gamma, \mathsf{C}(u)} \mathbb{I}(u) + (1-\eta')\mu^d C^{t-d}_{\nu'\beta}$$

The measures described above are based on what β says. In negotiation what was *not* said but *could have* been said may be equally significant. A *confidentiality* measure described in Sierra and Debenham (2008) addresses this issue.

In addition, if $\text{val}_\alpha(\cdot)$ is α's utilitarian evaluation function that is used to evaluate both the contract and the enactment *in context* then the observations

$$\nu^t(\Gamma) = \text{val}_\alpha((a',b')|H^t) - \text{val}_\alpha((a,b)|H^{t-s})$$

update the variable $U^t_{\nu\beta}$ that estimates *utility gain* during Γ:

$$U^t_{\nu'\beta} = \eta' \left(\text{val}_\alpha((a',b')|H^t) - \text{val}_\alpha((a,b)|H^{t-s})\right) + (1-\eta')\mu^d U^{t-d}_{\nu'\beta}$$

Finally the LOGIC evaluation of a complete dialogue is assembled. Putting the six measures together define α's evaluation function, $\text{logic}^t(\Gamma)$, for a complete dialogue Γ in which the contract (a,b) is signed. With notation as above:

$$\text{logic}^t(\Gamma) = \Big(\sum_{u \in \Gamma, \mathsf{L}(u)} \mathbb{I}(u), \mathbb{H}^{t-s}(Y) - \mathbb{H}^t(Y), \text{Sim}(a,\nu), \max_\delta \text{Sim}(b,\delta),$$
$$\sum_{u \in \Gamma, \mathsf{C}(u)} \mathbb{I}(u), \text{val}_\alpha((a',b')|H^t) - \text{val}_\alpha((a,b)|H^{t-s}) \Big)$$

We model our expectation of observing any particular value $\text{logic}^t(\Gamma)$ with the six-dimensional random variable $\mathbf{E}^t_{\nu\beta}$ where $(E^t_{\nu\beta})_k$ is the expectation for $L^t_{\nu'\beta}$, $O^t_{\nu'\beta}$, $G^t_{\nu'\beta}$, $I^t_{\nu'\beta}$, $C^t_{\nu'\beta}$, $U^t_{\nu'\beta}$ respectively, $k = 1,\ldots,6$.

29.5 Negotiation

If α prefers to deal with trusted partners then because trust is established by interaction α needs to determine the pool of agents to interact with who are then potential negotiation partners for each generic need. If the pool is large then the integrity of the trust estimates will be low, and if the pool is small then α may deny itself access to new partners. The *pool selection* problem is to manage the size and composition of the pool of partners for each generic need so as to balance these conflicting values. Pool selection is addressed followed by the offer strategy, and finally the strategic use of argumentation to build strong and trusted relationships.

29.5.1 Pool Selection

The aim of the pool *selection* phase is to select a strategically *diverse* pool of agents, $\mathscr{P}_\nu$, for each of α's needs ν. Let $\mathscr{B}_n$ be the set of n-element subsets of $\{\beta_1, \dots, \beta_o\}$, then

$$\mathscr{P}_\nu = \arg\max_n \{B \in \mathscr{B}_m \mid \\ \forall bb' \in B : \mathbb{P}((\mathbf{E}^t_{\nu b})_k > e_k) > c_k, \mathbb{H}((\mathbf{E}^t_{\nu b})_k) < h_k, \text{div}(b, b') > d\}$$

where: **e**, **h**, **c** and d are selected constants, $k = 1, \dots, 6$, and $\text{div}(\beta_i, \beta_j)$ is a measure of: geographic, political, economic and/or functional *agent diversity*. Suppose that α's *needs model* is such that the probability that need ν is triggered at any time is ε_ν.

The *uniform selection strategy* selects an agent from $\mathscr{P}_\nu$ when ν is triggered by: $\mathbb{P}^t(\text{Select } \beta | \nu) = \frac{1}{n}$, and each $\beta \in \mathscr{P}_\nu$ expects to be selected each $m = \frac{1}{n\varepsilon_\nu}$ time steps. If β is selected at time $t - s$ and if the value $\text{logic}^t(\Gamma)$ is observed for the resulting negotiation dialogue then:

$$\mathbb{P}(\mathbf{E}^t_{\nu\beta} = \text{logic}^t(\Gamma)) = \eta + (1 - \eta) \times \mathbb{P}(\mathbf{E}^{t-1}_{\nu\beta} = \text{logic}^t(\Gamma))$$

The full distribution for $\mathbf{E}^t_{\nu\beta}$ is then calculated using the MRE (minimum relative entropy) process described in Sect. 29.3.2 using Eq. 29.5.1 as the constraint. By time $t + m$ full distribution for $\mathbf{E}^t_{\nu\beta}$ will have decayed in line with Eq. 29.3.2 and:

$$\mathbb{P}(\mathbf{E}^{t+m}_{\nu\beta} = \text{logic}^t(\Gamma)) = \\ (1 - \mu^m)\mathbb{P}(\overline{\mathbf{E}^t_{\nu\beta}} = \text{logic}^t(\Gamma)) + \mu^m(\eta + (1 - \eta)\mathbb{P}(\mathbf{E}^{t-1}_{\nu\beta} = \text{logic}^t(\Gamma)))$$

To ensure decreasing entropy: $\mathbb{P}(\mathbf{E}^{t+m}_{\nu\beta} = \text{logic}^t(\Gamma)) > \mathbb{P}(\mathbf{E}^{t-1}_{\nu\beta} = \text{logic}^t(\Gamma))$. Suppose $\mathbf{p} = \mathbb{P}(\overline{\mathbf{E}^t_{\nu\beta}} = \text{logic}^t(\Gamma))$ and $\mathbb{P}(\mathbf{E}^{t-1}_{\nu\beta} = \text{logic}^t(\Gamma)) = \kappa \cdot \mathbf{p}$; i.e. expect $\kappa_k > 1$ and $\kappa_k \mathbf{p}_k < 1$ for $k = 1, \dots, 6$. Let $\kappa = \kappa_k$ and $p = \mathbf{p}_k$ for some value of k. Then the expected least value of m to prevent integrity decay is such that: $\kappa p = (1 - \mu^m)p + \mu^m(\eta + (1 - \eta)\kappa p)$, and so:

$$m = \frac{\log(p(\kappa - 1)) - \log(\eta - p + (1 - \eta)\kappa p)}{\log \mu}$$

e.g. suppose $p = 0.2$, $\kappa = 3$, $\eta = 0.7$, $\mu = 0.98$ then $m = 26$. Alternatively, solving for η: $\eta = \frac{(\kappa-1)(1-\mu^{-m})p}{\kappa p - 1}$. The lower limit for m in Eq. 29.5.1 and a value for ε_ν gives an upper limit for n the size of the pool $\mathscr{P}_\nu$.

A *stochastic selection strategy* selects an agent from $\mathscr{P}_\nu$ when ν triggers by:

$$\mathbb{P}^t(\text{Select } \beta | \nu) = \mathbb{P}(\mathbf{E}^t_{\nu\beta} \gg)$$

where $\mathbb{P}^t(\mathbf{E}^t_{\nu\beta} \gg)$ denotes the probability that β is better than for all the others in the following sense. If the six-dimensional sample space for $E^t_{\nu\beta}$ is linearly ordered in increasing degree of satisfaction, then the probability that the evaluation of a dialogue for ν with β will be more satisfactory that, β' $\mathbb{P}^t(\mathbf{E}^t_{\nu\beta} > \mathbf{E}^t_{\nu\beta'})$, may be estimated. To prevent integrity decay of $\mathscr{P}_\nu$ for this strategy repeat the calculation above for the worst choice for ν that will expect to be selected every: $m' = \frac{1}{\varepsilon_\nu}\mathbb{P}(\mathbf{E}^t_{\nu\beta} \ll)$ time steps. For any stochastic strategy denote $\mathbb{P}^t(\text{Select } \beta \,|\, \nu)$ by $\mathbb{P}^t(S_\nu = s_{\nu,i})$ for random variable S_ν then $\mathbb{H}(S_\nu)$, $i = 1,\ldots,n$, measures *selection strategy diversity*, or normalised as: $\frac{1}{\log n}\mathbb{H}(S_\nu)$ (Acar and Troutt 2008).

29.5.2 *Offer Strategy*

The previous section analysed the intuition if an agent maintains too great a choice of trading partners then its certainty in their behaviour will decay—no matter whether their behaviour is good or bad. Having determined which negotiation partners to interact with the *offer strategy* that determines what offers to make is considered, and so this section is concerned with the options component of the LOGIC model, $O^t_{\nu\beta}$. In the following Sect. 29.5.3 considers *argumentation*, that 'wraps' utterances with rhetorical argumentation, and will address the remaining LOGIC components.

α is assumed to have a utilitarian negotiation strategy (Osborne and Rubinstein 1994) that the following ideas are intended to embellish. That strategy may reference the estimate that β will accept the contract (a,b): $\mathbb{P}^t(\text{Accept}(\beta,\alpha,(a,b)))$—an estimate[15] is derived in Sierra and Debenham (2007). This leads to a variation of the issue-tradeoff strategy where α makes the offer that is acceptable to her that β is most likely to accept. If $\text{Accept}^t(\alpha,\beta,c)$ denotes that c is acceptable to α then offer c^* where:

$$c^* = \arg\max_c \{\mathbb{P}^t(\text{Accept}(\beta,\alpha,c)) \mid \text{Accept}^t(\alpha,\beta,c)\}$$

Setting utilitarian considerations aside for a moment estimate which offer to make for which β's response, accept or reject, gives α greatest information gain. If β was prepared to answer repeated questions of the form then "Is contract y acceptable to you?" then the expected shortest question sequence has a Shannon encoding that is optimum with respect to the prior expectation of offer acceptance.

We show that if there is one issue and if the prior is the maximum entropy distribution then the sequence with greatest information gain will select the 'mid-

[15] If α assumes the each dimension of the contract space may be ordered to reflect β's preferences and interprets β's illocutionary actions of `offer` as willingness to *accept* whilst *rejecting* α's previous offers then a probabilistic model of β's limit contracts is derived using maximum entropy inference.

value' at each stage. Denote β's expected limit contract by random variable Y. Suppose Y's sample space is $(0,\ldots,n)$ and β's preferences are known to be monotonic increasing over this space with n known to be acceptable and 0 known to be unacceptable. The prior for Y is the maximum entropy distribution over $(1,\ldots,n)$ with $\mathbb{H}(Y) = \log_2 n$, and $\mathbb{P}(\text{Accept}(\beta,\alpha,y) = \frac{y}{n}$. If β reports that y is acceptable then $\mathbb{H}(Y|y \text{ acceptable}) = \log_2 y$, and the information gain is $\log_2[\frac{n}{y}]$. Likewise $\mathbb{H}(Y|y \text{ unacceptable}) = \log_2(n-y)$. Solving the continuous model for maximal expected information gain:

$$\frac{d}{dy}\left(y\log_2\frac{n}{y} + (n-y)\log_2\frac{n}{n-y}\right) = 1 - \log_2\frac{n}{n-y} = 0, \text{ and } y = \frac{n}{2}$$

Consideration of the offer with maximal expected information gain is more interesting in multi-issue negotiation where α may have a set of potential offers D_v all with similar material value v, and may then wish to priorities them on the basis of expected information gain. Given an estimate for $\mathbb{P}(\text{Accept}(\beta,\alpha,y)), y \in D_v$ (see Sierra and Debenham 2007) the preceding ideas may be used to enumerate the expected information gain for each $y \in D_v$ and so to make the maximal offer.

This section takes both utilitarian gain and information gain into account in managing the offer sequence. Within a single negotiation dialogue utilitarian gain is what matters most. Information gain on the other hand is concerned with strengthening the relationship and trust models and so underpins the agent's long-term strategies to build secure trading relationships for the future. Information-based agents aim to strike a balance between short term gains and long term security.

29.5.3 Argumentation and Relationship Building

This section is concerned with trust and relationships between agents. Relationships are built through dialogical interaction that is modelled using the LOGIC framework. Argumentation strategies take account of bluff and counter-bluff in the cut and thrust of competitive interaction, and contribute to relationships in each of the five LOGIC categories. We discuss what an argumentation strategy should aim to achieve from the LOGIC model point of view—the construction of the illocutionary sequences to achieve this aim is beyond the scope of this discussion.

Rhetoric argumentation aims to alter the beliefs of the recipient; it is also an information acquisition and revelation process as measured using the LOGIC framework. Equation 29.4.2 is α's evaluation function that applies to both contract enactment and argumentation, it is *also* the basis for α's *relationship-building strategies* that aim to influence the strength of β's relationship through argumentation and offer acceptance.

For each generic need v α maintains a pool of potential partners (Sect. 29.5), and for each negotiation partner β, α has a model of their relationship summarised as: $L^t_{\nu\beta}$, $O^t_{\nu\beta}$, $G^t_{\nu\beta}$, $I^t_{\nu\beta}$, $C^t_{\nu\beta}$ and $U^t_{\nu\beta}$. The idea is that for each agent in a pool α has a *target intimacy* that is its desired LOGIC model for that agent: $TL^t_{\nu\beta}$, $TO^t_{\nu\beta}$, $TG^t_{\nu\beta}$, $TI^t_{\nu\beta}$, $TC^t_{\nu\beta}$ and $TU^t_{\nu\beta}$. The prior to commencing an interaction dialogue Γ, α constructs a target LOGIC model for that dialogue: $DL^t_{\nu\beta}$, $DO^t_{\nu\beta}$, $DG^t_{\nu\beta}$, $DI^t_{\nu\beta}$, $DC^t_{\nu\beta}$ and $DU^t_{\nu\beta}$. The dialogue target then becomes a constraint on the argumentation strategy.

α does not give private information away freely, and seeks a level of *balance* in information revelation. This is achieved by building a speculative model of β's model of α—after all, α should have a fairly good idea of what β knows about α—this is the *reflection model*. As the dialogue proceeds information in the five logic categories is exchanged (or, 'traded') and whilst attempting to maintain a reasonable level of balance α aims to achieve its dialogue target. Conversely, α may deliberatively diverge from a balanced information exchange to send a (positive or negative) signal to β.

Contract enactment is α's final opportunity to adjust the balance of an interaction dialogue by enacting minor variations of the signed commitment or by further information revelation. This mechanism is used widely by human agents who may "add a little extra" to impress their partner, or may otherwise diverge from their commitment to signal their intent.

The preceding discussion is at a high level but given the detailed measurement of information exchange in the LOGIC framework it tightly constrains α's utterances possibly to the extent of making α's behaviour appear to be predictable. *Stance* is common device used by human agents to conceal their interaction strategies. Stance randomly varies along the axis 'tough guy'/'nice guy'[16] and is applied as a filter on outgoing utterances to add strategic noise that aims to prevent its underlying interaction strategies from being decrypted by β.

29.6 Conclusions

This chapter has drawn together two major threads: trust in the enactment of contracts and the relationships between agents. Trust has been defined in terms of the expected *value* derived from signing a contract—this is in contrast to defining trust as the expected variation between commitment and enactment. The definition chosen is more general in that it assumes some time delay between the enactment and the valuation, and that the valuation reflects the personal preferences of the agent. For example, if a car is purchased it may be delivered exactly as specified but after driving the car for some time the agent may come to value the purchase as being imperfect in some way. This notion of trust treats commitment as not simply "acting

[16]When questioning suspects the police may have two officers present each with a deliberately different stance.

as specified" but as attempting to act in the interests of the contractual partner. This is achieved with a model of the relationships between agents that enables agents to build relationships with trust.

References

Acar, W., and M. D. Troutt. 2008. A methodological analysis of the normalisation, calibration and linearity of continuous diversity measures. *International Journal of Operational Research* 3(1–2): 52–76.

Adams, J. S. 1965. Inequity in social exchange. In *Advances in experimental social psychology*, vol. 2, ed. L. Berkowitz. New York: Academic.

Arcos, J. L., M. Esteva, P. Noriega, J. A. Rodríguez, and C. Sierra. 2005. Environment engineering for multiagent systems. *Journal on Engineering Applications of Artificial Intelligence* 18(2): 191–204.

Bazerman, M. H., G. F. Loewenstein, and S. B. White. 1992. Reversal of preference in allocation decisions: Judging an alternative versus choosing among alternatives. *Administration Science Quarterly* 37: 220–240.

Behrens, T. E. J., M. W. Woolrich, M. E. Walton, and M. F. S. Rushworth. 2007. Learning the value of information in an uncertain world. *Nature Neuroscience* 10: 1214–1221.

Kalfoglou, Y., and M. Schorlemmer. 2003. IF-Map: An ontology-mapping method based on information-flow theory. In *Journal on Data Semantics I*. Lecture Notes in Computer Science, vol. 2800, ed. S. Spaccapietra, S. March, and K. Aberer, 98–127. Heidelberg: Springer.

Li, Y., Z. A. Bandar, and D. McLean. 2003. An approach for measuring semantic similarity between words using multiple information sources. *IEEE Transactions on Knowledge and Data Engineering* 15(4): 871–882.

MacKay, D. 2003. *Information theory, inference and learning algorithms*. Cambridge: UK.

Osborne, M., and A. Rubinstein. 1994. *A course in game theory*. Cambridge, MA: MIT.

Sierra, C., and J. Debenham. 2007. Information-based agency. In *Twentieth international joint conference on AI, IJCAI-07*, ed. M. Veloso, 1513–1518. AAAI Press.

Sierra, C., and J. Debenham. 2007. The LOGIC negotiation model. In *Proceedings sixth international conference on autonomous agents and multi agent systems AAMAS-2007*, 1026–1033. Honolulu, Hawai'i.

Sierra, C., and J. Debenham. 2008. Information-based deliberation. In *Proceedings seventh international conference on autonomous agents and multi agent systems AAMAS-2008*, ed. L. Padgham, D. Parkes, J. Müller, and S. Parsons. New York/Estoril: ACM.

Sierra, C., and J. Debenham. 2009. Information-based reputation. In *First international conference on reputation: Theory and technology (ICORE'09)*, Gargonza, Italy, ed. M. Paolucci, 5–19.

Sondak, H., M. A. Neale, and R. Pinkley. 1995. The negotiated allocations of benefits and burdens: The impact of outcome valence, contribution, and relationship. *Organizational Behaviour and Human Decision Processes* 64(3): 249–260.

Valley, K. L., M. A. Neale, and E. A. Mannix. 1995. Friends, lovers, colleagues, strangers: The effects of relationships on the process and outcome of negotiations. In *Research in negotiation in organizations*, vol. 5, ed. R. Bies, R. Lewicki, and B. Sheppard, 65–93. Greenwich, CT: JAI.

Part VII Applications

The research efforts described in the previous parts of this book concentrated on the development of tools, models and techniques for the field of Agreement Technologies. In this part, different authors present applications that demonstrate the use of many of these technologies in a variety of real-world application scenarios.

Chapter 30, by Stella Heras et al. presents a case-based argumentation system that allows the technicians of a call centre to reach agreements and provide a high quality customer support. In Chapter 31, by Paul Davidsson et al. the use of agreement technologies in the planning and execution of goods transports is analyzed. In particular, the chapter studies the application of the five key technologies (semantics, norms, organizations, argumentation and negotiation, and trust), in the context of an agent-based solution for transport management. The next chapter, by Henrique Lopes Cardoso et al. presents the ANTE framework, a general platform that supports agent negotiation as a mechanism for finding mutually acceptable agreements as well as the enactment of such agreements. Two application cases of the platform are presented: automated B2B electronic contracting and disruption management in the context of an airline company operational control. The fourth chapter in the list (Chap. 33), by Antonio Garrido et al. proposes an electronic institution approach to building virtual markets as an instance of the approach to the real case of a water-right market. The next chapter (Chap. 34), by Pablo Almajano et al. proposes to combine 3D Virtual Worlds with electronic institutions as a means to facilitate a more direct human participation in organization-based multiagent systems. As a case study, the example of the water-right market shown in the previous section is used. Chapter 35, by Marin Lujak and Holger Billhardt, presents an organization-based multiagent application for the management of emergency medical assistance (EMA). The chapter shows how the use of technologies like trust and auction-based negotiation can improve the efficiency (arrival times to emergency patients) of a system with a predefined organizational structure. The next chapter (Chap. 36), by Toni Penya-Alba et al. exhibits an environment to support the rapid assembly of agent-oriented business collaborations. This environment focuses on the creation of supply chains and the follow-up of the whole business collaboration from the early stages of its creation to the final steps of its realization. Finally, the chapter presented by Fabien Delecroix, Maxime Morge and Jean-Christophe Routier, presents a proposal for a proactive and adaptive virtual selling agent for e-commerce scenarios.

All presented applications and use cases have in common that they deal with open multiagent systems. These define environments that are regulated by norms and other organizational structures within which agents interact. In all the cases, agents have to reach agreements with others (e.g., by means of negotiation or argumentation) in order to achieve their individual or collective goals.

Vicente Botti, Holger Billhardt, Vicente Julián, and Juan A. Rodríguez-Aguilar
Editors Part "Applications"

Chapter 30
Arguing to Support Customers: The Call Centre Study Case

Stella Heras, Jaume Jordán, Vicente Botti, and Vicente Julián

30.1 Introduction

Nowadays, products, prices and quality are very similar and companies try to obtain an advantage over their competitors in the market by offering focused customer care. Most commercial activity is done via phone, with a call centre that manages the incoming calls, and it is necessary to provide a fast and high quality service. Good customer support depends, in many cases, on the experience and skills of its technicians. A quick and accurate response to the customers problems ensures their satisfaction and a good reputation for the company and, therefore, it can increase its profits. Moreover, less experienced technicians are cheaper for the company. Thus, it is interesting to provide them with a means for arguing, contrasting their views with other technicians and reaching agreements to solve (collaboratively if necessary) as many requests as possible. Also, storing and reusing later the final solution applied to each problem and the information about the problem-solving process could be a suitable way to improve the customer support offered by the company.

In this chapter, we present a case-based argumentation system that allows the technicians of a call centre to reach agreements and provide high quality customer support. Our application implements an argumentation framework that proposes individual knowledge resources for each agent to generate its positions and arguments (Heras 2011, Chap. 3). Case-Based Reasoning (CBR) systems have been widely applied to enhance the performance of call centre applications. A CBR system tries to solve a problem (case) by means of reusing the solution of an old similar case (Kolodner 1993). This solution is previously stored in a memory of cases (case-base) and it can either be retrieved and applied directly

S. Heras (✉) • J. Jordán • V. Botti • V. Julián
Departamento de Sistemas Informáticos y Computación, Universitat Politècnica de València, Valencia, Spain
e-mail: sheras@dsic.upv.es; jjordan@dsic.upv.es; vbotti@dsic.upv.es; vinglada@dsic.upv.es

S. Ossowski (ed.), *Agreement Technologies*, Law, Governance and Technology Series 8, DOI 10.1007/978-94-007-5583-3_30,

to the current problem, or revised and adapted to fit the new problem. The suitability of CBR systems to manage call centres has been guaranteed for the success of some of these systems from the 1990s to nowadays (Acorn and Walden 1992; Roth-Berghofer 2004; Watson 1997). These approaches propose systems for human-machine interaction where the CBR functionality helps the call centre technicians to solve problems more efficiently by providing them with potential solutions via helpdesk software.

The current implementation extends previous work that deployed a case-based multi-agent system in a real call centre (Heras et al. 2009). This system was implemented and is currently used by the company that runs the call centre to provide its technicians with potential solutions for the problems that they must solve. In the original implementation, agents were allowed to use their case-bases to provide experience-based customer support. However, although this proposal provided successful results, it also has some drawbacks. On the one hand, to integrate the knowledge of all technicians in a unique CBR module can be complex and costly in terms of data mining (due to extra large case-bases with possible out-of-date cases). On the other hand, to have a unique but distributed CBR could be a solution, but to assume that all technicians are willing to unselfishly share their knowledge with other technicians is not realistic. Note that in many companies, technicians are rewarded for outperforming their peers. In addition, they may have to sign confidentiality agreements that forbid them to share certain knowledge with technicians that do not work on their same project. Finally, several technicians could provide different solutions and hence, they need a mechanism to negotiate and reach an agreement about the best solution to apply.

In this work, we propose to automate the system by representing the technicians by means of software agents that can engage in an argumentation process to decide the best solution to apply to each new incidence that the call centre receives. Our approach is a hybrid system that integrates an argumentation framework for agent societies to provide agents with argumentation capabilities and individual knowledge resources. This provides a computational framework for the design and implementation of Multi-Agent Systems (MAS) in which the participating software agents are able to manage and exchange arguments between themselves by taking into account the agents' *social context* (their roles, dependency relations and preferences). The resulting system has been implemented and tested with real data. This chapter shows the results of the tests performed.

30.2 The Call Center Study Case

In our system, we consider a society of agents that act on behalf of a group of technicians that must solve problems in a Technology Management Centre (TMC). TMCs are entities which control every process implicated in the provision of technological and customer support services to private or public organisations. In a TMC, there are a number of technicians whose role is to provide the customers with technical assistance – microcomputing, security and network management among other services. This help is typically offered via a call centre. The call centre technicians have computers provided with helpdesk software and phone terminals connected to a telephone switchboard that manages and balances the calls among technicians. Usually, the staff of a call centre are divided into three levels:

- First level operators (or *Operators*), who receive customer queries and answer those ones from which they have background training or their solution is registered in the company manuals of action protocols.
- Second level operators (or *Experts*), who are expert technicians that have more specialised knowledge than the first level operators and are able to solve problems that the operators cannot solve.
- *Administrators*, who are in charge of organising working groups, of assigning problems to specific operators and of creating generic solutions, which will be registered and used later by the operators of lower levels.

Therefore, we consider a society of agents composed of call centre technicians with three possible roles: operator, expert and administrator. Also, each agent can have its own values that it wants to promote or demote. These values could explain the reasons that an agent has to give preference to certain decisions. Thus, they represent the motivation of agents to act in a specific way. For instance, an agent representing an administrator could prefer to promote the value of *wealth* (to increase the economic benefits of the company) over the value of *fairness* (to preserve the salaries of the call centre technicians). Technicians can have their own preferences over individual values and belong to different groups intended to solve specific types of problems or assigned to specific projects. Also, these groups can have their own social values. Furthermore, dependency relations between roles could imply that an agent must change or violate its value preference order. For instance, an administrator could impose its values on an expert, or an operator could have to adopt a certain preference order over values that its group imposes. In our system, we define the following dependency relations among roles, which capture the common relationships between the different technicians of a call centre:

- A *power* dependency relation of administrators over other roles, which commits experts and operators to accept the positions and arguments of administrators.
- An *authorisation* dependency relation of experts over operators, which commits operators to accept the positions and arguments of experts.
- A *charity* dependency relation among agents that play the same role, by which an agent has to accept positions and arguments from other agent with the same role only if it is willing to do it.

When the call centre receives a new request, the so-called incident register or *ticket* is generated with the customer data and a description of the incident. Hence, this ticket is the problem to be solved. Tickets are characterised by several parameters, such as the type or category of the incident (e.g. network error, OS exception, hardware failure, etc.), data about the actual problem occurred inside each category (e.g. OS, hardware brand, customer observations, etc.), to which group the ticket has been assigned or work-notes about the incident. In our system, each technician has a helpdesk application to manage the large amount of information that the call centre processes. We assume the complex case where a ticket must be solved by a group of agents representing technicians that argue to reach an agreement over the best solution to apply. Each agent has its own knowledge resources (acceded via its helpdesk) to generate a solution for the ticket. The data-flow for the problem-solving process (or argumentation process) to solve each ticket is the following:

1. The system presents a group of technicians with a new ticket to solve.
2. If possible, each technician generates his own solution (referred as position in this chapter) by using an argumentation module that implements the case-based argumentation framework presented in Heras (2011, Chap. 3).
3. All technicians that are willing to participate in the argumentation process are aware of the positions proposed in each moment.
4. The technicians argue to reach an agreement over the most suitable solution by following a *persuasion* dialogue with their peers, trying to convince them to accept their solution as the best way to solve the ticket received, while observing the common objective of providing the best solution for a ticket from their point of view.
5. The best solution is proposed to the user and feedback is provided and registered by each technician helpdesk.

In this section, we briefly introduce the case-based argumentation framework that our system implements. This framework allows agents to argue and reach agreements by taking into account their social context in the way agents can argue. In addition, the argumentation system developed in the call centre is also presented.

30.2.1 Argumentation Framework

The system presented in this chapter implements the case-based argumentation framework for agent societies proposed in Heras (2011). There, an *agent society* is defined in terms of a set of *agents* that play a set of *roles*, observe a set of *norms*, have a set of *dependency relations* between roles and use a *communication language* to collaborate and reach the global objectives of the *group*. Therefore, we consider that the values that individual agents or groups want to promote or demote and preference orders over them have a crucial importance in the definition of an argumentation framework for open MAS where agents form part of a society. As pointed out before, these values represent the motivation of agents to act in a specific way. Also, dependency relations between roles could imply that an agent must change or violate its value preference order. Therefore, we endorse the view of Bench-Capon and Atkinson (2009), who stress the importance of the audience in determining whether an argument is persuasive or not for accepting or rejecting someone else's proposals.

In open multi-agent argumentation systems the arguments that an agent generates to support its position can conflict with arguments of other agents. These conflicts can be solved by means of argumentation dialogues between them. In our framework, we propose two types of knowledge resources that the agents can use to generate, select and evaluate arguments in view of other arguments:

- Domain-cases database, with domain-cases that represent previous problems and their solutions. The structure of these cases is domain-dependent.
- Argument-cases database, with argument-cases that represent previous argumentation experiences and their final outcome.

These knowledge resources are case-based. Reasoning with cases is especially suitable when there is a weak (or even unknown) domain theory, but acquiring examples encountered in practice is easy. Most argumentation systems produce arguments by applying a set of inference rules. Rule-based systems require eliciting an explicit model of the domain. However, in open MAS the domain is highly dynamic and the set of rules that model it is difficult to specify in advance. However, tracking the arguments that agents put forward in argumentation processes could be relatively simple.

In addition, the knowledge resources of this argumentation framework are represented by using ontologies. Concretely, we have developed a domain-dependent ontology to represent the call centre domain-cases and a generic argumentation ontology, called ArgCBROnto,[1] to represent argument-cases and arguments that the agents interchange. This ontological representation allows heterogeneous agents to communicate and understand the arguments of other agents.

Arguments that agents interchange are defined as tuples:

Definition 30.1. $\text{Arg} = \{\phi, v, <S>\}$

where ϕ is the conclusion of the argument, v is the value (e.g. economy, quality) that the agent wants to promote with it and $<S>$ is a set of elements that support the argument (*support set*). A support set (S) is defined as a tuple:

Definition 30.2. $S = <\{P\}, \{DC\}, \{AC\}, \{DP\}, \{CE\}>$

where

- *Premises (P)* are features that describe the problem to solve. These are the features that characterise the problem and that the agent has used to retrieve similar domain-cases from its case-base. Note that the premises used might be all features of the problem description or a sub-set.
- *Domain cases (DC)* are cases that represent previous problems and their solutions whose features match some or all features of the problem description.

[1] The complete specification of the ArgCBROnto ontology can be found at http://users.dsic.upv.es/~vinglada/docs.

- *Argument-cases (AC)* are cases that represent past argumentation experiences with their final outcome. These cases are used to select the best position and argument to propose in view of the current context and the argumentation experience of the agent. Thus, argument-cases store information related to the domain and the social context where previous arguments (and their associated positions) were used. The information about the domain consists of a set of features to compare cases (e.g. the type of incident or the affected equipment) and information about the social context where the proposed solution was applied (e.g. the agents that participated in the dialogue to solve the problem, their roles or their value preferences). The latter information can determine if certain positions and arguments are more persuasive than others for a particular social context and hence, agents can select the best ones to propose in the current situation.
- *Distinguishing premises (DP)* are premises that can invalidate the application of a knowledge resource to generate a valid conclusion for an argument. These premises are extracted from a domain-case that propose a different solution for the argument to attack. They consist of features of the problem description of the argument to attack, that were not considered in drawing its conclusion.
- *Counter-examples (CE)* are cases that match the problem description of a case but propose a different solution.

Agents generate *support arguments* when they are asked to provide evidence to support a position since, by default, agents are not committed to showing evidence to justify their positions. Therefore, an opponent has to ask a proponent for an argument that justifies its position before attacking it. Then, if the proponent is willing to offer support evidences, it can generate a support argument which support set is the set of features (premises) that describe the problem and it has considered to generate its position and, optionally, the set of domain-cases and argument-cases that it has used to generate and select its position. Note that the set of premises could be a subset of the features that describe the problem (e.g. when a position has been generated from a domain-case that has a subset of features of the problem in addition to other different features).

When the proponent of a position generates an argument to justify it and an opponent wants to attack the argument (and hence, the position), it generates an *attack argument*. In our argumentation framework, arguments can be attacked by putting forward two types of attacks: *distinguishing premises* and *counter-examples*. The attack arguments that the opponent can generate depend on the elements of the support set of the argument of the proponent to attack:

- If the justification for the conclusion of the argument to attack is a set of premises, the opponent can generate an attack argument with a distinguishing premise that it knows. It can do it, for instance, if it is in a privileged situation and knows extra information about the problem (e.g. it plays the role of administrator or expert) or if it is implicit in a case that it used to generate its own position, which matches the problem specification.

- If the justification is a domain-case or an argument-case, then the opponent can check its case-bases and try to find counter-examples to generate an attack argument with them.

The agents of the framework need a mechanism to manage the arguments and perform the argumentation dialogue. Therefore, in Heras (2011, Chap. 4) a dialogue game protocol has been defined with this aim. This protocol is represented by a set of locutions that the agents use to communicate with each other and a state machine that determines the set of allowed locutions that an agent can put forward at each step the argumentation dialogue. The concrete *argumentation protocol* that the agents of the call centre application follow has also been defined in Jordán et al. (2011), which is a concrete instantiation of the dialogue game protocol cited before.

30.2.2 Argumentation System

Subsequently, we describe the different modules of the call centre system and their functionality:

- **Magentix2**: to develop this system we have used the Magentix2 agent platform.[2] Magentix2 is an agent platform that provides new services and tools that allow for the secure and optimised management of open MAS.
- **Domain CBR module**: consists of a CBR module with data about previous problems solved in the call centre (domain-cases). This CBR is initialised with past tickets reported to the call centre. The CBR module used to perform the tests is an improved version of the module used in Heras et al. (2009). To make a query to the domain CBR, the user has to provide a ticket and a threshold of similarity. The domain CBR module searches the domain case-base and returns a list of similar domain-cases to the given ticket. In addition, with every request attended and every CBR cycle performed, the module adds, modifies or deletes one or more domain-cases of the domain case-base. In the current version of the system, if the ticket that has been solved is similar enough (over certain similarity threshold) to a case of the domain-cases case-base, the update algorithm updates this case with the new data acquired. Otherwise, a new domain-case is created and added to the case-base.
- **Argumentation CBR module**: consists of a CBR module with argumentation data (previous arguments stored in the form of argument-cases). Once an agent has a list of potential solutions for a current ticket, it has to select the best position to put forward among them. Also, the agent can generate arguments to support its position and attack another agent's arguments and positions. Then, this module is used to look for previous argumentation experiences and use this knowledge to select the best positions and arguments to propose. As for the domain-cases

[2] http://users.dsic.upv.es/grupos/ia/sma/tools/magentix2/index.php

case base, if the argument-cases created during the problem solving process are similar enough to previous argument-cases stored in the argument-cases case-base, the update algorithm updates those cases with the new data acquired. Otherwise, new argument-cases are created and added to the case-base.

- **Ontology parsers**: The contents of the case-bases of the domain CBR and the argumentation CBR are stored as objects in OWL 2 ontologies. In this way, heterogeneous agents can use these ontologies as common language to interchange solutions and arguments generated from the case-bases of the argumentation framework. The main advantage of using ontologies is that the structures and features of the cases are well specified and agents can easily understand them. The ontology parsers developed provide an API to read and write data in the case-bases of the argumentation module.
- **Argumentative agents**: are agents with a domain CBR and an argumentation CBR that are able to engage in an argumentation dialogue to solve a ticket. These agents learn about the domain problem and the argumentation dialogue by adding and updating cases into the domain and argumentation case-bases with each CBR run. Moreover, argumentative agents can play any role defined before.
- **Commitment Store**: is a resource of the argumentation framework that stores all the information about the agents participating in the problem solving process, argumentation dialogues between them, positions and arguments. By making queries to this resource, every agent of the framework can read the information of the dialogues that it is involved in.

In order to show how the developed system works, the data-flow for the problem-solving process (or argumentation process) to solve each ticket is shown in Fig. 30.1 and described below (arrows in the figure are labelled with the number of the data-flow step that they represent):

1. First, we have some argumentation agents running in the platform and representing the technicians of the call centre. An agent of the group (randomly selected) acts as the *initiator* of the argumentation dialogue (an administrator in the case presented in the figure). This kind of agent has a special behaviour in receiving tickets to solve and create a new dialogue with the agents of its group. The process begins when a ticket that represents an incident to solve is received by the initiator agent. Then, this agent sends the ticket to their peers in the group.
2. Each agent evaluates individually if it can engage in the dialogue by offering a solution. To do that, the agent makes a query to its domain CBR to obtain potential solutions to the ticket based on previous solutions applied to similar tickets. To compute such similarity, agents use a *weighted Euclidean* algorithm that searches their domain-cases case-bases for previous problems that semantically match the category of the current ticket to solve. Thus, the algorithm retrieves all problems of the same category and of related categories and select those that syntactically match (assign the same values to the attributes that match the ticket attributes) and overpass a predefined *similarity threshold*. If one or more valid solutions can be generated from the selected domain-cases, the agent will be able to defend a position in the dialogue. We consider a valid solution any domain case from the

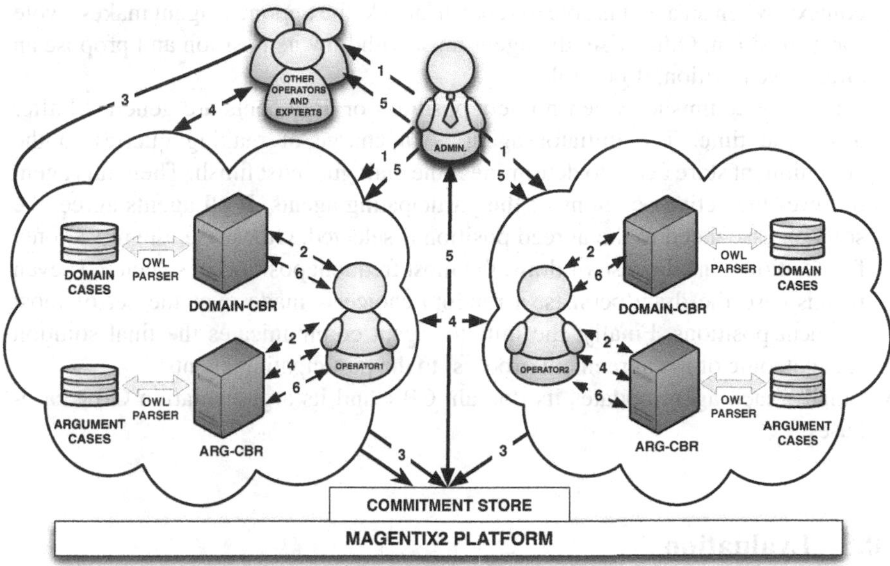

Fig. 30.1 Data-flow for the argumentation process of the call centre application

domain CBR with one or more solutions and with a similarity degree greater than the given threshold. Moreover, the agent makes a query to its argumentation CBR for each possible position to defend. With these queries the *suitability degree* of the positions is obtained as explained in Heras (2011, Chap. 3). This degree represents if a position will be easy to defend based on past similar argumentation experiences. Then, all possible positions to defend are ordered from greater to lesser degree of suitability.

3. When the agents have a position to defend (a proposed solution), these positions are stored by the commitment store, in a way that other agents can check the positions of all dialogue participants. Every agent tries to attack the positions that are different from its position.
4. The argumentation process consists of a series of steps by which agents try to defend its positions by generating counter-examples and distinguishing premises for the positions and arguments of other agents. A counter-example for a case is generated by retrieving from the domain case-base another case that matches the features of the former, but has a different conclusion. Similarly, distinguishing premises are computed by selecting such premises that the agent has taken into account to generate its positions, but that other agents did not consider. If different attacks can be generated, agents select the best attack to rebut the position of another agent by making a query to their argument-cases case-base, extending the characterisation of each case with the current social context. In this way, agents can gain knowledge about how each potential attack worked to rebut the position of an agent in a past argumentation experience with a similar social

context. When an agent is able to rebut an attack, the opponent agent makes a vote for its position. Otherwise, the agent must withdraw its position and propose an alternative position, if possible.

5. The dialogue finishes when no new positions or arguments are generated after a specific time. The initiator agent is in charge of making queries to the commitment store agent to determine if the dialogue must finish. Then, this agent retrieves the active positions of the participating agents. If all agents agree, the solution associated to the agreed position is selected. Otherwise, the most voted for position wins. In case of draw, the most frequent position in selected. If even in this case the draw persists, a random choice is made over the set of most frequent positions. Finally, the initiator agent communicates the final solution (the outcome of the agreement process) to the participating agents.
6. Finally, each agent updates its domain CBR and its argumentation CBR case-bases.

30.3 Evaluation

To evaluate the proposed call centre application, a set of empirical tests have been performed. For the tests, we assume that there are several agents engaged in an agreement process and that these agents have an individual argumentation system that complies with our case-based argumentation framework. Testing a CBR system involves two separated processes: verification (concerned with building the system right) and validation (concerned with building the right system) (Watson 1997). Validation is a complex socio-technical problem that involves ensuring that the developed system is the right system for the problem to solve. Here we cope with the verification problem and more concretely, with the problem of verifying the performance of the system.

For the tests, a real database of 200 tickets solved in the past is used as domain knowledge. Translating these tickets to domain-cases, we have obtained a tickets case-base with 48 cases. Despite the small size of this case-base, we have preferred to use actual data rather than a larger case-base with simulated data. The argument-cases case-bases of each agent are initially empty and populated with cases as the agents acquire argumentation experience in execution of the system.

To diminish the influence of random noise, for each round in each test, all results report the average and confidence interval of 48 simulation runs at a confidence level of 95 %, thus using a different ticket of the tickets case-base as the problem to solve in each run. The results report the mean of the sampling distribution (the population mean) by using the formula:

$$\mu = \bar{x} \pm t * \frac{s}{\sqrt{n}}$$

where, $\bar{x}$ is the sample mean (the mean of the 48 experiments), t is a parameter that increases or decreases the standard error of the sample mean ($\frac{s}{\sqrt{n}}$), s is the sample standard deviation and n is the number of experiments. For small samples, say below 100, t follows the *Student's t-distribution*, which specifies certain value for the t parameter to achieve a confidence level of 95 % for different sizes of population. In our case, with a population of 48 experiments the Student's t-distribution establishes a value of 2.0106 for t.

In each simulation experiment, an agent is selected randomly as initiator of the discussion. This agent has the additional function of collecting data for analysis. However, from the argumentation perspective, its behaviour is exactly the same as the rest of agents and its positions and arguments do not have any preference over others (unless there is a dependency relation that states it). The initiator agent receives one problem to solve per run. Then, it contacts its peers (the agents of its group) to report them the problem to solve. If the agents do not reach an agreement after a maximum time, the initiator chooses the most supported (the most voted for) solution as the final decision (or the most frequent in case of draw). If the draw persists, the initiator makes a random choice among the most frequent solutions.

The case-based argumentation system proposed in this chapter has been evaluated from different perspectives. On the one hand, the *performance* of the system has been tested and analysed. On the other hand, the ability of the system to take into account the *social context* of the participating agents is also verified.

30.3.1 Testing the Performance

The performance tests have been repeated and their results compared for the following decision policies:

- Random policy (CBR-R): each agent uses its domain CBR module to propose a solution for the problem to solve. Then, a random choice among all solutions proposed by the agents is made. Agents do not have an argumentation CBR module.
- Majority policy (CBR-M): each agent uses its domain CBR module to propose a solution for the problem to solve. Then, the system selects the most frequently proposed solution. Agents do not have an argumentation CBR module.
- Argumentation policy (CBR-ARG): agents have domain and argumentation CBR modules. Each agent uses its domain CBR module to propose a solution for the problem to solve and its argumentation CBR module to select the best positions and arguments to propose in view of its argumentation experience. Then, agents perform an argumentation dialogue to select the final solution to apply.

To evaluate the effect of the available argumentative knowledge that agents have, some tests are also repeated for the following specific settings of the argumentation policy. These settings cover the most interesting options regarding which agents have available previous argumentation knowledge:

- CBR-ARG All-Argument-Cases (CBR-ARG AAC): All participating agent have argument-cases in their argument-cases case-base.

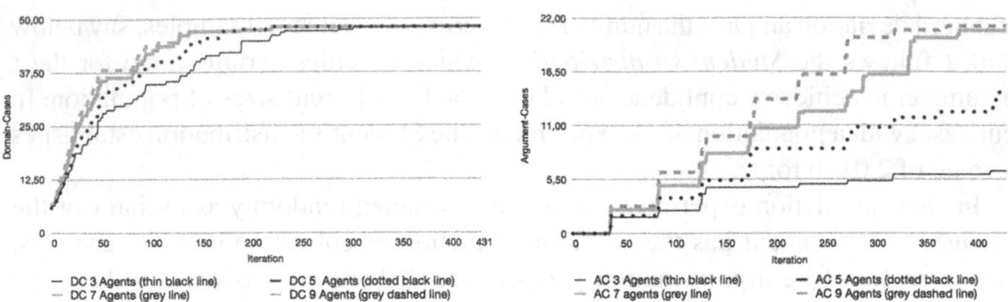

Fig. 30.2 (*Left*) Number of domain-cases that agents learn; (*right*) number of argument-cases that agents learn

- CBR-ARG Initiator-Argument-Cases (CBR-ARG IAC): Only one agent, say the initiator agent, has argument-cases in its argument-cases case-base. Note that the selection of the initiator as the agent that has argumentative knowledge is just made for the sake of simplicity in the nomenclature. The behaviour of this agent only differs from the other agents' in the fact that it is in charge of starting the dialogue process and conveying the information about the final outcome. This does not affect its performance as dialogue participant and does not grant this agent any privileges over their peers.
- CBR-ARG Others-Argument-Cases (CBR-ARG OAC): All agents except for one, say the initiator, have argument-cases in their argument-cases case-bases.

With these tests, we evaluate the efficiency of the system that implements our framework under the different decision policies. By default, all agents know each other, all are in the same group and the dependency relation between them is *charity*. The values of each agent have been randomly assigned and agents know the values of their peers. Also, all agents play the role of *operator*. The influence of the social context will be evaluated in the next section.

30.3.1.1 Number of Cases that the Framework Learns with Respect of Time

To perform this test, all agents follow the argumentation policy, with an initial number of five domain-cases in their domain-cases case-bases. The argument-cases case-base of all agents are initially empty. In each iteration, the agents use their CBR modules to propose and select positions and arguments and after this process, each agent updates its case-bases with the knowledge acquired.

If the system works properly, the knowledge acquired about past problem solving processes should increase with time up to some threshold, where the learning process should stabilize (because the cases in the case-bases of the agents cover most possible problems and arguments in the domain). To perform this test, we have executed several rounds to simulate the use of the system over a certain period of time. For each repetition, we compute the average number of domain-cases and argument-cases in the case-bases of the agents. Figure 30.2 shows the results obtained in this test. The experiment has been repeated for 3, 5, 7 and 9 agents and the average number of domain-cases (DC) and argument-cases (AC) that all agents learn in each iteration has been computed. As expected, in all cases, the agents are able to learn the 48 domain-cases of the tickets case-base. However, if more agents participate in the dialogue, the quantity of domain knowledge that agents have available and exchange among themselves increases and the domain-cases case-bases are more quickly populated. Also, the quantity of argument-cases that agents are able to learn increases with the number of agents, since more potential positions and arguments give rise to more complex argumentation dialogues. As shown in the figure, the learning curve for the argument-cases is softer than for the domain-cases, presenting peaks at some points. This is due to the fact that at some points of the dialogue, the agents can learn a specific domain-case that change its opinion about the best solution to apply for a specific category of problem. Therefore, the outcome of subsequent dialogues differ from the outcome that could be expected by taking into account past similar dialogues and the argument-cases learning rate of the agents in those situations notably increases.

The results of this test have helped us to set the value of some parameters of the subsequent evaluation tests. The test shows that in 48 simulation runs, 3 agents are able to learn an average of 54.8 % of the domain-cases of the tickets case-base, 5 agents 56.6 %, 7 agents 66.9 % and 9 agents 73.1 %. The maximum number of argument-cases that agents are able to learn reaches an average of 20 argument-cases when 9 agents participate in the dialogue (18 argument-cases in the worst case).

Therefore, due to the small size of the whole tickets case-base and the learning rates obtained in this test, the evaluation tests have been executed with a number of 7 agents participating in the dialogue, with domain-cases case-bases populated with a maximum number of 45 domain-cases and argument-cases case-bases populated with a maximum number of 20 argument-cases (except for the social context tests, where a more varied choice of social contexts enables the learning of a larger number of argument-cases). This number of agents allow complex enough argumentation dialogues where the use of argument-cases can be useful, while having a reasonable case learning rate to avoid filling the case-bases with all the available knowledge for this case of study with a small number of simulations.

Also, the domain-cases of the case-bases of the agents will be randomly populated and increased from 5 to 45 cases in each experimental round. The argument-cases case-bases of the agents for the argumentation-based policy are populated with 20 randomly selected argument-cases (from those acquired during the performance of the present test). Also, to evaluate the influence of the quantity of argumentative knowledge that the agents have in some tests, those tests are repeated by setting the number of domain-cases of the case-bases of the agents to 20 (approximately the half part of the available cases in the tickets case-base), while varying the number or argument-cases of the argumentative agents from 0 to 18 cases, with an increase of 2 randomly selected argument-cases in each round.

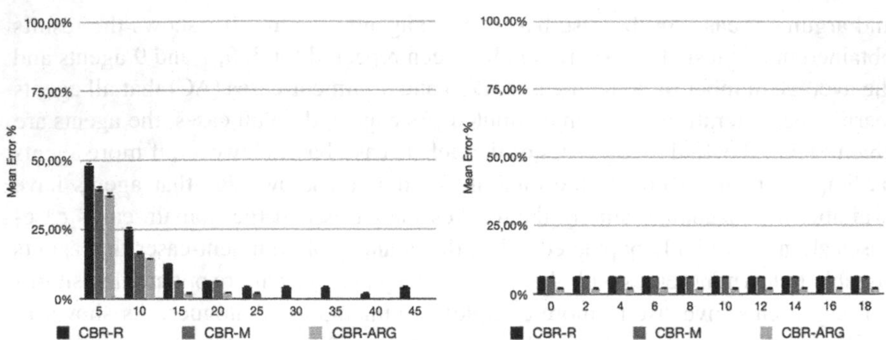

Fig. 30.3 (*Left*) Solution prediction accuracy achieved by 7 agents ([5, 45]Δ5 domain-cases; 20 argument-cases); (*right*) solution prediction accuracy achieved by 7 agents (20 domain-cases; [0, 18]Δ2 argument-cases)

30.3.1.2 Percentage of Problems that Were Properly Solved with Respect to the Knowledge of the Agents

In this test, the percentage of problems that the system is able to solve, providing a correct solution, are computed. To check the solution accuracy, the solution agreed by the agents for each ticket requested is compared with its original solution, stored in the tickets case-base. One can expect that with more knowledge stored in the case-bases the number of problems that were correctly solved should increase. Figure 30.3 (left) shows how, as the number of domain-cases of the agent's case-base increases, the solution they propose is more appropriate and similar to the actual solution registered in the tickets case-base for the ticket that has been requested to the agents (the mean error percentage in the solution predicted decreases). Obviously, if agents have more domain knowledge, the probability that one or more of them have a suitable domain-case that can be used to provide a solution for the current problem increases.

The results achieved by the argumentation policy improve those achieved by the other policies, even when the domain-cases case-bases are populated with a small number of cases. The argumentation policy achieves more than a 50 % improvement for a domain-cases case-base size up to 15 cases. These results demonstrate that if agents have the ability to argue, the agents whose solutions are more supported by evidence have more possibilities of winning the argumentation dialogue and hence, the quality of the final solution selected among all potential solution proposed by the agents increases. Finally, Fig. 30.3 (right) shows the results of this test if the number of domain-cases is set to 20 and the number of argument-cases that the agents have is increased in each round. The results show that the argumentative knowledge has no substantial influence on the accuracy of the solution proposed, at least for the data used in this case study.

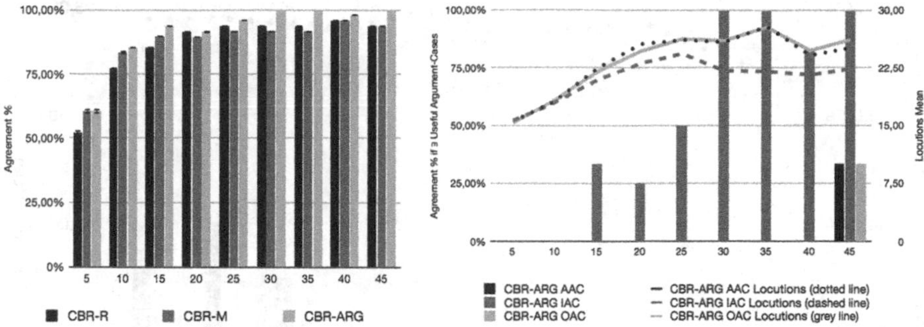

Fig. 30.4 (*Left*) Percentage of agreement reached by 7 agents ([5, 45]Δ5 domain-cases; 20 argument-cases); (right) percentage of agreement reached by 7 agents when useful argument-cases are available ([5, 45]Δ5 domain-cases; 20 argument-cases)

30.3.1.3 Percentage of Agreements Reached with Respect to the Knowledge of the Agents

In this test, we evaluate the percentage of times that an agreement is reached and a frequency-based or a random choice among all possible solutions proposed by the agents is not necessary. Figure 30.4 (left) shows the results obtained. For all policies, the overall trend of the agreement percentage is to increase as the knowledge about the domain that agents have increases. Nevertheless, the figure shows slight fluctuations between results. This behaviour can be explained since the addition of a small quantity of new domain-cases between two simulation rounds can give rise to temporary situations, such as some agents temporarily changing their opinions until new information is gained or obtaining the same *suitability degree* for several positions and arguments. In the last case random choices are made, which can have a slightly negative effect on the overall performance of the system. In addition, the improvement on the agreement percentage reaches more than 80 % with little knowledge about the domain (e.g. 10 domain-cases).

More interesting results can be observed if we compare the agreement percentage that the argumentation policy achieves when useful argument-cases are available. To perform this test, the percentage of agreement that agents reach in those cases that they have been able to find useful argument-cases (argument-cases where the problem description matches the current situation) has been computed. Note that the fact that agents have argument-cases in their argument-cases case-bases does not necessarily mean that these cases match the current dialogue context and are actually used by the agents to make their decisions. Therefore, Fig. 30.4 (right) shows the percentage of agreements that the argumentation policy achieves when one or more agents use their argumentative knowledge. In these tests, the fluctuations between subsequent simulation rounds are notably greater than in the previous tests. These fluctuations are due to the fact that the percentage of useful argument-cases highly depends on the domain knowledge that agents have and on the dialogue context.

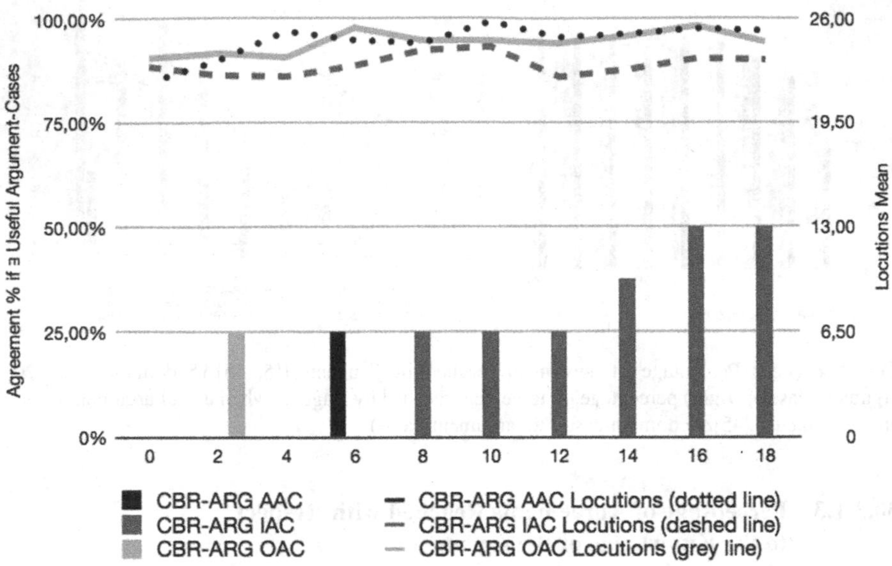

Fig. 30.5 Percentage of agreement reached by 7 agents when useful argument-cases are available (20 domain-cases; [0, 18]Δ2 argument-cases)

We can observe that when enough domain knowledge is available and agents engage in more complex dialogues (up to 15 domain-cases), the agreement percentage has a general trend towards increasing when the initiator agent is the only agent that has useful argument-cases. This behaviour shows how the use of argumentative knowledge allows the initiator to argue better and persuade the other agents to accept their positions and reach an agreement. However, if more agents are also able to improve their argumentation skills by using their argumentative knowledge (CBR-ARG AAC and CBR-ARG OAC policies), fewer agents are persuaded to accept other agents' positions and hence, no agreement is reached in almost all simulations (except for the case of 45 domain-cases in the agents domain-cases case-bases).

Figure 30.4 (right) also shows the average number of locutions exchanged among the agents during the argumentation dialogue. The number of interchanged locutions seems to stabilize when the percentage of agreements reached approaches 100 %. Also, when only one agent has argumentative knowledge, the number of locutions (or let us say, the number of dialogue steps) that are necessary to reach a final decision among agents is more stable than in the cases where more agents use their argument-cases. Therefore, the CBR-ARG IAC policy is also the more efficient policy, achieving the best performance results with shorter argumentation dialogues among the agents.

Finally, to evaluate the influence of the amount of argumentative knowledge of the agents on the agreement percentage, Fig. 30.5 shows the results obtained by the argumentation policy when the number of argument-cases available for one or more agents is increased. When the initiator agent is the only agent that uses argumentative knowledge, as this knowledge increases, the probability of finding useful argument-cases to apply in each argumentation dialogue also increases. Therefore, this agent improves its argumentation skills and it is able to persuade the others to reach an agreement and accept its position as the best solution to apply for the ticket to solve. However, when several agents have a small quantity of argument-cases, the probability of finding a useful argument-case is very low. In these cases (CBR-ARG AAC with 6 argument-cases and CBR-ARG OAC with two argument-cases), the performance of the system suffers from a high randomness, and this agent that finds a useful argument-case has a greater advantage over the others, being able to persuade them to reach an agreement that favours its preferences. Regarding the number of locutions exchanged among the agents, Fig. 30.5 shows how the number of locutions to reach the agreement is stable for all policies and does not depend on the argumentation knowledge that agents have. Thus, as pointed out before, the CBR-ARG IAC policy gets higher percentage of agreement when useful argument-cases are actually used.

30.3.2 Testing the Social Context

The ability of the system to represent the social context of the system has also been evaluated. To perform these tests, the system has been executed with seven participating agents, following the argumentative policy (CBR-ARG). The knowledge about the domain that each agent has is increased by 5 domain-cases in each round, from 5 to 45 domain-cases. Argumentative agents have a full argument-cases case-base populated with 20 cases. By default, all agents know each other, all are in the same group and the dependency relation between them depends on the specific test. The influence of different degrees of friendship and group membership are difficult to evaluate with the limited amount of data of our tickets case-base and remains future work. The values of each agent have been randomly assigned from a set of pre-defined values (*efficiency* of the problem solving process, *accuracy* of the solution provided and *savings* in the resources used to solve the ticket).

Subsequently, the influence of the presence of an expert and the knowledge about the values of other agents in the system performance is evaluated.

30.3.2.1 Presence of an Expert

In this test, an agent has been allowed to play the role of an *expert*, while the rest of agents play the role of *operators*. An expert is an agent that has specific knowledge to solve certain types (categories) of problems and has its case-base of domain-cases populated with cases that solve them. Thus, the expert domain-cases case-base has as much knowledge as possible about the solution of past problems of the same type. That is, if the expert is configured to have five domain-cases in its domain-cases case-base, and there is enough suitable information in the original tickets case-base,

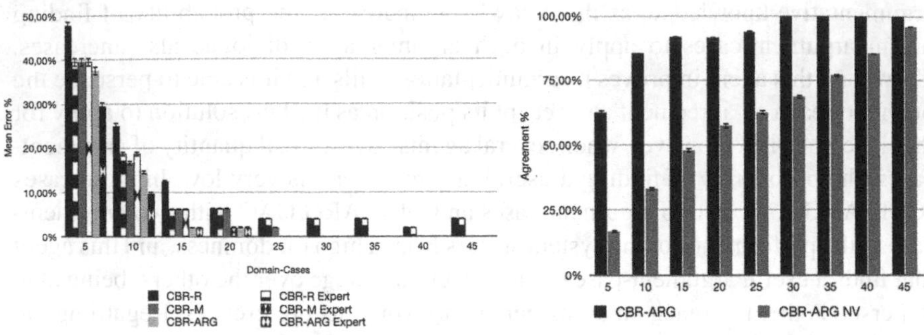

Fig. 30.6 (*Left*) Accuracy of the predictions of 1 expert and 6 operators ([5, 45] $\Delta 5$ domain-cases; 20 argument-cases); (*right*) percentage of agreement reached by 7 agents ([5, 45] $\Delta 5$ domain-cases; 20 argument-cases) when they have (CBR-ARG) and do not have (CBR-ARG NV) knowledge about the preference over values of their peers

these cases represent instances of the same type of problems. In the case that the tickets case-base has fewer than five cases representing such category of problems, three for instance, the remaining two cases are of the same category (if possible). In our case, the expert agent has an *authorisation* dependency relation over operators. Therefore, if it is able to propose a solution for the ticket requested, it can generate arguments that support its position and that will defeat other operators' arguments.

All simulation tests have been executed and their results compared for the random based decision policy (CBR-R Expert), the majority based decision policy (CBR-M Expert) and the argumentation based policy (CBR-ARG Expert). For these policies, the domain-cases case-base of the expert has been populated with expert domain knowledge. To evaluate the overall effect of this expert knowledge, the results obtained for the accuracy of predictions when the domain-cases case-base of all agents are populated with random data are also shown for each policy (CBR-R, CBR-M and CBR-ARG).

Figure 30.6 (left) shows how the accuracy of predictions is higher if agents are allowed to argue following the CBR-ARG Expert policy. Comparing the results obtained when the initiator has (CBR-R Expert, CBR-M Expert and CBR-ARG Expert) or does not have expert knowledge (CBR-R, CBR-M and CBR-ARG), as expected, agents are able to achieve better accuracy in their final prediction when they are able to argue and there is an expert participating in the argumentation dialogue (CBR-ARG Expert). This demonstrates that the decisions of the expert prevail and, as it has more specialised domain-knowledge to propose solutions, the predictions of the system are more accurate.

30.3.2.2 Knowledge About Other Agents' Social Context

With these tests, we have evaluated the influence that the knowledge about the social context has in the performance of the system. Therefore, we have compared the performance of the system when the participating agents follow an argumentation policy and have full information about the social context of their peers (CBR-ARG), or on the contrary, do not know the preference over values that their peers have (CBR-ARG NV). In a real company, the dependency relations over technicians and the group that they belong are known by the staff. Hence, we assume that agents know this information about their peers.

In our evaluation domain, if an agent does not know the value preferences of their peers, on many occasions it uses argument-cases that are not suitable for the current situation. This causes the agent to make wrong decisions that worsen the overall performance of the system. Figure 30.6 (right) shows how the system presents a poor performance in terms of the agreement percentage when argumentative agents ignore the values of their peers. The use of wrong argument-cases makes argumentative agents propose solutions and arguments that hinder agreement reaching. This could be avoided if the system assigns less importance to the argumentative knowledge. In this way, a system that supports our framework can also perform well in domains where acquiring social context information about competitors is difficult, although this would significantly reduce the advantages of learning this type of information.

30.4 Conclusions

In this chapter, several tests to evaluate the case-based argumentation system proposed have been developed. With this aim, the system has been implemented and tested in a real call centre application currently run by a company. This company receives tickets about user problems that have to be solved by a group of technicians. The system has been integrated as an argumentation module that agents that represent technicians can use to argue and persuade other agents to accept their proposed solutions as the best way to solve each problem reported to the call centre.

To perform the tests we have used a 48 tickets case-base with real domain knowledge. The small size of this case-base has influenced the choice of several evaluation parameters, such as the number of agents to make the tests and the number of simulations. Also, in the company the group that the operators belong and their dependency relations are known by all technicians. Concretely, we have assumed that all agents belong to the same group to allow them to populate their domain-case bases with random cases extracted from the same tickets case-base. We plan to extend the evaluation of our system by updating the tickets case-base, as the company provides us with new information, and by applying them to different projects, where different assumptions need to be made.

Furthermore, the performance of the system has been evaluated under different settings. The tests show how those agents that follow an argumentation policy are able to provide more accurate solutions to the problems that the system receives. The ability of the agents to argue allows those who have better arguments to support their decisions to win the argumentation dialogue. Therefore, the higher quality solutions are selected from among those proposed.

In terms of the percentage of agreement, the argumentative agents get better results than agents following other policies. In this case, agents that have proposed less accurate solutions are persuaded to withdraw them and accept other agents' proposals, resulting in more agreements reached. The influence of the amount of argumentation knowledge that argumentative agents have has also been evaluated. If only one agent has argumentation knowledge that matches the context of current argumentation processes, as this knowledge increases, the number of agreements reached also increases. This demonstrates that this agent is effectively using its argumentation knowledge to select the best positions and arguments to put forward in a dialogue with other agents. Thus, the more useful arguments an agent has, the more proficient the agent is in persuading other agents to accept its proposals. However, if all or most agents have the ability to learn from argumentation dialogues, all of them have the same (high) persuasive power to defend their decisions and agreement is difficult to reach.

Finally, the influence of the knowledge that an agent has about the social context of their peers has been also evaluated. Results show that if an expert actually is better informed to assign better solutions to specific types of problems, the performance of the system improves. The quantity of knowledge that agents have about the values of other agents also determines the good performance of the system. Therefore, if an agent does not know the value preferences of their partners, on many occasions the agent uses argument-cases that are not suitable for the current situation. This causes the agent to make wrong decisions that worsen the overall performance of the system.

We have assumed in this example that agents do their best to win the argumentation dialogue, thus following a persuasion dialogue, since in this way they get economical rewards and increase prestige. Despite that, those solutions that are better supported prevail. This assumption has allowed us to perform more comprehensive tests with the small amount of data that we have and to check the advantages of the amount of available knowledge about the preferences of other agents. However, a cooperative approach where agents do not pursue their individual benefit and collaborate to reach the best agreement would be appropriate for this example and will be implemented and evaluated in the future.

In addition, the framework is flexible enough to be applied to different domains where a group of agents must reach an agreement about the best solution to apply for a given problem. Thus, we have also tested the formal properties of the case-based argumentation framework used in this work by applying it in a system that manages water-rights in a river basin (Heras 2011, Chap. 5).

References

Acorn T., and S. Walden. 1992. Smart – Support management automated reasoning technology for compaq customer service. In *Proceedings of the 4th conference on innovative applications of artificial intelligence*, vol. 4, 3–18. Menlo Park: AAAI.

Bench-Capon T., and K. Atkinson. 2009. Abstract argumentation and values. In *Argumentation in artificial intelligence*, ed. I. Rahwan, G.R. Simari, 45–64. Dordrecht/New York: Springer.

Heras S. 2011. *Case-based argumentation framework for agent societies*. Ph.D. thesis, Departamento de Sistemas Informáticos y Computación. Universitat Politècnica de València. http://hdl.handle.net/10251/12497, http://hdl.handle.net/10251/12497.

Heras S., J.A. García-Pardo, R. Ramos-Garijo, A. Palomares, V. Botti, M. Rebollo, and V. Julián. 2009. Multi-domain case-based module for customer support. *Expert Systems with Applications* 36(3): 6866–6873.

Jordán J., S. Heras, S. Valero, V. Julián. 2011. An argumentation framework for supporting agreements in agent societies applied to customer support. In *Proceedings of the 6th international conference on hybrid artificial intelligence systems (HAIS-11)*, Lecture notes in computer science, vol. 6678, 396–403. Berlin/Heidelberg: Springer.

Kolodner J. 1993. *Case-based reasoning*. San Mateo: Morgan Kaufmann.

Roth-Berghofer T.R. 2004. Learning from HOMER, a case-based help-desk support system. In *Proceedings of the Advances in learning software organisations*, Banff, 88–97.

Watson I. 1997. *Applying case-based reasoning: Techniques for enterprise systems*. San Francisco: Morgan Kaufmann.

Chapter 31
Agreement Technologies for Supporting the Planning and Execution of Transports

Paul Davidsson, Marie Gustafsson Friberger, Johan Holmgren, Andreas Jacobsson, and Jan A. Persson

31.1 Introduction

In order to achieve efficient intermodal transports of goods, there is a need for organized collaboration between the different actors involved, e.g., transport users, transport coordinators, transport operators, and infrastructure operators. We have previously proposed an approach, called *Plug and Play Transport Chain Management* (PnP TCM) (Davidsson et al. 2011), which provides support for the planning of transport solutions between multiple actors, as well as for activity coordination and administrative information transactions during the execution of transports.

The PnP TCM approach can be seen as an instantiation of the more general *Plug and Play Business* concept (Davidsson et al. 2006) and aims at:

- Making information about available transport services easily accessible,
- Providing support for finding the "best" set of transport services for a particular transport, including a match-making functionality that makes it easier for potential transport chain actors to find each other and negotiate with potential collaborators,

---

P. Davidsson (✉)
Malmö University, Malmö, Sweden

Blekinge Institute of Technology, Karlskrona, Sweden
e-mail: paul.davidsson@mah.se

M.G. Friberger • A. Jacobsson • J. A. Persson
Malmö University, Malmö, Sweden
e-mail: marie.friberger@mah.se; andreas.jacobsson@mah.se; Jan.A.Persson@mah.se

J. Holmgren
Blekinge Institute of Technology, Karlskrona, Sweden
e-mail: johan.holmgren@bth.se

S. Ossowski (ed.), *Agreement Technologies*, Law, Governance and Technology Series 8, DOI 10.1007/978-94-007-5583-3_31,

- Supporting the negotiation and collaboration between actors in a transport chain (see Sect. 31.4 for the definition of a transport chain), and
- Lowering the entry barriers for small-sized companies to participate in highly integrated transport chains by providing low cost and easy-to-use software tools.

Ideally, PnP TCM should be implemented in a completely distributed fashion, both with respect to control and information, and it should be seamlessly interoperable with relevant legacy Enterprise Resource Planning (ERP) systems of the participating actors. The PnP TCM software has two types of user interfaces, one that interacts directly with legacy ERP systems, or other relevant information systems, and the other is a web browser interface, which may be particularly useful for small enterprises.

PnP TCM is based on the FREIGHTWISE Framework (FWF), which will be described in the next section. Then some key components of the PnP TCM software are introduced. This is followed by an analysis of how different types of agreement technologies are applied (or in some cases may be applied) to the PnP TCM software.

31.2 The FREIGHTWISE Framework

PnP TCM is based on the FREIGHTWISE framework (FWF) (Fjørtoft et al. 2009) whose main purpose is to simplify the phases of planning, executing and following up transport services. An important aim is to do this without interfering with the internal processes and systems in the organizations corresponding to the users and providers of transport services. The FWF identifies four transport chain roles. A *Transport User* (TU) is anyone who wants to transport some goods. A *Transport Service Provider* (TSP) carries out the transport of the cargo, including the management of the transport services and the operation of the transport means and handling equipment. The *Transport Network Manager* (TNM) is responsible for providing information regarding the infrastructure related to planning and execution of transports. Finally, the *Transport Regulator* (TR) monitors that all transport services are completed according to existing regulations. All interaction between these actors makes use of a small set of well-defined *information packages*, for which the responsibilities and requirements for use are specified (see Fjørtoft et al. 2009).

The interaction between the transport chain actors is illustrated in Fig. 31.1. The figure shows what happens during the planning, execution and completion of a certain goods transport. Initially, the Transport Service Provider interacts with the Transport Network Managers using Transport Network Status (TNS) information packages in order to take into account information about the transport network. Based on this information it plans what transport services it should offer, which are then specified in terms of Transport Service Descriptions (TSDs) that are published to the Transport Users.

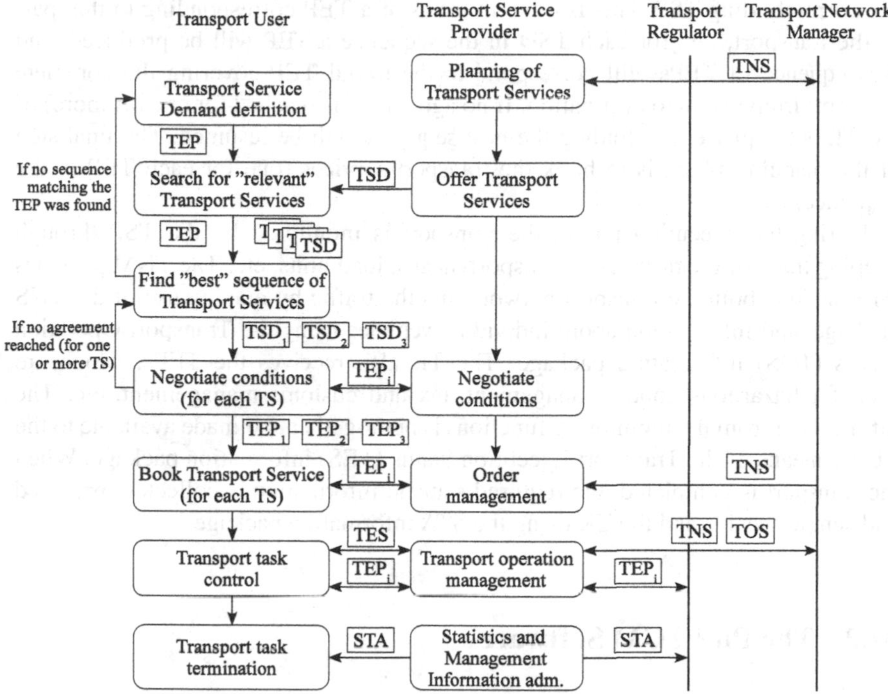

Fig. 31.1 The interaction between transport chain actors

At the beginning of the planning process for a goods transport, the TU specifies its transport demands, which result in an initial Transport Execution Plan (TEP) covering the complete transport from origin to destination. The TEP is initial, or preliminary in the sense that it specifies the items that are to be transported, the desired time and date of pickup and delivery, the origin and destination, and the condition requirements of the items during the transport (e.g., ambient temperature), but not which Transport Service(s) to use. The next step is to identify those transport services that potentially can be used to meet the transport demands specified in the initial TEP. This is done by searching among the TSDs published by the TSPs (which could be a locally stored subset of all TSDs as the TU subscribes for potentially relevant TSDs) and selecting those TSDs that are considered relevant for fulfilling the requirements of the TEP.

The set of selected TSDs then provides the input to the next step, which is to find the sequence of TSDs that satisfies the requirements of the TEP. If more than one such sequence is found, the one that is "best" according to one or more criteria, such as, cost, reliability, environmental impact, etc., is chosen. If no sequence that satisfies the requirements is found, the TEP needs to be revised, e.g., with respect to desired time of delivery (or, additional TSDs need to be found). When a sequence is found, it is time to negotiate the detailed conditions for each of the TSD with the corresponding TSP. This is done in terms of a TEP corresponding to that part of the transport, i.e., for each TSD in the sequence a TEP will be produced, and the sequence of TEPs will correspond to the initial TEP covering the complete transport from origin to destination. If no agreement is reached for one (or more) of the TEPs the process of finding the best sequence will be resumed. The final step of the planning phase is to book the transport services (one for each TEP in the sequence).

During the execution phase, the transport is monitored by the TSP through keeping track of the driver, the transport means, load units, etc. The TNM provides information about the transport network and the traffic by making use of the TNS package, and information about individual vehicles using the Transport Operation Status (TOS) information package. The TR also receives the TEPs, which are used for hazardous goods management, tax and customs management, etc. The information from the monitoring functions is put together and made available to the TU by means of the Transport Execution Status (TES) information package. When the transport is completed, the required statistic information is collected, prepared and sent to the TU and the TR using the STA information package.

31.3 The PnP TCM Software

For the design of the PnP TCM system, we applied the Gaia methodology (Zambonelli et al. 2003). We here give a brief overview of the PnP TCM system, a more detailed description of the approach, including an overview of the design process, is available in Davidsson et al. (2011).

On the system level, the PnP TCM system mainly has a distributed architecture, in which software clients that represent different transport chain actors, runs locally and interacts directly with each other in a peer-to-peer fashion. In addition, there is a Gatekeeper facility that decides who should be allowed to enter the PnP TCM system, provides basic information about connected actors, etc.

We specify the PnP TCM software clients as multi-agent systems. In Fig. 31.2, simplified versions of the multi-agent systems for the TU and TSP clients are illustrated. Full versions of the clients are presented in Davidsson et al. (2011).

Optimizer. From the set of locally stored TSDs, the task of the Optimizer (TU) is to find the "best" sequence of TSDs that satisfies the requirements of a TEP, according to one or more criteria, such as, cost, reliability, environmental impact, etc.

The TSD Announcers and Finders. The task of the Announcer (TSP) is to distribute TSDs to those TUs who find them relevant, i.e., subscribers of TSDs (and to notify the TUs if TSDs are no longer valid or have changed). The task of the Finder (TU) is to provide the Optimizer with all currently relevant TSDs.

Negotiation, Booking and Order Managers. The task of the Negotiation and Booking Manager (TU) is to book a transport service for each TSD in the sequence

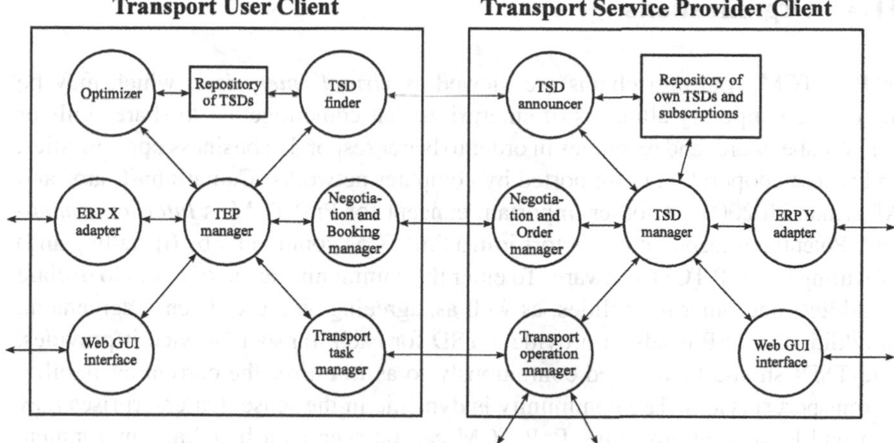

Fig. 31.2 Simplified architectures of the TU and TSP (PnP TCM) software clients

of TSDs provided by the Optimizer (which has been converted to a sequence of TEPs by the TEP Manager) according to the preferences of the TU. Thus, the output is a sequence of TEPs that are agreed upon with those TSPs that provide the transport services included in the transport solution. The task of the Negotiation and Order Manager (TSP) is to secure agreements with TUs according to the preferences of the TSP.

Transport Task and Transport Operation Managers. These agents manage the information exchange between the TU, TSP and TNM during the execution of transports.

Interface Agents. From the users' perspective, the complexity of the process of setting up a transport chain should be hidden by the PnP TCM software. As mentioned earlier, there are, at least, two types of interfaces:

- A web-based interface, which can be used by all types of users, independently of company size and IT maturity. One version for TUs, which consists of a number of different views specialized for each of the phases in the process, and one version for the TSPs, also with a number of different views.
- An adapter agent interface, which makes the PnP TCM software interoperable with the user's ERP or other legacy systems. An adapter may have to be developed for each ERP system, but once it is developed it can be re-used by other organizations using the same system. One approach to implementing the adapters is the general wrapper agent solution based on open source freeware introduced by Davidsson et al. (2006) that makes it possible for any business system to exchange (administrational) information with any other business system.

31.4 Organizations

In PnP TCM, transport chains are viewed as *virtual enterprises*, which may be defined as temporary alliances of enterprises that come together to share skills or core competencies and resources in order to better respond to business opportunities, and whose cooperation is supported by computer networks (Camarinha-Matos and Afsarmanesh 2003). Another important concept for PnP TCM is *Internet community*. Potential transport chain actors join a PnP TCM community by (installing and) executing the PnP TCM software. To enter the community, an actor needs to declare its address and other formalities, as well as, agreeing on a user license agreement. In addition, a TSP needs to provide a TSD for each transport service it provides. The TSDs should be updated continuously so as to mirror the current availability of transport services. The community is dynamic in the sense that enterprises may join and leave it at any time. PnP TCM can be seen as a breeding environment (Camarinha-Matos and Afsarmanesh 2003) for transport chains, i.e., an association of enterprises that have both the potential and the ambition to collaborate with each other through the establishment of long-term cooperation agreements and through an interoperable infrastructure.

The set of installed PnP TCM software clients can be viewed to form an *artificial society*. Davidsson (2001) has identified four types of artificial societies: open, closed, semi-closed, and semi-open. These categories balance the trade-off between important society properties, such as, openness, flexibility, robustness, and trustfulness. In open societies there are no restrictions at all for joining the society, which makes it very open and flexible, but not robust and trustworthy. In an FWF setting, this may correspond to that all interaction is performed in an ad-hoc fashion, e.g., TSDs are published openly on the WWW and the TUs need to find transport offers, e.g., through the use of general WWW search engines. The opposite is true for closed societies where all members must be known when the society is initiated. In an FWF setting, a closed society solution may be a completely centralized system in which all information is stored and through which all interaction between the transport chain actors is mediated. In many situations, such as in breeding environments for transport chains, there is a need for societies that balance the trade-off between the society properties. We will therefore limit our discussion to the two intermediate categories.

An important actor in the context of artificial societies is the "owner" of the society, or environment owner. By this we mean, the person or organization that has the power to decide which software entities may enter, which roles they are allowed to occupy, what communication language should be used, the set of norms and rules that are valid within the society, etc.

In semi-closed artificial societies, external software agents are not allowed to enter. However, actors have the possibility to initiate new software agents in the society, which will act on behalf of the actor. In semi-closed societies, there is a (central) physical environment, in which the agents (representing their owners) execute and communicate with other agents. This requires that the actors' agents can access some level of mutual communication properties, which are included in the breeding environment. Semi-closed societies convey almost the same degree of openness as semi-open societies, but are less flexible. From a FWF perspective, they fail to meet the requirement of a distributed solution. On the other hand, they have a larger potential for implementing important society attributes, such as, security and trustfulness.

The main difference to semi-closed artificial societies is that, in semi-open societies, agents execute locally on the clients individual computer systems. Another distinction is that the environment owner is no longer in control of the agents even though the environment owner still has the power e.g., to dictate the rules of engagement within the society. In order to meet security-related requirements, semi-open societies are equipped with a *Gatekeeper*, to which every agent needs to connect before entering the society. In addition, the Gatekeeper, being a trusted third party, may also mediate the payment of transport services, provide contract validation, etc.

31.5 Argumentation and Negotiation

Argumentation and negotiation occurs in PnP TCM in order to enable the TU and TSP clients to agree upon the particular conditions of the transport services (a sequence of TEPs) that represent a transport solution. The TSDs, as specified by the TSP, may sometimes not specify all information that are needed when building transport solutions and the Optimizer therefore may have to make particular assumptions, which need to be negotiated before a contract can be signed, e.g., concerning prices of transport services.

There is a long tradition in the area of agent-based systems of studying the automation of reaching agreements. From work in the negotiation area (cf. Jennings et al. 2001), we identify four different components as relevant for the PnP TCM setting, namely:

- A negotiation set, representing the space of possible obligations agents can make,
- A protocol, which defines the legal obligations that the agents can make,
- A collection of strategies, one for each agent, which determines what obligations the enterprises will make, and
- A rule that determines when the negotiation is over and a deal has been closed.

In the negotiation between a TU and TSP the negotiation set consists of the different terms and conditions specified in the TEP (and the possible values they can assume).

The protocol has two components, the pre-booking agreement as specified by a TEP, and the actual order (or booking), which is also specified as a TEP. The negotiation results in an electronic contract, in this case a TEP, which govern the collaboration process. Electronic contracts are to be regarded as virtual representations of traditional contracts, i.e., “formalizations of the behavior of a

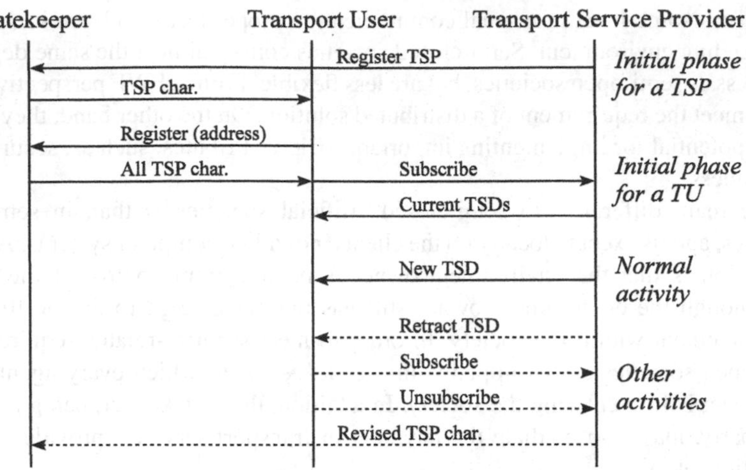

Fig. 31.3 Illustration of the interactions involved in the TSD subscription process

group of agents that jointly agree on a specific business activity" (Lopes Cardoso and Oliveira 2004). Electronic contracts usually have a set of identified roles, obligations or prohibitions to be fulfilled by the parties involved in the relationship. The FREIGHTWISE framework focuses on obligations, i.e., that an agent's role is defined by the obligations it has towards other agents to bring about a certain state of affairs before a certain deadline.

The general strategy of the Negotiation Manager of a TU is to first reach pre-booking agreements for all the TEPs in the sequence, and then to place actual orders for each of the TEPs. If agreement cannot be reached for one or more of the TEPs (and the alternative choices that may have been provided by the Optimizer has been tried), this is reported to the TEP Manager who then asks the Optimizer to find a new sequence of TSDs (or possibly just replace the ones for which negotiation failed). To be able to find a new sequence of TSDs, it might be necessary to update the initial TEP and to extend the local repository of TSDs, e.g., by subscribing to new types of TSDs or to TSDs from TSPs for which the TU is not already subscribing. An illustration of the interactions (between the Gatekeeper, TUs and TSPs) involved in the TSD subscription process is given in Fig. 31.3.

The use of a pre-booking phase in PnP TCM is a solution to a rather general problem concerning when it is appropriate to allocate resources in a negotiation situation. For instance, in the Contract Net Protocol (Smith 1980), bidders for a contract allocate their resources already when they send proposals. This would in PnP TCM correspond to that TSPs would allocate transport resources to a TU already when a negotiation starts concerning a particular TEP, with the consequence that a TSP would not be able to participate in parallel negotiations for the same resource. Several solutions have been proposed for dealing with the problem of when to allocate resources, e.g., levelled commitment (Sandholm and Lesser 2001), in which contract breaching is allowed if a penalty is paid. However, none of the

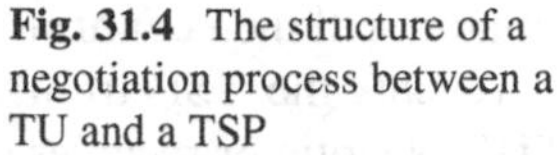

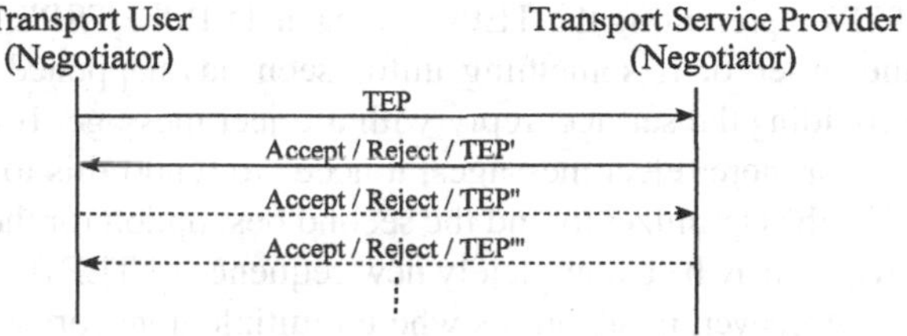

Fig. 31.4 The structure of a negotiation process between a TU and a TSP

suggested solutions has the potential to work in the PnP TCM context, mainly because multiple negotiations typically appear in parallel and different negotiations often depend on each other, e.g., when several TUs may need to negotiate in parallel for the same transport service (TSD).

The pre-booking phase starts when the Negotiation Manager of the TU sends the first version of the TEP to the Negotiation Manager of the TSP (for each of the TEPs in the sequence). The TSP's Negotiator then has three options: (i) to accept the TEP as it is, thus confirming the pre-booking of the transport service, (ii) to reject the request, or (iii) to modify the TEP by changing one or more terms or conditions, let us denote this revised version for TEP'. The two first options will end the negotiation (by sending an accept or reject message to the TU), whereas the third option will give back the initiative to the TU. The TU's Negotiator now has the same three options as the TSP's Negotiator had: to accept TEP', to reject it, or to modify it. As before, the two first options will terminate the negotiation, whereas the third will provide a new bid (TEP") to the TSP to consider. The negotiation will continue until either the TU or the TSP accepts or rejects the current TEP, as illustrated in Fig. 31.4. There should also be a time-out mechanism so that a negotiation process automatically ends if an agreement concerning a TEP has not been reached, e.g., within a certain number of negotiation iterations.

The Negotiators may be given limits for what is acceptable by their "owners" (the humans/organizations on whose behalf they negotiate) regarding the terms and conditions that are subject to negotiation. This can make the negotiation automated to a large extent. However, when such directives are not available, it may be necessary for a Negotiator to check with its owner whether a certain bid is acceptable or not. Moreover, it may be necessary for the TU's Negotiator to coordinate a number of negotiations. For instance, it may have been given a limit on the total cost for a transport solution. It should be emphasized here that different owners might want their agents to operate in different levels of autonomy; for example, one owner might want to delegate the responsibility of contract signing to the booking manager agent while another owner may want a human to take care of that responsibility. Therefore it might be necessary in PnP TCM to develop different negotiation and booking strategies for different agents.

After agreements (pre-bookings) have been reached for all transport services in a transport solution, the next phase is to book (order) all the services. The TU's Negotiator initiates the booking phase by sending the agreed-upon, final version of the TEPs (one for each transport service in the solution) to the Negotiators of the

TSPs representing the TEPs. For each TEP, the TSP's Negotiator, will then confirm the order, or if something unforeseen has happened that prevents the TSP from providing the service, reply with a reject message. If the TU's Negotiator receives one or more reject messages, it needs to report this to the TEP Manager, who then asks the Optimizer to find the second best option for the missing transport service(s) (which may be a completely new sequence of TEPs).

Moreover, in situations where multiple transport services in a transport solution (sequence of TEPs) is provided by the same TSP, it is possible to negotiate multiple TEPs in the same negotiation. This will typically make the behaviors of the Negotiators considerably more complex as they need to consider dependencies between TEPs in the same negotiation. However, a potential gain is that there will be fewer complex dependencies between negotiation protocols.

31.6 Semantics

In order for the actors of the PnP TCM to exchange and act on information exchanged among them, interoperability issues need to be addressed. At a syntactic level, this includes having a common data format. However, to enable combining information from several sources, semantic interoperability needs to be addressed.

The FREIGHTWISE framework defines a set of information packages (Fjørtoft et al. 2009), e.g., TSD and TEP, which have been harmonized with the Universal Business Language (UBL) (Bosak et al. 2006). While this work has provided a basis for what information needs to be exchanged as part of PnP TCM, much of the semantics of the domain are not explicitly modeled. Thus, information packages are of use when it comes to the transfer of documents between partners and may enable syntactic interoperability. However, to properly interpret this information, align it with other conceptualizations, and to infer new facts, further development is necessary.

For example, in its current conception, strings are often used to model aspects that could be more usefully modeled as classes or instances, with an identification scheme that could be reused by all TCM actors. The use of identifications does not mean that all partners have to use the same naming, but makes it possible to explicitly state that two identifications refer to the same real world object (for example, when two names exist for a city). Such modeling would also include arranging the classes in subclass hierarchies and could include defining necessary and sufficient conditions for these classes. It can also include a clearer modeling of part-of relations between geographic regions. More specifically, if the information packages of FREIGTWISE are examined, for the TSD, it is possible to more clearly model categories of transportation, goods, and environmental profiles.

A clarification of the semantics related to TCM can also be seen a building block for the modeling of norms and agreements. For example, both the TU and the TSP need to use the same terminology, or there needs to be a way to translate from one to another. Using semantic technologies is one way of achieving this. Further, to match between requests and offerings, it is necessary to be able to model and reason with, e.g., part-of and subclass relations.

An elaboration of the semantics of the FREIGHTWISE information packages could be further informed by work by others on semantic representation of logistics services (e.g., Hoxha et al. 2010) and on adding semantics based customization to UBL document schemes (e.g., Yarimagan and Dogac 2007).

31.7 Norms

When agreements between the actors in a transport chain are reached, as well as, when subscribing for TSDs, publishing TSDs, etc., the application of norms as rules that govern behavior and interaction is important. Two types of norms can be distinguished, regulative norms, often described as obligations, prohibitions and permissions, and constitutive norms, such that regulate the creation of institutional facts. Often, regulative norms are formalized as goals of individual actors or agents, and constitutive norms as beliefs of the system. Regulative norms are based on the notion of a conditional obligation with an associated sanction. This sanction may be specified as an economic fine, but it may also be in the shape of non-specified sanction of, e.g., blame and reputation degradation. Obligations are defined in terms of goals of the agent, prohibitions are obligations concerning negated variables, and permissions are specified as exceptions to obligations.

In PnP TCM, a constitutive norm may be that a contract must be signed by all parties when an agreement has been reached, and that the contract is to be valid and carried out. Another type of constitutive norm may be that sensitive information may only be shared with intended parties (to avoid information leakage in, e.g., negotiation processes). In a contract structure, such as the one that may occur in the TEP between TSP and TU, regulative norms can be applied to enforce agreements. To a TSP, an obligation is defined as a goal of ensuring that a certain good is delivered at the agreed price and on time. Accordingly, it is prohibited for a TSP to break that obligation. However, a situation may arise when an actor bound by an agreement is permitted by the counteracting part to break the obligation, and, for instance, deliver the good at a later time than agreed upon. In such a case, no sanctions may by enforced upon the actor. However, if the obligation is broken without permission, the gatekeeper facility may enforce a penalty upon the actor.

In order to ensure that the norms are not broken or violated, the gatekeeper facility could also be equipped with a norm-enhancing functionality in the shape of a promoter capacity that monitors and rewards norm compliance among the interacting actors. Functionality to deliver sanctions or punishments, for instance, in the form of a fine (or blame), when norms are broken could also be included in the gatekeeper facility.

Since intelligent agents, such as the ones in the PnP TCM system, can be designed to cope with individual goals and conflicting behavior, norms that govern the rules of encounter, as well as mechanisms set to enforce those, are instrumental means of reaching agreements, as well as, interacting in a sound, organized and just manner.

31.8 Trust

Trust is typically connected to the perception of another part, e.g., a potential business partner, and thereby to the willingness of getting involved in business with that partner. For anyone using the PnP TCM approach, there is a need to establish trust both in the system and in the actors that a certain user may get involved with. A company's reputation is one type of information that influence the perception of trust, security-enhancing mechanisms such as authentication and encryption is another. In other words, there are several aspects that potentially could affect the perception of trust in the context of the PnP TCM approach, which will now be discussed.

Since the PnP TCM software clients typically run on a company's local computer, it is important that there is no leakage of information, i.e., information should not be exchanged with other types of software, e.g., ERP systems, residing on the computer. This requires careful design, which among many things promotes transparency of the ERP adapter agents in PnP TCM while at the same time ensuring confidentiality and integrity of the information.

As a PnP TCM software client exchanges information with the clients of other organizations, it is important that the user of the software has a clear understanding of what the information is composed of and to what extent it can be shared with other users. The specified information packages and the associated semantics could help to raise the user's understanding of the content of information, as well as, the limits of sharing it.

The PnP TCM software client should be able to handle dedicated information exchanges with certain other PnP TCM users without accidentally or deliberately sharing the information with all the PnP TCM community members. For instance, it may be the case that information about special offers or conditions during a negotiation about a transport should only be shared with a particular member. The design of the PnP software client with direct client-to-client information exchange supports this. Information should not be revealed or modified by unauthorized parties. Identification, authentication and encryption are important mechanisms to ensure confidentially, integrity and availability of the information in this context.

In order for a TSP to reserve, negotiate and accept a booking of a service, it is vital that the user can trust the identity of the TU. This requires a mechanism of confirming the identity of a PnP TCM user and its associated information. Important functions in this respect are identification and authentication protocols.

This concerns the internal handling of the identity, within the community, i.e., a user should typically not be able to have multiple identities and assume new identities within the PnP TCM community. Furthermore, the identity should be certified (when possible) with respect to external information, such as, official postal address, corporate identification number, and other types of relevant company information. The gatekeeper facility has an important role in this context. Moreover, norms could support the maintenance of identities by deploying rules, which encourage users to inform the gatekeeper of suspicious handling of identities.

In order to increase the willingness of a TU to use a particular transport service, access to information connected to a reputation of the corresponding TSP could be provided. Such information is ideally provided by other TUs in the PnP TCM community that have done business together with that TSP in the past. There are many potential information types to consider for inclusion in a reputation like this, e.g., general types for agreements-related information, such as, role fulfillment, relationship, knowledge, experience, credential, competence, honesty, favorability, and faith (Bagheri and Ghorbani 2006). Other interesting aspects include quality of service in freight transport-related information, such as, cost, transport time, punctuality, etc.

Interestingly, the defined information packages in FWF include information, which can be used for creating reputation-based information, and hence can be gathered by the PnP TCM system without the explicit interaction or consent of the user, i.e., the user need not actively agree to or provide any additional information. Examples of such reputation-based information that can be computed from the information packages are, for instance, delivery time deviation and amount of delivery units of a certain type (by STA and by accepted TEPs). Other types of reputation-based information cannot directly be handled by the information packages in FWF, but require extensions to them. Such reputations may concern different dimensions, such as, efficiency and honesty during negotiation and booking, as well as, reliability and efficiency during execution.

To sum up, in order to increase the trust level of the PnP TCM system we have adopted a semi-open approach. The Gatekeeper, being a trusted third party, may also mediate the payment of transport services, provide authentication of identity and contract validation, etc. Moreover, the Gatekeeper may be responsible for a reputation system concerning the TUs and TSPs. For instance, if a TSP (or TU) has refused to act according to the agreement between two parties, the other part can inform the Gatekeeper, who keeps track of the complaints, and if necessary takes an appropriate action. It could also be the case that a TSP (or TU) refuses to follow the rules of the community, e.g., not replying to requests.

Since the PnP TCM TU client includes an Optimizer agent with the task to provide the most relevant transport solution for the user, there can be a risk that the users (both TSP and TU) suspect that it may be tweaked to suggest a particular type of transport solution or favoring a particular provider. The integrity of the optimization algorithms included in the PnP TCM TU clients must thus be ensured, for instance, by the deployment of encryption schemes.

31.9 Concluding Remarks

We have analyzed the use of agreement technologies in a concrete application concerning the planning and execution of intermodal goods transport. The conclusion is that all five considered agreement technologies, i.e., semantics, norms, organizations, argumentation and negotiation, and trust, play critical roles in the realization of PnP TCM. The analysis also provided pointers to further research and development of the PnP TCM system.

References

Bagheri, E., and A.A. Ghorbani. 2006. Behavior analysis through reputation propagation in a multi-context environment. In *Proceedings of the 2006 international conference on privacy, security and trust: Bridge the gap between PST technologies and business services, PST '06*, 40:1–40:7. New York: ACM. http://doi.acm.org/10.1145/1501434.1501482.

Bosak, J., T. McGrath, and G.K. Holman. 2006. Universal business language v2.0. Organization for the advancement of structured information standards (OASIS), standard. http://docs.oasis-open.org/ubl/.

Camarinha-Matos, L., and H. Afsarmanesh. 2003. Elements of a base VE infrastructure. *Journal of Computers in Industry* 51(2): 139–163.

Davidsson, P. 2001. Categories of artificial societies. Engineering societies in the agents world II. Lecture notes in computer science, vol. 2203, ed. A. Omicini, P. Petta and R. Tolksdorf, 1–9. Berlin/New York: Springer.

Davidsson, P., A. Hederstierna, A. Jacobsson, J.A. Persson, B. Carlsson, S.J. Johansson, A. Nilsson, G. Ågren, and S. Östholm. 2006. The concept and technology of plug and play business. In *Proceedings of the 8th international conference on enterprise information systems*, Paphos, ed. Y. Manolopoulos, J. Filipe, P. Constantopoulos and J. Cordeiro, 213–217.

Davidsson, P., J. Holmgren, J.A. Persson, and A. Jacobsson. 2011. Plug and play transport chain management: Agent-based support to the planning and execution of transports. In *e-Business and telecommunications*, Communications in computer and information science, vol. 130, ed. M.S. Obaidat and J. Filipe, 139–155. Berlin/Heidelberg/New York: Springer.

Davidsson, P., L. Ramstedt, and J. Törnquist. 2006. Inter-organization interoperability in transport chains using adapters based on open source freeware. In *Interoperability of enterprise software and applications*, ed. D. Konstantas, et al. 35–43. London: Springer.

Fjørtoft, K., H. Westerheim, A. Vannesland, and M. Hagaseth. 2009. Deliverable D13.2 – FREIGHTWISE framework architecture, release 3. http://www.freightwise.info.

Hoxha, J., A. Scheuermann, and S. Bloehdorn. 2010. An approach to formal and semantic representation of logistics services. In *Proceedings of the workshop on artificial intelligence and logistics (AILog) at the 19th European conference on artificial intelligence (ECAI 2010)*, Lisbon, ed. K. Schill, B. Scholz-Reiter and L. Frommberger.

Jennings, N., P. Faratin, A. Lomuscio, S. Parsons, C. Sierra, and M. Wooldridge. 2001. Automated negotiation: Prospects, methods and challenges. *International Journal of Group Decision and Negotiation* 10(2): 199–215.

Lopes Cardoso, H., and E.C. Oliveira. 2004. Virtual enterprise normative framework within electronic institutions. Engineering societies in the agents world V. In *Proceedings of the ESAW*, Lecture notes in computer science, vol. 3451, ed. M.P. Gleizes, A. Omicini and F. Zambonelli, 14–32. Berlin/New York: Springer.

Sandholm, T.W., and V.R. Lesser. 2001. Leveled commitments contracts and strategic breach. *Games and Economic Behaviour* 35: 212–270.

Smith, R.G. 1980. The contract net protocol: High-level communication and control in a distributed problem solver. *IEEE Transactions on Computers* C-29(12): 1104–1113.

Yarimagan, Y., and A. Dogac. 2007. Semantics based customization of UBL document schemas. *Distributed and Parallel Databases* 22(2–3): 107–131.

Zambonelli, F., N.R. Jennings, and M. Wooldridge. 2003. Developing multiagent systems: The gaia methodology. *ACM Transactions on Software Engineering and Methodologies* 12(3): 317–370.

Chapter 32
ANTE: Agreement Negotiation in Normative and Trust-Enabled Environments

Henrique Lopes Cardoso, Joana Urbano, Ana Paula Rocha, António J.M. Castro, and Eugénio Oliveira

32.1 Introduction

Negotiation and task allocation have been in the multi-agent systems realm since its inception as a research field. More recently, social aspects of agenthood have received increasing attention, namely developments in the fields of normative and trust systems.

The ANTE[1] framework encompasses results of research efforts on three main agreement technology concepts, namely negotiation, normative environments and computational trust. ANTE is therefore the corollary of an ongoing long-term research project, which has been targeting the domain of B2B electronic contracting, although having been conceived as a more general framework with a wider range of applications in mind.

This chapter provides an overview of the main guidelines of this project, together with a brief description of its most important research contributions. Furthermore, two application domains for this framework are explored: automated B2B electronic contracting, and disruption management in the context of an airline company operational control.

Section 32.2 describes in broad lines the main concepts of the ANTE framework, and identifies the main research contributions in each of its main research areas: automatic negotiation, normative environments and computational trust.

[1] Agreement Negotiation in Normative and Trust-enabled Environments.

H. Lopes Cardoso (✉) • J. Urbano, • A.P. Rocha, • A.J.M. Castro and E. Oliveira
LIACC, Department of Engineering, Informática, Faculdade de Engenharia, Universidade do Porto, Rua Dr. Roberto Frias, 4200-465 Porto, Portugal
e-mail: hlc@fe.up.pt; joana.urbano@fe.up.pt; arocha@fe.up.pt; antonio.castro@fe.up.pt; eco@fe.up.pt

S. Ossowski (ed.), *Agreement Technologies*, Law, Governance and Technology Series 8, DOI 10.1007/978-94-007-5583-3_32,

Section 32.3 describes the two application domains identified above and provides details regarding how ANTE has been exploited to fit those domains. Section 32.4 concludes the chapter.

32.2 The ANTE Framework

ANTE addresses the issue of multi-agent collective work in a comprehensive way, covering both negotiation as a mechanism for finding mutually acceptable agreements, and the enactment of such agreements. Furthermore, the framework also includes the evaluation of the enactment phase, with the aim of improving future negotiations.

Taking a broad perspective, an agreement can in this context be a solution obtained using a distributed cooperative problem solving approach. Therefore, a wide range of problems can be tackled. The agreement binds each negotiation participant to its contribution to the overall solution. It is therefore useful to represent the outcome of a successful negotiation process in a way that allows for checking if the contributions of each participant do in fact contribute to a successful execution of the agreement. A normative environment, within which agent interactions that are needed to enact the agreement will take place, takes care of this monitoring stage. Assessing the performance of each contribution is essential to enhance future negotiations. Computational trust may therefore be used to appropriately capture the trustworthiness of negotiation participants, both in terms of the quality of their proposals when building the solution (i.e. the practicability of the approach) and in terms of their ability to successfully enact their share.

In the following we provide some insight to the most important contributions of our developments in each of the aforementioned agreement technologies.

32.2.1 Negotiation

Negotiation is a form of decision-making where two or more parties jointly search a space of possible solutions with the goal of reaching a consensus. People use negotiation as a means of compromise in order to reach mutual agreements. In general, negotiation is defined as an interactive process whose goal is to achieve an agreement between interested parties. In competitive environments (as it is the case of e-business), self-interested agents have their own goals and are thus intrinsically competitive among each other; but even in this case it is also desirable for negotiating agents to have an incentive to cooperate in order to achieve efficient and mutually beneficial solutions. In cooperative environments, agents work together to find an optimal solution, e.g. by merging a set of multiple partial solutions. In ANTE, we have developed a negotiation protocol (Q-Negotiation) suitable for both competitive and cooperative environments that conducts to the selection of the best possible solutions (Rocha et al. 2005). Using this protocol, negotiation participants engage themselves in a sequential negotiation process composed of multiple rounds, by exchanging multi-attribute proposals and counter-proposals, trying to convince each other to modify the values for attributes they evaluate the most. The negotiation protocol selects the participants that, based on their capabilities and availability, will be able to make the best possible deal. However, since agents are autonomous entities, they are free to quit negotiation whenever they feel that no further concession is in their own interest.

It encompasses two important features:

- A multi-attribute evaluation to select the most favorable proposals at each round.
- A learning capability in order to enable agents to make the best possible deals even when faced with incomplete information and when operating in dynamic environments.

Attaching utility values to different attributes helps to solve the problem of multi-attribute evaluation. Generally, an evaluation formula is a linear combination of the current attribute values weighted by their corresponding utility values. However, in some cases, it can be a very difficult task to attach absolute values to attributes' utilities. A more natural and realistic situation is to simply impose a preference order over attributes' values and/or attributes themselves. Q-Negotiation adopts a multi-attribute evaluation based on a qualitative, as opposed to quantitative, measure. A learning capability is included through a Reinforcement Learning algorithm. The choice of this kind of learning algorithm has two main reasons. First, reinforcement learning algorithms support continuous, on-line learning during the negotiation process itself by making decisions according to the environment reactions in the past. The history of a negotiation (past rounds) is a crucial piece of information to be considered when deciding what to do in the next round. Second, reinforcement learning includes not only exploitation but also exploration facilities. In dynamic environments or in the presence of incomplete information, exploration (i.e. trying out new different possibilities) becomes a powerful technique. Learning is done through a qualitative comment that an agent receives, concerning its last proposal, from negotiating partners. The negotiation process results in the selection of a set of agents that commit themselves to the issues discussed during negotiation. This agreement may be formalized into a contract and subject to monitoring by a normative environment, as discussed in the following section.

32.2.2 Normative Environment

The normative dimension of a multi-agent system may, in general, encompass two perspectives on the interactions that norms are supposed to govern. Norms regulating pre-established interactions apply to the agent population as a whole, e.g. by specifying appropriate interaction conventions for negotiation. On the other hand, run-time norms are those that come into force when agents negotiate or adopt them to govern subsequent interactions (e.g. negotiated contracts). Within ANTE we are mostly concerned with the latter case, i.e., with norms that are agreed upon through a negotiation process.

In the context of agreement technologies, the role of a *normative environment* (Lopes Cardoso 2010) is twofold. Given the agreement on a possible solution as obtained from the negotiation phase, it is necessary to check if the partial contributions of individual agents make their way in enabling a successful overall resolution of the problem. In many cases, the execution of the solution is itself distributed, which requires agents to enact by themselves their part of the agreement. *Monitoring* this phase is therefore an important task. Furthermore, in non-cooperative or dynamic scenarios, it is possible that after successfully negotiating an agreement self-interested agents are no longer willing to fulfill their commitments. This puts in evidence the second role of a normative environment, that of *enforcing* norms by coercing agents to stand for their commitments.

The notion of norm has been used with different meanings. In ANTE, a norm is a rule prescribing some behavior that agents governed by that norm must meet in certain circumstances. Given that these norms will govern previously negotiated agreements, the normative environment should enable the run-time establishment of new normative relationships. The "normative shape" of the environment will therefore evolve and adapt to the actual normative relationships that are established. In order to make this feasible, we believe it is important to provide some infrastructure that facilitates the establishment of norm governed relationships: a supportive and extensible *normative framework* (Lopes Cardoso and Oliveira 2008) for framing the agreements that might be achieved. The main aim of this infrastructure is to assist software agents in the task of negotiating and establishing agreements that need an explicit representation for monitoring and enforcement purposes.

32.2.3 Trust

In Sect. 32.2.2, we addressed the role of normative environments for agreement technologies. In fact, control, legal norms and monitoring are common governance mechanisms used to reduce opportunism in business transactions (Bachmann 2001; Luhmann 1979; Sako 1998; Wathne and Heide 2000). However, the drafting and monitoring of detailed contracts is sometimes costly and ineffective, and trust is often seen as a complementary, or even supplementary, governance mechanism that helps reduce the risk associated with business transactions (Das and Teng 1998; Ireland and Webb 2007; Mayer et al. 1995; Wathne and Heide 2000; Williamson 1979).

Although trust is typically associated with uncertainty (for instance, in business transactions), it is an ubiquitous social concept present in everyday life. In fact, trust has been studied in several research areas in distinct fields such as close relationships, political relationships between countries, social networks, and even cooperative relationships. Computer science scholars, especially in the area of multi-agent systems, have been proposing *computational models of trust* that can be used to assist the decision making of agents when negotiating agreements, particularly in the phase of resource allocation.

Current research on computational trust models addresses the estimation of the trustworthiness of the target entities (individuals, groups, institutions, or things) by aggregating past evidence on these entities. These models tend to focus on some particular problem of computational trust, such as the modeling of the dynamics of trust (Jonker and Treur 1999), the context in which the evidence was produced (Urbano et al. 2011a), the use of reputation as a trust antecedent (Josang et al. 2007), and the modeling of trust in a socio-cognitive perspective (Castelfranchi and Falcone 2010).

Our approach to computational trust has as it main desideratum the ability to compute adequate estimations of trustworthiness in several different environments, including those of high dynamicity, where evidence on the agent in evaluation is scarce or even inexistent. Our model is composed of two basic components. The first one is Sinalpha, which computes general values of trustworthiness by relying on different properties of the dynamics of trust. Sinalpha models the trustworthiness of an agent using a function of α that presents a sinusoidal shape (see Eq. (32.1)). By setting $\delta = +0.5$, the trustworthiness value is restricted to the range $[0,1]$.

$$trustworthiness = \delta * (\sin \alpha + 1) \tag{32.1}$$

The trustworthiness score of the agent is minimum when $\alpha = 3\pi/2$ and maximum at $\alpha = 5\pi/2$. This score is updated using $\alpha_{i+1} = \alpha_i + \lambda \cdot \omega$, where λ reflects the outcome associated with the piece of evidence being aggregated (it assumes positive values for evidences with positive outcomes and negative values for evidences with negative outcomes, where $|\lambda^+| < |\lambda^-|$), and parameter ω is used to define the size of the ascending/descending step in the trustworthiness path. A detailed description of Sinalpha is given in Urbano et al. (2009).

The second component of our computational model is Contextual Fitness, a situation-aware tuner that downgrades the trustworthiness scores computed by Sinalpha in cases where the agent in evaluation has proved to behave poorly in the situation in assessment. Its mode of operation is based on the dynamic extraction of *tendencies of failure* from the past evidence of the agent, using the *information gain* metric (Quinlan 1986). This approach differs from other situation-aware computational trust approaches by its flexibility and ability to reason in terms of context even when the evidence on the agent in evaluation is scarce (Urbano et al. 2010b, 2011a).

32.3 Application Domains

In this Section we will describe two application domains being addressed by the technologies that integrate the ANTE framework.

32.3.1 B2B E-contracting

The first scenario addressed by ANTE is that of B2B electronic contracting. With a strong automation perspective, the scenario envisages the use of software agents negotiating on behalf of their principals, which are buyers or suppliers in a B2B network. Negotiation is therefore used to select, among a group of potential suppliers, the best ones to fit a particular business opportunity. Contracts resulting from successful negotiations are validated, registered and digitally signed, before being handed to the normative environment for monitoring and enforcement purposes. Finally, the way agents enact their contracts provides important information for trust building. A repository of trust and reputation information may then complete the circle by providing relevant inputs for future negotiations. The integration of all these stages is depicted in Fig. 32.1.

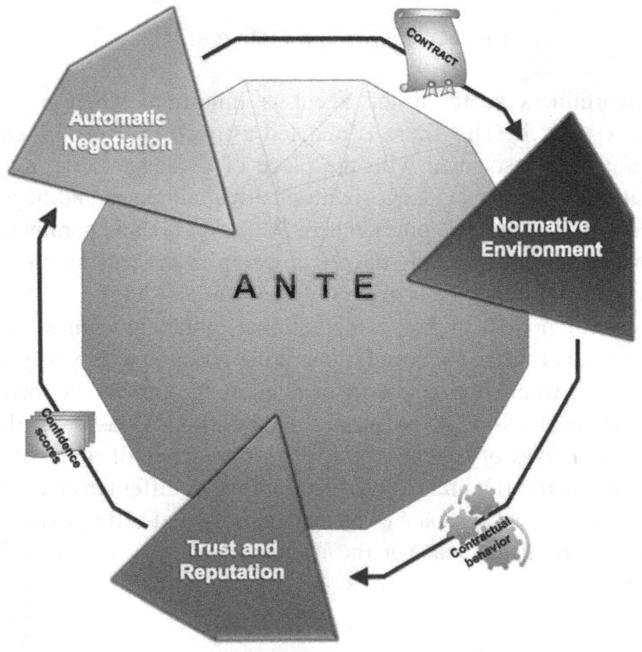

Fig. 32.1 ANTE

Important synergies are obtained from the integration of the three main research domains identified in Fig. 32.1. Negotiation is informed by trustworthiness assessments of negotiation participants. In ANTE, this may be put in practice in three different ways: using trust for preselecting the partners with whom to negotiate; evaluating negotiation proposals taking into account the trustworthiness of proposal issuers; or exploiting trust information when drafting a contract with a selected supplier, e.g. by proposing a sanction in case the supplier breaches the contract (thus trying to reduce the risk associated with doing business with a not fully trustworthy agent).

Connecting the monitoring facility of the normative environment with a computational trust engine means that we can use contractual evidences regarding the behavior of agents when enacting their contracts to build trust assessments. Our approach to modeling contractual obligations (Lopes Cardoso and Oliveira 2010) allows for a rich set of possible contract enactment outcomes (fulfillments, delays, breaches, and so on), which in turn enables a trust engine to weight differently the possible sub-optimal states that might be obtained (Urbano et al. 2010a, 2012a).

As mentioned in Sect. 32.2.2, connecting negotiation with a normative environment that provides a monitoring service opens up the possibility of providing some normative infrastructure that facilitates contract establishment. For that, the normative environment should provide a supportive and extensible normative framework. Inspired by notions from contract law theory, namely the use of "default rules" (Craswell 2000), we have proposed a model for this normative structure based on a hierarchy of *contexts* (Lopes Cardoso and Oliveira 2009), within which norms are created that may apply to sub-contexts. The context hierarchy tries to mimic the fact that in business it is often the case that a B2B contractual agreement forms the business context for more specific contracts that may be created. Each contract establishes a new context for norm applicability. A *norm defeasibility* approach (Lopes Cardoso and Oliveira 2008) is used to determine whether a norm should be inherited, for a specific situation, from an upper context. This feature allows the normative framework to be adapted (to better fit a particular contract case) and extended (allowing new contract types to be defined). The rationale behind this design is based on the assumption that "default rules" should be seen as facilitating rather than constraining contractual activity (Kaplow 2000).

32.3.1.1 Prototype

The ANTE framework has been realized as a JADE-based FIPA-compliant platform. In the case of the e-contracting application domain, as can be seen in Fig. 32.2, there are three kinds of agents in the platform: those that provide contracting services (upper part of the figure), namely negotiator, computational trust, ontology mapping, notary and normative environment; external agents whose role is to make a connection to real-world contract enactment events (e.g. deliveries, payments); and users of the system (lower part of the figure), representing buyers and suppliers.

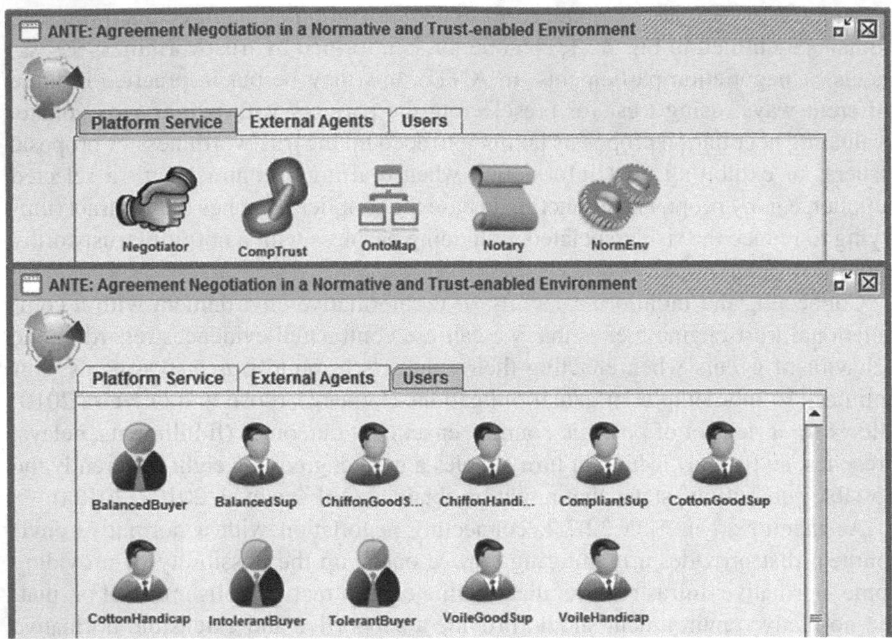

Fig. 32.2 ANTE main screen

Figure 32.3 shows a buyer interface for specifying its needs (left side) and for configuring a multi-attribute negotiation (right side) to take place using the negotiator service. Options include how trust is to be used in each of the negotiation steps, as described earlier in this section. Also, the buyer may indicate the type of contract that is to be created should negotiation succeed; norms governing specific contract types are already available in the normative environment, thus making it easier to establish a contract.

Figure 32.4 shows, on the buyer interface, the contracts it has already established (upper part) and a set of events related to their enactment (lower part). These events are automatically reported by the normative environment in the contract monitoring phase.

Turning to the supplier interface, in Fig. 32.5 we can inspect the negotiations that took place, together with the messages exchanged using the Q-Negotiation protocol described in Sect. 32.2.1.

The negotiator interface (see Fig. 32.6) shows the evolution of the proposals exchanged during a negotiation protocol in terms of their utility for the buyer that started the negotiation process.

The interface for the computational trust service (shown in Fig. 32.7) allows us to inspect how trustworthiness assessments are being computed, including the contractual evidences that are used as input for each agent. It also allows us to choose the mapping method that associates different weights to each of the possible contract enactment outcomes.

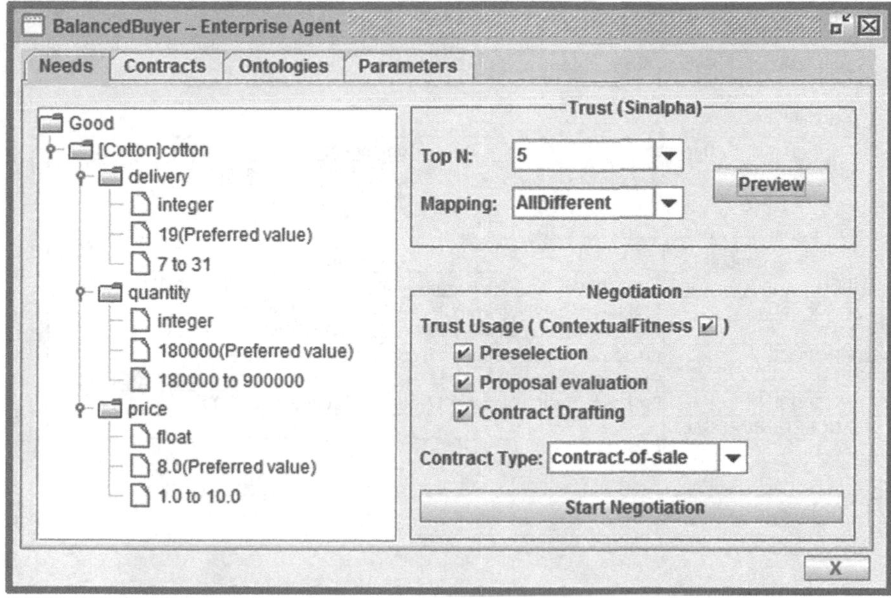

Fig. 32.3 Buyer's needs and negotiation configuration

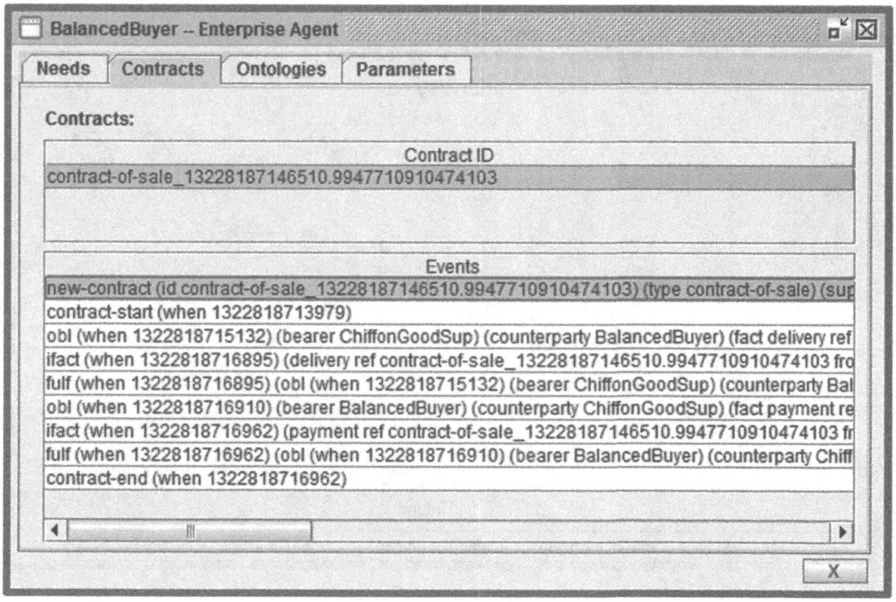

BalancedBuyer -- Enterprise Agent

Needs | Contracts | Ontologies | Parameters

Contracts:

Contract ID
contract-of-sale_13228187146510.9947710910474103

Events
new-contract (id contract-of-sale_13228187146510.9947710910474103) (type contract-of-sale) (sup
contract-start (when 1322818713979)
obl (when 1322818715132) (bearer ChiffonGoodSup) (counterparty BalancedBuyer) (fact delivery ref
ifact (when 1322818716895) (delivery ref contract-of-sale_13228187146510.9947710910474103 fro
fulf (when 1322818716895) (obl (when 1322818715132) (bearer ChiffonGoodSup) (counterparty Bal
obl (when 1322818716910) (bearer BalancedBuyer) (counterparty ChiffonGoodSup) (fact payment re
ifact (when 1322818716962) (payment ref contract-of-sale_13228187146510.9947710910474103 fr
fulf (when 1322818716962) (obl (when 1322818716910) (bearer BalancedBuyer) (counterparty Chiff
contract-end (when 1322818716962)

X

Fig. 32.4 Buyer's established contracts and their enactment

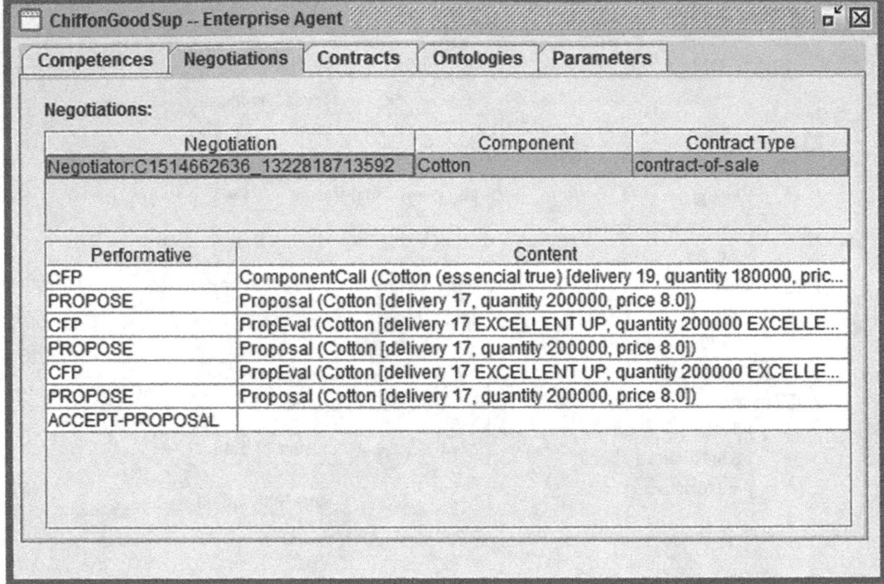

Negotiation	Component	Contract Type
Negotiator:C1514662636_1322818713592	Cotton	contract-of-sale

Performative	Content
CFP	ComponentCall (Cotton (essencial true) [delivery 19, quantity 180000, pric...
PROPOSE	Proposal (Cotton [delivery 17, quantity 200000, price 8.0])
CFP	PropEval (Cotton [delivery 17 EXCELLENT UP, quantity 200000 EXCELLE...
PROPOSE	Proposal (Cotton [delivery 17, quantity 200000, price 8.0])
CFP	PropEval (Cotton [delivery 17 EXCELLENT UP, quantity 200000 EXCELLE...
PROPOSE	Proposal (Cotton [delivery 17, quantity 200000, price 8.0])
ACCEPT-PROPOSAL	

Fig. 32.5 Supplier's negotiations

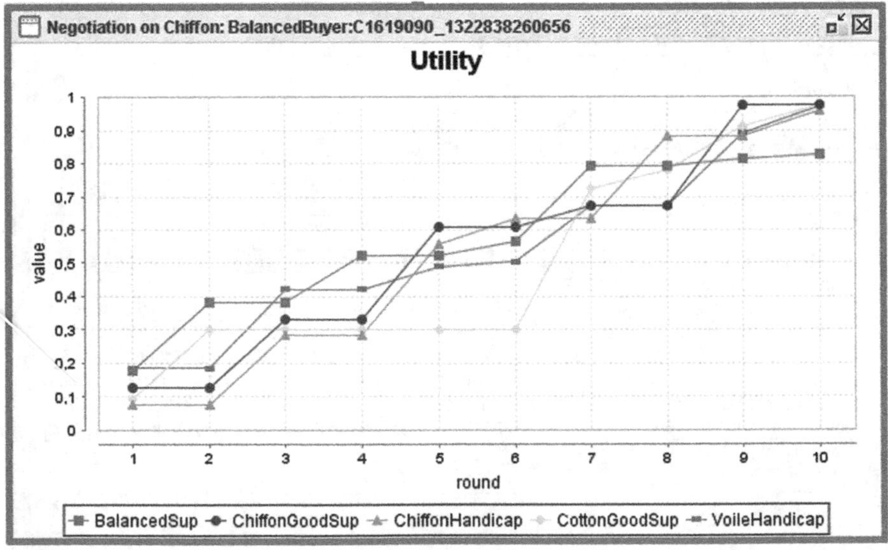

Fig. 32.6 Negotiator: proposal evolution in a particular negotiation

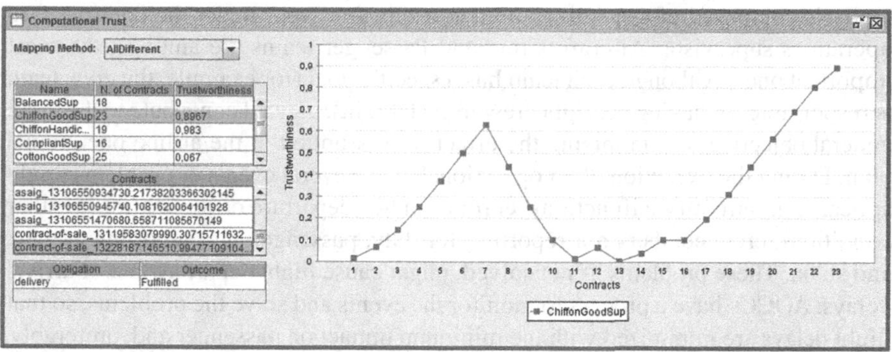

Fig. 32.7 Computational trust: computing trustworthiness assessments from contractual evidences

The scenario that is illustrated throughout this sequence of screenshots is from the textile industry domain. We have run several experiments with the aim of trying to figure out the best ways of integrating negotiation, norms and trust (Urbano et al. 2011b, 2012a,b).

32.3.2 *MASDIMA*

The second scenario addressed by ANTE is related to disruption management in Airline Operations Control. MASDIMA[2] is an agent-based application that represents the Airline Operations Control Centre (AOCC) of an airline company. The AOCC is the organization responsible for monitoring and solving operational problems that might occur during the execution of the airline operational plan. It includes teams of human experts specialized in solving problems related to aircrafts and flights, crewmembers and passengers, in a process called Disruption Management. In this section we will briefly introduce the Airline Operations Control Problem (AOCP) and we will present our solution to this problem, i.e., the agent based application MASDIMA (Castro and Oliveira 2011). Although we present a high level view of the system architecture we will give more emphasis on how we used the ANTE Framework (described in Sect. 32.2) to implement this application.

Airline companies developed a set of operations control mechanisms to monitor the flights and check the execution of the schedule. During this monitoring phase, several problems may appear related to aircrafts, crewmembers and passengers (Clausen et al. 2005). According to Kohl et al. (2004), disruption management is the process of solving these problems. To be able to manage disruptions, airline companies have an entity called Airline Operations Control Centre (AOCC). This

[2]Multi-Agent System for DIsruption MAnagement.

entity is composed of specialized human teams that work under the control of an operations supervisor. Aircraft, Crew and Passenger teams are amongst the most important ones. Although each team has a specific goal (for example, the crew team is responsible for having the right crew in each flight), they all contribute to the more general objective of minimizing the effects of disruption in the airline operational plan. During the execution of an operational plan, several events or problems might appear, e.g., aircraft malfunctions, enroute and/or departure or destination weather conditions, crewmembers not reporting for duty, passengers not reporting at gate, and so on. These problems, if not solved, might cause flight departure and/or arrival delays. AOCCs have a process to monitor the events and solve the problems, so that flight delays are minimized with the minimum impact on passenger and, preferably, with the minimum operational cost. Typically, the main costs to consider are: (1) Crew Costs, (2) Flight Costs and (3) Passenger Costs. There is also a less easily quantifiable cost that is also included: the cost of delaying or cancelling a flight from the passenger point of view. Most airlines use some kind of rule-of-thumb when they are evaluating the impact of the decisions on passengers. Others just assign a monetary cost to each minute of delay and evaluate the solutions taking into consideration this value. When faced with a disruption, the AOCC needs to find the best solution that minimizes the delay and costs of the flights, crewmembers and passengers affected returning, as soon as possible, to the previous operational plan.

As in the B2B scenario presented in Sect. 32.3.1, important synergies are obtained from the integration of the three main research domains identified in Fig. 32.1. It is important to point out that in the disruption management scenario we have a closed and cooperative environment that contrasts with the open and competitive environment of the B2B scenario. Figure 32.8 shows the MASDIMA architecture. The agents *Tracking* (keep log of negotiation messages), *Learning* (increase robustness of future plans) and *Event Information* (system that registers the event information on the environment), although implemented, are not relevant for the scope of this chapter. The agent *Data Visualization* is responsible to update the user interface (Fig. 32.9) with information so that the users can interact with the system. The *Monitor* agent is responsible for the runtime execution of the problem and is the counterpart of the normative environment as modeled in the scenario presented in Sect. 32.3.1.

The main negotiation takes place between the *Supervisor* and the *A/C, Crew and Pax* manager agents and the negotiation protocol used has the characteristics identified in Sect. 32.2.1. The Supervisor acts as the organizer agent and the managers as respondents. Since we are in a cooperative environment, each manager does not possess the full expertize to be able to propose a solution to the supervisor. As such, each manager needs to start an inter-manager negotiation to be able to complete their proposal and participate in the main negotiation. Although we are in a cooperative environment each manager wants to maximize its own utility and act according to its preferences. In this scenario the number of participants is defined according to the problem we want to tackle. As a minimum we need to have at least one manager for each part (or dimension) of the problem. Nevertheless, we can have more than one agent with the same expertize in the same dimension of the problem.

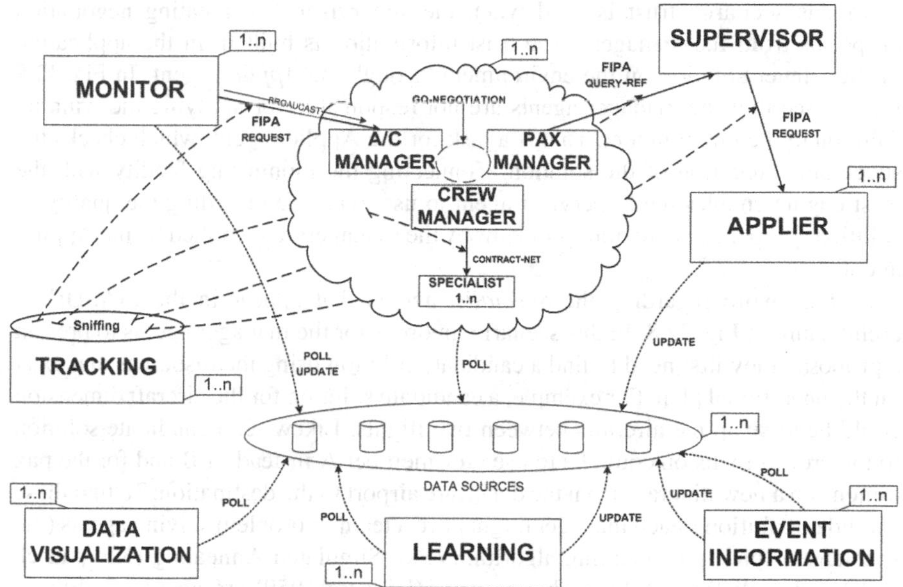

Fig. 32.8 MASDIMA architecture

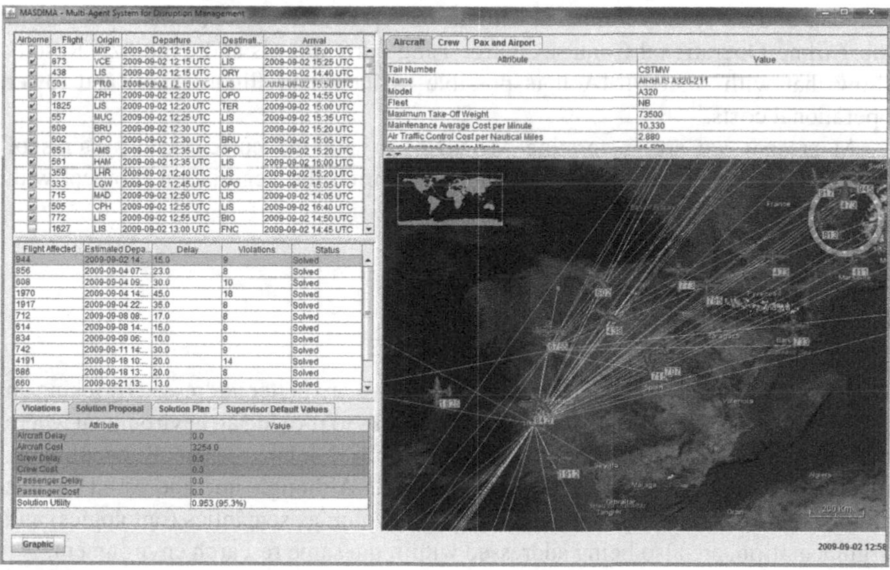

Fig. 32.9 MASDIMA user interface

In this scenario, trust is used when the supervisor is evaluating negotiation proposals from the managers. The trust information is built from the application of the winner solution on the environment through the *Applier* agent. In Fig. 32.8 we can see that the manager agents are not responsible for applying the winning solution to the environment. That is a task for the Applier agent, which checks the successful execution of the solution. Connecting the monitoring facility with the trust engine enables the Supervisor agent to use evidence regarding the quality of solutions proposed in previous problems by the managers and applied by the Applier agent.

A final word regarding the *Specialist* agents that appear in the MASDIMA architecture in Fig. 32.8. In this scenario, in order for the manager agents to present a proposal, they first need to find a candidate solution using the resources that exist on the operational plan. For example, a candidate solution for the aircraft dimension could be to swap the aircrafts between two flights. Likewise, a candidate solution to the crew dimension could be to use crewmember A instead of B and for the pax dimension a new itinerary from the departure airport to the destination. To find these candidate solutions, each manager might have a team of problem solving agents (the specialists) that, implementing algorithms like Simulated Annealing (Kirkpatrick and Vecchi 1983) or Dijkstra shortest-path (Dijkstra 1959) are able to find those solutions. It is from these candidate solutions that the managers take the attribute values necessary to present a proposal during the main negotiation.

MASDIMA is being tested at TAP Portugal (the major Portuguese airline) using real data and the results compared with the ones provided by the human operators in the Airline Operational Control Centre, using current tools and expertize. Results show that with MASDIMA it is possible to have less flight delays and lower operational costs.

At present we are integrating MASDIMA with the current end systems of the airline company and we are planning to enrich the negotiation protocol with arguments.

32.4 Conclusions

Real world applications of agreement technologies are better addressed by taking an integrative approach. The ANTE framework seeks to provide an environment where the interdependencies between different research domains – namely negotiation, norms and trust – can be experimented with. Although not addressed in this chapter, other areas of agreement technologies, such as semantics (ontologies) and argumentation, are also being addressed within the same research environment.

The quite disparate application domains described here demonstrate the effort that is being put into applying our research results in different areas. Having a strong initial focus on the formation of virtual enterprises, and later to general B2B electronic contracting, part of the framework (mostly negotiation) is being used to address the problem of disruption management in an airline operational control, together with all the issues that this problem raises.

Acknowledgements This research is supported by Fundação para a Ciência e a Tecnologia (FCT), under project PTDC/EIA-EIA/104420/2008, and by QREN under project RESPLAN. The authors would also like to thank Pedro Brandão for his work on the implementation of the ANTE prototype.

References

Bachmann, R. 2001. Trust, power and control in trans-organizational relations. *Organization Studies* 22(2): 341–369.

Castelfranchi, C., and R. Falcone. 2010. *Trust theory: A socio-cognitive and computational model*, Wiley Series in Agent Technology. Chichester: Wiley.

Castro, A., and E. Oliveira. 2011. A new concept for disruption management in airline operations control. *Proceedings of the Institution of Mechanical Engineers, Part G: Journal of Aerospace Engineering* 3(3): 269–290. doi:10.1243/09544100JAERO864.

Clausen, J., A. Larsen, and J. Larsen. 2005. *Disruption management in the airline industry – concepts, models and methods*. Technical report, Informatics and Mathematical Modelling, Technical University of Denmark, DTU, Richard Petersens Plads, Building 321, DK-2800 Kgs, Lyngby. http://www2.imm.dtu.dk/pubdb/p.php?3763.

Craswell, R. 2000. Contract law: General theories. In *Encyclopedia of law and economics*, vol. III, ed. B. Bouckaert and G. De Geest, 1–24. Cheltenham: Edward Elgar.

Das, T.K., Teng, B. 1998. Between trust and control: Developing confidence in partner cooperation in alliances. *Academy of Management Review* 23(3): 491–512.

Dijkstra, E.W. 1959. A note on two problems in connexion with graphs. *Numerische Mathematik* 1: 269–271.

Ireland, R.D., and J.W. Webb. 2007. A multi-theoretic perspective on trust and power in strategic supply chains. *Journal of Operations Management* 25(2): 482–497.

Jonker, C.M., J. Treur. 1999. Formal analysis of models for the dynamics of trust based on experiences. In *MultiAgent system engineering, 9th European workshop on modelling autonomous agents in a multi-agent world*, 221–231. Berlin: Springer.

Josang, A., R. Ismail, C. Boyd. 2007. A survey of trust and reputation systems for online service provision. *Decision Support Systems* 43(2): 618–644.

Kaplow, L. 2000. General characteristics of rules. In: *Encyclopedia of law and economics*, vol. Volume V: The economics of crime and litigation, ed. B. Bouckaert and G. De Geest, 502–528. Cheltenham: Edward Elgar.

Kirkpatrick, S., C.Gelatt Jr, M. Vecchi. 1983. Optimization by simulated annealing. *Science* 220(4598): 671–680.

Kohl, N., A. Larsen, J. Larsen, A. Ross, S. Tiourline. 2004. *Airline disruption management: Perspectives, experiences and outlook*. Technical report CRTR-0407, Carmen Research.

Lopes Cardoso, H. 2010. *Electronic institutions with normative environments for agent-based e-contracting*. Ph.D. thesis, Universidade do Porto.

Lopes Cardoso, H., and E. Oliveira. 2008. Norm defeasibility in an institutional normative framework. In *Proceedings of the 18th European conference on artificial intelligence (ECAI 2008)*, ed. M. Ghallab, C. Spyropoulos, N. Fakotakis, and N. Avouris, 468–472. Patras: IOS Press.

Lopes Cardoso, H., and E. Oliveira. 2009. A context-based institutional normative environment. In *Coordination, organizations, institutions, and norms in agent systems IV*, LNAI, vol. 5428, ed. J. Hubner, E. Matson, O. Boissier, V. Dignum, 140–155. Berlin: Springer.

Lopes Cardoso, H., and E. Oliveira. 2010. Directed deadline obligations in agent-based business contracts. In *Coordination, organizations, institutions, and norms in agent systems V*, LNAI, vol. 6069, ed. J. Padget, A. Artikis, W. Vasconcelos, K. Stathis, V. Torres da Silva, E. Matson, A. Polleres pp. 225–240. Berlin: Springer.

Luhmann, N. 1979 *Trust and power*. New York: Wiley.

Mayer, R.C., J.H. Davis, and F.D. Schoorman. 1995. An integrative model of organizational trust. *The Academy of Management Review* 20(3): 709–734.

Quinlan, J.R. 1986. Induction of decision trees. *Machine Learning* 1: 81–106.

Rocha, A., H. Lopes Cardoso, and E. Oliveira. 2005. *Virtual enterprise integration: Technological and organizational perspectives*, chap. Contributions to an electronic institution supporting virtual Enterprises' life cycle, chapter XI, 229–246. Hershey: Idea Group.

Sako, M. 1998. Does trust improve business performance? In *Trust within and between organizations: Conceptual issues and empirical applications*, ed. C. Lane and R. Bachmann. New York: Oxford University Press.

Urbano, J., A. Rocha, and E. Oliveira. 2009. Computing confidence values: Does trust dynamics matter? In *14th Portuguese conference on artificial intelligence (EPIA 2009)*, LNAI, 520–531. Aveiro: Springer.

Urbano, J., H. Lopes Cardoso, and E. Oliveira. 2010a. Making electronic contracting operational and trustworthy. In *12th Ibero-American conference on artificial intelligence*. Bahia Blanca: Springer.

Urbano, J., A. Rocha, and E. Oliveira. 2010b. Trustworthiness tendency incremental extraction using information gain. In *2010 IEEE/WIC/ACM international conference on web intelligence and intelligent agent technology (WI-IAT)*, Toronto, vol. 2, pp. 411–414. doi:10.1109/WI-IAT.2010.151.

Urbano, J., A. Rocha, and E. Oliveira. 2011a. A situation-aware computational trust model for selecting partners. *Transactions on computational collective intelligence V* pp. 84–105. Berlin: Springer.

Urbano, J., A. Rocha, and E. Oliveira. 2011b. Trust-based selection of partners. In *E-Commerce and web technologies*, Lecture notes in business information processing, vol. 85, ed. C. Huemer, T. Setzer, W. Aalst, J. Mylopoulos, M. Rosemann, M.J. Shaw, and C. Szyperski, 221–232. Berlin/Heidelberg: Springer.

Urbano, J., LH. Lopes Cardoso, E. Oliveira, and A. Rocha. 2012a. Normative and trust-based systems as enabler technologies for automated negotiation. In *Negotiation and argumentation in MAS*, ed. F. Lopes and H. Coelho. Bentham Science Publishers: Sharjah (United Arab Emirates).

Urbano, J., H. Lopes Cardoso, A. Rocha, and E. Oliveira. 2012b. Trust and normative control in multi-agent systems: An empirical study. In *10th International conference on practical applications of agents and multi-agent systems (PAAMS 2012)*, Special sessio on trust, incentives and norms in open multi-agent systems (TINMAS). Salamanca: Springer.

Wathne, K.H., and J.B. Heide. 2000. Opportunism in interfirm relationships: Forms, outcomes, and solutions. *The Journal of Marketing* 64(4): 36–51.

Williamson, O.E. 1979. Transaction-cost economics: The governance of contractual relations. *Journal of Law and Economics* 22: 233–261.

Chapter 33
mWater, a Case Study for Modeling Virtual Markets

Antonio Garrido, Adriana Giret, Vicente Botti, and Pablo Noriega

33.1 Introduction

As previously discussed in this book, virtual organisations are an emerging means to model, enact, and manage large-scale computations. They are composed of a dynamic collection of semi-independent autonomous entities, each of which has a range of problem solving capabilities and resources at their disposal (Norman et al. 2004). These entities exhibit complex behaviours; they usually co-exist, collaborate and agree on some computational activity, but sometimes they compete with one another in a ubiquitous virtual marketplace.

Virtual markets appear because of the electronic-commerce phenomenon and provide a flexible architecture for autonomous, or semi-autonomous, agents playing different roles (standard participants, such as buyers or sellers, and market mediators/facilitators) and protocols governing the interaction of self-interested agents engaged in the market transaction sessions. Interactions among agents, realised as Multi-Agent Systems (MASs), aim at achieving individual and global goals, and are structured via collaboration, argumentation, negotiation and, eventually, via AT, and contracts, which are modeled as a set of (formal) commitments that can have complex nested structures.

The transition from a regulated monopolistic system to a decentralised open virtual market raises many questions, particularly as markets evolve. First, how to develop negotiated semantic alignments between different ontologies meeting the new requirements of the organisation. Second, how to recruit agents or services

A. Garrido (✉) • A. Giret • V. Botti
Departamento de Sistemas Informáticos y Computación, Universitat Politècnica de València, Valencia, Spain,
e-mail: agarridot@dsic.upv.es, agiret@dsic.upv.es, vbotti@dsic.upv.es

P. Noriega
IIIA - CSIC, Barcelona, Spain,
e-mail: pablo@iiia.csic.es

S. Ossowski (ed.), *Agreement Technologies*, Law, Governance and Technology Series 8, DOI 10.1007/978-94-007-5583-3_33,

to form teams or compound services for the market, and how they negotiate in these emerging organisations. Third, how the conventions, norms and negotiation protocols of the market change over time, and how participants in these markets react to these changes. Four, how to extrapolate the empirical outcomes of the market, in terms of economic and environmental impact, to deal with the social (welfare) aspect of the market. On the other hand, existing works about virtual markets put special emphasis on the construction of formal conceptual models, such as goods markets, stock markets, electricity markets and water markets (Gomez-Limon and Martinez 2006; Thobani 1997; Ventosa et al. 2005), but they do not always report significant advances from a social point of view or a collaborative AI perspective.

In summary, virtual markets provide new areas of opportunities for users (buyers and sellers), while also changing the relationships among users and market facilitators, making them more agile. But building these markets involves facing important challenges to achieving efficient management of the operation rules, and new capabilities are required: (i) rich ontology and semantics; (ii) norm reasoning, enforcing and regulating entities; (iii) flexible organisation schemes; (iv) coordination and cooperation (even dynamic group formation); (v) rules for negotiation, argumentation theories and conflict resolution techniques; (vi) trust models and reputation mechanisms; (vii) control and security; and, finally, (viii) a seamless way to integrate all these components. Although this chapter is far from being the last word on this integration, we try to push forward the agenda for innovative disciplines within virtual markets using *mWater*, a real-world water-right market, as a case study (Botti et al. 2009, 2010). Thus, this chapter is clearly multi-disciplinary and deals with many components from both AI and AT that offer the foundations for an agreement computing solution, including agility, scalability, heterogeneity and reconfigurability issues (Sierra et al. 2011). The main objective of this chapter is to provide a fundamental study of the means of constructing a formal conceptual model for a virtual market (using water rights as an application example) under a multi-agent perspective.

33.2 A Virtual Market Scenario for Water Rights

A virtual market, as part of a virtual organisation with a general structure, can be seen as a set of entities and roles regulated by mechanisms of social order and created by more or less autonomous actors to achieve some goals.

33.2.1 Description and Objectives

Water scarcity is a significant concern in most countries, not only because it threatens the economic viability of current agricultural practices, but because it is likely to alter an already precarious balance among its different types of use. Also, good water management involves a complex balance between economic, administrative, environmental and social factors. This balance is partially determined by physical conditions like rainfall, water supply and distribution infrastructure, population distribution, land use and main economic activities. However, actual water demand is the determining balancing condition, and actual water use is the outcome to measure the success of an adequate water management policy.

More efficient uses of water may be achieved within an institutional framework where water rights may be exchanged more freely under different market conditions (Thobani 1997). The willingness of irrigators to buy or sell water highly depends on the difference between the price of water and net revenue each farmer expects to earn by irrigating, and similarly for other stakeholders like utility companies or municipalities. Nevertheless, it is not always a matter of price expectations alone that motivates users to trade water rights. Policy-makers may wish to promote trading that favours outcomes that may not necessarily be directly associated with price expectations. But formulating market regulations that have the intended effects is not straightforward. There are many aspects that may be regulated and many parameters involved and, therefore, the consequences of the many combinations are difficult to foresee, not to mention the oftconflicting interests of the many stakeholders.

In hydrological terms, a water market can be defined as an institutional, decentralised framework where users with water rights are allowed to voluntarily trade them, always fulfilling some pre-established norms (legislation), to other users in exchange of some compensation (Gomez-Limon and Martinez 2006; Thobani 1997). Water-right markets allow rapid changes in allocation in response to changes in water supply and demand, and ideally allow the stimulation of investment and employment when users are assured access to secure supplies of water. Because of water's unique characteristics, such markets do not work everywhere, they are not homogeneous since they operate under different organisational and institutional schemata, nor do they solve all water-related issues (Marinho and Kemper 1999; Thobani 1997). Some experiences have shown that more flexible regulations may be desirable but policy-makers need means and methodologies that allow them to visualise the potential consequences of new regulations and fine-tune them before enacting them, in order to avoid undesirable outcomes. Underneath this situation, the crude reality of conflicts over water rights and the need of accurate assessment of water needs become more salient than ever. In order to deal with these issues, the main objectives in *mWater* are to help:

- Find the best conditions and taking the best decisions on the design of the market; even subtle changes are very costly. Since they are difficult and delicate tasks, and cannot be freely applied in the real world, a virtual market provides a valuable environment for testing.
- Deploy a virtual market to simulate the interplay among intelligent agents, rule enforcing and performance indicators. This market also provides a playground for the agreement computing paradigm to easily plug in new techniques, such

as trust mechanisms, negotiation, cooperations, argumentation, etc., and assess their impact in the market indicators, which is very interesting.

- Offer a mechanism for policy-makers to evaluate the effects of norms in the market. In general, a policy-maker has little control over the hydrographical features of a basin but (s)he has legal power to regulate water user behaviour to a larger extent by means of: (i) government laws, (ii) basin or local norms, and (iii) social norms. Consequently, one aim of a policy-maker in using such a virtual market is to design appropriate water laws that regulate users actions and, in particular, give users the possibility of exchanging water resources.

It should also be mentioned that, from a performance standpoint, it is unclear which quality indicator of water management is the best as it cannot be measured in terms of one factor. Furthermore, many outcome functions have singularities that are hard to identify, test and visualise by existing analytical tools.

33.2.2 Related Work

Sophisticated basin simulation models are present in literature, particularly decision support systems for water resources planning, sustainable planning of water supply, and use of shared visions for negotiation and conflict resolution (Andreu et al. 1996; Cai et al. 2004; Palmer et al. 1999; Smajgl et al. 2009). From a hydrological perspective, these works have successfully bridged the gap between the state of the art in water-resource systems analysis and the usage by practitioners at the real-world level. However, the gap is still wide from a social perspective. The need is not only to model hydraulic factors, but also norm typology, human (mis)conducts, trust criteria and users willingness to agree on water-right trading, which may lead to a more efficient use of water.

Most water management models are based on equational descriptions of aggregate supply and demand in a water basin; only a few include a multi-agent-based perspective. This perspective allows us to emulate social behaviour and organisations, where the system is used to mimic the behaviour of autonomous rational individuals and groups of individuals (Smajgl et al. 2009). In this way, complex behavioural patterns are observed from simulation tests in which autonomous entities interact, cooperate, and/or compete. This offers several advantages: (i) the ability to model and implement complex systems formed by autonomous agents, capable of pro-active and social behaviour; (ii) the flexibility of MAS applications to add and/or delete computational entities, in order to achieve new functionalities or behaviours in the system, without altering its overall structure; (iii) the ability to use notions such as organisation, norms, negotiation, agreement, trust, etc. to implement computational systems that benefit from these human-like concepts and processes among others (Sierra et al. 2011); and finally (iv) the possibility to use 3D Virtual Worlds to provide all the necessary means for direct human inclusion into software systems, as proposed in Chap. 34 of this book.

Under this perspective, we explore an approach in which individual and collective agents are essential components because their behaviour, and effects, may be influenced by regulations. *mWater* is inspired by the MAELIA (http://www.iaai-maelia.eu) and NEGOWAT projects (http://www.negowat.org) that simulate the socio-environmental impact of norms for water and how to support negotiation in areas where water conflicts arise.

From a technical perspective, there are several approaches to implementing MAS applications. Some approaches are centered and guided by the agents that will populate the systems, while others are guided by the organisations that the constituent agents may form. Other approaches rely on the development process on the regulation that defines the MAS behaviour, which is usually encoded as an Electronic Institution (EI) (Almajano et al. 2011; Esteva 2003; Rodriguez-Aguilar 2001). We are interested in this latter approach due to the requirements imposed by the environment, which is presented in the next section. In particular, *mWater*—from the standpoint of a MAS simulation tool, later described in Sect. 33.4.2—implements a regulated market environment as an EI, in which different water users (intelligent agents) trade with water rights under different basin regulations.

33.2.3 An EI Framework for mWater

Our conceptual model for *mWater* virtual market follows the IIIA EI description (Arcos et al. 2005). In short, an EI is a type of regulated MAS that combines a workflow (scenes and networks of scenes, namely performative structures), and regulation on structural norms. EIs are a way of expressing and implementing the conventions that regulate agent interactions. They may be understood as an interface between the internal decision-making capabilities of an agent and the external problem domain where those agents interact to achieve some goals.

33.2.3.1 Performative Structures

Procedural conventions in the *mWater* institution are specified through a nested performative structure (see Fig. 33.1[1]) with multiple processes. This top structure describes the overall market environment, and includes other performative structures and scene protocols as follows.

[1]At a glance, a performative structure represents complex interaction models and procedural prescriptions. The dynamic execution is modeled trough arcs and transitions, by which the different participating roles of the institution may navigate synchronously (AND transitions) or asynchronously (OR/XOR transitions). See Arcos et al. (2005) for further details on this type of notation.

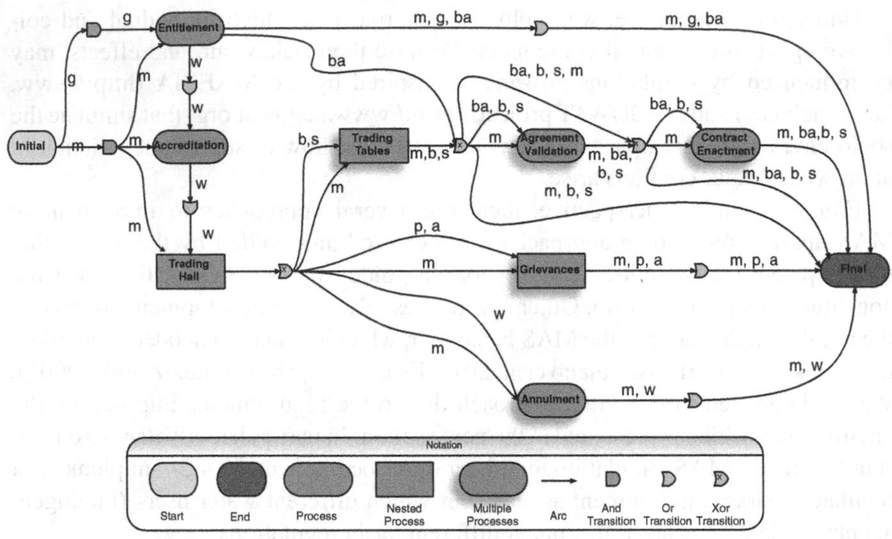

Fig. 33.1 *mWater* performative structure. Participating roles: *g* guest, *w* water user, *b* buyer, *s* seller, *p* third party, *m* market facilitator, *ba* basin authority

Top performative structure of the market (Fig. 33.1).

Entitlement. Only bona fide right-holders may trade water rights in the market and there are only two ways of becoming the owner of a right. Firstly when an existing right is legally acquired from its previous owner outside of *mWater* (through inheritance or pecuniary compensation for example). Secondly when a new right is created by the *mWater* authorities and an eligible holder claims it and gets it granted. *Entitlement* scene gives access to the market to new right holders who prove they are entitled to trade. It is also used to bootstrap the market.

Accreditation. This scene allows legally entitled right-holders to enter the market and trade by registering their rights and individual data for management and enforcement purposes.

Agreement Validation and Contract Enactment. Once an agreement on transferring a water right has been reached, it is managed according to the market conventions. *mWater* staff check whether or not the agreement satisfies formal conditions and the hydrological plan normative conventions. If the agreement complies with these, a transfer contract is agreed upon and signed by the parties involved in the *Contract Enactment* scene, and then the agreement becomes active.

Annulment. This scene in the *mWater* performative structure deals with anomalies that deserve a temporary or permanent withdrawal of rights.

***TradingHall* performative structure (Fig. 33.2).** Intuitively, in this complex performative structure right-holders become aware of the market activity (*Open Trades*

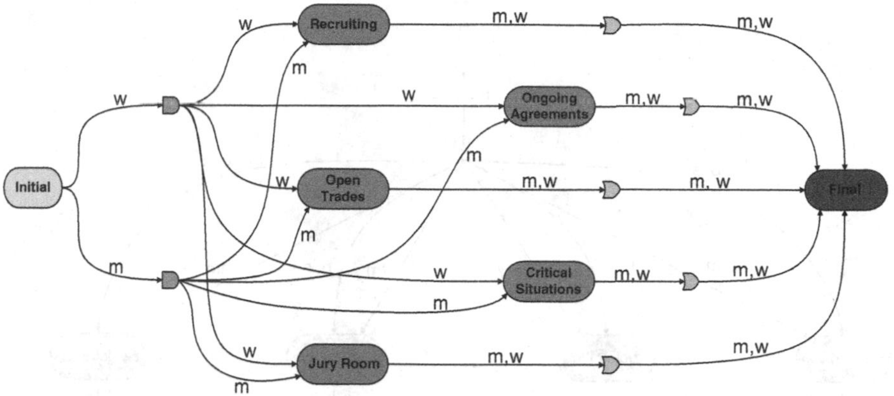

Fig. 33.2 *TradingHall* performative structure

and *Ongoing Agreements* scenes), and initiate concurrent activities: get invitations to trade and/or initiate trading processes (*Recruiting* scene), initiate grievance procedures (*Ongoing Agreements* scene), and get informed about anomalous situations (*Critical Situations* scene), for example severe drought situations. Actual trading starts inside the *TradingHall* scene. On the one hand, updated information about existing tradeable rights, as well as ongoing deals, active contracts and grievances is made available here to all participants. On the other, as shown in Fig. 33.2, users and trading staff can initiate most trading and ancillary operations here (from the *Recruiting* scene): open, request trading parties and enter a trading table; query about different agreements; and initiate a grievance procedure from the *Ongoing Agreements* scene or, in the same scene, get informed about a dispute in which the water user is affected. Members of the Jury may also be required to mediate in a dispute at the *Jury Room* scene. Technically speaking, all these scenes are "stay-and-go" scenes. While the users are inside the market, they have to *stay* permanently in these scenes but they may also *go* (as *alteroids*, clone-like instantiations of the same agent that allow the agent to be active simultaneously in different scenes) to trading table scenes and contract enactment scenes where they are involved. The scenes where user alteroids become involved are created (as a new *instance* of the corresponding performative structures) when a staff agent creates one at the request of a user, of an authority, or because of a pre-established convention (like weekly auctions).

***TradingTable* performative structure (Fig. 33.3).** In our *mWater* performative structure (recall Fig. 33.1), a market facilitator can open a new trading table whenever a new auction period starts or whenever a right-holder requests to trade a right outside the auction hall. In such a case, a right-holder chooses a negotiation protocol from a set of available ones In order to accommodate different trading mechanisms, we assemble the *TradingTable* performative structure as a list of different scenes, each corresponding to a valid trading mechanism or negotiation

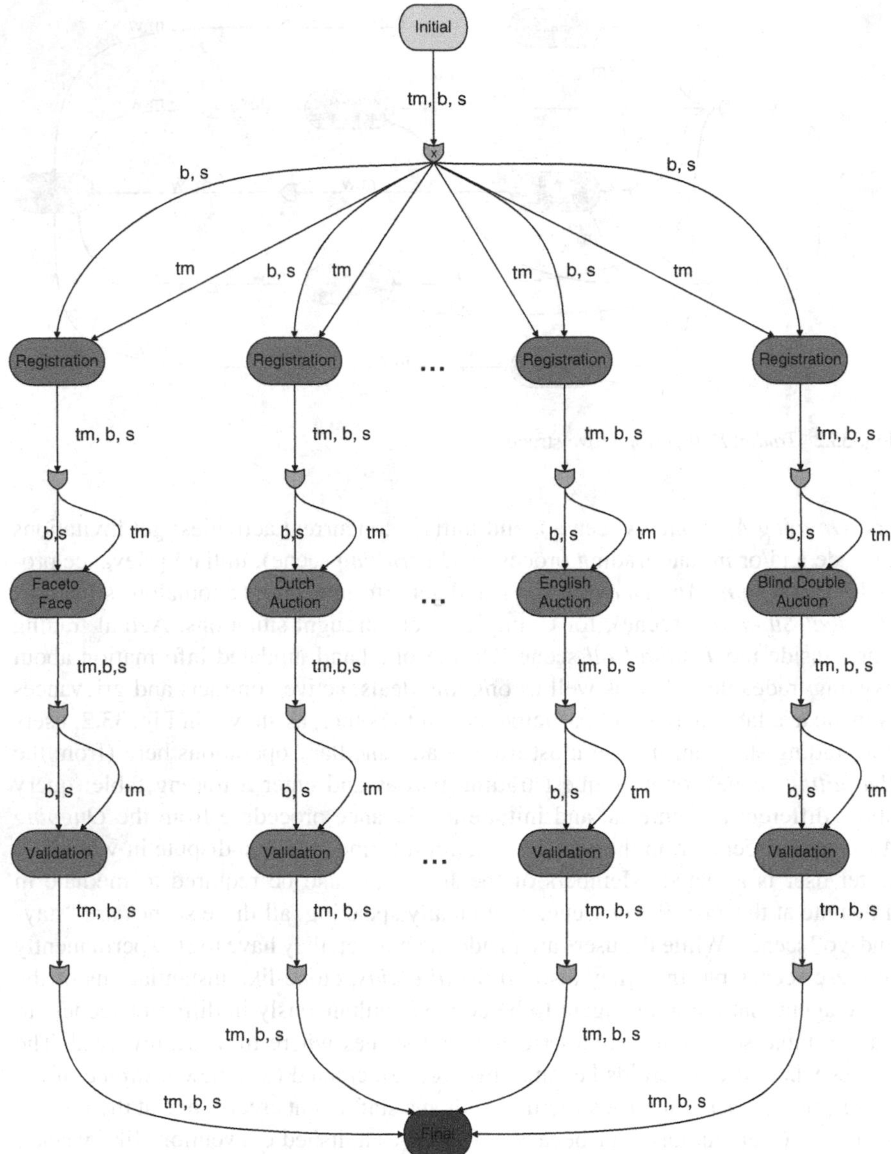

Fig. 33.3 *TradingTable* performative structure

protocol. Each instance of a *TradingTable* scene is managed by a *Table Manager*, *tm*, who knows the structure, specific data and management protocol of the given negotiation protocol.

Every *TradingTable* is defined as a three-scene performative structure. The first scene is *Registration*, in which the *tm* applies a filtering process to assure that only

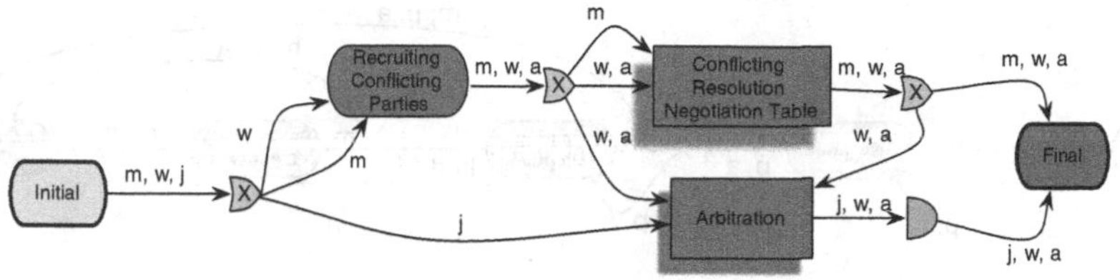

Fig. 33.4 *Grievances* performative structure

valid water users can enter a given trading table. The specific filtering process will depend on the given trading protocol and possibly on domain specific features. The second scene is the trading protocol itself, in which the set of steps of the given protocol are specified. Finally, in the last scene, *Validation*, a set of closing activities are executed, for example registering the final deals or stating the following steps for the agreement settlement.

***Grievances* performative structure (Fig. 33.4).** Once an agreement is active, it may be executed by the new right-holder and, consequently, other right-holders and some external stakeholders may initiate a grievance procedure that may overturn or modify the transfer agreement. Even if there are no grievances that modify a contract, parties might not fulfill the contract properly and there might be some contract reparation actions. If things proceed smoothly, the right subsists until maturity. In this structure any conflict can be solved by means of two alternative processes (these processes are similar to those used in Alternative Dispute Resolutions and Online Dispute Resolutions (Schultz et al. 2001; Slate 2002)). On the one hand, conflict resolution can be solved by means of negotiation tables (*Conflict Resolution Negotiation Table* performative structure). In this mechanism, a negotiation table is created on demand whenever any water user wants to solve a conflict with other/s water user/s, negotiating with them with or without mediator. Such a negotiation table can use a different negotiation protocol, such as face-to-face, standard double auction, etc., analogously to the *TradingTable* performative structure. On the other hand, arbitration mechanisms for conflict resolution can also be employed (*Arbitration* performative structure). In this last mechanism, a jury solves the conflict sanctioning the offenses. The difference among the two mechanisms for conflict resolution is that the arbitration process is binding, meanwhile the negotiation is not. In this way, if any of the conflicting parties is not satisfied with the negotiation results (s)he can activate an arbitration process in order to solve the conflict.

***Arbitration* performative structure (Fig. 33.5).** There are three steps in the arbitration process. First, the *Grievance* is stated by the plaintive water user. Second, the different conflicting parties present their allegations to the jury (*Hearing Dispute*). Third, the jury, after hearing the dispute, passes a sentence on the conflict.

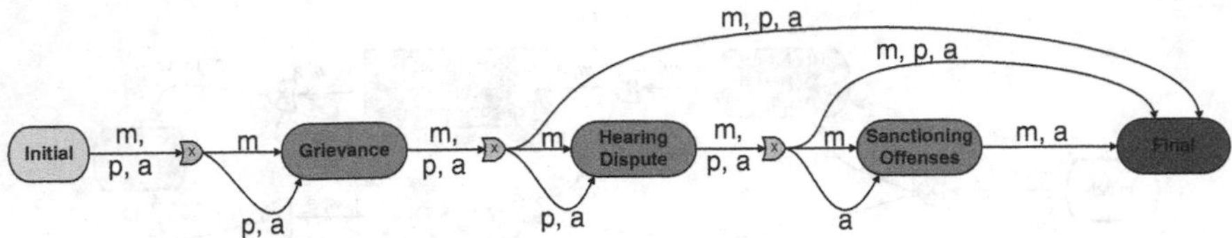

Fig. 33.5 *Arbitration* performative structure

33.2.3.2 Users and Roles

There are seven roles, which are depicted in Fig. 33.1. This number is not arbitrary and represents the natural interaction of the institution. First, the guest role (*g*) is the user that wants to enter the process. After admission, the guest is specialised into a water user (*w*), which is later specialised as a buyer or seller (*b*/*s*, respectively). There are two staff roles throughout the process. The market facilitator (*m*) represents institutional agents who start the trading activities, such as managing the users data, the specific parameters of the trading protocols, etc. The basin authority role (*ba*) represents institutional agents who are in charge of the last activities, such as agreement validation and contract enactments that are executed as a result of a successful negotiation process. Finally, there is a third party (*p*) role that appears when a grievance is started in the system.

33.2.4 Implementation

mWater uses a flexible multi-tier architecture (Botti et al. 2011; Giret et al. 2011), which relies on the EI model presented in Fig. 33.1. It has been implemented within a higher level architecture depicted in Fig. 33.6 that also includes a policy simulation module explained in Sect. 33.4.2. The persistence tier implements a *mySQL* database with more than 60 relational tables that store the information about basins, markets and grievances. The business tier is the core of the system and allows us to embed different AI techniques (e.g. trust and data mining for participants selection, planning to navigate through the institution, collaboration and negotiation to enhance agreements and minimise conflicts, etc.), thus ranging from a simple to a very elaborate market. *mWater* implements a schema of agents that include both the internal and external roles. There is a JADE (Java Agent DEvelopment Framework, http://jade.tilab.com) definition for each class that represents the roles in the scenes. The underlying idea is to offer open and flexible templates to simulate different agents and norms, which provides more opportunities to the analyst to evaluate the market indicators under different regulations and types of agents. These templates also offer an important advantage: we can extend them and implement as many different agents (with different behaviours) as necessary, and assess their impact in the market simulation.

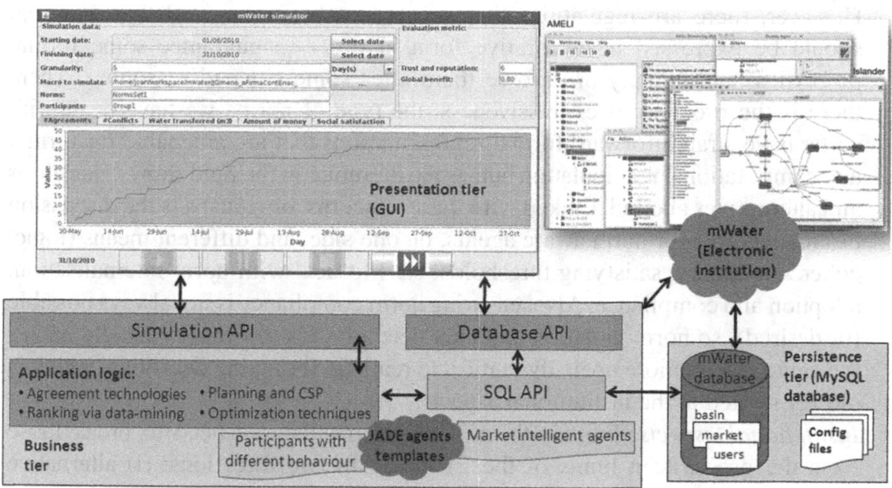

Fig. 33.6 Multi-tier architecture of the *mWater* system

In order to simulate how regulations and norms modify the market behaviour and to evaluate their effects (see Sect. 33.4.2), we include a deliberative module in the staff agents to reason on regulation matters. The presentation (GUI) tier is very intuitive and highly interactive, as it offers an effective way for the user to configure a given simulation, ranging from different time periods, participants and current legislation (Botti et al. 2010, 2011). The GUI displays graphical statistical information, which is also recorded in the database, which indicates how the market reacts to the input data in terms of the number of transfer agreements signed in the market, volume of water transferred, number of conflicts generated, together with quality indicators based on social functions to asses the trust and reputation levels of the market, and degree of water user satisfaction.

33.3 *mWater* as a Testbed for AT

mWater provides a flexible and still powerful infrastructure for a virtual (water-right) market. This way, it can be used as a testbed, i.e. a platform for experimentation of further development projects, to explore techniques and technologies from the agreement computing standpoint. In summary, *mWater* provides answers to different issues:

Norms. How to model and reason about norms within the market, how the regulations evolve and how to include new dispute resolution mechanisms? Current regulations impose certain constitutive restrictions and constitutive regimentations that may be readily regimented into the institutional specification.

However, there are regulations that should not be regimented that way and should be expressed in declarative form in order to guarantee some formal properties, and comply or enforce them after some situated reasoning. Then, there is the problem of expressiveness: the type of norms we have dealt with so far have straightforward formal representations that are amenable for formal and computational manipulation but, as the literature in the field shows, questions and alternatives abound. Linked with these concerns, obviously, is the discussion of architectures for norm aware agents, on one side, and different means (logic, coherence theory, satisfying thresholds, etc.) to deal with norm internalisation, adoption and compliance. Also, ensuring norm compliance is not always possible (or desired), so norm violation and later detection via grievances usually makes the environment more open, dynamic and realistic for taking decisions, which is closely related to the institutional aspects.

Institutional aspects. From a theoretical perspective, we need to break loose from the procrustean limits of the EI model in two directions: (i) alternative enforcement mechanisms (in addition to internal agent enforcers which are already available), and (ii) the evolution of regulations (beyond parameterised protocols and re-usable scenes).

Organisational issues. How beneficial is the inclusion of collective roles, their collaboration (and trust theories) and how the policies for group formation affect the market behaviour? In order to do this, we need to capture all those roles currently recognised by legislation that have any impact on trading and agreement management, specially in grievances and conflict resolution. This involves dealing with ad-hoc and dynamic coalitions to trade and to intervene in conflicts and with a special focus on the by-laws, goal-oriented groupings and goal-achievement features of such organisations. On the other hand, it is also necessary to study the roles and operations of non-trading organisations that somehow affect demand (e.g., water treatment plants, water distribution companies, municipality services, water transport firms and infrastructure).

Collective decision-making, social issues and coordination. Argumentation (rhetorical and strategic aspects), judgement aggregation (not only from the social choice perspective), reputation, prestige and multi-party negotiation (negotiation involving more than two parties, multiple-stages, reconfiguration of parties and mediating roles) are essential elements that have a relevant impact in the market performance.

Integration with other tools. mWater, used as a policy-simulator (see Sect. 33.4.2), allows water policy-makers to easily predict and measure the suitability and accuracy of modified regulations for the overall water market, before using other operational tools for the real floor. Our experiments shed light on the benefits that a collaborative AI perspective for a water-right market may bring to the policy-makers, general public and public administrators.

Applicability to other markets and inclusion of new features. This framework can be the basis for new developments. In particular, Almajano presents *amWater* (Almajano et al. 2011), a simplification of *mWater* that provides an assistance scenario, which has been subsequently extended with 3D graphical environments functionality where humans participate (represented as avatars) and interact by using intuitive control facilities—see Chap. 34 later in this book for further details. Also, our experiences show that this approach is general enough, as described in Sect. 33.4.1, and can be valid for other markets.

33.4 Further Applications of *mWater*

In this section, we present two further applications we have deployed for our *mWater* case study. First, we have extrapolated our water-right market to a generic negotiation framework that condenses both the trading and the conflict resolution process. Second, we introduce our work on how this type of MAS can be used to enhance policy-making simulation within the setting of a decision support tool (Botti et al. 2010, 2011; Giret et al. 2011).

33.4.1 A Formal Framework for Generic Negotiation

Picture our water-right market (or any other produce market) where customers are involved in face-to-face negotiation or participate in auctions that must obey different policies. Picture, also, the various ways that conflicts among the users of water resources of a single basin are being solved. These are just two examples of institutions that share some standard features which can be captured in a generic negotiation framework with common roles.

33.4.1.1 Revisiting the Original Performative Structures

As pictured above, in many situations we can establish a metaphor with an institution that comprises several negotiation scenarios. Interestingly, the common denominator in all these situations is the negotiation process, e.g. price-fixing encounters or solving conflict resolution, each with a specific negotiation protocol that expresses how scenes are interrelated and how agents playing a given role move from one scene to another. While most negotiations restrict access, there is a large public hall (the market floor or the legislative environment of a hydrographic basin) where participants exchange information, request to open or enter a negotiation table, invite participants or are invited/requested, and where they reconvene after leaving such a table. For this last purpose, they may go to another private encounter to carry other institutional businesses, like enacting agreements, creating/dissolving coalitions, etc. We have integrated this global arrangement as a generic institution for negotiation with generic roles, as shown in the ISLANDER specification of

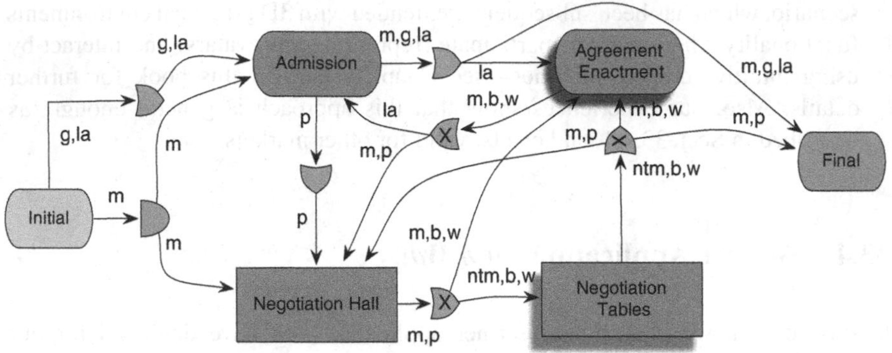

Fig. 33.7 Performative structure of a generic electronic institution for negotiation. Roles: *g* guest, *p* participant, *b* black, *w* white, *m* mediator, *ntm* negotiation table manager, *la* legal authority

Fig. 33.7—which is a generalisation of the original one depicted in Fig. 33.1. Procedural conventions in this negotiation institution are specified through a top performative structure which includes both the generic *NegotiationHall* and the *NegotiationTables*. At a glance, *NegotiationHall* captures the public activity that surrounds negotiation, that is, where participants (now *black* and *white*) become aware of any activity by exchanging information, initiate concurrent activities and deal with critical situations. On the other hand, *NegotiationTables* is the core of the institutional framework because it mirrors the conventions and policies that allow different protocols (e.g. auction mechanisms) to negotiate about a deal and co-exist. Specificity is embedded in the negotiation tables and gets propagated all the way to the main performative structure of Fig. 33.7 by the generic negotiation framework. Once negotiation tables are specified in detail, the end product would be one specific EI for some type of negotiation.

33.4.1.2 Discussion

mWater has allowed us to establish the foundations for the specification of an agent-based negotiation framework that handles multiple negotiation protocols in a coherent and flexible fashion. Although it may be used to implement one single type of agreement mechanism—like a blind double auction or argumentation-based negotiation—, it has been designed in such a way that multiple mechanisms may be available at any given time, to be activated and tailored on demand by participating agents. The underlying objective is to have a generic EI that may be tailored to specific needs and grafted into other EIs. As a by-product, we have created a repertoire of light-weight agreement mechanisms that may be used as "scene-modules" in other EIs and, in particular, as stand-alone interaction plug-ins in peer-to-peer architectures.

33.4.2 mWater *as a MAS for Policy Simulation*

Policy-making is a hard task and it usually changes throughout time due to variations in the economic situation, population distribution and physical conditions. To make things even more complex, the outcome of measuring the success of a given policy is not always intuitive. It is, therefore, essential to have mechanisms and/or simulation tools in the early phases of the policy cycle, i.e. before the legislators fix the legislation—and policies are really applied in the real world—, to analyse the impact and assess the expected success. In this line of work, *mWater* is implemented as a component of a larger institutional framework designed as a demand module for water management. It also simulates (negotiation) regulations and is enabled with tools to specify performance indicators, to spawn agent populations and allow humans as well as software agents to participate in simulations of virtual trading (Botti et al. 2011; Giret et al. 2011).

33.4.2.1 *mWater* as a Simulator

When the *mWater* simulator is in action (see Figs. 33.8 and 33.9), it allows the water policy-maker to create different configurations (input values that involve simulation dates, participants, legislation, in the form of protocols used during the trading negotiation, and some decision points that can affect the behaviour of the participants[2]) and study the market performance indicators. We have also implemented a specific decision tier for comparing and analysing the indicators of such configurations, as observed in Fig. 33.9. This is very valuable assistant to decision making as we can easy and efficiently compare the results of dozens of configurations, which is prohibitive when done manually.

From the experts evaluation, we can conclude that a simulation tool like this provides nice advantages: (i) it successfully incorporates the model for concepts on water regulation, water institutions and individual behaviour of water users; (ii) it formally represents the multiple interactions between regulations, institutions and individuals; (iii) it puts strong emphasis on user participation in decision making; and (iv) it finally provides a promising tool to evaluate changes in current legislation, and at no cost, which will surely help to build a more efficient water market with more dynamic norms. Note, however, that the simulation tool is currently mainly policy-maker-oriented rather than stakeholder-oriented. The reason for this is that we have focused on the possibility of changing the norms within the market and evaluating their outcomes—which is the policy-makers labour—, but not in the participation of stakeholders to change the model of the market itself. But clearly, in a social context of water-right management it is important to include tools for letting

[2]In our current implementation, these additional decision points rely on a random basis, but we want to extend them to include other issues such as short-term planning, trust, argumentation and ethical values.

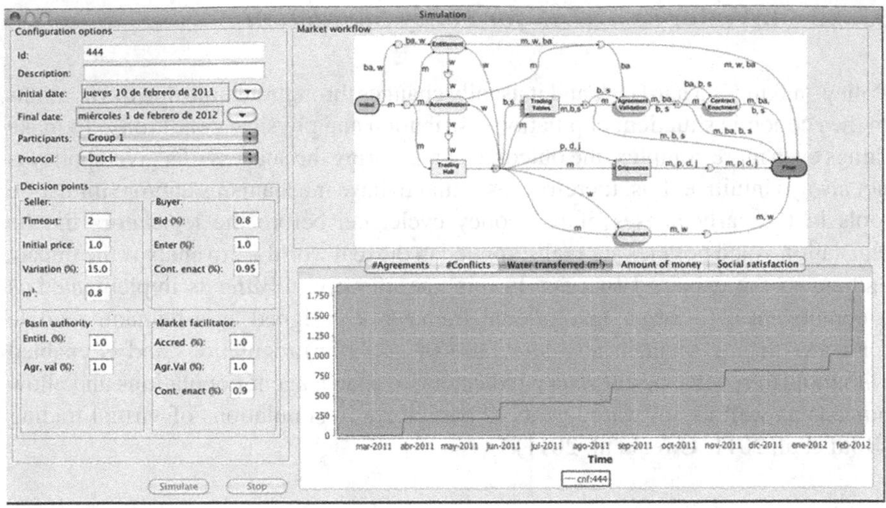

Fig. 33.8 The *mWater* simulator in action

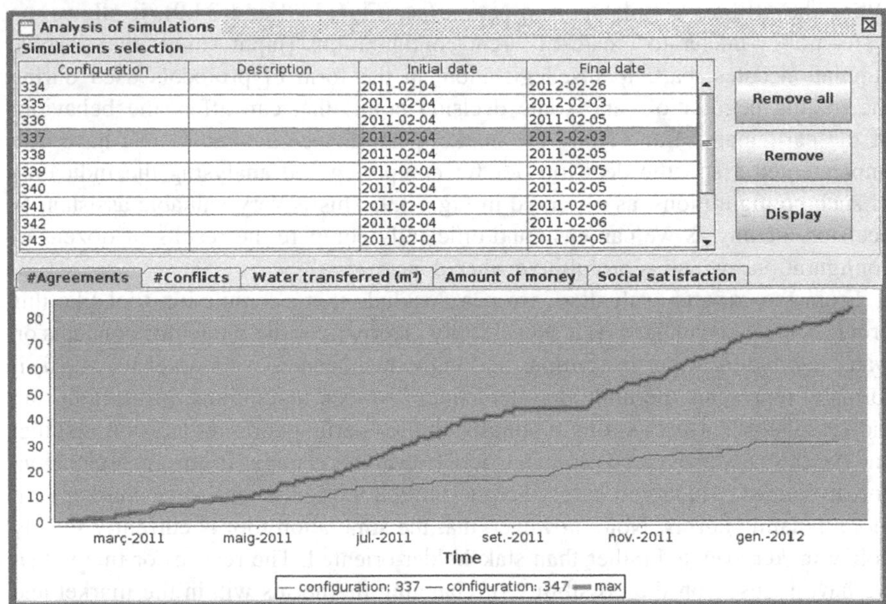

Fig. 33.9 Analysis of different configurations. *Thick line* represents the optimal solution, in this case the max number of agreements

stakeholders themselves use the system. In other words, the framework should be also able to include the participation of relevant stakeholders, thus helping validate results, which is our current work.

33.4.2.2 Discussion

One of the key problems in policy content modeling is the gap between policy proposals and formulations that are expressed in quantitative and narrative forms. Furthermore, it is difficult to find formal models that can be used to systematically represent and reason with the information contained in the proposals and formulations. As a by-product, *mWater* offers a tool designed so that policy-makers may explore, monitor and visualise the interplay between: (i) market regulations, (ii) trader profiles and market composition, (iii) the aggregated outcomes of trading under those set conditions, and finally (iv) the impact of these multi-agent policy simulations (and arguments about policies) on the outcomes of the market at no real cost. This provides an appealing scenario to managing the water resources effectively, both in the short and medium term.

33.5 Conclusions

This chapter has presented *mWater*, a virtual market that is intended as a MAS implementation to support institutional foundations for further markets and AT developments. *mWater* grasps the components of an electronic market, where rights are traded with flexibility under different price-fixing mechanisms and norms. In addition to trading, *mWater* also includes those tasks that follow trading. The main contribution is that it has been designed around a realistic institutional core with multiple functional add-ons that may be readily adapted to eventual regulations on one hand, and market-design and testing requirements, on the other.

mWater has been thought not only as a test case for a potential actual market but also as a sandbox for testing, development and demonstration of AT techniques, including norms reasoning, virtual organisations, argumentation, trust, use of 3D virtual interfaces, etc. In this line, some authors have used *mWater* as the basis for developing execution infrastructures that facilitate agents' interactions and visual representations (Almajano et al. 2011). As a by-product, this market has allowed us first to provide a generic negotiation framework as a general multi-agent-based specification. Second, it provides a decision-support tool constructed around a water-right market that integrates a wide range of subcomponents. With such a tool, water policy-makers can visualise and measure the suitability of new or modified regulations for the overall water market.

Acknowledgements This work was partially funded by the Consolider AT project CSD2007-0022 INGENIO 2010 of the Spanish Ministry of Science and Innovation; the MICINN project TIN2011-27652-C03-01; and the Valencian Prometeo project 2008/051.

References

Almajano, P., M. Lopez-Sanchez, M. Esteva, and I. Rodriguez. 2011. An assistance infrastructure for open MAS. In *Proceedings 14th international conference of the Catalan association for artificial intelligence (CCIA 2011)*, 1–10. Amsterdam/Washington, DC: IOS Press: Frontiers in Artificial Intelligence.

Andreu, J., J. Capilla, and E. Sanchis. 1996. AQUATOOL, a generalized decision-support system for water-resources planning and operational management. *Journal of Hydrology* 177(3–4): 269–291.

Arcos, J., M. Esteva, P. Noriega, J. Rodriguez-Aguilar, and C. Sierra. 2005. Engineering open environments with electronic institutions. *Engineering Applications of Artificial Intelligence* 18(2): 191–204.

Botti, V., A. Garrido, A. Giret, F. Igual, and P. Noriega. 2009. On the design of mwater: A case study for agreement technologies. In *Proceedings of the 7th European workshop on multi-agent systems (EUMAS 2009)*, Ayia Napa (Cyprus).

Botti, V., A. Garrido, J. Gimeno, A. Giret, F. Igual, and P. Noriega. 2010. An electronic institution for simulating water-right markets. In *Proceedings of the III workshop on agreement technologies (WAT@IBERAMIA)*, Universidad Nacional del Sur, Bahía Blanca (Argentina).

Botti, V., A. Garrido, J.A. Gimeno, A. Giret, and P. Noriega. 2011. The role of MAS as a decision support tool in a water-rights market. In *AAMAS 2011 workshops*, LNAI, vol. 7068, 35–49. Berlin/London: Springer.

Cai, X., L. Lasdon, and A. Michelsen. 2004. Group decision making in water resources planning using multiple objective analysis. *Journal of Water Resources Planning and Management* 130(1): 4–14.

Esteva, M. 2003. *Electronic institutions: From specification to development*. IIIA. Ph.D. Monography 19.

Giret, A., A. Garrido, J.A. Gimeno, V. Botti, and P. Noriega. 2011. A MAS decision support tool for water-right markets. In *Proceedings of the tenth international conference on autonomous agents and multiagent systems (Demonstrations@AAMAS)*, 1305–1306. New York: ACM.

Gomez-Limon, J., and Y. Martinez. 2006. Multi-criteria modelling of irrigation water market at basin level: A Spanish case study. *European Journal of Operational Research* 173: 313–336

Marinho, M., and K. Kemper. 1999. Institutional frameworks in successful water markets: Brazil, Spain, and Colorado, USA. World Bank technical paper no. 427.

Norman, T., et al. 2004. Agent-based formation of virtual organisations. *Knowledge Based Systems* 17: 103–111.

Palmer, R., W. Werick, A. MacEwan, and A. Woods. 1999. Modeling water resources opportunities, challenges and trade-offs: The use of shared vision modeling for negotiation and conflict resolution. In *Proceedings of the water resources planning and management conference*. New York: ASCE.

Rodriguez-Aguilar, J. 2001. On the design and construction of agent-mediated electronic institutions. IIIA. Ph.d. Monography 14. Universitat Autònoma de Barcelona.

Schultz, T., G. Kaufmann-Kohler, D. Langer, and V. Bonnet. 2001. Online dispute resolution: The state of the art and the issues. In *SSRN*. http://ssrn.com/abstarct=899079.

Sierra, C., V. Botti, and S. Ossowski. 2011. Agreement computing. *KI – Künstliche Intelligenz* 25(1): 57–61.

Slate, W. 2002. Online dispute resolution: Click here to settle your dispute. *Dispute Resolution Journal* 56(4): 8–14.

Smajgl, A., S. Heckbert, and A. Straton. 2009. Simulating impacts of water trading in an institutional perspective. *Environmental Modelling and Software* 24: 191–201.

Thobani, M. 1997. Formal water markets: Why, when and how to introduce tradable water rights. *The World Bank Research Observer* 12(2): 161–179.

Ventosa, M., A. Baillo, A. Ramos, and M. Rivier. 2005. Electricity market modeling trends. *Energy Policy* 33: 897–913.

Chapter 34
v-mWater: An e-Government Application for Water Rights Agreements

Pablo Almajano, Tomas Trescak, Marc Esteva, Inmaculada Rodríguez, and Maite López-Sánchez

34.1 Introduction

e-Government is the use of information and communication technologies (ICT) with the aim of providing government services over the internet to citizens, businesses, employees and agencies (e.g. tax returns, virtual offices or help desk applications) (Almarabeh and AbuAli 2010). We argue that *e-Government* applications can take advantage of Organisation Centred Multiagent Systems (OCMAS) to model these services as structured interactions between stakeholders and to enforce government norms (Ferber et al. 2004; Jennings et al. 1998). In particular we are interested in those systems where participants can be both humans and software agents.

Virtual Institutions (VI) combine Electronic Institutions (an OCMAS) and Virtual Worlds technologies (Bartle 2003; Esteva 2003). They represent 3D virtual spaces where both human and software agents can interact. They offer interesting possibilities to both MAS and 3D virtual environments (Bogdanovych 2007). First, thanks to the regulation imposed by an OCMAS – in our case an Electronic Institution (EI) (Arcos et al. 2005) –, the 3D environment becomes a normative virtual world where norms are enforced at runtime. Second, a 3D real-time representation of the system allows humans to participate in MAS by controlling its 3D representation (avatar) in an immersive environment. We advocate that VIs can enhance the participation of citizens and business representatives in *e-Government* applications compared to traditional web-based user interfaces (WUI) or 2D graphical user interfaces (GUI).

P. Almajano (✉) • T. Trescak • M. Esteva
IIIA – CSIC, Barcelona, Spain
e-mail: palmajano@iiia.csic.es; ttrescak@iiia.csic.es; marc@iiia.csic.es

I. Rodríguez • M. López-Sánchez
University of Barcelona, Barcelona, Spain
e-mail: inma@maia.ub.es; maite@maia.ub.es

S. Ossowski (ed.), *Agreement Technologies*, Law, Governance and Technology Series 8, DOI 10.1007/978-94-007-5583-3_34,

In this chapter we show an *e-Government* application for the negotiation of water rights. Governments are employing water markets with the objective of encouraging more efficient use of water for irrigation, above all, in countries with water scarcity problems (e.g. Australia Bjornlund and Rossini 2010). Our *virtual market* based on trading *Water* (*v-mWater*) is modelled as a VI and facilitates human participation (in our case, citizens and business representatives). It is a simplification of mWater (Giret et al. 2011) and has been deployed using VIXEE, a robust VI eXEcution Environment that provides interesting features such as multi-verse communication and dynamic manipulation of the virtual world content (Trescak et al. 2011). VIXEE is a generic and domain-independent solution. Although *v-mWater* is an *e-Government* application, VI can also be used in other domains which may benefit from structured interactions and norms enforcement such as *e-Learning* and *e-Commerce* (Bogdanovych 2007; Bogdanovych et al. 2010).

This chapter is structured as follows. First, Sect. 34.2 provides some background concepts. Second, Sect. 34.3 specifies *v-mWater* model. Next, Sect. 34.4 explains the infrastructure used. Afterwards, Sect. 34.5 discusses the engineering process and shows an example execution. Then, Sect. 34.6 provides some related work. Finally, Sect. 34.7 draws the conclusions and proposes future work.

34.2 Background

34.2.1 Electronic Institutions

Organisation Centred MAS (OCMAS) approaches are MAS whose foundation lies in organisational concepts (Ferber et al. 2004). Electronic Institution (EI) is a particular OCMAS that we have used in our application. EIs structure agent interactions by establishing what actions agents are permitted and forbidden to perform as well as their consequences (Esteva 2003). In particular, interactions are grouped in several dialogic *activities* (also referred as scenes) where agents participate enacting different *roles*. Interactions for each activity follow well-defined *protocols* which are specified by directed graphs whose nodes represent the states and the arcs are labelled with illocution schemes (i.e. events defined as messages) or time-outs. In an activity, participants may change over time, agents may enter or leave.

The so-called *performative structure* defines how agents can legally move among activities depending on their role. It also defines if an activity can be executed several times at run time and when its execution starts. Specifically, a performative structure is specified as a graph where the nodes represent both activities and transitions – i.e. activity connectives – linked by directed arcs.

34.2.2 Virtual Worlds

Virtual worlds (VW) are three-dimensional (3D) social spaces where people interact by controlling embodied characters (Bartle 2003) (Messinger et al. 2009). One of their main features is the immersive experience provided to their participants. They can walk around the world to explore it as they would in real spaces. Moreover, they can also fly or even teleport to other places in the VW. Participants interact by using multi-modal communication such as *text-based* interfaces (e.g. chat windows), *voice* chat (e.g. using headsets and microphones) or *actions* performed by avatars (e.g. making gestures or touching objects). Moreover, the immersive experience can be still increased by incorporating sounds (e.g. birds singing in a virtual forest). Furthermore, they can provide an intuitive graphical representation of the progress of activities that participants are engaged in.

34.2.3 Virtual Institutions

Virtual Institutions (VI) combine EIs to regulate the participants' interactions and VWs to facilitate human participation in the institution (Bogdanovych 2007). This way, humans participate in the system by controlling an avatar in the VW, while software agents are directly connected to the EI and can be displayed as bots in the VW to emphasize their artificial nature.

Both EI and VW are causally connected because whenever one of them changes, the other one changes in order to maintain a consistent state (Maes and Nardi 1988). Notice that EI and VI have a conceptual difference. EIs define what is permitted and the rest is prohibited. On the contrary, in VIs, only those actions in the virtual world platform that have institutional meaning are regulated, while everything else is permitted.

34.3 v-mWater Model

The *v*irtual *m*arket based on trading *Water* (*v-mWater*) is a VI which models an electronic market of water rights. This market is a simplification of mWater which is an Electronic Institution (EI) focusing on a general water market that includes conflict resolution features (see previous Chap. 33 of this part). While mWater includes generic water uses such as human consumption or industrial, we restrict our model to water trading for agricultural purposes, where irrigators are the only actors using the water.

34.3.1 Water Market

Some governments are using markets to regulate the consumption of water from their managed water resources. As introduced in Sect. 33.2 of previous chapter, in *water markets*, the goods to negotiate are *water rights* and the traders are the *right-holders*. The result of a negotiation is an *agreement* where a seller agrees to reallocate (part of) the water from her/his rights to a buyer for a fixed period of time in exchange for a certain amount of money.

We model our market in the agriculture domain. More specifically, we consider farmlands that irrigate from water resources totally controlled by public governments. *Assigned water rights* in this domain are associated to the farmlands. The *right-holders* are either the owners or the lessees of the farmlands, namely, the *irrigators*. At the beginning of the *irrigation season*, the authorities estimate the water reserves and assign the quantity of water to the rights. *Tradable water rights*[1] contain the surplus of water the irrigators expect to have on their *assigned water rights* and decide to sell them. We define an irrigation *area* as a group of farmlands which can irrigate from the very same water resource – e.g. a reservoir of a basin–. We assume that one farmland only belongs to one *area*.

Our market opens at the beginning of the irrigation season. Only those irrigators holding rights are allowed to join it. We group the negotiations of water rights by irrigation areas. That means all the requested rights' trades for an area are negotiated in the same activity under the same negotiation protocol. Only irrigators holding rights in this area can participate in the negotiation. Moreover, in order to avoid speculation, it is not permitted to resell rights. In order to prevent monopolist strategies, the authorities may establish a maximum water quantity that one irrigator is allowed to buy in a particular area. For example, we can consider a norm such as "one irrigator only can buy a maximum of the 40 % of the total amount of water under negotiation".

34.3.2 EI Specification

From the market defined in previous Sect. 34.3.1 and using ISLANDER, the EIs specification editor (Esteva 2003), we have defined (1) the ontology of the application, (2) the roles played by participants, (3) the activities involved in the market and the transitions between them (i.e. the performative structure), and (4) the protocols enacting such activities.

The ontology specifies domain concepts such as *water right*, *land*, *area* or *agreement*. With respect to the roles, agents may adopt a number of them. Irrigator agents can participate as either *buyer* or *seller* subroles while *market facilitator* and *basin authority* correspond to staff agents. Figure 34.1 shows the performative structure of *v-mWater* (Almajano et al. 2011). Besides the obligated initial and final

[1]From now on, we will refer to these as water rights.

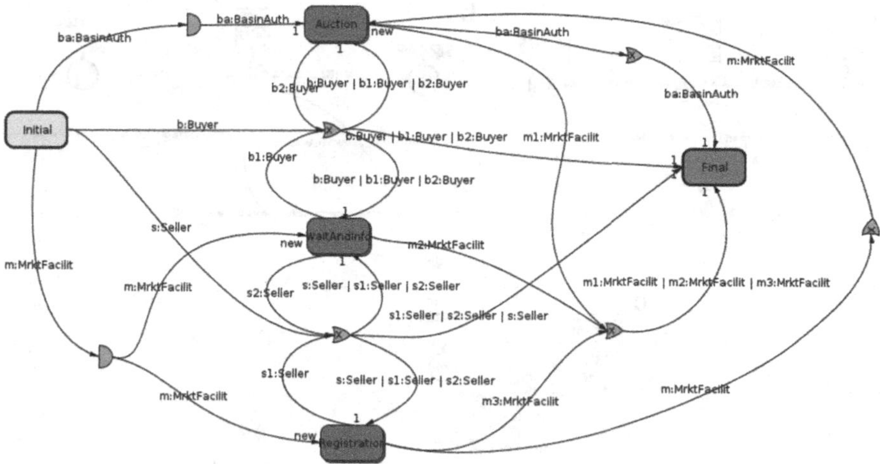

Fig. 34.1 *v-mWater* performative structure

activities to enter and exit the institution, there are three activities which enact the market: *Registration*, *Waiting and Information* and *Auction*. The *market facilitator* is responsible for starting the execution of each activity. The *basin authority* is only allowed to enter the *Auction* activity to validate the results. *Seller* participants can move from the *Registration* to the *Waiting and Information* activity and the other way around. On the other hand, *buyer* agents movements are restricted between *Waiting and Information* and *Auction* activities.

34.3.3 Registration

In this activity the market facilitator is in charge of registering sellers' rights. The interactions between participants are regulated following the protocol represented in Fig. 34.2a. First, a seller asks for registering a right indicating the water quantity to trade. Second, the market facilitator checks whether it is valid or not. Finally, the seller is informed about the result of the process (i.e. with an agree or failure message).

34.3.4 Waiting and Information

This activity follows the protocol depicted in Fig. 34.2b. It permits irrigators (buyers and sellers) to request information about negotiations from the market facilitator. Moreover, all participants within the activity are proactively informed when: (i) a new auction has been opened, so buyers are able to enter; (ii) an auction round is finished, giving information about reached agreements; and (iii) a seller

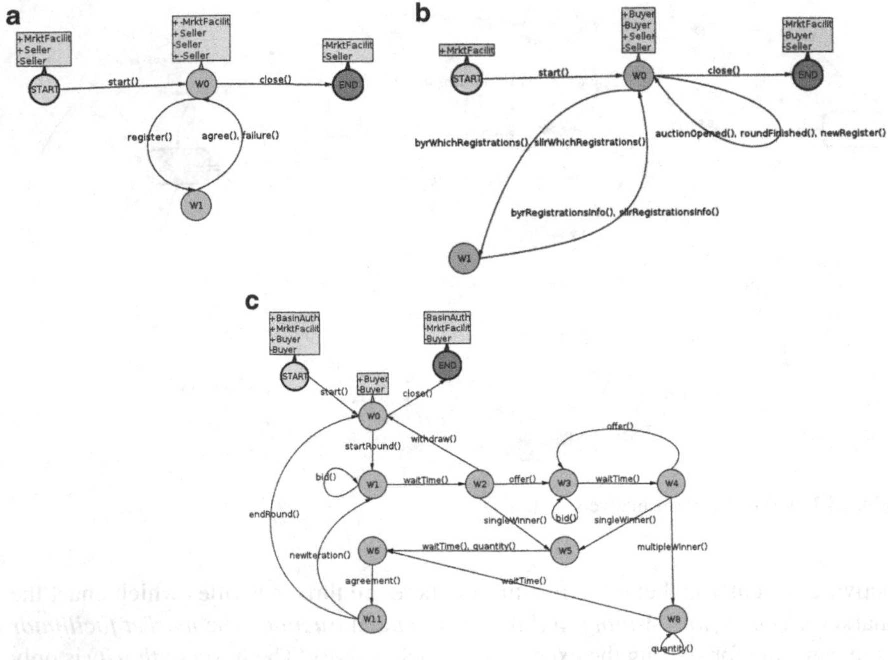

Fig. 34.2 Activities' protocols: (a) Registration; (b) Waiting and Information; (c) Auction

has successfully registered a new right that will be negotiated later on in the corresponding auction activity. Therefore, sellers can wait within this activity for the result of the negotiations of their rights after registering them, and buyers can wait until the auction they are interested in opens.

34.3.5 Auction

The negotiation of water rights takes place in this activity. There are three roles involved. The market facilitator conducts the auction, buyers bid for water rights and the basin authority announces the valid agreements. All (previously registered) rights belonging to the same area are negotiated within the same activity. Therefore, one auction activity is created for each area that has available water rights to negotiate.

A multi-unit Japanese auction protocol enacts the activity (see Fig. 34.2c). In this protocol, registered water rights – composed of several litres of water – are auctioned in consecutive *rounds*, i.e. one *round* per registered water right. Buyers can only join and leave the auction between *rounds*. The market facilitator starts a new *round* at a previously established price. It is divided in several *iterations* following these four rules: (1) the price goes up in regular *increments*; (2) only buyers that bid at a previous *increment* are allowed to place bids (all of them in case of first *increment*) (3) the *iteration* ends when (i) just one buyer bids at current *increment* (single winner) or (ii) no bids are performed, so the winners are the buyers that bid at previous *increment*; (4) winner(s) request the amount of water desired. If there is more than one winner, then the water is assigned by following a proportional allocation algorithm. Once an *iteration* is finished, the basin authority validates the result(s) – winner(s) have requested a minimum quantity of water and have enough credit – and announces the agreement(s). The *round* ends either when there was no bid in the last *iteration* or the water right under negotiation has no more water available. The negotiation is over when all rights have been traded.

The activities explained above have the following correspondences with *mWater* Performative Structures (PS) defined in Sect. 33.2.3 of the previous chapter: (1) Registration is a simplification of *Accreditation*; (2) in Waiting and information, water users may obtain information about negotiations as in *Open Trades* and *Ongoing Agreements* – both located in the *TradingHall PS* –; and (3) Auction activity includes *Agreement Validation* as well as a particular *trading protocol* of the *TradingTable PS*.

34.4 VIXEE Architecture

We have deployed *v-mWater* model using the Virtual Institution eXEcution Environment (VIXEE) (Trescak et al. 2011). Figure 34.3 depicts its architecture which is composed of three layers: (i) normative, (ii) visual interaction and (iii) causal connection.

The **normative** layer is based on AMELI, the electronic institutions infrastructure that mediates agents' interactions while enforcing institutional rules (Esteva 2003). AMELI can be regarded as domain-independent because it can interpret any institution specification generated by ISLANDER tool (Esteva 2003). In our case, it interprets the specification defined in Sect. 34.3.2. It is implemented in JAVA and uses two TCP ports for communication with the causal connection layer.

The **visual interaction** at the top layer comprises several 3D virtual worlds. Each Virtual World (VW) can be implemented in a different programming language using a different graphics technology. The usual parts of a VW are a VW client and a VW server. Such a server communicates with the causal connection layer using a standard protocol (e.g. UDP, TCP or HTTP). In our application we employ *Open Simulator*, an open source multi-platform, multi-user 3D VW server (OpenSimulator 2011).

The **causal connection** layer causally connects the visual interaction and the normative layers, i.e. whenever one of them changes, the other one changes in order to maintain a consistent state (Maes and Nardi 1988). This layer implements a *multi-verse communication* mechanism that allows users from different virtual worlds to participate in the same VI. The mapping between VW actions and AMELI protocol messages – and vice versa – is defined by a *movie script* mechanism. Moreover, VIXEE uses the Virtual World Grammar (VWG) mechanism and its implementation

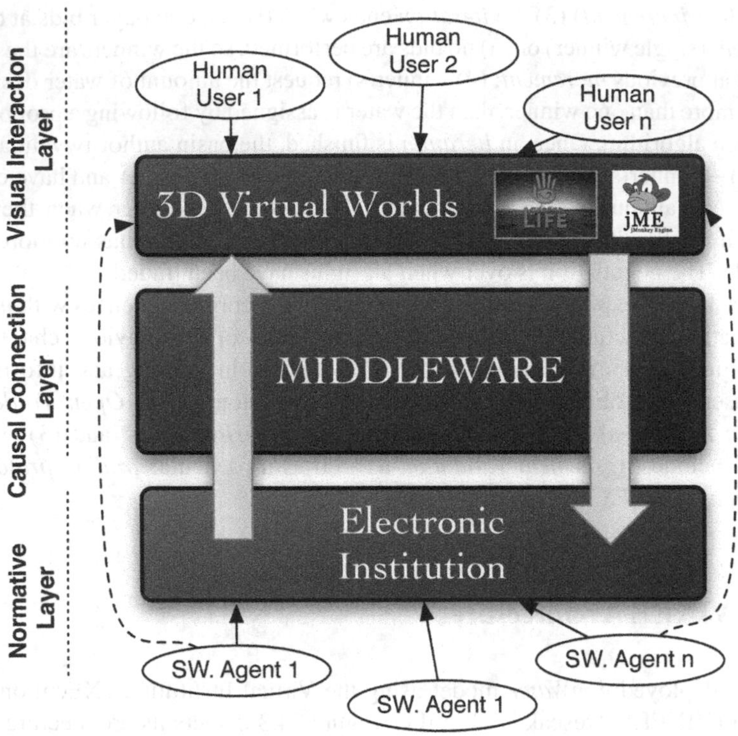

Fig. 34.3 Overview of VIXEE architecture

in the Virtual World Builder Toolkit (VWBT) to dynamically manipulate the 3D representation of all connected virtual worlds (Trescak et al. 2010).

34.5 The Application

34.5.1 Setting Up the Model

In order to engineer *v-mWater*, we define the three following steps:

First, we specify the normative control layer of the virtual institution – that is an electronic institution – using ISLANDER tool (Esteva 2003). The output is the electronic institution specification introduced in Sect. 34.3.2.

Second, using the VWBT tool, we generate the 3D representation from *v-mWater* specification. Figure 34.4a depicts the resulted generation in Open Simulator (OpenSimulator 2011). In particular, it shows an aerial view of three rooms located at an open space that correspond to the three main activities in *v-mWater*. Participants join and leave these activities by opening (and crossing) the doors of these rooms. Moreover, transitions between activities are experienced as movements in the open space.

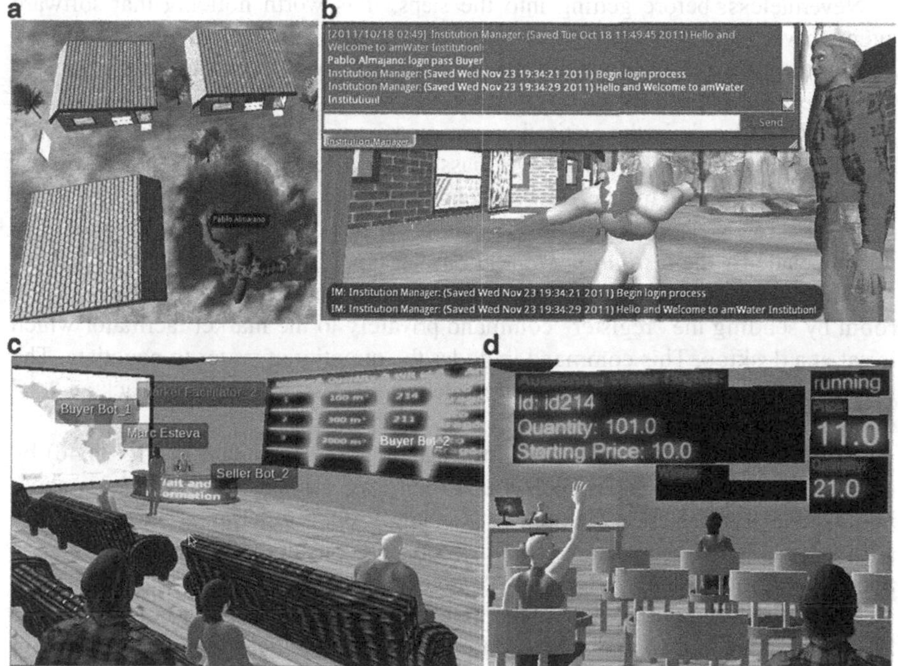

Fig. 34.4 Examples of *v-mWater* running. (**a**) Initial aerial view. (**b**) Human avatar login: interaction with a software agent by means of a chat window. (**c**) The inside of the *Waiting and Information* room. (**d**) Bot bidding in a running auction

Third, using the *movie script* mechanism we define the mapping between VW actions and EI messages and vice versa. In this first prototype, some actions in the VW (such as touching a door to open it) are mapped to EI messages (join the activity taking place in the room). Additionally, commands typed on chat windows in the VW (e.g., the login chat represented in Fig. 34.4b) have been mapped to protocol messages in the EI. On the other hand, some of the bot messages in the EI are represented as gestures made by its respective avatar in the VW. Thus, for instance, a "bid" message is mapped to a "raise hand" gesture as depicted in Fig. 34.4d.

34.5.2 Running the Application

In this section we comment on key aspects of the result of the engineering process mentioned above. They are introduced by following a particular sequence that a given participant may follow.[2]

[2] Watch video at youtube http://www.youtube.com/watch?v=OisCys8q_i8 for a complete visualization of such a participation sequence.

Nevertheless, before getting into the steps, it is worth noticing that software agents have been characterized as bots with the aim of enhancing their artificial nature: they are bold and have differentiated artificial skin colours that represent their roles (see Fig. 34.4b–d).

In order to Login in the institution, we send a private message to the *Institution Manager* bot with the content "login pass role". Where "pass" is replaced by our password and "role" by the desired role to play in the institution (either seller or buyer). The welcome event to the institution has been mapped to a "greeting" gesture made by the *Institution Manager* avatar (see Fig. 34.4b).

When playing a seller role, we can register a water right in the Registration room by sending the "register" command privately to the market facilitator which is sat at a desktop. This command includes the quantity of water to negotiate. The market facilitator then performs the registering process and sends us back an "ok" or "failure" message.

We can access the Waiting and Information room (depicted in Fig. 34.4c) by enacting a seller or a buyer role. In this room, we can ask for information about negotiations to the market facilitator sat at a desktop. Furthermore, we can wait by sitting down on the sofas arranged in the room and consult the available information about negotiations displayed on the dynamic information panels.

In the Auction room the market facilitator and the basin authority bots are located at their respective desktops and several chairs are available within the room for buyer participants. Figure 34.4d shows how human participation in the auction has been improved by providing a comprehensive environment that includes dynamic information panels. Moreover, the bots' bid actions can be also easily identified by human participants since they are displayed as raising hands.

34.6 Related Work

Public administrations are increasing the use of e-Governments to provide a variety of services over the internet to citizens such as, for instance, tax returns, administrative process, personal information update and voting (Chadwick and May 2003). A water market is a government service available in many countries with water scarcity problems that can be provided as an e-Government application. For instance, *Waterfind* is an intermediary private company which offers web-based tools to access the national market in Australia (e.g., place online buy or sell water rights orders, buy from or sell to a previous registered order or see real-time information about orders) (WaterFind 2011). *v-mWater* can provide such tools (because it is an electronic market for water rights) and also improve human participation by means of an interactive and immersive 3D environment.

A research work models a MAS for the management of e-Government services. It improves citizens' access to government information distributed among agencies following strict interactions (De Meo et al. 2005). *v-mWater* is modelled as an OCMAS which structures agent interactions as well as enforce government norms.

With respect to MAS and VW combination, Ranathunga et al provide a framework which connects a BDI agent platform to the VW server Second Life[3] (Ranathunga and Cranefield 2011). This framework includes an online monitor of social expectations that notifies agents when their expectations of others (i.e. actions performed in the virtual world) have been fulfilled or violated (Cranefield and Li 2009). Another work integrates a MAS developed in JADE with the VW server Open Wonderland (http://openwonderland.org/) by modifying an existing Open Wonderland module that starts a JADE agent (Blair and Lin 2011). *v-mWater* is a Virtual Institution that uses a robust infrastructure which causally connect a domain independent OCMAS platform (EI) with VWs.

Gartner et al. combine an EI and a VW to deploy an e-Commerce virtual organisation in the tourism domain by using the 3D Electronic Institution framework architecture (Gärtner et al. 2010). Regarding Virtual Institutions, an e-Learning application simulates the culture of the ancient City of Uruk (Bogdanovych et al. 2010). Both infrastructures allow the connection of an EI to a given VW, while *v-mWater* uses VIXEE architecture that allows the connection to multiple VWs as well as the dynamic manipulation of the 3D representation of all connected VWs.

34.7 Conclusions and Future Work

In this chapter we use Virtual Institutions (VI), which combine both multi-agent systems and 3D interfaces, to engineer e-* applications. A VI is composed of (i) a normative layer which structures participants interactions, (ii) a visual interaction layer which provides a 3D interface for direct human participation in the system, (iii) and a communication layer.

We present an e-government prototype for water rights agreements named *v-mWater*, a *v*irtual *m*arket based on trading *Water*. First, we specify the normative layer, i.e. the Electronic Institution (EI) which defines agent roles, activities' protocols and roles' workflow between activities. Then, from this specification we generate the visual interaction layer, i.e. a 3D Virtual World (VW) representation using the Virtual World Builder Toolkit (VWBT). And finally, we use the Virtual Institution eXEcution Environment (VIXEE) to deploy *v-mWater*, connecting the normative (i.e. EI) and the visual interaction (i.e. VW) layers.

We proposed an immersive environment where humans participate in the institution by controlling an avatar which allows their interaction with the environment and other participants, software or human agents. Software agents are directly connected to the institution and can be represented as bots in the VW in order to highlight their artificial nature. As result, our system has favoured direct human participation in MAS.

[3] http://secondlife.com/

As future work, we will extend *v-mWater* with assistance services to participants, and so make their participation in the system more efficient. Moreover, we plan to evaluate the usability of the prototype by measuring interface effectiveness, efficiency and user experience.

Acknowledgements This work is partially funded by EVE (TIN2009-14702-C02-01/TIN2009-14702-C02-02) and AT (CONSOLIDER CSD2007-0022) Spanish research projects, EU-FEDER funds and the Catalan government (Grant 2005-SGR-00093).

In memoriam of Marc Esteva, who actively contributed to our research line. With his passing we have lost a great colleague and supervisor. It will be an honour to continue working on his scientific seed.

References

Almajano, P., M. López-Sánchez, M. Esteva, and I. Rodriguez. 2011. An assistance infrastructure for open MAS. In *Artificial intelligence research and development – proceedings of the 14th international conference of the Catalan association for artificial intelligence*, Lleida, Catalonia, Spain, vol. 232, ed. C. Fernández, H. Geffner and F. Manyà, 1–10. Amsterdam: IOS Press.

Almarabeh, T., and A. AbuAli. 2010. A general framework for E-government: Definition maturity challenges, opportunities, and success. *European Journal of Scientific Research*, 39(1): 29–42.

Arcos, J., M. Esteva, P. Noriega, J. Rodríguez-Aguilar, and C. Sierra. 2005. An integrated development environment for electronic institutions. In *Software agent-based applications, platforms and development kits*, 121–142. Basel/Boston: Birkhäuser.

Bartle, R. 2003. Designing virtual worlds. *New riders games*, vol. 7. Indianapolis, USA: New Riders.

Bjornlund, H., and P. Rossini. 2010. Climate change, water scarcity and water markets: Implications for farmers' Wealth and farm succession. In *Proceedings from the 16th annual conference of the Pacific Rim Real Estate Society*, Wellington, New Zealand.

Blair, J., and F. Lin. 2011. An approach for integrating 3D virtual worlds with multiagent systems. In *Proceedings of the IEEE workshops of the international conference on advanced information networking and applications*, 580–585. Washington, DC, USA: IEEE Computer Society.

Bogdanovych, A. 2007. *Virtual institutions*. Ph.D. thesis, University of Technology, Sydney.

Bogdanovych, A., J.A. Rodriguez-Aguilar, S. Simoff, and A. Cohen. 2010. Authentic interactive reenactment of cultural heritage with 3d virtual worlds and artificial intelligence. *Applications of Artificial Intelligence* 24: 617–647.

Chadwick, A., and C. May. 2003. Interaction between states and citizens in the age of the internet: "e-government" in the United States, Britain, and the European Union. *Governance* 16(2): 271–300.

Cranefield, S., and G. Li. 2009. Monitoring social expectations in Second Life (Extended Abstract). In *Proceedings of The 8th international conference on autonomous agents and multiagent systems*, AAMAS '09, vol. 2, 1303–1304. Budapest, Hungary. Richland: International Foundation for Autonomous Agents and Multiagent Systems.

De Meo, P., G. Quattrone, D. Ursino, and G. Terracina. 2005. A multi-agent system for the management of E-government services. In *Proceedings of the IEEE/WIC/ACM international conference on intelligent agent technology*, IAT '05, 718–724. Washington, DC, USA: IEEE Computer Society. http://dx.doi.org/10.1109/IAT.2005.14.

Esteva, M. 2003. *Electronic institutions. From specification to development*. Ph.D. thesis, UPC.

Ferber, J., O. Gutknecht, and F. Michel. 2004. From agents to organizations: An organizational view of multi-agent systems. In *Agent-oriented software engineering IV*, ed. Giorgini, P.,

Müller, J. and Odell, J., Lecture Notes in Computer Science, vol. 2935, 214–230. Berlin/New York: Springer Berlin Heidelberg. http://dx.doi.org/10.1007/978-3-540-24620-6_15.

Gärtner, M., I. Seidel, J. Froschauer, and H. Berger. 2010. The formation of virtual organizations by means of electronic institutions in a 3d e-tourism environment. *Information Sciences* 180: 3157–3169.

Giret, A., A. Garrido, J. A. Gimeno, V. Botti, and P. Noriega. 2011. A MAS decision support tool for water-right markets. In *The 10th international conference on autonomous agents and multiagent systems*, vol. 3, AAMAS '11, Taipei, Taiwan, 1305–1306. International Foundation for Autonomous Agents and Multiagent Systems.

Jennings, N.R., K. Sycara, and M. Wooldridge. 1998. A roadmap of agent research and development. *Autonomous Agents and Multi-Agent Systems* 1: 7–38.

Maes, P., and D. Nardi, (ed.). 1988. *Meta-level architectures and reflection*. New York: Elsevier Science Inc.

Messinger, P.R., E. Stroulia, K. Lyons, M. Bone, R.H. Niu, K. Smirnov, and S. Perelgut. 2009. Virtual worlds – past, present, and future: New directions in social computing. *Decision Support Systems*, 47(3): 204–228.

OpenSimulator. 2011. http://opensimulator.org.

Ranathunga, S., S. Cranefield, and M. Purvis. 2012. Agents for educational games and simulations. Lecture Notes in Computer Science, ed. M. Beer, C. Brom, F. Dignum, S. Von-Wun, vol. 7471, 1–21. Berlin/Heidelberg: Springer.

Trescak, T., M. Esteva, and I. Rodriguez. 2010. A virtual world grammar for automatic generation of virtual worlds. *The Visual Computer*, 26: 521–531.

Trescak, T., M. Esteva, and I. Rodriguez. 2011. VIXEE an innovative communication infrastructure for virtual institutions (extended abstract). In *The 10th international conference on autonomous agents and multiagent systems*, vol. 3, AAMAS '11, Taipei, Taiwan. 1131–1132. International Foundation for Autonomous Agents and Multiagent Systems.

WaterFind. 2011. Water market specialists. http://www.waterfind.com.au/.

Chapter 35
Coordinating Emergency Medical Assistance

Marin Lujak and Holger Billhardt

35.1 Introduction

The domain of medical assistance in general, and of emergency situations in particular, includes many tasks that require flexible on-demand negotiation, initiation, coordination, information exchange and supervision among the different entities involved (e.g., ambulances, emergency centres, hospitals, patients, physicians, etc.). Furthermore, it is a domain in which the involved parties, especially patients and medical professionals, can benefit from the introduction of new informatic services. Services that aid in the process of getting medical help in case of a sudden disease or emergency have a clear benefit for patients. Such services may consist of locating the nearest hospital or medical centre, including the description of the route to get there, or in calling the local emergency centre in order to order an ambulance. From the point of view of medical professionals, they could be liberated from certain standard decision and negotiation tasks that are currently carried out by humans but that could be delegated to artificial agents. Such tasks include, for instance, the assignment of ambulances to emergency patients, or finding an appropriate hospital for a patient. Finally, augmenting the possibilities of exchanging data on-demand among different parties, e.g., medical records, will be beneficial for the whole system, because it allows for more personalized and, thus, more effective medical treatments.

In this Chapter we present our multi-agent organization-based application for the integrated management of emergency medical assistance (EMA): the processes involved in attending people that suffer sudden illnesses at any possible location

---

M. Lujak (✉) • H. Billhardt
CETINIA, University Rey Juan Carlos, Madrid, Spain
e-mail: marin.lujak@urjc.es; holger.billhardt@urjc.es

S. Ossowski (ed.), *Agreement Technologies*, Law, Governance and Technology Series 8, DOI 10.1007/978-94-007-5583-3_35,

within an area of influence – including a possible in-situ assistance and the transfer to a medical centre. The application is based on the operation of the Emergency Medical Coordination Centre *SUMMA112*; the centre responsible for out-of-hospital medical assistance in the Autonomous Region of Madrid in Spain. The application has two main objectives. On one hand, it aims to provide a seamless interaction between the participating entities assuring that the specified protocols and norms that regulate the assistance processes are fulfilled. Furthermore, the application provides access to remote medical data of an emergency patient, if such data is available, and thus, allows medical professionals to make better decisions about the appropriate treatment of a patient. On the other hand, the application employs coordination mechanisms that aim at an efficient use of the available resources (ambulances) from a global point of view. The main goal here is to improve overall key performance indicators, in particular to reduce the average response times to emergency calls (time a patient has to wait for an ambulances) and to increase the percentage of patients with short or acceptable response times.

Regarding the second objective, EMA managers are faced with two main problems: allocation and a redeployment of ambulances. The allocation problem consists of determining that an ambulance that should be sent to assist a given patient. Redeployment consists of, whenever an available ambulance gets allocated to a new patient or a busy ambulance becomes idle again, relocating the available ambulances to locations where emergencies will occur with high probability. While we are still working on integrating mechanisms for the redeployment of ambulances, in this Chapter we present three different approaches for the ambulance allocation problem: (i) trust-based selection, (ii) auction-based negotiation, and (iii) auction-based negotiation with trust information. The trust-based selection takes into account possible differences among ambulances in driving performance influenced by driver's skills and driving characteristics inherent to each individual ambulance vehicle. Regarding auction-based negotiation, it tends to optimize the overall travel times when different ambulances have to be allocated at the same time and taking into account the dynamic evolution of the system.

The outline of the Chapter is as follows. In Sect. 35.2, we present some related work. In Sect. 35.3, we analyse the general structure of EMA services. Section 35.4 contains the overall description of our EMA application and focuses on some of its key features. In Sect. 35.5, we present the coordination mechanisms we employ to provide a solution to the ambulance allocation problem. We briefly describe the problem and the three different approaches we have used: trust-based selection, auction-based negotiation, and of auction-based negotiation with trust information. Section 35.6 presents an experimental evaluation of the different ambulance allocation mechanisms in comparison to a standard first-come first-served (FSFS) model. Finally, Sect. 35.7 gives some conclusions and points out some aspects of our current and future research.

35.2 Related Work

The current state of EMA services can be summarised as follows. There exist several commercial software applications for emergency medical services, mainly on the US market (e.g., RescueNet Data Management Suite for EMS, National EMS Information System, Medical Response Emergency Software), that usually combine different tools for different parts of the emergency assistance process (e.g., computer aided dispatching, management of calls, billing software, etc.). On the other hand, especially in public health care systems as they are often present in Europe, many emergency services have their own proprietary software systems. In practice, most of the employed software solutions do not integrate and provide support to all participants in the assistance process (patients, coordination centres, hospitals, ambulance crews) and do not take into account their specific needs and preferences. Furthermore, there is a lack of integration of remote medical data, even though such data might be accessible through the Internet. In many systems, the selection of ambulances and/or hospitals is done manually or is only partially supported by the software tools. Some proposals of more integrated solutions have been presented in Ciampolini et al. (2004) and Centeno et al. (2009a,b).

In the research community, there have been many proposals regarding the allocation and the redeployment of ambulances. Brotcorne et al. provides a good review of ambulance allocation and redeployment strategies from the early 1970s through 2003 (Brotcorne et al. 2003). Most of the state-of-the-art approaches are either static or probabilistic. Some of the models consider allocation and redeployment together, while others concentrate only on the redeployment of ambulances (see, e.g., Gendreau et al. 2001; Glover 1986). In Henderson and Mason (2005), authors apply a statistical model using historical data of emergency calls.

More recent research has focused on developing dynamic optimization models to repeatedly relocate ambulances throughout the day (see, e.g., Gendreau et al. 2001; Rajagopalan et al. 2008). The dynamic multi-agent model is better than static and probabilistic ones since it produces a solution which depends on the current state of the system and adapts adequately and quickly to unpredicted new situations. The model developed by Gendreau et al. (2001) makes use of the deterministic static model which in addition to the standard coverage and site capacity constraints, takes into account a number of practical considerations inherent to the dynamic nature of the problem. However, in the case of too little time between two patient occurrences, the model does not find a solution and no reallocation takes place.

35.3 Emergency Medical Assistance Services

EMA services might have different forms of operation. However, there are some main lines of emergency management common to all of them. The assistance procedure typically starts when a patient calls an Emergency Coordination Centre asking for assistance. The call is received by an operator who screens the call and gathers initial data from the patient. The operator, maybe together with a physician, assigns one of several levels of severity to incoming calls. Usually there are four levels of severity, e.g. from zero to three: level zero, urgent life-threatening calls; level one, urgent but not life-threatening calls; level two, less urgent calls, and level three representing none-urgent calls. The number of levels and their description may vary for different EMA services. According to the evaluation of the severity of a call, a specific type and number of ambulances is assigned, taking into account their availability, distance, and the estimated time to reach the patient. When the ambulance arrives at the patient's location, the crew provides first aid and in some cases in-situ assistance. According to the conditions of the patient, he/she is transported or not to hospital.

The assignment of ambulances and hospitals is usually done using the closest method rule based on the first-come/first-served (FCFS) principle and taking into account the severity level of a patient. That is, the first patient of a given level is assigned to the closest ambulance, then the next patient is assigned to the next closest ambulance, and so on, taking as candidates always the ambulances that are available at each time.

EMA services typically work with at least two types of ambulances having basic life support (BLS) and advanced life support (ALS) units. In the most severe cases, the time a patient has to wait until an ambulance arrives is directly related with the chances of saving his/her life. This is why ambulances should be at all times located in the positions which guarantee a quick average response time. The positions of ambulances are usually available to the Coordination Centre through a Geographic Positioning System (GPS).

35.4 Emergency Medical Assistance Application

The application proposed in this work is designed as an organization-based Service-Oriented Multi-Agent System that integrates access to external (e.g., web) services and provides itself services to external agents (e.g., patients). The EMA organisation is the core of the system. Besides different types of agents, it incorporates two organisational or coordination mechanisms (*trust mechanism* and *auction-based negotiation*) that can be seen as environmental artifacts providing additional services to agents. The overall architecture is presented in Fig. 35.1.

35.4.1 EMA Multi-agent Organisation

Inspired by the operation of SUMMA112, five different agent roles are defined in the system:

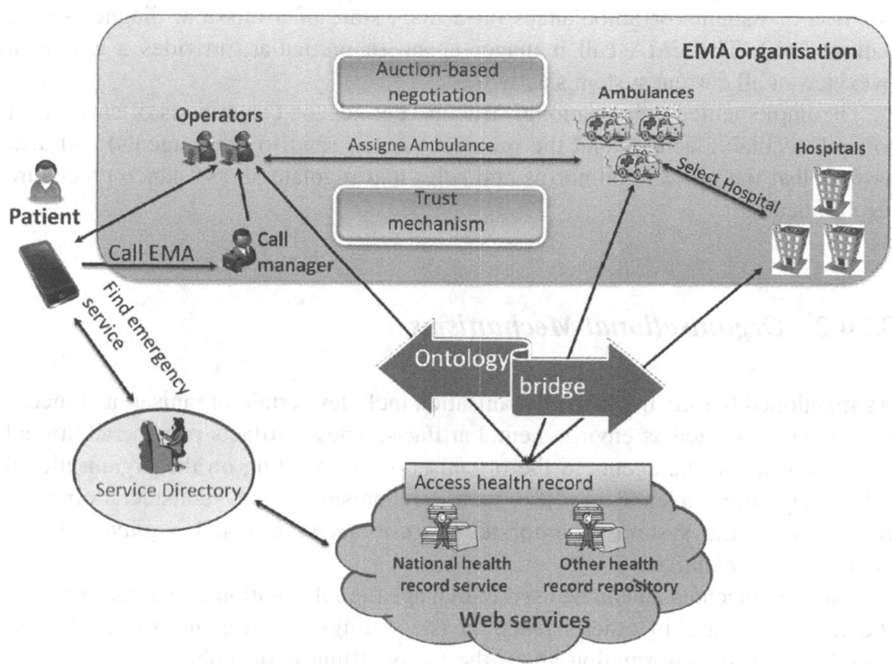

Fig. 35.1 Medical emergency transportation: AT architecture

- *EMA Call manager*: represents the call centre of the system and is in charge of receiving incoming emergency calls, and assigning them to available operators.
- *Operator*: attends the incoming emergency calls, determines the first diagnosis for the calling patient and passes the mission to the *ambulance allocation mechanism*.
- *Ambulance*: represents an ambulance vehicle with its crew. It may be categorized within different ambulance types and it is responsible for the missions assigned to it (moving to the patients location, providing in-situ assistance and transferring the patient to a hospital, if necessary).
- *Hospital*: represents a hospital within the system. It provides information about the availability of each of its services and receives information of arriving patients sent by ambulance agents.
- *Patient*: represents a person with a medical problem, who requests medical assistance from the EMA service. Patient agents are external agents that use the services provided by the EMA organisation. The patient agent is installed on a person's mobile phone, thereby allowing agent-to-agent communication with the Call manager.

Each agent in the system provides a user interface that presents relevant information to the medical professionals involved in the assistance process (e.g., position of patients or ambulances on a map, state of a mission, diagnosis of a patient, etc.). The EMA call manager agent, in particular, provides a graphical overview of all current system's activities.

The implemented organisational structure defines the capabilities of each agent role (its available actions and the messages it can send to other agents) and also assures that the operational norms and rules that regulate an assistance procedure are fulfilled.

35.4.2 Organisational Mechanisms

As mentioned before, the EMA organisation includes certain organisational mechanisms implemented as environmental artifacts. These artifacts provide additional services to assist the agents in the organisation. Depending on the organisational rules and norms, agents may use such mechanisms if they consider doing so. In particular, the system incorporates a *trust mechanism* and a *auction-based negotiation mechanism*.

The trust mechanism can be used to manage the information of agents regarding the trust they have in other agents. In our settings, we use this mechanism to establish and use information about the trustworthiness of ambulances regarding their efficiency in arriving faster at patient's location. This information can be taken into account when ambulances are assigned to patients.

The auction-based negotiation mechanism allows the assignment of ambulances to patients to be coordinated through an iterative auction-based negotiation process. Operators may use this mechanism to (re)assign ambulance to patients. The mechanism performs the patient assignment taking into consideration all currently present assignments and reassigns ambulances if needed to lower the average travel time. A more detailed description of different ambulance allocation methods is given in Sect. 35.5.

35.4.3 External Services

The EMA organisation may be accessed by external agents (e.g., patients) as an EMA service. In this regard, it may publish the provision of the EMA service in any service directory. Patient agents, can then find this service by querying such directories.

One important feature of the system is the usage of external services to access remote medical data from patients (if such information is available). To facilitate this task, a patient agent, when calling the EMA service, may provide access information to his/her medical record on remote repositories (e.g., URL and authorization information). This access information is passed to all agents that have to deal with the patient. In order to overcome the semantic heterogeneity of different formats of medical health records (or other patient related medical information) we employ *ontology bridges*. These modules, after accessing the corresponding repository and receiving the patients medical data, perform a process of semantic filtering in order to extract relevant information for the emergency case. The module extracts all data regarding allergies, vaccines, medications and procedures. The filtering process is supported by *mappings*. The latter include descriptions on how to interpret the data format of external repositories and relate concepts of the internal representation of medical data to concepts in the representation language of the external source. In order to interpret data from a new external source, it is sufficient to specify new mappings for that source. This can be done either manually, or by using some automatic semantic alignment techniques.

35.5 Ambulance Allocation Methods

One of the tasks of the system is to assign ambulances to emergency patients in an automatic way. Formally, the allocation problem can be defined as follows. Considering a time horizon made of T time periods $1,\ldots,T$, given is a group of n collaborative ambulance agents $A = \{a_1,\ldots,a_n\}$. Furthermore, let $\Theta(t) = \{\theta_1,\ldots\theta_m\}$ denotes the set of patients to be attended at time t. Ambulances and patients are positioned, w.l.o.g., in a square environment $E = [0,l]^2 \subset \mathbf{R}^2$ of side length $l > 0$. $p(a_i,t)$ and $p(\theta_k,t)$ denote the position of ambulance a_i and patient θ_k at time t.

The situation of an ambulance a_i at time t can be described as a tuple:

$$a_i(t) = \{p(a_i,t),\ v_{a_i}, pat_{a_i}(t)\}\ ,$$

where $p(a_i,t)$ is the ambulances position, v_{a_i} is its velocity and $pat_{a_i}(t)$ represents the patient assigned to ambulance a_i at time t ($pat_{a_i}(t) = 0$ if no patient is assigned).

Let $c(a_i,\theta_k,t)$ be the distance between the positions of ambulance a_i and patient θ_k at time t.

The assignment problem consists of determining which ambulances should be assigned to each patient so as to dynamically minimize the average travel time for all the appearing patients from the momentary positions of ambulances at each time step t. In our approach we assume that ambulances have a constant velocity, thus, the optimization can be carried out based on distances.

The standard strategy used in many real world EMA services is the fist come/first serve approach. It works as follows: at each time t, the first patient θ_1 is assigned to the available ambulance a_i that minimizes $c(a_i,\theta_1,t)$. Then, the next patient θ_2 is assigned to the available ambulance a_j that minimizes $c(a_j,\theta_2,t)$. The process is repeated until all patients have been assigned.

In the following subsections we briefly present three alternative methods that improve the overall travel times.

35.5.1 Trust-Based Ambulance Allocation

In this case, we assume that ambulances may have inherent performance differences in terms of speed. Such differences, reflect different reliability levels of ambulances and may be due to multiple tangible and intangible factors like, for example, driver's driving skills, structural characteristics of an ambulance (e.g., a model, age), and traffic situation on the road. Such different reliability levels may be reflected through the notion of trust.

Let $trust_{a_i}(t) \in [0\ldots 1]$ denote the trust the assignment mechanism has in ambulance a_i at time t based on the ambulances previous behaviour. $trust_{a_i}(t) = 0$ implies no trust and $trust_{a_i}(t) = 1$ complete trust. The trust value is the same regarding all possible patients, e.g., the reliability of an ambulance regarding travel times does not depend on the assigned patient and, thus, we can include the trust as an additional factor in the cost of the ambulance assignments. Based on this idea, we modify the classical first come/first serve strategy by selecting for each patient θ_j the ambulance a_i that minimizes $c(a_i, \theta_j, t)/trust_{a_i}(t)$. That is, we chose the closest ambulance to a patient with respect to a trust-weighted distance.

35.5.2 Auction-Based Negotiation

The classical FCFS approach to the assignment problem is not optimal in cases where more than one patient have to be attended at the same time. From an overall perspective, on certain occasions, the average response time may be improved by reassigning an ambulance that has already been assigned to attend a patient to another patient that appeared later. This may occur if no available ambulance is close to the new patient, but there are other ambulances close to the first patient. Based on this, we propose a continuous dynamic (re)assignment of patients. In particular, whenever a new patient appears or any ambulance becomes available again, we start the (re)assignment of all patients to ambulances (including patients that have been already assigned, but where the ambulance has not yet reached the patient).

With this approach, the allocation problem defines the assignment of m patients to n ambulances, $m \leq n$, such that the overall average distance is minimized. We solve this problem by employing the dynamic iterative auction algorithm with mobility described in Lujak and Giordani (2011) and inspired by the Bertsekas auction algorithm (Bertsekas 1992). The former algorithm is stable in the case of communication network breakdown, providing an optimal solution if the communication network remains fully connected and a near-optimal solution if the network partially breaks down.

Table 35.1 Comparison of trust-based and standard FCFS allocation

	Trust-based	Standard FCFS
Average waiting time, [min]	14:58	15:35
Patients assisted faster, [%]	18.1	11.3

35.5.3 Auction-Based Negotiation with Trust

In this approach we enhance the auction-based negotiation with trust information. In particular, the dynamics of the method and the algorithm to solve the $m \times n$ assignment problem is the same as in the one used in the previous strategy. However, the cost function applied in the auction algorithm (the distance of an ambulance to a patient $c(a_i, \theta_j, t)$) is weighted, giving rise to the new function: $c_{trust}(a_i, \theta_j, t) = c(a_i, \theta_j, t)/trust_{a_i}(t)$.

35.6 Experimental Results

We tested the performance of the three allocation methods in different experiments and compared their results with the standard FCFS allocation approach. For the experiments we used a semi-realistic simulation tool. This tool allows for a semi-realistic simulation of time intervals of the normal operation of an EMA service. All movements are simulated using Google Maps technology. That means, ambulances "move" on the actual road network with a velocity adapted to the type of road. External factors, like traffic conditions or others, are ignored.

35.6.1 Trust-Based Ambulance Allocation

In this case we compared the performance of the trust-based allocation with the standard FCFS approach. In the experiment we simulated the operation of SUMMA112 with real patient data of the 12th of January 2009 (a day with 221 patients, the highest number of level 0 patients during 2009). In the simulation we only considered level 0 patients. We used 29 ambulances and 29 hospitals (the real data from the Madrid region). Each ambulance has an assigned speed factor (randomly chosen between 0.6 and 1.0) which is applied in their movements. That is, an ambulance with factor 0.8 has a velocity of 0.8 times the standard velocity calculated by Google Maps. Initially, the trust values of ambulances are set to 0.8. During operation these values are updated when new observations are available. For this, we compare the estimated travel time with the actual travel time.

The results of the experiment are presented in Table 35.1 and Fig. 35.2.

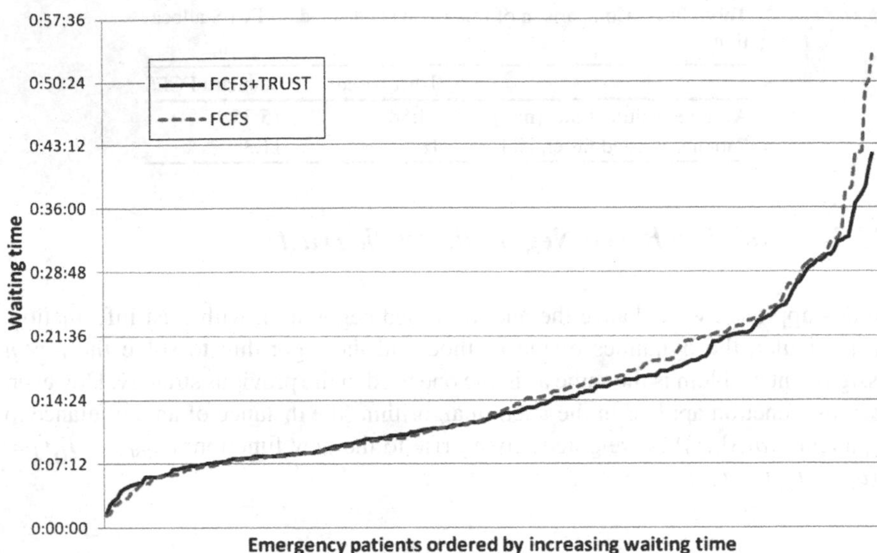

Fig. 35.2 Comparison of trust-based and standard FCFS allocation

As can be seen, trust-based allocation improves the average travel times of ambulances to patients by about half a minute. Also, analysing Fig. 35.2 it can be observed that the improvements are slightly higher for medium and longer travel times (e.g., patients located in more remote regions).

35.6.2 Auction-Based Negotiation of Ambulance Allocation

To test the auction-based negotiation we used the same experimental setting as before (same number and initial positions of ambulances and hospitals, same patient data, same speed factors for ambulances). The auction-based ambulance allocation mechanism is activated each time an ambulance becomes idle (after a previous mission) and each time a new patient appears. In these cases, it may reassign all current missions in a way that the overall distance from ambulances assigned to patients is minimized. In the peak hours of the simulated operation day (12th of January 2009) up to about ten patients have to be attended at the same time and, especially in these cases, more efficient assignments may be found. Assuming that a reassignment may have an additional cost, we employ a threshold to avoid reassignments that provide only small improvements. A current ambulance/patient assignment is only changed if this improves the overall distance (sum of all distances of ambulances to their assigned patients) by at least 800 m.

The results of the experiment are presented in Table 35.2 and in Fig. 35.3.

These results confirm that the auction-based approach performs better than the standard FCFS method. This only occurs if there are intervals of time where more

Table 35.2 Comparison of auction-based negotiation (with and without trust) and standard FCFS allocation

	Auction	Auction + trust	Standard FCFS
Average waiting time, [min]	14:56	14:42	15:35
Patients assisted faster (as compared to FCFS), [%]	19.0	24.9	
Patients assisted slower (as compared to FCFS), [%]	11.7	17.2	

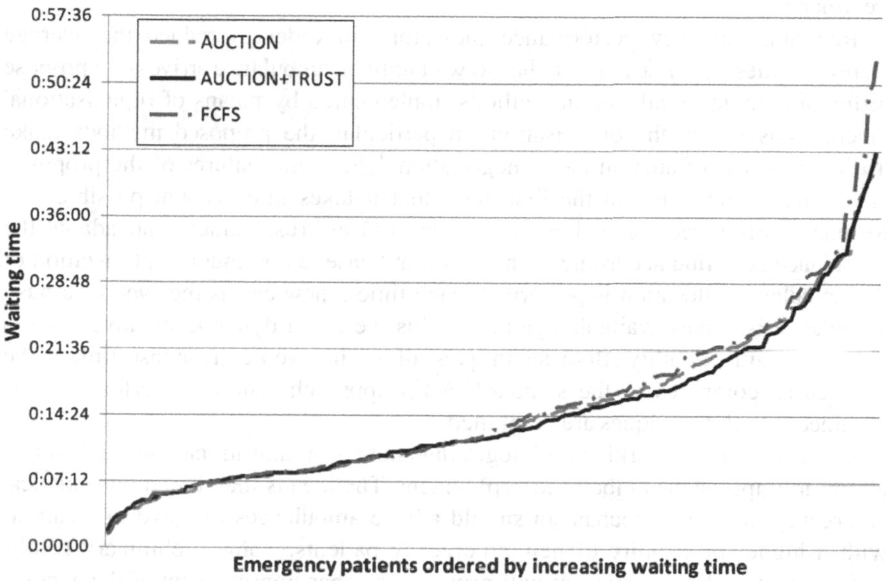

Fig. 35.3 Comparison of auction-based negotiation (with and without trust) and standard FCFS allocation

than one patient has to be attended. The average waiting times of patients is reduced even more (about 1 min in average) if auction-based negotiation is used together with a trust model. Similar to the previous results, the improvements are concentrated on patients that require medium and longer travel times. In addition, the average daily travel distance of the 29 ambulances is also reduced from about 130 km to about 120 km (per day).

35.7 Conclusions

In this Chapter, we presented an application to support EMA services. This application uses different AT related methods to provide support to the whole emergency assistance procedure and to all involved participants. The application is conceived as an organisation-based multi agent system. Organisational structures define the capabilities of the participating agents and the norms and rules that regulate the interactions and assure that those norms are fulfilled by the agents. The system uses semantic-based technologies. The organisation itself provides services to external agents (e.g., assistance service for patients) and can be accessed through service directories. Furthermore, the system uses ontology bridges to integrate medical data of patients (e.g., health record) with potentially different formats and that may be located at remote repositories. Providing such data at the right time and the right place allows for more personalized and, thus, more effective medical treatments.

Regarding the key performance indicators, in order to reduce the average response times (the time a patient has to wait until an ambulance arrives) we propose different ambulance allocation methods implemented by means of organisational mechanisms within the organisation. In particular, the proposed methods make use of trust and of auction-based negotiation. The main features of the proposed allocation methods are, in the first case, that it takes into account possible performance differences of ambulances (measured as trust values) and adapts the ambulance selection accordingly. In the second case, a continuous optimization of the ambulance allocation is performed each time a new call is received or a busy ambulance becomes available again. For this we use a dynamic iterative auction algorithm with mobility. Both techniques allow the average response time to be reduced as compared to the standard FCFS approach. The best performance is obtained if both techniques are combined.

Currently we are working on integrating another organisational mechanism that allows to improve the ambulance deployment. The idea is that, based on statistical emergency data, this mechanism should advice ambulances to move to locations with a higher probability of new emergency patients. Some preliminary results confirm that such a mechanism will provide a further improvement of the average response times, especially in the "difficult" cases (e.g., patients appearing at remote, low density locations).

Acknowledgements We thank the professionals from SUMMA112, especially Vicente Sánchez-Brunete and Pedro Huertas, for their support and helpful comments. This work was supported in part by the Spanish Ministry of Science and Innovation through the projects "AT" (Grant CONSOLIDER CSD2007-0022, INGENIO 2010) and "OVAMAH" (Grant TIN2009-13839-C03-02) co-funded by Plan E.

References

Bertsekas, D. 1992. Auction algorithms for network flow problems: A tutorial introduction. *Computational Optimization and Applications* 1(1): 7–66.

Brotcorne, L., G. Laporte, and F. Semet. 2003. Ambulance location and relocation models. *European Journal of Operational Research* 147(3): 451–463.

Centeno, R., M. Fagundes, H. Billhardt, and S. Ossowski. 2009a. Supporting medical emergencies by mas. In *Proceedings of the third KES international symposium on agent and multi-agent systems: Technologies and applications*, 823–833. Berlin/New York: Springer.

Centeno, R., M. Fagundes, H. Billhardt, S. Ossowski, J. Corchado, V. Julian, and A. Fernandez. 2009b. An organisation-based multiagent system for medical emergency assistance. In *Proceedings of IWANN 2009, bio-inspired systems: Computational and ambient intelligence*, 561–568. Berlin/New York: Springer.

Ciampolini, A., P. Mello, and S. Storari. 2004. A multi-agent system for medical services synergy and coordination. In *International ECAI 2004 workshop on agents applied in health care*, ed. J. Nealon, U. Cortes, J. Fox, and A. Moreno, 38–46. Valencia: Spain.

Gendreau, M., G. Laporte, and F. Semet. 2001. A dynamic model and parallel tabu search heuristic for real-time ambulance relocation. *Parallel Computing* 27(12): 1641–1653.

Glover, F. 1986. Future paths for integer programming and links to artificial intelligence. *Computers and Operations Research* 13(5): 533–549.

Henderson, S., and A. Mason. 2005. Ambulance service planning: Simulation and data visualisation. *Operations Research and Health Care* 70: 77–102.

Lujak, M., and S. Giordani. 2011. On the communication range in auction-based multi-agent target assignment. In: *IWSOS'11: Proceedings of the 5th international conference on Self-organizing systems*, LNCS, vol. 6557, 32–43. Berlin/New York: Springer.

Rajagopalan, H., C. Saydam, and J. Xiao. 2008. A multiperiod set covering location model for dynamic redeployment of ambulances. *Computers and Operations Research* 35(3): 814–826.

Chapter 36
An Environment to Build and Track Agent-Based Business Collaborations

Toni Penya-Alba, Boris Mikhaylov, Marc Pujol-González, Bruno Rosell, Jesús Cerquides, Juan A. Rodríguez-Aguilar, Marc Esteva, Àngela Fàbregues, Jordi Madrenas, Carles Sierra, Carlos Carrascosa, Vicente Julián, Mario Rodrigo, and Matteo Vasirani

36.1 Introduction

Globalisation and technological innovation are driving the creation of the extended enterprise – the dynamic network of interconnected organizations, from suppliers' suppliers to customers' customers, which work collaboratively to bring value to the marketplace. That is, today's companies are in need for support to swiftly create *business collaborations* that allow them to readily respond to changing market needs. Furthermore, they are also in need of tools that allow them to quickly react to collaboration exceptions so that their goals can still be achieved. To summarise, the capability of forming and sustaining collaboration has become central for companies.

Several works have focused on guaranteeing temporal constraints in dynamic environments allowing agent decommitment (usually with a penalty). On one hand, with MAGNET (Collins et al. 2002), Collins et al. propose a solution for business collaborations based on contracts. In their approach, agents reach

T. Penya-Alba (✉) • B. Mikhaylov • M. Pujol-González • B. Rosell • J. Cerquides •
J.A. Rodríguez-Aguilar • M. Esteva • À. Fàbregues • J. Madrenas • C. Sierra
IIIA – CISC, Barcelona, Spain
e-mail: tonipenya@iiia.csic.es; boris@iiia.csic.es; mpujol@iiia.csic.es; rosell@iiia.csic.es; cerquide@iiia.csic.es; jar@iiia.csic.es; marc@iiia.csic.es; fabregues@iiia.csic.es; jmadrenas@iiia.csic.es; sierra@iiia.csic.es

C. Carrascosa • V. Julián • M. Rodrigo
Departamento de Sistemas Informáticos y Computación, Universitat Politècnica de València, Valencia, Spain
e-mail: carrasco@dsic.upv.es; vinglada@dsic.upv.es; mrodrigo@dsic.upv.es

M. Vasirani
CETINIA, University Rey Juan Carlos, Madrid, Spain
e-mail: matteo.vasirani@urjc.es

S. Ossowski (ed.), *Agreement Technologies*, Law, Governance and Technology Series 8, DOI 10.1007/978-94-007-5583-3_36,

agreements through a negotiation protocol. Moreover, all interactions between agents are supervised and coordinated by a central entity. Thus, the existence of this central entity discourages fraud and simplifies communication between agents. On the other hand, Norman et al., with CONOISE (Norman et al. 2003), propose an approach based on virtual organizations. In CONOISE, agents reach agreements through a series of combinatorial auctions over requested goods or services. Moreover, agents bidding to provide a service are allowed to create virtual organizations themselves. Thus, CONOISE allows the decomposition of a collaboration in subcollaborations thanks to this mechanism of creating virtual organizations within virtual organizations.

In this chapter we present a novel approach to enable business collaborations that is based on concepts introduced in Part IV. Unlike MAGNET and CONOISE, our work focuses in the creation of supply chains and the follow-up of the whole business collaboration from the early stages of its creation to the final steps of its realisation. In our environment agents can request and offer services thus creating virtual organizations that represent market places. From those market places we create supply chains that allow the requested goods or services to be produced. After asserting a supply chain, the actual performance of the participants can be tracked in real time. Data gathered during the execution of the tasks is fed into the environment and can be used in future collaborations.

The rest of this chapter is structured as follows. In Sect. 36.2, we introduce mixed auctions as a mechanism to solve the problem of supply chain formation. Next, Sect. 36.3 introduces the readily available base technology upon which the platform is built. Finally, we present the architecture of the platform in Sect. 36.4, and give an overview of possible future improvements in Sect. 36.5.

36.2 Mixed Auctions for Supply Chain Formation

According to Walsh and Wellman (2003), "Supply Chain Formation (SCF) is the process of determining the participants in a supply chain, who will exchange what with whom, and the terms of the exchanges". Combinatorial Auctions (CAs) (cramton et al. 2006) are a negotiation mechanism well suited to dealing with complementarities among the goods at trade. Since production technologies often have to deal with strong complementarities, SCF automation appears as a very promising application area for CAs. However, whilst in CAs the complementarities can be simply represented as relationships among goods, in SCF the complementarities involve not only goods, but also *transformations* (production relationships) along several levels of the supply chain.

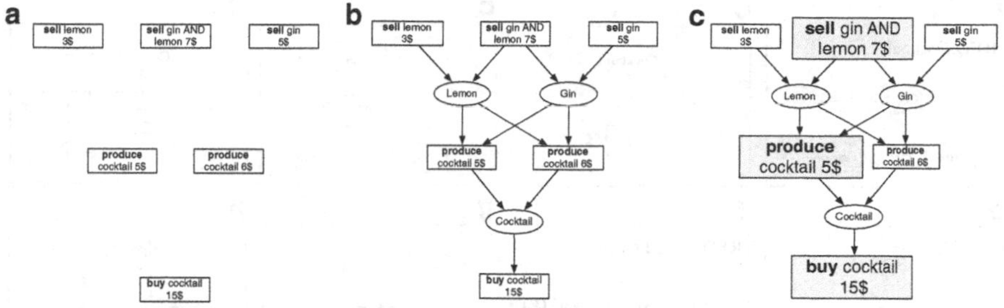

Fig. 36.1 Example of MMUCA. (**a**) Market. (**b**) Supply chain problem. (**c**) Supply chain solution

36.2.1 Mixed Multi-unit Combinatorial Auctions

The first attempt to deal with the SCF problem by means of CAs was made by Walsh and Wellman in (2003). Then, Mixed Multi-Unit Combinatorial Auctions (MMUCAs), a generalisation of the standard model of CAs, are introduced in Cerquides et al. (2007a). Rather than negotiating over goods, in MMUCAs the auctioneer and the bidders can negotiate over *transformations*, each one characterised by a set of input goods and a set of output goods. A bidder offering a transformation is willing to produce its output goods after having received its input goods along with the payment specified in the bid.

While in standard CAs, a solution to the Winner Determination Problem (WDP) is a set of atomic bids to accept, in MMUCAs, the *order* in which the auctioneer "uses" the accepted transformations matters. Thus, a *solution* to the WDP is a *sequence of transformations*. For instance, suppose the market in Fig. 36.1a where a bidder offers to sell one kilogram of lemons for 3 $, another bidder offers to sell one litre of gin for 5 $, a third one offers to sell one kilogram of lemon and one litre of gin together for 7 $; there are bids for making a cocktail given one kilogram of lemons and one litre of gin for 5 $ and 6 $ respectively; and there is a bidder willing to pay 15 $ for the cocktail. Such a market and its dependencies can be expressed graphically as in Fig. 36.1b, where goods are represented as ellipses and transformations over goods as boxes. Solving the WDP for this market is equal to choosing the bids that maximise the auctioneer revenue (the bidder offering to buy the cocktail). Notice that a solution for this problem will be the sequence of highlighted transformations in Fig. 36.1c. According to this solution, task "sell gin AND lemon" must be executed before "produce cocktail" which, in turn, needs to be executed before "buy cocktail".

Unfortunately, the MMUCA WDP has been proved to be NP-complete (Cerquides et al. 2007a). Although reasonably fast solvers have been introduced (Giovannucci et al. 2008), MMUCA still turns out to be impractical in high complexity scenarios. Furthermore, a bidder in MMUCA only knows the desired

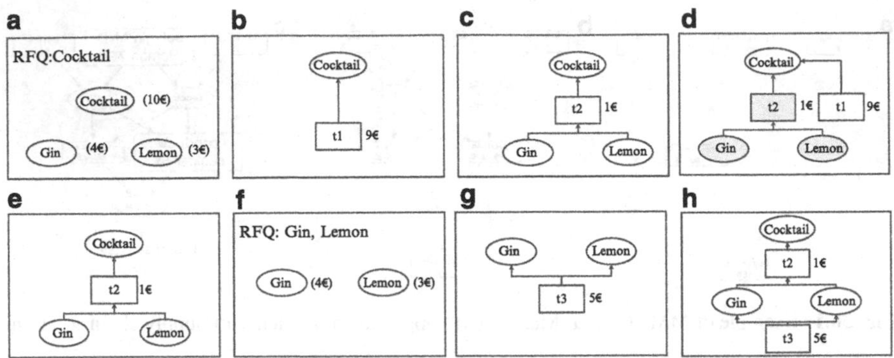

Fig. 36.2 Example of sequential mixed auction. (**a**) First auction. (**b**) Bid for good. (**c**) Bid for transformation. (**d**) All bids. (**e**) Winning bid. (**f**) Second auction. (**g**) Combinatorial bid for goods. (**h**) Resulting supply chain

outcome of the supply chain and the current stock goods. Hence, it is difficult, especially for providers placed in the intermediate levels of the supply chain, to decide what to bid for. Therefore, in order for mixed auctions to be effectively applied to SCF, we must ensure computational tractability and reduce bidder uncertainty.

36.2.2 Sequential Mixed Auctions

Aiming to alleviate MMUCA's complexity and uncertainty problems, Sequential Mixed Auctions (SMAs) were introduced in Mikhaylov et al. (2011), a novel auction model conceived to help bidders collaboratively discover supply chain structures.

SMAs propose solving a SCF problem by means of a sequence of auctions. The first auctioning round starts with the desired outcome of the supply chain as requested goods and the stock goods as available goods. During the first auction, bidders are only allowed to bid for transformations that either (i) produce goods in the set of requested goods or (ii) consume goods from the available goods. After selecting the best set of transformations, the auctioneer updates the set of requested and available goods after the execution of these transformations and then starts a new auction. The process continues until no bids can be found that improve the supply chain.

Figure 36.2 illustrates the operation of an SMA. Say that a cocktail bar intends to form a supply chain using an SMA to produce a gin & lemon cocktail. Assume that the bar knows approximate market prices for a gin & lemon cocktail as well as for its ingredients. The auctioneer starts the first auction issuing a Request For Quotation (RFQ) for a gin & lemon cocktail (Fig. 36.2a). During the first auction, the auctioneer receives two bids: one offering to deliver a cocktail for 9 € (Fig. 36.2b); and another one to make a cocktail for 1 € when provided with lemon and gin (Fig. 36.2c). The auctioneer must now choose the winning bid out of the bids in Fig. 36.2d. Since the expected price of the second bid is $8(=1+4+3)$ €, the auctioneer chooses this bid.

At this point, the structure of the supply chain is the one depicted in Fig. 36.2e. Nonetheless, the auctioneer must still find providers of gin and lemon. With this aim, the auctioneer starts a new auction by issuing an RFQ for gin and lemon (Fig. 36.2f). This time the auctioneer only receives the combinatorial bid in Fig. 36.2g, which offers both lemon and gin for 5 €. This bid is selected as the winning bid of the second auction. Figure 36.2h shows the resulting structure of the supply chain after the second auction. Since there are no further goods to allocate, the auctioneer closes the SMA. The resulting supply chain produces a cocktail at the cost of 6 €.

Notice that each auction in the sequence involves only a small part of the supply chain, instead of the whole supply chain as MMUCAs do. Thus, auctions in an SMA are much less computationally demanding than a MMUCA. Moreover, the incremental nature of an SMA provides its participants with valuable information at the end of each auction round to guide their bidding.

36.3 Base Technology

The Assembling Business Collaborations for Multi Agent Systems (ABC4MAS) platform (Penya-Alba et al. 2011) is built upon four readily available modules, each managing a different aspect of supply chain formation and maintenance processes. In this section we briefly present each of these building blocks, along with a general description of their functionalities.

36.3.1 MMUCATS

MMUCATS (Giovannucci et al. 2009; Vinyals et al. 2008) is a test suite for MMUCAs that allows researchers to test, compare, and improve their WDP algorithms for mixed auctions. MMUCATS provides several graphical facilities for the structural analysis of WDP instances. Thus, it allows the depiction of: (i) the supply chain structure along with the distribution of goods and transformations between tiers (Fig. 36.3); (ii) the bid graph structure capturing the relationships among bids, goods, stock goods, and goods required as a result of the supply chain operation; (iii) the transformation dependency graph showing the dependencies among transformations; and (iv) the strongly connected components of the transformation dependency graph.

MMUCATS interprets the solutions provided by the solver in order to graphically display the optimal structure of the supply chain, the net benefit of the formation process, the time employed by the solver, and the number of decision variables employed.

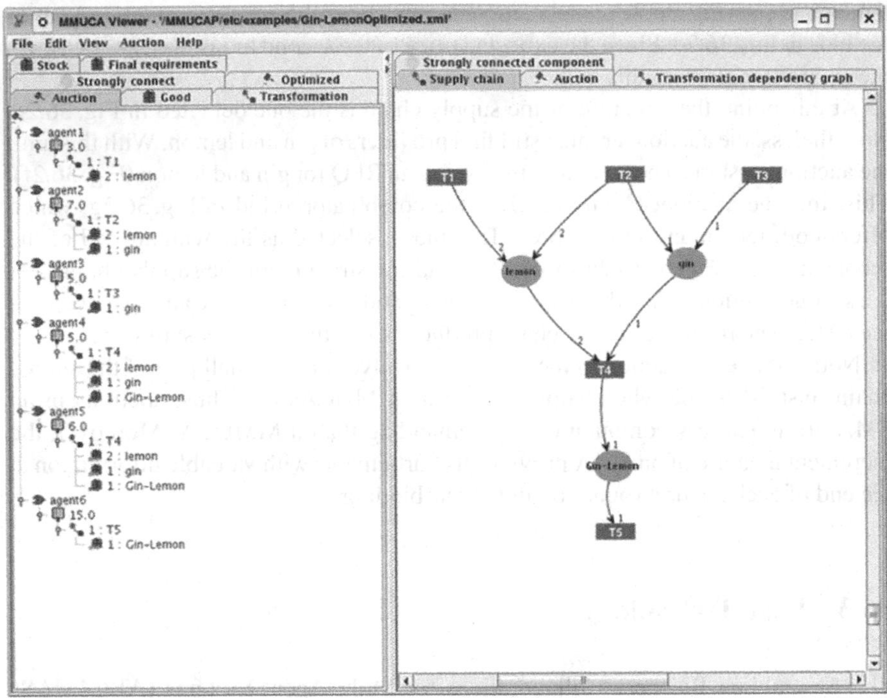

Fig. 36.3 Mixed multi-unit combinatorial auctions test suite

36.3.2 Virtual Organizations

The THOMAS framework (Argente et al. 2010) allows any agent to create a virtual organization with the structure and norms needed along with the demanded and offered services (see also Part IV). Virtual Organisations (VOs) are a set of individuals and institutions that need to coordinate resources and services across institutional boundaries (Argente et al. 2004). In addition, system functionalities should be modelled as services in order to allow heterogeneous agents or other entities to interact in a standardised way. The integration of MAS and service technologies has been proposed as the basis for these new and complex systems (Luck and McBurney 2008).

The THOMAS framework is able to manage the organization structure, norms and life cycle, as well as controlling the visibility of the offered and demanded services and the fulfilment of the conditions to use them. All the functionalities of the framework are offered as *semantic web services* which are classified into two different entities: the Service Facilitator (SF) and the Organisation Management System (OMS).

Firstly, the service facilitator is a mechanism and support by which organizations and agents can offer and discover services. The SF provides a place in which the

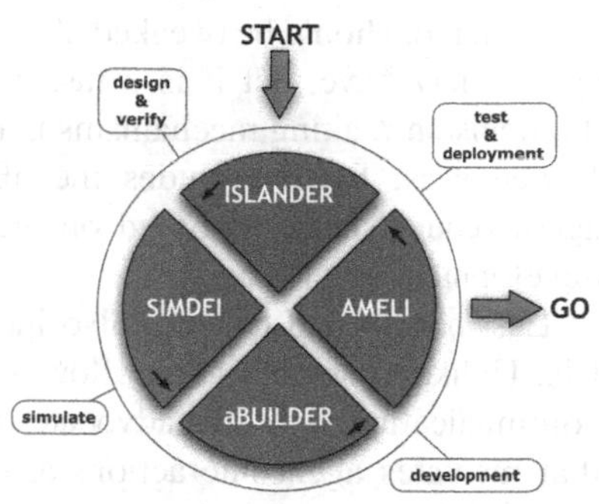

Fig. 36.4 Electronic institutions development cycle

autonomous entities can register service descriptions as directory entries, acting as a gateway to access the THOMAS platform. The SF can find services by searching either for a given service profile, or based on the goals to be achieved by the execution of the services. This is done using the matchmaking and service composition mechanisms that are provided by the SF.

Secondly, the organization management system is in charge of the organization life-cycle management, including specification and administration of both the structural components of the organization (roles, units and norms) and its execution components (participant agents and roles they play). Hence, the OMS keeps records on which are the organizational units of the system, the roles defined in each unit and their attributes, the entities participating inside each organizational unit and the roles that they enact through time. Moreover, the OMS also stores which norms are defined in the system. Thus, it includes services for creating new organizations, admitting new members within those organizations and members resigning.

36.3.3 Electronic Institutions

Electronic Institutions Development Environment (EIDE) (Arcos et al. 2005b) is a set of software tools that support all the stages of an Electronic Institution (EI) engineering. An electronic institution defines a set of rules that establish what agents are permitted and forbidden to do, and the consequences of agent's actions. Hence, an EI can be regarded as a coordination artifact that mediates agent interactions. Figure 36.4 depicts the role of the EIDE tools in an EI engineering cycle.

To support the engineering of EIs, ISLANDER allows designers to define a formal specification of the institutional rules according to its formalisation presented in Arcos et al. (2005a). ISLANDER combines both graphical and textual specifications of EI components. In addition, the tool also supports the static verification of specified EIs, which amounts to checking the structural correctness of specifications. The second tool, SIMDEI, allows EI simulations to be run with different agent populations. Thus, SIMDEI enables EI designers to analyse simulation results and decide whether the institutional rules yield the expected behaviour or should be tweaked. An EI specification defines the possible behaviours agents may have, but it is a task of agent designers to incorporate agents with the decision making mechanisms that will determine the specific agent behaviour. Nonetheless, EIDE includes the aBUILDER tool that automatically generates agent (code) skeletons based on the graphical specifications, thereby easing the development of such agents.

Last but not least, EIDE also includes AMELI, an execution environment for EIs. Unlike approaches that allow agents to openly interact with their peers via a communication layer, we advocate for the introduction of a social layer (AMELI) that mediates agent interactions at run time. On the one hand, AMELI provides participating agents with information about the current execution. On the other hand, it enforces whenever possible the institutional rules to the participating agents. With this aim, AMELI keeps track of the execution state, and uses it along with the institutional rules encoded in the specification to validate agents actions. Additionally, an EI execution can be monitored thanks to the monitoring tool that graphically depicts all the events occurring during an EI execution. Fairness, trust and accountability are the main motivations for the development of a monitoring tool that registers all interactions in a given enactment of an EI.

36.3.4 Supplier Relationship Management

Supplier Relationship Management (SRM) (Fabregues and Madrenas-Ciurana 2008) is an application that gives support to a company in the task of deciding which supplier to choose when a new supply has to be ordered. It is based on a measure of trust and provides several tools that visualise that measure and support its use in decision making.

The trust model used, extensively described in Sierra and Debenham (2005), can deal with multiple requirements, including: (i) importance of each order's characteristics, (ii) how accurately the supplied goods match the specification and (iii) preferences. The model is based on a knowledge base populated with past experiences with the suppliers. Each experience is composed of an order commitment and the observation of the execution of this commitment.

This model is then used to provide the following four analysis tools. The trust tool allows the analysis of the trust evolution over time for a supplier and a given commitment. The supplier analysis tool, shown in Fig. 36.5a, analyses suppliers by similarity or satisfaction based on the interaction history. The critical order tool allows suppliers to be ranked based on their trust level for a desired order and the relative importance of each characteristic of the order. The minimal cost tool, shown in Fig. 36.5b, enables users to obtain a division of orders along suppliers so that certain user levels of satisfaction are guaranteed whilst minimising the overall cost.

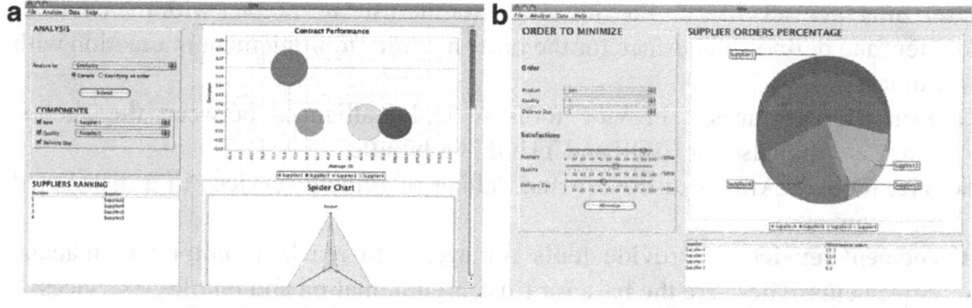

Supplier analysis. Minimal cost analysis.

Fig. 36.5 Supplier relationship management tool suite. (**a**) Supplier analysis. (**b**) Minimal cost analysis

Fig. 36.6 ATE services and tools

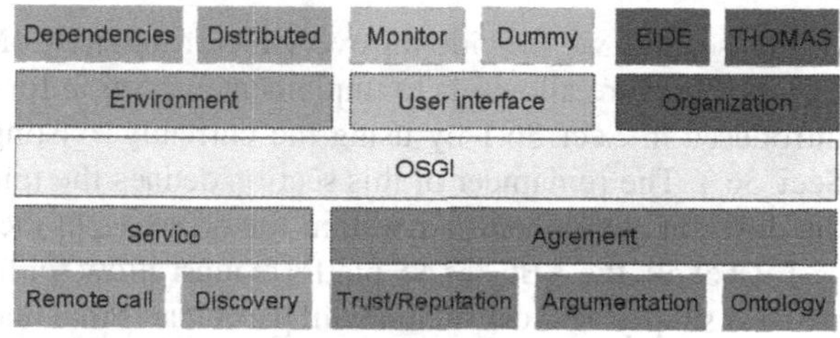

36.3.5 Agreement Technologies Environment

The Agreement Technologies Environment (ATE) is an environment that provides the seamless interplay of agents and services. We choose OSGi as the technological framework to support the development of ATE as a service-based environment. This choice allows us to follow the *de facto* industry standard software, providing a way to create modules (bundles) facilitating the collaboration between different groups. We have implemented all previously mentioned technologies (MMUCA, THOMAS, EIDE and SRM) as OSGi bundles allowing them to interact as ATE modules.

By default the OSGi framework provides us with a way to: (i) install, start or stop bundles, and (ii) register, deregister, search and access services enabled by bundles. However, OSGi does not provide all the services needed to have seamless interaction between agents. In order to overcome OSGi's limitations we build a series of services on top of it that constitute the core of the ATE (Fig. 36.6). We group these new services into:

Environment services. Manage the ATE environment by ensuring that dependencies between modules are met and facilitate collaborations in a distributed environment.

User interface services. Provide a way for the user to interact with the environment and define an interface for the other modules to implement interaction with humans.

Organisation services. Provide tools to make alliances between the agents. These are the base for EIDE and THOMAS bundles.

Service tools. Allows discovery and calling of remote services in a distributed environment.

Agreement services. Provide tools for agents to reach, monitor and manage agreements. These are the base for trust, argumentation and ontology services.

36.4 Architecture

In this section we provide an overview of the ABC4MAS platform architecture. This architecture allows us to implement a solution for collaboration environments introduced in Sect. 36.1 by using the currently existing technologies presented in Sect. 36.3. The remainder of this section defines the functional integration between the different components, as well as the objective of their interactions.

First of all, the ABC4MAS platform must allow for the definition of a supply network. A supply network includes all participants that may take part in the production of the requested goods, including both external and internal resources/companies. Additionally, the entity requesting the goods must be able to specify which roles each participant can play. These definitions will be fed into the THOMAS service, which will in turn create a virtual organization representing the whole supply network, as shown in Fig. 36.7a.

Thereafter, when a customer order is received, the system must define the supply chain to serve it. Hence, the auctioneer agent inside the global virtual organization receives the customer order specification and initiates the auction. Whenever the auctioneer needs to resolve the supply chain according to current supplier's bids, it calls the Mixed Auctions (MA) service. MA is readily available to resolve the winner determination problem, as well as to represent it as an ISLANDER

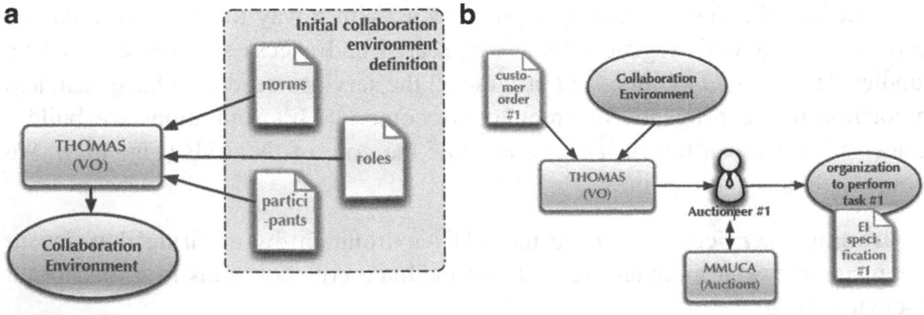

Fig. 36.7 Main processes. (**a**) Collaboration environment creation. (**b**) Collaboration formation

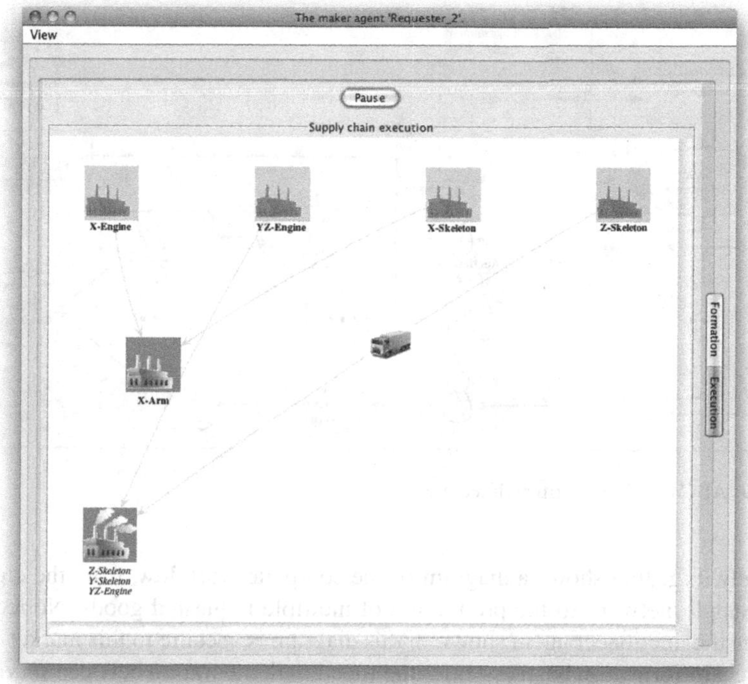

Fig. 36.8 AMELI execution environment

specification. Hence, the MA service replies to the auctioneer with a full-fledged ISLANDER specification. Once the auctioneer decides to end the auction process, it creates a new virtual organization whose participants and roles correspond to those in the resolved supply chain. To clarify, the whole process of determining the supply chain for a given customer order is depicted in Fig. 36.7b.

Once the supply chain has been defined, it is time to start the production process. Thus, the auctioneer launches an electronic institution using the AMELI service. AMELI then tracks each and every action as defined in the supply chain, allowing the auctioneer to monitor: (1) which entity is performing each task, (2) that all the agreements are being fulfilled, and (3) that no task is overdue. AMELI has been modified to report the execution of each task graphically with the data obtained in real time (Fig. 36.8). Additionally, AMELI generates reports about all the transactions being made in the form of events, that are stored in a central event database shared among all organizations within the platform. When AMELI detects that the production process has finished, both the EI and the machine-specific virtual organization are terminated.

During the production, the SRM service interacts with the central event database to feed its trust and reputation model. Hence, the different SRM tools can be used to evaluate the suppliers' performance.

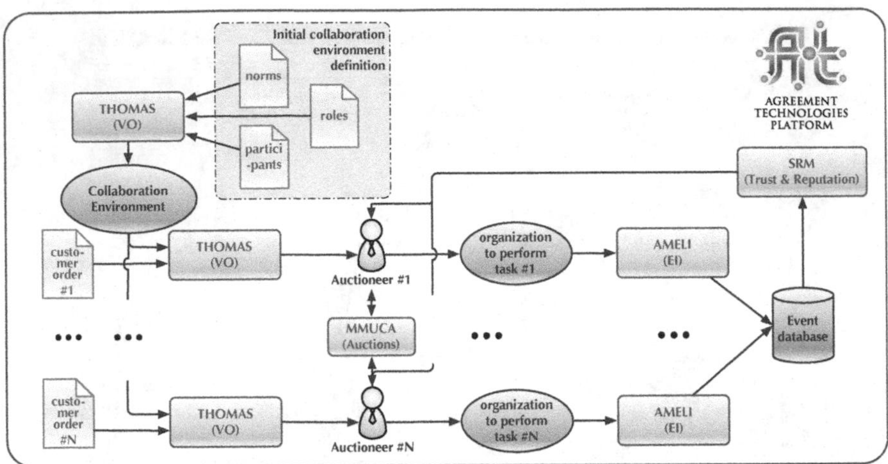

Fig. 36.9 ABC4MAS platform architecture

Finally, Fig. 36.9 shows a diagram of the complete workflow, from the creation of the supply network to the production of multiple requested goods. Notice that, although the auctioneer agent shown in this diagram is specific to this market-based supply chain formation business case, the functional integration between services is usable in any other scenario.

36.5 Future Work

Firstly, a key aspect to be taken into account in future versions of the platform is robustness. Although the ABC4MAS platform tracks how well each agent performs the tasks it is committed to, that information has limited effect on future interactions. At present, the trust information collected during the execution of supply chains is only employed by the auctioneer to filter out low-performing agents. However, we plan to employ trust information as part of the auction mechanism along the lines of Ramchurn et al. (2009) (see also Part VI).

Secondly, at present the negotiation process takes into account a single attribute: price. In actual-world scenarios, it is common practice to negotiate over further attributes (e.g. delivery time, quality, or features of the tasks/goods at auction) (Cerquides et al. 2007b). Hence, we plan to extend mixed auctions to cope with multi-attribute negotiations.

Acknowledgements This work was partially funded by Agreement Technologies (CONSOLIDER CSD2007-0022), EVE (TIN2009-14702-C02), the Secretaría de Estado de Investigación, the EU FEDER funds, the Generalitat de Catalunya (grant 2009-SGR-1434) and the proyecto intramural CSIC 201050I008.

References

Arcos, J., M. Esteva, P. Noriega, J. Rodriguez, and C. Sierra. 2005a. Environment engineering for multiagent systems. *Journal on Engineering Applications of Artificial Intelligence* 18(2): 191–204.

Arcos, J., M. Esteva, P. Noriega, J. Rodríguez-Aguilar, and C. Sierra. 2005b. An integrated development environment for electronic institutions. In *Software agent-based applications, platforms and development kits*, 121–142. Switzerland: Birkhäuser.

Argente, E., A. Giret, S. Valero, V. Julian, and V. Botti. 2004. Survey of MAS methods and platforms focusing on organizational concepts. *Frontiers in Artificial Intelligence and Applications* 113: 309–316.

Argente, E., V. Botti, C. Carrascosa, A. Giret, V. Julian, and M. Rebollo. 2010. An abstract architecture for virtual organizations: The THOMAS approach. *Knowledge and Information Systems* 29(2): 379–403. http://www.springerlink.com/index/10.1007/s10115-010-0349-1.

Cerquides, J., U. Endriss, A. Giovannucci, and J. Rodriguez-Aguilar. 2007a. Bidding languages and winner determination for mixed multi-unit combinatorial auctions. In *IJCAI*, Hyderabad, 1221–1226.

Cerquides, J., M. Lopez-Sanchez, A. Reyes-Moro, and J. Rodriguez-Aguilar. 2007b. Enabling assisted strategic negotiations in actual-world procurement scenarios. *Electronic Commerce Research* 7(3): 189–220.

Collins, J., W. Ketter, and M. Gini. 2002. A multi-agent negotiation testbed for contracting tasks with temporal and precedence constraints. *International Journal of Electronic Commerce* 7(1): 35–57.

Cramton, P., Y. Shoham, and R. Steinberg (eds.). 2006. Combinatorial Auctions. Cambridge: MIT.

Fabregues, A., and J. Madrenas-Ciurana. 2008. SRM: A tool for supplier performance. In *Proceedings of the 8th international conference on autonomous agents and multiagent systems*, Estoril, vol. 2, 1375–1376.

Giovannucci, A., M. Vinyals, J. Cerquides, and J. Rodriguez-Aguilar. 2008. Computationally-efficient winner determination for mixed multi-unit combinatorial auctions. In *AAMAS*, Estoril, 1071–1078.

Giovannucci, A., J. Cerquides, U. Endriss, M. Vinyals, J. Rodriguez, and B. Rosell. 2009. A mixed multi-unit combinatorial auctions test suite. In *Proceedings of the 8th international conference on autonomous agents and multiagent systems*, vol. 2, 1389–1390. Richland: International Foundation for Autonomous Agents and Multiagent Systems. Budapest.

Luck, M., and P. McBurney. 2008. Computing as interaction: Agent and agreement technologies. In *Proceedings of the 2008 IEEE international conference on distributed human-machine systems*. Citeseer, Athens: Greece.

Mikhaylov, B., J. Cerquides, and J. Rodriguez-Aguilar. 2011. Solving sequential mixed auctions with integer programming. In *Advances in artificial intelligence: 14th conference of the spanish association for artificial intelligence*, 42–53. Berlin/New York: Springer. Tenerife.

Norman, T., A. Preece, S. Chalmers, N. Jennings, M. Luck, V. Dang, T. Nguyen, V. Deora, J. Shao, and A. Gray et al. 2003. CONOISE: Agent-based formation of virtual organisations. In *23rd SGAI international conference on innovative techniques and applications of AI*, 353–366. Cambridge: UK.

Penya-Alba, T., M. Pujol-Gonzalez, M. Esteva, B. Rosell, J. Cerquides, J.A. Rodriguez-Aguilar, C. Sierra, C. Carrascosa, V. Julian, M. Rebollo, M. Rodrigo, and M. Vassirani. 2011. ABC4MAS: Assembling business collaborations for MAS. In *2011 IEEE/WIC/ACM international conference on web intelligence and intelligent agent technology (WI-IAT)*, vol. 2, 431–432. Washington, DC: IEEE. Lyon.

Ramchurn, S., C. Mezzetti, A. Giovannucci, J. Rodriguez-Aguilar, R. Dash, and N. Jennings. 2009. Trust-based mechanisms for robust and efficient task allocation in the presence of execution uncertainty. *Journal of Artificial Intelligence Research (JAIR)* 35(1): 119–159.

Sierra, C., and J. Debenham. 2005. An information-based model for trust. In *Proceedings of the fourth international joint conference on autonomous agents and multiagent systems*, 504. New York: ACM. Utrecht.

Vinyals, M., A. Giovannucci, J. Cerquides, P. Meseguer, and J. Odriguez-Aguilar. 2008. A test suite for the evaluation of mixed multi-unit combinatorial auctions. *Journal of Algorithms* 63(1–3): 130–150. doi: 10.1016/j.jalgor.2008.02.008. http://linkinghub.elsevier.com/retrieve/pii/S0196677408000102.

Walsh, W., and M. Wellman. 2003. Decentralized supply chain formation: A market protocol and competitive equilibrium analysis. *Journal of Artificial Intelligence Research (JAIR)* 19: 513–567.

Chapter 37
A Virtual Selling Agent Which Is Persuasive and Adaptive

Fabien Delecroix, Maxime Morge, and Jean-Christophe Routier

37.1 Introduction

Within the last 12 years e-commerce has succeeded in persuading a massive number of shoppers to change their idea of buying. Several existing businesses have taken an advantage of this boom by adding a virtual presence to their physical one by means of an e-commerce website, moreover, new companies that exist only through the web have also appeared (e.g., Amazon). Although the online presence of companies is cost-efficient, the lack of a persuading salesman still affects the transformation ratio (sales vs. visits). Several companies have started to embody a virtual assistant to aid potential online shoppers.

Most of the agents available on the e-commerce websites consists of intuitive interfaces for consulting catalogues by using the customer language (cf. Anna on www.ikea.com). The use of natural language and multi-modal virtual agents increase the expectations of customers who are quite often disappointed by the poor linguistic and the poor selling abilities of the agents (Mimoun and Poncin 2010). This corresponds to the uncanny valley phenomenon. Currently, these agents play the role of interactive FAQ. They are purely reactive agents responding in one-shot interactions (i.e. query/inform) with predefined answers.

In this chapter, we claim that the online selling process can be improved if the experience of the customer is closer to the one in a retailing store. For this purpose, we provide a virtual selling agent that is persuasive, adaptive and that behaves as an adviser. Our Persuasive Selling Agent[1] (PSA) initiates the dialogue and drives

[1] Available online at the following url: http://vvutest.lille1.fr/

F. Delecroix (✉) • M. Morge • J.-C. Routier
Laboratoire d'Informatique Fondamentale de Lille, Université Lille 1, Bat M3,
F-59655 Villeneuve d'Ascq, France,
e-mail: Fabien.Delecroix@lifl.fr; Maxime.Morge@lifl.fr; Jean-Christophe.Routier@lifl.fr

S. Ossowski (ed.), *Agreement Technologies*, Law, Governance and Technology Series 8, DOI 10.1007/978-94-007-5583-3_37,

it in order to simultaneously advance two processes: customer profiling and the identification of the product to sell. Additionally, our virtual seller is adaptive since the selection of the next utterance in the dialogue depends on the customer profile. The PSA is an extended version of Proactive Dialogical Agent (PDA) proposed in Delecroix et al. (2012a) and demonstrated in Delecroix et al. (2012b). First at all, our prototype is now populated with real-world data. Moreover, the PSA is persuasive since her proposals are supported by arguments which fit the customer profile.

The chapter is organized as follows. Firstly, we introduce a walk-through example in Sect. 37.2. Secondly, we present the knowledge representation language embedded by our agent in Sect. 37.3. Section 37.4 introduces the dialogue framework and the corresponding strategies. We describe the agent behaviour in Sect. 37.8 and the arguments in Sect. 37.6. Our implementation is briefly described in Sects. 37.7 and 37.8 discusses some related works. Section 37.9 concludes with some directions for future works.

37.2 Walk-Through Scenario

We motivate our approach with the following scenario. A buyer is surfing on a commercial website. He is looking for a digital camera. Since he does not find the appropriate product, he spends some time on the website and so, the PSA is triggered. Then the conversation presented in Fig. 37.1 occurs.

This specific case run illustrates the main features exhibited by the virtual seller:

- **Initiative.** The PSA has initiative since she starts the conversation in order to support the customer (cf. utterance #1).

1. PSA: what is your budget?
2. Customer: small.
3. PSA: are you a beginner, a fan or an expert?
4. Customer: beginner.
5. PSA: which kind of models are you looking for?
6. Customer: the most efficient.
7. PSA: which kind of pictures are you taking?
8. Customer: family.
9. PSA: May I suggest can on digital ixus 1100 hs. The technology at the best value for money.
10. Customer: No thanks.
11. PSA: May I suggest nikon coolpix s6200. The compact at the best price.
12. Customer: ...

Fig. 37.1 Persuasive seller agent vs. customer: a sale scenario

- **Adaptability.** The PSA reaction depends on the utterance #2. The following questions and proposals depends on the customer's replies.
- **Profiling.** The PSA asks questions to the customer in order to identify him and propose the most relevant products.
- **Persuasion.** The proposals are supported by arguments adapted to the products and the customer profile (cf. utterances #9 and #11).
- **Reasoning.** The proposals and their arguments are not directly linked to the previous answers but they are the results of inferences over the whole conversation.

37.3 Knowledge Representation

In this section, we provide the Knowledge Representation (KR) language which is adopted by our PSA.

In our simple KR language, concepts are patterns defined by a set of attributes. A concepts defines constituent members which enable its instances to have values.

Definition 37.1 (Concept). Let $(Att_i)_{1 \leq i \leq n}$ an indexed family of sets, called **attributes**. A **concept** is the Cartesian product $C = \Pi_{i=1}^{n} Att_i$. An **instance** $o \in C$ a tuple $\langle v_1, \ldots, v_n \rangle$ where $\forall i,\ 1 \leq i \leq n,\ v_i \in Att_i$.

Our PSA has an explicit representation of the products (cf. Sect. 37.3.1) and the customers (cf. Sect. 37.3.2).

37.3.1 Product

The PSA supports the choice between products of the same kind. The product category can be described as a concept where product features are attributes.

Definition 37.2 (Product). Let $P = \Pi_{i=1}^{n} F_i$ a concept representing a **product category** with n attributes called **features**. A **product** is an object $p \in P$.

It is worth noticing that the KR language requires that the domains of values are discrete but it does not require that they are ordered.

The product we consider in our use case are digital cameras. They are defined by a set of features (type, zoom, etc.) Each feature is associated with a set of values (for the type, the values are compact, hybrid, bridge and SLR). It is worth noticing that the values can be n/a (i.e. not applicable). For instance, the zoom feature is not relevant for SLR cameras which have a lens. Products can be represented by vectors of Boolean values as in Table 37.1. If a feature is n/a for a product, then all the Boolean values for this feature are 0. For instance, all the zoom values are 0 for the SLR cameras. The products have been chosen so that every kind of digital cameras are represented.

Table 37.1 The digital cameras and their feature. For instance, LX5 is a compact digital camera with a resolution between 8 and 12 MP and a zoom which is medium

Features	Values	LX5	s6200	Cyber	VG130	ixus	RS1500	PetShop	iTwist	Aqua	J1	GF3	NEX	P500	FZ	FinePix	L120	EOS	K-r	E5	D300s
Type	Compact	1	1	1	1	1	1	1	1	1	0	0	0	0	0	0	0	0	0	0	0
	Hybrid	0	0	0	0	0	0	0	0	0	1	1	1	0	0	0	0	0	0	0	0
	Bridge	0	0	0	0	0	0	0	0	0	0	0	0	1	1	1	1	0	0	0	0
	SLR	0	0	0	0	0	0	0	0	0	0	0	0	0	0	0	0	1	1	1	1
Resolution	<8 MP	0	0	0	0	0	0	1	1	1	0	0	0	0	0	0	0	0	0	0	0
	8≤ ≤12 MP	1	1	0	0	1	0	0	0	0	1	1	0	1	1	0	0	0	1	1	1
	>12 MP	0	0	1	1	0	1	0	0	0	0	0	1	0	0	1	1	1	0	0	0
Zoom	Basic	0	0	0	0	0	0	1	1	1	0	0	0	0	0	0	0	0	0	0	0
	Medium	1	0	0	0	0	1	0	0	0	0	0	0	0	0	0	0	0	0	0	0
	Powerfull	0	1	1	1	0	0	0	0	0	0	0	0	0	0	0	0	0	0	0	0
	Innovative	0	0	0	0	1	0	0	0	0	0	0	0	1	1	1	1	0	0	0	0
Setting	None	0	0	0	0	0	0	1	1	1	0	0	0	0	0	0	0	0	0	0	0
	Medium	0	1	1	1	1	1	0	0	0	0	0	0	0	0	0	0	0	0	0	0
	Innovative	0	0	0	0	0	0	0	0	0	1	1	1	1	1	1	1	0	0	0	0
	Advanced	1	0	0	0	0	0	0	0	0	0	0	0	0	0	0	0	1	1	1	1
ScreenSize	<3 inch	0	1	0	0	0	0	1	1	1	0	0	0	0	0	0	0	0	0	0	0
	>3 inch	1	0	1	1	1	1	0	0	0	1	1	1	1	1	1	1	1	1	1	1
Size	Verycompact	0	0	1	0	0	1	0	1	0	0	0	0	0	0	0	0	0	0	0	0
	Compact	1	1	0	1	1	0	1	0	0	1	1	1	0	0	0	0	0	0	0	0
	Ergonomic	0	0	0	0	0	0	0	0	1	0	0	0	1	1	1	1	1	1	0	0
	Bulky	0	0	0	0	0	0	0	0	0	0	0	0	0	0	0	0	0	0	1	1
Weight	Verylight	0	1	1	1	0	1	1	1	1	0	0	0	0	0	0	0	0	0	0	0
	Light	1	0	0	0	1	0	0	0	0	1	1	1	0	0	0	0	0	0	0	
	Normal	0	0	0	0	0	0	0	0	0	0	0	0	1	1	1	1	1	1	0	0
	Heavy	0	0	0	0	0	0	0	0	0	0	0	0	0	0	0	0	0	0	1	1
Price	Small	0	0	0	1	0	1	1	1	1	0	0	0	0	0	1	1	0	1	0	0
	Medium	1	1	1	0	1	0	0	0	0	0	1	0	1	0	0	0	1	0	0	0
	Large	0	0	0	0	0	0	0	0	0	1	0	1	0	1	0	0	0	0	1	1

Sensor	Classical	1	1	0	1	0	1	1	1	1	0	0	0	0	0	1	1	0	0	0	
	Innovative	0	0	1	0	1	0	0	0	0	1	1	1	1	1	0	0	1	1	1	1
ISO	Low	0	0	0	0	0	0	1	1	1	0	0	0	0	0	0	0	0	0	0	0
	Standard	0	0	0	1	0	0	0	0	0	0	0	0	0	0	1	1	0	0	0	0
	High	1	1	1	0	1	0	0	0	0	1	0	0	1	1	0	0	0	0	0	1
	Veryhigh	0	0	0	0	0	1	0	0	0	0	1	1	0	0	0	0	1	1	1	0
SensorSize	Small	0	1	1	1	1	1	1	1	1	0	0	0	0	0	0	0	0	0	0	0
	Medium	1	0	0	0	0	0	0	0	0	1	0	0	1	1	1	1	0	0	0	0
	Large	0	0	0	0	0	0	0	0	0	0	1	0	0	0	0	0	0	0	1	0
	Verylarge	0	0	0	0	0	0	0	0	0	0	0	1	0	0	0	0	1	1	0	1
Definition	Classical	0	0	0	0	0	0	1	1	1	0	0	0	0	0	0	0	0	0	0	0
	hd	1	1	0	1	0	1	0	0	0	0	0	0	0	0	1	1	1	1	1	1
	Fullhd	0	0	1	0	1	0	0	0	0	1	1	1	1	1	0	0	0	0	0	0
Speed	<4 pps	0	0	0	1	1	1	0	1	0	0	0	1	0	0	1	0	0	0	0	0
	$4\leq\ \leq 12$ pps	1	1	0	0	0	0	0	0	0	0	1	0	1	0	0	0	1	1	1	1
	>12 pps	0	0	1	0	0	0	0	0	0	1	0	0	0	1	0	1	0	0	0	0
Stablizer	Numerical	0	0	0	1	0	1	1	1	1	0	0	0	0	0	0	0	0	0	0	0
	Optical	1	1	1	0	1	0	0	0	0	1	1	1	0	1	0	0	1	0	0	1
	Mechanical	0	0	0	0	0	0	0	0	0	0	0	0	0	0	0	0	0	1	1	0
	Both	0	0	0	0	0	0	0	0	0	0	0	0	1	0	1	1	0	0	0	0
WideAngle	Standard	0	0	0	0	0	0	1	1	1	0	0	0	0	0	0	0	0	0	0	0
	Wide	0	0	0	0	1	1	0	0	0	0	1	0	0	0	0	0	1	0	0	0
	Verywide	1	1	1	1	0	0	0	0	0	1	0	1	1	1	1	1	0	1	0	1
Telephoto	Standard	0	0	0	0	0	0	1	1	1	0	0	0	0	0	0	0	0	0	0	0
	Telephoto	1	1	1	1	0	1	0	0	0	1	1	1	0	0	0	0	1	1	0	1
	Super	0	0	0	0	1	0	0	0	0	0	0	0	1	1	1	1	0	0	0	0
Memory	No	0	0	0	0	1	0	0	0	0	1	1	1	0	0	1	0	1	1	1	1
	<50 mo	1	0	1	1	0	1	1	1	1	0	0	0	0	0	0	1	0	0	0	0
	≥ 50 mo	0	1	0	0	0	0	0	0	0	0	0	0	1	1	0	0	0	0	0	0
ViewFinder	Screen	1	1	1	1	1	1	1	1	1	1	1	1	0	0	0	1	0	0	0	0
	Electronical	0	0	0	0	0	0	0	0	0	0	0	0	1	1	1	0	0	0	0	0
	Optical	0	0	0	0	0	0	0	0	0	0	0	0	0	0	0	0	1	1	1	1

(continued)

Table 37.1 (continued)

Features	Values	LX5	s6200	Cyber	VG130	ixus	RS1500	PetShop	iTwist	Aqua	J1	GF3	NEX	P500	FZ	FinePix	L120	EOS	K-r	E5	D300s
ScreenType	Standard	1	1	0	1	0	1	1	0	1	1	0	0	0	0	1	1	1	1	0	1
	Moveable	0	0	0	0	0	0	0	1	0	0	0	1	1	1	0	0	0	0	1	0
	Tactical	0	0	1	0	1	0	0	0	0	0	1	0	0	0	0	0	0	0	0	0
	Face	0	0	0	1	0	0	0	0	0	1	0	0	0	1	0	0	0	0	0	0
	Smile	0	0	0	0	0	0	0	0	0	0	0	0	0	0	0	0	0	0	0	0
	Both	0	1	1	0	1	1	0	0	0	0	1	0	1	0	1	1	0	0	0	0
PictBridge	No	0	0	1	0	0	0	1	0	1	1	0	1	0	0	0	0	0	0	1	0
	Yes	1	1	0	1	1	1	0	1	0	0	1	0	1	1	1	1	1	1	0	1
Power	Standard	0	0	0	0	0	0	1	1	0	0	0	0	0	0	1	1	0	0	0	0
	Builtin	1	1	1	1	1	1	0	0	1	1	1	1	1	1	0	0	1	1	1	1
Solidity	Standard	1	1	0	1	1	1	1	1	0	1	1	1	1	1	1	1	1	1	0	0
	Tropicalbody	0	0	0	0	0	0	0	0	0	0	0	0	0	0	0	0	0	0	1	1
	Shockproof	0	0	1	0	0	0	0	0	1	0	0	0	0	0	0	0	0	0	0	0
Mode	<10	0	0	0	0	0	0	1	1	1	0	1	1	0	1	1	0	1	1	1	1
	≥ 10	1	1	1	1	1	1	0	0	0	1	0	0	1	0	0	1	0	0	0	0
Landscape	No	1	1	0	0	1	0	1	1	1	1	1	0	0	1	0	1	1	1	1	1
	Yes	0	0	1	1	0	1	0	0	0	0	0	1	1	0	1	0	0	0	0	0
3D	No	1	1	0	1	1	1	1	1	1	1	0	0	1	1	1	1	1	1	1	0
	Yes	0	0	0	0	0	0	0	0	0	0	1	1	0	0	0	0	0	0	0	0
	Optional	0	0	1	0	0	0	0	0	0	0	0	0	0	0	0	0	0	0	0	0
LeicaLens	No	0	1	1	1	1	1	1	1	1	1	0	1	1	0	1	1	1	1	1	1
	Yes	1	0	0	0	0	0	0	0	0	0	1	0	0	1	0	0	0	0	0	0
Brand	No	0	0	0	0	1	0	0	0	0	1	1	1	0	0	1	0	1	1	1	1
	Yes	1	0	1	1	0	1	1	1	1	0	0	0	0	0	0	1	0	0	0	0
	Trusted	0	1	0	0	0	0	0	0	0	0	0	0	1	1	0	0	0	0	0	0
Warranty	2 year	1	1	1	1	1	1	1	1	1	1	1	1	1	1	1	1	1	1	1	1
Design	Yes	1	1	1	1	1	1	1	1	1	1	1	1	1	1	1	1	1	1	1	1

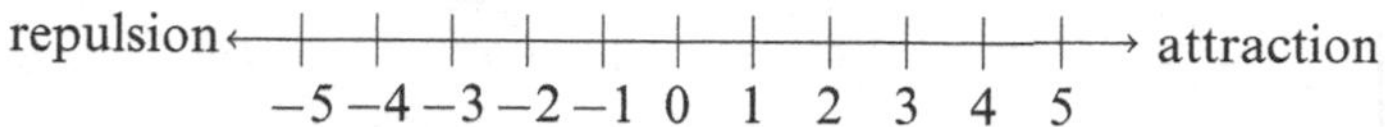

Fig. 37.2 Likert scale for the weights

37.3.2 Customer

We make the assumption that the choice of the customer is based on a multi-attribute decision-making process. Therefore, the customer choice depends on the feature values of the products and the relative importance of these values.

Definition 37.3 (Profile). Let $P = \Pi_{i=1}^{n} F_i$ a product category with n features. A **profile** is a weight vector $p = (w_1, \ldots, w_m)$ with $m = \Sigma_{i=1}^{n} |F_i|$. For all the values v_j of the feature F_i, there exists a corresponding weight.

At any time in the conversation, the need of the customer is represented by the PSA with a profile, called **customer profile**. These weights are numbers on a Likert scale. In this way, we measure the approval or the disapproval of a customer with respect to the corresponding feature value. A weight is within the interval $[-5;5]$ (cf. Fig. 37.2). A zero means an indifference with respect to the feature value. A strictly positive number captures the attraction of the customer through the feature value, and a strictly negative weight means that this value is repulsive.

In order to identify the customer needs during the conversation, the PSA knows some **stereotype profiles**. These profiles are defined a priori by marketing experts and they correspond to typical existing customers.

In our use case, the customer is captured by a concept composed of three attributes. The attribute called **buyer** representing the values promoted by the products to which the buyer is sensitive: safety, self-Esteem, novelty, convenience, price or affinity. This categorization is classical in the marketing literature (e.g. David and Machon 2006). The second attribute, called **user level** (beginner, fan or expert), and the third attribute, called **use** (family, globetrotter, clubber, sport-fan, reporter or multipurpose), represents the possible usages of digital cameras. The KR of the customers is domain-specific and defined by the marketing expert but it can be easily adapted to a different product category. Actually, we have successfully tested similar KR of the customers with two other real-world use cases: one about mobile phones and another one about bedding. As shown in Table 37.2, a stereotype profile is a vector of weights where the special character * means that the feature value is not relevant for this stereotype (the value 0 in the Likert scale). For instance, a beginner prefers a compact with less than 12M pixels.

The customer profile is computed from the stereotype profiles collected during the dialogue.

Table 37.2 The stereotype profiles corresponding the typical existing customers. For instance, a secure customer (promoting safety) prefers a compact or a bridge rather than a hybrid or a SLR and the resolution is not relevant for him

Features	Values	Safety	SelfEsteem	Novelty	Convenience	Price	Affinity	Beginner	Fan	Expert	Family	Globetrotter	Clubber	Sportfan	Reporter	Multipurpose
Type	Compact	3	1	3	5	3	3	5	1	1	5	3	2	1	*	3
	Hybrid	*	3	5	3	1	3	*	5	5	−3	3	2	1	1	3
	Bridge	3	3	3	5	3	3	1	5	1	3	3	2	5	3	5
	slr	*	5	3	3	1	1	−5	3	5	−5	1	2	1	5	3
Resolution	<8 MP	*	−3	*	*	*	*	2	−3	−3	2	−2	−2	−5	−5	−5
	8≤ ≤12 MP	*	*	*	*	*	*	2	*	*	2	*	*	*	*	*
	>12 MP	*	*	*	*	*	*	*	3	3	*	3	*	3	*	*
Zoom	Basic	1	−3	*	3	3	*	3	−3	−3	3	*	*	−3	−3	−3
	Medium	3	*	3	3	3	3	3	1	1	3	*	3	−3	*	*
	Powerfull	3	3	3	3	1	3	3	3	3	3	3	3	*	*	1
	Innovative	*	3	3	*	*	3	*	3	3	*	3	*	5	3	3
Setting	None	3	*	*	5	3	3	5	*	−3	5	3	3	−3	−3	*
	Medium	3	3	5	3	1	5	3	3	*	3	3	3	3	*	3
	Innovative	*	3	3	*	*	*	*	5	3	−3	1	*	3	3	5
	Advanced	*	5	3	*	*	*	−3	3	5	−3	1	*	3	5	3
ScreenSize	<3 inch	*	*	*	*	*	*	*	*	*	*	*	*	*	*	*
	>3 inch	*	*	*	5	*	*	*	*	*	*	*	*	*	*	*
Size	Verycompact	1	1	3	*	*	1	1	*	*	1	3	1	*	*	1
	Compact	3	*	1	1	3	1	3	*	*	3	3	3	1	*	1
	Ergonomic	1	*	*	3	1	*	*	3	1	1	1	1	3	1	1
	Bulky	*	1	*	*	*	*	*	1	3	*	*	*	*	3	*
Weight	Verylight	1	1	3	*	*	1	1	*	*	1	3	1	*	*	1
	Light	3	*	1	1	3	1	3	*	*	3	3	3	1	*	1
	Normal	1	*	*	3	1	*	*	3	1	1	1	1	3	1	1
	Heavy	*	1	*	*	*	*	*	1	3	*	*	*	*	3	*
Price	Small	*	*	*	*	5	*	3	*	*	3	1	1	1	*	1
	Medium	3	1	3	1	1	3	1	3	1	1	3	3	3	1	3
	Large	1	3	1	1	−3	1	*	1	3	*	*	1	1	3	3

Sensor	Classical	1	*	*	*	1	1	3	*	1	3	1	1	1	*	*
	Innovative	*	3	3	1	*	3	*	3	3	*	3	3	3	1	1
ISO	Low	*	−3	*	*	1	1	1	*	*	*	*	*	*	*	*
	Standard	1	*	*	3	1	1	3	*	*	3	1	*	*	*	1
	High	3	1	3	1	*	3	*	3	3	1	3	5	3	5	3
	Veryhigh	*	3	1	*	*	1	*	3	3	*	1	5	3	3	3
SensorSize	Small	3	*	*	1	3	1	3	3	1	3	*	*	3	1	1
	Medium	1	1	*	*	*	*	*	3	3	*	1	*	3	3	3
	Large	*	3	*	*	*	*	*	3	5	*	1	1	3	5	3
	Verylarge	*	3	*	*	*	*	*	3	5	*	1	1	3	5	3
Definition	Classical	*	−3	-3	*	*	*	*	*	*	*	*	*	*	*	*
	hd	3	1	*	3	1	1	3	3	3	1	1	1	3	3	1
	Fullhd	*	3	5	1	*	3	*	1	*	1	3	1	1	1	3
Speed	<4 pps	3	−3	-3	*	3	*	3	*	−3	3	1	*	−3	*	*
	4≤ ≤12 pps	*	3	3	3	1	3	*	3	3	*	1	1	3	1	3
	>12 pps	*	3	3	1	*	1	*	3	3	*	*	*	5	3	3
Stablizer	Numerical	1	−3	*	1	3	1	5	*	−3	3	1	1	−3	−3	1
	Optical	3	3	1	3	1	1	1	5	3	1	5	3	3	5	5
	Mechanical	*	3	*	*	*	*	*	1	3	*	*	*	3	5	3
	Both	3	3	1	*	*	1	*	3	3	1	3	1	3	3	5
WideAngle	Standard	1	−3	*	*	3	1	3	−3	−3	1	*	−3	−3	−3	−3
	Wide	3	1	1	3	1	3	1	3	1	3	3	3	3	3	3
	Verywide	1	3	3	3	*	1	1	3	3	1	5	5	5	1	5
Telephoto	Standard	1	−3	*	*	3	1	3	−3	−3	1	*	−3	−3	−3	−3
	Telephoto	3	1	1	3	1	3	1	3	1	3	3	3	3	3	3
	Super	1	3	3	3	*	1	1	3	3	1	3	1	5	1	5
Memory	No	*	*	*	*	*	*	*	*	*	*	*	*	*	*	*
	<50 mo	1	*	*	*	*	*	1	1	*	1	1	*	1	1	*
	≥50 mo	1	*	*	*	*	*	1	1	*	1	1	*	1	1	*
ViewFinder	Screen	1	1	1	1	3	3	3	*	1	3	1	1	*	*	*
	Electronical	3	1	*	1	1	*	*	3	*	*	1	1	3	1	3
	Optical	1	3	*	3	*	*	−3	1	5	−3	*	1	3	5	*

(continued)

Table 37.2 (continued)

Features	Values	Safety	SelfEsteem	Novelty	Convenience	Price	Affinity	Beginner	Fan	Expert	Family	Globetrotter	Clubber	Sportfan	Reporter	Multipurpose
ScreenType	Standard	3	*	*	*	3	*	3	*	*	3	1	1	1	1	1
	Moveable	*	1	1	3	1	1	1	3	3	1	3	*	3	3	1
	Tactical	*	3	5	1	*	3	1	*	*	1	*	*	*	*	*
FaceDetector	None	*	*	*	*	*	*	*	*	1	*	*	*	1	1	*
	Face	1	*	1	1	*	1	*	*	*	*	1	3	*	*	*
	Smile	1	*	1	1	*	1	*	*	*	*	1	3	*	*	*
	Both	3	1	3	5	*	3	1	*	*	5	1	3	*	*	1
PictBridge	No	*	*	*	*	*	*	*	*	*	*	*	*	*	*	*
	Yes	3	1	*	3	1	3	3	1	*	3	1	1	1	*	1
Power	Standard	*	*	*	*	*	*	*	*	*	*	*	*	*	*	*
	Builtin	*	*	*	*	*	*	*	*	*	*	*	*	*	*	*
Solidity	Standard	1	1	3	3	1	3	3	3	1	3	1	3	1	1	1
	Tropicalbody	5	3	*	*	*	*	−3	1	3	*	1	*	1	3	*
	Shockproof	5	1	*	*	*	*	1	1	1	*	3	*	3	1	1
Mode	<10	1	*	*	5	1	*	1	1	*	3	1	1	1	*	1
	≥10	3	1	3	1	*	5	3	*	*	1	3	3	1	*	3
Landscape	No	*	*	*	*	1	*	*	*	*	*	*	*	*	*	*
	Yes	1	1	5	1	*	3	1	3	1	1	5	1	3	*	1
3D	No	*	*	*	*	1	*	*	*	*	*	*	*	*	*	*
	Yes	*	1	3	1	*	1	*	3	*	*	1	*	*	1	3
	Optional	*	3	5	*	*	3	3	1	*	1	1	1	1	*	1
LeicaLens	No	*	*	*	*	*	*	*	*	*	*	*	*	*	*	*
	Yes	3	5	*	*	*	*	*	3	3	*	1	1	1	1	*
Brand	No	−3	−3	*	*	1	*	1	−3	−3	1	*	*	−3	−3	−3
	Yes	1	*	1	3	1	3	3	1	*	3	1	3	3	1	3
	Trusted	5	5	1	1	*	1	*	3	5	*	3	1	1	3	1
Warranty	2 year	*	*	*	*	*	*	*	*	*	*	*	*	*	*	*
Design	Yes	*	1	1	*	*	5	1	*	*	*	*	*	*	*	*

37.4 Dialogue Framework

Our approach for dialogue modelling considers that the exchange of utterances is regulated by a protocol. Our approach is based upon the notion of dialogue which aims to move from an initial state to achieving the goals of the participants (Walton and Krabbe 1995). For instance, **information seeking** appears when a participant (the PSA) aims to get knowledge from its interlocutor (the customer). The **deliberation** begins with an open problem. The discussion is about a future action, i.e. the product to sell. Actually, we distinguish two dialogues in our scenario. Firstly, the need identification is performed with the help of an information seeking dialogue about the customer concept where the PSA asks questions. Secondly, the sale is performed by a dialogue where the aim is to "*make a deal*". In this deliberation dialogue, the PSA makes some proposals and the customer accepts or rejects them.

In order to communicate, the participants share the same KR language – denoted $\mathscr{L}$ – (cf. Sect. 37.3) and the same agent communication language – denote $\mathscr{ACL}$ – in which each move has a unique id $M_k \in \mathscr{ACL}$.

Definition 37.4 (Move). Let $\mathscr{L}$ be a knowledge representation language. A **move** $M_k \in \mathscr{ACL}$ is defined as $M_k = \langle S_k, H_k, P_k, R_k, A_k \rangle$ s.t.:

- $S_k = \texttt{speaker}(M_k)$ is the speaker;
- $H_k = \texttt{hearer}(M_k)$ is the hearer;
- $P_k = \texttt{protocol}(M_k)$ is the protocol used;
- $R_k = \texttt{reply}(M_k) \in \mathscr{ACL}$ is the identifier of the move to which M_k responds, eventually θ if the move do not reply to a previous one;
- $A_k = \texttt{act}(M_k)$ consists of a speech act, i.e. a locution (denoted $\texttt{locution}(M_k)$) and a content (denoted $\texttt{content}(M_k)$), i.c an attribute, a value or an object in $\mathscr{L}$. The potential locutions are: `query`, `assert`, `unknow`, `propose`, `withdraw`, `accept` and `reject`.

The protocols we use can be summarized by the deterministic finite-state automaton represented in Fig. 37.3. An information-seeking dialogue begins with a `query`. The legal responding speech acts are `assert` and `unknow`. Such a dialogue consists of an arbitrary number of questions. Additionally, two questions cannot be built on the same attribute.The dialogue is closed by an `assert` or an `unknow`. A deliberation dialogue begins with a set of proposals through the speech act `propose`. It is worth noticing that the proposals are supported by arguments. The legal responding speech acts are `accept` and `reject`. Such a dialogue consists of an arbitrary number of different proposals. The dialogue is closed by an `accept` or a `withdraw` when the proposer has no more proposals.

In our e-commerce application, the PSA and the customer interact through a conversation. The PSA has the initiative, he speaks first. At each turn, the PSA produces an utterance (either a question or a proposal) based on the history. The information-seeking dialogue aims to capture the customer's needs (cf. Sect. 37.4.1) and the deliberation aims to reach an agreement over a product (cf. Sect. 37.4.2).

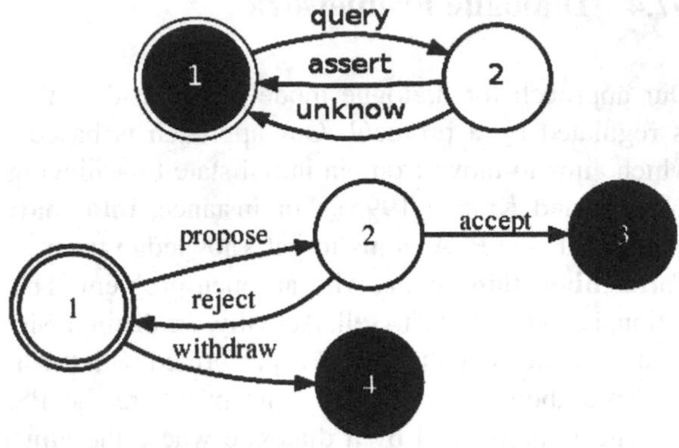

Fig. 37.3 Dialogue-game protocol for information-seeking (*on top*), and deliberation (*on bottom*). An information-seeking dialogue ends with an assertion or an admission of ignorance while a deliberation dialogue ends with an acceptance or a withdrawal

Our scenario (cf. Fig. 37.1) can be formalized in the following way:

- $M_1 = \langle PSA, Customer, IS, \theta, \texttt{query}(price(x))\rangle$
- $M_2 = \langle Customer, PSA, IS, M_1, \texttt{assert}(price(small))\rangle$
- $M_3 = \langle PSA, Customer, IS, \theta, \texttt{query}(userLevel(x))\rangle$
- $M_4 = \langle Customer, PSA, IS, M_3, \texttt{assert}(userLevel(beginner))\rangle$
- $M_5 = \langle PSA, Customer, IS, \theta, \texttt{query}(buyer(x))\rangle$
- $M_6 = \langle Customer, PSA, IS, M_5, \texttt{assert}(buyer(selfEsteem))\rangle$
- $M_7 = \langle PSA, Customer, IS, \theta, \texttt{query}(use(x))\rangle$
- $M_8 = \langle Customer, PSA, IS, M_7, \texttt{assert}(use(family))\rangle$
- $M_9 = \langle PSA, Customer, Del, \theta, \texttt{propose}(ixus,$ “The technology at the best value for money” $)\rangle$
- $M_{10} = \langle Customer, PSA, Del, M_7, \texttt{reject}(ixus)\rangle$
- $M_{11} = \langle PSA, Customer, Del, \theta, \texttt{propose}(s6200,$ “The compact at the best price” $)\rangle$
- ...

IS stands for information-seeking while Del stands for deliberation.

37.4.1 *Information Seeking*

The information-seeking dialogue is a process driven by the PSA for profiling the customer. For this purpose, the PSA asks questions on the customer concept (i.e. the attributes buyer, userLevel and use) and indirectly *via* feature products. For instance, if the PSA asks a question about the type of the device, then the customer will reply that he prefers a compact, a hybrid, a bridge, or a SLR. Each answer contains an object associated with a stereotype profile. For the customer concepts, the stereotypes are represented in Table 37.2. When a question is related to a feature, the profile of the answer is a vector where all the values are 0 excepted the corresponding feature values which is 5 if the value is the right one and -5 otherwise. Obviously, the natural language translation of the questions and their answers have been performed manually.

All the stereotype profiles collected during the conversation are memorized. At each step of the conversation, the customer profile is the internal representation of the customer embedded by the PSA. Initially, the weights for all the feature values are unknown. We denote "?" this unknown weight. The computation of the customer profile is based on the history (cf. Algorithm 1).

```
Data: ph: set of stereotype profiles in the history
Result: cp: customer profile
foreach fv: feature values do
  | cp.setWeight(aggregate(ph,fv));
end
```

Algorithm 1: Computation of the current profile

The aggregation of weights for a feature value is performed by the Algorithm 2. For each feature value, the weight in the customer profile is the average of the weights in the stereotype profiles. If a customer answer corresponds to a profile for which the feature value is not relevant, then this weight is not taken into account for this feature value. The weight for a feature value is unknown when no stereotype profile in the history is relevant for this feature value. This aggregation operator corresponds to a moderate attitude. A skeptical attitude consists of taking the minimum weight and a credulous one the maximum weight.

```
Data: ph: stereotype profiles in the history value: feature value
Result: weight
sum = 0;
nbWeight = 0;
foreach profile: ph do
  | weight = profile.getWeight(value);
  | if weight ≠ * then
  |   | sum += weight;
  |   | nbWeight++;
  |
end
if nbWeight ≠ 0 then Return(sum/nbWeight);
else
  | Return(?);
end
```

Algorithm 2: Aggregation of weights for a feature value

The **strategy for IS** is the mechanism for selecting the next question within the set of available questions. For this purpose, the strategy must take into account the dialogue history in order to select the question which advances the best the customer profiling. Actually, each question can potentially bring some information. The **informational payoff** of a question measures the quantity of additional information. The PSA selects the question with the largest informational payoff (see Algorithm 3). The payoff of a question depends on the payoffs of its answers. The informational payoffs for a question is calculated a priori based on the profiles corresponding to the potential answers.

```
Data: cp: customer profile setOfQuestions: set of available questions
Result: question to ask
max=0;
question=null;
foreach q: setOfQuestions do
    setOfAnswers=q.getAnswers();
    payoff=aggregation(cp,setOfAnswers);
    if payoff > max then
        max =payoff;
        question=q;
end
Return(question);
```

Algorithm 3: IS strategy

As shown in Algorithm 4, we consider that the informational payoff of a question is the average payoff of the possible answers, i.e. the corresponding stereotype profiles. This aggregation operator is a moderate attitude. An optimistic attitude consists of taking the maximum payoff and a pessimistic one takes the minimum.

```
Data: cp: customer profile setOfAnswers: set of stereotype profiles
Result: payoff
sum = 0;
nbProfile = 0;
foreach p: setOfAnswers do
    sum += p.getPayoff(cp);
    nbProfile++;
end
Return(sum/nbProfile);
```

Algorithm 4: Aggregation of payoffs for a question

A stereotype profile brings information if it determines the unknown weights of the current profile. We consider here that the informational payoff of a stereotype profile is the number of feature values for which the weight is informed. In other words, the payoff is incremented for each feature value on which we had no information until then (see Algorithm 5). This metric can be refined by taking into account the values of the weights in the stereotype profile. Intuitively, a stereotype vector which allows a definite opinion on a feature value is more informative than another one which corresponds to an indifference on this feature value.

```
Data: p: stereotype profile cp: customer profile
Result: payoff
payoff = 0;
foreach v: feature value do
    weightP = p.getWeight(v);
    weightC = c.getWeight(v);
    if weightP ≠ * and weightC = ? then
        payoff+=1;

end
Return(payoff);
```

Algorithm 5: Informational payoff for a stereotype profile

The customer profile built during the information-seeking allows to push the adequate products during the deliberation.

37.4.2 *Deliberation*

The deliberation dialogue aims to reach an agreement about a product. For this purpose the PSA make some proposals which can be accepted or rejected. The deliberation strategy interfaces with the deliberation protocol through the condition mechanism of utterances for a move.

The deliberation strategy consists of selecting the products based on the customer profile. For this purpose, we define the **utility of a product** as the adequacy between the customer profile and the product. As shown in Algorithm 6, the utility of a product is the sum of the weights for all the feature values satisfied by the product (e.g. greater than 3 on the Likert scale). It may be noted that the calculation of utility does not consider the feature values for which the current profile is not informed.

```
Data: p: product cp: customer profile
Result: utility
utility = 0;
foreach fv: feature value do
    weight= cp.getWeight(fv) ;
    if p.isSatisfying(fv) and weight ≠ ? then
        utility+= weight;
    Return(utility);
end
```

Algorithm 6: Utility of a product

37.5 Behaviour

The behaviour of the PSA connects the information-seeking phase and the deliberation one and so, it determines the utterance at each turn.

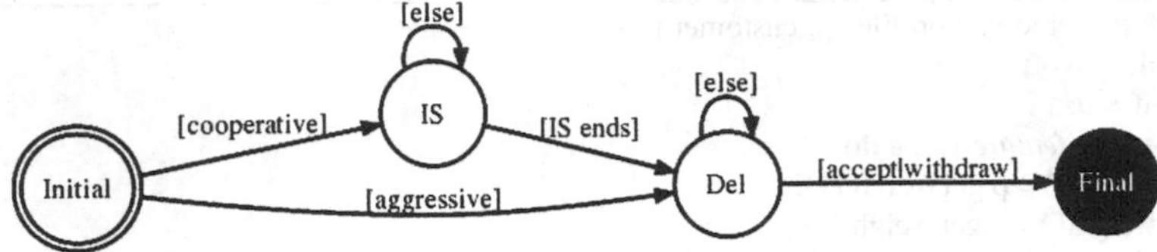

Fig. 37.4 The behaviour of the PSA

The behaviour can be summarized by the deterministic finite-state automata represented in Fig. 37.4. This automaton contains four states: the initial state, the final state, the information-seeking state and the deliberation one. In the two latter ones, the PSA uses the appropriate dialogue strategy. While the PSA aims to model the customer in the IS phase, the PSA tries to identify the product in the deliberation one. Since our agent is cooperative, the PSA starts with an information-seeking process. Several agent behaviours have been tested. The PSA behaviour deployed in our case run has been selected as the most relevant by the marketing experts. According to this behaviour, the information-seeking process starts with a predefined initial question about the budget. The three following questions are computed dynamically by the information-seeking strategy and after these, the deliberation phase starts. The latter consists of three proposals. The conversation ends as soon as one proposal is accepted or when the three proposals are rejected.

37.6 Argumentation

The PSA can support the proposals with some arguments. They are of three kinds:

- A **summary argument** simulates the principle of active listening by reformulating the answers. For instance, the argument associated with the stereotype security is "you look for a device of great quality";
- A **feature argument** pushes forward one feature value of the product. For instance, the argument associated with type–compact is: "small and lightweight, it is the perfect companion for all your travels";
- A **stereotype argument** is associated with each couple product-stereotype. In our scenario, the argument supporting the product s6200 which is adapted for a customer promoting safety is: "the compact at the best price".

It is worth noticing that the stereotype ones depends on the proposal and the customer, i.e. the customer profile. That is the reason why these arguments are the most specific and relevant ones. The stereotype arguments pushed forward by the PSA are not implicitly mentioned during the conversation but they are the output of the reasoning process. These arguments emerge from the sequence of answers. For this purpose, we introduce the notion of **revealed profile**, i.e. the stereotype profile which is the one most similar to the customer profile. For this purpose, we specify how to compute the dissimilarity between a customer profile and a stereotype profile as shown in Algorithm 7. The dissimilarity between a customer profile and a stereotype profile is the sum of the distances between the weights of these profiles over all the feature values. If one feature value is not relevant for the stereotype profile (the character *), this feature value is not taken into account. If one feature value is unknown within the customer profile the distance is the average one: $(|\text{ Likert scale size }| - 1)/2$.

```
Data: sp: stereotype profile cp: customer profile
Result: dissimilarity
dissimilarity=0;
nbFeatures= 0;
foreach f: features do
    nbFeatureValues = 0;
    featuresValues = product.getFeatureValues(f);
    tmp=0;
    foreach v: feature values do
        weightS = sp.getWeight(v);
        weightC = cp.getWeight(v);
        if weightS ≠ * then
            nbFeatureValues++;
            if weightC ≠ ? then
                tmp+ = ||weightC − weightS|| ;
            else
                tmp+ = (| Likert scale size | −1)/2
            end
        end
        dissimilarity=+tmp/nbFeatureValues;
        if nbFeatureValues≠0 then
            nbFeature++;
        end
    end
    dissimilarity=dissimilarity/nbFeatures;
    Return(dissimilarity);
end
```

Algorithm 7: Dissimilarity between a customer and a stereotype

37.7 Implementation

The dialogue does not take place in a natural language but with the help of a classical web form (cf. Fig. 37.5) where the user has the choice between several predefined answers for each question asked by the software agent. The user interface is written with AJAX technologies. For this purpose, we have defined a specific XML-based language describing the query/inform (cf. Fig. 37.6).

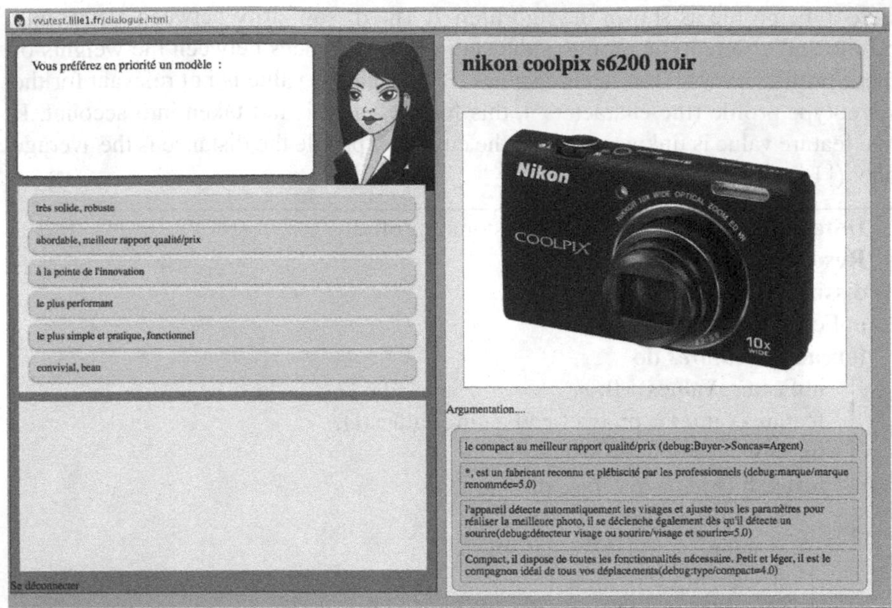

Fig. 37.5 Web interface with a container for the questions and a container for the proposals

The PSA is deployed on the server side with a prototype agent platform written in Java which can support interaction between the customer's agent and the PSA. For each specific case, the following data must be setup with the help of the retailing company:

- The product database containing the description of potential proposals;
- The stereotype profiles, i.e. the domain-specific information at the semantic level;
- The agent behaviour, i.e. the marketing strategy of the retailing company;
- The natural language query/inform (cf. Fig. 37.6);
- The list of arguments.

37.8 Related Works

Lin and Kraus (2010) present the challenges and current state-of-the-art of automated solutions for proficient negotiations with humans. They observe that research in AI has neglected this issue, at the expense of designing automated agents that negotiate with perfect rational agents. In this perspective, different approaches to automated negotiation have been investigated, including game-theoretic approaches (Rosenschein and Zlotkin 1994) (which usually assume complete information and unlimited computation capabilities), heuristic-based approaches

```
<?xml version="1.0" encoding="UTF-8" ?>
<questionAnswer>
<question>
<nlQuestion>which kind of models are you looking for ?
</nlQuestion>
<concept>customer</concept>
<attributeName>buyer</attributName>
</question>
<answers>
<answer>
<nlAnswer>very strong , robust</nlAnswer>
<attributeValue>safety</attributValue>
</answer>
<answer>
<nlAnswer>affordable , best quality/price</nlAnswer>
<attributeValue>price</attributValue>
</answer>
<answer>
<nlAnswer>at the forefront of innovation</nlAnswer>
<attributeValue>novelty</attributValue>
</answer>
<answer>
<nlAnswer>the most efficient</nlAnswer>
<attributeValue>selfEsteem</attributValue>
</answer>
<answer>
<nlAnswer>the most simple , convenient and functional</nlAnswer>
<attributeValue>convenience</attributValue>
</answer>
<answer>
<nlAnswer>friendly , beautiful</nlAnswer>
<attributeValue>affinity</attributValue>
</answer>
<answer>
<nlAnswer>I do not know.</nlAnswer>
<attributeValue>null</attributValue>
</answer>
</answers>
</questionAnswer>
```


Fig. 37.6 XML data for the question #5 and its 7 possible answers

(Faratin et al. 1998) (which try to cope with these limitations) and argumentation-based approaches (Amgoud et al. 2007; Morge and Mancarella 2010) (which allow for more sophisticated forms of interaction). Moreover, Lin and Kraus suggest that adopting non-classical methods such as argumentation-based decision making and learning mechanism for modelling the opponent may allow greater flexibility and more effective outcomes to be achieved. Along this line of research we have proposed a persuasive selling agent arguing her proposals and adapting her behaviour and her arguments to the customer profile learned during the conversation.

In the field of Artificial Intelligence, dialectical argumentation has been put forward as a very general approach to support decision-making. Thus, the decision aiding process can be modelled by a dialogue between an analyst (the PSA) and a decision maker (the customer) where the preference statements of the former are elaborated using some methodology by the latter (see Ouerdane et al. 2010 for a survey). On the contrary, our PSA can be considered as a persuasive technology (Fogg 2003) since it aims to influence the customer behaviour by providing suitable arguments. Contrary to Amgoud et al. (2007) and Morge and Mancarella (2010), our system is not built upon an argumentation theoretic model of deliberation. However, by justifying why products were recommended and providing explanations, the PSA may help to inspire customers' trust, increase the effectiveness of the selling process and persuade them to purchase a recommended product. As suggested in Tintarev and Masthoff (2007):

- The summary arguments promote transparency and scrutability by explaining why the product has been proposed;
- The feature arguments help the customer to make good decisions by presenting the full range of options;
- The stereotype arguments try to convince the customer to purchase the product.

Most existing recommender systems focus on how to use information rather than how to obtain this information (Montaner et al. 2003). Our PSA does not require prior data, she dynamically models the user. Our customer modelling is still limited since it is an explicit representation which is canonical, static and for the short term (McTear 1993): we model the buyer profile (e.g. does he prefer novelty or price), the user level (beginner, fan or expert), and the use (family, globetrotter, clubber, sport-fan, reporter or multipurpose). The user modelling allows the PSA to personalize the interaction, i.e. be adaptive. As stated in Paramythis et al. (2010), the adaptation requires (in our case): collecting input data (the customer's answers), interpreting data (the interpretation of the customer's utterances), modelling the current state of the world (update the customer profile), deciding upon adaptation, and applying adaptation (the selection of the utterance).

37.9 Conclusion

In this chapter we have proposed a persuasive selling agent which initiates the dialogue and drives it in order to collect information to make relevant proposals which are supported by arguments. Furthermore, our agent is adaptive since the strategies dynamically select the next utterance by taking into account the dialogue history in order to advance the best customer profiling and identification of the products. Additionally, the argumentation is suitable to the product and personalized since it depends on the revealed profile inferred during the dialogue. We have populated our prototype with real-world data from a retailing company: product database, domain-specific information at the semantic level, marketing strategies and natural language query/inform. We have worked with some experts and researchers in marketing who are quite enthusiastic about this approach (Mimoun and Poncin 2010). We have successfully tested the PSA with two other real-world use cases: one about mobile phones and another one about bedding. The PSA can be easily deployed whatever the channels is, in particular for mobile commerce (m-commerce). Finally, the PSA behaviour is fully configurable by the retailing company. In future, we plan to use machine learning techniques to improve agent behaviour in the long run.

Acknowledgements This work is supported by the Ubiquitous Virtual Seller (VVU) project that was initiated by the Competitivity Institute on Trading Industries (PICOM). We thanks Bruno Beaufils, Laurent Deslandres, Adrien Nouveau, Isabelle Pialaprat, and the anonymous reviewers for their comments on this chapter.

References

Amgoud, L., Y. Dimopoulos, and P. Moraitis. 2007. A unified and general framework for argumentation-based negotiation. In *Proceedings of AAMAS*, Honolulu, 963–970.

David, P., and J.N. Machon. 2006. *La négociation commerciale en pratique*. Paris: Eyrolles.

Delecroix, F., M. Morge, J.C. Routier. 2012a. A virtual selling agent which is proactive and adaptive. In *Proceedings of the 10th international conference on practical applications of agents and multi-agent systems (PAAMS 12), advances in intelligent and soft-computing*, 57–66. Salamanca: Springer.

Delecroix, F., M. Morge, and J.C. Routier. 2012b. A virtual selling agent which is proactive and adaptive: Demonstration. In *Proceedings of the 10th international conference on practical applications of agents and multi-agent systems (PAAMS 12), advances in intelligent and soft-computing*, 231–236. Salamanca: Springer.

Faratin, P., C. Sierra, and N.R. Jennings. 1998. Negotiation decision functions for autonomous agents. *International Journal of Robotics and Autonomous Systems* 24: 3–4.

Fogg, B.J. 2003. *Persuasive technology: Using computers to change what we think and do.* Amsterdam/Boston: Morgan Kaufmann.

Lin, R., and S. Kraus. 2010. Can automated agents proficiently negotiate with humans? *Communications of the ACM* 53(1): 78–88.

McTear, M.F. 1993. User modelling for adaptive computer systems: A survey of recent developments. *Artificial Intelligence Review* 7: 157–184.

Mimoun, M.B., and I. Poncin. 2010. Agents virtuels vendeurs: Que veulent les consommateurs? In *Proceedings of the workshop sur les agents conversationnels animés*, 99–106. Lille.

Montaner, M., B. López, and J.L. De La Rosa. 2003. A taxonomy of recommender agents on the Internet. *Artificial Intelligence Review* 19: 285–330.

Morge, M., and P. Mancarella. 2010. Assumption-based argumentation for the minimal concession strategy. In *Proceedings of ArgMAS 2009*, LNCS, vol. 6057, 114–133. Berlin: Springer.

Ouerdane, W., N. Maudet, and A. Tsoukiàs. 2010. Argumentation theory and decision aiding. *International Series in Operations Research and Management Science* 142: 177–208.

Paramythis, A., S. Weibelzahl, and J. Masthoff. 2010. Layered evaluation of interactive adaptive systems: Framework and formative methods. *User Modeling and User-Adapted Interaction* 20(5): 383–453.

Rosenschein, J.S., and G. Zlotkin. 1994. *Rules of encounter: Designing conventions for automated negotiation among Computers*, The MIT Press Series of Artificial Intelligence. Cambridge: MIT.

Tintarev, N., and J. Masthoff. 2007. A survey of explanations in recommender systems. In *Proceedings of the 23rd international conference on data engineering workshops*, Istanbul, 801–810.

Walton, D., and E. Krabbe. 1995. *Commitment in dialogue*. Albany: SUNY Press.